3 November 1988

Mary,

Congratulations on your selection to attend this institution! It is a pleasure for me to see the Army recognize your talents. You are superbly qualified, will represent the AMEDD well, and will continue your professional growth through this school year.

I am pleased to share the joy of your successes, and look forward to many more.

With all my love,
Me

OF RESPONSIBLE COMMAND

OF RESPONSIBLE COMMAND

A HISTORY OF THE
U.S. ARMY WAR COLLEGE

by: Harry P. Ball
Colonel
United States Army, Retired

**THE ALUMNI ASSOCIATION OF THE
UNITED STATES ARMY WAR COLLEGE
CARLISLE BARRACKS, PENNSYLVANIA**

Library of Congress Catalog Card Number 84-070402

Library of Congress Cataloging in Publication Data

ISBN 0-961-33010-4

First Printing.   1984

Typesetting: Batsch Company, Inc., Camp Hill, PA
Jacket design and chapter headings: Stone House Studio, Carlisle, PA
Printing and binding: Taylor Publishing Company, Dallas, TX

CONTENTS

Preface

Historians of American public and military affairs have long recognized and generally applauded the watershed reforms initiated by Secretary of War Elihu Root between 1899 and 1904. Among Secretary Root's initiatives was the founding of the United States Army War College, perhaps the most visible and enduring product of the statesman's efforts. Except for a period of two years during World War I and another of ten years during and following World War II, the Army War College has had a continuous existence since Mr. Root's stewardship of the War Department.

Were this work the biography of an individual rather than the history of an institution, it would have to carry the title of "The Life and Times of —." But if the "times" are important to the growth of an individual, even more critical are they to the development of a public institution. This has been particularly true in the case of the Army War College. It was not altogether by coincidence that the establishment of the Army War College followed by just a few years the launching of America's early twentieth century overseas empire, nor that the growth and development of the Army War College paralleled the evolution of the United States into the world's leading economic, industrial, and military power.

Understanding the United States Army War College, however, requires an appreciation of the impulse toward Army reform and professionalism in the late decades of the nineteenth century, when Eilhu Root's interests were still confined to building a private law practice in the city of New York. During this period a small but articulate segment of the officer corps attempted to emulate the professionalism developing both in various sectors of American society and within the military establishments of Europe. Most attractive to American military reformers, as well as to those of Europe, was the Prussian military system encompassing a General Staff and professional military education. Secretary Root built upon the thinking and earlier accomplishments of these officers, using the Prussian pattern without proposing to duplicate it. The earlier achievements and Root's adaptations constitute the early portion of this book.

The second portion of the history concerns itself with the initial attempt at an Army War College, carried forth between 1903 and 1917. During those years the college was officially and intellectually an adjunct to the newly formed War Department General Staff, an organizational attempt to apply the benefits of the Prussian system to the American situation. It was not an entirely successful experience. Acting as the war plans agency of the War Department, the War College learned to handle effectively planning for limited contingencies, but as an educational institution it was not able to progress much beyond a school of higher tactics. In neither role did it adequately prepare the Army and the senior officer corps for the enormity of the military problem presented by America's entry into the First World War.

The next part of the history deals with the Army War College from 1919 through 1940. Given a fresh start, separated organizationally from the War Department General Staff, and provided two decades of stability by the nation's neutralist and isolationist bent, the Army War College became the capstone of the professional education system originally envisioned. By 1940 it was rare indeed for an American Army officer to be chosen for a position of high command or staff responsibility unless he had graduated from the Army War College. During the Second World War all the most senior Army commanders—with the notable exceptions of Douglas MacArthur and George Marshall—were graduates.

During the early years of the Cold War and the Korean War the same pattern held true. Indeed, a few graduates of the prewar classes were still occupying pivotal positions as late as the Cuban missile crisis of 1962 and the early phases of America's Southeast Asia involvement. The common educational experience of this group of men destined to become influential in the nation's wartime and postwar security policies is in itself worthy of historical examination.

In an admirable but somewhat naive post-World War II effort to establish a joint-services professional educational system comparable to that built by the Army before the war, George Marshall and Dwight Eisenhower sacrificed in the early postwar years the Army War College, its building, its library, and its traditions. Despite their efforts, within a few years thoughtful officers were recommending, even pleading for, a reactivated Army War College. In 1950 Chief of Staff J. Lawton Collins reopened the college temporarily at Fort Leavenworth, then moved it the next year to its permanent home at Carlisle Barracks, Pennsylvania. Understanding the rationales behind both the disestablishment and the reestablishment of the Army War College is necessary to an appreciation of what the third version of the Army War College was to become.

The final part of this history, the thirty years since the reestablishment of the Army War College in 1950, offers no convenient or sharp points for division. An early debate on just where the instructional center of gravity should be was soon overtaken by the need to meet the intellectual challenge presented by President Eisenhower's "New Look" at defense policy. In response to this challenge to the very utility of land forces, the Army War College program by 1958 was built solidly on the theme "a national strategy and its supporting military program." The academic horizon was national military policy in its broadest sense.

The national military policy focus survived for more than a decade, although subject to increasing criticism. After the appointment of Robert S. McNamara to the position of Secretary of Defense in 1961, the Army War College gradually but reluctantly made room in its program for two phenomena of the McNamara period, counterinsurgency and scientific methods of management. The latter innovation in particular was neither well understood nor gracefully received, but by the late 1960s "management" had become a major facet of the educational effort.

Also in the late 1960s and early 1970s, the war in Vietnam with its range of international and domestic ramifications was influencing all that the Army and its educational system were attempting. At the direction of Chief of Staff William C. Westmoreland, the Army War College became a primary agency for the study of the internal problems of the Army. Taking its lead from this effort, the academic program began to draw on contributions of the behavioral sciences and to focus additional attention on matters that fall within the broad category of civil-military relations.

In the early 1970s the War College made a formal attempt to consolidate and reconcile into one whole the national military policy focus of the 1950s, the management thrust of the 1960s, and the more recent behaviorist and civil-military relation inclinations. But time would not stand still; by the late 1970s a growing body of opinion within the Army—and within the Army War College as well—called for the War College to become what it had not been for decades, an institution for the study of higher tactics and campaign strategy.

In a way, Secretary Root had both created and foreseen the dilemma the Army War College now faced. At its founding Root admonished the Army War College to become an institution for the study of three great problems, that of national defense, that of military science, and that of responsible command. The history of the Army War College is the story of how and how well the institution has responded to Eilhu Root's call.

Acknowledgements

The initiative for the writing of this history was that of the Board of Trustees of the Alumni Association of the United States Army War College. I am indebted to Brigadier General Alfred L. Sanderson, in 1980 a member of the Board and Deputy Commandant of the Army War College, for his confidence in providing me the opportunity to undertake the task. General Sanderson assured me at the time that I would have full freedom of thought and expression. It was a promise that the Board has fulfilled without deviation. Funds for research and administrative costs were provided by the Board of Trustees. The support and tolerance of the Board is appreciated, particularly that of its President, General Richard G. Stilwell, U.S. Army (Retired), and its Executive Secretary-Treasurer, Colonel George W. Aux, U.S. Army (Retired).

Assistance in preparation of the history has come from a number of sources and individuals. The U.S. Army Military History Institute at Carlisle Barracks, Pennsylvania, where the bulk of the records of the Army War College are held, provided critical and willing assistance. The Director of the Institute, Colonel Donald P. Shaw, granted me full access to the Institute's holdings. In addition, Colonel Shaw read and provided important comment on the draft manuscript. Dr. Richard J. Sommers, archivist of the Institute, and his staff were at all times most interested and helpful.

Dr. Harold C. Deutsch of the Army War College faculty read portions of the manuscript, as did Brigadier General Oliver B. Patton, U.S. Army (Retired), and members of the professional staff of the U.S. Army Center for Military History. Their comments reduced error and improved the text. Remaining deficiencies are my responsibility alone. A number of current and former faculty members of the Army War College have provided insights into events described in the text. Their contributions are cited in the notes on sources and their time and effort are appreciated.

At the University of Virginia I am indebted to the faculty of the Corcoran Department of History, particularly to Professors Norman A. Graebner, William H. Harbaugh, and Enno E. Kraehe, who without flinching assumed the unlikely task of retraining an infantry officer of thirty years into a student of history.

Mrs. Edith Stivers of Mint Spring, Virginia, and Mrs. Judy Lewis of Carlisle, Pennsylvania, typed and corrected numerous drafts. Mr. Gregory N. Todd of Carlisle edited the final copy. Their patience, perseverance, and skill were admirable and are gratefully acknowledged. Finally, this project may well have never been undertaken or might have been abandoned on any of several occasions had it not been for the support and encouragement of Helen Moore Ball.

It is my deepest regret that my faculty colleague at the Army War College and my friend of many years, the late Colonel William Francis Schless, will not read this book. His contributions to the War College as a serving officer were many. His counsel in the preparation of this history was invaluable.

Basye, Virginia
1983

Prussian Model and
American Practice

In May of 1900 the Congress of the United States appropriated for the first time monies to support a war college for the United States Army. The following year, on November 27th, the War Department issued General Order Number 155, the document which officially established the Army War College. To the proponents of the institution, however, November 27, 1901, was as much a date of culmination as of beginning, for the founding of the War College represented a significant victory in a long and often discouraging struggle to modernize, reform, and professionalize the officer corps of the Army. By 1901 the concept of a war college for the professional education of military officers was hardly new. It was not an idea whose time had come; it was an idea whose time was long past due. The roots of the concept reached down not only into American military history but deeply into the fundamentals of continental European military thought. To understand the Army War College, its original purposes, its subsequent successes, and its failures, one must look back almost a century prior to the issuing of General Order Number 155, back to those who conceived and developed the idea.

The Prussian System

In 1802 Colonel Christian von Massenbach served on the staff of the Quartermaster General of the Prussian Army. If one German historian is accurate, Massenbach was a most unattractive man in appearance, personality, and character. Small, squat, and bald, of unstable temperament, and unable to resist his own eloquence, Massenbach was not a popular officer. Colleagues found insufferable his driving ambition, dogmatism, and slanderous exaggerations. But Massenbach had talent; in many ways he was a remarkable officer. Equipped with a restless but first-rate mind, he was imaginative and possessed to an unusual degree the ability to organize. If it is necessary to name a man and a time that marked the beginning of what was to become a revolution in military

1

organization, a strong argument can be made that the man was Massenbach and the time was 1802.[1]

From Massenbach's early concepts evolved over the next seventy years the Prussian general staff, an organization that would develop and then direct an army that in a span of five years would defeat decisively both Austria and France, unify Germany and, for good or ill, alter dramatically the power structure of Europe.

Massenbach emphasized to his superiors that Prussia's strategic position demanded, even in peacetime, that operational plans must be available for any eventuality. Massenbach therefore recommended the formation of a permanent general staff, to be organized around the three threats to Prussia's existence—Russia, Austria, and France. The general staff would be the agency for this operational planning; but it would also be a school, and its curriculum would include reconnaissance of all possible areas of operations within and beyond the borders of Prussia. Massenbach suggested two other features: rotating the assignment of officers between general staff duty and service with troops, and providing direct access for the head of the general staff to the supreme war lord, the King. Frederick William III approved all but this last feature. In 1803 the Quartermaster General's staff was reorganized in line with Massenbach's suggestions.[2]

Whatever the advantages that accrued from Frederick William's directed staff reorganization, they came too late. Napoleon smashed the Prussian armies at Jena and Auerstadt in 1806, and the nation was humiliated in the Peace of Tilsit in 1807, dictating broader reform for both nation and army. Led by an unusual group of officers—among whom the names of Boyen, Gneisenau, Scharnhorst, Grolman, and Clausewitz are the most important and familiar—the Prussian Army set out, as a recent historian has put it, "to institutionalize military excellence." Massenbach's concepts were revived, and a general staff manned by a small number of carefully selected officers became the heart of the War Ministry. Officer professional education was revitalized and improved with strong emphasis placed on military history and on scientific training and method.[3]

The final defeat of Napoleon diminished neither the pace of Prussian military planning and education nor the steady growth of the general staff concept. In 1821 the general staff of the War Ministry was designated *Grossen Generalstab* to distinguish it from the staffs of combined arms formations, the *Truppengeneralstab*. That same year both were placed under the control of one man, the *Chef des Generalstabes*, General von Muffling.* Muffling won considerable extension of general staff

*To insure a distinction between the German (Prussian) general staff system and the American general staff system that later evolved, the German term will be used throughout the text when referring to the German concepts.

authority and greater autonomy within the War Ministry. The greatest accomplishment of the Muffling era (1821-29), however, stemmed from his concentration on military education. He revised the practice of staff rides over possible operational areas and introduced the *Kriegspiel*, or war game, for the training of individual officers and staff teams and for the development and testing of war plans.[4]

Prussia's general staff system reached its full development after 1857 when Helmut von Moltke became *Chef des Generalstabes*. In 1859, he organized a Railways Department in addition to the three geographical departments. These four planning departments were served by a supporting establishment of non-general staff specialists who compiled statistics, performed geographical studies, did surveying and topographical work, and kept a war room. Within the supporting establishment was included a military history element, traditionally a feature of the general staff, to respond to requests for information and to analyze strategy and tactics.[5]

It was Moltke's general staff system that defeated in turn the Danes, the Austrians, and the French. With the great prestige flowing from those victories, Moltke was able to expand his authority. He won full control over the *Kriegsakademie*, the superior military academy, and in 1883 finally gained the right of direct access to the sovereign, now not only Prussian King but also German Emperor.[6] Moltke made the Prussian system the model for military organization. The French organized a general staff in 1872; the Russians and Austrians soon followed.[7]

Also to Berlin during the last three decades of the nineteenth century, to study and perhaps to borrow, came a number of officers representing the army of the distant North American republic. Among them were men important to this history: Emory Upton, Joseph P. Sanger, Tasker H. Bliss, Arthur L. Wagner, Theodore Schwan, William Ludlow. These officers proved to be not unthinking copiers, but what they saw in Berlin and what they later related and recommended in the United States was the strongest single influence on attempts to reform the staff and officer education systems of the United States Army. The evidence is strong that the American observers understood not only the Prussian staff system, but the nineteenth-century changes in the art of war that had brought it about. They were fully aware from their study of Napoleon and of their own Civil War that with improved weapons infantry had the ability to defend itself without massing, that an army could be safely subdivided and subdivided again, and that all-weather roads and railroads, together with advances in cartography, allowed maneuvering of the subdivisions. The art of war had become "an art to be pursued on a map, and with immensely greater permutations and combinations possible than ever before."[8] If warfare was now to be characterized by speed, mobility, and complexity, then a premium had to be placed on comprehensive campaign planning and on rapid command reaction, two requirements the Prussian general staff system had been designed to meet.

The Prussians had paid a near fatal price to learn that armies must prepare in peace. They found that adequate preparation required accurate maps, prior reconnaissance of terrain, and knowledge of the capabilities of possible enemies. They found that rapid reaction required not only staff officers of technical specialities but also a new type of staff officer, one trained in the art of conducting war upon a map using intelligence reports and written operations orders. In western Europe the proliferation of railways not only permitted but required comprehensive planning for the commitment of forces immediately upon the outbreak of war.[9] Central to Prussian planning was the general staff, an organization and a system whose purpose was not to administer the army, but to prepare it for war.

The preparation was intense; it included mapping in detail the entire realm, studying the armies of neighbors, preparing operational and mobilization plans, and providing education and scientific training for the higher officers of the future. Understanding military theory and principles was necessary but not enough. The ability to perform intelligently in accordance with theory had to be ingrained. The intellectual result of the Prussian military organization was more important then the organization itself. The intellectual result was a systematic and disciplined method of formulating and solving military problems and a body of highly selected officers thoroughly trained in the method.[10] The preparation, the training, the organization, and the method—all were encompassed in the concept of "general staff."

In the later decades of the nineteenth century, the American military observer found in Germany a general staff apparatus with five interlocking elements. At the top was the *Chef des Generalstabes*, who was the principal military advisor to the Emperor and, as his title indicates, the director of the apparatus. Closely associated with him was a second element, the *Grosse Generalstab*, an agency neither superior nor subordinate to the War Ministry, charged with preparing the army for war. Its functions were planning, coordination and supervision, and assurance of what would now be called operational readiness.

Planning began with campaign plans, from which flowed plans for concentration and mobilization and plans for the maintenance and sustenance of the army once committed to campaign. The coordinating and supervising function focused on maintaining operational readiness and on insuring that plans of subordinate echelons were in harmony. Assuring operational readiness involved both officer education and the organization and conduct of maneuvers. It also involved developing new operational doctrine and influencing training and weapon procurement to support the requirements of doctrine and war plans.[11] This last function was akin to what the American Army many years later would attempt to formalize as "combat developments"—the lacing together of war planning, materiel development, operational doctrine, and tactical organization.

Administration of the army was not the business of the general staff but was left to the War Ministry. Personnel matters were the responsibility of the Kaiser's Military Cabinet. The ultimate aim of the general staff was to rapidly deploy an army superior in skill and in quality of weapons, and prepared to execute an established campaign plan. Execution of the plan would be under the general direction of the *Chef des Generalstabes*, but detailed execution, according to German thinking, was best decentralized and left to the initiative of subordinates. For this reason a third element of the apparatus, the *Truppengeneralstab*, was placed in subordinate headquarters. Its duties in peacetime were to insure operational readiness and to prepare the detailed plans supporting those of the *Grosse Generalstab*. In campaign it assisted and advised field commanders, insuring that operations were carried forth in accordance with overall campaign strategy.[12]

The fourth element in the apparatus was an elite corps of officers, carefully selected and rigorously trained through formal schooling and careful career assignments which provided experience on the *Grosse Generalstab*, *Truppengeneralstab*, and in command of troops. Once selected, officers were assigned permanently to the General Staff Corps and their careers were guided by its chief.

The fifth element of the system was the *Kriegsakademie*, located in Berlin. Because the German officer corps was not recruited from university graduates, much of the curriculum of the *Kriegsakademie* necessarily had to be on an undergraduate level: general history, physical sciences, and foreign languages. Concurrently, there was a strong emphasis on the study of military history and operations. As an officer progressed through the three-year course (more exactly, through three one-year courses taken without interruption), studies focused on an increasingly higher operational level. Entrance into the *Kriegsakademie* was through recommendation by regimental commanders and competitive examination. Attrition was heavy; perhaps one-third of the aspirants completed the three years. After graduation the officer served with the *Grosse Generalstab* under the tutelage and direction of a permanently assigned general staff officer. There he participated for two years in topographical work, map exercises, and war games, and made the annual staff rides led personally by the *Chef des Generalstabes*. Only then would the candidate be appointed to the General Staff Corps—if he had been found worthy.[13] The system was harsh. It was also effective.

The Prussian general staff system was devised and developed to meet

Prussia's military problem. That problem was not simple, but it was clear-cut. It was France, Austria, and Russia, and no frontiers of natural defensive strength.

The American Arrangement

That most fortunate of late-nineteenth-century powers, the United States of America, had no security problem comparable to that of Prussia. Its central security concern was Great Britain, the power that controlled the Atlantic, but against whom the United States had twice successfully defended itself—and without raising large armies. During the distraction of the American Civil War, Napoleon III had been so bold as to introduce an expeditionary force into Mexico, but after the United States had demonstrated its military potential during the Civil War, Napoleon abandoned the project. The Mexican republicans gained control, and the Habsburg archduke and erstwhile Mexican Emperor, Maximilian, was executed by firing squad on a barren hillside near a Mexican provincial town. By June 1867 the threat had evaporated.

Contemplating Maximilian's destruction with its demonstration of republican compassion, justice, and resolve, the Congress of the United States correctly reasoned that the danger of European monarchial penetration of the Western Hemisphere had passed. It thereupon reduced by more than a third (from 56,641 to 37,313) the authorized strength of the United States Army. Then, increasingly persuaded that indeed the South would not rise again and that military support of Reconstruction was a necessity no longer, succeeding Congresses continued Army reductions. By the end of the second Grant administration in 1877, the Army's authorized strength was less than 28,000. Until the war with Spain at the end of the century, that figure was not exceeded.[14]

The history of the United States Army War College begins with those 28,000 that represented the military power of the United States during the last two decades of the nineteenth century, from approximately the end of Reconstruction to the Spanish-American War. More precisely, it begins with an impulse toward reform that seized a segment of the officer corps of that small force and sent its representatives to Berlin.

The Army represented was hardly an army at all in the conventional sense. The "line" of the Army, its infantry, cavalry, and artillery, was divided by mission but not by organization into two parts. The more numerous part, the infantry, cavalry, and field batteries of artillery, was deployed as a frontier constabulary, charged with the prevention and punishment of depredations by the sorely pressed plains and mountain Indians and with assisting in the maintenance of law and order in the western territories. Another part of the "line," the heavy or foot artillery, less celebrated by popular artists, novelists, cinema producers, and historians, served as fortress troops manning obsolete and decaying harbor defense installations principally along the Atlantic seaboard.

In Chicago was located the headquarters most involved in the constabulary mission, the Division of the Missouri. From 1866, when it was formed, until 1891 when inactivated, its commanders were in turn Sherman, Sheridan, and Schofield of Civil War fame, followed by Terry, Crook, and Miles with reputations as Indian fighters. All but Terry and Crook would become the Commanding General of the Army. Subordinate to the Division of the Missouri were geographical "departments" which varied over time in both number and boundary. The troop units were dispersed into small, widely separate garrisons generally along the routes of communication of the western territories. Although those units were designated companies of permanently established regiments, they were rarely employed operationally as regiments. The brigades, divisions, army corps, and field armies of the great Civil War had long since disappeared.[15]

The two commands coequal with the Division of the Missouri were the Division of the Atlantic and the Division of the Pacific. Together these two commands held responsibility for the fortress troops, for the defense of America's more important seaports. The Division of the Pacific was committed heavily to the constabulary mission, as was the Division of the Missouri. The Division of the Atlantic was a more tranquil command but by location was more critical to the basic security problem of the United States. By 1889 the frontier constabulary and the fortress troops occupied 134 posts, none with a garrison of over 700.[16]

A third part of the Army was the supply and service support elements known (incorrectly, by later terminology) as the "staff." The "staff" consisted of ten departments or bureaus. Three dealt with procurement and supply: the Quartermaster, Subsistence, and Ordnance Departments. Three provided services: the Corps of Engineers, the Signal Corps, and the Medical Department. Four provided administrative support: the Paymaster, the Adjutant General, the Inspector General, and the Judge Advocate General Departments. All but the Judge Advocate General and the Inspector General Departments had a command as well as advisory role, each directing the operations and personnel involved in the performance of its assigned functions. The system made frequent conflict between "line" and "staff" inevitable.[17]

Although each bureau was in theory responsible to the Secretary of War, in practice each had become essentially autonomous. Officers were assigned to a bureau permanently, and the chief of bureau remained chief until removed by death or extreme disability. Resident in Washington, these tenured chiefs cultivated strong congressional ties with which the relatively short-termed Secretaries could not compete. Whether the motive was the worthy one of civil and legislative control of the republic's standing army, or the less worthy one of patronage and pork-barrel, the Congress over the years had legislated a protective fence around the bureaus. Appropriations were made directly to them for specific purposes. Resource allocation, that primary means of control, rested with the Congress, not with the Secretary.[18]

Even had the Secretary of War possessed real control over the bureaus, he would have been unable to exercise it. There was no coordinating nor supervisory body extant to assist him and his office staff. Neither was there an agency able or charged with the responsibility to assist the Secretary through long-term planning.[19] In addition, if these conditions were not discouraging enough for the Secretary, he had a competitor for the role of directing the Army in the person of the Commanding General of the Army.

Created by Secretary of War John C. Calhoun in 1821, the position of Commanding General of the Army had long been a frustrating one to the senior Army officer. While in Army regulations the division of responsibility between the Secretary and the Commanding General seemed clear, in practice it was not. All orders and instructions from the President or the Secretary of War relating to military operations, control, or discipline were to be issued, according to regulation, through the Commanding General. The Secretary of War, on the other hand, was to conduct the fiscal affairs of the Army through the several staff bureaus. With resource allocation and fiscal authority resting elsewhere, the Commanding General, despite his title and the implementing regulation, had no real command authority over either the bureaus or the subordinate territorial commands.[20] Commanding General William T. Sherman sized up the situation to his successor in 1883 as, "the President commands, the Secretary of War commands, and the real General is a mere figurehead."[21]

In sum, the organization of the War Department was seriously flawed in at least three ways. Neither the Secretary of War nor the Commanding General of the Army had real authority over the bureaus; there were no means by which the activities of the bureaus could be supervised or coordinated; and there was no provision for long-term planning. Moreover, the Secretary of War and the Commanding General were rivals. In Washington there was no *Chef des Generalstabes*, no *Grosse Generalstab*, no *Kriegsakademie*. Nor was there a War Ministry capable of central administration of the Army. In the field there was no *Truppengeneralstab* nor General Staff Corps. In 1887 the Commanding General of the Division of the Atlantic, John M. Schofield, put it bluntly: "It is self-evident that military operations cannot possibly be conducted with success under such a system."[22] But with no threatening neighbors, and with Britain looking with increased concern to the security of its global empire, there were very few who cared—even within the

Army. There was no compelling reason to care. The United States was a most fortunate nation indeed.

A Changing America

Fortunate as the United States may have been from the perspective of national security, fundamental changes were taking place in America nonetheless, changes that were unsettling, stressful, and at times violent. In his last annual report as Commanding General in 1883, Sherman announced, "I now regard the Indians as substantially eliminated from the problems of the army." This condition he attributed not just to past work of the Army, but to immigration, occupation of land by farmers and miners, and particularly to the railroad, both symbol and engine of the industrial revolution.[23]

Although the industrial revolution had profound long-term effects upon America's Army, its immediate consequence for the post-Civil War Army was minor. Industrial strife periodically called the Army away from its frontier and fortress garrisons to establish order where local authority and militia had either failed to do so or were not trusted to do so. In 1877 the Army was employed in the great railroad strike; in 1892, 1894, and 1899 in the mine strikes in Idaho; and in 1894 in diverting the so-called "industrial armies" from seizing railroad property in the west. The major commitment of 1894, however, was the Pullman strike, which for two months required troops from every military department west of the Mississippi except the Department of Texas.[24] These were major commitments for the small and dispersed Army, commitments that were sometimes used as the rationale for regular Army expansion.[25] The rationale was not convincing; instead, labor strife sparked renewed interest in the long-neglected militia, now beginning to call itself a "national guard." Organizing itself politically to enhance its prospects with Congress, the National Guard eventually was to become, in the minds of some regular Army as well as militia officers, a competitive military system.[26]

The Army, with meager funds for procurement, was not able to share in any major way in the technological progress of the late nineteenth century. It was aware of the impact of that progress, however. The appearance of steam-powered, armor-protected, sea-keeping warships mounting breech-loading, rifled guns caused great concern for harbor defense. The masonry forts of the pre-Civil War era became as obsolete as the Civil War ordnance they contained. Major expenditures and concentrated effort were required if America's ports were to be defended. That was the only visible mission remaining, and Army leadership was eager to give the problem attention. The Congress was less eager.[27]

The expansion of American industry in the post-Civil War period would by the beginning of the twentieth century provide the United States with the industrial base of a world power. It would also result in the development of new instruments and methods that could plan for, organize, and control enterprises of immense scale. A managerial revolution was an integral part of America's industrial revolution. But the Army did not share immediately in this revolution, either. The efficiency of the management of the great industrial enterprises, however, was not lost on those officers, administrators, and congressmen who one day were to become truly interested in reforming the administration of the War Department and the Army.[28]

Another change, or perhaps a manifestation of change, in American society in the last several decades of the nineteenth century was the phenomenon of "professionalization." This phenomenon is more easily recognized and described than defined and explained, though sociologists have not been reluctant to attempt both definition and explanation. Evidence of a "professional" includes expertise in a specific, reasonably well-defined body of knowledge, service or activity, and the banding together of those who share this expertise, often into formally organized "professional associations." Entrance into the "profession" is the prerogative of the association; and the conduct of its members is guided by some formal or informal, or at least widely understood, statement of desirable behavior or "code of ethics," violation of which brings sanction. Two additional evidences of a professional are an effort to gain public recognition of the "profession," to win legitimacy, and the impulse to improve professional "standards" through formal education and training, and through the exchange of knowledge and information using symposia, seminars, and publications.[29] "Professionalizing" took a firm hold in the United States as it approached the twentieth century. In this the officer corps of the Army did share.

In 1878 the Army established examinations as a means of controlling the direct commissioning of officers from civil life. In 1882 mandatory retirement at age sixty-four was instituted, and in the next decade reports on how well individual officers performed their duties were initiated. Through these three measures it was believed, or hoped, that the effectiveness of the officer corps would be improved. Following the lead of the Navy, and the British, the Military Service Institution was founded in 1879, publishing a journal and conducting colloquia where ideas and concepts on professional matters were presented, critiqued, and argued. During this period schools for the post-commissioning training of officers also began to appear. The "professionalizing" of the Army's officer corps was just beginning, however. The virtue of continuing professional education for officers was not yet widely accepted. The graduate schools and doctoral programs on the German model that were appearing for other professions were not yet available to the military profession.[30]

The effects of the industrialization of the United States would extend eventually beyond domestic problems and policies. The increasing productivity of American industry (and agriculture) would raise concern over American access to overseas markets. That concern in turn would contribute to the growing realization that the United States was, will it or not, part of an international system and that it must interact with other powers. In the final analysis, it was America's position in that system that would determine the usefulness, and the degree of excellence required, of its military power.

The Changing International Scene

The international system of which the United States was becoming an often-unrecognized part was undergoing fundamental change in the last two decades of the nineteenth century. Central to American security since the colonial period had been the capability of Great Britain to control the Atlantic. From the American viewpoint there were three facets to British control: it constituted a British threat to the United States and to the Western Hemisphere; it afforded protection from other European powers; and it acted as a restraint on American freedom of action in the Caribbean. In response to the threat of British seapower, the United States had with varying degrees of attention or neglect followed a security policy that combined coastal defense with retaliation. Coastal defense was to be provided by a Navy designed for that purpose, backed up by fixed harbor fortifications. Retaliation encompassed a capability to attack and cripple British commerce on the high seas in the event of war. Probably with more effect, it also involved holding Canada hostage to the military potential of the United States.[31]

Britain's ability to control the Atlantic, to act as both threat and protector, was determined by the condition of the balance of military power on the European continent and the condition of the balance of naval power between Britain and some possible combination of hostile European states. The balance on the Continent in the late nineteenth century was changing from the flexible and shifting systems associated with the names of Metternich and Bismarck into inflexible blocs underwritten by formal military alliances. The Prussian defeats of Austria and then France, followed by the formation of the German Empire in 1871, had created a new central European power with a strength comparable to that of the flanking powers, France and Russia. Moreover, the Triple Alliance negotiated by Bismarck with Austria and Italy in 1882 became, after the Iron Chancellor's departure in 1890, a bedrock of European diplomacy. In response to the Triple Alliance, republican France

11

and tsarist Russia drew closer together. In 1894 a positive military alliance was arranged, providing for mutual support against Germany.[32]

The rise of a powerful Germany had also influenced France and Russia to direct their expansionist ambitions outside of Europe; Russia toward central Asia and the Far East, France toward an overseas empire extending from the Mediterranean to Africa and on to Indochina. Those moves threatened British imperial interests in the Mediterranean, on the Afghanistan approach to India, and in the Far East. Isolated from Europe partially by design and partially by neglect, its Empire threatened by the growing concert between France and Russia and their naval construction programs, Britain turned to its traditional and proven instrument, the Royal Navy.[33]

With the Naval Defence Act of 1889, Britain, aiming specifically at France and Russia, formally adopted the "two-power standard" for naval construction. With Germany joining in overseas colonialism, the specter of a French-Russian-German coalition began to haunt British navalists. By 1893 they were pressing for a three-power standard. Both the absolute growth of British naval power and its decline relative to its commitments and competition influenced American foreign and naval policy. The absolute growth provided a rationale for reviving the United States Navy. The relative decline loosened the restraint on American freedom of action in the Caribbean.[34]

The foreign policy of the United States in the last two decades of the nineteenth century was an amalgam of reaction to European colonialism and British naval power and America's own growing tendencies toward overseas expansion. Britain remained the central concern. From the Civil War until the 1890s, British-American disputes had been limited to the problems of access to the northeast Canadian fisheries and Canadian activities in the sealing grounds of the Bering Sea. But in the 1890s, British activity in Latin America, particularly in the Caribbean, caused alarm. The United States was habitually suspicious of British motives in Latin America. In 1881 Secretary of State Blaine had categorized the War of the Pacific as an "English War" against Peru. Similarly, in 1893 Britain was portrayed as the culprit in a monarchist revolt against the Brazilian republic.[35]

The Royal Navy's landing of marines during the "Corinto Affair" dispute with Nicaragua in early 1895 set the stage for a more serious confrontation with the United States later that year when President Cleveland intervened in the British-Venezuelan squabble over the boundary between Venezuela and British Guiana. It was then that Secretary of State Olney, in his famous note, chose to inform Britain that "the United States is practically sovereign on this continent, and its fiat is law." As undiplomatic as Olney may have been, his statement reflected a great deal of truth. The globally stretched Royal Navy had missions elsewhere more critical to British interests. By conceding to American demands for arbitration, Britain tacitly accepted American hegemony in the Caribbean. The United States on its part replaced Great Britain in the role of protector of the Caribbean. With greater freedom of action had come increased responsibility.[36]

American sensitivity to events in the Caribbean was in large measure the result of a long-held interest in an isthmian canal under American control. Generally recognizing that such control required supremacy over the sea approaches to the isthmus, American statesmen were concerned with the Caribbean republics astride and flanking the eastern approach. They were also concerned with the status of Hawaii, strategically located on the Pacific approach. Secretary of State Daniel Webster had argued the strategic importance of Hawaii as early as 1851. In 1873 Major General John M. Schofield, then Commanding General of the Division of the Pacific, was sent to Hawaii to locate a defensible naval base. As a result of his recommendation that the government obtain the "Pearl River Harbor," the United States initially acquired coaling station rights to that place and then, in 1887, exclusive rights .[37]

In Hawaii the United States again came into conflict with British interests and also with those of the new Asiatic power, Japan. Beginning in 1886 Hawaii had imported Japanese labor to the extent that within ten years Japanese constituted 22 percent of the population. In 1893 when, at the behest of the American minister, US warships and Marines assisted a revolt against the Hawaiian monarchy (an action soon disavowed by the incoming Cleveland administration), both Britain and Japan dispatched warships to Honolulu. Disputes between the Republic of Hawaii and Japan over immigration policy brought Japanese warships to Honolulu again in 1897. By that date Britain was interposing no objection to American annexation of the Islands.[38]

A New American Strategy

Despite expressions ranging from concern to outrage, American statesmen of the late nineteenth century did not really see imminent danger to the security of the United States in British interests in the Caribbean and Hawaii nor in the rejuvenation of the Royal Navy. On this such diverse personages as General Phil Sheridan and Carl Schurz could agree.[39] There was true concern, however, that the spread of European colonialism would jeopardize access to foreign markets. Ideas and ambitions underlying the view that America should emulate European expansionism often reinforced such concerns.[40] Reflecting both the concerns and the ambitions was the naval construction program begun with hesitation in the Garfield and Arthur administrations but receiving its greatest impetus from the powerful leadership of President Harrison's Secretary of the Navy, Benjamin F. Tracy. Between 1885 and 1900 the

United States Navy was to grow in world rank from twelfth to third.[41]

Concurrently with fleet construction a new naval strategy was taking hold within the Navy and among its civilian supporters. American naval policy heretofore had stressed two missions: coast defense and commerce raiding. In peacetime the cruisers that in war were to attack an enemy's maritime trade were dispersed about the globe showing the flag and offering protection to perceived American interests overseas. The Army shared the coast defense role. Protection of harbors by fortress artillery and naval monitors in theory freed the cruisers to range afar and to destroy enemy commerce. Moreover, harbor defenses would protect coastal cities from raids and divert enemy landings to less vital areas, there to be contained and disposed of by the militia.[42]

The new naval strategy, the product of many minds but notably that of Commodore Stephen B. Luce, was codified and popularized in the last decade of the century primarily by Captain Alfred Thayer Mahan. The new theory saw the Navy as an offensive instrument emphasizing a sea-keeping fleet of battleships that would defend the United States by intercepting and destroying on the high seas its true object, the enemy's fleet. To those of this school the ultimate purpose of a navy was to gain control of the seas. Specifically, for the American fleet, it was to control those seas that provided approach to the prospective isthmian canal.[43]

The new naval policy did not markedly alter the purpose of fortress artillery, although according to the theory priority for protection had to be given to the naval operating bases that provided the fleet its sanctuaries. The Navy was to become less interested in coast defense, devoting its resources instead to strengthening the deep-water fleet. Congressional supporters of the new policy termed the first battleships "sea-going coastal" to satisfy those colleagues who were reluctant to embrace the new concept.[44]

The Army accepted the new naval strategy and the passive role allotted it. There is no evidence that Army officers made any intellectual contribution to the theory. They apparently saw their problem solely as one of modernizing harbor defenses to meet the technological advances in ship design and naval ordnance. A complicating problem was the absence of American manufacturers capable of fabricating modern artillery. This situation led to the establishment of an Army and Navy Gun Foundry Board in 1883. Two years later a second joint body with a more comprehensive charter was formed under the chairmanship of Secretary of War William C. Endicott. The Endicott Board recommended a highly ambitious program to construct modern fortifications at twenty-seven ports, including three on the Great Lakes.[45]

In 1888, two years after the Endicott Board's report was submitted, Congress took its first action. It established within the Army a Board of Ordnance and Fortification to be headed by the Commanding General of the Army, then Major General Schofield. This body was to oversee implementation of the Endicott recommendations. Though some work was started, the Endicott program remained largely on paper because of limited appropriations. Despite the slow progress in giving substance to harbor defense, however, it became a primary concern of the Army, perhaps an obsession. Mahan's theory in even its most grandiose form, calling for naval operating bases overseas, did not include a strategically mobile army prepared and trained for overseas expeditions.[46]

On its part the Army had goals much less ambitious than those of the Navy. From the time it became apparent that the Indian mission was fading in significance, the War Department consistently attempted to concentrate its frontier constabulary into fewer but larger garrisons. The motives for the recommended concentration, however, had little to do with the strategy of the Mahan or any other school. The pragmatic aim was simply to promote economy and efficiency and to improve morale and discipline. Despite local oppositions that resisted losing "their" Army post, the War Department enjoyed some success in this endeavor. By 1895 the number of posts had been reduced to 77 from the 119 of 1885. Nonetheless, as Walter Millis has assessed the situation on the eve of the Spanish-American War "the truest symbol of American military policy was still the heavy, immovable and purely defensive seacoast gun."[47]

But concentration of the frontier force contained the seeds of converting the constabulary into a true field army, and there were individual Army officers who were looking beyond the Indian fighting and beyond the passive role of harbor defense. Their stress was on war as an inevitable historical phenomenon for which the nation should be prepared.[48] Their intellectual effort focused not on *why* and *where* national policy might require an army, but on *how* one might be raised if required. Because the emphasis was on structure rather than strategy, discussion of what was termed "military policy" often degenerated into an emotional dialogue between those who favored an "expansible" regular army and those who held that a citizen army of mobilized militia was the preferred and only true American way. Both sides built their rationale more on the Civil War mobilization experience than on future requirements. Without consensus on the future mission of the Army, there was no possible resolution of the debate.[49]

Despite the lack of consensus on future roles and missions and despite the dispersal of much of the strength of the officer corps throughout the western states and territories, a significant portion of the officer corps appears to have been fully aware of the currents of change both within and outside the United States. As Walter Millis described it, this was a "time whose extraordinary achievement it was to combine a frontier conquest with an industrial revolution."[50] The Army's officer corps was

15

a major participant in the frontier conquest. It had experienced at first hand the stresses and resulting violence brought about by both the closing of the frontier and the industrialization of America. A not inarticulate segment of the officer corps sensed the increasing possibility of international conflict stemming from the competitions for markets, trade, and colonies. They believed, as did many of their countrymen of the era, in the virtues of science, technology, and expertness.

These officers were well within the mainstream of late-nineteenth-century American thought when they began to call for reform, for professionalism and all that concept implied.[51] Primarily but not exclusively a product of post-Civil War service, these thoughtful officers were encouraged and supported by Commanding General Sherman and later by Commanding General Schofield. An early and still tentative push in the direction of reform and professionalism was the founding and nurturing of modest institutions for the study of what was rather grandly called "military art and science."

NOTES

1. Walter Gorlitz, *The German General Staff 1657-1945*, trans. Brian Battershaw (New York: Praeger, 1953), 20, 22, 30.
2. Ibid., 20-21.
3. Hubert Rosinski, *The German Army* (Washington: The Infantry Journal Press, 1944), 71-73. Colonel T. N. Dupuy, USA Ret., *A Genius for War: The German Army and General Staff, 1807-1945* (Englewood Cliffs, N.J.: Prentice-Hall, 1977), 24, 37, 39. Quote from Dupuy.
4. Gorlitz, *German General Staff*, 57, 59-60. Dupuy, *Genius for War*, 51.
5. Dupuy, *Genius for War*, 64-65, 92. For the impact of railroads see Theodore Ropp, *War in the Modern World*, new rev. ed. (New York: Collier Books, 1959), 143-44.
6. Gordon A. Craig, *The Politics of the Prussian Army, 1640-1945* (New York: Oxford University Press, 1956), 45. Rosinski, *German Army*, 164. Gorlitz, *German General Staff*, 97.
7. Dupuy, *Genius for War*, 113-14.
8. Dallas D. Irvine, "The Origins of Capital Staffs," *The Journal of Modern History* X (June 1938): 171-73.
9. Ibid., 177-78.
10. Gorlitz, *German General Staff*, 49. Dupuy, *Genius for War*, 115. Ropp, *War*, 177.
11. Dupuy, *Genius for War*, 46.
12. For an excellent analogy see Ropp, *War*, 138.
13. Ibid., 47-48.
14. The legislative enactments governing the strength of the Army are cited in Frederick L. Huidekoper, *The Military Unpreparedness of the United States* (New York: Macmillan, 1916), 151.
15. Arthur P. Wade, "The Military Command Structure: The Great Plains, 1853-1891," *Journal of the West* XV (July 1976): 5-21. Russell P. Weigley, *Towards an American Army: Military Thought from Washington to Marshall* (New York: Columbia University Press, 1962), 137.
16. James A. Huston, *The Sinews of War: Army Logistics, 1775-1953* (Washington: Office of the Chief of Military History, United States Army, 1966), 268.
17. James E. Hewes, Jr., *From Root to McNamara: Army Organization and Administration, 1900-1963* (Washington: Center of Military History, United States Army, 1975), 4.
18. Leonard D. White, *The Republican Era 1869-1901: A Study in Administrative History* (New York: Macmillan, 1958), 142-43.
19. Ibid., 144.

20. William B. Skelton, "The Commanding General and the Problem of Command in the United States Army, 1821-1841," *Military Affairs* XXXIV (December 1970): 117-22. Hewes, *Root to McNamara*, 4-5.
21. Letter, Sherman to Sheridan, November 17, 1883, cited in Richard A. Andrews, *Years of Frustration: William T. Sherman, the Army and Reform, 1869-1883* (Ann Arbor, Mich.: University Microfilms, 1968), 293.
22. "Report of Major-General Schofield, Headquarters, Division of the Atlantic, September 20, 1887," in *Report of the Lieutenant-General of the Army to the Secretary of War, 1887* (Washington: GPO, 1887), 49.
23. *Annual Report of the General of the Army to The Secretary of War for the Year 1883* (Washington: GPO, 1883), 5-6.
24. Barton Hacker, "The United States Army as a National Police Force: The Federal Policing of Labor Disputes, 1877-1898," *Military Affairs* XXXIII (1970): 256-61. Jerry M. Cooper, *The Army and Civil Disorder: Federal Military Intervention in Labor Disputes, 1877-1900* (Westport, Ct.: Greenwood Press, 1980), 45-66, 101-14, 144-96.
25. For example, see Lieutenant Colonel Henry C. Egbert, "Is an Increase in the Regular Army Necessary?" *United Service* VI (1896): 380-82, and Major George Wilson, "The Army: Its Employment in Time of Peace and the Necessity for its Increase," *Journal of the Military Service Institution of the United States* (Hereafter *JMSI*) XVIII (1896): 483.
26. Weigley, *Towards an American Army*, 146. For an argument that the National Guard was the nation's true instrument of defense see J. C. Kelton, "Requirements for National Defense," *The Forum* VIII (1889): 317-25. The National Guard Association was founded in 1879. See also Cooper, *Army and Civil Disorder*, 215-17, 256-57.
27. Emmanuel R. Lewis, *Seacoast Fortifications of the United States: An Introductory History* (Washington: Smithsonian Institution Press, 1970), 66-76. Weigley, *Towards an American Army*, 140-42.
28. Paul Y. Hammond, *Organizing for Defense: The American Military Establishment in the Twentieth Century* (Princeton: Princeton University Press, 1961), 23-24.
29. On professionalism see Wilbert E. Moore, *The Professions: Roles and Rules* (New York: Russell Sage Foundation, 1970), 3-20. On professionalization see H. L. Wilensky, "The Professionalization of Everyone?" *American Journal of Sociology* LXX (September 1964): 137-58.
30. John M. Schofield in the inaugural address to the Military Service Institution held the new institution to be a "scientific association" and that "military science should be a subject of never-ceasing and most diligent study," *JMSI* I (1880): 1. On military professionalization see Allan R. Millett, *Military Professionalism and Officership in America* (Columbus: Ohio State University Press, 1977) and Samuel P. Huntington, *The Soldier and the State: The Theory and Politics of Civil-Military Relations* (Cambridge: Belknap Press, 1957), 7-79, 222-82. On naval professionalism see Ronald Spector, "The Triumph of Professional Ideology: The United States Navy in the 1890's" in *In Peace and War: Interpretations of American Naval History, 1775-1978*, Kenneth J. Hagan, ed. (Westport, Ct.: Greenwood Press, 1978), 174-85. On the growth of graduate education, see Robert L. Church and Michael W. Sedlack, *Education in the United States: An Interpretive History* (New York: The Free Press, 1976), 227-30, 242-46.
31. Walter Millis, *Arms and Men: A Study in American Military History* (New York: Putnam, 1956), 147-48. Henry Cabot Lodge expressed the hostage idea well in 1895: "War with Britain . . . would mean the end of the British Empire in North America." John A. Garraty, *Henry Cabot Lodge* (New York: A. A. Knopf, 1953), 154.
32. Laurence Lafore, *The Long Fuse: An Interpretation of the Origins of World War I* (Philadelphia: Lippencott, 2nd ed., 1971), 96-104.
33. Rene Albrecht-Carre, *A Diplomatic History of Europe Since the Congress of Vienna* (New York: Harper & Row, rev. ed., 1973), 186-92. Arthur J. Marder, *The Anatomy of British Sea Power: A History of British Naval Policy in the Pre-Dreadnought Era, 1880-1905* (New York: A. A. Knopf, 1940), 121-22.
34. Ibid., 105-06, 131, 146, 162-64, 259. Millis, *Arms and Men*, 157. Charles S. Campbell, *The Transformation of American Foreign Relations, 1865-1900* (New York: Harper & Row, 1976), 221.

35. Ibid., 60, 122-27, 133-36, for a discussion of the American drift toward expansionism during the Harrison administration. David M. Pletcher, *The Awkward Years: American Foreign Policy under Garfield and Arthur* (Columbia, Mo.: University of Missouri, 1962), 356, concludes that imperialism germinated even before the first Cleveland administration. Herbert Millington, *American Diplomacy and the War of the Pacific* (New York: Columbia University Press, 1948), 42. Walter LaFeber, "American Depression Diplomacy and the Brazilian Revolution, 1893-1894," *Hispanic American Historical Review* XL (February 1960): 108, 112, 116.

36. Nelson M. Blake, "Background of Cleveland's Venezuelan Policy," *American Historical Review* XLVII (January 1942): 263. Walter LaFeber, "The Background of Cleveland's Venezuelan Policy: A Reinterpretation," *American Historical Review* LXVI (July 1961): 947. Marder, *Anatomy*, 255. Campbell, *The Transformation*, 221, 335.

37. William R. Adams, "Strategy, Diplomacy, and Isthmian Canal Security, 1880-1917," (unpublished Ph.D. dissertation, Florida State University, 1974), 9-25, 32-39. Hugh B. Hammett, "The Cleveland Administration and Anglo-American Naval Friction in Hawaii, 1893-1894," *Military Affairs* XL (February 1976): 28. Letter, Major General J. M. Schofield and Bvt. Brigadier General B. S. Alexander to Secretary of War Belknap, 8 May 1873, reprinted in "Documents," *American Historical Review* XXX (April 1925): 560-65.

38. Thomas A. Bailey, "Japan's Protest Against the Annexation of Hawaii," *Journal of Modern History* III (March 1931): 46-48. Hammett, "Naval Friction," 28-29.

39. "It would require more than a million and a half men to make campaign upon land against us. It would demand a large part of the shipping of all Europe." *Annual Report of the Lieutenant-General of the Army to the Secretary of War* (Washington: GPO, 1884), 7. "We are the only [great nation] that is not in any of its parts threatened." Carl Schurz, "Manifest Destiny," *Harper's New Monthly Magazine* LXXXVII (October 1893): 743.

40. A good synthesis of this type of rationale is Alfred Thayer Mahan, "The United States Looking Outward," *Atlantic Monthly* LXVI (December 1890): 816-24.

41. Robert Seager, "Ten Years Before Mahan: The Unofficial Case for the New Navy, 1880-1890," *Mississippi Valley Historical Review* XL (December 1953): 502. Seager believes the most effective argument for naval expansion in the eighties was an exaggerated concern as to the vulnerability of the American coastline. Seager, *Alfred Thayer Mahan: The Man and His Letters* (Annapolis: Naval Institute Press, 1977), 142. On Tracy as Secretary of the Navy see Benjamin F. Cooling, *Benjamin Franklin Tracy: Father of the Modern American Fighting Navy* (Hamden, Ct.: Archon Books, 1973), 62-149.

42. Kenneth J. Hagan, *American Gunboat Diplomacy and the Old Navy, 1877-1889* (Westport, Ct.: Greenwood, 1973), 7-10.

43. John A. S. Grenville and George B. Young, *Politics, Strategy, and American Diplomacy: Studies in Foreign Policy, 1873-1917* (New Haven: Yale University Press, 1966), 32-38. Alfred Thayer Mahan, "The Isthmus and Sea Power," *Atlantic Monthly* LXXII (October 1893): 459-72.

44. Cooling, *Tracy*, 87.

45. U.S. Congress, 49th Congress, 1st Session, House Document No. 49: Report dated January 23, 1886 (hereafter *Endicott Report*).

46. Weigley, *Towards an American Army*, 140. In a specific plan in the event of war with Britain, Mahan did envision a major overseas movement by the Army directed at Halifax. Kenneth Bourne and Carl Boyd, "Captain Mahan's 'War' with Great Britain," *United States Naval Institute Proceedings* (hereafter *USNIP*) XCIV (1968): 71-78.

47. Figures from "Report of the Inspector-General, September 17, 1885" in *Report of the Lieutenant-General of the Army to the Secretary of War, 1885* (Washington: GPO, 1885), 53. "Report of the Inspector-General, September 1895," in *Report of the Major-General of the Army to the Secretary of War 1895* (Washington: GPO, 1895), 49. Superb plates showing the location of posts and distribution of troops are in Francis P. Prucha, *A Guide to Military Posts of the United States, 1789-1895* (Madison: The State Historical Society of Wisconsin, 1964). For other efforts to improve morale and discipline see Jack D. Foner, *The American Soldier Between Two Wars: Army Life and*

Reforms, 1865-1898 (New York: Humanities Press, 1970). Millis, *Arms and Men*, 167.

48. For example, see Captain Arthur Williams, "Readiness for War," *JMSI* XXI (September 1897): 229-30.

49. See the discussion of Emory Upton and John A. Logan in Weigley, *Towards an American Army*, 100-36. Also Major William C. Sanger, "An Army Organization Best Adapted to a Republican Form of Government which will Result in an Effective Force," *JMSI* XIV (November 1893): 1145.

50. Walter Millis, *The Martial Spirit: A Study of Our War with Spain* (New York: Houghton Mifflin, 1931), 3.

51. In his *Soldier and the State* (1957), Samuel Huntington put forth the thesis that military professionalism was a result of the isolation of the officer corps from society. This thesis has been convincingly disputed in John M. Gates, "The Alleged Isolation of U.S. Army Officers in the Late 19th Century," *Parameters: Journal of the U.S. Army War College* X (September 1980): 32-45, and James L. Abrahamson, *American Arms for a New Century: The Making of a Great Military Power* (New York: Free Press, 1981), 130-35.

Monroe, Newport and Leavenworth

In 1823 John Quincy Adams, Secretary of State, persuaded the President to announce what became a basic tenet of United States foreign policy, the Monroe Doctrine. The next year John C. Calhoun, Secretary of War, established at Old Point Comfort, Virginia, a school for artillery officers on the post of Fortress Monroe. That the first American war school beyond the cadet academy at West Point was established at approximately the same time as an ambitious and somewhat belligerent foreign policy was announced may have been coincidence. But it also may have been a reflection of the understanding of the statesmen of that era of the relationship between policy and power. Calhoun's school continued with periodic interruptions until the Civil War forced it to close. In 1867 General Ulysses S. Grant, Commanding General of the Army, reestablished the school. Its reopening was a first step in a three-decade-long process of tentative military professionalizing carried forth by Grant's successors, Sherman, Sheridan, and Schofield.

The Artillery School and Emory Upton

The post-Civil War Artillery School provided junior officers of the five United States Army artillery regiments a course of instruction with the declared purpose of training them in the techniques of their arm. The course was conducted with skill and imagination and appears to have accomplished well its mission of producing competent artillerists. In 1875 the course length was increased from one to two years. The commandant, Colonel and Brevet Major General George W. Getty, and his faculty did not confine themselves thereafter to training technicians. Within the first decade after reestablishment the school organization included not only a "Department of Artillery," but also a "Department of Engineering," a "Department of Military Law and Administration," and a "Department of Military Art and Science, Military History and Geography." In March 1877 the latter three departments were placed

21

under the supervision of Emory Upton, Lieutenant Colonel of the Fourth Artillery.[1]

Upton arrived at Fort Monroe with a well-deserved reputation as both combat leader and military theoretician. An 1861 graduate of West Point, Upton had commanded during the Civil War an artillery battery and brigade; an infantry regiment, brigade, and division; and a cavalry division. He had been twice wounded and when the war ended was a twenty-six-year-old major general of volunteers. In late 1865 and early 1866, while commanding the military district of Colorado from Denver, Upton produced the work that first established him as a military intellectual. Upton had set out to create a new formal tactical system for infantry. Reverting to a lieutenant colonelcy in the regular Army, Upton lost his western command in April 1866 and spent the remainder of that year and much of 1867 demonstrating and defending his tactical system before a board of officers at West Point. By August Upton had convinced the board. The War Department officially adopted Upton's infantry system.[2]

In July 1870, William Tecumseh Sherman, then Commanding General of the Army, appointed Upton commandant of cadets at West Point, a position he was to hold for the next five years. At Upton's instigation, Sherman formed a board of officers at West Point in 1873 to assimilate the new infantry tactics into the artillery and cavalry. He appointed Upton the chairman. In 1873 also a revised edition of *Infantry Tactics* appeared and in 1874, without credit line, came the text on cavalry tactics. The following year, again without credit line, the text on artillery tactics was published. Upton enhanced his reputation further through his contributions to the influential *Army and Navy Journal*, for which he acted as tactical editor.[3]

During the year before he reported to the Artillery School, Upton traveled to Asia and Europe to study the military systems of selected nations. General Sherman apparently was primarily interested in Britain's Indian Army, believing that the United States Army was already well enough acquainted with the European military systems. Secretary of War William W. Belknap, on the other hand, directed Upton to pay particular attention to the German schools established "for the instruction of officers, in strategy, grand tactics, applied tactics, and the higher duties in the art of war."[4] From Berlin in October 1876 Upton reported that he had "been permitted to see the military schools and had learned much of the military system of Germany." Ideas of reform were beginning to take shape in his thoughts. He wrote, "We cannot maintain a great army in peace, but we can provide a scheme for officering a large force in time of war, and such a scheme is deserving of study."[5]

Upton returned to the United States in the fall of 1876. He spent most of the winter preparing his formal report for General Sherman, a report he had decided could serve as a vehicle for reform. As a first move in what would become a campaign, and with Sherman's encouragement, Upton published in February extracts of a letter from himself to Sherman. There he outlined the evolving features of the expansible army scheme with which his name would be historically associated. In order to prepare officers for the high command and staff positions created by wartime expansion, Upton urged that a "war school" be established at Fort Leavenworth. Only officers with two years of service in the line would be admitted to the school. There they would study "the great campaigns and all the details of war."[6]

At that stage in the preparation of his proposed work on the armies of Asia and Europe, Upton considered including a history of the military policy of the United States, emphasizing what in his view were its historical failings. Sherman discouraged the idea, however, and Upton decided to save the review of United States military policy for a later work. The last chapter of his report on foreign armies did include a series of recommendations for improvement of the United States Army, but without detailed historical support.[7] In December his report was published.

Upton's *Armies of Asia and Europe* admiringly describes the postgraduate military education systems of Europe, particularly that of Prussia. The thrust of his treatment of the European schools is that war is a distinct body of knowledge that can be taught and learned in an academic environment. He pointed out that in Europe the theory was universal that "the art of war should be studied only after an officer has reached full manhood." In accord with that theory, postgraduate institutions had been established "where meritorious officers may study strategy, grand tactics, and all the science of war." Upton then commended the curriculum of the Artillery School at Fort Monroe, offering the opinion that lengthening the course to two years and thereby making time available to devote to "history, strategy, law, and the art of war [would] obviate, as far as the artillery is concerned, any necessity for a war academy." He then proposed a like school for infantry officers at Atlanta and one for cavalry officers at Fort Leavenworth.[8] If Upton was not yet clear in his own mind as to the specifics of substance and method, as a senior supervisor at the Artillery School he had the opportunity to experiment.

Upton took up his duties at Fort Monroe while still working on the *Armies of Asia and Europe*. The book did not lessen his enthusiasm for duty at the school, particularly for supervising the division of the Department of Military Art responsible for instruction in strategy and grand tactics. A month after his arrival at Fort Monroe, Upton wrote,

> In the department of strategy and grand tactics I shall hope to repay the Government all of the expense incurred in sending me

abroad. . . . [We] have nothing to compare to the war academies of Europe, except the Artillery School, but here we have the opportunity to form a corps of officers who in any future contest may prove the chief reliance of the Government.[9]

Upton's rationale for higher military education of relatively junior officers in peacetime was to provide the professional leadership of an expanded wartime army. With Sherman's encouragement Upton's goal was to broaden the course at the Artillery School until it too could be considered a "war academy."

During Upton's first year at Fort Monroe, the class of 1878 was in its second year of the course. Two and one-half months of that academic year were allocated to the "Department of Military Art and Science, Military History and Geography." The instruction covered both general history and military history, the latter focusing on the handling of armies on campaign. The students recited from textbooks and received lectures from Upton and the department head, Captain John H. Calef. The lectures covered Civil War campaigns and were intended to illustrate "the great principles of warfare." Each student was required to submit an original essay. Of the essay topics chosen by the twenty-one students, ten involved "strategic and tactical deductions" from various Civil War campaigns. Students made similar deductions from four European campaigns (Marlborough, Frederick the Great, the Eckmuhl campaign, the Austro-Prussian War of 1866) and from Greene's Carolina campaigns of the Revolutionary War. There was one study of "ancient and modern tactics," one on the use of cavalry during the Civil War, and another on "the extent and value of the cooperation of the Navy during the Civil War." One on the "Use and Influence of the Telegraph and Railroads in Modern War" demonstrated recognition of the importance of technological progress. Upton's own ongoing analysis of American military policy may have been assisted by two essays: "The War of 1812 and Causes for its Protraction" and "Organization and Recruitment of the Armies of the Revolution and Their Influence on the Conduct of the War."[10] Certainly Getty, Upton, and Calef were carrying these artillery subalterns far beyond techniques of gunnery.

The significance of the Artillery School of Getty and Upton was greater, however, than that of broadening the military horizons of a few artillery lieutenants and preparing them for higher wartime duties. Upton's reputation brought attention and prestige to the institution. The active support of Sherman, a great captain in his own right, muted criticism stemming from the belief that the only adequate school of war is war itself, and it encouraged acceptance of the European theory of war as a distinct body of knowledge from which principles could be derived. By the 1880s the Artillery School at Fort Monroe had become the American model for professional military education. Upon this model two additional institutions would be built, institutions which were to play major roles in the development of American military thought: the Infantry and Cavalry School at Fort Leavenworth and the Naval War College at Newport, Rhode Island.

Stephen B. Luce and the Naval War College

The man most responsible for the founding of the Naval War College was its first president, Commodore Stephen B. Luce. On January 5, 1865, Luce was commanding the monitor *Pontiac* participating in the blockade of Charleston. On that date he was ordered to report to the headquarters of General William T. Sherman at Savannah. Sherman had completed his march to the sea and was preparing to attack north into the Carolinas. *Pontiac* was to support the Army's crossing of the Savannah River. Luce commented later that observing Sherman planning the campaign and issuing instructions for the coming offensive was to have "the scales fall from my eyes . . . there were certain fundamental principles underlying military operations. . . . I learned there was such a thing as a military problem—and there was a way of solving it, or a way of learning whether it was susceptible to solution." Luce related this experience nearly forty years after the event while arguing for the establishment of a naval general staff. Invoking the name of the great Sherman strengthened his case. But seeing Sherman in battle and watching his systematic approach to command apparently did make a lasting impression on the naval officer.[11]

After Emory Upton's arrival at the Artillery School, Luce sought him out, perhaps at the suggestion of Sherman, perhaps at the suggestion of William C. Church, a mutual friend and publisher of the *Army and Navy Journal*. Luce made himself thoroughly familiar with the program of the Artillery School and corresponded with Upton until the latter's death in 1881. In 1877 Luce urged Secretary of the Navy Richard W. Thompson to send an officer abroad for a purpose similar to that for which Upton had traveled the previous year, "to study the systems of naval education in foreign countries with a view to establishing a postgraduate course." The officer was sent, but his report had no effect upon the Navy Department.[12]

By 1879 Luce had convinced Admiral of the Navy David D. Porter, the grand old man of the Navy, but one essentially powerless, of the need for higher naval education. Porter subsequently published an argument that the "art of war" is the study of a lifetime and that "the system of education in a naval or military service had much better be general than exclusive."[13] Four more years passed before Luce launched his successful campaign for the establishment of a naval war college. In an article entitled "War Schools" Luce reviewed in detail the 1882 report of General John C. Tidball, commandant of the Artillery School. He quoted with obvious admiration remarks that the course "was not limited to what is necessary for merely expert artillerists, but one which aims to qualify officers for any duty they may be called upon to perform, or for any position, however high in rank or command, they may aspire to in service." Luce called his readers' attention particularly to the program of the Department of Military Art and Science which Upton had formerly supervised. In conclusion Luce announced, "This is just what we need for the navy."[14] Luce, of course, was not influenced solely by Sherman, Upton, or the Artillery School. He was well aware of the progress in Great Britain in the systematizing and analyzing of naval history.[15]

In 1884, through Admiral of the Navy Porter, Luce obtained an audience with Secretary of the Navy William E. Chandler. After a long interview, Chandler became receptive and promised Luce a hearing before the chiefs of the line bureaus of the Navy. There he won the support of the chief of the powerful Bureau of Navigation, Commodore John G. Walker. In May of 1884 Chandler appointed a board of officers consisting of Luce as chairman and two other sympathetic officers to make recommendations pertaining to a naval war college. Not surprisingly, the Luce Board recommended "a place where our officers will not only be encouraged but required to study their proper profession: war." On October 6, 1884, Chandler ordered the college established, "an advanced course of professional study."[16] By then commander of the North Atlantic Squadron, Luce was detached from the fleet and appointed president.

Luce had his appointment, and the Navy provided as a facility a former alms house situated on Narragansett Bay, Rhode Island. Except for a theory as to what was to be done, Luce had little else with which to start his war college. His aim was to create a science of naval warfare. Believing that there were immutable principles of strategy as applicable to sea warfare as to land warfare, Luce theorized a "comparative method" for the study of naval science. In the study of military strategy, naval operations would be compared to military operations. In the study of naval history, present situations would be compared to historical situations.[17] Luce was describing a naval war college that was as much an institute for original research as it was a teaching institution.

His proposed method dictated the talent that he must have on his faculty. He must have a naval historian. Though not his first choice, Luce secured the services of Captain Alfred Thayer Mahan, then commanding the wooden sloop *Wachusett* off the coast of Peru. Mahan had no reputation either as theorist or as historian, but he had written *The Gulf and Inland Waters*, a narrative of Civil War naval operations. To complement the naval historian and to make the comparative method work, Luce sought a military strategist from the Army, "an officer learned in military science.''[18] The officer provided was First Lieutenant Tasker Howard Bliss, the adjutant of the Artillery School.

Tasker Bliss was hardly typical of the late-nineteenth-century American Army officer. Son of a Baptist pastor and Professor of Greek at the Baptist college at Lewisburg, Pennsylvania (later to become Bucknell University), Bliss developed early a taste for classical studies, an interest he maintained for the remainder of his life. A cadet at West Point while Upton was commandant, Bliss graduated in 1875. He attended the Artillery School the next year, then returned to West Point as an instructor in French and a lecturer on military science. In 1878 the superintendent of the Military Academy, General Schofield, had Lieutenant Bliss prepare lectures for the cadets on the ongoing Russian-Turkish War. Bliss found that he could not treat the war adequately without understanding the political background of the "Eastern Question," an understanding that Bliss felt required a reading knowledge of German and Russian, and so he set out to acquire that ability. Bliss's tour of duty at West Point ended in 1880. After duty with his regiment on the Pacific Coast, he returned to the Artillery School in 1883.[19]

When the first Naval War College class convened for its one-month session in September of 1885, Mahan had but recently returned from southern waters and had removed himself to the New York Public Library to prepare his lectures. Bliss delivered three lectures to that first class. The spectacle of a thirty-year-old Army lieutenant lecturing to naval officers was considered in some Navy circles as scandalous. Luce explained to his critics once again the comparative method and the essentiality of Bliss to its success.[20] At the close of the 1885 session Bliss was dispatched to Europe to collect information on the military schools of England, France, and Germany as "no proper textbooks on Military Science exist." As it had Upton ten years before, the *Kriegsakademie* in Berlin most impressed Bliss. During his investigations, Bliss's reports went both to Commodore Luce (who passed them on to Mahan in New York) and to the Adjutant General of the Army.[21]

When Bliss returned to Newport in 1886 for the second summer session, Luce had been reassigned to the fleet and Mahan was president. Indeed, at the time Mahan and Bliss constituted the entire permanently assigned faculty. The lack of faculty was but one of many obstacles the Naval War College had to overcome. Powerful and intense opposition to the institution existed within both the Congress and the Navy Department. It was questionable whether the college would survive. Bliss had departed Newport in 1888 and no sessions were convened in 1890, 1891 or 1893. Mahan and Luce, particularly the latter, lobbied energetically to win congressional sympathizers, making the War College something of a minor political issue. After Mahan was ordered to sea in 1893, his successor, Captain Henry Clay Taylor, initiated a public relations campaign to win support for the college. Lectures, addresses, newspaper interviews, and journal articles were all used in an attempt to gain acceptance of the institution and its purposes. But it was probably the growing national and international reputation of Mahan as a naval historian and philosopher, born of his published works on sea power, that was most instrumental in directing attention to the college and lending it prestige.[22]

Under Taylor's administration the length of the course was extended and fixed at four months. Approximately twenty students appeared for each annual session. A permanent staff was assigned. Lectures received less emphasis and a reading course was introduced that focused on the broad political and military aspects of naval warfare. But it was as an institute for original research rather than as a teaching institution that the Naval War College first began to exert influence. Beginning in 1893 a scheme known as the "main problem" provided the framework for each session. The main problem was a hypothetical war situation which required strategic analysis and solution by the staff and students.[23] Of even greater significance to the future role of the War College was the introduction of naval war games.

William McCarty Little, a resident of Newport when the Naval War College was founded, was a former naval officer who had been retired because of a physical disability. Luce brought him onto the War College faculty, where he served for almost thirty years, at times without compensation. In 1886 Little presented the first instruction in war gaming. From his study of land warfare games Little eventually devised games simulating action between two ships and between fleets, and finally a strategic game. His original intent was to find a way that naval officers could practice the profession of war in peacetime, but he soon discovered that war games could serve also as useful analytical tools for deriving tactical doctrine and even for determining the required characteristics of warships. Little's war games, together with the main problem, inevitably drew attention to the nature of future war and strategy. It was a short and logical step to move from strategic war gaming to war planning. From the crisis with Chile in 1890 through the preparations for war with Spain over Cuba, war planning was a major endeavor at the Naval War College.[24] In its short life until the outbreak of war with Spain, the War College's principal contribution to the Navy was probably its war planning capability. Clearly Taylor and Little had taken the Naval War College far beyond the Artillery School model with which Luce had begun. They had also taken it also far beyond the search by Luce and Mahan for abstract principles of naval strategy.

The congressional and public lobbying of Luce and Taylor, the acclaim accorded Mahan, and the utility of strategic analysis and war planning all heightened awareness and appreciation of the institution. The evolution of the early Naval War College provided a reservoir of experience from which the Army would later draw. The Army officer centrally involved in its beginnings, Tasker Bliss, would return to lecture at Newport periodically through 1895. He would also become the first president of the Army War College.[25]

Leavenworth: The Infantry and Cavalry School

While Luce, Mahan, Taylor, and company were building their school and war planning agency on Narragansett Bay, another institution was under development on the banks of the Missouri. Upton had recommended infantry and cavalry schools in 1877. In 1880 his friend and eventual biographer, Professor Peter S. Michie at West Point, recommended that schools for infantry and cavalry be located on the larger Army posts. The following year Commanding General Sherman ordered a "school of application for infantry and cavalry" be established at Fort Leavenworth similar to the Artillery School at Fort Monroe. Sherman envisioned a two-year course, with each class to consist of one officer from each of the infantry and cavalry regiments of the Army. Sherman saw the Leavenworth school as completing the Army's educational system.[26]

Sherman had introduced some ambivalence, however, at least in the mind of the appointed commandant, when he called for a "school of application" while at the same time directing instruction in "the military art" and stressing a broad education. Colonel Elwell S. Otis, in his first report as commandant, stated that "the course is not as comprehensive as might be desired, but it is probably as broad as the average intelligence of the officers receiving instruction here can master in the period of time allocated for instruction." Both Sherman and Otis thought of the school initially as an experiment. From its founding until 1887 it was geared primarily to preparing lieutenants for company-grade duties.[27]

General Philip H. Sheridan succeeded Sherman as Commanding General of the Army in 1883 and held that post for five years until his death in 1888. Sheridan was a supporter of the fledgling school system and initiated an additional school at Fort Riley, Kansas, a school "of instruction for drill and practice of the mounted arms," (the cavalry and light artillery). Congress authorized this additional school in 1887, but it was not formally organized until 1892. Since the new school at Riley would be concentrating on the lowest levels of tactical activity, at least for the mounted arms, the aim of the already established Infantry and Cavalry School at Fort Leavenworth could be raised. The Leavenworth course was therefore reorganized; a two-year course with seven academic departments was put into place. Although the Leavenworth course was still built around the duties of company-grade officers of the infantry and cavalry, a "Department of Military Art" was formed and the second year of the course included instruction in international law and in military history.[28]

Sheridan's reorganization was significant to the future direction of Leavenworth, but just as significant was the assignment to the faculty in 1886 of Lieutenant Arthur L. Wagner. Like his West Point classmate Tasker Bliss, Wagner was an officer of uncommon intellectual energy. Unlike Bliss, he had performed much of his service with his regiment in the western territories. His only prolonged detached service had been a three-year tour of duty as Professor of Military Science at Louisiana State University. In 1884, while on that duty, Wagner had won the Gold Medal Prize of the Military Service Institution for his essay "The Military Necessities of the United States and the Best Provisions for Meeting Them." In that essay he had shown an interest in and some talent for strategic assessment.[29]

At Leavenworth Wagner was assigned to the Department of Military Art, where he would remain for the next eleven years, becoming head of the department in 1893. Believing, as did Luce, that the road to an understanding of military science began with the study of military history, Wagner arranged to be sent to Germany to make a detailed study of von Moltke's campaigns. That study resulted in Wagner's first book, *The Campaign of Koniggratz: A Study of the Austro-Prussian Conflict in the Light of the American Civil War* (1889). Wagner's interests and concerns were primarily with tactics and how they might be taught. There were few texts on tactics, fewer in English. This situation Wagner set out to correct, writing in turn *The Service of Security and Information* (1893) and *Organization and Tactics* (1894).[30]

Wagner began also to contribute regularly to the professional military journals. In 1889 he published an article in which he compared the curriculum of the American Infantry and Cavalry School to those of the German *Kriegsschule* and the more advanced German *Kriegsakademie*. He found the Infantry and Cavalry School not wanting; like the *Kriegsakademie*, it instructed in strategy and grand tactics. He pointed out that at Leavenworth map problems involved army corps, divisions, and brigades. He expressed some doubt about war gaming. Of his map problems he stated, "This instruction (which in its main features savors much of the *Kriegsspiel*) is continued only so long as the similitude of war could reasonably be expected to exist, and does not include a game of battle, in which no war game can adequately provide." What Wagner failed to point out was that the *Kriegsakademie* curriculum included "General Staff duties," while the Infantry and Cavalry School did not. The relationship between a war college and a general staff was perhaps not yet recognized, though Wagner predicted, "The time will come when the seed planted at Fort Leavenworth will have grown into a great tree."[31]

The year that Wagner took charge of the Department of Military Art, he was joined on the faculty by Lieutenant Eben Swift. Wagner and Swift proved to be a harmonious team. In effect, while Wagner was developing tactical doctrine, Swift began to devise ways to teach that doctrine and methods by which it would be applied in a standard way. Borrowing liberally from German Army practice, Wagner and Swift developed and began to teach a systematic approach to solving tactical problems and to making and expressing tactical decisions. They developed for the American Army the formal and standard "Estimate of the Situation." They also developed from German practice a standard and systematic format for issuing orders to initiate tactical operations. From the concept of the *Kriegsspiel*, Swift developed teaching schemes such as map problems, map maneuvers, and "tactical rides." All these they termed the "applicatory system of military instruction."[32] Theirs was a significant accomplishment: the development of systematic, formal command procedures and a means by which officers could be schooled in those procedures. As McCarty Little had done at Newport, Wagner and Swift moved professional military education beyond a historical search for principles. They also "moved Leavenworth beyond a mere school of application that trained officers for their next assignment."[33]

In the 1890s there was growing applause for the broader approach being taken at Leavenworth. William Harding Carter, of the faculty at Fort Leavenworth and an officer who would play a major role in post-Spanish War reforms, opined that the schools had come to stay. As they became more firmly established they could "extend themselves beyond the elementary stage."[34] Lieutenant E. M. Weaver wrote in 1890 that "the school at Fort Leavenworth . . . bids fair to develop into a general war school for the combined instruction of officers of all arms of the service in the highest applications of the military art."[35] In an 1892 article on the Prussian Great General Staff, Captain T. A. Bingham argued that the United States Army carried out the officer training requirements of the Prussian General Staff "more or less thoroughly at West Point and the various army schools of application."[36] The Secretary of War apparently agreed. In his annual report of 1892 he stated, with probable exaggeration, that the Infantry and Cavalry School at Fort Leavenworth "has already assumed the appearance and form of a war academy . . . [and] in the near future it will be safe to describe [the Leavenworth school] as a war college of the highest character."[37] By 1894 Carter had reached the conclusion that "if service schools do not produce a great general, they will at least provide a body of trained staff officers capable of taking rank next after the natural masters of war."[38] As a historian of the turn-of-the-century American Army has concluded, by the mid-1890s the "Infantry and Cavalry School had begun to teach that most important and least understood of the new technical specialities—the science of high command."[39]

But there were also articulate critics who argued that it was all moving too far and too fast and at the expense of neglect of more basic Army problems. As early as 1887, Charles F. Benjamin urged that the Artillery School be restored "to its proper uses;" that it had become "not a school of artillery but was serving the general purposes of the army as an annex to the Military Academy." He was concerned for the artillerymen "not learning to be generals, lawyers, statesmen, and scientists at the Fort Monroe Annex."[40] There was apparently enough of this type of criticism to cause the commandant of the Artillery School, in his annual report of 1894, to defend his "military science or the art of war" course, stating that "while not an essential part of a curriculum of an artillery course, a knowledge of those subjects is indispensable to every military officer."[41]

Another critic was Captain James S. Pettit, Professor of Military Science at Yale University, who himself had compiled a text on military science.[42] Citing Leavenworth's Infantry and Cavalry School instruction in military policy and institutions, strategy, logistics, military geography, and staff duties and administration, Pettit remarked that "if this course is thoroughly taught there will not be much time for individual training in infantry and cavalry, and the name of the school should be changed to War College, and it should be opened to officers of all arms." He continued, "The tendency of an elaborate system of theoretical instruction is to make war appear complicated and abstruse; and to divert the attention of the student from his present rank and duties, to an idle contemplation of the remote possibilities of the future." Wagner responded rather petulantly that he had no objection to changing the name to War College. But Pettit was not stilled. "If [Leavenworth] is to be made a War College in the usual and accepted meaning of the terms, then it should have selected students, officers of rank and experience, who can demonstrate that they can give two years' time to the study and investigation of the highest and most intricate features of military art and science." "Personally," added Pettit, "I do not think our service training has reached the stage where a War College is a necessity."[43]

Benjamin and Pettit had seen one issue clearly. If the schools at Monroe and Leavenworth continued to broaden their courses and concerns with "military art and science," it would be at the expense of the more mundane training of the officer corps. The sense was growing that perhaps Sherman's system was not complete, that something called a war college would be a necessity in the future, if not now. The sense was also growing, as demonstrated by Carter, that the cause of higher military education was somehow linked to the establishment of an American general staff. This sense was best expressed by Major Edward Field in a letter to the *New York Times*. Citing the Naval War College, he said that their work fell into two general categories: "Acquisition of Military Information" and "Strategy." The latter could not be taught by recitation, but could be taught through war games. Field went on to say, "Nowadays an army without a general staff is an army without a brain." A school should be founded for this "corps d'elite of intellect." "A real general staff does the silent, inconspicuous, never ending work which molds and fashions the instruments. . . . It is a Staff College that we want—to educate a fighting staff."[44] Major Field in 1896 was merely the latest in a long line of American officers who had been calling for a "real general staff." While the details of what they wanted were not always precisely spelled out, it was evident that the Prussian model was widely admired.

Antecedents of a General Staff

Major General Winfield Scott Hancock had demonstrated in 1869 his good understanding of the role of a *grosser Generalstab* in testimony before the Military Affairs Committee of the House. He called the lack of such a staff "one of our greatest deficiencies in time of war," but the status quo recommendations of his Civil War colleagues won out. The chairman, former Major General and future President James A. Garfield, and the committee did not follow Hancock's recommendation. Based on his study of the French Army before the Franco-Prussian War, Brigadier General Thomas M. Vincent in 1870 expressed the opinion, not compelling in the Indian-fighting Army, that the peacetime mission of the Army was to prepare for war.[45]

Emory Upton had reported accurately and admiringly on the Prussian General Staff system and had recommended consolidation of the offices of the Adjutant General and Inspector General as a start. His proposed organization was to serve both the Secretary of War and the Commanding General, but in clearly separate functional areas. Through Sherman, Upton's thoughts were impressed upon the so-called "Burnside Committee," a joint congressional committee considering reorganization of the Army in 1878. Testimony by Colonel William B. Hazen before the committee echoed the recommendation of Upton. The legislation proposed by Burnside, but never passed into law, did recommend an American general staff but one more administrative in function than was the Prussian *grosser Generalstab*. In an address to National Guard officers, Brevet Major Joseph P. Sanger, who had accompanied Upton on his world tour, showed thorough understanding of the Prussian system. He claimed in 1880 that attempts to remodel the Army failed because "the changes necessary . . . would affect the interests of too many influential persons."[46]

Despite failure of attempts to formally reorganize the War Department, the department was nonetheless performing many of the functions of war planning and preparation generally accepted as those of a European-style general staff. The work of the Army and Navy Gun Foundry Board established in 1883 clearly involved combat developments and preparation for war. In 1884, just prior to his assignment to the Naval War College, Tasker Bliss had served as recorder on a board to investigate interior coastline waterways for the defense of the Atlantic and Gulf seaboards.[47] The recommendations of this board, its members primarily from the Corps of Engineers, included construction of canals across the Florida peninsula, between Chesapeake Bay and the Delaware River, and across Cape Cod. These recommendations found their way into those of the Endicott Board, itself a war planning agency, although the strategy on which its work was based was purely defensive. When Congress designated the Commanding General of the Army to head the Board on Ordnance and Fortifications and charged him with coordinating efforts of and allocating resources between the Chief of Ordnance and the Chief of Engineers in implementing the Endicott program, in a real sense it directed him to act as a chief of staff.[48]

Elements within the Navy, however, became the leaders in war planning, just as they had been in establishing an institution for the higher professional education of officers and in deriving a more ambitious strategic concept. In June 1881, President Garfield's Secretary of the Navy, William H. Hunt, appointed a Naval Advisory Board for the purpose of preparing plans for the rebuilding of the Navy. A second advisory board for this purpose was formed in the fall of 1882; it in turn was replaced by a Board of Construction in 1885. Also in 1882, the Office of Naval Intelligence was established, its duties to include not only intelligence but war planning. Apparently little planning was accomplished, however, at least initially. In 1888 the forward-looking Stephen Luce, having launched the Naval War College, was calling for a "Chief of the General Staff" for the Navy.[49]

A beginning was made in that direction in 1890 when the Assistant Secretary of the Navy was charged with the supervision of both the Office of Naval Intelligence and the Naval War College, the latter already engaging itself in strategic war games and planning. That same year Secretary of the Navy Tracy informally appointed a "secret strategy board," to which he named Mahan, the President of the Naval War College, and Assistant Secretary John R. Soley, an early member of the War College faculty. The strategy board's initial efforts addressed possible operations against Chile, followed by plans for operations in the event of war with Spain, Germany, or Great Britain. With President Cleveland's aggressive stand on the Venezuelan-British Guiana boundary dispute, the possibility of war with Britain took precedence. Henry

C. Taylor, Mahan's successor at Newport, was directed to draw up new plans for that contingency.[50]

With the passing of the Venezuelan crisis, American naval planners assumed war with Spain over the future of Cuba to be the more likely contingency. Planning apparently began in the summer of 1896. The Office of Naval Intelligence and the Naval War College were involved, but the long-standing opposition to the War College within the Navy Department led to appointment of a senior board to control the two agencies. When the McKinley administration assumed office in 1897, a new board under Admiral Montgomery Sicard was convened to review previous planning. Again the president of the War College, then Commander Caspar F. Goodrich, was included. The Sicard Board produced a revised plan for war with Spain. Additionally, it drew up plans for possible war with Japan.[51] Luce and Taylor had not achieved the general staff they desired for the Navy, but it is clear that on the eve of the Spanish-American War the Navy did have in place working instrumentalities for war planning under the direct control of the civilian Secretary and his assistant. The function paralleled that of Moltke and his successors in Berlin, even if the organization did not. The Navy also had in place an academic institution to train the planners.

The Army made less progress than the Navy, but progress there was. In 1885, Adjutant General Richard C. Drum, on his own initiative, formed a Military Information Division within his office with functions similar to the mapping and military statistics elements of European general staffs, collecting and arranging information on both United States and foreign geography and military resources. The division was formally recognized and funded by Congress in 1888. That same year military attaches under the control of the Military Information Division were dispatched to five major European capitals. In 1892 the mission of the division was made more specific, including the "study and preparation of plans for the mobilization and transportation of militia and volunteers and their disbandment and for the concentration of the military forces of the United States at the various strategic points on or near the frontier of the country."[52]

That mission was *Grosser Generalstab* in every sense. The division followed the Prussian example by organizing into sections on militia, military progress, frontiers, mapping, and Latin America. Quality personnel were also assigned. Major Arthur MacArthur, later to command American forces in the Philippines, was an assistant division chief. Also a member was Major Theodore Schwan; born in Germany, Schwan returned to study the Prussian system and then published a pamphlet on the German Army which served as an authoritative reference when the War Department began to seriously consider reorganization after the

Spanish-American War. In 1897 Wagner came from Leavenworth to head the division. At the outbreak of war with Spain, Tasker Bliss was attache in Madrid.[53]

The Military Information Division also had a role in military education. When examinations for officer promotion below the grade of major were introduced in 1890, "lyceums" were established on all posts to provide a course of instruction to assist officers in their preparation. Additionally, each member of the lyceum was required to submit annually a professional paper reflecting original research. The Military Information Division supported the lyceums by acting as a sort of central library, providing research material and publishing deserving papers. It also prepared and published monographs with such titles as "The Hawaiian Islands," "The German Army," "The Militia," and "Notes of Military Interest." At the outbreak of the war with Spain, the division had twelve officers and twelve civilians assigned, had compiled more than 40,000 index cards, had established contact with the insurgent forces in Cuba, and had made accurate estimates of the strength and disposition of Spanish forces in Cuba.[54]

Growth of the Military Information Division and establishment of the Board of Ordnance and Fortification, while partially filling the void of a *Grosse Generalstab*, did not solve the problem of the relationship between the Secretary of War and the Commanding General nor that of directing and coordinating the semi-autonomous bureaus. Nonetheless the pragmatism and good sense of Major General John M. Schofield, Commanding General from 1888 to 1895, went far to ameliorate those problems during his tenure. Unlike Sherman and Sheridan, Schofield accepted his subordination to the Secretary of War. He saw his position literally as that of a chief of staff to the Secretary and through him to the President and Commander-in-Chief. Although under Schofield's arrangement neither he nor the three Secretaries he served had unchallenged control of the bureau chiefs, Schofield achieved what he later claimed to be "perfect harmony . . . between the War Department and the headquarters of the army." The Army gained professional leadership, but civilian control was retained.[55]

Schofield also informally created a means to accomplish the *Grosser Generalstab* function of determining and guiding the operational readiness of Army units. While commander of the Division of the Atlantic, Schofield had designated his aide-de-camp (and Upton's travelling companion), J. P. Sanger, "Inspector of Artillery and Small Arms Target Practice." In 1888, when Schofield became the Army's Commanding General, Tasker Bliss was brought from the Naval War College to replace Sanger. Under Schofield's direction Bliss had designated in each major subordinate command an equivalent "Inspector." From the correspondence contained in the letter books of Bliss during the seven years he served as aide to Schofield, it is apparent that Schofield's purpose extended beyond "target practice" to standardization of doctrine and to what is now known as operational readiness. Moreover, the network of inspectors provided a link between Army headquarters and the field, and between the field and the schools at Monroe and Leavenworth. In a rather rudimentary way, at least in the troop readiness area, these inspectors were general staff corps officers serving with troops, not unlike those in the Prussian system.[56]

To summarize, on the eve of the Spanish-American War neither the United States Navy nor the United States Army had a general staff on the Prussian or other European national model. Each service was performing some general staff functions, however, at least those associated with a general staff. Each had an intelligence or information agency and various organs or boards to address specific war-preparation problems. Although his successor reversed the pattern, Schofield had demonstrated a chief-of-staff concept that could accommodate both professional leadership and civilian control. He had also devised a system for monitoring and improving operational readiness.

The officer education systems that supported these activities, although based originally on the Prussian *Kriegsakademie* and with the common precedent of the Artillery School, had evolved differently. Under the leadership of Mahan, Taylor, and Little, the Naval War College had become an adjunct to the Navy Department. As such, it emphasized strategy and national-level deployment of the fleet. On the other hand, the Army's closest counterpart to the *Kriegsakademie*, the Infantry and Cavalry School at Leavenworth, under the influence of Wagner and Swift, had not become associated with War Department functions. It had concentrated on tactics and to a lesser extent on campaign strategy. To use the German nomenclature, the Naval War College instructed more nearly on the level of the *Grosse Generalstab*, the Infantry and Cavalry School at that of the *Truppengeneralstab*. When compared to the German education system, both were primitive.

To speculate on how the Army's staff and educational system might have evolved had the Spanish-American War not occurred is interesting but not particularly useful. The near-disasters and the embarrassments that the Army experienced in that conflict came to overshadow much of the progress that had been made. The Spanish-American War was the catalyst that encouraged conversion of the thinking and informal arrangements of the late nineteenth century into the foundations of real reform and modernization of the United States Army, its staff, and its officer education system.

NOTES

1. Robert Arthur, *Historical Sketch of the Coast Artillery School* (Fort Monroe, Va.: The Coast Artillery School, 1930), 46. Headquarters, United States Artillery School, General Order No. 12, May 7, 1878, in *Annual Report of the General of the Army to the Secretary of War for the Year 1879* (Washington: GPO, 1879), 177. Upton's specific assignment was "Superintendent of studies in mathematics, engineering, military art and science, etc., law and military administration, applied tactics, infantry and grand tactics, also of practice in the same."

2. Biographical information on Upton is from Stephen E. Ambrose, *Upton and the Army* (Baton Rouge: Louisiana State University Press, 1964), 16-62. The tactical system was published in Emory Upton, *A New System of Infantry Tactics: Double and Single Rank* (New York: Appleton & Co., 1873).

3. Ambrose, *Upton*, 76-79. The other members of the board were Colonels Henry A. duPont and John A. Tourtelotte and Captain Alfred E. Bates. Donald N. Bigelow, *William Conant Church and the "Army and Navy Journal"* (New York: Columbia University Press, 1952), 125.

4. Letter, Sherman to Upton, July 12, 1875, and letter, Belknap to Upton, June 23, 1875, in Emory Upton, *The Armies of Asia and Europe* (New York: Appleton, 1878), iii-vi. Captains Joseph P. Sanger and Major George A. Forsyth accompanied Upton.

5. Peter S. Michie, *Life and Letters of General Upton* (New York: Appleton, 1885), 385-87.

6. Emory Upton, "Extracts from a Letter to General Sherman," *Army and Navy Journal* XIV (February 3, 1877): 405.

7. Ambrose, *Upton*, 97-98. The proposed later work became Upton's most influential book, published posthumously by the War Department in 1904 as *The Military Policy of the United States*. Upton, *Armies of Asia and Europe*, 317-70.

8. Ibid., 362-66.

9. Quotes in Michie, *Life of Upton*, 418.

10. *Annual Report of the General of the Army*, 1879, 180-81.

11. Stephen B. Luce, "Naval Administration III," *USNIP* XXIX (December 1903): 819-21.

12. John D. Hayes, "Stephen B. Luce and the Beginning of the Naval War College," *Naval War College Review* XXIII (January 1971): 52. Ronald Spector, *Professors of War: The Naval War College and the Development of the Naval Profession* (Newport, R.I.: Naval War College Press, 1977), 17, 23.

13. Ibid., 21. Kenneth J. Hagan, "Admiral David Dixon Porter: Strategist for a Navy in Transition," *USNIP* XCIV (July 1968): 143. David D. Porter, "Naval Education and Organization," *United Service* I (July 1879): 482-84.

14. Stephen B. Luce, "War Schools," *USNIP* IX (1883): 635-36, 647, 655.

15. For example, John K. Laughton, "The Scientific Study of Naval History," *Journal of the Royal Service Institution* XVIII (1874): 508-527. Luce acknowledges indebtedness to Laughton in a lecture at the Naval War College in September 1886, "On the Study of Naval History (Grand Tactics)," *USNIP* XIII (1887): 187. For the status of British work see the chapters on Laughton, Captain Sir John Colomb and Vice Admiral Philip Colomb in Donald M. Schurman, *The Education of a Navy: The Development of British Naval Strategic Thought, 1867-1914* (Chicago: University of Chicago Press, 1965).

16. Spector, *Professors of War*, 21-25. The other officers were Captain William T. Sampson and Commander Caspar F. Goodrich. Goodrich became president of the War College in 1896. Both of these naval officers also served on the Endicott Board.

17. Stephen B. Luce, "The United States Naval War College," *United Service* XII (January, 1885): 81.

18. Hayes, "Luce and the Beginning," 57.

19. Frederick Palmer, *Bliss, Peacemaker: The Life and Times of General Tasker H. Bliss* (New York: Dodd, Mead & Co., 1934), 5-30.

20. Robert Seager II, *Alfred Thayer Mahan: The Man and His Letters* (Annapolis: Naval Institute Press, 1977), 163. Spector, *Professors of War*, 28-29. Luce cautioned the class of 1886 that the position of Bliss was "one of extreme delicacy." Stephen B. Luce, "On the Study of Naval Warfare as a Science," *USNIP* XII (1886): 544.

21. Letter, Acting Secretary of the Navy Walker to Secretary of War Endicott, October 7, 1885, and letter, Adjutant General Drum to Bliss, October 12, 1885, Bliss Papers, U.S. Army Military History Institute Collection (hereafter MHI), Carlisle Barracks, Pa. Bliss was abroad from October 1885 until July 1886. Letter, Mahan to Luce, January 6, 1886, in *Letters and Papers of Alfred Thayer Mahan, Vol. 1, 1847-1889* Robert Seager II and Doris D. Maguire, eds. (Annapolis: Naval Institute Press, 1975): 619. Letter, Adjutant General Drum to Bliss, October 12, 1885, Bliss Papers, MHI.

22. Alfred Thayer Mahan, *From Sail to Steam, Recollections of Naval Life* (New York: Harper, 1907), 293. On the problems of the early years of the Naval War College see Spector, *Professors of War,* Chapter V, "A Sea of Troubles," 50-70. Mahan's lectures at the War College were published as *The Influence of Sea Power Upon History, 1660-1783* (1890), and *The Influence of Sea Power Upon the French Revolution and Empire, 1793-1812* (1892).

23. Spector, *Professors of War,* 71-74.

24. Ibid., 74-82, 88-97. The works that Spector determined to have most influenced Little were one by a British Army officer, Colonel John Middleton, *Explanation and Application of the English Rules of Playing the War Games* (London: W. Mitchell, 1873), and two by American Army officers, Major William R. Livermore, *The American Kriegsspiel* (Boston: Houghton Mifflin, 1882), and Lieutenant C. A. L. Totten, "Strategies, the American Game of War," *JMSI* I (1880): 185-202. All three drew from German Army efforts.

25. Letter, Bliss to Taylor, June 18, 1895, "Letter Book from May 25, 1895," 27, Bliss Papers, MHI.

26. Peter S. Michie, "Education and Its Relation to the Military Profession," *JMSI* I (1880): 176. *Annual Report of the General of the Army to the Secretary of War for the Year 1881* (Washington: GPO, 1881), 11. There was also an Engineer School at Willett's Point, New York, and a Signal School at Ft. Myer, Va.

27. Report of Colonel E. S. Otis, October 11, 1882, in *Annual Report of the General of the Army to the Secretary of War for the Year 1882* (Washington: GPO, 1882), 175. Otis, a graduate of Harvard Law School, was later commander of American Army forces in the Philippines from August 1898 to May 1900. Timothy K. Nenninger, *The Leavenworth Schools and the Old Army: Education, Professionalism and the Officer Corps of the U.S. Army, 1881-1918* (Westport, Ct.: Greenwood, 1978), 23, 26.

28. Ibid., 30. Also instrumental in the founding of the Fort Riley school was Schofield, who in 1887 commanded the Division of the Missouri, and Senator Preston B. Plumb of Kansas. John M. Schofield, *Forty-Six Years in the Army* (New York: Century, 1897), 426-27.

29. Arthur L. Wagner, "On Military Necessities of the United States and the Best Provisions for Meeting Them," *JMSI* V (1884): 237-71.

30. Eben Swift, "An American Pioneer in the Cause of Military Education: Arthur L. Wagner," *JMSI* XLIV (1909): 69.

31. Arthur L. Wagner, "An American War College," *JMSI* X (1889): 288-96.

32. Nenninger, *Leavenworth,* 45-48. Swift, "American Pioneer," 70.

33. Nenninger, *Leavenworth,* 48.

34. William H. Carter, "One View of the Army Question," *United Service* II (December 1889): 578.

35. E. M. Weaver, "The Military Schools of the United States," *United Service* III (May 1890): 464.

36. T. A. Bingham, "The Prussian Great General Staff and What it Contains that is Practical from an American Standpoint," *JMSI* VIII (July 1892): 671.

37. *Annual Report of the Secretary of War for the Year 1892,* Vol. I (Washington: GPO, 1892), 11.

38. William H. Carter, "The Infantry and Cavalry School at Fort Leavenworth," *JMSI* XV (1894): 759.

39. Graham A. Cosmos, *An Army for Empire: The United States Army in the Spanish-American War* (Columbia, Mo.: University of Missouri Press, 1971), 9.

40. Charles F. Benjamin, "The Artillery and Ordnance," *JMSI* VIII (December 1887): 365-66.

41. Report of the Commandant of the United States Artillery School, August 25, 1894 in *Annual Report of the Secretary of War for the Year 1894* (Washington: GPO, 1894), 173.
42. James S. Pettit, *Elements of Military Science, for the Use of Students in Colleges and Universities*, revised edition (New Haven, Ct.: Tuttle, Morehouse and Taylor, 1895).
43. Pettit, "The Proper Military Instruction for our Officers. The Method to be Employed, its Scope and Full Development," *JMSI* XX (January 1897): 31. Arthur L. Wagner, "Proper Military Instruction: Comment and Criticism," *JMSI* XX (March 1897): 424. Pettit, "Comments and Criticisms: Reply to Wagner's Comments on 'Proper Military Education,'" *JMSI* XX (May 1897): 632.
44. Edward Field, "Wanted, A War College," *New York Times*, August 9, 1896: 24.
45. U.S. Congress. House Military Affairs Committee, 40th Congress, 3rd Session, Report No. 33, "Army Organization," February 27, 1869, 88. For tabulation of the views of military leaders as expressed before congressional committees between 1869 and 1878, see Herman D. Reeve, *The Staff Departments of the United States Army* (Washington: GPO, 190,: 195-99. Brigadier General Thomas M. Vincent, "Staff Organization: A Plea for the Staff of the Army of the United States," March 1870, Military Pamphlets 15, Pamphlet No. 2, MHI Library.
46. Upton, *Armies*, 329-30. U.S. Congress, Joint Committee on the Reorganization of the Army, 45th Congress, 3rd Session, Senate Report No. 555 to accompany Senate Bill 1491, December 12, 1878, 453, 2, 15. Senator Ambrose E. Burnside, former Major General, commanded the Army of the Potomac at the Battle of Fredericksburg. Sanger's address was published as "Duties of Staff Officers," *United Service* II (June 1880): 756-59.
47. War Department Special Orders No. 111, May 13, 1884.
48. Edward Ramson, "The Endicott Board of 1885-1886 and the Coast Defense," *Military Affairs* XXXI (Summer 1967): 74-84.
49. Henry P. Beers, "The Development of the Office of Chief of Naval Operations, Part I," *Military Affairs* XI (Spring 1946): 40-47. Stephen B. Luce, "Naval Administration, *USNIP* XIV (1888): 586.
50. Henry C. Taylor, "Memorandum on General Staff for the United States Navy," *USNIP* XXVI (September 1900): 441-42. For the Chilean crisis see Frederick B. Pike, *Chile and the United States, 1880-1962* (Notre Dame, Ind.: University of Notre Dame Press, 1963), 66-81. Bourne and Boyd, "Mahan's 'War,' " 71-78. The Army also was directed to plan for operations against Chile. Commanding General Schofield complied but apparently disapproved of the idea, believing it akin to beating a mongrel just to hear him yelp. Schofield, *Forty-six Years*, 489-90.
51. John A. S. Grenville, "American Naval Preparations for War With Spain," *Journal of American Studies* II (1968): 34-38, 41-47. Also Ronald Spector, "Who Planned the Attack on Manila Bay?" *Mid-America* LIII (April 1971): 97-101. David M. Trask, *The War With Spain in 1898* (New York: Macmillan, 1981), 73-78.
52. Elizabeth Bethel, "The Military Information Division: Origin of the Intelligence Division," *Military Affairs* XI (Spring 1947): 20.
53. Ibid., 17-21.
54. Ibid., 22-24. Wagner dispatched Lieutenant Andrew S. Rowan with the "Message to Garcia" in late 1897.
55. Schofield, *Forty-six Years*, 423. Weigley, *Towards an American Army*, 171-73.
56. Schofield, *Forty-six Years*, 458-60. Letter Books for 1888-1895, Bliss Papers, MHI.

War, Scandal and Investigation 1898-1899

In 1895 revolt broke out in Cuba for the second time since the end of the American Civil War. The Cleveland administration declared a policy of nonintervention. William McKinley's accession to the presidency did not change that policy. Indeed, by the end of 1897, McKinley's efforts to resolve the Cuban issue by diplomacy appeared to be meeting with success, but in striving to prevent conflict, McKinley did not provide for fighting a war. Even after the destruction of the *Maine* on February 15, 1898, and the resulting public clamor, the President attempted to avoid provocation.[1]

Plans for a War with Spain

Within the Navy Department, however, planning for the contingency of war with Spain had begun as early as 1896. By the middle of June 1897 the Navy had produced the "Sicard Plan" which envisioned a primarily naval war, the decisive instrument to be blockade of Cuba. As outlined in this plan, the Army's role was to occupy, after naval seizure, the port of Matanzas some twenty miles east of Havana. From that place the Army would arm and equip the insurgents and also mount an operation to take Havana. Subsequently, and if necessary, a similar move would be made on the coast west of Havana. The Sicard Plan included a recommendation for an attack on Spanish naval forces in the Philippine Islands but saw no need there for Army forces. Finally the plan called for Army garrisoning of Puerto Rican ports captured by the Navy.[2]

During the same period that Navy plans were evolving, the Military Information Division of the Adjutant General's Office was toiling hard and effectively at producing intelligence on Cuba and the Spanish forces there. The Army's planning was less formal than that of the Navy and also more dependent upon the administration's political objectives. However, if McKinley had objectives, he did not reveal them. In March the Secretaries of the two armed service departments appointed a board of two officers to coordinate planning for both coast defense and an assault on Cuba. The Army representative was Lieutenant Colonel Arthur L. Wagner, formerly of the Leavenworth school and then chief of the Military Information Division.

Wagner and his naval colleague, Captain Albert S. Barker, submitted their plan to the Secretary of War on April 4th. It was similar to the Sicard Plan. It relied upon blockade, but a small Army expedition was to seize a Cuban port for the purpose of supplying the insurgents. Barker and Wagner saw no military necessity for a large-scale invasion of Cuba, but if political considerations so dictated, a 50,000-man assault on Havana was recommended. They also advised the occupation of Puerto Rico to deprive the Spanish Navy of Caribbean operating bases. The Army's missions in essence were to protect the Navy's continental operating bases while the fleet was away, to provide logistical support to the Cubans, and to furnish small expeditionary forces to assist the Navy in seizing and securing forward bases.[3]

In support of the Barker-Wagner concept, an Army board consisting of Wagner, Lieutenant Colonel Theodore Schwan, and Major William Harding Carter was directed on April 13 to make plans for the mobilization of a volunteer force of up to 40,000 for active field service, and of 20,000 more for reserve seacoast service. The board reported back the next day, recommending concentration of an expeditionary force and its subsequent embarkation from three points: Tampa, Mobile, and New Orleans. The plan called for three Army corps. The entire regular Army mobile force structure, with the exception of one infantry regiment, would be employed in the expeditionary force.[4] With each regular regiment would be brigaded two volunteer regiments.

The Army in the War with Spain

Neither the Barker-Wagner plan nor the Wagner-Schwan-Carter plan was executed as drawn. On April 22nd President McKinley, with the authorization of Congress, ordered the Navy to blockade Cuba. From that first act of war until hostilities against Spain ceased in August, some 112 days later, the Army was engaged in five missions. First, to strengthen the defenses of the Atlantic seaboard. Second, to mobilize a land force that at peak strength would exceed 270,000 men. Third, beginning in May, to deploy an expeditionary force to the Philippines. Fourth, in June and July to seize Santiago de Cuba. Finally, in July and August, to occupy the island of Puèrto Rico. All missions were successfully, if not always efficiently, accomplished by mid-August. In the Philippines, however, American forces controlled only the town of Cavite and the city of Manila.

The strengthening of coastal defense began on March 9th, when Congress made a special appropriation of $50 million for "national defense." The Army's share, less than $20 million, McKinley and Secretary of War Russell A. Alger devoted in the main to accelerating the harbor defense program of the Endicott Board. In hindsight this was money spent in the wrong direction. On the other hand, since the President was still seeking a peaceful solution to the Cuban issue, coast defense improvement avoided a warlike act. Moreover, the decision probably saved the administration embarrassment in May when there was popular alarm along the eastern seaboard as to the whereabouts and intentions of the Spanish fleet.[5]

Mobilization increased the size of the Army, not by the 60,000 assumed by Wagner, Schwan, and Carter, but sixfold by the end of May, tenfold by the end of August. The Army was not prepared to manage efficiently nor to support this buildup. The Commander-in-Chief, however, had found it necessary to accommodate the martial spirit abroad in the land, particularly that of the leadership of the National Guard. The first call for volunteers was 125,000, the approximate authorized strength of the National Guard.[6] The Army mobilized into seven, not three, Army corps and concentrated at locations in Virginia, Florida, Georgia, Alabama, and near San Francisco. The largest concentration was at Camp Thomas near Chickamauga, Georgia, where by July there were 56,000 men.[7] The extent of the mobilization had little relation to operations, either as planned or executed. A large majority of the volunteers never left the United States.

The requirement for Army forces in the Philippines was entirely unforeseen by the Commander-in-Chief, the Navy and War Departments, and the local commander, Admiral Dewey. When news of the Manila Bay victory arrived in Washington, Major General Nelson A. Miles, Commanding General of the Army, recommended dispatch of an expeditionary force. Dewey called for a force of 5,000, and McKinley responded by ordering a concentration of forces near San Francisco. On May 19 McKinley made specific the Army's mission in the Philippines: "completing the reduction of the Spanish power in that quarter and . . . giving order and security to the islands while in the possession of the United States." On the 25th the first contingent of troops sailed. By the end of July seven increments had departed for the Far East, a total of some 16,000 troops. By mid-August sufficient force was deployed south of Manila to convince the Spanish commander to relinquish the city without serious resistance.[8] The troop strength in the Philippines was adequate for negotiation with the Spanish; for fighting Filipinos greater strength would soon be needed.

The expeditionary force under Major General William R. Shafter, which in July received the surrender of Santiago, had experienced repeated changes in mission. Initially Shafter was to conduct a reconnaissance in force near Havana with some 4,000 to 5,000 men. The troop strength for that operation was then increased to 10,000. Early in May new instructions directed Shafter to seize Mariel, a town twenty miles from Havana, and from there to attack the capital. A force of 40,000 to 50,000, later increased to 70,000, was contemplated for this operation. Finally, on May 30th, the War Department instructed Shafter to seize Santiago, where the Navy had cornered the Spanish fleet.[9] For this mission Shafter embarked a force of 17,000, sailed for Cuba on the 14th of June, and landed over the beach on the 22nd. On July 1st he drove in the outer defenses of Santiago at the Battle of El Caney/San Juan Hill, invested the city, and on the 17th accepted its surrender. Soon after, debilitated by dysentery and malarial diseases and threatened by an outbreak of yellow fever, Shafter's force was relieved by fresh troops and redeployed to an isolated, hastily established camp at Montauk Point, Long Island. By the end of August the Army had transported over 27,000 men to Cuba.

The seizure of Puerto Rico was a scheme favored by General Miles. When the operation was ultimately mounted, he was in personal command. Three separate landings were made during the period from July 25th to August 5th, with little resistance encountered. Over 14,000 American troops were on the island when hostilities ceased on the 12th of August.[10] In all, the War Department within a period of four months had mobilized an Army of 270,000 and established three expeditionary forces overseas totaling twice as many men as had been on active duty when the war began. It was a remarkable logistical and administrative achievement. Nonetheless, it was a performance that was to receive severe and bitter public criticism in the months to come.

If from a broad perspective the Army had done and done well all that its political masters had asked, on closer inspection its performance was at best marginal.[11] Its tactical skill was tested in but one day of battle, but that test revealed on the part of the corps, division, and brigade commanders an inability to control and maneuver the force in any coherent and purposeful way, even accepting the difficulty of the terrain. The methods of command and troop leadership derived and taught by Wagner and Swift at Leavenworth had little influence, at least little that reached into the chain of command of Shafter's corps. But tactical flaws were minor when compared to logistical failures. Due partially to terrain but also to lack of system and plan, resupply and medical evacuation of the forward regiments were at the point of breakdown after one day of combat.[12]

Causes of the logistical problems extended back to the movement from the United States. The debarkation in Cuba was marked by confusion, the embarkation at Tampa by chaos. The vacillating and delayed political and military decisions as to Shafter's mission certainly contributed to the condition, as did the absence of a stock of supplies available for war emergency. As basic to the poor results, however, was the lack of experience and training at all levels from Washington to Tampa in the intricacies of deploying a combatant force overseas. Moreover, responsibility for the movement was not clearly defined; no one man assisted by a planning, coordinating, and supervising staff was in charge.[13] Tampa illustrated almost tragically the truth of General Schofield's prediction of eleven years before as to the effectiveness of the American staff system.

The projection of a contingency force into a hostile underdeveloped area was then, and is now, a complex enterprise. The collection and maintenance of troops in temporary camps within the United States is far less complex, but here also the Army came close to failure. Ill-equipped, ill-trained, and ill-disciplined upon arrival at the southern camps, and inadequately supported by the War Department after arrival, the volunteer regiments were decimated by dysentery and typhoid by July. By the end of September, 425 soldiers had died at Camp Thomas; 246 at a camp near Jacksonville, Florida; 107 at Falls Church, Virginia; and 139 at the camp near San Francisco. In the late summer Shafter's force, sick and dispirited, returned from Cuba and was isolated on Long Island.[14]

The Postwar Problem: The War Department

With no campaigns left to critique, the hyperactive late-nineteenth-century press turned its attention to conditions within the camps. For a scapegoat the press selected the War Department, and specifically its head, the hapless Secretary Alger. The Democratic opposition was delighted to join in; suddenly and unexpectedly the administration faced a serious political problem. Rather than accolades for the outcome of a short and victorious war, the administration received abuse for mismanagement of that war. As a recently discharged colonel of a volunteer cavalry regiment, but now the Republican nominee for the governorship of New York, lamented, "Algerism is a heavy load to carry."[15] And the mid-term elections were only weeks away.

Unable to sacrifice Alger without admitting to deficiencies in his own administration, McKinley chose to convene a presidential commission "to investigate the conduct of the War Department in the war with Spain." In particular the commission was "to fix the responsibility for any failure or fault by reason of neglect, incompetency or maladministration upon the officers and bureaus responsible therefor, if it should be found that the evils complained of had existed." To chair the commission, McKinley appointed Grenville Dodge, a Civil War major general of engineers and postwar transcontinental railroad builder. Dodge and the other members of the commission performed their task with all the careful deliberation that it was due. Indeed, so careful and deliberate was the commission that it was unable to complete its task until January, two months after the elections.[16]

For most Americans the war was over in August and the Dodge Commission was aftermath; not so for the Army and the War Department. As the Dodge Commission convened, there were still substantial Army forces on Puerto Rico, Cuba, and Luzon. On all three islands there were also Spanish forces to be repatriated and military government to be exercised pending the outcome of peace negotiations with Spain. In Cuba and the Philippines, moreover, there were armed insurgent forces who had been fighting Spaniards long before the Americans arrived and whose interests were not necessarily well represented at the negotiations. As winter approached it was becoming apparent that any American attempt to occupy the Philippine archipelago beyond Manila would be actively resisted by Emilio Aguinaldo and his Filipino army. Major General Wesley Merritt, first commander of the Philippine expedition, estimated in October that it would take 20,000 to 25,000 troops to occupy Luzon alone. The next month his successor in Manila, Major General Elwell S. Otis, recommended that "all troops here and soon to arrive" be retained. Though six more regiments arrived in January, law required that the regiments that had volunteered for the war with Spain be mustered out. As the Dodge Commission finished its work that same month, the danger of a new war in the Philippines was real indeed.[17] If it occurred, there would come with it the requirement to raise a new army.

The Dodge Commission neither exonerated nor condemned Secretary Alger, but it found "lacking in the general administration of the War Department . . . that complete grasp of the situation that was essential."[18] Nor did the work of the commission completely defuse the political problem. Alger remained a discredited official, bitter, defensive, and ineffectual in directing the Army in the tasks of colonial administration (and war) that lay ahead. Of as little use as Alger in directing the Army was its Commanding General, Nelson A. Miles. Upon Schofield's retirement in 1895, Miles being the next senior officer, automatically succeeded him. Too vain and ambitious to subordinate himself in the chief-of-staff role that Schofield had adopted, Miles had dissipated much of his influence even before the war.[19]

Early in the war Miles' military instincts were sound. He opposed sending troops into Cuba until after the fever season and until they could be trained. He opposed the quarter-million-man buildup as unnecessary and beyond the Army's ability to support. To those students of strategy who admire the "indirect approach," his recommendation to seize Puerto Rico before landing in Cuba may have merit. Frustrated perhaps by having his advice repeatedly rejected by the President and the Secretary of War, or by the lack of acclaim for his wartime contributions, Miles' object after the war seems to have been to embarrass the administration whenever possible. It was Miles, during testimony before the Dodge Commission, who brought up the unsubstantiated charge of "embalmed beef" being supplied to the troops, a charge that reignited public outcry. Miles continued to create problems until his retirement in 1903. He is a difficult personality to explain. Without formal education, Miles had been a "boy general" during the Civil War, had stayed in the Army, and had won a not-altogether-deserved reputation as a skillful Indian fighter in the West. He was liked and respected by his subordinates but distrusted by his colleagues, who looked upon his inflated ambitions with deep suspicion. Perhaps the most generous thing that can be said of Nelson Miles is that he was an excellent regimental commander who was far beyond his ethical and intellectual depth in a positions of higher command.[20]

The report submitted to the President by the Dodge Commission consists of eight volumes. Seven of those volumes contain long, repetitive, sometimes contradictory, sometimes irrelevant testimony. Only a minor part of the remaining volume purports to be a report of findings. If the report reflects the deliberations of the body, the commission was long on gathering data but very short on deriving from the data fundamental causes of the conditions it discovered. Moreover, despite Dodge's personal conviction that War Department reform was necessary, the commission made only the mildest suggestions on how the Army might be improved. In fairness, the commission was not asked to propose a program of reform. The result, however, is that savoring the full flavor of the Army's problems during the War with Spain requires tedious reading of the testimony. But even cursory examination reveals the utter lack of planning and unified direction of the Army's war effort. Also apparent are the sad results of senior officers unequipped to handle large bodies of troops, and of junior officers and noncommissioned officers unaware of the basics of caring for troops in the field.[21]

The effects of the Dodge Commission and of the notoriety that accompanied its deliberations proved to be more indirect than direct. Probably the commission's greatest contribution was in providing a documented case study of Army deficiencies. Opponents of Army reform would henceforth bear the burden of proof. Moreover, the report of the commission confirmed that the welfare of the Republican Party, and probably that of the Army and the nation as well, demanded that the unlucky Alger be replaced. Public sentiment would expect whoever replaced him to reestablish direction to the Army. At least the appearance of reform, if not its substance, would be necessary. In June 1899, President McKinley, at long last and to the great relief of his party, secured the resignation of Secretary Alger. As his replacement McKinley nominated Elihu Root, a lawyer engaged in private practice in the city of New York.

When Root became titular head of the War Department in August 1899, Army missions were far broader in scope than they had been but fifteen months before. From the routine of administering its numerous small posts and stations, the Army had been put to the task of administering overseas colonies composed of millions of culturally different peoples. As the governing instrumentalities in the former Spanish islands, major generals were proconsuls: James R. Brooke in Havana, George W. Davis in San Juan, and Elwell S. Otis in Manila.[22] By the end of the year all Spanish troops had been repatriated from Cuba, American military control there was complete, and the Cuban population was generally cooperative, though suspicious. Puerto Rico was a lesser problem, but as Root settled into office, a massive Army relief operation was underway there as the result of extensive destruction caused by a hurricane. In the Philippines, Otis had on his hands a major colonial war, but one that in August 1899 he seemed to be winning. After the first clash between American and Filipino forces outside Manila in early February, American forces had driven out into Luzon and landed on Panay, Negros, and Cebu islands. By April Aguinaldo's capital had been seized and his government scattered. The successes were not without cost. Through June, 225 American soldiers had been killed and 1,357 wounded.[23]

At the War Department the year's major trial was the mustering out of one army and the building of another. Ratification of the peace treaty with Spain in April dictated the discharge of 35,000 regulars and 110,000 volunteers. To meet the requirement of subduing Aguinaldo, Congress authorized on March 2, 1899, a regular Army of 65,000 and the raising of 35,000 volunteers from the country at large. By the end of the year the volunteer state regiments of the Spanish War were disbanded and new volunteer regiments raised, trained, and either deployed or deploying to the Philippines. At the end of November the new Secretary reported an Army of almost 99,000—two-thirds of it in the Philippines, 11,000 troops in Cuba, and another 3,000 in Puerto Rico.[24]

Elihu Root: Colonial and War Secretary

Root has told of his amazement at being asked to serve as Secretary of War, of his ignorance of armies and war, and of the President's selection of him as the lawyer to administer the new colonies. There is no reason to doubt this story. Colonial administration was obviously a major new task for both the Army and the nation, a task riddled with unprecedented constitutional and legal questions. But there can be little doubt either that the President had been sorely tried by his War Department since the beginning of the Spanish War. In addition to the political embarrassment, McKinley too often for his taste had been forced to perform actively the duties of Commander-in-Chief. Secretary Alger was a liability; General Miles was distrusted. In Elihu Root the President had made a happier choice than he anticipated if he was looking merely for a colonial secretary.[25]

In addition to legal acumen, Root brought qualities to the cabinet post that had been sadly lacking: an analytical, orderly, and retentive mind; an attractive personality and persuasive manner; and a capacity and will to work. His political credentials were also correct. He was a conservative Republican, perhaps a neo-Federalist, an influence in New York politics but not a national figure, and decidedly not a political hack. Son of a mathematics professor at Hamilton College in upstate New York, Root was a self-made man to be admired, the founder of what became under his direction a prestigious and profitable New York City law firm. His clients were corporations. Though without executive experience, Root had dealt with bigness and how to organize it efficiently and, of course, legally. Elihu Root proved to have one additional quality badly needed in the War Department. He would not tolerate either incompetence or disloyalty.[26]

As Secretary of War, Root worked, studied, and learned. From the beginning he sought control. For an executive officer he had another man with great capacity for hard work, the Adjutant General, Brigadier General Henry C. Corbin. Corbin from 1862 to 1880 had been an infantry officer and a good one. In 1880, as a major, he transferred to the Adjutant General's department, becoming its chief two months before the outbreak of the war. Corbin was from Ohio, and he was friendly with and appreciated by the Ohio Republican group that had raised McKinley to the Presidency. During the Spanish War it was upon Adjutant General Corbin that the Commander-in-Chief had come to rely as his principal military advisor, really as his chief of staff. Corbin was neither innovator nor reformer, but he was an unusually capable administrator who served Root both loyally and well.[27]

The role of Root's military tutor eventually fell to Lieutenant Colonel William Harding Carter, an assistant Adjutant General. Originally a cavalry officer, Carter was an instructor at the Infantry and Cavalry School at Fort Leavenworth in the 1890s. In 1897 he was moved to the Adjutant General's department in Washington to work on revising the system of examinations for officer promotion. His talents took him beyond that limited role. With Wagner and Schwan he planned the concentration of the Army for the Cuban campaign. In early 1899, again with Schwan, he helped negotiate through Congress the bill that provided an Army for pacifying the Philippines. Articulate and persuasive, Carter was a reformer; he was an early advocate of a general staff and of a more effective system of officer education. Moreover, Carter was thoroughly familiar with the problems of the War Department and he knew Capitol Hill. To administer the current Army, Root used Corbin; to plan the future Army, he used Carter.[28]

Elihu Root brought to the War Department no new strategic ideas. He accepted the view of the United States as an emerging world power and Mahan's concepts of maritime strategy supporting that emergence. To Root the Army's mission in a maritime strategy was as Schofield had described it: defensive. He therefore gave high priority to improving materially and organizationally the system of coast defense. For the remainder of the Army, now being termed the "mobile army," Root had no fixed long-term mission, assuming simply that a world power would inevitably have conflicts of interest with other powers that could, and eventually would, lead to war. For that war the Army should be prepared.[29]

The immediate problem facing Root, however, was neither military strategy nor Army reform; it was colonial administration. The Secretary of War in effect was both Army secretary and colonial secretary. Root separated the two functions by organizing administratively within the War Department a Division (later Bureau) of Insular Affairs, and by ending military governments as early as possible; a course that proved wise in view of Root's later difficulties with Brooke and Wood in Cuba, and with Otis and MacArthur in the Philippines. In May 1900 the government in Puerto Rico was transferred to civil authority; in May 1902 Wood transferred authority to the government of the new Cuban republic; and on the Fourth of July 1902 military government in the Philippines was ended. In judging Elihu Root's service as Secretary of War, it is important to appreciate his contributions as colonial secretary and the fact that colonial affairs frequently had to take precedence over Army reforms.

The new Secretary did not move into his War Department office carrying in his briefcase a comprehensive or definitive program of reform, but within a few months he was beginning to articulate the outlines of such a program. A patient and thorough investigator, Root tackled in its entirety the report of the Dodge Commission during his term. He studied Emory Upton's works, *The Armies of Asia and Europe* and *The Military Policy of the United States*. He saw to it that the latter work was finally published, and at War Department expense. To Root, *Military Policy* was an example of how a comprehensive, guiding, and unifying military policy could be derived logically from historical understanding and evaluation of America's world position. He gained understanding of the Prussian military system through Schwan's monograph on the German Army, a translation of Bronsart von Schellendorf, and a British work, *Brain of an Army*. In addition to the German model of military organization there was the precedent of the United States Navy, which had established a War Board during the conflict with Spain and in 1900 a General Board "to insure efficient preparation of the fleet in case of war." Root also knew of Schofield's view on how the perennial conflict between Secretary and Commanding General could be resolved. Within the Army he came to understand the importance of the functions of the Military Information Division. He drew on his own experience as a corporation counsel, and from that of his good friends in corporate America, for examples of organizational management.[30]

The reforms that Elihu Root was to champion were not original. Thoughtful Army officers and congressmen since the 1870s had been calling for systematic strategic planning, improved officer education, merit promotion, a streamlined coast defense organization, federal direction of the militia, and resolution of the conflicts in authority between the Secretary, Commanding General, and bureau chiefs. Many of those issues had been debated recently, though not resolved, when the Congress from December 1898 to March 1899 considered the bill that provided a force for the Philippine operations.[31] Each proposal for change had its advocates and its opponents within the Army and in Congress, in the latter often divided along party lines. Root's contributions were not in original ideas, but in his ability to judge concepts, and particularly in the leadership he provided to reform efforts. His sense of legislative timing and his understanding of the need to concurrently inform and educate the officer corps, the Congress, and the public were important aspects of that leadership.[32]

Root served four and a half years as Secretary. Within the first few months he established broad objectives for the Army, and he held to these objectives throughout his term, although the organizational structures and methods he proposed shifted as he met opposition and as his own thinking matured. At the core of what have come to be known as the "Root reforms" were two mutually reinforcing goals. First, and paramount, a unity of effort needed to be achieved within the War Department, throughout the Army, and between the regular and non-regular forces; a unity of effort subject to the civilian Secretary's direction. Second, the United States needed to be able to field a more proficient and competent force. From these two objectives Root derived his specific proposals, but he knew that he faced serious conflicts and tensions: between civilian control and military efficiency, between the executive and legislative branches of government, between the Secretary and the Commanding General, between the line of the Army and the "staff" departments, and between the regular Army and the militia.

To achieve unity of effort Root began by attempting to win acceptance in Congress and throughout the Army of the idea that there was one overriding purpose for having an Army. That single purpose was to prepare for war, a concept long and well established in continental Europe.[33] The Army and the War Department had to orient themselves on future operations, not on current administration. Root's problem therefore became one of establishing organizationally a body dedicated to planning for the future, a body that would set the goals and establish the program for a unified effort. Concurrently, the body would become the primary source of professional military advice reaching the Secretary, and through him the President and the Congress.

For the coast defense mission, Root inherited both the Endicott Board program and the Board of Ordnance and Fortification to keep abreast of technological advances and changed strategic requirements brought about by the creation of an American overseas empire. Root sought to improve the coast defense organization in two ways. First, he established a Corps of Artillery to replace the regimental structure. Second, he designated a major general as Chief of Artillery to provide the corps with representation equal to that of the Chief of Engineers and the Chief of Ordnance in the process of deciding where and how fortifications would be built and armed.[34] The mission of the rest of the Army, "the mobile army," was not as clear-cut, and the proper organization for its direction and support was less apparent.

Root recognized that some organizational entities in existence before the Spanish War had dealt to some degree with future requirements and plans: the Military Information Division, which was still active, and the several Army service schools that had been inactive since the start of the war. These entities should and could be strengthened. But Root sensed two deficiencies remaining even if that were done. The first was that the Secretary, owing to a lack of staff assistance, would remain unequipped to manage effectively and direct a unified effort; that is, he would remain unable to coordinate the activities of the various implementing commands and bureaus and to supervise their execution of programs.[35] The second deficiency was the lack of a body of officers educated and trained to plan and solve problems from the perspective of the Army as a whole. Root recognized that there were many good officers in the Army, some even superb: infantrymen, cavalrymen, artillerists, engineers, quartermasters. But what the brief campaigns of the Spanish War had demonstrated was a lack in the field of effective commanders of the combined arms and services, and in Washington of officers whose thinking took them beyond the narrow concerns of their own departments. Some correction of these conditions could be accomplished through maneuvers and exercises with large bodies of troops, through merit promotion of officers, and through rotating assignments so that officers gained experience in both the line and "staff" departments. But Root ultimately came to realize that to meet the need, a broadened officer education system, an overall scheme of progressively higher level study, was required.[36]

After four years of deliberation, experimental prototypes, and legislative defeats and victories, Root was able to put in place organizations that could produce unity of effort and a more competent Army in wartime, given their further development. His struggle to provide the Secretary with non-parochial staff assistance resulted in a "War Department General Staff," a uniquely American version of an established European practice. One of the solutions to improving the conduct of operations by combined arms and services was a "General Staff with Troops," officers trained to be operational specialists at a "General Service and Staff College." Related to all of this and central to future-oriented planning and progressive education was the concept of an Army War College.

NOTES

1. For assessment of McKinley's diplomacy see H. Wayne Morgan, *William McKinley and His America* (Syracuse, N.Y.: Syracuse University Press, 1963), 375-77.
2. The "Sicard Plan" is reprinted and discussed in Grenville, "American Naval Preparations," 37-38, 41-47.
3. Cosmas, *Army for Empire*, 74-76, 81-82. Trask, *War with Spain*, 148-49, 153-54.
4. Instructions to and report of the board are reprinted in William Harding Carter, *The American Army* (Indianapolis: Bobbs-Merrill, 1915), 206-11.
5. Cosmas, *Army for Empire*, 83-87. Trask, *War with Spain*, 149.
6. Graham A. Cosmas, "From Order to Chaos: The War Department, the National Guard and Military Policy, 1898," *Military Affairs* XXIX (Fall 1965): 118-19. National Guardsmen were expected to volunteer as individuals to serve with their state units. Trask, *War with Spain*, 151-52.
7. Strength figures throughout this discussion are from U.S. Senate, 56th Congress, 1st Session, Document No. 221: *Report of the Commission Appointed by the President to Investigate the Conduct of the War with Spain* (1899) (hereafter, *Report of Commission*) 8 vols. I "Reply of the Adjutant General": 254-66.
8. Cosmas, *Army for Empire*, 118-21, 238-42. Trask, *War with Spain*, 166-67.
9. Cosmas, *Army for Empire*, 111-12, 125-26, 130, 181. Trask, *War with Spain*, 172-74.
10. Cosmas, *Army for Empire*, 197-98, 230-34. Frank B. Freidel, *The Splendid Little War* (Boston: Little, Brown, 1958), 261-68. For campaign in Puerto Rico see Trask, *War with Spain*, Chap. 15.
11. There was close, but not always expert, inspection. For every ten officers in Shafter's expedition, there was one newspaper correspondent (815 officers, 89 correspondents). Millis, *Martial Spirit*, 255.
12. Ibid., 287. Trask, *War with Spain*, Chap. 9.
13. Millis, *Martial Spirit*, 243-44. Trask, *War with Spain*, Chap. 8. For photographs of the movement to Cuba, see Freidel, *Splendid Little War*, 59-97.
14. Cosmas, *Army for Empire*, 264-75.
15. Theodore Roosevelt to Henry Cabot Lodge, quoted in Millis, *Martial Spirit*, 82. For the political impact of "Algerism," see Margaret Leech, *In The Days of McKinley* (New York: Harper and Brothers, 1959), 297, 311-16.
16. *Report of Commission* I: 107. Cosmas, *Army for Empire*, 282-84. The Republicans lost seats in the House, but retained control.
17. Recommendations of Merritt and Otis are quoted in Millis, *Martial Spirit*, 377-78, 387. Impending danger of war in the Philippines is discussed in Leech, *Days of McKinley*, 345-47 and in John M. Gates, *Schoolbooks and Krags: The United States Army in the Philippines, 1898-1902* (Westport, Ct.: Greenwood Press, 1973), 34-42.
18. *Report of Commission* I: 116.
19. Twenty years earlier General Sherman, the uncle of Miles' wife, wrote of Miles, "I know no way to satisfy his ambitions but to surrender to him absolute power over the

whole Army with President and Congress thrown in." Sherman to Sheridan, May 9, 1879, cited in Richard N. Ellis, "The Humanitarian Generals," *The Western Historical Quarterly* III (April 1972): 177.

20. Edward Ransom, "Nelson A. Miles as Commanding General," *Military Affairs* XXIX (Winter 1965-66): 179-200, discusses Miles' controversies with Secretary Alger and Secretary Root and provides a balanced evaluation of the man. Less useful is Virginia W. Johnson, *The Unregimented General: A Biography of Nelson A. Miles* (Boston: Houghton Mifflin, 1962). For the "embalmed beef" charges and subsequent attacks by Miles on the Army see Cosmas, *Army for Empire*, 284-94.

21. For comments on the command problem see *Report of Commission* I: 115-16. For planlessness see testimony of Miles, Corbin and Shafter, Ibid. VII: 3241, 3249, 3281-82, 3284-88, 3191. For comment on the impact of the commission, see H. Wayne Morgan, *America's Road to Empire: Our War with Spain and Overseas Expansionism* (New York: John Wiley, 1965), 79.

22. The island of Guam was placed under Navy control.

23. Gates, *Schoolbooks and Krags*, 76-102.

24. Elihu Root, *Five Years at the War Department, 1899-1903, As Shown In the Annual Reports of the Secretary of War* (Washington: GPO, 1904), "Report for 1899," 6.

25. On Root's acceptance of the position, see Philip C. Jessup, *Elihu Root*, 2 Vols (New York: Dodd, Mead, 1938) I: 215-22. For McKinley and the War Department, see Ernest R. May, *The Ultimate Decision: The President as Commander-in-Chief* (New York: George Braziller, 1960), 94-107, and Cosmas, *Army for Empire*, 304.

26. Richard W. Leopold, *Elihu Root and the Conservative Tradition* (Boston: Little, Brown, 1954), 15-17. Horace S. and Marion G. Merrill, *The Republican Command: 1897-1913* (Lexington, Ky.: University of Kentucky Press, 1971), 98.

27. Jessup, *Root*, 223-25. Cosmas, *Army for Empire*, 62-64, 304.

28. U.S. Senate, 68th Congress, 1st Session, Document No. 119, *Creation of the American General Staff: Personal Narrative of the General Staff System of the American Army*, by Major General William Harding Carter (hereafter Carter, *Personal Narrative*) (Washington: GPO, 1924), 1. Carter, *American Army*, 206-11. Graham A. Cosmas, "Military Reform after the Spanish-American War: The Army Reorganization Fight of 1898-99," *Military Affairs* XXXV (February 1971): 16. Carter, "One View of the Army Question," 573-78. Carter was not the sole advisor to Root on reform, and in later writing he may have overemphasized his role. Nonetheless, in his 1903 annual report, Root gives "special credit" to Carter for bringing about the general staff law. Root, *Five Years*, 333.

29. For example, see remarks of Root at a General Staff dinner in 1903 quoted in William H. Carter, "Elihu Root — His Services as Secretary of War," *The North American Review* CLXXVIII (January 1904): 121.

30. It is mistaken to conclude, as many officers appeared to, that in publishing *Military Policy* Root endorsed all of Upton's recommendations. Root's remarks on Upton were in the context of the need in peace to prepare for war and to preserve and build on past military thought, "Address at the Marquette Club, Chicago, October 7, 1899," in Elihu Root, *The Military and Colonial Policy of the United States*, Robert Bacon and James B. Scott, eds. (Cambridge, Mass.: Harvard University Press, 1916), 108. In addition to those of Upton, works that may have influenced Root were Henry Spenser Wilkinson, *The Brain of an Army: A Popular Account of the German General Staff*, New ed. with letters from Count Moltke and Lord Roberts (London: Constable, 1895); Theodore Schwan, *Report on the Organization of the German Army* (Washington: GPO, 1894); and the introduction to a translation of General Bronsart von Schellendorf, *The Duties of the General Staff*, 3rd ed. (London: HMSO, 1895) reprinted in Military Information Division, *Staffs of Various Armies* (Washington: GPO, 1899). On Root's studies see Jessup, *Root*, I: 241-43, and Allan R. Millett, "The General Staff and the Cuban Intervention of 1906," *Military Affairs* XXXI (Fall 1967): 113. For Navy organization see Jarvis Butler, "The General Board of the Navy," *USNIP* LVI (August 1930): 700-05.

31. Graham A. Cosmas, "Military Reform: 1898-99," 12-18.

32. For support and opposition of the press regarding Root's Army reforms see Philip L. Semsch, "Elihu Root and the General Staff," *Military Affairs* XXVII (Spring 1963): 22-26.
33. Root, "Report for 1899," *Five Years*, 58.
34. Ibid., 66.
35. Ibid., 60-61.
36. Ibid., 61-65.

The Military Education
of Elihu Root
1899-1902

After only two months in office, Elihu Root began to call for reform. In a public address he termed the Army a "machine [that] today is defective," one that ought to be improved.[1] In November 1899 in his first annual report as Secretary of War, Root recommended that an army war college be established. Reaction was not exactly immediate; it was not until five years and three quarters of a million dollars in appropriations later, after Root had left office, that the first students arrived—all nine of them. One tangible result of the money Congress appropriated can be viewed today at Fort Lesley J. McNair, in the District of Columbia. Overlooking the Potomac is the edifice of the National War College. The reasons why five years elapsed between Root's announced intention and the arrival of the initial class are manifold. They range from simple resistance within the Army and the Congress to the multiple responsibilities that the new American empire imposed upon the Army.

The Root Proposals of 1899
In his 1899 report, Root pointed out that the legislation of March providing for a 65,000-man regular Army and 35,000 volunteers would expire on July 1, 1901. He argued that troop requirements of the Philippines and of coast defense would necessitate "reasonable enlargement" of the regular Army beyond that authorized before the Spanish War. Root suggested at the same time enlargement was being considered, "some improvements should be made in the organization of the Army."[2]

Starting with the proposition "that the real object of having an Army is to prepare for war," Root derived four measures fundamental to preparedness: modern weapons and equipment, a stockpile of supplies, exercises conducted with large bodies of troops, and a merit system for the promotion of officers.[3] Preparation for war demanded also, as Root put it,

Systematic study by responsible officers of plans for action under

> all contingencies of possible conflict, and with this . . . study of the arrangement of territorial and tactical organizations, and the establishment of depots, camps, fortifications and lines of communication with reference to these plans. . . .

And, moreover,

> study of the larger problem of military science and the most complete information of the state of the art, study of the constant improvements in implements and methods of warfare, and of the adaptability of improvements and inventions for the purpose of carrying out the plans devised. . . .

The happy result would be unity of effort and efficiency,

> so that all expenditures for each separate step of development may contribute toward the practical realization of a comprehensive and consistent scheme.

Whether he realized it or not, Root had summed up succinctly and well two important functions of the Prussian *Grosse Generalstab*, war planning and combat developments, and he understood that the two must be pointed toward a common goal.[4]

But having brought himself to that point, Root did not take the next logical step. He did not recommend the establishment of a general staff; he recommended only an "Army war college." The officers who made up the "college" would be charged with the duty

> to acquire the information, devise the plans and study the subjects above indicated, and to advise the Commander in Chief upon all questions of plans, armament, transportation, mobilization, and military preparation and movement.

Root then included an additional duty: "to direct the instruction and intellectual exercise of the the Army." To carry this out the college

> should not supersede but should incorporate, continue and bring under the same general management the present service schools, supplementing where it is necessary their courses, which now, so far as instruction is concerned, largely cover the ground. Its instruction at the outset and perhaps permanently, would be given through these schools, but it would give unity, influence, authority, and effectiveness in military affairs to the work and thought developed in them, aside from mere instruction.

By including among its duties management of the several service schools, Root was suggesting that the "war college" go beyond pure *Grosser Generalstab* functions. Moreover, since the service schools "aside from mere instruction" would develop "thought" and give "authority," Root was suggesting for them also a research and combat developments role.[5]

To this point Root seems to have played down the instructional role of the college itself, but then he recommended:

> That every officer of the Army below the rank of a field officer, and not already a graduate of one of the service schools should be detailed for some fixed period during his service to receive instruction at this college in the science of war, including the duties of the staff, and in all matters pertaining to the application of military science to national defense; that provision should be made for the continuance of such instruction by correspondence after expiration of the period of each officer's detail, and that all officers should be invited and entitled to present . . . as a part of the regular course . . . the results of their investigations, explorations, reflections, and professional and scientific work, and upon such subjects as may be prescribed by the college.[6]

The college would, after all, have an instructional role, to include providing continuing education through correspondence. Its curriculum would be theoretical ("the science of war") as well as applicatory ("duties of the staff") and would be at a high level ("application of military science to national defense"). Moreover, officers would be expected to engage in original research.

As Root outlined it further the "college" would consist of the Commanding General of the Army, the bureau chiefs, and "a number of the ablest and most competent officers of high rank in the Army, these officers to be detailed for service in the college for limited periods." The Military Information Division would be combined with the college and provide its office of record and archive.[7] What Root appears to have envisioned was a council of senior officers, assisted by the Military Information Division, which would perform *Grosser Generalstab* functions. The council also would supervise an officer education system that would conduct combat developments activities as well as provide instruction. The system would encompass a new academic institution for higher military study. All this Root enveloped into the term "army war college."

So despite his call for repair of the defective machine, Secretary Root had not recommended reorganization of the War Department. He had not recommended an American general staff nor even, as Upton had suggested and as Representative George B. McClellan, Jr., had attempted to include in the Army bill the previous year, the combining of the Adjutant General's office and that of the Inspector General to serve *Grosser Generalstab* purposes.[8] In fact Root was far from precise in describing his "army war college." So early in his incumbency, he may have been unclear himself as to how to organize for the results desired. Or he may have been only testing the wind to determine Army and congressional reaction to new concepts of staff and officer education. Or finally, by neither calling directly for a general staff nor proposing reorganization, he may have been simply attempting to get a general staff without creating opposition.

One of the Secretary's associates, William Harding Carter, explained that Root's scheme in 1899 was to establish "a War College with General Staff powers, so far as might be possible,"[9] as "the first step forward." If Carter was correct, it follows that in addition to the benefit that Root saw resulting from a high-level academic institution, he saw at least as much, if not more, resulting from an agency with "General Staff powers." His motives at the time, however, are not as important as the fact that very early he came to realize that critical *Grosser Generalstab* functions were not being performed at the War Department. It is also important that Root recognized that the prewar service schools and the Military Information Division were the two foundation blocks upon which some sort of structure could be built to perform *Grosser Generalstab* and other important functions. At the least, Elihu Root was demonstrating that Algerism was dead, that the defective machine was to be improved, and that the Republican Party was in charge.

As the War Department approached the year 1900, however, it faced more pressing problems than reform. In Cuba just before the turn of the year, Root replaced the military governor, Brooke, with Leonard Wood. By June, Wood had held municipal elections, and by November he had convened a constitutional convention. In Puerto Rico organic legislation took effect on May 1st, ending military government and the War Department's responsibility for the island. In the Philippines, Otis was coming under increasing criticism both from his subordinates and from the press. At the end of 1899, Aguinaldo had turned to guerrilla warfare and the conflict was taking on an ugly, more frustrating form. At his own request Otis was relieved in May, and Major General Arthur MacArthur was appointed in his place. During the spring, Secretary Root prepared instructions for a new Philippine Commission headed by Judge William Howard Taft, a commission that on September 1 assumed legislative functions in the islands, MacArthur retaining executive functions. Meanwhile the pacification campaign wore on, MacArthur achieving results no more visible than those of Otis. By the end of the year MacArthur was commanding 74,000 troops.[10]

But not only the former Spanish islands were draining Army energy and resources. In January the War Department had been required to send more than a thousand troops to Alaska to keep order among the miners and adventurers responding to the lure of gold.[11] In May the

Boxer Rebellion broke out in China; by mid-June foreign legations in Peking were under siege. A movement of some 16,000 troops from the Philippines and the United States to China was begun, but only five to six thousand had arrived before the siege was lifted in mid-August. The rest were diverted to the Philippines, and by the end of September only a legation guard of some two thousand remained.[12] The diversion of troops to the Philippines, however, did not compensate MacArthur for the 28,000 volunteers he was instructed in December to return to the United States. Indeed, the entire manpower situation of the Army during 1900 was in flux; over a third of the regular Army was discharged due to expiring enlistments.[13]

The year 1900 was also a presidential election year. Root for a time received serious Republican vice presidential consideration, but he discouraged the move. Theodore Roosevelt became the nominee. As a cabinet officer Root of course turned to aiding the Republican cause, vigorously defending the administration against the anti-imperialists. In October he delivered a slashing attack on the Democratic nominee, William Jennings Bryan. Root's campaigning may have helped reelect McKinley, but it probably did not assist in gaining future bipartisan support for Army reform. McKinley won reelection and the Republicans retained control of the Congress. Elihu Root would remain as Secretary of War.[14]

The Ludlow Board

With all that political and military activity, it is surprising that the wheels of Army reform turned at all, but slowly they did and progress was made. In late February 1900, three months after Root first sketched out the organization and purpose of his proposed war college, he appointed a board of three officers and charged it in effect with arriving at terms of reference for the war college and additionally with taking "preliminary measures toward [its] organization." Root apparently had made the decision to have a war college even if he did not know exactly what he wanted it to be. The instructions to the board were silent on the composition of the college other than stating that the Military Information Division, "reinforced and enlarged in its scope and effectiveness," would be combined with the college. The earlier idea of a council of senior officers was missing. The purpose of the war college with respect to education did not change. The college was "to supervise and direct" the service schools, which "as far as practicable" were "to cover the entire field of military instruction." The door was still open, however, for the war college itself to conduct instruction through providing "means for advance and special instruction" for "graduates of the service schools and others found qualified."[15]

The duties of the college other than in the area of education included more than had been described in the annual report of 1899. War planning was again directed, but this time special mention was made of planning for the employment of the "instructed reserve" and for cooperation with the Navy. Root directed "close and effective relations between the Army War College and the Naval War College." The instructions to the board were less specific on combat developments, but performance of that function clearly was implied. Significantly, the scope of the college as a "coordinating and authoritative agency through which all means of professional military information shall be . . . at the disposal of the War Department" was considerably broadened. The college was "to consider and report upon *all questions affecting the welfare and efficiency of the Army*" [emphasis added]. A broader area of interest could hardly have been prescribed. It was certainly broader than that of the *grosse Generalstab*. There was no indication, however, that the war college should serve as a supervising staff in any field other than officer education.[16]

Root appointed Brigadier General William Ludlow, a distinguished engineer and Civil War veteran who had commanded a brigade during the Santiago campaign, to head the board. Ludlow's duties between the wars were primarily with civil works, although he had served as military attache to Britain and had investigated European military systems while on that duty. More recently he had commanded the Department of Havana. Colonel Henry C. Hasbrouck, an artilleryman with experience at Fort Monroe, was the second member of the board, and Carter was the third. In June, Lieutenant Colonel Joseph P. Sanger, Upton's companion on the world tour of twenty years before, once Schofield's aide, and then a member of the Inspector General's department, was added. All the board members were advocates of reform. All but Hasbrouck had written for publication on the need for a general staff.

Ludlow was a man who saw things in black and white. His career in civil works was shot through with controversies in which he had taken strong and uncompromising positions. Soon after formation of the board Ludlow sailed for Europe once again to study European systems. In July, Root wrote him requesting his views on what should be included in the next year's legislation. Root asked and he received. Ludlow sent back from Berlin recommendations that ranged in subject from the preferred color of chevrons to the size of the Army (larger). They included a proposal for one general and five lieutenant generals in the Army, one of the five to be Chief of the General Staff, a staff to be composed of a major general, six colonels, and 58 other officers. Root did not include this recommendation in his legislative request. Upon Ludlow's return to the United States, according to Carter, he did not place the results of his overseas investigations before his board. He did make a separate individual report on these investigations to the Adjutant General some months later.[17]

The Ludlow Board was active for seven months, though it appears that service on the board excused only the chairman from other duties. Its report was submitted in October. The functions of the war college as recommended by the board understandably reflected those that Root had spelled out in the letter of instruction. The concept that the war college should supervise officer education throughout the school system was retained. The board apparently did not agree, however, that the existing (but recessed) service schools could be made to "cover the entire field of military instruction," as Root had suggested. The war college itself, the board recommended, should "provide higher and special training." To train "student officers," there should be assigned to the college "assistants and instructors." This recommendation was the most definitive statement to date that a primary function of the war college would be academic instruction. Also significant was the recommendation that the "higher and special training" was to be "for the command and management of troops and the conduct of military operations." If Root accepted this recommendation, the war college would be focusing its instruction not on affairs of the *grosse Generalstab*, but on those of the *Truppengeneralstab*.[18]

According to the Ludlow Board, however, supervising military education and conducting instruction should not be the sole functions of the war college. It should also provide "original consideration and report upon the various aspects of military administration in general" constituting "an authority, capable of furnishing the War Department expert professional opinion . . . upon any question, general or technical." It would deal with the "consideration and disposition of professional matters and the coordination and regulation of the military administration." The war college would include, as Root had directed, the Military Information Division with its traditional intelligence and planning functions. The college would become, in the words of the board, "a body charged in some respects with the duties and responsibilities imposed upon what is known in foreign services as the General Staff, as well as others in addition." That final clause is interesting. The Ludlow Board apparently recognized full well that in calling for an agency with responsibility in the area of "coordination and regulation of the military administration," it was recommending a broader scope than the war planning and combat developments activity associated with the *grosse Generalstab*.[19]

In sum, the war college that Ludlow and his colleagues described for Root was to be both an academic institution, concentrating on the command and management of troops and the conduct of military operations, and a staff with coordinating responsibility as well as intelligence, war planning, and combat developments responsibilities. But much of the Ludlow Board's report consists of argument as to why the war college should not be considered an adequate substitute for a true general staff element within the War Department, even though the board conceded that the proposed war college's efforts "would be found to inure in a marked degree to an improved administration, a higher efficiency, a greater coherence and unity, and an advantageous and desirable economy." With the war college a creature of the executive, Ludlow argued, fiscal support from the Congress might be withheld or withdrawn. As a creature of the current executive, the war college could be disbanded by a future executive.

The board had responded to Root's instructions; its members had described a war college to perform the functions outlined. But embodied in the board's response were two warnings. The first was that the prewar school system did *not* "pretty much cover the ground." The second was that nothing less than a statutory general staff could provide the desired direction and control of the War Department. Implied was the idea that there were no shortcuts, no cheap solutions; Root must ask for legislation establishing a general staff.[20]

The Ludlow Board's report was provided to Root just a month before the election; it is not surprising that no immediate action was taken to implement its recommendations. Moreover, a need much more critical to McKinley and Root than legislation proposing a general staff was legislation to provide an Army to continue pacification of the Philippines. The March 1899 emergency legislation would expire at the end of June 1901; if new legislation was not forthcoming, the Army would revert to its pre-Spanish War strength. McKinley and Root decided, undoubtedly wisely, to take as risk-free a course as possible. They decided to include nothing in the upcoming Army bill that was not acceptable to the military affairs committees of the Senate and the House. If Root's concept that the role of the Army was to prepare for war required legislation, then implementing that concept would just have to await the outcome of the war at hand. The "war college" Root had described in his 1899 annual report and in his 1900 instructions to General Ludlow did not require legislation; nonetheless, Root was cautious and did not activate a war college. The $20,000 appropriation for support of the college that Root had received shortly after appointing the Ludlow Board was allowed to lapse, the money reverting to the treasury.[21]

During 1900 Carter, in addition to his service on the Ludlow Board, was engaged in preparing the 1901 legislation needed to keep adequate forces in the Philippines. At Root's direction he had sent questionnaires to all general officers and colonels to obtain their views on measures to be included in the legislation. To Carter the responses were disappointing, most only calling for a larger Army, few providing ideas to improve effectiveness and efficiency. The Military Service Institution announced that its prize essay would be on the subject "The Organization of a Staff

Best Adapted to the United States Army." No entry was deemed worthy of the award. Either the officer corps was too busy, or the urge for reform was waning. Root's attempt to organize a corps of artillery passed the Senate but failed in the House. The year 1900 had not been one of major reform.[22]

Root had been able, however, to obtain appropriations for refurbishing the facilities of the prewar schools at Forts Monroe, Riley, and Leavenworth. New construction began in February 1901. He was also able to get a new appropriation of $10,000 for support of the nonexistent war college, and several officers were sent to Newport for the summer session of the Naval War College. Because of the requirements for officers for the Philippine campaign and for the expanding coastal defense works, however, there was a lack of officers to serve at the schools, either as faculty or as students. The Artillery School was able to reopen, but its supporters had to settle for a one-year course instead of the desired prewar two-year course. In his annual report of 1900, Secretary Root lamented that the Army was sadly short of officers.[23]

The legislative year 1901 began successfully. An expanded regular Army was authorized and the President given the discretion to vary its strength between 65,000 and 100,000. Root settled on approximately 89,000, which left the Army with 1,135 officer vacancies. Root also won authorization for artillery reorganization and for his scheme to rotate officer assignments between the line and the "staff departments."[24] Overseas, problems began to diminish. In the Philippines, Aguinaldo was captured in March; his movement soon began to deteriorate. On the 4th of July, Taft became governor with both executive and legislative functions. MacArthur departed the same day, replaced as troop commander by Major General Adna R. Chaffee, who had led American forces in China. The Philippine war was not over yet, however. In September insurgency broke out again on Samar and in southern Luzon. Chaffee struck back vigorously and harshly at these last two pockets of resistance. In Cuba, Leonard Wood saw the constitutional convention finish its work in March, but then had to negotiate (and force) Cuban acceptance of the provisions of the Platt Amendment, which under certain conditions permitted American intervention in the new republic. In December, Wood successfully supervised national elections for president and congress.[25] A new overseas problem for the Army and the nation came onto the horizon, however, when the Hay-Pauncefote Treaty was negotiated with Great Britain. It removed any treaty obstacles to the construction and maintenance of a Central American canal under the sole auspices of the United States.

On September 6, 1901, President McKinley was shot while attending an exposition in Buffalo, New York. For a few days it appeared that he would recover, but on the 13th Secretary of War Elihu Root, acting for the Cabinet, summoned the Vice President. On the 14th, William McKinley died. Theodore Roosevelt was President.

The Concepts of William Harding Carter

After Congress passed the critical 1901 Army bill in May, Carter, the only member of the Ludlow Board still at the War Department, sensing perhaps that the board had not provided Secretary Root what he needed, began to make new proposals for the school system and for a general staff. Taking a leaf from Root's book he opened with a subject other than that of the need for a general staff. He recommended revitalization of the lyceum system. In Carter's view that system had become a farce, threatening not only the examination feature of officer promotion but also the quality of the students who would be entering the service schools. Carter recommended the lyceum program be made formal and a board of officers be established on each post to determine an officer's successful completion of prescribed standard courses. Moreover, the lyceums should concern themselves only with regimental duties. The present system, according to Carter, "discusses too much the duties of generals and teaches too little the duties of subalterns."[26]

In Carter's scheme the lyceums were to be the starting point for the entire school system. Properly conducted, they would eliminate unfit officers and recognize talented officers qualified for the service schools. The school at Fort Riley to be called the "Cavalry and Field Artillery School" should present the model of a properly organized and administered post. During the late months of summer the Riley reservation should be used for brigade and division maneuvers. National Guard officers should be invited to attend. In Carter's view the school at Fort Leavenworth needed a title other than "Infantry and Cavalry School." It could be either "war college" or "staff college." Whatever the name, in addition to military studies, its students should gain proficiency and be tested in Spanish or French before graduation. Leavenworth graduates, after a brief tour with the line, would be detailed to Washington to serve either with the war college or the Military Information Division.[27]

At the war college in Washington (or "Staff College" if Leavenworth were named "War College") selected officers would study under advisors and familiarize themselves with the work of military attaches and the military systems of other nations. The Washington-based school should be "run on the lines of the Naval War College . . . under the direction of the General Staff." Carter recommended two categories of students: younger officers who would remain in Washington to continue their studies as candidates for the General Staff, and a class of more senior officers (up to the rank of colonel) who would participate in the work of the college for only a portion of the year, perhaps for four months as at the Naval War College.[28]

Carter also began to write of a "General Staff Corps." Eligible for such a corps would be officers who had distinguished themselves in the school system and who had shown a "high order of practical ability to command troops." Detail to the General Staff Corps would be for a period of four years. Members might also be required to serve in a branch of the line or in a "staff department" in which they were not originally commissioned. The duties of the "General Staff" as Carter described them were similar to those Root had specified for a "war college" in his letter of instructions to the Ludlow Board the previous year. The General Staff would engage in war planning and combat developments, but it would also be charged with the inspection of troops to determine the state of discipline and efficiency. Two General Staff Corps officers would be assigned to each subordinate territorial headquarters. At the War Department the Military Information Division would be transferred from the Adjutant General's office to the General Staff. A lieutenant general, "Chief of the General Staff," would supervise the General Staff at the War Department and coordinate the work of the various "staff departments." Carter in effect was suggesting a move back toward the Prussian system. At the same time he was reinforcing the distinction that he felt was necessary between the role of a "general staff" and that of a "war college."[29]

By October, Carter had won approval of his plans in concept, if not in detail. The Secretary approved a school system that would consist of an officers' school at each post (replacing the lyceum), where lieutenants would study the duties of lieutenants, and graduation would be recognized and recorded. The service schools, except for the one at Leavenworth, would be reestablished as before the war. The school at Fort Leavenworth would be converted to a "staff school." Qualified officers of all arms would be sent to Leavenworth regardless of whether they had attended one of the other service schools. Distinguished graduates of Leavenworth and selected officers of higher rank would be sent to the war college in Washington. At each stage, except for the war college students of higher rank, formal examinations would be conducted. Graduates of the war college of junior rank would be assigned to the General Staff, assuming one came into existence. If one did not, the graduates would be assigned either to the Military Information Division or as attaches abroad.[30]

Carter warned, as had the Ludlow Board, against trying "to imbue the war college with General Staff functions." He insisted that any such attempt would be "doomed to failure." Carter wanted both a war college and a general staff, and he wanted a general staff organization extending beyond the War Department, to include a General Staff Corps and *Truppengeneralstab*.[31] Carter's persistent staff work bore fruit; on November 27, 1901, Secretary Root published War Department General

Order Number 155. It directed the establishment of a formal tiered system of officer education, including a war college. On February 14, 1902, Root forwarded a legislative proposal to the Fifty-Seventh Congress, "A Bill to Increase the Efficiency of the Army." The proposal asked for authority to establish a General Staff Corps.

General Order Number 155

War Department General Order Number 155 of November 27, 1901, is a benchmark in the professionalization of the officer corps of the United States Army. For the first time the Army would have in place a systematic and progressive program of professional education. The starting point in the progression was to be officer schools established on each post "for elementary instruction in theory and practice," designed to produce regimental officers who were truly expert in the administration and handling of small units. At another level would be institutions to be known as "special service" schools. Their goal would be to produce technically proficient officers for what were considered the more complex military functions: engineering, medicine, coast artillery and harbor defense, and the mounted arms—cavalry and field artillery.

At a higher level would be the school at Fort Leavenworth. The former Infantry and Cavalry School would be considered a "general service" school and redesignated as the "General Service and Staff College." Leavenworth was to provide instruction in every branch of the military service. There would be sent "every officer who displays superior qualities in the lower schools," officers in the rank of lieutenant. Qualified National Guard and former volunteer officers were eligible to attend the schools at all three levels, the post officer schools, the "special service" schools, and the "general service" school. The academic performance of each officer attending a school would be made a matter of official record of the War Department.[32]

At the highest level General Order Number 155 directed that a War College be established at Washington Barracks, District of Columbia, "for the most advanced instruction." Root discussed the War College in his annual report submitted at the end of 1901. It would "ultimately be in effect a post-graduate course for the study of the greater problems of military science and national defense." It would embrace "the higher branches of professional study." Officer detailed to the War College would be of two categories: distinguished graduates of the General Service and Staff College and "such field officers and captains as may be specially designated by the War Department."

General Order Number 155 made it abundantly clear that the road to career success followed the route of distinguished performance at first the post officer school, next at the General Service and Staff College, and finally at the War College. Root explained that those officers who had "uniformly shown the greatest interest and most proficiency" through these three trials would "have high consideration . . . with a view to utilization of their abilities as military attaches or on special missions abroad and for the higher duties of general staff work."[33]

As directed by General Order Number 155, the War College was to be under the immediate supervision of a board of five officers with four additional ex officio members: the Superintendent of the Military Academy at West Point, the Commanding Officer of the General Service and Staff College, the Chief of Engineers, and the Chief of Artillery. This "War College Board" was charged additionally with exercising "general supervision and inspection of all the other enumerated schools" and with "maintaining through them a complete system of military education." Additional officers, as necessary, might be detailed to assist the board.[34]

In 1902 the War Department began to implement General Order Number 155. The Engineer School of Application, displaced from its Willets Point location by the Coast Artillery, moved into old buildings at Washington Barracks and began to instruct eleven student officers. The Coast Artillery assembled ten students for the course of the School of Submarine Defense at Fort Totten, New York, and thirty for the course at the Artillery School at Fort Monroe. In September, the General Service and Staff College opened at Fort Leavenworth with a class of ninety-seven. In June, Congress authorized Root to use $400,000 of the unexpended portion of the emergency 1899 appropriation to construct a suitable building for the War College at Washington Barracks. Congress appropriated an additional $15,000 to support the operation of the War College.[35]

In his 1901 report Root did not propose, as he had in 1899, to give *Grosser Generalstab* functions to the War College or to its governing board. Moreover, with its $15,000 appropriation, Congress stated that the object of the Army War College was "the direction and coordination of the instruction in the various service schools [and] extension of the opportunities for investigation and study in the Army and Militia." Significantly missing from the appropriations bill language as an object for the War College was "the collection and dissemination of military information," a phrase that had been included in the language of the two previous appropriations.[36] These omissions tend to indicate that by November 1901 Secretary Root wanted to project the War College as functioning primarily in the field of officer education and not as a substitute or prototype for a general staff.

The First General Staff Bill

The second important product of Carter's staff work in 1901 was the proposed legislation implementing the concept of a general staff. Root treated the subject very briefly in the 1901 report and separately from his discussion of the War College. He cited the creation of the War College Board and "the duties that will be imposed upon it," as indicated in his 1899 report. He then opined that the War College Board as described in 1899 was "probably as near an approach to the establishment of a general staff as is practical under existing law." As he continued his discussion, however, Root appears to have said that he had been overly optimistic in 1899, that he had reconsidered and concluded that the War College Board's work in the field of education was heavy enough by itself to preclude the board from adequately performing "all the duties of a general staff."[37]

Secretary Root then recommended, as Ludlow and his colleagues had urged him to do the previous year, that a general staff be established by law. A general staff, in Root's 1901 version, would provide

> opportunity and provision for the study of great questions, the consideration and formation of plans, comprehensive forethought against future contingencies, and coordination of the various branches of the service with a view to harmonious action.

A general staff, Root explained, was "a body of competent military experts . . . charged with these matters of the highest importance." As for the War College Board, it would become part of that general staff.[38] In sum, the Secretary was now asking for both an academic institution to provide highest-level professional education, and a planning and coordinating staff. The governing body of the institution, the War College Board, would be part of both the institution and the staff and would serve as the connecting link between the two.

The first call for general staff legislation came in December when President Roosevelt sent his first annual message to the Congress. Root probably had no difficulty selling the general staff concept to a Commander-in-Chief who had experienced (and had contributed to) the confusion at Tampa and during the march to Santiago.[39] The bill itself was introduced in Congress on February 14, 1902. In the bill Root asked for a "General Staff Corps" of thirty-seven officers. There would be a "Chief of the General Staff" to supervise those General Staff Corps officers on duty at the War Department. General Staff Corps officers assigned to duty with geographical departments and divisions and with troops in the field, however, would be under the control of the commanders of those departments, divisions, and troops. In a major departure from the Prussian system, officers would not be permanently appointed as General Staff Corps members.[40]

The duties of the General Staff Corps as outlined in the bill were practically identical to those Root had specified for the War College in his instructions to General Ludlow two years earlier. The same wording was frequently used. Only two duties that might be considered new were added: "to consider military policy of the country" and "to prepare and to supervise the preparation and arrangement of material for the military history of the United States." The duty to "consider and report on all questions affecting the welfare and efficiency of the Army" was retained. Root apparently still had in mind an agency with a breadth of interest wider than that normally associated with the intelligence, war planning, and combat developments functions of the *grosse Generalstab*.[41]

To the detriment of its legislative chances, the bill included subjects other than the establishment of a General Staff Corps. It called for the creation of a "Department of Supply," consolidating the Quartermaster, Subsistence, and Pay Departments, and it called for a new "Division of Transportation." These proposals made inevitable opposition to the bill from the three bureau chiefs concerned and their congressional allies. The bill also proposed to disestablish the Inspector General's Department, its auditing function going to the Treasury Department and its readiness inspection function to the General Staff Corps. The Inspector General thereby was added to the list of the bill's foes. The role of the Adjutant General also was to be greatly diminished. As Root put it in a letter to the Chairman of the Military Affairs Committee of the Senate, the Adjutant General would "be relieved from the consideration of important questions."[42] The loyal Corbin accepted this. In later years a successor very definitely would not.

Additionally, the position of Commanding General of the Army was to be abolished, but not until after General Miles left active service. Until that time Miles would retain the title of Commanding General but perform the duties of a Chief of General Staff.[43] John Schofield would not merely have accepted this change, he would have welcomed it. Nelson Miles' priorities were different. He became the most outspoken and perhaps the most influential opponent of the general staff system. Playing upon the emotions of the Civil War veterans who made up the military committees, Miles formed up and paraded by the memories of Washington, Steuben, Winfield Scott, Grant, and Sherman. This European, monarchist idea of a general staff would not only Prussianize but Russianize the gallant American Army of Yorktown, Gettysburg, and San Juan Hill. Behind Miles rallied all the bureau chiefs except the Adjutant General and the Chief of Engineers. Their congressional friends added to the intensity of the opposition. It was all too much. Faced with so much opposition from within the War Department, opposition led by the Commanding General himself, the Chairman of the Military Affairs Committee of the Senate sent word to Root in April that the bill would not leave committee during the session.[44]

Despite the setback on the general staff bill, the year 1902 proved to be one of progress in Root's efforts to turn the attention of the Army toward its real but elusive purpose of preparing for war. In May, General Wood turned over his authority in Cuba to President T. Estrada Palma and the elected government of the new republic. By that same month, after three and a half years of warfare in the Philippines, the Army had pacified all but the Moro-populated provinces of the southern islands. Congress enacted on July 1st the first organic Philippine government act. By the end of the year Root had cause for satisfaction in his diminishing role as colonial secretary. As a result of the lower level of activity in the archipelago, he began to reduce the Army from a strength of more than 80,000 to its statutory minimum of 65,000.[45]

Within the United States the War and Navy Departments scheduled a joint coast defense exercise along the New England seaboard. Planning went forward also for maneuvers of division size to be held at Fort Riley, maneuvers which would involve both regular Army and National Guard units. Working closely with the National Guard Association, Root successfully moved new militia legislation forward in the legislative process during the year. What would one day be known as the "Root reforms" were beginning to take shape. But the general staff problem remained.[46]

The War College Board

When Congress failed to take action on the general staff bill, Root found himself caught in a dilemma of his own making. In 1899 he had promised the benefits of a general staff while proposing only a war college. In 1902, after apparently acceding to the uncompromising position taken by General Ludlow and his reformist advisory board and to the arguments of Carter, Root was on record that a war college could not perform after all the true function of a general staff. It would be too busy with its educational duties. Root's choices were either to go back to his 1899 scheme and reorient the prospective War College Board toward what he conceived to be general staff duties, or to keep the War College Board focused on the educational system, fight the good legislative fight for a true general staff, and hope for the best. Root straddled the choices. He kept the War College Board pointed at educational affairs but at the same time gave it "a wide range of general staff duties . . . in absence of any more complete organization."[47]

Although Root had announced in November 1901 the formation of the War College Board, it was not until seven months later, in July of the next year, that he actually detailed officers to serve on it. His stated reason for the delay was the unavailability of the selected officers. When the composition of the board was finally announced, it included Carter, by then a brigadier general, and another very appropriate choice, Tasker Bliss, also a brigadier general. Since his return from Madrid upon the outbreak of the war, Bliss had served as chief of staff of an infantry

72

division during the operation in Puerto Rico and, from December 1898 to May 1902, as the Chief of Customs Service with the military government of Cuba. To lead the board, Major General S. B. M. Young was named. Young was a new personality on the War Department scene. A veteran of the Indian wars, Young had commanded a brigade in the Santiago campaign, where one of his subordinates was Lieutenant Colonel Theodore Roosevelt of the 1st Volunteer Cavalry. Young had enhanced his fighting reputation as a commander in the Philippine campaigns, but he had little understanding of the issues facing the War Department. Two majors were assigned to complete the board: Henry A. Greene and William D. Beach.[48]

The board first met on July 10, 1902, and soon thereafter rented and equipped a house at 20 Jackson Place on LaFayette Square. All but some $85 of the $10,000 fiscal year 1902 appropriation was spent for that purpose.[49] Since the same order that assigned officers to the War College Board announced that the General Service and Staff College would open on September 1, the first task of the War College Board was to draft regulations as guidance for the Fort Leavenworth school. This was done rather hastily by appointing a subordinate board of five officers to select faculty and lay out a course of instruction.[50] Appropriate regulations were published on August 1, a month before the first students were to arrive. The regulations for Leavenworth were followed on August 9 by regulations to guide the conduct of military instruction at those undergraduate military schools and colleges throughout the country where Army officers were detailed as instructors. By the end of September the War College Board had also drawn and distributed regulations that covered the foundation of the education system, the post officers' schools.[51] These regulations all followed closely the scheme for education proposed by Carter the previous year. During this early period in its life, the War College Board also worked with the Corps of Engineers on planning the interior arrangement of the new War College building to be constructed at Washington Barracks.[52]

In matters not directly related to officer education, the War College Board began to study the appropriate organization of the General Staff Corps—if one was eventually to be authorized by law—and the steps required to implement the militia bill that had passed the House but was still before committee in the Senate.[53] The War College Board's major involvement as an embryonic or prototype general staff engaged in true *Grosser Generalstab* work, however, was due to a circumstance beyond Root's control, the diplomatic style of Theodore Roosevelt.

Two foreign policy crises had been taking form since Roosevelt had become President, one in Alaska and one in the Caribbean. The trace of the boundary between southern Alaska and Canada had been disputed ever since the purchase of Alaska. It was of no consequence until 1901, when it was suspected that gold might be discovered in the disputed area. In March 1902 Roosevelt told a representative of the *London Times* that in case of bloodshed in the area he would "run our line as we assert it" and "send troops to guard and hold it." Later in March he instructed his Secretary of War to move "additional troops . . . as quietly and unostentatiously as possible to Southern Alaska." The President, convinced that the Canadian claims had no validity, refused through the summer and fall to submit the matter to arbitration.[54]

On the southern front, Roosevelt was informed in December 1901 that Great Britain and Germany intended to blockade Venezuela in a move designed to collect debts owed their nationals. The presence of German warships in a hostile posture in the Caribbean was a new and worrisome phenomenon. By late summer the President was sufficiently concerned to take precautions. The Navy began planning for a concentration of the fleet in the Caribbean, going so far as to investigate possible landing sites for troops on the Venezuelan coast.[55] As for Root, he had come into the War Department, among other reasons, to eradicate Algerism; it would not do to be caught in 1902, as Alger had been in 1898, without plan or preparation. The War College Board was the only planning staff Root had, and to it he turned.

In October Secretary Root directed the War College Board to make a study of what today would be called "war reserve stocks." It was a major tasking. Root wanted to know not only the current supply situation but the requirements for an Army of 150,000 and an Army of 250,000 in two situations: operations in a cold climate and operations in a hot climate. He also wanted to know the domestic sources for the production of war reserve material, the capacity of those sources, the Army's storage capacity, and where stocks should be located in reference to strategic requirements. While much of the work involved in answering Root's questions consisted of gathering data, a complete answer required assumptions as to threats; estimations of political, economic, geographical, and military conditions; and, above all, some policy-driven strategic concept within which war plans could be drawn.[56] None of these things were the stuff of which War Department deliberations were made in 1902.

Only infrequently did the board formally meet during its existence. At times it was shorthanded. Young, in company with Generals Corbin and Wood, went to Germany in the autumn to observe the annual maneuvers of the Prussian Army. During November and December, under the direction of the Department of State, Bliss was negotiating a trade reciprocity treaty with the Republic of Cuba.[57]

The Second General Staff Bill

Concurrently with the establishment and early efforts of the War College Board, Root and his supporters were working hard at getting from the next session of Congress a more favorable response to their proposal for a general staff. Root launched an educational campaign directed at the Congress, the public, and the officer corps. To counter General Miles' testimony, he had retired Generals Schofield and Merritt testify in favor of a general staff, and he submitted evidence that active general officers favored the measure. He and the President took the added precaution of getting Nelson Miles out of town by sending him on an inspection trip to the Philippines with return via the trans-Siberian railroad. Corbin, for his part, worked at getting sympathetic understanding from the press. Carter published two articles in the professional journal *United Service*, explaining the benefits to date of Root's reforms and the need for a general staff and a war college.[58]

At the next session of Congress, Root had a revised general staff bill introduced. Unlike the previous bill it addressed only the general staff. Omitted was the scheme to create a Department of Supply, although once again the Inspector General's department was to be disestablished in favor of the General Staff Corps. There were other differences from the earlier bill. The role of the General Staff Corps included, as before, preparing plans for the national defense and for mobilization in time of war, but its duties as an advisory body were made more specific: "to render professional aid and assistance to the Secretary of War, general officers and other superior commanders and to act as their agents in informing and coordinating the action of all the different officers engaged in carrying out their orders."[59]

Ironically the new bill made the position of the senior member of the General Staff Corps stronger than the bill to which Miles and the objecting bureau chiefs had taken exception. The title "Chief of General Staff" became "Chief of Staff of the Army." The Chief's role was expanded from that of supervision of "the employment and operations of the General Staff officers on duty at the War Department," giving him "under the direction of the President and Secretary of War supervision of all troops of the line and the several administrative staff and supply departments."[60]

Embedded in the proposed legislation was the basis for an American General Staff that could, and eventually would, evolve into an agency with far broader responsibilities than the *Grosse Generalstab* upon which it was modeled, responsibilities which in Germany were performed by the War Ministry. If the planning responsibilities were Prussian, the concept of a centralized executive body was that of American industry.[61]

Secretary Root, in order to soften the opposition of Miles' congressional admirers and thereby ease passage of the bill, recommended that the proposed law not become effective until after Miles' retirement in

August. This concession meant another six months of life for the War College Board as a central planning agency. On February 14, 1903, a year from the day when the initial general staff proposal was introduced in Congress, the General Staff Act was approved, authorizing forty-two officers to be detailed to the General Staff Corps. The pen used by the President to sign the act was graciously presented by Root to Brigadier General Carter.[62]

NOTES

1. Root, *Colonial and Military Policy*, 8.
2. Elihu Root, *Five Years of the War Department, 1899-1903: As Shown in the Annual Reports of the Secretary of War* (Washington: GPO, 1904), "Report of the Secretary of War for 1899," 56-57.
3. Ibid., 58, 61-62.
4. Quotes from Ibid., 59-60.
5. Quotes from Ibid., 62-63.
6. Ibid., 63.
7. Ibid., 62-63.
8. Cosmas, "Military Reform: 1898-99," 14.
9. Carter, *Personal Narrative*, 2.
10. For the Army in Cuba see David J. Healy, *The United States in Cuba, 1898-1902: Generals, Politicians and the Search for Policy* (Madison: University of Wisconsin Press, 1963), 117-53, and Graham A. Cosmas, "Securing the Fruits of Victory: The U.S. Army Occupies Cuba, 1898-99," *Military Affairs* XXXVIII (October 1974): 85-91. For Puerto Rico, Root, "Report for 1900," *Five Years*, 116-21. For the Philippines, Gates, *Schoolbooks and Krags*, 156-78. For the appointment and instructions to Taft, Ralph E. Minger, *William Howard Taft and United States Foreign Policy: The Apprenticeship Years, 1900-1908* (Urbana: University of Illinois Press, 1975), 1-6, 20-23, 31.
11. Root, "Report for 1900," *Five Years*, 78-79, 121-23.
12. Ibid., 86-98.
13. Ibid., 80.
14. For Root's vice-presidential possibilities see Carter, "Elihu Root—His Services," 117-19, and Jessup, *Root*, 230-32. For attack on Bryan see Root, "The United States and the Philippines, October 24, 1900," *Colonial and Military Policy*, 27-69.
15. Corbin to Ludlow, Letter of Instructions, February 20, 1900, in "The Army War College: Memoranda Pertaining to the Establishment and Operation of the Army War College," compiled and arranged by M. Bartow Mercer under the direction of Brigadier General W. W. Wotherspoon, President, Army War College, 1907, 3-4 (hereafter Mercer, "Memoranda"), unpublished document, MHI.
16. Ibid.
17. Eugene V. McAndrews, *William Ludlow: Engineer, Governor, Soldier* (Ann Arbor, Mich.: University Microfilms, 1976) is a laudatory account of the career of Ludlow (and the Corps of Engineers). For Ludlow's ideas on Army reform see 215-20. For Ludlow's individual report see 221 and Carter, *Personal Narrative*, 4. Ill feeling later developed between friends of Ludlow and those of Carter, McAndrews, *Ludlow*, 224.
18. "Ludlow to Adjutant General, October 31, 1900," in Mercer, "Memoranda," 5-6. Student officers were to include Army, Navy, and militia officers.
19. Ibid., 5, 7.
20. Ibid., 5-6.
21. Carter, *Personal Narrative*, 5. Mercer, "Memoranda," 9.
22. Ibid., 5, 2.
23. Root, "Report for 1900," *Five Years*, 131, 138-39.
24. Root, "Report for 1901," *Five Years*, 146-48, 151-53.
25. Gates, *Schoolbooks and Krags*, 225-65. Healy, *The U.S. in Cuba*, 153-77.

26. William H. Carter, "Memorandum for the Adjutant General, May 25, 1901," in *Personal Narrative*, 5-7.
27. William H. Carter, "Memorandum No. 1, Subject: Instruction of the Regular Army," undated in *Personal Narrative*, 7-10.
28. Ibid., 10.
29. Ibid., 10-13.
30. William H. Carter, "Memorandum for the Secretary of War, October 14, 1901," in *Personal Narrative*, 13-15.
31. Ibid., 14.
32. Adjutant General's Office, General Orders No. 155, November 27, 1901.
33. Root, "Report for 1901," *Five Years*, 163. GO No. 155.
34. GO No. 155.
35. Root, "Report for 1902," *Five Years*, 278. Mercer, "Memoranda," 12.
36. Mercer, "Memoranda," 12.
37. Root, "Report for 1901," *Five Years*, 165.
38. Ibid.
39. Theodore Roosevelt, "First Annual Message," *The Works of Theodore Roosevelt*, national ed., 20 vols. (New York: Charles Scribner's Sons, 1926): 123. Roosevelt had called for a general staff before becoming Vice President, "Address before the Hamilton Club, Chicago, April 10, 1899," in *The Works of Theodore Roosevelt* memorial edition, 24 vols. (New York: Charles Scribner, 1923-26), XV: 276-77. Roosevelt's testimony on the Santiago campaign is in *Report of Commission*, V: 2255-72.
40. U.S. Congress, Senate, *A Bill to Increase the Efficiency of the Army*, S.3917, 57th Cong., lst Sess., 1902, reprinted in Carter, *Personal Narrative*, 32-38.
41. Ibid., 34-35.
42. Ibid., 32-35. Letter, Root to Chairman, Committee on Military Affairs, The Senate, March 3, 1902, reprinted in Carter, *Personal Narrative*, 38-43.
43. Ibid., 40.
44. Carter, *Personal Narrative*, 46-47, 53.
45. Root, "Report for 1902," *Five Years*, 252-53, 256-57, 261, 246-48.
46. Ibid., 271-72, 290. The militia legislation ultimately became in 1903 the "Dick Act." Louis Cantor, "Elihu Root and the National Guard: Friend or Foe?" *Military Affairs* XXXIII (December 1969): 361-73.
47. Root, "Report for 1903," *Five Years*, 335.
48. Root, "Report for 1902," *Five Years*, 278. Adjutant General's Office General Orders No. 64, July 1, 1902.
49. Mercer, "Memoranda," 13. Suppliers were requested to back date their bills prior to 1 July, the date the fiscal year ended.
50. Nenninger, *Leavenworth* (1975), 113-15.
51. Root, "Report for 1902," *Five Years*, 279.
52. Mercer, "Memoranda," 13.
53. Ibid.
54. Howard K. Beale, *Theodore Roosevelt and the Rise of America to World Power* (Baltimore: Johns Hopkins Press, 1956), 110-16, 130.
55. Ibid., 396-98, 416-17. Richard D. Challener, *Admirals, Generals and American Foreign Policy, 1898-1914* (Princeton, N.J.: Princeton University Press, 1973), 111-19.
56. Elihu Root, Memorandum for the War College Board, October 18, 1902, in Elihu Root, *Establishment of a General Staff in the Army* (Washington: GPO, 1902), 53. Lytle Brown, "The United States Army War College," *The Military Engineer* XIX (July-August 1927): 294-95.
57. Root, "Report for 1902," *Five Years*, 305-06. Palmer, *Bliss*, 80.
58. Carter, *Personal Narrative*, 53-64. Jessup, *Root*, 254-57, 260-61. For removal of Miles see Ransom, "Miles as Commanding General," 197-98. For press reaction see Semsch, "Root and the General Staff," 22-26. Carter's articles are "Recent Army Reorganization," *United Service* II (August 1902): 113-20 and "The Training of Army Officers," *United Service* II (October 1902): 337-42.
59. U.S. Congress, House, *A Bill to Increase the Efficiency of the Army*, H.R. 15449, 57th Cong., 2nd Sess., 1902, reprinted in Carter, *Personal Narrative*, 68-69.

60. Ibid.
61. On development of centralized management in industry see Alfred D. Chandler, "The Large Industrial Corporation and the Making of the Modern American Economy," in *Institutions in Modern America: Innovations in St: ucture and Process*, ed. Stephen B. Ambrose (Baltimore: Johns Hopkins Press, 1967), 71-101.
62. Carter, *Personal Narrative*, 74-75.

The Collegium
of Tasker Bliss
1903-1907

While Secretary Root was maneuvering the General Staff bill through the Congress, the War College Board found that its initial quarters were too confining. In December 1902 it moved its offices next door to a larger house at 22 Jackson Place. From that location the War College Board continued to function as a prototype General Staff, and there also it began the academic work of the college until the new structure at Washington Barracks was completed.

A week after the President signed the General Staff bill into law, Root had the additional pleasure of dedicating the cornerstone of the Army War College building. The elaborate dedication ceremony emphasized the importance that Elihu Root attached to the institution and its future work. The Chief of Engineers acted as the master of ceremonies and members of the Grand Lodge of Masons of the District of Columbia (with appropriate rites and the same trowel used for dedication of the Capitol) laid the stone. Present was a most distinguished audience including justices of the Supreme Court, members of the diplomatic corps, the Cabinet, and both houses of Congress. President Theodore Roosevelt attended and made fitting remarks, but the Secretary of War delivered the principal address.[1]

Ambitious Beginning: War College and General Staff

Elihu Root's dedication speech is his clearest and most eloquent expression of what he intended in establishing the Army War College. Distinguishing between the War College and its governing body, the War College Board, Root termed the latter a part of the General Staff. As such, it would inspect and supervise a general system of military education. Additionally, it would supplement the work of the lower schools by having the War College conduct a "post-graduate course." The Army War College itself was to be "a great adjunct to the General Staff."[2]

Comparing the Army War College to the "great universities and technical schools," Root charged it with providing "education in the science of war" and continuity to American military thought:

> Only an institution perpetual but always changing in its individual elements, in which by conference and discussion a consensus of matured opinion can be reached, can perpetuate the results of individual effort, secure continuity of military policy, and command . . . the respect to which [military] judgement is entitled.

Membership in the War College would mean "honor and opportunity." Root put the duty of the War College simply but strongly: "to study and confer on the great problems of national defense, of military science, and of responsible command."[3]

Before the study of the three great problems could begin, however, there remained work to be done by the War College Board as a planning body. In January, while the General Staff bill was still pending before Congress, Root had charged the board with the responsibility for the officer schooling system "in all matters of instruction." A few weeks after enactment of the General Staff bill, the Secretary referred to the board the question of allocating a large appropriation for barracks and quarters. The board responded with a recommendation on the distribution and size of garrisons within the United States based on probable requirements of defense, mobilization, and training. Root was beginning to achieve the future-oriented deliberations that had been his aim since taking office.[4]

The greater portion of the War College Board's work after passage of the General Staff bill, however, involved planning for the authorized General Staff Corps. Within days of the bill's approval, Root directed the board to derive a scheme for the selection of officers who would serve in the General Staff Corps and who, until the corps was active, would work out its organization and procedures. On the question of officers to serve in the corps, the War College Board recommended they be designated by a selection board of six general officers. Generals Young, Carter, and Bliss were members of this selection board; by mid-April it had designated the authorized forty-two officers. The War Department ordered all the selected officers except for those serving in the Philippines to report immediately to Washington.[5]

The War College Board also addressed the relationship between the General Staff and the War College. Not surprisingly, the board followed the ideas that Root had expressed at the cornerstone ceremony. In responding to the Secretary, the board pointed out "that upon complete establishment of the General Staff Corps many of the duties now performed by the War College Board will be performed by the General Staff." Further:

Employment of the officers composing the War College board will, in the future, partake of the duties of an academic faculty rather than that of a General Staff board. [The work of the War College Board] together with that of the classes which may from time to time be ordered to the War College, will be of great advantage to the General Staff Corps, and the War College will thus in fact, as in name, be an adjunct to the General Staff Corps.

The board recommended that one of the general officers detailed to the General Staff Corps serve concurrently as President of the Army War College.[6] It is clear that the board intended the War College to be tied both organizationally and intellectually to the General Staff Corps.

By May 9th a sufficient number of the prospective General Staff Corps officers were present in Washington to enable Root to organize an experimental or provisional General Staff. The provisional staff was to work out a permanent organization and operational procedures for the General Staff Corps. It would also be assigned tasks and problems thought appropriate for General Staff action. Although the personnel of the War College Board became members of the provisional staff and the board retained its identity, the War College Board ceased to act as a planning group except for those matters pertaining to establishing the Army War College.[7]

One of the tasks assigned the War College Board was to review and provide recommendations to Secretary Root on the architectural plans for the new War College building, plans which the Chief of Engineers had engaged the distinguished firm of McKim, Mead, and White to provide. In May, Secretary Root approved the plans for a structure that in siting and architecture would reflect fully the serious activity to take place within.[8]

On June 20, 1903, the names of the general officers to be detailed to the General Staff Corps were announced, to become effective August 15. General Young was to be the first Chief of Staff, even though he was to retire the coming January. Corbin and Carter were to be his two assistants. Tasker Bliss was named President-designate of the Army War College.[9] The following month establishment of the Army and Navy Joint Board was also announced. According to its charter, the Joint Board would be the final recommending authority to the two service Secretaries and presumably through them to the Commander-in-Chief. Young, Corbin, and Bliss were appointed to the Joint Board, as was the Chief of Artillery, Brigadier General Wallace F. Randolph. The Navy members included Admiral of the Navy George Dewey and a former President of the Naval War College, Rear Admiral Henry C. Taylor.[10]

By early August the provisional General Staff had completed its work as to organization and functions of the General Staff Corps. Following the Prussian pattern, the General Staff Corps would have two components: the "War Department General Staff" and the "General Staff Serving with Troops." The War Department General Staff was to be organized into three divisions. The First Division would be responsible for mobilization planning; combat developments for the infantry, cavalry, and field artillery; and supervision of the officer education system. The Second Division was to be the former Military Information Division of the Adjutant General's Office, which would be transferred to the War Department General Staff. The Third Division would be responsible for campaign and contingency planning, joint operations with the Navy, and combat developments for coast artillery and the technical services. The Third Division would also assume the functions of the Board of Ordnance and Fortification. After but a few years of operation, this organization of the War Department General Staff would be found to have both duplications and omissions and it would be changed.[11] More important than its organization, however, was the range of functions that were to be assigned to the new General Staff Corps.

As a separate staff organization the General Staff Corps was charged "with supervision, under superior authority, over all branches of the military service, line and staff, . . . with a view to their coordination and harmonious cooperation in the execution of authorized military policies." It had the duty of "investigating and reporting upon all questions affecting the efficiency of the Army and its state of preparation for military operations." It was to prepare "plans for the national defense and for the mobilization of the military forces . . . [and] plans of campaign." In sum, the General Staff Corps was to be a supervising, coordinating, investigating, advising, and planning organization. If the language of the regulation was interpreted liberally, the General Staff Corps would have an almost unlimited area of interest.[12]

The General Staff bill, as finally enacted, mentioned neither the Army War College nor the War College Board. The War Department, without statutory limitation, would be able to arrange as it saw fit the relationship between General Staff and War College. The importance of the General Staff legislation to the future War College, however, can scarcely be overemphasized. Attendance at the War College was conceived as the final step in preparing officers for higher General Staff duties. The curriculum and method of the War College, therefore, were manifestly dependent upon those functions to be performed by the General Staff Corps. If this new organization was confined to war preparation activities on the *Grosse Generalstab* model or to broad strategic planning on the model of the Navy's General Board, that was one thing. If the new General Staff Corps was to interpret its mission more broadly, it was quite another thing. As the General Staff Corps went, so the War College must follow. The broader the role assumed by the General Staff

Corps, the more complex would be the task of preparing officers to serve with that body. The scope of the War College's program inevitably would remain ambiguous until experience established an accepted role for the General Staff Corps in its American version.

Although the American General Staff system could not yet draw upon experience, it now had a legislative charter and formal regulations to guide its initial efforts. In name at least the system would have all of the five elements of the Prussian system: a chief, a corps of trained officers, a capital staff, staffs serving major subordinate commanders, and an educational institution. The fifth element, the concept of the *Kriegsakademie*, was not yet completely in place. As the American system had evolved, however, the function of the *Kriegsakademie* was not to be performed by one institution alone, but by a system of institutions that began at the Military Academy at West Point, proceeded through post officer schools and the General Service and Staff College at Fort Leavenworth, and ended with the War College at the national capital. All parts of the American version of the *Kriegsakademie* were already existent in some form but one, the War College. The proposed institution, in addition to being a "great adjunct" to the General Staff Corps, also had to be an integral part of a formal education system. The work performed would have to build upon the education and training that the prospective General Staff officers had already received, particularly upon that received at the General Service and Staff College. To Brigadier General Tasker H. Bliss, the President-designate, fell the duty of creating the War College as both a General Staff adjunct and an institution, as Elihu Root had mandated, for the study of the great problems of national defense, of military science, and of responsible command.

Tasker Bliss officially became President of the Army War College on August 15, 1903. He was much more favorably positioned than had been his naval counterpart, Stephen B. Luce, some twenty years before. Bliss had the unqualified support of an able and strong Secretary, Congress was sympathetic, no powerfully placed opposition to professional education existed within his service, and a fine new building was under construction. The timing of the start of the War College appeared propitious also. After five years of turbulence involving two wars, military government, emergency legislation, and sudden overseas troop deployments, the Army perhaps could look forward to a period of stability during which its new staff organization and education system might take hold. But whether such a period of stability would in fact occur was not for the Army to determine.

Imperial America

With its excursion into the arena of imperialism, the United States had forfeited its former privilege of indifference to shifts in the global balance of power. The Army's Commander-in-Chief, Theodore Roosevelt, saw this more clearly than most. Throughout his presidency, Roosevelt concerned himself with all the international rivalries that might result in general war if the world balance were not maintained. He understood that Far Eastern problems were part of world problems, that the same imperial rivals faced each other in Asia as in Europe. The struggle in Eastern Asia was closely related to the struggle for supremacy in Europe; each was a component of a world struggle involving more than Europe or the Far East alone. Imbalance in either theater, Roosevelt reasoned, could seriously affect America. If the United States could not escape the consequences of world decisions, it had the responsibility to participate in those decisions.[13]

Moreover, Roosevelt saw world events and international politics in terms of power. Germany's continuing challenge to British naval supremacy and its suspected colonial ambitions, particularly as they might be directed toward Latin America, were of special concern. The progressive withdrawal of British seapower from the western Atlantic and Caribbean left a vacuum. Clearly it was critical that the United States fill that void, especially after the events of November 1903 that led first to the independence of Panama and two weeks later to a treaty with that new nation permitting American construction of the long-sought isthmian canal. In May 1904 Roosevelt charged the War Department with the responsibility for building that canal. That same month Roosevelt announced his so-called "corollary" to the Monroe Doctrine. The United States would henceforth police the Caribbean. In the spring of the next year Roosevelt proved good on his word. The United States began to administer the internal affairs of Santo Domingo.[14]

Roosevelt saw Russia as the great threat to the balance of power in the Far East and to perceived American interests there. He favored (and approached becoming a silent partner to) the Anglo-Japanese alliance of 1902. He believed Japan the appropriate counterweight to Russia in Manchuria and North China and was not unhappy with Japanese successes in its 1904-05 war with Russia until it appeared that Russia might be expelled from East Asia altogether. Concurrently, Roosevelt grew increasingly aware of the extended American position in the western Pacific and the terrible vulnerability of the Philippine possession the Army had struggled so long to secure.

Theodore Roosevelt, despite his activism in foreign affairs, was no bluffer. On the contrary he was cautious and careful, taking firm stands only when he believed he had the strategic naval and military advantage. He took the leadership in advocating a powerful Navy not simply to protect America but to provide a means of exerting American influence in international decisions. He saw, in addition to the need for a first-class Navy, the requirement for a small but efficient Army.[15] For the employment of these two instruments in support of policy, Roosevelt respected and sought the advice of professional leadership, but he demanded advice as carefully and cautiously considered as his own policy decisions. At the Navy Department he drew upon the General Board; from the Army he would expect timely and considered advice from its new General Staff and its War College adjunct. It was therefore not accident nor eccentricity on the part of the Army's leaders that caused the new War College to turn its early attention more to contingency planning than to the theoretical education of student officers.

The Grand Design of Tasker Bliss

The original War College Board went out of existence the day the General Staff Corps was established, August 15, 1903, and a new board for the direction of the prospective War College formed. In addition to Bliss, it consisted of two officers of the new General Staff Corps: Colonel Alexander Mackenzie, Chief of the Third Division of the War Department General Staff, and Major William D. Beach, a member of the original War College Board, but since June head of the Military Information Division and then Chief of the Second Division of the War Department General Staff. Several days later Major Samuel Reber, General Staff Corps, was appointed Secretary of the Army War College.[16]

The initial organization of the War College and the officers assigned to it were in accord with recommendations Bliss had made to General Young in early August. Bliss had felt that for the first few months of the War College's life its officers should be detailed from the General Staff in order to establish a routine of work for those who were to follow. In the same memorandum Bliss had outlined certain other characteristics for the War College. War College instruction should not repeat that of the other service schools, and the War College student already should have learned all that he needed to know of the theory of the art of war. Ultimately it would be the duty of the Leavenworth school to qualify officers "for the most important staff duties in time of war." After Leavenworth he should *"learn things by doing things"* (Bliss's emphasis).[17]

Bliss pointed out that the Naval War College had long since passed the stage of professors delivering lectures and assigning books for study; rather, it was an instrument of the General Board of the Navy. When the Naval War College and the General Board reached agreement, the product was a contingency plan of operation to meet an assumed emergency. Bliss "assumed that the Army War College will be an institution of the General Staff to take up the solution of practical military problems" for subsequent approval by the Chief of Staff and the Secretary. As a former faculty member and lecturer at the Naval War College and a current member of the Joint Army and Navy Board, Bliss felt keenly the need for the two war colleges to work in tandem on the same operational problems.[18]

In outlining his approach Bliss had isolated one issue that would recur to his successors in later years: just how the War College fit between the Staff College at Leavenworth and the War Department General Staff. Clearly, Bliss saw Leavenworth's role to be that of teaching the duties of a *Truppengeneralstab*, "the more important *staff duties in time of war*" (emphasis added). The role of the War College as "an institution of the General Staff" would be to teach the duties of the *Grosse Generalstab*. These duties would be learned by "*doing things*." Bliss was following closely the model of the Naval War College, but he added also a flavor of the Prussian system in his school whereby junior staff officers of the *Grosse Generalstab* worked in a kind of apprentice or internship relation with a more experienced general staff officer.

Secretary Root and General Young apparently approved of Bliss's general approach. On October 27 Young assigned three additional General Staff Corps officers of the Third Division to the War College, giving Bliss the services of all the officers of that division. The Third Division became known informally as the "War College Division." Young also ordered Bliss to organize the college immediately, the work of the college to be continuous, beginning on the 1st of July each year and ending on June 30. Young directed that Bliss submit not later than the end of March a detailed scheme of lectures and practical work suggested by the projects the War College would have completed by that time. Unlike Bliss, Young saw a requirement for "the theoretical instruction of classes of detailed officers," but such instruction was to be in connection with the practical work. Bliss now had five months to get the work of the college started and to arrive at a permanent program.[19]

A month after receiving General Young's instructions, Bliss submitted a ten-page report expanding upon his earlier views. Secretary Root apparently approved of the recommendations in that report. He appended it to his own annual report of 1903 and commended it to his readers. The formal report from Bliss, reasoned, detailed, and lucid, is the strongest expression of what the founders of the War College originally had in mind. Bliss built his analysis around the fundamental question "What is the object and true line of work of the Army War College?" He then asked three subordinate questions: "What shall be taught? How shall it be taught? How shall the teaching be extended to the greatest number?" To determine the answers to his questions Bliss reviewed the purposes of the War College as expressed in the language of congressional appropriations supporting the college from 1900 through 1903. He then covered foreign systems of military education and pointed out why the European situation was too different from the American to be of assistance. Next he elaborated upon the American

Army's system of military education as it theoretically would evolve from General Order Number 155 drafted by Carter two years before. He addressed Root's annual report of 1899 as it pertained to the establishment of a war college. Finally he remarked on the role of the Naval War College.

In the language of earlier appropriations bills Bliss found two objects for the War College, "direction and coordination of the instruction of the various service schools" and "extension of the opportunities for investigation and study in the Army and Militia of the United States." Bliss saw two requirements common to both the European and American military education systems. The first was to produce a "well-trained corps of regimental officers, a corps which is the very spinal cord of efficiency in any army." What a regimental officer needed to learn, Bliss thought could "be taught in no other school but experience." Here the United States Army was at a disadvantage compared to those European armies maintained at near wartime strength. But experience could be supplemented by the post officers' schools. Those schools must offer more than one course, however; they must offer successively more advanced courses, "graded courses." Bliss insisted there be no letup in exercising an officer's intellect in the study of his profession. Additionally, junior regimental officers could be trained with a complete regimental organization and field officers with a complete brigade organization if the Army could consolidate garrisons and hold annual maneuvers. Officers of "the special troops" (to Bliss this included cavalry and coast and field artillery) needed technical instruction that would be provided by what Carter had called special service schools. What training was necessary in those schools for a good lieutenant was, "given certain qualities of mind," enough for a good colonel.

After providing the spinal cord of efficiency, the second requirement of an educational system was to produce officers "for General Staff work performing duty outside of and of higher character than those of the regiment." Moreover, the object was "to train the officers who will form the leaven of a great army in time of war" for "we cannot be content merely with training a lieutenant to be a good lieutenant or a captain to be a good captain, or in training staff officers to the efficient performance of duty in peace which they will continue to perform in the same grade in time of war." The large European standing armies could be so content, the small American Army could not.

According to Bliss the task of meeting this second requirement fell primarily to the General Service and Staff College, where officers would be fitted "for general utility in the administration and handling of higher commands of all arms" and for "field service in any staff, corps, or department, as well as in the General Staff." Bliss obviously felt the *Truppengeneralstab* belonged to Leavenworth. Bliss concluded that the system of post officers' schools, special service schools, and the General Service and Staff College (itself a special school for the advanced training of selected officers) "exhausts the useful possibilities of scholastic training." The two- and three-year courses provided in the European institutions were a "tacit confession of the inadequacy, for the purpose of staff officers and officers of higher command, of the preliminary scholastic and professional training as compared with what, in theory, constitutes our system."

Bliss found the "truest and soundest idea of what [a war college] should be and do" in an extract from Secretary Root's annual report of 1899: A war college "should give unity, influence, authority, and effectiveness in military affairs to the work and thought developed in [the service schools] aside from mere instruction, etc." Bliss arrived finally at two conclusions. The first was that the word "college" was used in the Latin sense of "collegium—-that is to say, a body of men associated together by a community of interest and object for doing something rather than to learn how to do it, or, at the most, the 'learning how' is a mere incident of the 'doing.' " Second, noting that Root had assigned functions of a general staff to the proposed War College, Bliss concluded that an Army War College "properly developed and doing things which it should do, is . . . both the creation and the creature of the General Staff."

Bliss then held up for inspection the experience of the United States Navy. Quoting a former President of the Naval War College, Rear Admiral F. E. Chadwick, Bliss demonstrated that the Naval War College, together with the Office of Naval Intelligence and the General Board of the Navy, were all parts of what might be called a general staff system. With that system the Navy had achieved strategic and tactical success during the war with Spain (implying that the Army had not, perhaps).

From his analysis, Bliss defined first the things that the Army War College should *not* do. It should not collect military information; that was to be the duty of the Second Division of the War Department General Staff. It should not conduct "special study of the preparation of material of war," which was the job of the special service schools. Further, the service schools, not the War College, should teach such subjects as history, arms, construction of fortifications, mapping and sketching, military hygiene, military law, physics, geology, mathematics, surveying, and chemistry, even though these subjects constituted most of the courses at foreign war colleges.

Instead, the War College should "take up the detailed study of the military problems confronting the United States," producing complete and detailed plans for contingencies. Periodically the officers who would be responsible for carrying out those contingency plans should be assembled to study them through "the working out of a great war game."

The experts of the War College who prepared the plans would brief (Bliss used "lecture") the participants of the "great war game" on the strategy antecedent to the problem; logistical problems such as construction, embarkation, debarkation, transportation, and supply; peculiar tactical problems; and the issues of international law that might be involved. Bliss was describing an exercise long practiced in the Prussian Army.

In closing his report, Bliss proposed a brief regulation to govern the Army War College. It should be located in Washington. It should be under the direct control of the Chief of Staff, managed by a president assisted by two directors and a secretary. The Chief of Staff would define the problems to be studied, the War College would report their solutions back to the Chief of Staff. When appropriate, those solutions approved by the Chief of Staff would be submitted to the Joint Army and Navy Board. The work of the college would be confidential. From time to time suitable officers, in numbers as deemed necessary, would be detailed to work under the president and the two directors. Also, from time to time, selected officers would be assembled at the War College for detailed study of projects formulated by the War College. Bliss put it concisely: "The special duty of the college shall be to assist the Chief of Staff and the General Staff in the preparation of plans for the national defense."

In his cornerstone dedication address in February, Secretary Root had called for the War College to study the great problems of national defense, of military science, and of responsible command. Bliss, in his report of November, made very clear how he intended for the college to study the problems of national defense. He seemed prepared, however, to leave the study of military science to the lower schools in the educational system, stating bluntly, "There is nothing recondite in the art of war." On the third great problem, that of responsible command, Bliss was silent.[20]

The success of the entire scheme rested on the validity of two assumptions. First, the War Department General Staff must resemble either the General Board of the Navy, concerning itself with the problems of higher-level strategy, or the Prussian *Grosse Generalstab* in its necessary obsession with the minute details of planning for the opening phase of a continental war. The second assumption was that the school system below the War College could indeed "exhaust the possibilities of scholastic training." The difficulty with these assumptions, of course, was that neither the War Department General Staff nor the education system had yet proven that they could or would do what their designers envisioned.

The architects and foundation builders of the General Staff Corps departed the War Department in the winter of 1903-04. Elihu Root resigned in January to be replaced by the affable William Howard Taft,

Governor of the Philippines. Corbin was given a command, and Carter departed at the end of 1903 for duty in the Philippines. General Young retired on January 9th and was replaced by Major General Adna R. Chaffee, who had led the China expedition, had been commander in the Philippines, and since August had been Young's "first assistant." The direction, interest, vigor, but most of all, the understanding of the new team in the War Department toward the General Staff Corps was critical to the success of Bliss's scheme.

J. Franklin Bell and the Leavenworth College

On Bliss's other flank the connector between the War College and the school system, the General Service and Staff College, had gotten off to an inauspicious start in the academic year 1902-03. The Commandant-designate, Brigadier General J. Franklin Bell, the harsh suppressor of insurrection in southern Luzon, was delayed in the Philippines and did not arrive at Leavenworth until the summer of 1903. In addition, the selection by the War College Board in 1902 of the first class of Leavenworth was poorly done. Rather than consisting of officers with promise for higher duties, the class consisted of officers generally without prior formal professional or academic training. They were not up to the work. Approximately half the class failed at least one of the six mid-year examinations. The course took on aspects more akin to what Carter had envisioned for the post officers' schools. At the end of the academic year, Root found it necessary to prefer charges against several student officers as a result of their lack of diligence and zeal in the pursuit of their studies.[21]

After General Bell's arrival, however, things began to change. Bell had been a lieutenant with twenty years of service when the Spanish War began. During that time he had once served as the adjutant of the Cavalry and Field Artillery School at Fort Riley. He believed in the professional education of officers. He was a vigorous, enthusiastic, and driving officer, as his rise in five years from lieutenant to brigadier general indicated. He conferred with General Chaffee and the staff in Washington and decided early that what was needed was to get back to the high standard that the Infantry and Cavalry School had attained prior to the war. In this he was assisted by the two men who had been largely responsible for that achievement, Arthur Wagner and Eben Swift. Colonel Wagner had become Chief of the Third Division of the War Department General Staff in January 1904, and he concurrently served Bliss as the senior director of the Army War College. In May, Bell was successful in having Major Swift transferred from Washington to Leavenworth to become first the head of the Department of Military Art and subsequently the Assistant Commandant.[22]

The 1903-04 academic year at Fort Leavenworth was an improvement primarily because officers of higher qualification were chosen to attend. Bell, however, was aiming at the 1904-05 year. In May 1904 Wagner, in coordination with Bell, had drafted and obtained War Department approval of a plan that would subdivide the General Service and Staff College into two schools, an "Infantry and Cavalry School" (within a few years to be retitled "School of the Line") and, for distinguished graduates of that school, an "Army Staff College." Each school was to provide a one-year course. Bell revised the curriculum as well as the organization of the General Service and Staff College. For 1904-05 Bell planned a full return to the "applicatory method" of Wagner and Swift with its map problems, tactical rides, and stress on the writing of orders. At the Staff College level Swift's Department of Military Art would emphasize grand tactics, general staff duties, original research in strategy and military history, logistics, and military geography; it would even provide lectures on naval warfare.[23] If Bell and Swift were successful at Leavenworth, then Bliss and his successors at the future War College would be able to draw from a pool of officers who could be relied upon as competent in military science and able to handle those "great problems of national defense."

Year One: War College Without Students

While Bell was reorienting and energizing the General Service and Staff College to fill the role the system designers had contemplated for it, Bliss directed the War College's substantive work in two general areas, war planning and joint operations. In February the War College completed major planning projects and sent them to subordinate territorial commands for solution. To the Atlantic and Northern Divisions (responsible for the Canadian frontier) went instructions to assume a war with Great Britain. The Atlantic Division was to prepare plans for limited-objective attacks into eastern Canada to protect Buffalo and Niagara Falls and to destroy the locks on the Welland Canal. West of the Great Lakes, the Northern Division was to plan for the interdiction of the Canadian Pacific railroad to prevent British reinforcement from India or elsewhere.[24]

The Southwestern Division, responsible for the Mexican border, was to assume a war with Mexico and plan an invasion of that country using the routes of Zachary Taylor and Winfield Scott. The Philippine Division was to prepare plans for the redeployment on short notice of a force of seven regiments from the Islands. The War College did not simply ask for broad concepts but expected the subordinate commands to respond with detailed plans for mobilization, concentration, and transportation of troops, and with operations schedules and logistical estimates. This concept of detailed planning by subordinate commands and subsequent review by the War Department General Staff was of course in line with the standard German practice. Moreover, the concept brought into the problems the few officers of the "General Staff serving with Troops" who had been detailed to the subordinate territorial commands. Bliss informed Admiral of the Navy George Dewey, president of the Navy's General Board, of the planning now in progress. The War College also prepared a project calling for the deployment of an expeditionary force to Panama to support the United States' obligations to the new republic as called for in the treaty of November 1903.[25]

On joint matters the Army War College worked closely with the Naval War College, as Bliss had intended. The two institutions agreed upon rules for joint maneuvers, standard symbols for charts and maps, and plans for a joint maneuver to be held in Chesapeake Bay during the summer of 1905.[26] Whether the war planning and joint cooperation efforts were done by the "Army War College" or the "Third Division of the War Department General Staff" seems to be a matter of what label to use. The same officers manned the two organizations. No "students" or officers temporarily detailed to the War College were as yet assigned. In April the Congress continued to demonstrate its support of the Army War College, appropriating $15,000 for its operation and an additional $300,000 for its building. The appropriation for the building, however, contained the proviso that this sum would in fact complete the construction, implying that more would not be forthcoming. The War College was not without challenge, however. Upon inquiry from the Chairman of the Military Affairs Committee of the House, Bliss had to explain that, yes, the War College did in fact exist, that it was different from a conventional school, that "without pomp or parade" it produced plans "thought out by many minds of what the [Army] could best do tomorrow if the emergency contemplated . . . should arise."[27]

Despite his assurances to the House committee, Bliss was not satisfied with what was being accomplished. He wrote the Chief of Staff in April that progress had been "slow and unsatisfactory." At least ten officers were needed to do the work at hand. All ten should be assigned to the Third Division, and all should understand that the Third Division was the War College and should be assigned no unrelated tasks. To Bliss it was critical that the War College be part of the General Staff. He foresaw, accurately as it turned out, future hostility in Congress toward the General Staff, and he feared that financial support of the General Staff would be withdrawn. But appropriations would be forthcoming for the War College. Unless the War College was part of the General Staff, it would not be legal to use War College appropriations to perform General Staff work.[28]

Year Two: Students Assigned

As the end of the first "session" approached, plans were being made for the next session (1904-05) during which Bliss would not only have the services of the officers of the Third Division but also of the officers temporarily detailed to the War College. A memorandum from General Chaffee dated June 16, 1904, attempted to sort out the functions of the elements of the War Department General Staff. Chaffee treated the War College, even though it constituted the entire Third Division, as a section of that division. The other section included Third Division officers working on "purely technical questions." In other words, the assigned officers were "War College" if doing one type of work, and "Third Division" if doing something else. As would be expected, Chaffee charged the War College with the functions of war planning, supervision of the school system, and the related duty of preparing strategical and grand tactical problems to be worked out by "officers of the Army at large as the Chief of Staff may direct." Also it was to prepare tactical problems, one for each grade of officer, for solution by individual officers. The War College would examine and pass on those solutions. Finally, Chaffee directed the duty of "the annual preparation of a course of work at the War College of such officers of the army as may be assembled for the purpose."[29]

General Chaffee's memorandum referred to a "course of work," not a course of *instruction*, but the latter term was used later in the month when the War Department published a new and more detailed general order (Number 115, June 27, 1904) governing the entire system of military education. The order contained six paragraphs pertaining to the Army War College. The organization of the college was in line with Bliss's earlier recommendations. It would consist of a general officer president, two directors (a colonel and a lieutenant colonel), a secretary, and the officers of the Third Division. These officers were all categorized as "permanent personnel." The War College would consist additionally of "such students as may from time to time be detailed." This was the first official mention of "students" at the War College. Nonetheless, the intent was clear that the War College was not to be a conventional academic institution: "The object of the War College is not to impart academic instruction, but to make practical application of military knowledge already acquired." Bliss's interpretation that "college" meant "collegium" without academic trappings was reinforced. Formal opening and closing of the "term of instruction," examinations, and diplomas were all forbidden. "Selection for this advanced work is deemed sufficient recognition of [an officer's] professional attainments."[30]

The general orders made a distinction, however, between the work of the permanent personnel and that of the students, assigning ten specific tasks to the permanent personnel. Two pertained to war planning and six to supervision of the Army's education system; the remaining two might be considered as additional to those that Carter, Bliss, and Chaffee had previously listed. One was "critical analysis of foreign military systems;" the other was "the regulation and conduct of maneuvers." The activities spelled out for the students fell into three general categories: war plans, war games, and informal lectures and discussion. In regard to war planning, the students were to review critically an approved plan of operations and suggest modifications. They would then take up the same situation and, with the same assumptions underlying the approved plan, independently prepare a new plan. The two plans would then be compared and discussed.

After studying the approved plan and drawing up one of their own, the students would then in effect war-game the two plans in detail, carrying the plans through an appropriate number of days of operations and issuing the necessary orders to maneuver elements of the forces and to provide for their logistical support. Tactical and logistical problems in the plans could thus be isolated and discussed. A second type of war game called for in the course was the study of an actual campaign of a past war (the Civil War was suggested), refighting that campaign on the map using present-day organizations, armament, equipment, and tactical methods. Supplementing the work in war plans and war games were to be informal lectures and discussion of current military events and developments. The "course of instruction" was to begin on the first of November each year and close at the end of May, with a ten-day break at Christmas.

The seven-month course had one obvious advantage: it neatly avoided the Washington summer. It also fitted into the Naval War College program, which held its student session from June through October (avoiding Newport's winters), thereby facilitating exchange between the two institutions. Student officers were to be majors and captains selected by the Chief of Staff, and he was to give preference to graduates of Leavenworth's Staff College.

Under the authority of the above general orders, the first session began as scheduled on November 1, 1904. The building at Washington Barracks was not yet completed; the size of the first group of temporarily detailed officers therefore was limited by the space in the house at 22 Jackson Place. General orders assigned nine officers to the War College, three majors and six captains. Four were infantrymen, three cavalrymen, one an artilleryman, and one an engineer. Four had already been designated members of the General Staff Corps. Under President Bliss there were two directors, Colonel Arthur L. Wagner and Lieutenant Colonel William W. Wotherspoon. The Navy provided a representative, Commander Sydney A. Staunton, and Major Samuel Reber remained as Secretary. Six additional permanent personnel of the Third Division were assigned—two majors and four captains.[31] The subsequent accomplishments of this band of twenty who constituted the membership of

94

the 1904-05 Army War College attest to their promise. Bliss would gain international reputation as the American representative to the Allied Supreme War Council in 1918 and as a peace commissioner at Paris in 1919. A member of the Third Division, Major George W. Goethals, would be the engineer in charge of construction of the Panama Canal. Of the sixteen officers who lived to participate in the First World War, ten would serve as general officers. A student, Captain John J. Pershing, would command the American Expeditionary Force. (Pershing actually remained at the War College for only two months. During that short period he sought and obtained assignment as military attaché to Japan and married the daughter of Senator Francis E. Warren.[32])

Bliss organized the officers of the War College into five committees of three or four officers, each including both permanent and student officers. He assigned each committee, in keeping with the German pattern, specific geographical areas for which it would prepare a strategic plan or plans. One committee was to concern itself with the military resources of the United States and with Canada, a second committee with home defense and the Philippines and the Orient. A third committee was charged with the West Indies, Panama, Colombia, and Venezuela; a fourth with Mexico and Central America (except Panama); and a fifth with South America (except Colombia and Venezuela). Bliss, Wagner, and Wotherspoon would act as "The Board of Direction," a sort of steering group, and would also serve with the four majors as a "General Board" to pass on all completed work before it was submitted to the Chief of Staff.[33]

Bliss saw this organization as experimental and suspected that experience might indicate a better one. He desired not only "speedy and accurate solution, in all its details" but that officers "have reasonable opportunity for mind-broadening study, for independent and original investigation." Each Saturday the entire War College would meet in conference to discuss the progress of solutions to problems assigned to the committees.[34]

The problems presented to the 1904-05 session were all designed to support the Commander-in-Chief's active Caribbean policy. The first problem had been suggested by the Navy's General Board and involved preventing the use of Haiti and Santo Domingo as a base by a foreign maritime power. The second assumed United States military intervention in Santo Domingo to implement the "Roosevelt corollary." Two problems involved expeditions in Venezuela, one with a force of 9,000 and another with a force of 12,000 combatants. The fifth problem was a series of exercises requiring structuring of expeditionary forces ranging in size from 5,000 to 30,000 troops. A sixth problem called for an expedition to Panama to repel an invasion from Colombia. Additionally, the War College drew up a project for solution by the Pacific Division, calling for plans for the defense of the Puget Sound area in the event of war with Britain and Canada.[35]

Bliss also assigned six special studies to individual officers. Two involved the effects of technological developments (machine guns, "traction engines," and motor vehicles) on military operations. The other studies were of a manpower and organizational nature: should regiments of the regular Army be recruited from and permanently associated with specific geographical regions, consideration of a proposed mobilization reserve, and organization of a volunteer army. Finally, Bliss directed a study on military railroad management. Although thirty-five lectures had been planned, only twenty-three were actually delivered. Those presented included ten on international law and six on the campaigns of the ongoing Russo-Japanese War in Manchuria; the remainder were on the military geography of certain countries, on technological developments, and on logistical matters. In all cases but one the lecturers were military officers. The subjects, except for an undelivered lecture by Bliss on the Monroe Doctrine, were all of purely military content.[36]

Tasker Bliss had followed with apparent success the educational philosophy that he had advocated and Root had supported. During its first session, whether considered as a course of work or as a course of instruction, the War College acted very much as an adjunct of the General Staff. Its focus, as Root had demanded, was preparation for war; its orientation, the future; its emphasis, unity of effort. How much learning actually took place is impossible to measure, but it is not extreme to say that those officers who underwent the experience could no longer take a parochial view. They had been required to consider war and military operations as an integrated whole involving strategy, logistics, and tactics—and all the arms and services. Moreover, it must have been apparent that the military operations they planned were all designed to support the possible requirements of the President's foreign policy.

Year Three: Wotherspoon and Barry

After the close of the session in June 1905, General Bliss departed the War College to take command of the Department of Luzon. That same month Colonel Wagner died while on leave in Asheville, North Carolina, a loss that neither the War College nor the Army's educational system could afford at this stage in their development. Bliss was not immediately replaced. The task of readying the War College for its second true session fell to Lieutenant Colonel Wotherspoon, the junior director, who was designated Acting President.[37]

Wotherspoon had been detailed to the General Staff Corps in October 1904 to serve as a director of the Army War College. The year before that he had been head of the Department of Tactics at Leavenworth and then Assistant Commandant to General Bell. Son of an Army contract surgeon, he had served three years as an enlisted man in the Navy, then in 1873 was commissioned in the infantry. Except for a three-year tour of duty as professor of military science at Rhode Island College of Agricultural and Mechanical Arts, his service prior to the Spanish War was with infantry regiments. In 1899 his regiment deployed to the Philippines where, like General Bell, he remained until 1903.

Acting President Wotherspoon was shorthanded during the five months between the departure of the Class of 1905 and the arrival of that of 1906. In addition to receiving no immediate replacements for Bliss and Wagner, two officers of the Third Division spent the summer attending the four-month session of the Naval War College. Two officers of the permanent staff who had been reassigned were replaced, however, by retaining permanently two officers of the Class of 1905. Wotherspoon's guiding directive continued to be General Order No. 115. He made no major changes in the general scheme that Bliss had used the previous year, though he reduced in number the planning problems, special studies, and lectures attempted. The cancellation during the 1904-05 session of roughly half the lectures that had been scheduled and the reduced workload that Wotherspoon proposed indicates that perhaps Bliss had overestimated how much could be accomplished in seven months and had piled the platter a bit high.[38]

Another major problem had surfaced during the first year. The Army War College was not merely an adjunct to the War Department General Staff but as its Third Division was an integral part of that staff. Its work could not go forward independently of the other two divisions. The Second (Military Information) Division was the War College's source of intelligence and other planning data. The War College's requests for information may have overloaded that division. Wotherspoon found it necessary to direct that all requests placed on the Second Division must be made in writing and routed through his office. Moreover, while the Second Division was located in the same neighborhood, it was in a separate building, and coordination was difficult.[39]

Working with the First Division proved even more difficult. That division was responsible for producing studies involving organization, training, distribution, armament, and equipment of the Army, as well as troop movements by land or sea, the movement of supplies, and supply levels for troops, camps, and depots. These matters were not only pertinent but critical to the contingency planning and special studies being done by the War College. The First Division, due to "the pressure of other work," had not completed these studies. Wotherspoon saw no way through this problem other than for the War College to go ahead and make tentative working plans itself in these areas.[40] It is true that the War College with its "temporary personnel" had the other staff divisions out-manned, but the indication is that the War Department General Staff was already beginning to get itself involved in current administrative affairs, rather than concentrating on planning activities as its designers had hoped it could.

The Class of 1905-06 consisted of seven officers whom the Chief of Staff had selected from a list of officers recommended by Wotherspoon. There were four infantrymen, two cavalrymen, and an artilleryman. In October, just before the opening of the session, Lieutenant Colonel Smith S. Leach arrived for assignment at the War College from Leavenworth where he, like Wotherspoon before him, had been Assistant Commandant under General Bell. He and Major Goethals served as senior and junior directors, respectively, until Brigadier General Thomas H. Barry took over as President in December and Wotherspoon assumed the position of senior director.[41]

The War College organization remained as established by Bliss. Once again the main thrust of the work was planning for contingencies. Of the six problems of the year before, one was continued, that of intervention in Santo Domingo under the "Roosevelt Corollary." The college assumed that the situation on the island had escalated into a crisis involving a European maritime power, with the Atlantic and Gulf coasts of the United States threatened. Wotherspoon introduced an additional project, which required planning a live exercise in which 3,000 troops of the regular Army would practice embarkation and debarkation procedures. He also added a planning problem calling for intervention in Mexico "to restore normal conditions" (thereby anticipating the overthrow of dictator Porfirio Diaz in 1911) and a problem asking for the proper distribution of coast artillery under what was certainly a worst-case scenario, war with England, Japan, or the two in combination with allies.[42]

The college also undertook a problem that had not been planned. In July 1905 Chinese resentment of the United States because of its exclusive immigration policy and treatment of Chinese in both the United States and China resulted in a boycott of American goods in all the treaty ports of southern China. President Roosevelt, while attempting to get more reasonable policies passed by the Congress, decided to break the boycott by putting pressure, including military, on the Chinese government. In November he ordered as strong a naval force as could be spared to Chinese waters. In January he directed that Army forces be dispatched to the Philippines for possible subsequent use in China. The question put to the War College was how military force could be used to compel the government of China to prevent the boycott, protect the lives of Americans in China, and comply with American demands. Derivative questions were how many troops would be needed, how many could be taken from the Philippines, and how quickly could they be moved? The result was the deployment of two regiments from the

United States to the Philippines, an action which may or may not have had some effect on the eventual diplomatic solution of the issue. Concurrently, the Chief of Staff asked the War College to restudy the size and needs of the legation guard in Peking.[43]

Wotherspoon reduced the number of special studies by the Class of 1905-06 and had them performed by committees or by the War College as a whole rather than by individual officers. These studies spanned a wide variety of subjects. One group seems to have concentrated on mobilization questions: the manpower resources of the United States and the past effectiveness, current condition, and future required support of the organized militia. Another group was of a combat developments nature: organization of railway troops, defense of seacoast forts from land attack, and tables of supply for tactical formations of various sizes. A series of monographs was undertaken, in effect studies of the five Central American republics between Panama and Mexico. Two studies involved future troop exercises and one the best site for a brigade post in upstate New York. In cooperation with the Naval War College, a study was conducted to establish rules for troop transports sailing under naval convoy.[44]

The program included nineteen lectures. Eleven concerned the Russo-Japanese War, covering specific topics such as the siege of Port Arthur, Russian mapmaking, and Japanese field sanitation practices. The remaining eight lectures were on the employment of infantry, cavalry, artillery, and engineers and on developments in mortars and signal communication. The lecturers were officers who were either serving on the General Staff or who had recently returned from observation tours in Manchuria. Despite the lecture program General Barry had to once again explain, this time to the Senate Military Affairs Committee, that no instruction took place at the Army War College.[45]

In his report to the Chief of Staff at the end of the year, Barry expressed satisfaction with what had been accomplished: "While the experience and instruction which the officers gain by doing the work is very great, the practical value to the service and to the government is, if possible, greater." Barry proposed, however, that the detail of the temporary personnel be extended from seven months to a full year by beginning their detail on June 1 rather than on November 1. This would allow "studies of military histories, strategy and tactics on the ground, with such indoor work as may be necessary." According to General Barry the major difficulty was the inadequacy and inconvenience of the Jackson Place house. Barry hoped to get into the new building sometime during the coming session.[46]

Problems in the Empire

Because Barry had arrived on the scene after the 1905-06 session was well along, the summer of 1906 was his first opportunity to truly influence the work of the college. But the requirements of foreign policy once again took precedence. National elections had been held in Cuba in 1905, with the incumbent moderates retaining power. The defeated liberals were satisfied with neither the results nor the manner in which the elections had been conducted. By August 1906 armed uprising broke out against President Palma's government; in September Palma admitted to Washington that it was a revolt he could not quell. Roosevelt was not eager to intervene, though the Platt Amendment technically would have legitimized intervention. He dispatched Secretary of War Taft and Assistant Secretary of State Robert Bacon to Havana. On the way from Roosevelt's home on Long Island to Cuba, Taft learned from the Chief of Staff that 6,000 troops were available for immediate movement to Cuba and another 18,000 could be provided in a month. On September 17 the Chief of Staff provided the President with a completed contingency plan.[47] The work performed over the past several years on Caribbean deployments had not been in vain.

On September 28, with Taft in Havana, President Palma resigned, as did his vice president and entire cabinet. The next day, upon receiving Roosevelt's approval, Taft issued a proclamation of intervention under the authority of the Platt Amendment and named himself provisional governor. The War Department was ordered to execute its contingency plan. On October 6th, while Taft was attempting to bring about a peace between the two Cuban parties, a US Army expeditionary force of 5,600, the "Army of Cuban Pacification," sailed from Newport News. The Chief of Staff of the expeditionary force was the senior director of the War College, Lieutenant Colonel Wotherspoon. With him were three officers of the Third Division.[48] Barry's small War College staff had been decimated. Remaining from the previous year were only the Secretary, Major Reber, and the junior director, Lieutenant Colonel Leach, who had passed the summer at Newport attending the Naval War College. None of the temporary personnel of 1905-06 had been retained. All other officers of the Third Division were new.[49]

Year Four: Introduction of Military Art

One of these new officers, however, was Major Eben Swift. In August 1906 Swift had arrived from his previous assignment as Assistant Commandant of the General Service and Staff College. Swift brought with him all the years of experience he had accumulated as instructor at the prewar Infantry and Cavalry School and the postwar Army General Service and Staff College. He also brought with him an intense conviction in the efficacy of the "applicatory method" that he and Wagner had derived from the Germans, and a strong belief that military history, particularly that of the American Civil War, was the medium for learning the military art. Just as important, Swift had the support of a believer in the applicatory method, the new Chief of Staff, Major General J. Franklin Bell. Bell was the first Chief of Staff to serve a full four-year tour of duty; he and Swift were to have a profound effect on the War College during those years. The Infantry and Cavalry School model had arrived at the Army War College to compete with if not supplant that of the Naval War College used by Tasker Bliss.

Despite the limitation of time (the course of instruction remained seven months) and the poor accommodations of the Jackson Place residence, Swift was able to insert three innovations into the 1906-07 course. In the lecture phase of the course, Swift presented four lectures on "Military History" and one on "The Battle of Antietam." This last lecture introduced the second innovation, a week's tactical ride over the Antietam battle area. War College officers were required to draw up plans and orders for the opposing forces using the 1862 situation but with the formations, methods, equipment, and weapons of 1907. More of an indication of what was to come, however, was a third innovation, the introduction of thirty-one map problems into the curriculum. Fifteen of these problems were from the old Leavenworth reliable, Griepenkerl's *Applied Tactics*. They ranged from small-unit tactics to those of the division. The solutions were discussed at length by the college and a "proper" (not "approved") solution agreed upon and filed.[50]

The remainder of the course of instruction followed closely what had been established by Bliss and carried on by Wotherspoon: contingency planning, special studies, and lectures. The contingency planning effort centered on Cuba. In November the college completed a plan for the evacuation of American forces and in March won approval of a revised evacuation plan. In addition to the two evacuation plans the college also drew up plans for a 5,000-troop reinforcement. All this Wotherspoon had suggested writing from Havana, but the work was performed primarily by the permanent personnel of the Third Division. The special studies portion of the curriculum took on an added but not exclusive combat developments flavor. Studies involved street fighting and riot control; reduction in caliber of weapons; field service regulations; use of mobile heavy artillery, portable searchlights, wireless telegraphy, and ballooning; and procedures and techniques for overseas movement. The special studies were not high-priority work. Officers were to perform the studies when not engaged "in tactical subjects or special emergency work." Twenty lectures were presented during the year, including the five by Swift. The naval representative delivered three, as did Lieutenant Colonel Leach. Lecture topics covering the Russo-Japanese War disappeared from the program; one was added on "The Army in the San Francisco

Disaster." Lectures on "Remounts" and "Military Aeronautics" may have provided a contrast between what was passing and what was to come.[51]

The class consisted of eleven officers, again majors and captains, all of the line. With so many Third Division officers in Cuba, 22 Jackson Place could accommodate the enlarged class. In February 1907 General Barry left the War College to assume command of the Army of Cuban Pacification. At the same time Wotherspoon returned from Cuba to assume for the second time the title of Acting President. In June, the month after the temporary personnel departed, Lieutenant Colonel Wotherspoon had the satisfaction of moving the Army War College to its new spacious building at Washington Barracks. In October he had the additional satisfactions of being promoted to brigadier general and being designated President of the Army War College. He was the only officer remaining at the War College who had been with Bliss to receive the first class just three years earlier.[52]

NOTES

1. George P. Ahern, "A Chronicle of the Army War College, 1899-1919," (Army War College: June 24, 1919), 14, MHI Library.
2. Elihu Root, "The Army War College, Address at the Laying of the Cornerstone, Washington, D.C., February 21, 1903," in Root, *Military and Colonial Policy*, 121-27.
3. Ibid.
4. Carter, *Personal Narrative*, 75-76, 78.
5. Root, "Report for 1903," *Five Years*, 329.
6. "Report of the War College Board," March 9, 1903, reprinted in Carter, *Personal Narrative*, 81.
7. Ahern, "A Chronicle," 15-16. Root, "Report for 1903," *Five Years*, 329. Bliss was appointed head of a subordinate board to recommend the provisional organization of the General Staff. Young to Bliss, 13 May 1903, *Bliss Papers*, MHI Collection.
8. Mercer, "Memoranda," 13-14.
9. Adjutant General's Office, General Order No. 88, 20 June 1903 and General Order No. 107, 27 July 1903.
10. Root, "Report for 1903," *Five Years*, 333-35.
11. Otto L. Nelson, Jr., *National Security and the General Staff* (Washington: Infantry Journal Press, 1946), 66-68. An early change was to shift responsibility for officer education from the First to Third Division.
12. War Department, "General Staff Corps," August 3, 1903, reprinted in Root, *Five Years*, "Appendixes to 1903 Report," 483-87.
13. Beale, *Roosevelt*, 253, 255, 355-36.
14. Ibid., 448-49. William H. Harbaugh, *The Life and Times of Theodore Roosevelt*, new revised edition (New York: Oxford University Press, 1975), 189-93.
15. Beale, *Roosevelt*, 337, 451-52.
16. War Department General Order No. 2, August 15, 1903, and Special Order No. 5, August 20, 1903.
17. Tasker Bliss, Memorandum as to the Proper Line and Work of the Army War College, August 3, 1903, extracted in Ahern, "Chronicle," 17-20. A barely legible draft of this document is in the letter book August 1902 - November 1903, 18-37, *Bliss Papers*, MHI Collection.
18. Ibid.
19. Letter, Young to Bliss, October 27, 1903, copy in letter book 29 October 1902 - 8 January 1904, 347, *Young Papers*, MHI Collection.

20. Report of Brig. Gen. Tasker H. Bliss, U.S. Army, President of the Army War College, Washington, November 11, 1903, appended to *Annual Report of the Secretary of War for 1903*, 89-98.
21. Nenninger, *Leavenworth*, 59-62.
22. Ibid., 68-71, 73.
23. Ibid., 63-64, 70-73.
24. Mercer, "Memoranda," 19.
25. Ibid., 18-20. Ahern, "Chronicle," 27.
26. Mercer, "Memoranda," 20.
27. Ibid., 21. Ahern, "Chronicle," 27-28. Bliss, Memorandum Report for the Chief of Staff, January 15, 1904, reprinted in 58th Congress, 2nd Session, *Congressional Record*, Vol. 38, Pt. 2, 1156-57.
28. Bliss to Chief of Staff, 6 April 1904, Vol. 39, 443, *Bliss Papers*, Library of Congress.
29. Memorandum of June 16, 1904, from Office of the Chief of Staff announcing the distribution of business of the War Department General Staff, Box 1903-1909, *Bliss Papers*, MHI Collection.
30. War Department General Order No. 115, June 27, 1904.
31. War Department General Order No. 155, September 17, 1904.
32. Data are derived from *U.S. Army War College Directory, 1905-1980* (Carlisle Barracks, Pa.: U.S. Army War College, 19 May 1980). Frank E. Vandiver, *Black Jack: The Life and Times of John J. Pershing*, 2 vols. (College Station, Tex.: Texas A&M Press, 1977), I: 344-46. The War College Class of 1925 made General of the Armies Pershing an honorary member. On that occasion he made complimentary remarks as to the institution he so hastily departed twenty years earlier, George E. Pappas, *Prudens Futuri: The US Army War College, 1901—1967* (Carlisle Barracks, Pa.: The Alumni Association of the US Army War College, 1967), 46, 119-21.
33. Army War College, Memorandum No. 1, 26 September 1904, Letter Book, 405-09, Box "1900-1909," *Bliss Papers*, MHI Collection. Bliss initially called the General Board the "Strategy Board."
34. Ahern, "Chronicle," 39-40. Mercer, "Memoranda," 26.
35. Mercer, "Memoranda," 26-27.
36. Ibid., 27-29. The one civilian lecturer was James F. J. Archibald of *Collier's Weekly*, who related his observations as a war correspondent with the Russian Army in Manchuria.
37. Ibid., 45-46.
38. Ahern, "Chronicle," 44-45, 50-54. Army War College, Memorandum: Course of Study and Research at the Army War College for the term commencing on November 1, 1905, and ending May 31, 1906, July 15, 1905, in Mercer, "Memoranda," 30-31.
39. Army War College, Memorandum No. 1, October 20, 1905, in Mercer, "Memoranda," 31-33.
40. Ibid.
41. Ahern, "Chronicle," 48-49.
42. Mercer, "Memoranda," 34.
43. Harbaugh, *Roosevelt*, 283-85. Minger, *Taft*, 167-70. Mercer, "Memoranda," 34-36. Since the War College knew next to nothing about China, this problem caused consternation. Challener, *Admirals, Generals*, 25.
44. Mercer, "Memoranda," 34-35.
45. Ibid., 35-36. *Army and Navy Journal*, "Functions of the Army War College," (7 April 1906): 883.
46. Army War College, Memorandum for the Chief of Staff, October 12, 1906, in Mercer, "Memoranda," 38-39.
47. Minger, *Taft*, 121-24.
48. Ibid., 124-28. Mercer, "Memoranda," 37a. Allan R. Millett, "The General Staff and the Cuban Intervention of 1906," *Military Affairs* XXXI (Fall 1967): 114-18.
49. Ahern, "Chronicle," 60.
50. Ibid., 63. Mercer, "Memoranda," 41. Army War College, "Course for 1906-1907: Problems and Exercises," 2. Army War College Curricular Files (hereafter AWC-CF), MHI Collection.

51. Ibid., 6, 74. Millett, "Cuban Intervention of 1906," 118. Army War College, Memorandum: Assignment of Subjects, November 1, 1906 in Mercer, "Memoranda," 39-40. Ahern, "Chronicle," 61-63.
52. Mercer, "Memoranda," 42, 49. Ahern, "Chronicle," 70.

A Decade
of Progress
1907-1917

With the exception of the first formal session of 1904-05, the 1907-08 session of the Army War College was probably the most significant to the future nature of the institution until after the First World War. A major shift in the curriculum occurred, a shift that indicates a revision in thinking as to the very purpose of the college. General Barry had suggested earlier that the course be extended in length from seven to twelve months. That extension went into effect for the 1907-08 year; the session would begin as usual on November 1, but last through the summer until the end of October. The additional time, as well as the additional space provided by the new building, gave Wotherspoon the opportunity to attempt a program of much broader scope. He also won a new charter that provided much more flexibility than had General Order No. 115 of 1904.

The Influence of J. Franklin Bell

The new directive did not change the stated purpose of the War College. It remained "to make practical application of knowledge already acquired, not to impart academic instruction." But missing were the specific instructions of the earlier charter pertaining to war planning and war games. In their place were but two broad objectives. First, the college was to continue to direct and coordinate the military education of the Army. Second, it was "to promote advanced study of military subjects and to formulate the opinions of the college body on the subjects studied for the information of the Chief of Staff." Almost any program devised could be made to fit the term "advanced study of military subjects."[1]

With Major Swift (by then the junior director of the college) as the principal instructor, Wotherspoon instituted a comprehensive course in tactics. The "applicatory method" that Chief of Staff Bell believed had been so successful at Leavenworth was to be used throughout the tactical instruction, later to be termed the "Course of Military Art." Beginning with relatively simple map problems, Swift moved the class progressively through more complex situations, increasing the number of map problems to forty-six from the thirty-one of the year before. Swift next had the class take up map maneuvers, then led them outdoors into the Virginia and Maryland countryside for instruction through what were variously termed terrain exercises, tactical rides, staff rides, or historical rides and battlefield studies. Throughout the year Swift and his instructor colleagues introduced and complemented the map and terrain exercises with lectures on the employment of the several arms and services and on lessons to be deduced from past battles and campaigns.[2]

Swift continued to refine the course in military art during the next two sessions. His last year of service at the War College was 1909-10, but the year following his departure marks both the culmination of his efforts and the end of a transitional period during which War College emphasis gradually shifted from war planning to the conduct of military operations. By 1910-11 the course ran from September 1 to June 30. September was the "preliminary" month, involving map problems and a few map maneuvers. From then until Christmas additional and more complex map problems and map maneuvers were conducted, some of the latter being based upon existing war plans. During these first four months the class progressed from the study of small-unit tactics through the study of division and army corps operations, including work on Army-Navy cooperation.

Reconvening after Christmas, the students were expected to apply the knowledge they had gained to the "War Plan of the Year," a scheme reminiscent of the pre-Spanish War "Main Problem" of the Naval War College. The month of March was devoted to the study of military history to provide a basis for the historical rides and battlefield studies that would be conducted later in the spring. During April the class was outdoors for most of its work, taking up military engineering, field fortifications, and the laying out of lines of defense. May and June saw combined historical and staff rides into Virginia, with members of the class playing the roles of commanders and staff officers as several campaigns of the Civil War were followed on the ground. In all, the class attempted sixty-nine map problems and twenty-five map maneuvers, completed one war plan, and traveled 550 miles on horseback during historical and staff rides. It also heard twenty-six lectures, and each member researched and prepared a monograph on a "topic of military importance."[3]

The 1910-11 session was representative of the War College program from 1908 through 1917. The program was ambitious. By design it duplicated much of the course of the Staff College at Fort Leavenworth. Clearly it required a near full-time faculty for its preparation, presentation, and management. Unlike the collegium of Tasker Bliss, the program was directed not at producing staff plans and papers and with learning only incident to doing, but at development of the individual student officer. Officially expressed, "The object of the course was to prepare a limited number of selected officers for the duties of higher command in war, and in peace while preparing for war."[4] The collegium had eroded. "The general adjunct to the General Staff" had become adjunct only in the *Kriegsakademie* sense, a trainer of prospective General Staff Corps officers, not only for the *grosser Generalstab*, but for the *Truppengeneralstab*. The model of the Infantry and Cavalry School had won out over that of the Naval War College.

The influence behind this reorientation of the War College was that of the Chief of Staff, Major General J. Franklin Bell. He came to that position after almost three years as Commandant of the General Service and Staff College. He had worked closely with the Third Division of the War Department General Staff on officer education matters, and he was familiar with the overall education system and with Bliss's philosophy for the War College. But the military backgrounds of Bliss and Bell were strikingly different. The career of Bliss had been unique. He had served only briefly with troops. His professional associates had been men of unusual intelligence and capacity: Luce, Mahan, and Taylor at Newport; Schofield at West Point and in Washington; Ludlow and Wood in Cuba; and Root, Carter, and Wagner in the earliest days of the War College. Bliss was a man who read in four foreign languages and translated Greek and Latin classics for recreation. He had been military attache in Madrid at the outbreak of the war, had been an influential military government official in Havana, and had negotiated a trade treaty for the State Department. Moreover, he was essentially a modest man who saw nothing particularly significant in his achievements.[5] Bliss may have overestimated grossly the professional and intellectual capabilities and attainments of the officers who would be detailed to attend the Army War College.

J. Franklin Bell, several years behind Bliss at West Point, came from what was almost a different world. He had done little for more than twenty years other than serve with troops. Until Leavenworth his reputation was that of a fighter. If he had any illusions about the intellectual interest and energy of the officer corps, the early classes at the General Service and Staff College must have dispelled them. He knew full well, or at least sensed, that more was needed than the learning gained incident to doing staff work at the War Department.[6] Bell may have realized also that the Army's educational system, as it was operating, would inevitably create a dangerous generation gap within the officer corps. The junior officers would have the benefit of the courses of the post officers' schools and of the special service schools or the General Service and Staff College, while their seniors would remain without formal schooling. When he became Chief of Staff, Bell set out to see that the seniors would be schooled, and he brought Eben Swift along to assist.

General Bell introduced the study of tactics via the "applicatory method" in the first War College session he could influence, that of 1906-07. Swift was brought from Fort Leavenworth and assigned to the Third (War College) Division in August 1906. Next Bell approved extending the course to a full year. Then in May 1908 he directed the Second (Military Information) Division, despite its protests, to move out of downtown Washington and into the War College building at Washington Barracks. The following month he reorganized the War Department General Staff by combining the Second and Third Divisions into the Second Section. With this reorganization Wotherspoon became both President of the Army War College and Chief of the Second Section of the War Department General Staff.[7] In addition to being the Army's chief educator and chief planner, he was now its chief intelligence officer. Under Wotherspoon's control were sixteen of the thirty-one General Staff Corps officers stationed in Washington.

With the personnel as well as the records and archives of the former Military Information Division under his control, Wotherspoon would be able to meet his war planning responsibilities without having to rely heavily on the temporary personnel detailed to the War College. To provide Wotherspoon even more manpower, Bell approved the retention of a few selected graduates of each War College class for an additional year to serve as "assistant instructors," but without detailing them to the General Staff Corps, whose number of course was limited by law.[8]

The immediate effect of all these actions was not only to redirect the course of instruction, but to make redirection possible by permitting division of the permanent personnel of the Second Section and Army War College into those whose primary duty was to serve as faculty and those whose primary duty was to perform General Staff functions. Furthermore, the nature of the revised course required a distinction between instructor and student. The War College was no longer a place where, as Bliss had once put it, "each officer is a student and all are on the same plane."[9]

Tasker Bliss returned from four years of command duty to reassume the presidency of the War College (and to become Chief of the Second Section) on June 19, 1909. If he disapproved of what the War College had become during his absence, he kept his opinion to himself, although when congratulated by a friend on the assignment, he replied only, "I do not like Washington."[10] There is no evidence, however, that Bliss attempted to reverse or slow the trend of the program as it had evolved since his departure in 1905. Nor did he remain long. In August he was absent on maneuvers, and after three months back in Washington he was on his way to another command, this one on the Mexican border. At the War College he was once again replaced by William Wotherspoon.

More Problems of Empire

The astute Bliss may have recognized another fundamental influence that favored the revised course of instruction. The war planning collegium that he had installed originally had not done badly, particularly since such an endeavor had never before been attempted by the American Army. The War College was understandably and justifiably proud of its role in planning and executing the 1906 deployment to Cuba. But war planning under Theodore Roosevelt had become emergency contingency planning. In 1902 and 1903 there had been the Alaskan boundary and Venezuelan crises, and in 1904 that of Santo Domingo. The Chinese boycott affair followed in 1905, and in 1906 there was not only emergency planning for Cuba, but members of the staff of the War College were actually deployed as General Staff officers with the force.[11]

Contingencies of that sort could not be anticipated precisely as to either circumstance or time of occurrence. When they did occur, the War College, as a planning agency, could meet the Commander-in-Chief's needs only by responding promptly to constantly changing conditions. Rapid and flexible response is not among the virtues of a collegium. It is a task for a close-knit group of trained and experienced practitioners under the direction of strong leadership. It is not surprising that this work fell more and more to the permanent personnel of initially the Third Division and then the Second Section of the reorganized War Department General Staff.

The desirability of having a permanent planning group was brought out forcefully by the Japanese "war scare" of 1907. At the request of President Roosevelt in the early summer of that year, after the temporary personnel of the 1906-07 session had departed, the Chief of Staff instructed the War College to prepare plans based upon the assumption of a war with Japan. The background of the President's request was the growing indignation in Japan over the treatment of their nationals in California, treatment typified by the San Francisco Board of Education order of October 1906 that required children of Oriental parentage to attend segregated schools.[12]

On June 12, 1907, the Chief of Staff's instruction became War College Problem No. 12: "Measures to be taken to meet a sudden attack by Japan under existing conditions." Two days later a preliminary plan had been drawn up. It was endorsed by the Army and Navy Joint Board on the 18th. Wotherspoon and naval representatives to the Joint Board traveled to Roosevelt's Oyster Bay home and discussed the problem with the President on the 27th.[13] These discussions proved to be the genesis of a number of actions and events of the following years: the world cruise of the "Great White Fleet," the resurrection of a controversy between the Navy and the Army as to whether Subic Bay or Manila Bay was the proper locale for a naval base in the Philippines, and the decision to build a base at Pearl Harbor and fortify Oahu. Problem No. 12 was also the beginning of Army planning participation in "Plan Orange" for war with Japan, a plan that would keep more than a generation of planners employed.[14] The War College had once again responded promptly to a presidential concern, but it was the permanent personnel alone who had done so. The interest in this problem at the highest level, its initial crisis nature, and its long-term impact all favored having a group of full-time planners. After 1907-08 the temporary personnel of the War College (the students) ceased to perform more than a supporting role in actual contingency and war planning.

General Bell's efforts to prevent a generation gap and the new emphasis on the study of "military art" did not mean that Bell, Wotherspoon, and Swift merely moved Leavenworth east and instituted a replica of the Staff College course at Washington Barracks. The locus of interest at the War College was on a higher operational level, on the "tactical and strategical handling of troops with special reference to those including and larger than a division." Moreover, there remained an interest in war planning and in "questions of national policy, both offensive and defensive, for which armies are called into service."[15] The treatment of war planning now had the purpose of training an officer in how to plan as much as on developing the plan itself.

In 1907-08 members of the class worked to revise the plan for a deployment to Venezuela and continued the work on the plan for war with Japan. They conducted a war game of the latter plan, "Orange vs. Blue," that resulted in a scheme for the initial defense of the Pacific Coast. This was not a superficial exercise. The plan included details of rail loadings, movement schedules throughout the continental United States, mobilization plans for the National Guard, and even plans for relocating Japanese aliens in camps in Utah.[16] The next year similar work was done, the idea being for the class to appreciate the difficulties of "the passage of the country from a state of peace to a state of war," and for the class to test current plans through war-gaming.[17] But the members of the permanent party, not the temporary personnel, were ultimately responsible for having any plan "put in shape for future use . . . fully revised and edited." For this purpose the permanent personnel of the War College constituted the "War Plans Committee" of the War Department General Staff.[18]

Commencing with the 1908-09 session, work on war planning did not begin until late in the session because "the class needed to learn to make proper estimates of military situations, to weigh difficulties, and to give correct solutions."[19] However, in the map exercises conducted in the fall of the year, the situations were based in part on active war plans. In 1910-11 the Venezuelan problem was studied as the "War Plan of the Year." For the three classes of 1912 through 1914, the months of January and February were devoted to a "War Plan of the Year." For the classes of 1915 and 1916 the time expended on war planning was considerably reduced. Lectures to familiarize the class with current plans were used to compensate.[20]

The Use and Abuse of Military History

Eben Swift's enthusiasm for the "applicatory method" was matched only by his enthusiasm for military history. He was considered by his colleagues as an authority on military history, particularly on the campaigns of the Civil War.[21] During the sessions that Swift served at the War College, he carried on his own shoulders the main instructor load in military history. He introduced to the War College the "historical ride" which, when combined with the "staff ride," came to be known as "Modern Application to the Historical Situation." In the sessions of 1910-11 and 1911-12, the month of March was devoted to studying phases of American military history, primarily those of the Civil War in the east, in preparation for the "rides" that followed in June.[22]

During the session of 1912-13 the War College set for itself the objective of producing a War College "History of the Civil War," which was to reflect the results of its historical work at both Washington Barracks and in the field. At the annual meeting of the American Historical Association in December 1912, Major James W. McAndrew, a student, represented the War College and presented a paper, "Military History," to the first conference the association had held on military history as a specialty field. On the historical ride the next summer, R. M. Johnston, Professor of History at Harvard University, rode with the War College class for several days while it studied the Manassas battlefield. The conclusion at the end of the year was that the studies in military history and the attempts at original historical research were not satisfactory, that nothing of permanent value had resulted.[23]

The War College then began to question whether the benefits of the historical rides were really worth the time and effort, although the staff rides were considered most worthwhile. But a harsh judgment was not conceded. The Class of 1914 devoted March to the study of military history and to further work on the desired Civil War volume. A need for expert guidance was recognized, and Professor Johnston was invited to address the class at the beginning of its historical work. In Johnston's view efficient and adequate military organization had as its basis the "methodical study of military history, [but] such methodical study required expert direction to secure results." After Johnston's presentation, Captain Arthur L. Conger of the Staff College faculty was invited

111

to the War College to confer with the class on historical research and method. Conger was reputed to have established an excellent course in military history at Leavenworth.[24]

Conger was frank: the methods of the War College "were not what they should be." He may have been encouraged in his frankness by a report of the second conference on military history held at the 1913 meeting of the American Historical Association, at which he had read a paper, "The Teaching of Military History." The report of the association commended the Fort Leavenworth methods and recommended the adoption of similar work at the War College. With no expert to lead, the progress toward a Civil War volume was as disappointing in 1914 as it had been in 1913. Professor Johnston returned to address the Class of 1915. This time he delivered three lectures, one on historical method and two illustrating how military history could be used to help guide military organization and strategy. Lieutenant Colonel Clement A. F. Flager, a member of the faculty, also lectured on historical method. In February 1916 the President of the War College himself, Brigadier General Montgomery M. Macomb, lectured on "The Scientific Study of Military History." Nonetheless, the chronicler of the War College of the prewar era concluded several years later that these lectures only showed "how the trained historian uses his art to make important deductions from the record of past events which remain a sealed book to casual readers who imagine they are studying history."

By the spring of 1915, however, the War College, yet a creature of the General Staff, was swept up in matters more urgent than Civil War history.[25]

Attempts at Original Research

With the first session of the College, Bliss had inaugurated the requirement for original research in military subjects. By necessity Wotherspoon had given this requirement low priority—after emergency work. Yet Wotherspoon warned the student of the Class of 1908 that his capacity would be largely judged by the quality of his research. Each member of that class and of the one following was assigned one of a number of "Special Studies of Military Importance," which he was to carefully research throughout the year. Those subjects of a strategic nature (for example, the need for advance bases, the strategic importance of Hawaii, and the means for defense of Guantanamo) were assigned not to individuals, however, but to committees led by one of the permanent personnel. Purely general staff studies intended for permanent record, moreover, were to be "attended to" by the permanent personnel of the Second Section.[26]

The requirement for original research survived for only two years after the introduction of Swift's course in "military art." Interestingly for

112

the 1909-10 session, the only one Bliss could have influenced on his second assignment to the War College, the whole idea of students attempting original research (other than in military history) was abandoned. It was not resurrected until the session of 1914-15. Through the 1916-17 session "compilation of military monographs" was a task to be performed in the month of January. These monographs, however, were exclusively studies of the geography and military resources of designated countries. In 1915-16 the selection of subjects was based on requests made by the various committees of the War Department General Staff, an indication that in the years just prior to World War I, the workload of the permanent personnel of the General Staff was exceeding their capacity. Only then were War College students called in to help.[27]

The War College and Annual Field Exercises

One of the measures that Elihu Root had believed critical to having a more expert Army was the holding of annual maneuvers or camps of instruction where the regular Army and the organized militia could train together and where officers could gain experience in the handling of large bodies of troops. To capitalize on the annual maneuvers Wotherspoon recommended that the War College course be extended from seven months to a year. He wanted officers of the War College to participate in the maneuvers, particularly to serve with arms of the service other than their own. Wotherspoon's idea was adopted in the summer of 1909 when the President of the War College, General Bliss, commanded one "army" in a two-sided maneuver in Massachusetts. Five of the permanent personnel and twelve of the temporary personnel of the War College accompanied Bliss, constituting the staff of his force and almost the entire umpire staff.[28]

The success of the Massachusetts experience persuaded Bliss to include a special series of lectures and practical exercises in the War College curriculum on the preparation of maneuver problems and the duties of umpires. He assumed that the War College class would go as a body to the maneuver camps. In the summer of 1910 the historical ride ended on the Gettysburg battlefield. The class remained there during the month of July, acting as staff officers, observers, and umpires for maneuvers being held for the regular Army and the militia. General Wotherspoon, since December again President of the War College, commanded this Camp of Instruction. The class then returned to Washington Barracks for two more months of work.[29]

If using War College personnel for the camps of instruction was to become the practice, and Wotherspoon thought it should, then it would be more efficient to end the War College course on June 30 and have the class participate in the summer encampments on the way to their post-War College assignments. For this reason and others (including standardization with with other schools in the education system and giving the permanent personnel some "rest") Wotherspoon recommended having the War College year begin on September 1 and end on June 30. The War Department approved this recommendation to take effect in the summer of 1911. It detailed all but four of the June 1911 graduating class as inspector-instructors at Organized Militia camps during July and August. The next year, after the graduation of the Class of 1912, the President of the War College, Brigadier General Albert L. Mills, commanded one side on maneuvers held in Connecticut, taking with him one of the permanent officers of the college, Major Guy Carleton. Neither Mills nor Carleton, however, returned for duty at the War College. The study concerning preparation of maneuver problems and umpiring that Bliss began in 1909 remained part of the course through 1917, but by that time the emphasis had lessened and only three days were dedicated to the subject.[31]

The Faculty

No matter how well or imaginatively conceived the program of an educational institution might be, the degree of success rests ultimately with the quality of the faculty members who conduct the program and the quality of the students selected to participate. In general, the pre-World War I Army War College was more fortunate with its faculty than with its students. The War Department habitually provided the War College with a faculty composed of officers it considered to be of high quality and great potential. The department's expectations were borne out: thirty-four of the pre-World War I faculty members became general officers subsequent to their service at the War College; three became Chiefs of Staff of the Army. From the organization of the college in 1903 until 1909, all the officers selected for the faculty came from that elite group already designated to serve in the General Staff Corps. Beginning in 1909, as was mentioned earlier, it became policy to retain four members of the just-graduated class for an additional year as either "instructors" or "assistant instructors," but without detailing them to the General Staff Corps. The positions of President, Director, Assistant Director and Secretary, however, remained designated as part of the General Staff Corps. After 1909 three to five students were held over each year.

In 1914 the system partially failed; three General Staff officers had to serve as instructors for the Class of 1915 in addition to their General Staff duties. The year 1913-14 is the best example of the goal being sought. All members of the faculty, including the President, Brigadier General Hunter Liggett, were graduates of the War College. Four General Staff officers served as the directing group, and four recent graduates served as instructors. Additionally, from the years 1913 through

114

1916, there was a Medical Corps officer attached to the faculty to instruct and advise on medical support questions.[32]

War Department assignment policy also provided continuity in leadership. Wotherspoon had been a Director under Bliss in 1904-05. Except for two breaks of less than a year each, he served at the War College through January 1912. One of those breaks was from June through November 1909 when Bliss returned as President. Eben Swift served on the faculty during four sessions, 1907-10, and was replaced by Hunter Liggett, a member of the Class of 1910. Liggett was promoted to colonel and made Director for the Classes of 1911, 1912, and 1913, then was promoted again and served as President during the 1913-14 session. Major Benjamin A. Poore, of the Class of 1909, returned as a Director for the Class of 1913 and remained until January 1916.

The Navy also provided an officer for the faculty, even through the close relationship that Bliss had begun to build between the Army War College and the Naval War College changed after the Army War College became less active in war planning. The relationship became more one of liaison than of active joint planing. A United States Navy representative was on the Army War College faculty continuously from the first session in 1904-05 until after the graduation of the Class of 1913. Due to the worsening crisis in Mexico, the Navy was able to furnish a representative only briefly for the Class of 1914 and not at all for the Class of 1915. During the last two prewar years members of the Naval War College faculty attended the Army War College as students and served concurrently as naval representatives.[33]

Beginning in 1905 two Army officer from the General Staff attended the summer session of the Naval War College each year. After 1911 the War Department selected those two officers from the graduating class of the Army War College and from among the four who had been previously designated to remain as instructors or assistant instructors. In 1914 the Naval War College held no summer session, and restructured its program into a year-long course. Two members from each of the Army War College classes of 1915 and 1916 were sent to Newport for a second year of war college work.[34]

The Students

With regard to its student body the pre-World War I War College was almost exclusively an institution for the instruction of line officers. Infantry and cavalry officers dominated each class in number. The Corps of Engineers normally sent one representative per class. The permanent staff departments were represented during the entire period by only one Signal Corps, two Commissary, and four Quartermaster officers. No Ordnance, Medical, or Judge Advocate General Corps officers attended. The course was opened briefly to a National Guard officer, Major General John F. O'Ryan of New York. Authorized by President Wilson to attend, O'Ryan graduated with the Class of 1914. Root's idea that the War College would instruct militia as well as regular Army officers had not taken hold. Three naval officers were given credit as graduating from the Army War College, and all three were to achieve flag rank, two becoming full admirals. After 1907 one or two Marine Corps officers attended the Army War College as students each year. Eleven were graduated before World War I; seven became general officers.[35]

In May 1907, with the move into the new building and the expanded course pending, General Wotherspoon was concerned about the size, composition, and qualifications of the class. Acknowledging that the new building could accommodate a class of from forty to fifty students, Wotherspoon nonetheless recommended that the Class of 1907-08 be limited to sixteen so the War College could "adapt itself to its new surroundings." What was unsaid was that a small class would also allow a high permanent-to-temporary personnel ratio during the year of transition to the new military art emphasis. Wotherspoon also recommended that the class "be apportioned amongst the several arms of the service in proportion to their total strength in officers." He strongly favored putting the course "within reach of at least a certain number of officers who will, in the near future, reach high command." Dealing with the first three classes he had discovered majors to be as industrious, energetic, and conscientious as captains, and he had found their maturity and wider experience to be of value. He therefore recommended a class of three lieutenant colonels, five majors, and eight captains.[36] His new charter of 1907, General Order No. 116, had removed the earlier prohibition on officers above the grade of major.

Wotherspoon was not entirely successful. Only eleven rather than sixteen officers were detailed to the Class of 1908; four were majors and seven were captains. His experience with that class impressed upon him that the qualifications of the students posed a greater problem than the composition of the class by grade and arm of the service. In February he complained that those officers who were not graduates of one of the two schools of the General Service and Staff College at Leavenworth (the School of the Line or the Staff College) were not proficient in map reading, methods of issuing orders, conducting map exercises, participation in war games and tactical rides, and the umpiring and managing of maneuvers and field exercises. The problem was the impossibility of finding many students who were both field officers and graduates of the Staff College. Staff College graduates were still captains and were fated to remain so for a number of years. Field officers avoided entering into the intense competition at the School of the Line, a competition that General Bell had instituted as the sole process of gaining entrance to the Staff College for a second year of study at Leavenworth.[37]

116

In accordance with Wotherspoon's recommendation, the Secretary of War in August 1908 approved new rules for admission to the War College which would attract older officers. Those of the line of the mobile army (infantry, cavalry, and field artillery) who attended the Leavenworth's School of the Line after more than fifteen years of service could be detailed to attend the War College without competing for or attending the Staff College if the academic board of the School of the Line pronounced them qualified. Graduates of the School of the Line with less than fifteen years of service, however, would have to win appointment to and successfully complete the Staff College before attending the War College. Officers of the Coast Artillery who aspired to attend the War College would have to complete the Coast Artillery School and be recommended by that institution. Officers of the technical services, of which there would be only one student per class, would be individually selected by the Secretary of War. Officers with more than twenty years of service might apply and be accepted at the War College if their professional record justified it. Bell and Wotherspoon did not wish to abandon the competitive educational system originally outlined by Carter, but they realized that it would be at least five years until the college would be able to accept only Staff College graduates or graduates of the second year advanced work at the Coast Artillery School.[38] In the meantime the class at the War College would be less qualified than thought desirable.

The solution Wotherspoon arrived at was to provide a preparatory course for field-grade officers. For the Class of 1909 both the War College and Leavenworth offered two-month preliminary courses for officers prior to their entering the War College. Fifteen officers of the Class of 1909 attended these courses; an additional four were graduates of the School of the Line, but three had no special preparation. Of the last category, one was an officer of the Subsistence Department, the first non-combat arms officer to attend the War College. Wotherspoon was successful in getting three lieutenant colonels into the class, but only half the class was field grade. The War College continued to offer a preparatory course for the Classes of 1910 and 1911, though Leavenworth did not. The Class of 1910 had one Staff College graduate and twenty-one officers who had attended the preparatory course. The Class of 1911 had eight Staff College graduates and ten officers who had attended the preparatory course. About half the members of each class were field officers. The Class of 1911 included the first officer to graduate in the rank of colonel.[39]

Wotherspoon remained dissatisfied, however, with the level of professional competence of the officers selected for the War College. To Wotherspoon, Leavenworth was the proper place to conduct the "Leavenworth training" every officer should have before appearing at

Washington Barracks. Under the regulations, the Staff College was the only true preparatory school for the War College, a diploma from the Staff College being accepted as qualification without question. Wotherspoon was convinced that a field officers' course at Leavenworth was needed. He sent Colonel Hunter Liggett, newly appointed Director of the college, to Leavenworth in August 1910 to consult with the faculty there. After coordinating with the Acting Commandant, Colonel John F. Morrison, a member of the War College Class of 1906, Liggett recommended that Leavenworth conduct a three-month preparatory course in military art for field officers from January through March each year. Of the officers who completed this course, perhaps ten would be available each year for attendance at the War College. Liggett and Morrison agreed that any captain who attended the War College must be a graduate of the Staff College, and any field officer to attend must be a graduate of either the Staff College or the proposed field officers' course. This system would provide a well-prepared, homogeneous class so that at the War College "every hour may be utilized in the best way at legitimate War College work."[40]

Wotherspoon and Bell's replacement as Chief of Staff, Leonard Wood, supported this scheme. Wood directed in September that the field officers' course be established. Morrison conducted a ten-week course from January through March 1911 with a class of fourteen field officers of the line, including two of the Coast Artillery and an additional two from the Marine Corps. Wood's order did not require, however, that all officers attending the War College be graduates of either the Staff College or the new course. The Class of 1912, with thirty officers, was the largest pre-World War I class. It had six graduates of the field officers' course and four graduates of the technical schools of the Coast Artillery and Corps of Engineers, but twelve members had no special schooling. Like its predecessors this class lacked homogeneity. The experience level was rising, however. Of the thirty officers, only nine were captains, while three were promoted to colonel before graduation.[41]

The faculty found that the Staff College graduates were the best prepared for War College work, but that graduates of the field officers' course had a marked advantage over nongraduates. Moreover, the War Department recognized that the field officers' course had value beyond being a preparatory course for the War College. It became an established feature of the Leavenworth schools, convening yearly with classes of not more than twenty officers. The War Department arranged that officers detailed to the field officers' course be from among those considered as potential candidates for the War College.[42]

The War College Class of 1913 drew fourteen officers from the eighteen who attended the field officers' course and was the first class composed solely of field officers. Only two had no special preparation for

War College work, but three were graduates of the Staff College. The Class of 1913 was by far the highest qualified and most homogeneous class to date. The Class of 1914 was a slip backward, however. All students were of field grade, but there was only one Staff College graduate and ten graduates of the field officers' course. Eleven members of the class had no such schooling. As a result of this development, in September 1913 the Chief of Staff authorized the President of the War College to return to their regiments any officers who by December 1 had demonstrated that they were not up to the work. No students were relieved, but three were denied certificates of graduation upon completion of the course.[43]

While the Class of 1914 was in session, the War Department published a new regulation further tightening the rules for admission by requiring entrance examinations for all candidates except graduates of the Staff College, the one technical service officer admitted each year, and officers from the Navy and Marine Corps. Two years of service with troops after Leavenworth was required of Staff College graduates. The President of the War College retained the authority to relieve nonproductive officers. For the Class of 1915 examinations were administered in May prior to entrance, in April for the Class of 1916.[44] The examination consisted of four map problems (the candidate was given one day to complete each without use of references) and one original study to be written in two days using references.[45] The examination system seems to have had the desired effect. In the Class of 1915 there was only one Staff College graduate, but the other eighteen officers, including four who had completed the field officers' course, had passed the examination. The system had its drawbacks, however. The balance in the class between branches of the service was distorted. There were no field artillerymen in the Class of 1915. Moreover, despite the entrance test, two members of that class did not receive certificates of graduation.[46]

For the Class of 1916, twenty-four applicants took and passed the examination; twenty were selected, in addition to two Staff College graduates. For the 1917 class there were twenty-nine applicants approved for admission. Ten were Staff College graduates; the remaining qualified themselves through the examination route. The Class of 1917 was better qualified than any previous class.[47] The field officers' course, the entrance examinations, and time were curing the problem of qualifications. But time ran out. The Class of 1917 was the last for a while. There would not be another until after the defeat of Imperial Germany.

NOTES

1. War Department General Orders No. 116, May 28, 1907.
2. AWC, "Course for 1907-1908: Problems and Exercises," 1-15, *AWC-CF,* MHI Collection.
3. AWC, "Session 1910-11, Record of Work," 4 Vols. I, "Outline of Course," 3-14, Ibid.
4. Ibid., 3.
5. Characterization of Bliss is from Palmer, *Bliss,* 1-5. Among the Bliss papers in the MHI Collection are a number of samples of his translations from Latin.
6. For the early career of Bell see Edgar F. Raines, *Major General J. Franklin Bell and Military Reform: The Chief of Staff Years, 1906-1910* (Ann Arbor, Mich.: University Microfilms, 1977), 6-13.
7. War Department General Orders No. 128, August 12, 1908, para. 672-73.
8. Letter, Adjutant General to President of the Army War College, August 28, 1909, Box 1900-1909, *Bliss Papers,* MHI Collection.
9. Bliss, Memo Report for the Chief of Staff, January 15, 1904.
10. Cited in Palmer, *Bliss,* 99.
11. For the role of the General Staff in supervising the 1906 deployment to Cuba see Millett, "Cuban Intervention of 1906," 113-19.
12. For the President's view of this crisis see Harbaugh, *Roosevelt,* 285-87.
13. Wotherspoon to the Chief of Staff, Memorandum Relative to Conversations with the President in New York, "Army War College Course 1907-1908: Orange and Blue Problem," 65-70, *AWC-CF,* MHI Collection. The role of the Navy's General Board and the Army General Staff in this "crisis" is discussed in Challener, *Admirals, Generals,* 232-33, 244-48.
14. The Navy favored a base at Subic Bay, but the Army held that place to be indefensible and favored Manila Bay. Underlying the debate was the frustrating reality that the Philippines could not be defended by any military or naval force Congress reasonably could be expected to provide. Roosevelt began calling the Philippines "our Achilles heel." Challener, *Admirals, Generals,* 233-34. Work on Plan Orange remained in the student program for the Classes of 1909, 1910, and 1911, "Army War College Session, 1910-11: Record of Work." 4 Vols., I: 14, *AWC-CF,* MHI Collection.
15. "Session 1910-11," I: 3, Ibid.
16. "Course 1907-08: Orange and Blue Problems," Ibid.
17. AWC, "Course for 1908-1909: War College Problem," Ibid.
18. Report of the Chief of the Second Section, General Staff, to the Chief of Staff, August 31, 1910, in Ahern, "Chronicle," 132. Memorandum, Chief of the War College Division to the Chief of Staff, July 23, 1912, in Ibid., 184.
19. Report of Chief of the Second Section, August 31, 1910.
20. AWC, "Session 1910-1911," II: 14. "Outline of Course of Instruction: Session of 1911-1912," 5. "Outline of Course of Instruction: Session of 1912-1913," 3. "General Instructions and Schedules, Session of 1913-1914," 22-23. "General Instructions and Schedules, Session of 1914-1915," 22. "General Instructions and Schedules, Session of 1915-1916," 20. All in *AWC-CF,* MHI Collection.
21. One student at Leavenworth described Swift as "a saturated solution of Civil War History," cited in Nenninger, *Leavenworth,* 45.
22. AWC, "Session 1910-11," II: 5. "Session of 1911-1912," 5.
23. AWC, "Session of 1912-1913," 4. Ahern, "Chronicle," 188, 190-92.
24. AWC, "Session of 1913-1914," 24. Ahern, "Chronicle," 198-99, 204, 211-12. For an assessment of Conger's work at Ft. Leavenworth see Nenninger, *Leavenworth,* 96-99.
25. "Report on Conference on Military History," *The American Historical Review,* XX (April 1914): 482. Ahern, "Chronicle," 212, 224, 237-39, 246. Montgomery M. Macomb, "The Scientific Study of Military History," Opening address to Military History course, 15 February 1916, Army War College Session 1915-16, *AWC-CF,* MHI Collection.
26. Ahern, "Chronicle," 72, 78, 108, 116.
27. AWC, "Course, 1909-1910," 15 Vols., II: 4-18. "Session of 1914-1915," 23. "Session of 1915-1916," 21.
28. Ahern, "Chronicle," 73, 119-20.

29. Ibid., 133-34, 137.
30. Memorandum, President of the War College to Chief of Staff, April 15, 1910, paras. 1-4, in Ahern, "Chronicle," 148.
31. Ahern, "Chronicle," 180-82, 270. AWC, "Course, 1909-1910," II: 15-18.
32. Data from *War College Directory*, 12-14. Ahern, "Chronicle," 122, 201, 240.
33. Ahern, "Chronicle," 36, 194, 207.
34. Ibid., 44, 158, 229, 250, 274.
35. Branch of service data from *War College Directory*, 12-14. Ahern, "Chronicle," 200, 206, 252, 268. The Subsistence and Quartermaster departments were combined in 1912.
36. Wotherspoon, Memorandum for the Chief of Staff, Subject: The Army War College, May 28, 1907, in "Memoranda," 43.
37. Wotherspoon, Memorandum for the Chief of Staff, February 10, 1908, quoted in Ahern, "Chronicle," 95-97.
38. War Department Circular No. 69, August 22, 1908.
39. Ahern, "Chronicle," 97-98, 121, 145, 149. The colonel was Charles G. Treat, who during World War I was to command U.S. Army forces in Italy.
40. Ibid., 162-65.
41. Ibid., 165-66, 169-70.
42. Ibid., 178-79. For discussion of the field officers' course at Ft. Leavenworth (dubbed the "Get Rich Quick" course) see Nenninger, *Leavenworth*, 122-24.
43. Ahern, "Chronicle," 187-88, 202, 207. AWC, Regulation regarding the relief of student officers, September 26, 1913, in Ibid., 203.
44. War Department General Order No. 13, February 27, 1914.
45. War Department Bulletin No. 9, March 23, 1914.
46. Ahern, "Chronicle," 219-20, 229.
47. Ibid., 268-69.

And a Decade
of Distraction
1909-1918

The First Ten Years

The War College decade that began with Tasker Bliss gathering the officers of the Third Division into 22 Jackson Place in 1903 and ended with the graduation of the Class of 1913 was a period of growth and prosperity for the new institution. By 1913 the War College was regularly graduating a class of twenty-two Army officers and two of the Marine Corps each June. The directing faculty was small but stable, reinforced annually by selected members of the previous class serving a year's detail as instructors. The class was in session during a conventional academic year of ten months, and the college presented an established and familiar curriculum emphasizing "military art" and war planning. Almost two months of each year were spent in the field on the combined staff and historical rides—to the students the climax and most enjoyable phase of the program. War planning was studied, but in a fashion that provided realism without sweeping the students into the vortex of crisis management. Each year the students arrived with more and broader experience, and a preparatory course was in place to help assure that all students were at reasonably the same level.

The impressive building that had been occupied in the summer of 1907 was dedicated with ceremony on November 9, 1908. Notables of the three branches of the federal government, the diplomatic corps, and the naval and military services, with their ladies, were invited to attend. President Roosevelt and President-elect Taft had to send their regrets, but Secretary of State Elihu Root was present and delivered the principal address just as he had as Secretary of War at the laying of the cornerstone five years before.[1]

The building provided facilities not only for the faculty and students of the War College but also for half the War Department General Staff. Within its walls went forward not only the schooling of the Army's future leadership but all the military planning and intelligence activities of the War Department. The President of the War College was one of the Army's more influential officers. He was the chief planner, intelligence officer, and educator. As a member of the Joint Board, he consulted with the Navy's General Board and advised the President. The War College had the facilities, the people, and the financial support that gave it the potential to become the Army's true intellectual center for the study of war.

Just as the collegium concept instituted by Bliss had eroded, so also had his idea of abstinence from academic trappings. In 1904 Kaiser Wilhelm, undoubtedly unaware of Bliss's preferences, presented the War College with a statue of Frederick the Great. Accepted with ceremony by Theodore Roosevelt, the statue has survived precariously through two wars with Germany. In 1905, not content that selection for attendance at the War College was adequate professional recognition, participants in the first session gained approval of having their attendance noted in the *Army Register*. Beginning in 1911 the college presented a "Certificate of Graduation" as additional evidence of achievement. This parchment required an official seal, coat of arms, and motto, all of which the War Department had authorized the year before.[2]

Of greater significance than statues, diplomas, coats of arms, and mottoes was the consensus finally reached as to what the War College should be and what it could contribute to the American Army. Elihu Root, at his cornerstone address, had prescribed three great problems for study—national defense, military science, and responsible command. As the institution matured, General Wotherspoon described the object as "to prepare officers for the duties of the General Staff in campaigns and for the higher command."[3]

The emphasis by 1913 was clearly "duties . . . in campaigns." The applicatory method in use at the Infantry and Cavalry School, adapted from the Germans by Wagner and Swift before the Spanish War and transplanted to the War College between 1906 and 1910 by Bell, Wotherspoon, and Swift, dominated the curriculum. General Bell spoke of this instruction in tactics as a temporary expedient, but it was an expedient that no one in 1913 showed any inclination to discard. Original research in "topics of military importance" had survived only through 1909. The great problem of national defense had evolved into contingency planning to support first President Roosevelt's, and then President Taft's foreign policies. More and more, however, real planning became the responsibility of the permanent personnel of the General Staff acting not as faculty but as the War Plans Committee of the War Department General Staff. Student work on the problems was derivative and subordinate.

The third great problem, that of responsible command, the War College did not precisely define nor directly attack. If at all identifiable in the programs of instruction, study of this problem was inherent in the tactical decision-making called for by the map maneuvers and staff rides of the applicatory system. Although the War College was organizationally part of the War Department General Staff and to a degree remained intellectually connected to that body, its true intellectual milieu had become the *Truppengeneralstab* and its kinsmen were the schools of combined arms at Fort Leavenworth.

If the War College as an academic institution had found a comfortable niche in the scheme of things, the War Department General Staff, Root's other great creation, was still searching for a place. Commander-in-Chief to the final moment, Theodore Roosevelt's last bit of advice to his successor in 1909 was strategic: "Dear Will, one last legacy. Under no circumstances divide the battle fleet." Taft may not have had the interest and exuberance of things naval and military that the departing Rough Rider had, but if the planners of the fledgling General Staff thought the exit of Roosevelt would slacken their pace they were mistaken. Dollar diplomacy was to prove as crisis-ridden as *Realpolitik*. The world and its clash of interests was still out there, and power remained a part of it.

In the first year of his administration, Taft formally ended the second occupation of Cuba. That same year Tasker Bliss returned from the Philippines to become once again President of the War College and the Army's chief planner. A growing concern was the defense of Panama, where a member of the first collegium, George Goethals, had brought construction to the point that a canal was no longer a distant vision. Upon Bliss's transfer to the Mexican border later in the year, Wotherspoon completed the planning, but Taft would not agree to the stationing of four to five infantry regiments in the Canal Zone. He preferred to rely upon coast artillery batteries. Leonard Wood replaced Bell as Chief of Staff in 1910 and attempted the next year to reopen the Subic Bay controversy, but Taft was not interested. Revolutions in Mexico, China, and Cuba in March, October, and December of that year, however, did demand the President's attention.[4]

By March 1911 the probability of revolution in Mexico was clearly apparent. The pace of Navy and Army contingency planning quickened. Wotherspoon and his naval counterpart at Newport found common grounds of complaint in the dearth of policy guidance forthcoming from the State Department. Taft's decision was to mobilize and exercise in south Texas a "maneuver division" of 20,000 men. He believed this display might strengthen the hand of the Mexican government and deter acts of violence against American citizens and property south of the border. Captain Malin Craig of the War College faculty was absent from March to July with the division.[5]

The Mexican revolution erupted despite Taft's military demonstration. Francisco Madero replaced Porfirio Diaz as president, border inci-

125

dents increased, and additional Army units moved to the border. In February 1912 Taft officially authorized planning for a full-scale invasion of Mexico, to include the seizure of Mexico City. His intent was to avoid intervention, but if forced to it he did not want to "fool around with little expeditions." General Wood directed the War College Division to assume that the Mexican factions would unite against American intervention. In May the President approved the plan. It called for a 16-division, 130,000-man force to land at Vera Cruz, then move on Mexico City. Later the port of Tampico was added as an objective after an agent of the Standard Oil Company informed General William Crozier, who had succeeded Wotherspoon as President of the War College, of American interests in that area.[6]

In October 1911 revolt broke out in China against the Manchu dynasty. The War College Division was asked to report on the Army's capabilities to operate in China, specifically as part of an international force to secure the railroad to Peking. Wotherspoon was pessimistic. The Army could provide a force of only 25,000 to 30,000, and several months would be needed to get it on the scene. Wotherspoon wanted no part of attempting to influence the situation in the interior of China. He suggested instead the seizure of a port, preferably Shanghai. In January 1912, an American battalion was deployed to assist in guarding the Peking railroad.

Neither did the War College Division or Chief of Staff Wood want a third occupation of Cuba. When Secretary of State Philander Knox in early 1912 asked for four regiments for possible use in putting down turmoil on the island, Wood termed the measure "extreme and foolish." Knox backed off. Cuba was left to work out its own destiny without the assistance of the American Army.[7]

Nicaragua was yet another concern. In August 1912 President Taft went so far as to direct an infantry regiment to deploy to Nicaraugua to assist the Navy in settling revolt in that unhappy nation. But Henry L. Stimson, who had become Secretary of War the previous year, convinced the President that the State Department just did not understand the political implications, or the impact upon world opinion, of using soldiers rather than sailors and Marines. Stimson pointed out that the Mexican situation was much more critical to the United States and that Taft did not intend to use the Army there. Taft revoked the order; the sailors and Marines had Nicaraugua to themselves.[8]

The conservative approach of the War College planners during the Taft years is interesting. With a decade of experience in contingency planning behind them, they perhaps now better understood the operational and logistical difficulties of overseas intervention and political difficulty of extracting forces once committed. The second occupation of Cuba had lasted three years, and a large legation guard was still in

China a dozen years after the Boxer affair. Root's General Staff was maturing and so also was its "great adjunct," the War College.

Problems Within the War Department

It is now apparent that by 1910 the Root, Carter, and Young organization of the War Department General Staff, as modified in 1908 by General Bell, provided for *Grosser Generalstab* functions adequately if not well. The Second and Third Divisions, consolidated by Bell into the Second Section, grew increasingly competent in meeting their intelligence and planning responsibilities. What Root had not provided for was something analogous to the German War Ministry and Military Cabinet, something that could perform the functions of coordinating and supervising the personnel, administrative, supply, and service activities of the Army. Despite the warnings of Root and others that the General Staff must avoid "mere administration," there was no agency other than the General Staff to perform the necessary supervision and coordination of the still independent-minded bureaus. The First Division, later the First Section, moved rather clumsily into this vacuum as an executive agency of the Chief of Staff. General Staff supervision was becoming an attempt to manage, even to the point of meddling, a tendency that made conflict with the traditional staff departments or bureaus likely, if not inevitable. The struggle for supremacy within the War Department unfortunately did not cease with Root's creation of the War Department General Staff. Only the roster of claimants changed.[9]

The clash might not have come if a man of Root's vision, strength, and energy had replaced him. The amiable Judge Taft lacked those qualities. Taft looked upon the Chief of Staff as chief of only the General Staff, and he had a habit of dealing directly with the bureau chiefs without consulting the Chief of Staff. When disputes arose between Bell and the Adjutant General, Fred C. Ainsworth, Taft attempted to resolve them with appeals for harmony and peace. To be fair, Taft never really had the opportunity to establish his leadership at the War Department. President Roosevelt repeatedly sent him overseas on what were, in fact, diplomatic missions. Nor did Roosevelt himself strengthen the role of the General Staff. When Taft was away it was Roosevelt's practice to place (apparently with General Bell's concurrence) the more senior Ainsworth, not Bell, in charge at the War Department.[10]

A former Army surgeon, Ainsworth had entered the War Department by way of the Bureau of Records and Pensions. He rose to the position of Adjutant General through true talent as an administrator and even greater talent as a politically astute bureaucrat. As Adjutant General he had no intention of surrendering real or assumed powers to the General Staff. Ainsworth was able to deflect most of Bell's efforts at gaining control, but he found a more politically powerful, tenacious, and ruthless adversary in Bell's successor of 1910, another former Army surgeon, Major General Leonard Wood.Wood was a former commander and friend of Theodore Roosevelt. He had been military governor in Cuba and Commanding General in the Philippines. He had grown quite accustomed to being in charge. Moreover, to Wood controversy was the natural state of affairs. And Wood was not only a Republican, but an outspoken one.[11]

Observing the early work of the War Department General Staff from the Philippines, Wood became convinced that it was defective. Once Chief of Staff he began to reorganize. Eliminating "sections," Wood established four "divisions": a Mobile Army Division, a Coast Artillery Division, a Division of Militia Affairs, and a War College Division. In the eyes of his critics, Wood created with the War Department General Staff divisions new "super bureaus." All elements of the line army now had proponents on the War Department General Staff.[12]

The true *Grosser Generalstab* element of Bell's staff, the Second Section, Wood renamed the War College Division. It was not affected greatly by Wood's reorganization. Its functions and internal organization were not changed, nor was its location at Washington Barracks. The new name did cause some confusion. The appearance was of "a relatively small number of student officers . . . taught by a large number of instructors made up of General Staff officers and selected assistants." The President of the War College argued that this perception was inaccurate. He argued that the 1911-12 course "was conducted . . . by four General Staff officers and four assistants. . . . This body of instructors also makes up the War Plans Committee."[13] But with its name associated with a division of the War Department General Staff, the War College inadvertently was placed on the field of jurisdictional strife.

In that strife Wood gained a strong ally in 1911 when a protege of Elihu Root, Henry L. Stimson, was named Secretary of War. Stimson, as had Root, chose to support his Chief of Staff. The differences between Wood and Ainsworth reached an unseemly climax later in 1911. The immediate outcome was court-martial proceedings initiated against Ainsworth for insubordination, his retirement from the Army, and an investigation into the entire affair by the Military Affairs Committee of the House. The details of the affair are not of specific interest to the history of the War College, but its consequences are.[14]

If Wood was fortunate in having Henry Stimson as his Secretary of War, he and Stimson were unfortunate to an equal degree with regard to the person occupying the chair of the House Military Affairs Committee. In the election of 1910 the Democrats had gained control of the House, making the Honorable James Hay of Virginia committee Chairman. Hay was a rural Democrat of Jeffersonian persuasion. He distrusted standing armies, national armies, the concept of a general staff, and chiefs of staff who were Republicans. It is difficult to say which he distrusted the most; he made life unpleasant for all impartially. His committee's investigation exonerated Ainsworth. Hay then used the embittered former Adjutant General as an unofficial but willing consultant on future Army legislation.[15]

Congress and the General Staff

After the Ainsworth affair Congress began to demonstrate a decided hostility toward the general staff concept that had been authorized in 1902, much as Bliss had expected. The timing was unfortunate because in 1912 the War Department General Staff produced for the first time the sort of study that Elihu Root had originally hoped it might. Entitled "Report on the Organization of the Land Forces of the United States" and described by Secretary Stimson as a "broad outline of a comprehensive military policy," the study urged an Army organized for war. Recommended was a mobile force of eventually four divisions, an improved militia also organized on the divisional pattern, and a cadre of trained reserve officers about whom a volunteer force could be assembled in a major emergency. To rationalize its proposed organizations and policy, the War Department General Staff of necessity had been led to engage itself in what is now known as "requirements planning."

Heretofore, the War College Division had confined itself to planning the "little expeditions" that President Taft scorned as inappropriate to the Mexican problem. The War College Division had confined itself in other words (again using more modern terminology) to "capabilities planning"—what could and should be done with forces available to meet specific contingencies. Capabilities planning is fundamentally the solving of a military problem. Requirements planning, however, takes the planner into more nebulous political, social, and economic arenas.

Requirements planning must start with the definition of national interests and threats to those interests. From those definitions are deduced the missions the Army must be capable of performing. From missions the number and types of forces required are calculated. Finally, programs are developed, with estimates of the funds necessary to provide the forces in the number and configuration required. Merely to initiate requirements planning calls for an understanding of those fundamental trends in the international and domestic environment that will affect the security of the nation.

The first requirements plan under the label of "military policy" that Secretary Stimson presented so proudly to the Congress was not a sophisticated, lengthy, or detailed document; nonetheless it was a long-range program, "a broad chart for present guidance and for future progress." Stimson hoped it would serve as a document from which both the executive and legislative branches could work to provide for the common defense. That had been its original purpose. The Congress missed its significance entirely. Its members did not miss, however, the fact that the organization plan called for consolidation of military posts and the abandonment of a number of them, including, unhappily, Fort D. A. Russell in Wyoming, the state represented by Senator Francis E. Warren, Chairman of the Military Affairs Committee of the Senate. The "Report on the Organization of the Land Forces of the United States" proved to be a learning experience for its authors—in more ways than one.[16]

The Congress held the culpable party in both the Ainsworth affair and the post closure proposals to be the General Staff. Using the medium of the 1912 Army Appropriations Act, Congress reduced the General Staff Corps, already ridiculously small by European standards, from forty-five to thirty-six officers. The *Army and Navy Journal* reported that among the effects of the General Staff reduction would be a crippling of the War College. It would be almost impossible to provide the necessary officers for the college. The *Journal* was overly pessimistic. The workload of the remaining General Staff officers did increase, however, and the students of the War College organizationally and physically were conveniently located to provide some relief. In 1915 there appeared in the college curriculum the item "General Staff Work." In the War College President's report of 1916 was the comment that "the principle innovation after January was the assignment to detailed instructors and to student officers of certain current papers referred by the Chief of Staff to the War College Division of the General Staff for action."[17]

In August 1912 the Congress passed what came to be known within the Army as the "Manchu Law." This law prescribed that company-grade officers on "detached service" must have served at least two of their previous six years with troops. The provision was extended to field-grade officers in 1915. This statutory personnel assignment policy had a number of real virtues, but its effect on the War College was to reduce the number of officers available for selection to the faculty and annual class. It also limited the length of an officer's tour of duty with the War College, regardless of his value as a faculty member or the urgency of the requirement for his services elsewhere. There could be no tenure or permanent professors at the Army War College.[18]

The congressional hostility toward the General Staff did not cease with the departure of Stimson at the close of the Taft administration, nor with the later departure of General Wood in April 1914 at the conclusion of his four-year tour as Chief of Staff. The hostility would be vividly demonstrated again in 1915 and 1916 as it blended with the greater political controversy over "preparedness" that preceded America's entry into the European war. But by 1916 the Army had learned that liberal Democrats, as well as dollar-diplomacy Republicans, could put stress on the military planning system. Woodrow Wilson had become Commander-in-Chief in 1913.

The Problem of Mexico

Several months before Wilson's inauguration the Mexican Revolution had taken an ugly turn. In a coup led by his military chieftain, Victoriano Huerta, President Madero was murdered. Taft, now a lame-duck President, increased the naval watch in Mexican waters and moved an Army brigade from Omaha to Galveston. When Wilson became President, for reasons that had little to do with the security of the United States or even American economic interests, he chose to shape the outcome of the Mexican Revolution. Shaping the social revolutions of other nations is rarely a rewarding enterprise, but in 1913 Wilson did not know that. With characteristic persistence (or stubbornness) Wilson pursued his objective in Mexico for almost four years. During that time the Army would send two expeditions onto Mexican soil and concentrate all available forces, including almost the entire National Guard, on the Mexican border.[19]

Wilson's desires for Mexico were noble; he wanted there a freely elected democratic government of the American pattern. The government of Huerta was illegitimate, "a government of butchers," which he refused to recognize. Moreover, Huerta did not have complete control of the country. Revolution continued in the northern provinces, where the constitutionalists under Venustiano Carranza were gaining strength. In June 1913 Wilson made his first formal statement of policy. If Huerta would promise free elections and not be a candidate, the United States would attempt to bring the warring parties together. Both Huerta and Carranza reacted negatively and strongly against this uninvited interference in Mexican affairs. Repudiated, Wilson chose watchful waiting and neutrality, embargoing war material to either side. Then in October, Huerta imprisoned 110 members of the Chamber of Deputies and established unabashedly a military dictatorship. To Wilson this was almost a personal insult. From November 1913 to April 1914 he attempted to rid Mexico of Huerta by isolating him diplomatically and encouraging Carranza.[20]

Wilson proposed to Carranza that they cooperate jointly against Huerta, but Carranza rebuffed him. He wanted no American advice or support. He would oppose with force any entry of American forces into Mexico. He wanted only the right to purchase arms in the United States. Determined to expel Huerta, Wilson's options were reduced to military intervention or arms sales. In February, Wilson lifted the embargo, but Huerta remained in as strong a position as ever.[21]

In April 1914 President Wilson finally was presented with the justification (or pretext) for military intervention. On the 10th there occurred an incident between Huerta's police and a detachment of sailors of the American "naval watch" at the port of Tampico. Wilson supported his admiral, who was demanding apology and salute of the American flag. From Huerta neither apology nor salute was forthcoming. On the 18th Wilson went before a joint session of Congress and requested authority to use armed force. While Congress was considering the development, Wilson learned of a German ship, destination Vera Cruz, with a cargo of arms for Huerta. Wilson ordered the Navy to seize Vera Cruz. By April 22nd the city was under American control. Nineteen Americans and 126 Mexicans had been killed in its taking.[22]

An Army brigade sailed from Galveston on the 24th and on the 30th assumed responsibility for Vera Cruz. At Washington Barracks plans for the staff and historical rides into Virginia, Maryland, and Pennsylvania were canceled. On the day the Army assumed command in Vera Cruz, War College student officers were dismissed and instructed to report to their regiments. The Naval War College held no summer session.[23]

The plans of the War College Division had called for an advance from Vera Cruz to seize Mexico City. The orders of the President instead called for remaining in Vera Cruz and avoiding all provocative acts. This state of war that was not war was awkward and disconcerting. General Bliss, commanding the Southern Department (Texas and New Mexico) and thereby overall commander of the force at Vera Cruz, in June wrote an angry letter to Wotherspoon, now Chief of Staff. Bliss denounced the inflexibility and unrealistic assumptions of the plans for Mexico that the War College Division had provided him. According to Bliss the plan was politically naive and therefore militarily worthless.[24]

Huerta, Carranza, other powers, and an influential segment of American opinion all condemned Wilson's intervention. In May, however, Huerta agreed to negotiate. Carranza would not. He refused any American mediation to settle Mexico's own civil war, particularly since he was winning. In July, Huerta abdicated, and the next month Carranza established his government in Mexico City. September saw revolution once more, however, when an erstwhile Carranza supporter, Francisco Villa, "declared war" on the Carranza government. Believing Villa to be more likely than Carranza to establish a constitutional government, Wilson favored Villa's cause. With American encouragement a convention of all factions met in Mexico City during October and November. American troops were withdrawn from Vera Cruz. But Carranza would not relinquish in negotiation what he had won in battle. He moved his government to Vera Cruz, Villa entered Mexico City, and civil war began all over again.[25]

In the summer of 1914, believing now that the President did not contemplate full-scale operations in Mexico, the War Department convened the next War College class on schedule, just as total war was engulfing

Europe. While there was great interest in the massive European battles of the late summer and autumn of 1914, the faculty did not modify in any major way the curriculum that had become standard since the early Wotherspoon presidency.[26]

The Army's attention remained focused on Mexico. By the early months of 1915 President Wilson was coming under increasing public pressure to intervene once again. Villa had suffered major defeats, but neither faction appeared to be able to establish control over the bleeding country. More ominous, but not yet recognized as such, was the German declaration on February 4th that the waters adjacent to the British Isles and the coast of France were a war zone. Wilson's response was that he would hold Germany to a "strict accountability" for any violation of America's neutral rights.[27]

Toward April of 'Seventeen

Tasker Bliss returned to the War Department in February 1915 for duty as Assistant Chief of Staff and concurrently Chief of the Mobile Army Division of the War Department General Staff. In March he sought and gained the approval of the Chief of Staff, Hugh L. Scott, and the Secretary of War, Lindley S. Garrison, to have the War College Division prepare a "comprehensive military policy . . . with respect to the strength and organization of the armed land forces in peace with a view to the most rapid and efficient development of them to the extent that may be necessary in time of war." Bliss directed that where appropriate the policy should be based on Stimson's plan of 1912.[28]

By the end of May 1915 Wilson faced international crises on three fronts. Earlier, Japan had made its "Twenty-One Demands" of China, Villa had been driven into the mountains and desert of northern Mexico, and on May 7 a German submarine had sunk the British liner *Lusitania* without warning and with the loss of 128 American lives. Wilson wisely settled the problem with Japan through diplomacy, warned the Mexican factions to stop fighting or face American intervention, and in his third note to Germany on the *Lusitania* warned that a repetition of ruthless sinkings possibly would lead to war. Although it might be expected that an air of urgency would now surround the study on the "strength and organization of the armed land forces," the War College Division appeared unaffected—much to the annoyance of both Secretary Garrison and General Bliss.[29]

The War College Division had been requested to complete and submit the comprehensive military policy during May. In April the Secretary of War instructed the President of the War College to let nothing interrupt the work of the officers at the college in its preparation. Faculty and students alike were put on the project. The staff and historical rides were curtailed and postponed until June 1st. On May 22nd, still not in receipt of the paper, the Secretary overruled the appeals of the War College and directed "this ride will not be taken this year." At the end of June the class graduated as scheduled, but the policy paper was still not completed. The next month Bliss wrote Secretary Garrison that he was "beginning to despair of the War College."[30]

In July the results of the War College Division's efforts were at last provided to Secretary Garrison. He was not pleased. There was (and is) much to criticize in the study; fundamentally it simply bore no relation either to the diplomatic crises into which the nation had been maneuvered or to the international political and military situation that existed in 1915. Moreover, to carry out the plan would be shockingly expensive, at least in the view of the administration and Congress. The planners' eyes and minds had been fixed on some distant future and on an Army that would take years to construct. Garrison returned the study with a request for a more modest proposal. In 1915 the War Department General Staff had flunked its first major test in requirements planning. And time was running out. That summer the "preparedness movement" had become too strong for Woodrow Wilson to ignore.[31]

Bowing to preparedness pressures, on July 21 Wilson called on the War and Navy Departments for programs adequate to meet the needs of national security. The Navy responded with an ambitious program of shipbuilding that would have provided naval equality with the British by 1925. It was not until August 12 that the War Department responded with a revised War College work, an "Outline of Military Policy." Forwarded immediately to the President, Wilson found it "most superficial" and promptly returned it. Assistant Secretary Breckinridge, Scott, and Bliss personally worked on the paper, even over the Labor Day weekend, and in September resubmitted it as "A Statement of Proper Military Policy for the United States." Accepted then without modification, Wilson sent it to Congress in December, where it became known as the "Garrison Plan." It would become a centerpiece of the national preparedness debate.[32]

Meanwhile, the War College Class of 1916 assembled in mid-August. The curriculum planned for it did not differ from that of the previous year. As had been the practice during the Russo-Japanese War, officers who had served as observers with the belligerents in Europe addressed the class, presenting one lecture on French operations and three on Austrian. Using reports from the European fronts the faculty attempted to introduce into the map problems and map maneuvers what they saw as developments applicable to the American situation. Together with naval officers, the War College President, Brigadier General Macomb, who as Army commander in Hawaii had been involved in planning the defenses of Oahu, lectured on that problem.[33]

The "Garrison Plan" before Congress had as its core a federally controlled reserve force of 400,000 known as the "Continental Army," to be raised over a period of five years. Chairman Hay took exception. The distrusted General Staff was proposing a distasteful federal force that all but ignored the states' National Guard. Moreover, the Secretary and the Chief of Staff, General Scott, conceded in their testimony that conscription might be required to raise the federal force. Mr. Hay, supported by the majority leader of the House, Claude Kitchin of North Carolina, informed the President that the bill would have to be changed. When the President backed away and agreed to compromise, Secretary Garrison submitted his resignation.[34]

Newton D. Baker, reform mayor of Cleveland, Ohio, and a professed pacifist, succeeded to Garrison's position in March 1916. He was confronted immediately by crisis on the Mexican border. In October Wilson had reluctantly recognized Carranza as the de facto government of Mexico. The abandoned Villa turned terrorist. In January he removed seventeen Americans from a train in northern Mexico and murdered sixteen of them. On the night of March 8, with a band of five hundred, he crossed the border, surprised the garrison at Columbus, New Mexico, burned the town, and killed nineteen Americans. The force that would come to be known as the "Punitive Expedition" began to assemble at Columbus under the command of Brigadier General John J. Pershing.[35]

At the War College one instructor and three students whose regiments were involved in the concentration left immediately for New Mexico. Then, on May 3rd, Mexican bandits attacked two isolated Texas border towns. Pershing by then was 300 miles into Mexico, with Carranza making threats and demanding withdrawal of the expedition. On the recommendation of General Scott, the militias of Texas, New Mexico, and Arizona were called into service on May 9. The War College immediately canceled the two remaining months of the course and graduated the Class of 1916 without ceremony on May 10. The students departed to join their units. For the third consecutive year the staff rides climaxing the course did not occur.[36]

On Capitol Hill, the alternative to the "Garrison Plan," the "Hay Bill," was enacted into law on June 3rd. For a number of reasons, this "National Defense Act of 1916" is a milestone in the evolution of American defense legislation and organization. For the first time, a reasonably long-term program was established to guide the War Department in force development. Had it run its course, and had the United States not entered the European war, this five-year program would have put the Army in a better position to cope with the requirements of a postwar world. Its importance to this history, however, is that the act was James Hay's final salvo aimed at the General Staff. More than a few rounds fell on the Army War College.[37]

The "Garrison Plan" called for a General Staff Corps of ninety-one officers. Hay's new law permitted an increase from thirty-six to fifty-four, but the increase was to take place over a four-year period. Moreover, only half the General Staff Corps could be stationed in Washington. The immediate effect therefore was a reduction in the War Department General Staff to nineteen. The law abolished Wood's Mobile Army Division, its functions being transferred to the Adjutant General. The Coast Artillery Division became a bureau. Also in the law were provisions prohibiting the General Staff from interfering with the bureaus or in administration. Consultant Ainsworth had won his point. To prevent the Army War College from acting as a surrogate for a General Staff (per Root's scheme of 1899) the act prohibited any officer attached or assigned to the War College from serving in any capacity other than as president, director, instructor, or student. The War College Division, which since 1912 had been staffed with twenty-one General Staff Corps officers, was now authorized eleven. The War College was to remain under the supervision of the War Department General Staff, but only the president was required to be of the General Staff Corps, while the director was permitted to be. Instructors and students were not to be of the General Staff Corps.[38]

The intention of the Congress seems clear. The great adjunct to the General Staff was to be amputated from the body. The War College was to be solely an institution of higher military study and must discontinue functioning as a working subdivision of the War Department General Staff. Insofar as the classes were concerned, this of course had been the trend from 1907 to 1913. The General Staff reduction of 1912, however, and the desire of Bliss and Garrison for a national security program had wrenched the class back into general staff work—with unimpressive results.

Carranza had no interest in the problems of the Yankee War Department. He wanted American troops out of Mexico. On May 22nd he sent a virtual ultimatum to the State Department and reportedly was concentrating forces against the overextended Pershing. On June 16th the Chief of Staff directed the War College Division to update plans for the invasion of Mexico, and on the 18th, under the provisions of the new National Defense Act, Wilson called to active service almost the entire National Guard for duty on the border. Tension increased with news of an engagement between Carranzistas and elements of Pershing's force in which twelve Americans were killed and twenty-three captured. In midsummer Wilson finally gave up on the Mexican Revolution. His problem then was to arrange Pershing's withdrawal without appearing to accede to Carranza's demands. The two leaders agreed to negotiate.[39]

The mobilization on the border greatly affected the Army War College. In August 1916 the Chief of Staff directed a month's delay in the opening of the session, then directed another postponement. The class did not assemble until October 16th and was ten short of the planned twenty-nine students. Moreover, the college had no president. Macomb retired on October 12 and his replacement, Brigadier General Joseph E. Kuhn, was not released from the border until February 1917. Lieutenant Colonel Henry Jervey, a graduate of the previous year's class, and four instructors conducted the course. The curriculum was not changed from the past session, and the course was to be continued through July to make up for the late start.[40]

When Kuhn returned to Washington from the border, he found his Military Information Division overwhelmed with the volume of information coming from the European battle fronts. Despite the Defense Act strictures on the War College's performing general staff work, he put the class at the service of the swamped staff division. The members of the Class of 1917 spent the rest of their time at Washington Barracks reviewing and digesting information from Europe and compiling it into pamphlets for use in training American troops. In May, the month after the United States entered the war, Secretary Baker ordered the class graduated. The Class of 1917 had participated in less than four months of traditional War College work.[41] The study of the great problems of national defense, of military science, and of responsible command had come to this, the compiling and editing of training literature.

After the hurried departure of the Class of 1917 and while the Army bent its every effort to make the world safe for democracy, the War College was inactive. On May 12, 1917, the War College Division, reduced to eleven officers as a result of the National Defense Act of 1916, was authorized fifty officers. A week later Congress lifted any ceiling on the strength of the War Department General Staff. It grew to a thousand. The expanded and largely untrained War College Division planned the reception of the first draft and the organization, training, and transportation to France of the first thirty-eight divisions. On February 9, 1918, the War College Division was reorganized and renamed the War Plans Division, but it remained located in the Washington Barracks building. The director of the War Plans Division carried concurrently the title of President of the Army War College and remained the titular head of the inactive institution until June of 1919.[42]

The First Army War College: An Assessment

America's entry into the European war and the early dismissal of the Class of 1917 closes the first period of the Army War College's service. In its fourteen years it had graduated thirteen classes totalling 256 Army, eleven Marine Corps, and three Navy officers. Measurement of the contribution of those fourteen years to the quality of the officer corps or to the security of the nation cannot be made with any expectation of statistical certainty. Some fifty-seven percent of the Army graduates served before death or retirement as general officers. Thirty percent of the Army's general officers on November 11, 1918, were War College graduates, as were more than forty-five percent of the commanders of divisions or larger formations, and twenty percent of major unit chiefs of staff.[43] But these data reveal little. As a group these men agreed to go to the War College because they were interested and ambitious, and they were selected to go because they had already proven themselves effective officers. Given the expansion of mobilization, it is probable that a comparable percentage of the group would have become general officers without War College attendance. Nor is performance during the First World War alone a valid test. These men served elsewhere and they influenced the Army both before and after the war.

A reasonable, if not an exact, approach to measurement is to ask a more encompassing question. In retrospect, did the War College do what it should have, and did it do it well? The answer is complicated by the difficulty in considering the War College of 1903-17 as an isolated entity. The institution was part of two larger systems: both an element of the War Department General Staff and concurrently part of a progressive officer education process. It shared in the successes and failures of each.

Initially, there was doubt as to what the War College should attempt, even whether a distinct educational institution was needed at all. West Point, the Artillery School, and the Infantry and Cavalry School in combination appeared to Sherman, Upton, and Wagner to fulfill the purposes of a *Kriegsakademie*. Root and Carter in their proposals for a war college made qualified statements as to the need for formal education beyond the Staff College course planned for Leavenworth. Their equivocation stemmed in part from uncertainty as to what Congress might allow in the way of a general staff. Root's initial impulse was to create a war college and have it perform as a general staff. Ludlow and Carter argued against that. After two years' experience with the difficulties of managing the War Department, even with the assistance of a "War College Board," Root came to agree.

Tasker Bliss, ultimately charged with establishing the War College, drew from Root's early idea, from his own study of the Prussian system, and from his association with the Naval War College. He proposed and then instituted the scheme whereby the War College would serve as an important, but not the sole, element of the War Department General Staff. Concurrently the War College would educate officers through an amalgam of the Prussian master-apprentice system of staff officer training and the Naval War College "main problem" and war-gaming approach to the study of strategy. To Bliss the objective was to provide the Army with a competent *Grosser Generalstab* of which the War College would be the central element, and for which it would train the officers. The role of the Staff College at Leavenworth was to provide him officers already competent in the art of handling troops on campaign.

Bell and Wotherspoon saw what Bliss had not anticipated. The officers coming to the War College were not competent in the military art.
Remedial training may be too strong a term, but it is descriptive of what
Bell felt was needed. Field officers and company officers had to be
trained in the military art simultaneously, perhaps for a generation.
With the new building available and an additional five months authorized for instruction, an opportunity appeared to train officers for both
the *Grosser Generalstab* and *Truppengeneralstab* duties, for the latter
with Leavenworth. Bell put his protege Swift at Wotherspoon's disposal
to perform the task. Wotherspoon, on his part, continued to insist on
more-experienced and better-prepared officers being selected for War
College attendance.

Wotherspoon retained some of the Bliss flavor of learning *Grosser
Generalstab* duties by performing them, but emergency contingency
planning was not of a nature to be scheduled into a program of instruction. For true *Grosser Generalstab* work Wotherspoon and his successors came to rely on the permanent personnel, whether called "faculty"
or "War Plans Committee." In 1913, the last session that was able to
follow the program as planned, the class devoted only two of the ten
months to the preparation of war plans. The final outcome was a War
College attempting to do three things: to act as the war plans element of
the War Department General Staff, to train officers for that staff, and to
train officers to act as commanders and staff officers of larger troop
formations. The results in each of the three areas were mixed.

As a war plans agency the War College had to cope with a dynamic
world. Tasker Bliss served at the War Department during three different
periods. During each the military problem of the United States was significantly different. From 1888 to 1895 the United States was just beginning to recognize itself as a world power. Those few who had extra-
continental ambitions for the country were firmly rebuffed by the
Cleveland administration. Great Britain remained the central security
concern. The Army, not illogically, thought in terms of continental defense. Any war-planning work that was required could be performed
adequately by such instruments as the Endicott Board and the Board of
Ordnance and Fortification. Harbor defense was the first priority, and
the Army saw an increasing, not diminishing, role for it in the new
seapower theory of Mahan.

When Bliss returned to serve with the War College from 1902 to 1905,
and again in 1909, the United States was an imperial power. It had insular possessions in the Pacific and the Caribbean, and protectorates in
Panama, Cuba, and Santo Domingo. It was the policeman of the Caribbean and a minor, though active, participant in the balance of power in
the Far East. It was the world's third largest sea power. Though the

theory of sea power required continued emphasis on harbor defense, there were now two additional and more complex military problems. The first was defense of overseas possessions and protectorates; the second, the projection of power overseas.

During Bliss's last tour from 1915 to 1918 as Assistant Chief of Staff and then Chief of Staff, the European balance of power and therefore that also of the Far East was collapsing. The economic and potential military power of the United States was becoming critical to the structure of the warring and postwar world. The outcome of the war hinged on American policy, depended upon United States action or lack of action. The military problem then was how to organize and arrange the potential power of the United States to best support the nation's new and pivotal world role.

The changes in the military problem were gradual, more difficult to discern then than now. Bliss initially tasked his collegium with continental defense projects, but except for Plan Orange, introduced in 1907, little urgency was attached to keeping the work current. Power projection soon took priority. It was not a simple problem. It required rapid concentration of a force, its embarkation, coordination with the Navy, and movement overseas, all guided by assumptions subject to sudden change. The collegium learned to handle this problem. Those who worked on it were better staff officers for having done so. The expeditions to Cuba in 1906 and to Vera Cruz in 1914 brought no repetition of the embarrassments of Tampa. If the War College Division contributed to the conservatism of Stimson, Wood, and Wotherspoon during the Taft administration, then that was indication of a growing awareness of political as well as military limitations.

Yet the War College Division failed to appreciate the dimensions of the military problem presented them by the war in Europe. Its planning for power projection was limited to capabilities planning. Capabilities planning was essential, but it was not an appropriate response to the new problem. Only belatedly did the planners in any systematic way, or to useful result, progress into requirements planning.

This sort of political, economic, and military analysis was not the practice of the War College Division, nor was it in the curriculum of the Army War College. The near total unpreparedness of the United States in April 1917 to participate in the World War cannot, of course, be laid exclusively at the doorstep of the War Department or its General Staff, and certainly not before that handful of officers who while acting as the faculty of the Army War College also served as the War Plans Committee of the General Staff. Constitutional accountability rests with Woodrow Wilson and the Congress. The failure of the War College was represented by the intellectual unpreparedness of the more senior members of the officer corps, and of the War Department General Staff particularly, to either foresee or come to grips with the magnitude of the emerging military problem caused by the changing power structure in Europe. In May 1915, when Secretary Garrison and General Bliss were almost desperate for a requirements plan, the War College was responding with appeals to continue the historical ride. Whether priorities might have been different and horizons broader had the original collegium been allowed to mature is unknown. In any event it was six months after the declaration of war that any troop program to fight the war was approved—and that program had come from Pershing's headquarters in France.[44]

The War College taught war planning through the preparation of actual plans, or at least parts of actual plans. Similarly, it taught the conduct of field operations through the learning-by-doing applicatory method, considering operational situations necessarily contrived even though they might be based on a historical situation or on a situation expected to result from execution of a war plan. The applicatory method had (and has) a number of beneficial features. As Eben Swift promised, it taught "principles" in a way that made student retention more probable. It provided practice not feasible otherwise in peacetime in analyzing operational problems, solving them, and translating solutions into clear, comprehensive, and definitive orders for execution by subordinates. Furthermore, it standardized procedures and methods within the Army that would be of inestimable value in campaign and that permitted flexibility in organizing a force and handling it in the field. In sum, the applicatory method effectively taught and disseminated accepted doctrine.

The applicatory method also had serious limitations however. Directed at the teaching of principles and doctrine and at the acquisition of a habit of command, it could not take the student beyond the current state of the art. It discouraged innovation and encouraged the acceptance without challenge of contemporary methods, procedures, and doctrine. The practitioners could become very good at what they were doing, but there was no assurance that what they were doing was correct. Swift's distaste for the study of pure theory was proper. The disrespect for theory was unfortunate.

Though there were frequent references to "military science," the applicatory method is not scientific method. Emphasizing the derivation and application of "principles," the War College (and the Staff College, which used the same methodology) did not attempt to study land warfare by isolating its component elements of maneuver, firepower, intelligence, logistics, and control; then studying those elements individually; and next relating the influence of each on the others. The applicatory method, as derived by Wagner and Swift, had evolved from a tactical war game into a map maneuver that was terminated when opposing forces made contact and deployed for battle. Beyond that point Wagner and Swift had been unable to replicate "a similitude." This practice virtually eliminated from serious consideration the element of firepower and the effect of its range, accuracy, rate of fire, lethality, and survivability on maneuver, logistics, and control. Yet it was firepower that dominated the European battles of 1914-18, just as it had promised to do in the Russo-Japanese War of 1904-05. It was a serious omission.

The program of original research abandoned in 1909 might have compensated for the limitations of the applicatory method. But the decision to abandon it was probably correct. It was going nowhere because neither faculty nor students were trained in scientific method and time was not available for true research. The experience of the attempt at a Civil War history demonstrated that, if research was to be attempted, expert assistance from outside the War College and the Army would have to be brought in. Except for Professor Johnston, it was not.

The fascination with Civil War history is understandable. The Civil War was an American war, and many of its battlefields were convenient. There was still much to be learned from its campaigns. But nothing approaching a similar effort was made in regard to the Russo-Japanese War. The Boer War received scant attention. Less understandable was the apparent lack of any motivation to record, analyze, and thereby understand the experiences in the Philippine insurrection. Possibly considering it an aberration, the War College could not know that a half-century later the Philippine experience might have application in America's longest war.

Studying war through planning campaigns and through contrived operational situations was limited by the imagination of the planner and the contriver. The system did not force the student—indeed, it probably discouraged him—to consider war in its totality, to go beyond the purely military aspects to the consideration of war as a political, social, and economic phenomenon. Either the pre-World War I War College did not recognize the existence of nonmilitary aspects, did not consider them important, or did not believe them to be of concern to military officers. The War College, therefore, did not bring to bear on the problem of war any intellectual discipline other than that of military history as it was then understood. The War College produced no overarching strategic concept within which United States security policy might be developed. It produced neither a Clausewitz nor a Mahan nor a Wagner.

But to emphasize the omissions and limitations of the War College of 1903-17 is to risk neglect of its very real and important accomplishments and contributions. As a planning staff it made available to three Presidents, during a crucial period of American history, considered and generally sound military advice. Until it was faced with the unforeseen dimensions of the World War, it responded well to those Presidents when called upon, initiating and controlling effective and efficient military operations. As an educational institution it provided the American Expeditionary Force a nucleus of senior commanders and staff officers whose performance did not suffer in comparison with that of their counterparts in either associated or enemy armies. Many of those officers would return to provide the leadership that in the 1920s and 1930s would again take up the charge of Elihu Root that the true purpose of an army is to prepare for war.

Most significantly, in those first fourteen years, an important beginning had been made and much had been learned about the education of potential senior officers in the great problems of national defense, of military science, and of responsible command. The War College may have fallen short of reaching some ultimate goal, but if so it was not because it had attempted too little. J. Franklin Bell correctly understood the priorities in the education of the officer corps of the United States Army in the early years of the twentieth century. The officer corps had to learn first how to campaign and how to fight and win battles. Until that was done, all else must wait. To have expected more would have been to expect too much, too soon, and of too few.

NOTES

1. Mercer, "Memoranda," 74-75. Ahern, "Chronicle," 103-06.
2. "Programme at the Ceremonies Unveiling the Statue of Frederick The Great, Saturday, 19 November 1904," MHI Library. William H. Carter, *The Life of Lieutenant General Chaffee* (Chicago: University of Chicago Press, 1917), 264. Pappas, *Prudens Futuri*, 45-46, 68-71.
3. Ahern, "Chronicle," 162-64.
4. Challener, *Admirals, Generals*, 324-26, 277-78.
5. Ibid., 267-68, 345-48. Ahern, "Chronicle," 162.
6. Challener, *Admirals, Generals*, 350-52, 356-57. General Crozier was president of the War College from September 1912 to July 1913.
7. Ibid., 285-86,, 340-43.
8. Ibid., 304-06.
9. Root, *Colonial and Military Policy*, 127-29. Nelson, *National Security*, 111-12. John McA. Palmer, *America in Arms: The Experience of the United States with Military Organization* (New Haven: Yale University Press, 1941), 125.
10. Hewes, *Root to McNamara*, 13. Hammond, *Organizing for Defense*, 25. Raines, *Bell*, 200-01. For Taft's diplomatic missions see Minger, *Taft*, 102-78.
11. Mabel E. Deutrich, *Struggle for Supremacy: The Career of General Fred C. Ainsworth* (Washington: Public Affairs Press, 1962). Hermann Hagedorn, *Leonard Wood: A Biography.* 2 Vols. (New York: Harper and Brothers, 1931). Jack C. Lane, *Armed Progressive: General Leonard Wood* (San Rafael, Calif.: Presidio Press, 1978). Hewes, *Root to McNamara*, 14.
12. Wood to Bliss, 25 October 1904, Letter Book, August 1902-November 1903, 375, *Bliss Papers*, MHI. Hagedorn, *Wood*, 2:99-100. Hewes, *Root to McNamara*, 132-35. Hugh A. Drum, "Evolution of the General Staff," *The Reserve Officer* (November 1933): 19. Lane, *Armed Progressive*, 157, 168-69.
13. President of the War College to Chief of Staff, 23 July 1912, quoted in Ahern, "Chronicle," 184-85.
14. Versions of episode are in: Hewes, *Root to McNamara*, 17-18. Hammond, *Organizing for Defense*, 25-28. Nelson, *National Security*, 85-92, 138-66. Henry L. Stimson and

McGeorge Bundy, *On Active Service in Peace and War* (New York: Harper, 1947): 33-38. Deutrich, *Ainsworth*, 107-22. Hagedorn, *Wood*, 2:107-10, 120-25. Lane, *Armed Progressive*, 158-67.

15. George C. Herring, Jr., "James Hay and the Preparedness Controversy, 1915-1916," *Journal of Southern History*, 30 (November 1964): 383-88. Hewes, *Root to McNamara*, 19. Deutrich, *Ainsworth*, 124-27, 132.

16. *Secretary of War Report: War Department Annual Reports, 1912*, I. App. A. "Report on the Organization of the Land Forces of the United States," 69-128. Hewes, *Root to McNamara*, 16-17, 19. Hammond, *Organizing for Defense*, 31. John P. Finnegan, *Against the Specter of a Dragon: The Campaign for American Military Preparedness, 1914-1917* (Newport, Ct.: Greenwood Press, 1974), 17-19.

17. *Army and Navy Journal* (1 June 1912): 1244-45. AWC, "Session of 1914-1915," 22-23. Annual Report of the Army War College, 1916, quoted in Ahern, "Chronicle," 257.

18. Nelson, *National Security*, 175-76.

19. Challener, *Admirals, Generals*, 357-60. For Wilson's policy toward Mexico see Arthur S. Link, *Woodrow Wilson and the Progressive Era, 1910-1917* (New York: Harper and Row, 1954), 107-55.

20. Quotation cited in Ibid., 109.

21. Ibid., 120-22.

22. Ibid., 123-25. For details on the intervention see Robert Quirk, *An Affair of Honor: Woodrow Wilson and the Occupation of Vera Cruz* (Lexington: University of Kentucky Press, 1962) and Clarence C. Clendenen, *Blood on the Border: The United States and the Mexican Irregulars* (New York: Macmillan, 1969), 152-76.

23. Ahern, "Chronicle," 204-05, 207.

24. Challener, *Admirals, Generals*, 394-96.

25. Link, *Wilson*, 127-30.

26. Ahern, "Chronicle," 223-25. AWC, "Session of 1914-1915: General Instructions and Schedules."

27. Link, *Wilson*, 132-33.

28. Assistant Chief of Staff to Secretary of War, 15 February 1915, and Assistant Chief of Staff to Chief, War College Division, 17 March 1915. Copies in *Bliss Papers*, Vol. 189, Library of Congress. Finnegan, *Against the Specter*, 42-44.

29. Link, *Wilson*, 87-90, 132-33, 164-67. Finnegan, *Against the Specter*, 46-47.

30. Ahern, "Chronicle," 227-28. Assistant Chief of Staff to Chief, War College Division, 16 June 1915, *Bliss Papers*, Vol. 190, Library of Congress. Bliss to Garrison, 10 July 1916, *Bliss Papers, Vol. 191*, Ibid.

31. Finnegan, *Against the Specter*, 47-52.

32. Link, *Wilson*, 179-80. Wilson to Edith B. Galt, 18 August 1915, quoted in Link, *Wilson: Confusion and Crises* (Princeton: Princeton University Press, 1964), 16-17. U.S. Army War College, *Statement of a Proper Military Policy for the United States* (Washington: GPO, 1916).

33. Ahern, "Chronicle," 256-57.

34. U.S. House of Representatives, Committee on Military Affairs, *Hearings to Increase the Efficiency of the Military Establishment of the United States, January 6 to February 11, 1916* 64th Cong., 1st Sess., 16-114. Hewes, *Root to McNamara*, 19-20. Hammond, *Organizing for Defense*, 32-33. Herring, "Hay," 394-98. Finnegan, *Against the Specter*, 54-55, 74-90.

35. Link, *Wilson*, 136-37. For the details of Pershing's operations in Mexico see Clendenden, *Blood on the Border*, Chaps. 10-18.

36. Ibid., 137-40. Ahern, "Chronicle," 247-48.

37. Hewes, *Root to McNamara*, 19-21. Hammond, *Organizing for Defense*, 32-33. Nelson, *National Security*, 179. Finnegan, *Against the Specter*, 155-56.

38. *Acts and Resolutions Relating to the War Department passed during the Sixty-Fourth Congress First Session, December 6, 1915-September 8, 1916* (Washington: GPO, 1916), Vol. 20, "An Act Making Further and More Effectual Provision for the National Defense, June 3, 1916 [HR 12766]" (Hereafter "National Defense Act of 1916"), Sec. 5. Hewes, *Root to McNamara*, 19-21. Ahern, "Chronicle," 260-62.

39. Link, *Wilson*, 140-43.

40. Ahern, "Chronicle," 264-65, 267-70. AWC, "Session 1916-1917, Part I: Problems and Exercises."
41. Ahern, "Chronicle," 273, 277.
42. Ibid., 277-82. Nelson, *National Security*, 222-24. *Chief of Staff Report: War Department Annual Reports, 1919*, 23.
43. Data from Pappas, *Prudens Futuri*, 87.
44. This was the thirty division program. *Chief of Staff Report, 1919*, 239-40.

A Completely
New Edifice
1919-1920

In the nineteen months between America's declaration of war and the armistice, the United States accomplished a near miracle in military administration and logistics. From a base of only 100,000 soldiers on active duty, the country raised a mass Army of over four million. With critical assistance from the Allied Powers in shipping and supply, more than half that mass Army was deployed to Europe in an overseas movement unprecedented in scale and complexity. In Paris was General Tasker Bliss, American representative to the Supreme War Council, the agency that became the politico-military center of the Allied effort. To Bliss fell the delicate task of somehow reconciling the desire of Woodrow Wilson for diplomatic freedom of action, the need for unified military effort, the legitimate demands of the Allied Powers for an early and meaningful American military contribution, and the equally legitimate demand of the American Expeditionary Force (AEF) commander, General John J. Pershing, that his troops be committed only when trained and as a separate and distinct national army.[1]

The Great Winter Crisis of 1917-18

The American military miracle of 1917-1918, however, came very close to being a disaster beside which the Tampa-Santiago fiasco of twenty years before would appear as comic opera. In what could accurately be called the "Great Winter Crisis of 1917-1918" the Allied Powers, the United States, and the War Department all faced extraordinary difficulties. The Bolshevik revolution in November 1917 effectively took Russia out of the war, an event confirmed at Brest-Litovsk in early March. The coming spring promised renewed and reinforced German offensives on the western front against exhausted Allied armies. Meanwhile, the American war effort was mired in mismanagement. The volume of contracts from the Allied Powers, from the Navy, and from the five uncoordinated procurement bureaus of the War Department overwhelmed in-

147

dustrial plants. Railroad and shipping systems were hopelessly congested. Critical shortages were developing in fuel, power, and raw materials. Shortages in clothing, hospital equipment, and other supplies led to hardships and pneumonia in the Army training camps. Prices were skyrocketing.[2]

In July 1917 the Congress created a War Industries Board, but did not give it real power; the Secretary of War remained the President's principal advisor on mobilization. By December the Senate Military Affairs Committee was investigating; its investigation would continue throughout the "Great Winter Crisis." There were two schools of thought on what should be done. One favored a "Ministry of Munitions" on the British and French pattern. The other school favored simply strengthening the authority of the War Industries Board. The issue hinged on whether the procurement function should remain with the services or be vested in a civilian agency. The War Department, led by Secretary Baker, was the strongest opponent of a munitions ministry. Baker pleaded for the authority to control his procurement bureaus. In March Congress passed the Overman Act, granting Baker this authority. Concurrently Congress gave the War Industries Board broader powers and placed it directly under the President. That same month Bernard Baruch became head of the War Industries Board and Peyton C. March became Acting Chief of Staff of the Army.[3]

Baker had already taken steps to gain control. He had brought Major General George W. Goethals (AWC 1905) back from retirement and put him in charge of the Quartermaster Department. Goethals, in turn, recruited and brought in prominent industrialists. It is to Peyton March, however, that much credit must go for at long last opening the War Department to the managerial revolution. The General Staff became an operating agency, the central executive agency of the War Department. To avoid disaster, Secretary Baker established centralized control over the bureaus by means of a "Division of Procurement, Storage and Traffic," an element of the General Staff with Goethals as director. Reinforcing Goethals was a strong Assistant Secretary of War, Benedict Crowell, whom Baker charged specifically with overseeing the procurement effort.[4]

The "Great Winter Crisis" was overcome. The lesson was clear. Total war meant total mobilization of manpower, industry, transportation, agriculture—of the entire economy, not just mobilization of an army. Mobilization, like war itself, was national, not military, but the General Staff of 1917 had proven grossly inadequate for even the military dimension of total war. It would have proven so even had the Honorable Messrs. Hay and Kitchen restrained their anti-preparedness prejudices. After the "Great Winter Crisis" and the European adventure, the need for an adequate War Department General Staff composed of experienced and trained officers was no longer seriously questioned. The extent of the authority of that staff, however, would remain an issue.

Lessons from Over There

At the time of the armistice, Pershing's AEF consisted of two field armies and a theater logistical command called the "Services of Supply." Graduates of the Army War College commanded all three. Twenty-nine American divisions had participated in battle. To direct and coordinate this force Pershing had found a General Staff indispensable. He adopted for his own general headquarters (GHQ) and for subordinate tactical units the General Staff organization of the French Army, a decision that was to prove a major and enduring step in the evolution of American military practice. Pershing divided the responsibilities of his own GHQ staff functionally into five sections: administration, intelligence, operations, supply, and training. At the lower tactical levels administration and supply were combined, as were operations and training.[5]

Adopting the French staff system was one thing; providing officers adequately trained and in sufficient number to make the system work was quite another. In October 1917, Pershing established at Langres, France, a General Staff College. The college provided an intensive three-month course on staff organization and administration, the AEF system of supply, and the employment of the combined arms and services. Initially the faculty consisted of British and French officers, but they were gradually replaced by Americans. By the end of 1918 four classes totaling 537 staff officers had graduated. In the United States the dearth of trained staff officers had also been a major inhibitor of orderly mobilization, training, and deployment of the Army. An immediate impression, if not yet a considered lesson, of the experience of the World War was that the American Army must do much more than it had in the past to provide itself with skillful staffs. The impression held whether viewed through the lens of the Meuse-Argonne or the lens of the "Great Winter Crisis."[6]

Staff skill, however, was but one of many skills the American Army lacked when it embarked on its great European adventure. The General Staff College at Langres was only one of a number of schools the AEF established. Also at Langres were an officer candidate school, an infantry specialist school, a tank school, an intelligence school ("Army Center of Information"), and an Army Line School. Elsewhere in France the AEF conducted courses for the combat arms at corps centers of instruction and for enlisted specialists at base training centers. Pershing reported that 21,330 noncommissioned officers and 13,916 officers graduated from these schools.[7]

Schools had blossomed in the United States as they had in France, not only for the traditional arms and services, but also to support the new

Air Service, Chemical Warfare Service, Tank Corps, and Motor Transport Corps. A second immediate impression from the experience of the World War was that the quickest, most efficient, and most effective way, indeed in time of expansion the only way, to train individuals was through a formal system of schools. This impression held among those who had served in France or in the United States.[8]

Planning the Postwar Army

As the War Department entered its first postwar year, it was providing and supporting an army of occupation on the Rhine and two small expeditionary forces in Russia. However, to the American public and its congressional representatives, the urgent military problem was not Germany or Russia, it was returning the AEF to the United States and its conscripted soldiers to civilian life. Baker, March, and the General Staff, however, had to look beyond demobilization. Despite the pressures for demobilization, March had already directed his War Plans Division to begin developing plans for the postwar Army and a military policy to guide it.[9]

The planners had a difficult, almost impossible task. The structure of the peacetime Army depended upon a long-term national military policy. That policy depended in turn upon the postwar foreign policy of the United States, but the role America intended to play in a new international order was still an open question. The Peace Conference in Paris convened on January 12 with President Wilson in attendance assisted by four other Peace Commissioners, one of whom was General Bliss. The results of the conference and its effect on America's future foreign and military policies were great unknowns. Nonetheless, Baker and March needed permanent legislation. If they did not get it, current law required that the great majority of soldiers who had been drafted or who had enlisted for the emergency be discharged within four months after the peace treaty, regardless of what international obligations the United States might assume.

Four days after the Peace Conference convened, the War Department submitted its proposal to Congress for the Army's peacetime organization. With Wilson's concurrence, Baker and March requested authorization for a regular Army of 509,909, which could be expanded to one million in the event of emergency. They made no proposals relative to the National Guard; provisions for that institution would be guided by the National Defense Act of 1916. They also proposed a strong War Department General Staff with all the authority it had accumulated during the war. But in January 1919 the lame-duck 65th Congress was not satisfied with the War Department's proposals; it held only cursory hearings, talked about demobilization, and took no action. When the 66th Congress convened in March, its reins were in Republican hands.

150

At the end of June, almost concurrently with German acceptance of the Treaty of Versailles, the Congress approved an average force level of 325,000 for fiscal year 1920 in its Army appropriation act. The War Department expected that by September regular Army strength would level off at about 225,000. With the Versailles Treaty and a permanent military policy still to be debated, with demobilization accelerating rapidly, and with no long-term defense organization yet authorized, the War Department established "The Military Education System."[10]

The War Plans Division of the General Staff, directed by Brigadier General Lytle Brown, was the staff agency responsible for designing the new education system. The War Plans Division's goal was to consolidate into one coherent system all the various schools that had proliferated during the war. Brown's system for officer education did not deviate in its essentials from the prewar scheme designed by Harding Carter for Secretary Root, though there were significant differences. Major criticisms of prewar officer education were that instruction did not progress in step with an officer's advancement in rank and that continuity was lacking throughout the entire system. Primarily, however, the small capacity of the prewar schools had precluded them from exerting a major influence on the Army as a whole.[11]

The revised system also had to meet what Secretary Baker saw as a requirement to broaden the range of a senior officer's understanding. Still bearing scars of the "Great Winter Crisis," Baker concluded:

> It has been made specially apparent that General Staff officers for duty with the War Department and for larger expeditionary forces should have broader knowledge, not only of their purely military duties, but also a full comprehension of all agencies, governmental as well as industrial, necessarily involved in a nation at war, to the end that coordinated effort may be secured . . . both in the preparation for and during the war.[12]

In Baker's view, neither his staff nor that of Pershing had been properly prepared for the tasks they confronted. They had lacked a necessary understanding beyond their "purely military duties."

The War Plans Division's proposed officer education system, while similar to the prewar system, was made considerably more intense at the lower levels. Two categories of schools were envisioned, "Special Service Schools" and "General Service Schools." The Special Service Schools were those operated for and by the arms and services, the Coast Artillery School at Fort Monroe being the oldest example. Each Special Service School was to provide both a basic course for newly commissioned officers of the regular Army and an advanced course to prepare an officer for "performance of all [officer] duties . . . of the respective arm or service as a specialty." Two items in the plan for Special Service

Schools were of interest to the future of the Army War College. The War College's co-tenant, the Engineer School, was to move out of Washington Barracks, and a Medical Field Service School was to be established at Carlisle Barracks, Pennsylvania, using the site and facilities of the Indian Industrial School that had closed in 1918.[13]

The higher-level "General Service Schools" were part of a four-year officer education program comprising three institutions. At the lowest level the "School of the Line" was to be reestablished at Fort Leavenworth to train officers "in the combined use of all arms and services functioning with the division, including the functioning of corps and army troops and services." Officers attending the School of the Line were not to be "selected officers"; all line officers of appropriate length of service should receive this training. Officers attending the next school, however, were to be selected. The School of the Line, as before the war, was to be highly competitive, its Commandant selecting only the best students to remain at Leavenworth for a second year to attend the "General Staff School." The General Staff School would train these selected officers "for duty as General Staff officers with *tactical* units and for higher *tactical command*" (emphasis added).[14]

The year at the General Staff School was not intended to be as competitive as the year at the School of the Line, but its Commandant was to determine the qualification of an officer to continue in the General Service Schools program. After graduation from the General Staff School, the officer was to be detailed for a year to an arm or service other than that in which he was commissioned, a favorite Wotherspoon scheme never put into effect before the war. In the fourth and final year of the General Service Schools program, the officer was to attend the "General Staff College." This institution was to be located in Elihu Root's Army War College building in Washington, soon to be vacated by the War Plans Division of the General Staff.

In one sense the old "Army War College" had simply been renamed the "General Staff College," but the new name indicated that Secretary Baker had definite ideas as to the function this highest-level school was to perform.* To meet Baker's criticism of the performance of the War Department and AEF general staffs during the war, the General Staff College (Army War College) was to include in its course "studies of an economic nature in regard to supply in general and industrial activities employed in war." Its overall objective was to be "the training of selected officers for duty in the War Department General Staff and for high command." It might also conduct "special courses for general officers and selected officers of the technical and administrative services."[15]

The dividing line between Leavenworth and the highest school was

---

* As will be seen, the name "General Staff College" did not long endure. For clarity the expression General Staff College (Army War College) will be used.

thus returned to where Bliss had originally placed it, along the line between *Truppengeneralstab* and *grosser Generalstab*. Yet the War Plans Division did not contemplate making the General Staff College (Army War College) an "adjunct" to the War Department General Staff in the fashion of the earlier War College. The National Defense Act of 1916 had directed the War College to be solely a teaching institution; the War Plans Division took that stricture to be the intent of Congress still. The concept of the planners also reflected a general consensus that the old adjunct system had not worked well, that it had been a detriment to both the War Department General Staff and the War College.

The change in name of the highest school in the officer education system has additional significance. The National Defense Act of 1916 addressed the "Army War College" specifically, placing certain restrictions on what it might do regarding general staff work, and placing other restrictions on the assignment of General Staff Corps officers to the college, as well as requiring its President to be a detailed member of the General Staff Corps. A change in name skirted these potential problems, though if brought to a test the Congress might have considered the change in name meaningless, if not dissembling. Second, and probably of more significance, the role of the senior school was seen as having changed in major ways. A new name emphasized those changes. The new school was not to be the war-planning agency Bliss had made it in the collegium days, nor was it to be a school of tactics or military art, as Bell, Wotherspoon, and Swift had emphasized after 1908. If Baker's guidance held, the school would retain the war plans instruction of the 1908 through 1917 courses (only about two months of the work) but expand it into a full year's study of the problems of national mobilization and the relationship of those problems to the War Department General Staff and the staff of the GHQ in the field.

In the spring of 1919, General March began requesting of Pershing the release of a number of the senior commanders and staff officers of the AEF. March was losing many of the men who had come into the War Department from civilian pursuits for the emergency, and he also wanted the experience of those who had been "over there" to influence the direction taken by the postwar Army. For the position of Director of the War Plans Division, he asked for Major General James W. McAndrew, who since May 1918 had been Pershing's Chief of Staff. Pershing recommended instead that McAndrew be appointed Commandant of the General Staff College (Army War College). March agreed; there was no one in the Army with better credentials for the position.[16]

James McAndrew and the One Big Problem

McAndrew was an 1888 graduate of West Point, a classmate of Peyton March. He had fought at Santiago and had served in the Philippines during the insurrection. In 1910 he was an honor graduate of the School of the Line, and he graduated from the Staff College at Leavenworth the following year, remaining there for a year as an instructor in the Department of Military Art. He attended the Army War College in 1913, the year the institution was at its prewar apogee. He was the student officer who presented the paper on the battle of Gettysburg to the American Historical Association. He was selected to remain at the War College for an additional year as an instructor, and he attended the summer session of the Naval War College.

After the departure of the Army War College Class of 1914, McAndrew served two years with his regiment in Alaska, then in 1916 became Assistant Commandant, then Commandant, of the schools at Fort Leavenworth. McAndrew deployed to France with the 1st Division in the summer of 1917. In October, Pershing selected him to organize the AEF schools at Langres. McAndrew remained there until May of 1918, when Pershing made him GHQ Chief of Staff, a position McAndrew held during the most active phases of American participation on the western front. In April 1919 he received notice that he would be the first Commandant of the new General Staff College (Army War College).[17]

Pershing and March gave McAndrew high priority in the selection of faculty. McAndrew elected to choose officers currently in Europe, probably for two reasons. First, he was familiar with their wartime performance, and second, he could gather them together to begin work immediately on constructing what he was to call "a completely new edifice." The nineteen officers he selected had all earned reputation, decoration, and promotion in France. Nine had risen several grades to become brigadier generals, the remainder had reached the rank of colonel. If there was a common denominator among them other than successful performance in the brief campaigns of the AEF, it was successful experience in the prewar school system. In addition to McAndrew there were four graduates of the old Army War College—Malin Craig (1910), Campbell King (1911), Richard Williams (1912), and Edgar Collins (1917). Craig and King had also served as instructors at the War College. Ten were graduates of the Staff College at Leavenworth, of whom nine had remained there on the faculty. Among the latter was Harry A. Smith, the prospective Assistant Commandant, and Arthur L. Conger, the military historian who had criticized the War College attempts at a Civil War history. Smith had also been the Assistant Commandant at the AEF schools at Langres. Campbell King and Stuart Heintzelman were closely associated with Leavenworth, having served multiple tours there.[18]

McAndrew had collected a faculty that appeared to be first-rate, as good as the Army, or at least the AEF, could provide. From another perspective, however, they were not nearly as qualified as they seemed. Their experience with the problems of the War Department General

Staff was meager at best. Craig and Dennis E. Nolan had served on the War Department General Staff before the war. Service there during the war, however, amounted to only two months each by Smith and Harry G. Bishop, and five days by Edgar Collins; they were just passing through on their way to war. The experience at GHQ was only slightly more extensive. Nolan had been Pershing's Director of Intelligence, and Conger had also served at GHQ. Except for McAndrew that was the extent of the GHQ experience. Baker's purpose was to have the new General Staff College (Army War College) insure that there would be no repetition of the "Great Winter Crisis" in the future, but to this group that crisis was only hearsay—and what had gone on at GHQ was not much more. On the specifics of Baker's charge, they were no more qualified than the students they would teach. McAndrew had chosen quality but not necessarily expertise in the problem at hand.[19]

In April 1919 McAndrew gathered his faculty at Treves, Germany, to lay the foundations for the new edifice. When the prospective faculty adjourned in May, it had drafted the outline of a solution to what McAndrew termed a radically different mission from that of the pre-1918 War College. Since the mission was to conduct a general staff course, the Treves group logically organized the curriculum around general staff functions. They divided the general staff work into five parts: intelligence, operations, personnel, supply, and training. This organization did not reflect exactly the organization of the War Department General Staff nor that of GHQ, but McAndrew was experienced enough to realize that a staff's organization, the way that functions are grouped, is but a means toward the end. A staff might be organized in any of a number of ways. The important thing was to insure that the students understood the total range of General Staff work as the American Army had come to practice it. The planned program addressed and investigated in detail each functional area in sequence. It would lead off with an Intelligence Course, followed by an Operations Course which would include war planning, and then by courses in Personnel, Supply, and Training. War games would follow the five courses, and the entire session would close with a field exercise. The Operations Course and the Supply Course would require the most time, about two and a half months each.[20]

McAndrew and his faculty decided to use a magnified applicatory method. They would structure the entire course around solving one large problem—preparing the Army for war. During the Intelligence Course, students would be formed into committees to study international relations and the power position of designated nations. After about six weeks the class was to arrive at a consensus as to the most probable war the United States might have to fight. As it turned out, something of an unspoken assumption prevailed that the war envisioned must be one that required national mobilization. The remainder of the course depended upon that assumption. The war selected by the initial class was one in which the United States faced Britain and Japan in combination. In line with what had become a traditional color code, this was the "Red-Orange" scenario.[21]

Whatever in retrospect one might think about the Red-Orange scenario being probable, it did put in worst-case combination the only two world powers of 1919 that could conceivably threaten the United States and its overseas possessions. The two powers, moreover, had been partners in a defensive alliance since 1902. More importantly, a war with Red-Orange presented an almost infinite variety of sub-scenarios to exercise the students of the first and subsequent classes. All the problems of defending the insular possessions, the Canal Zone, and Alaska could be addressed. Opportunities were available to work on the problem of projecting power overseas with expeditionary force operations against Red's Caribbean possessions and bases in Bermuda and Halifax. This permitted joint planning with the Navy. Additionally, Mexico (Green) could be assumed to have joined Red-Orange or to be threatened by them.

The Red-Orange scenario could also be manipulated to present problems of continental warfare. By concentrating their attention on the Canadian border, the students could study the problems of a full-blown theater of operations with a GHQ controlling armies and groups of armies. The faculty and students appeared to be confident that the United States' European involvement would soon end, even though there was still an expeditionary force in eastern Siberia and an occupation force on the Rhine, and even though President Wilson in May had signed a guaranty treaty with France promising American intervention in the event of another German attack on France.

Based on the conclusions and the scenarios arrived at in the Intelligence Course, the class, again working as committees, would construct war plans as the central task of the Operations Course. Initially the committees would determine measures that should be taken external to the United States—for example, withdrawal from the Philippines, reinforcement of Oahu, perhaps an attempt to seize Halifax. The class was then to turn to measures to be taken to defend the continental United States. The students would identify priority areas for defense within the United States and select objectives for offensive action against Canada. Operational plans would then be written to implement the decisions. From these plans the force levels and structure required would be deduced. The General Staff College (Army War College), unlike its predecessor, was to attempt requirements planning. The results of each committee's work were to be exchanged with and explained to other committees. Finally, the faculty would select student plans from which the entire class would work for the remainder of the year.[22]

With agreement reached upon a common operations plan and a force structure to support it, the students could begin their work in the Personnel Course. Here the focus would be on manpower mobilization. Manpower requirements would be determined first, and then a variety of problems would be divided among committees concerning such matters as federalizing and concentrating the National Guard; calling reserve officers to active duty; and planning for selective service, to include determining the occupational skills needed by the Army, as well as physical, mental, and age criteria. The manpower needs of the Army were to be balanced against those of industry and agriculture. Further, internal personnel policies of the Army were not to be neglected. Questions of direct commissioning of officers, promotions, and decorations would be the subjects of student policy statements.

The Supply Course would deal with both industrial mobilization and logistic support within a theater of operations. Again McAndrew contemplated that the class would work in committees independently addressing questions as to the location and capacity of key industries and the availability of critical raw materials. The rail, highway, and inland waterway systems of the United States were to be studied, with emphasis on those regions of the United States that the intelligence and operations parts of the course had indicated would become the theater of operations. In the Supply Course different committees would deal with problems of construction, hospitalization, evacuation, and the statutes involved in leasing or purchasing real estate.

In the Training Course the class would begin with the study of the training systems of foreign armies, specifically those of the Swiss, French, German, British, and Japanese. An analysis would then be made of United States Army training methods. Then, going back to the Red-Orange scenario and the common war plan, committees would estimate such training requirements as the size and location of training facilities and specialist and officer schools. The assistance that might be provided by civilian vocational schools, universities, and colleges was to be investigated. Training programs were to be written for federalized National Guard units, expanded regular Army units, and newly activated units. Committee appraisals of these several aspects of training would then be briefed to the entire class and provided to other committees.

By the time the Training Course was completed, it would be mid-May. The operational plan would then be war-gamed. Weak points and omissions in the plan were to be isolated and the plans corrected. Students were to be impressed with the necessity of gaming real plans in order to improve and refine them. The field exercise that closed the academic year would be a "War Department General Staff Reconnaissance." The class was to test its plans once again by actually examining on the ground the prospective theater of operations. Not only was the terrain to be examined from a tactical viewpoint, but roads, railroads, and telephone and telegraph lines were to be investigated and locations selected for airfields, troop concentrations, hospital facilities, and supply installations.

Year One: The General Staff College

General McAndrew knew that difficulties would arise, commenting, "It is impossible to forecast clearly all our work for the first year." He also understood that the selection of faculty, of curriculum subjects, and of method could take him only so far in accomplishing the educational mission with which he had been charged. It was just as important that he create within the institution a climate that encouraged intellectual initiative and independent thought. He wanted the faculty and students to be "intimate and interwoven," though he avoided the term collegium. Basic responsibility for learning was put squarely on the student: "The benefits you secure from this course will depend largely on your own efforts. We shall endeavor to do our part to assist you." And academic competition, McAndrew believed, would defeat his purpose: "We shall have no system here of close numerical rating, but we must keep some record of the quality of the work you do."[23]

In June the War Department established the criteria for selection of students for the 1919-20 class. Graduates of the prewar Army War College were qualified, as were graduates of the former Staff College at Fort Leavenworth. So too were officers who had served as brigade commanders, division chiefs of staff, or the chiefs of general staff sections of army corps headquarters during the war and officers currently detailed to the General Staff Corps. There was a blanket escape clause for officers who met none of those criteria, but they had to establish their qualification to the satisfaction of the Commandant.[24]

The officers selected for the first General Staff College (Army War College) class had risen rapidly in rank during 1917 and 1918, as had the prospective faculty. In the summer of 1919 their decline was even faster. Reverting to their permanent regular Army grades, all lost at least one grade, most two, and some three. Four major generals became colonels, as did thirteen brigadier generals. Six additional brigadier generals became lieutenant colonels, and three dropped all the way to major. Had the class convened in the spring of 1919 it would have consisted of four major generals, twenty-six brigadier generals, forty-three colonels, and two lieutenant colonels. When the class did convene in September 1919, it consisted of nineteen colonels, twenty-three lieutenant colonels, twenty-nine majors, and four captains—a total of seventy-five Army officers. There were thirty-two infantry officers, thirteen coast artillerymen, twelve officers each from the cavalry and field artillery, three engineers, and one officer each from the Signal Corps, Medical Corps, and Judge Advocate General Corps. Fourteen of these officers had graduated from the prewar Army War College, going back as far as the Class of 1907. Forty-three had graduated from Leavenworth's Staff College. Three Marine Corps officers joined the group.[25]

When the Class of 1920 convened there was as yet no congressionally approved plan for the peacetime Army. The Senate Committee on Military Affairs had opened hearings early in August. The issues being defined extended beyond the mere size of the Regular Army. They involved the authority of the Chief of Staff and the War Department General Staff, the desirability of universal military training, and the place of the new branches that had come into being during the war, particularly that of the Air Service. The military policy that the Congress would debate was dependent on the outcome of the larger issue of American participation in the League of Nations. President Wilson had signed the Treaty of Versailles in late June, but the political battle for its Senate ratification was just beginning. President Wilson and Secretary Baker would make the argument that a large standing army would not be needed if the United States joined the League. The League's opponents argued the opposite; if America joined the League, a standing army would be required to meet the obligations of Article X of the Covenant. Chief of Staff March argued that the Army should be a half-million-men strong in either case.[26]

Until a military policy was established in statute, General McAndrew's one large study problem had no known starting point, no foundation on which to build. As long as the Congress continued to debate military policy, so long did the General Staff College (Army War College) problem have to proceed from assumption. It was becoming clear that on Capitol Hill the shadow of James Hay's philosophy still lingered. Elements in Congress, despite the lessons of the "Great Winter Crisis," were determined to reexert detailed legislative control over the Army and curtail the authority of the Chief of Staff and the War Department General Staff. Until Congress defined that authority it was difficult for McAndrew to proceed with the basic mission of teaching the role and function of the War Department General Staff. Moreover, the Army's senior leadership was divided. General Pershing and Chief of Staff March publicly disagreed on the required size of the regular Army, on the need and purpose of universal military training, on the authority of the General Staff, and on other less fundamental matters of policy. Congress did not resolve these issues until June 1920, the month the initial postwar class graduated.[27]

Despite the absence of a guiding policy, the relatively short period available to work out the ambitious program of instruction, and the faculty's lack of national-level experience, the General Staff College (Army

War College) attacked with considerable success the one large problem as conceived at Treves. The Secretary of War and the Chief of Staff attended the opening ceremonies, both addressing the class. Unlike the Presidents of the former War College, the Commandant's sole duty was the college; he could follow the work closely. After observing the students' initial efforts at intelligence estimates, McAndrew told the class that he was not fully satisfied with the results. There was "too much of a desire to embody the results of your study in an interesting lecture, such as might be delivered in a university or before a geographical or historical society," McAndrew said. "We want deductions rather than lectures." The class must perform as an intelligence section of a general staff should perform, providing its essential conclusions to the other general staff sections.[28]

As remarked earlier, the class elected the Red-Orange scenario as the "unlimited war" situation upon which the remainder of the year's work would be based. External to the continental United States, the class assumed that the Philippines would be lost; the defense of Oahu therefore received the most attention. On the continent, the "Montreal Question" was highlighted. The class was unable, however, to actually produce a completed war plan; a concept of such a plan was all that time and lack of experience permitted. The Personnel and Supply Courses required the gathering of massive data from the War Department, from other government agencies, and from the Library of Congress. This consumed an inordinate amount of time at the expense of analyzing what the data meant and how they could be used to solve the mobilization problem. The students were more comfortable and confident with the Training Course. Most had experienced aspects of this problem during the war. They also received some assistance here from an officer of the French Army, Colonel Jacques de Pinston Comte de Chabrun, assigned to the college as an observer and lecturer.[29]

Throughout the year guest lecturers were invited to address the class, usually on topics being studied at the time. Naval guests explained the Navy's strategy for the Pacific and the Atlantic. Men who had been deeply involved in the 1917-18 mobilization, such as Bernard Baruch and Benedict Crowell, appeared, as did the men responsible for mobilization planning in the War Department and in other executive departments. Industrialists were also heard, as was Samuel Gompers, President of the American Federation of Labor, whose topic was "Relations of Labor to the Army, Peace and War, Domestic and Foreign." The chiefs of the divisions of the War Department General Staff and bureau chiefs made presentations generally in the vein of "These are my problems and this is how I am solving them." In all, there were ninety-one lectures.[30]

With the class organized into eight "general staffs," two-sided war games were held, lasting nine days and involving operations on the "Ottawa Front," the "Montreal Front," and the "Maine Front." The class was then divided into three groups and, from Plattsburg Barracks and Watervliet Arsenal in New York and Fort Ethan Allen in Vermont, made the two-week "War Department General Staff Reconnaissance" of the theater of operations employed in the map games. McAndrew's historian bent came to the surface with two weekend trips to visit Gettysburg and the battlefields of the northern Shenandoah Valley. A one-day trip was made to visit the Tank Corps shops at Camp Meade, Maryland.[31]

The original guidance from Baker and March required the General Staff College (Army War College) to provide special courses for general officers and for officers of the administrative and technical services. Except for the numerous demoted general officers attending the regular course, the War Department did not ask McAndrew to provide any instruction for generals. Eighteen officers of the administrative and technical services did join the college for a "Special Course," however. This class included one officer each from the Adjutant General, Finance, and Inspector General departments and two from that of the Judge Advocate General. One Quartermaster and two Ordnance officers represented the Supply Services. The Signal Corps provided one officer. From the new corps and services, not yet permanently authorized by law, came two officers of the Motor Transport Corps, one of the Transportation Service, one of the Veterinary Corps, two of the Tank Corps, and two of the Air Service. There was also one Ordnance officer from the New York National Guard who attended at his own expense. He was the only non-regular officer associated that year with the General Staff College (Army War College).[32]

The Special Course convened in November at the time the regular class began its Operations Course. The Special Course students attended all lectures with the regular class and initially prepared papers on the roles, missions, and capabilities of the various administrative and technical services. During the Personnel and Supply phases of the regular course, the Special Course students acted as advisors and consultants in their specialities to the regular class committees. During April and May, while the regular students were engaged in the Training Course, the Special Course students familiarized themselves with the intelligence estimates and war plans written the previous fall. They again participated as advisors during the war games. They then departed and did not participate in the General Staff Reconnaissance. Since they had been at the college only from November through May and had been present at but three phases of the regular course, McAndrew recommended against their being considered graduates of the General Staff College (Army War College). They did not receive the accolade of having "General Staff College" noted by their names in the *Army Register.* However, McAndrew commended eleven of the officers to the Adjutant General as having performed "especially good work."[33]

During the first year of the General Staff College (Army War College), McAndrew had followed scrupulously the mission guidance provided by Baker and March. The judgment has to be that he was successful in meeting the objectives his superiors set forth. He forced the future general staff officers who attended the college to consider unfamiliar but important areas of concern, and he provided them an experience much broader than that provided students of the earlier War College and to contemporary general staff officers. The College had made a sincere effort to bring out and understand the full dimension of national mobilization and the omissions that had brought about the "Great Winter Crisis" and the wartime conflicts between the War Department and the AEF headquarters in France.

It had been a busy and taxing year. Ten officers, more than eleven percent of the class, did not complete the course.[34] Not unexpectedly, there were weak areas in the conduct of the course, the shallowness of the intelligence estimates and the sometimes aimless search for mobilization data being among them. No complete war plan or mobilization plan was produced. In the war games the students tended to lose sight of the larger problem and become enamored of local tactical situations. The very breadth of the course and the limited time available made inevitable incomplete solutions to the numerous problems posed.

McAndrew had challenged his faculty to "erect a completely new edifice," and he had promised his superiors and the class that they would do so. But McAndrew owed much to the legacy of Eben Swift and the War College of 1908-17, as well as to refinements of the applicatory method developed at the prewar schools at Fort Leavenworth. The techniques of map maneuver and field reconnaissance drew heavily on the earlier experiences, as did the basic concept of learning by solving problems. The "intimate and interwoven" relationship between faculty and class was a clear reflection of the spirit of Tasker Bliss.

In the conduct of the course there was, to be sure, a new edifice when compared to the pre-1918 War College of William Wotherspoon and Hunter Liggett, but the concept underlying the edifice was not really new. McAndrew's year-long problem was the preparation of the Army for war, exactly what Elihu Root had called for originally and what Bliss had attempted with his eight temporary personnel in the rented house. Bliss had failed to reach Root's goal because of the more urgent need to train officers in the military art, because of the contingency plan demands of Roosevelt's foreign policy and, as it turned out, because of a universally shared lack of appreciation for what mobilization for total war really involved. McAndrew faced none of these problems.

But the McAndrew concept and method really reached back beyond Bliss and Root. What McAndrew attempted with the Class of 1920 was nothing less than the *Grosser Generalstab* practice conceived by von Massenbach and perfected by Moltke. The detailed planning for the opening phase of war, the war games, and the reconnaissance were all part of the Prussian practice. Moltke and his predecessors of course had developed the method to meet the real problem of the survival of Prussia. Bliss had attempted to emulate them to meet the real military problems of the United States. McAndrew used the practice, on the other hand, simply for training general staff officers; he used a possible but not necessarily real military problem. McAndrew in 1919-20 came as close as the American version of a general staff ever had to duplicating a central practice of the German *Grosser Generalstab*.

NOTES
1. David M. Trask, *The United States in the Supreme War Council: American War Aims and Inter-Allied Strategy, 1917-1918* (Middleton, Ct.: Wesleyan University Press, 1961).
2. *Chief of Staff Report, 1919*, I: 245-48.
3. Paul A. C. Koistenen, "The Industrial Military Complex in Historical Perspective: World War I," *Business History Review*, 41 (Winter 1967): 378-403.
4. Hewes, *Root to McNamara*, 49. Hammond, *Organizing for Defense*, 43, 48.
5. *Final Report of Gen. John J. Pershing: War Department Annual Reports, 1919*, I:558.
6. Ibid., 559. Nenninger, *Leavenworth* (1975), 351-53. 69th Cong. 2nd Sess., *Historical Documents*, Statement of Colonel John McA. Palmer, 10 October 1919, 344-51, and Statement of General Pershing, 31 October 1919, 367, 412-14, 420.
7. Headquarters, American Expeditionary Forces, General Order #46, 10 October 1917. *Final Report of Pershing*, 559.
8. *Chief of Staff Report: War Department Annual Reports, 1920*, I:188-89, 306-20.
9. Edward M. Coffman, *The Hilt of the Sword: The Career of Peyton C. March* (Madison: University of Wisconsin Press, 1966), 174-75. 69th Cong., 2nd Sess., *Historical Documents*, Statement of Secretary Baker, 16 January 1919, 260, 263, 268-71, 278.
10. 65th Cong., 3rd Sess., HR 14560: A Bill to reorganize and increase the efficiency of the Regular Army, reprinted in 69th Cong., 2nd Sess., *Historical Documents*, 242-51. Coffman, *March*, 176-77, 193.
11. *Secretary of War Report: War Department Annual Reports, 1919*, I:28.
12. Ibid.
13. Ibid., 28-29. *Chief of Staff Report, 1920*, 188-90.
14. *Secretary of War Report, 1919*, 30. *Chief of Staff Report, 1920*, 190.
15. *Secretary of War Report, 1919*, 30.
16. Coffman, *March*, 165, 292.
17. George W. Cullum, *Biographical Register of the Officers and Graduates of the U.S. Military Academy at West Point, New York, since its establishment in 1802* (Hereafter *Cullum's Register*), Vol. VI A Supplement 1910-1920, Ed. Colonel Wirt Robinson. (Saginaw, Mich., 1920).
18. Biographical information from *Official Army Register, July 1, 1921*, and *Annual Reports of the Commandant, General Service and Staff College*, 1903 and 1904, *Annual Reports of the Commandant, Infantry and Cavalry School and Staff College*, 1905-1907, *Annual Reports of the Commandant, Army Service Schools*, 1908-1916, Fort Leavenworth, Kansas.
19. *Official Army Register, 1921*.
20. McAndrew, Address, 24 June 1920, AWC/CF 1919-20, VIII, 47. Commandant to Chief of Staff, 26 June 1919, AWC/CF 1919-20, "Outline of Course," 117.
21. AWC/CF 1919-20, "Outline of Course," 1-46.

22. Discussion that follows on proposed curriculum is from Ibid., 47-64, 74-327.
23. McAndrew, Address, 2 September 1919, AWC/CF 1919-20.
24. War Department Circular No. 286, 3 June 1919.
25. Data on grades and schools from *Army Register, 1921*. Army War College, "Chronicle of the Army War College, 1919/20-1930/31," 3-4, MHI Library.
26. Coffman, *March*, 197-98.
27. Ibid., 198-202. 69th Cong., 2nd Sess., *Historical Documents*, Statement of March, 16 January 1919, 280-303; Statement of Pershing, 31 October, 1 November, and 5 November 1919, 363-498.
28. McAndrew, Talk to the Class, 18 September 1919, AWC/CF 1919-20, II, Pt. 1.
29. AWC/CF 1919-20, "Outline of Course," 48, 144-65, 191-209, 245-67.
   30. Ibid., 10. "Chronicle 1919/20-1930/31," 5.
31. AWC/CF 1919-20, "Outline of Course," 209-23, and "Historical Staff Rides."
32. Commandant to the Adjutant General, Report on Special Class, 1919-1920, 29 June 1920, "Reports of the Operations of the Army War College, 1920-1940," MHI Library.
33. AWC/CF 1919-20, "Outline of Course," 65-73. Report on Special Class, 1919-1920.
34. "Chronicle 1919/20-1930/31," 4.

Command vs Staff
1920-1922

While the War College Class of 1920 was working its way through the one large problem, the United States was slowly arriving at those decisions that would set the course of its foreign and military policies for the decades ahead. By September 1919 the demobilization of the mass army of 1918 was all but complete. Pershing returned that month from France to receive the cheers of his countrymen, to be promoted to "General of the Armies," and perhaps to listen for the call that Zachary Taylor and Ulysses Grant had once heard and that Admiral of the Navy George Dewey had mistakenly thought that he too discerned. While Pershing listened, Secretary Baker and Chief of Staff March had a General of the Armies on their hands with no armies for him to command. By the end of the year the Army was down to a strength of 217,000.[1]

Pershing and Palmer: In Search of Policy
As part of a permanent military policy, March sought a 500,000-man Regular Army. With reluctance, because he thought the Congress would not approve, he proposed a three-month universal training program. To raise the 500,000-man Army the Recruiting Service began to depict the Army as a "national university," advertising opportunities for education and vocational training. Pershing, on his part, testified in favor of a 275,000- to 300,000-man Regular Army and a fully federalized National Guard as the primary reserve. He supported a six-month universal military training period with subsequent service in the reserves. Before and after Pershing's personal testimony his views were represented by a young, highly intelligent, and very articulate but somewhat theoretical staff officer from the War Plans Division, Colonel John McAuley Palmer. Palmer was on familiar ground. In 1912 he had been one of the principal authors of Secretary Stimson's "Report on the Organization of the Land Forces." Palmer struck responsive chords in the Congress. With rhetoric in the finest traditions of classical republicanism, Palmer

lauded citizen armies, pointed out the dangers of militarism, and condemned large standing armies and the legislation proposed by the Secretary of War that would have provided one. Palmer was soon a favorite of the Military Affairs Committee of the Senate and became its staff aide.[2]

An issue almost as emotional as that of the size of the Regular Army was that of the authority of the War Department General Staff. Baker and March sought to retain the central executive authority granted by Congress in the Overman Act during the "Great Winter Crisis." But the barons of the bureaus were back, struggling to reestablish their Magna Carta of 1916. The principal target was the "Purchase, Storage and Traffic Division," which under George Goethals had finally brought about order in 1918. Pershing testified that the AEF's General Staff did not "operate in the supply field," arguing that neither should the War Department General Staff. He failed to stress that he had found it necessary in France to establish a single controlling "Services of Supply." The General of the Armies, however, was less than adroit in responding to leading questions. Palmer also insisted that the General Staff not be an operating body. He provided the committee with an unsolicited but brief history of the general staff concept, beginning with Frederick the Great. Palmer favored a return to the 1903 General Staff Act, arguing that the Chief of Staff should not direct planning but rather act as a sort of presiding officer over a deliberative body. For the directing and controlling functions, according to Palmer, the Chief of Staff's role was essentially that of an executive officer carrying out approved policy.[3]

The National Defense Act of 1920

Throughout the spring Congress debated the Army reorganization bill. By June the bill had been passed and sent to the President. Wilson was inclined to veto it, but Baker convinced him that the bill was as good as any the administration was likely to get. The legislation technically was written as amendments to the National Defense Act of 1916, but it became known as the National Defense Act of 1920. Of the new branches created during wartime, the Chemical Warfare Service, a Finance Department, and the Air Service were made permanent, as was the position of Chief of Chaplains. General March had recommended a permanent Transportation Corps, but it was not included. The act set up a single-list promotion system to replace promotions by branch and created the positions of Chief of Infantry and Chief of Cavalry.[4]

The act made the General Staff a permanent agency, but congressional hostility toward the institution remained, reinforced by hostility toward the abrasive Peyton March. Congressional intent appears to have been that the War Department General Staff be only one bureau among others. It was to restrict itself to planning and coordination, to investigating and reporting on the Army's efficiency and preparedness, and to rendering professional aid and assistance to the Chief of Staff and Secretary of War. It was not to "engage in work of an administrative nature that pertains to established bureaus ... or that ... would involve impairment of the responsibility or initiative of such bureaus." The 1916 language restricting the Army War College disappeared however.[5]

Congress recognized that if the General Staff did not control the bureaus, then some other authority would have to. Taking its cue from the work performed by Assistant Secretary Benedict Crowell during the war, the Congress gave two statutory responsibilities to the Assistant Secretary of War, to supervise materiel procurement for the Army and to plan for industrial mobilization. The supply bureaus thus were permitted to bypass the Chief of Staff in those two areas. In effect, the responsibility for the supply function was divided between the Chief of Staff and the Assistant Secretary of War—to the Chief of Staff went the responsibilities for determination of supply requirements and for distribution; to the Assistant Secretary went the responsibility for procurement. The responsibility for mobilization planning was also divided. The Chief of Staff was responsible for all mobilization planning except industrial mobilization. At the General Staff College (Army War College), Commandant McAndrew had based his one large problem on the assumption of the General Staff having total responsibility. Future curricula would have to adjust to the new statutory scheme.[6]

While the Congress debated the Army bill, the Senate also debated ratification of the Versailles Treaty and American participation in the League of Nations. In March the treaty was rejected, with or without reservations. Also rejected was the guaranty treaty with France. The United States had decided to return to its traditional policy of no entangling alliances. The national security policy to support this aloofness was to rest primarily on a large Navy. The National Defense Act of 1920 made no provision for universal military training, the foundation of Palmer's citizen army concept. The citizens' representatives believed in a citizens' army, but not to the extent of compelling the citizens to be trained, however. Congress did not accept March's large standing army as an alternative. It authorized a Regular Army strength of 298,000, but appropriated funds to support only 200,000.

The National Defense Act of 1920 was the axis about which all Army activities—including those of the War College—revolved during the interwar years. A grasp of its underlying concepts is fundamental to understanding the War College program during those years. The basic assumption of the act was that wars are fought and won by mass armies. The military problem was how to produce a mass army most rapidly and efficiently in the event of war. John McAuley Palmer, the leading theoretician behind the solution to the problem, insisted that certain American traditions and circumstances be recognized and exploited. He insisted

167

that the historical republican distrust of standing armies be respected as well as its corollary, the militia tradition. Nonetheless, he pointed out that every American war had demonstrated the waste and the tragedy resulting from an untrained soldiery. Palmer called for not just a mass army of citizens, but for a mass army of *trained* citizens.

Although it did so in a distorted form, the National Guard of the several states represented the militia tradition. Therefore the National Guard was to have a prominent place in military policy. But Palmer and Pershing also attempted to draw upon the purer militia tradition, that of universal obligation for military training and, if need be, service. In this they failed, and the failure to provide universal military training created the critical gap in the whole scheme. The Palmer theory also held that a proper military policy should recognize the huge reservoir of citizens trained as officers during the war. Arrangements should be made to prevent this reservoir from draining and to refresh it as the years passed. The means of replenishment proposed was to expand and to include as a formal part of military policy the type of military training that had been carried on at some of the nation's colleges and universities since passage of the Morrill Act of 1862.

To rapidly and efficiently produce a mass army of citizens in wartime, five elements had to be set up in peacetime. First, there must be in place an organizational structure—companies, regiments, divisions—upon which to build. Second, trained officers would be needed to maintain the structure in peacetime, build it to strength in wartime, train the citizens, and lead them in battle. Third, stocks of arms, munitions, and other materiel had to be on hand to equip rapidly the fleshed-out structure. Fourth, American industry had to be able to convert in an orderly fashion to the early production of war material in order to meet the enormous consumption of modern war. Fifth, and critical to the overall concept, a high command had to be continuously planning to assemble the wartime mass army, then be able to effectively control its buildup during mobilization and give it strategic direction.

The National Defense Act of 1920 provided an organizational structure called the "Army of the United States" consisting of three elements, the Regular Army, the National Guard, and the Organized Reserve Corps. The Regular Army would man overseas garrisons and the coastal defenses, and it would be available for minor emergencies. The National Guard would remain under the control of the states but would receive federal assistance in exchange for availability in national emergencies and subject to meeting competency standards set forth by federal authority. Upon mobilization, Organized Reserve Corps units would complete the wartime structure. In peacetime these units would be provided a cadre of designated reserve officers in order to permit early activation and training.

The Regular Army was to assist the training of the two reserve components in important ways. Instructors from the Regular Army would be assigned to the National Guard and Organized Reserve organizations. Standardized doctrine in common texts would be provided, and reserve component personnel would be encouraged to attend Army schools. Extension courses designed for the reserve components would also be offered. Additionally, the Regular Army, through the Reserve Officers Training Corps (ROTC) at colleges and universities would conduct precommissioning training for the Organized Reserve Corps, thereby replenishing the pool of war-trained officers as they aged and left the service.

Training its own officers, as well as those of the reserve components, required the Regular Army to operate an elaborate and expensive school system comprehensive enough to address all the new skills demonstrated as needed during the World War. In the envisioned wartime Army, officers would be serving in grades higher than their peacetime rank. The system was therefore designed not to train officers in the duties of their present rank nor for peacetime assignments, but to train officers in the duties of the grade they would be expected to attain upon mobilization, the timing of which could not be forecast. Not the least important responsibilities of the school system were to keep alive the flame of knowledge in the realm of military art and science, to develop operational doctrine, and to recommend the organizations and the materiel required to support that doctrine.

To provide materiel for the wartime force, the Army retained large stocks remaining from the World War. These stocks were to be maintained by the technical services; replacement, when necessary, was to be made through modest production and purchases by the arsenals of the Ordnance Department and the depots of the other technical services. The problem of future obsolescence of the World War stocks was not yet fully apparent in the immediate postwar period. Planning for the early and orderly conversion of industry to wartime production was the responsibility of the Assistant Secretary of War.

The high command called for by the scheme underlying the act was embodied in the General Staff, or more accurately, in the General Staff Corps. While officers were not permanently assigned to the General Staff Corps, as was the German practice, detail to the General Staff Corps was highly selective and tightly controlled through the means of a "general staff eligible list." The law required that to be selected for this list an officer had to successfully progress through the General Staff School at Fort Leavenworth (admission to which was highly selective in itself) and then be selected by a board of officers. To serve on the War Department General Staff, the act required graduation from the General Staff College (Army War College) at Washington Barracks. Failure to be selected for the "general staff eligible list" meant a future career limited to regimental-level duties. The highest command echelon was of course the War Department; next subordinate were to be territorial commands within the United States and three overseas departments (the Philippines, Hawaii, and Panama). Eventually the War Department established nine commands in the United States called "Corps Areas." The headquarters of these twelve commands, manned by General Staff Corps officers, were responsible for war and mobilization planning within their respective areas. It was for service in these headquarters, as well as at the War Department, that the General Staff College (Army War College) was to prepare selected officers.

To make the scheme of the National Defense Act workable required first that the Congress provide the necessary financial support to maintain the structure and permit the necessary training. Second, it required what at first glance might appear to be an "over-officered" Regular Army. The criterion for the strength of the officer corps of the Regular Army could not be merely its enlisted strength nor the number of Regular Army units. Officers were needed not just for Regular Army units but in support of reserve components, in planning headquarters, and in the school system. In times of austerity various administrations and Congresses would fail to understand this point, even though it was fundamental to the success of the military policy stipulated by the 1920 act. Congress did authorize, however, an administrative arrangement of a "Detached Officer List" to account for those officers who were not serving with troop units.

The 1920 solution to the military policy problem was neither impressive nor expensive. But at least General McAndrew and his General Staff College (Army War College) could now see the direction that American foreign policy was taking and had a military policy upon which to base their deliberations. To solve the one large problem, all that remained to be clarified were the details of the General Staff (less potent than that of 1918-19) and its relation to a newly described entity, the Office of the Assistant Secretary of War.

The War Department issued General Order Number 48 on August 12, 1920, to implement the provisions of the National Defense Act as they pertained to the General Staff. It became the basic text for McAndrew in teaching the organization and function of the elements of the War Department and its General Staff. The "Purchase, Storage and Traffic Division" was renamed the "Supply Division," but its authority was markedly reduced. Since McAndrew's one large problem dealt more with planning than with the problems of controlling and directing, this change did not immediately affect his curriculum. But the issue of who was responsible for training those officers who were to serve in the office of the Assistant Secretary of War remained to be addressed.[7]

"Instruction in Higher Command"

Second thoughts about the school system itself arose within the War Department. In June 1919, in line with his policy to put AEF officers in pivotal positions, March replaced Lytle Brown as Director of the War Plans Division with Brigadier General William G. Haan. From 1903 through 1906 Haan had been assigned to the War Department General Staff, serving as a member of the War College in 1905 and as an observer during the Russo-Japanese War. In France he had been the commander of the successful 32d Division and, after the armistice, of a corps in Germany. The first change in the school system that Haan initiated was to eliminate without any real trial the third year of the four-year "General Service Schools" program. He believed that officers could become sufficiently familiar with branches other than their own merely by attending brief courses of observation and instruction at the "Special Service Schools."[8]

A second change that Haan initiated had more effect on the General Service Schools themselves. The General Service Schools, Haan insisted, "should cover and can cover more than General Staff instruction. Instruction in higher command is as clearly important and even more so." Observing that in France inexperienced General Staff officers had sometimes assumed the role of commander, Haan argued that "the line of demarcation between the functions of command and the functions of General Staff duties can and must be clearly defined by the teaching in our higher schools."[9]

To McAndrew this was not a new problem. Before the war he had published an article providing his version of the proper relationship between a commander and his chief of staff. The problem between command and staff in the AEF had turned out as J. Franklin Bell had feared—and had attempted to circumvent by turning the War College to the study of the *Truppengeneralstab*. The juniors, graduates of Leavenworth and Langres, were better schooled than their seniors. What is more, they knew they were. A large part of the solution was for commanders to better understand the intricacies of a general staff. However, the Chief of Staff apparently agreed with Haan. After all, no one could really argue against the primacy of command. On September 14, 1920, just after the Class of 1921 convened, the War Department published General Order Number 56, which added to the basic guidance given to McAndrew and the Commandant at Fort Leavenworth. Both must "amplify" and "extend" instruction in "command."[10]

The call for amplification and extension of instruction in "command" indicates that Haan did not fully understand what McAndrew was about; or if he did understand, he did not fully agree, though he had approved McAndrew's proposed program for the Class of 1920. The problem in France had developed at the tactical level among what came to be known as the "Leavenworth Clique," not at the level with which McAndrew was now concerned. Besides, there remained the problem of just what should be taught under the banner of "command." No less an authority than John McAuley Palmer insisted that properly translated *Generalstab* meant "generalship staff," that members of that staff were "general's assistants." It followed, according to Palmer, that training for and service on a general staff was in fact schooling in command. Either Palmer was in error, Haan did not understand the general staff concept, or the American general staff version was different from the German. Moreover, under the recently adopted French staff organization all functions of command were covered somewhere among the several general staff divisions. There seemed to be little left to teach that was not already being taught.[11]

At the General Staff College (Army War College), McAndrew inventoried all the topics he had introduced the previous year that might reasonably be considered as "command," collected them together, and declared them a "Command Course." The result was two full months of activity under that label, including the war games and the reconnaissance of a strategic area. Two war games would be played. In one the students would act as staff officers; in the second they would act as commanders. Through these games the students would learn the difference between "detail" and "direction." Also placed in the Command Course were the historical rides (now performed in hired automobiles) which were to be increased from two to four, adding the Antietam campaign and Grant's campaign of 1864 to the 1919-20 investigations of Gettysburg and Jackson in the Shenandoah Valley. Three lectures on leadership were also included, one by Major General John A. Lejeune, commander of the Marine Corps schools at Quantico, former commander of the 2d Division in France, and an Army War College graduate of the Class of 1910.[12]

The reorganization of the War Department General Staff and the addition of the Command Course forced some adjustments in the organization of both the curriculum and the faculty. The Personnel Course was dropped as a separate entity; the topics previously covered there were included in the Operations Course. By accommodating to his new guidance in this fashion, McAndrew appeared to preserve the integrity of his curriculum—at least the general scheme of one large problem.[13] In changing the *purpose* of the war games and the reconnaissance, however, from a means for teaching the established *grosser Generalstab* practice of testing war plans to a method for developing commanders, McAndrew made a subtle shift that began an erosion that over time would change the course considerably. The issue of "command" versus "staff" would not soon go away.

Year Two: 1920-21

General Haan's War Plans Division introduced additional complications into the 1920-21 course. In 1919 and 1920 the United States contracted an odious sickness referred to since as the Red Scare. Unhappily the War Department was not immune. General Haan appears to have been particularly sensitive to this internal threat. He urged the General Staff College (Army War College) to take up the study of this "new enemy of organized government." The college resisted and suggested that the topic be termed "Domestic Disturbance," not "Communist Warfare." Assistant Commandant Harry A. Smith, in orienting the class on the upcoming year, stated that an officer must know "not only the military conditions of the United States, but he must know its history, its political, industrial, and financial conditions, and the hopes and aspirations of its people." But the senior leadership of the Army apparently did not find palatable the hopes and aspirations of some of the nation's people. Smith went on to inform the class that "there would also be considerable time devoted to the internal conditions of the United States and how best to counteract the Red element."[14]

The class was to be required to draw up a War Plan White to deal with internal revolution. A representative of the Military Intelligence Division of the General Staff briefed the class on the dangers of anarchists and socialists. He admitted that these radicals were not numerous but in remarks with ugly anti-Semitic undertones reminded the class of the increasing immigration from Eastern Europe. War Plan White turned out to be a rather poor effort; the students did not get much beyond concluding that neither the Regular Army nor the National Guard was in a very good posture to counter the sort of threat described. The Red Scare passed into history and so did War Plan White. It did not appear in the curriculum again.[15]

The Class of 1921 began with eighty-four Army officers, an increase of nine over the previous year. Over half, forty-six, were colonels. The increase allowed the inclusion of seven officers from the administrative and technical services, including one from the Air Service. No "special course" was offered these noncombatant branches as in the first postwar year. To provide the technical expertise the special students theoretically had provided the year before and to facilitate the gathering of data, every chief of arm and service, as well as the Militia Bureau, named a representative (really a "point of contact") to the General Staff College (Army War College), whose duty it would be "to provide data and technical advice and information for the preparation of balanced problems and intelligent and constructive committee work." Another purpose was to inculcate in the future general staff officers the need to coordinate with and draw upon the expertise of the special branches. One purpose might also have been to reduce student traffic in the corridors of the War Department. The college intended that the branch representatives act somewhat in the fashion of part-time faculty.[16]

Cooperation with the Naval War College was also reestablished. At McAndrew's suggestion the Army and Navy Joint Board recommended in July 1920 that each year two graduates of the Naval War College be detailed for duty with the class at the General Staff College (Army War College), and that every other year two General Staff College (Army War College) graduates be detailed to the class at the Naval War College. The board also recommended that two officers of the Marine Corps be detailed to each college every year. During academic year 1920-21 two naval officers and two officers of the Marine Corps attended the General Staff College (Army War College), and three Army officers were at Newport. One was a 1917 graduate of the Army War College, and two were graduates of the 1920 General Staff College (Army War College).[17]

Among the provisions of the National Defense Act of 1920 was one that limited duty on the War Department General Staff to those officers who either had been selected for an "initial General Staff eligible list" or those who were graduates of the General Staff College (Army War College). General of the Armies Pershing chaired the selection board for the initial list, and McAndrew was a member of the board. The selection of the names for the General Staff eligible list was a matter of great career concern throughout the officer corps. All but one of McAndrew's original faculty was selected, but that unfortunate one was given credit as having graduated from the General Staff College (Army War College), as were all members of the 1919-20 faculty. The National Defense Act had not only made the General Staff College (Army War College) by statute the highest school in the Army's education system, but, if service on the War Department General Staff had become critical to career success, then so too had graduation from the General Staff College (Army War College).[18]

Not all who attended graduated, and not all who graduated did so with high marks. The Class of 1920 lost ten of its members during the year; the Class of 1921 lost four, two of them through death. Regulations required that the Commandant designate those graduates suitable for high command and those suitable for duty with the War Department General Staff. The college went beyond the required designations, however. For those recommended for high command the college further divided the category into command of divisions and command of brigades. Because of their youth, students in the grade of major were not considered for division command. Five students were recommended for command of divisions and fifty-four for command of brigades, but eighteen were not recommended for either because of "lack of initiative" or "temperamental characteristics" or, in the case of majors, "youth and inexperience." For those students recommended for duty on the War Department General Staff, the college made a further distinction between those suitable for duty in all sections and those suitable for duty only in specified sections. In the Class of 1921, forty-four of seventy-eight graduates were declared qualified for all sections, but three were declared not qualified for the War Department General Staff at all. Among the officers who made both the command list and the unspecified War Department General Staff list was a major, Walter Krueger, who was also selected to remain on the faculty.[19]

In November 1920 General McAndrew became ill and was admitted to Walter Reed Hospital. He did not regain his health, and for the remainder of the year the college was under the direction of the Assistant Commandant, Colonel Harry A. Smith. The absence of McAndrew was unfortunate. A senior major general and an associate of both March and Pershing, McAndrew was able to soften the impact on the college program of the suggestions flowing from the supervising War Plans Division. He accommodated without major disruption both the demand for emphasis on "command" and the alarm over the perceived internal threat. Colonel Smith was not as well established. He had to accept General Haan's admonitions on command and radicalism and add at Haan's request lectures on the "relationship of geology to military operations." Then, in the spring, General Haan instructed Smith to reduce the volume of student work. Haan held that it was poor practice to inculcate in future staff officers the habit of working more than eight hours a day and carrying work home at night. As a final blow, the War Department canceled the strategic reconnaissance. The class graduated a month early so that vacancies on the General Staff could be filled.[20]

Because of McAndrew's absence and the continual interference of the War Plans Division, the General Staff College (Army War College) was unable to correct all the weaknesses in the course revealed during the first year. What should have been a year of consolidation became a year of more experiment. Once again the class was unable to formulate a complete war plan, much less a comprehensive mobilization plan. In July, McAndrew, still a patient at Walter Reed, was relieved as Commandant. His guidance and direction during the early postwar period had been extremely important. The approach to senior officer education that he established in 1919 proved enduring. There were to be additions to and deletions from his curriculum, and modifications and changes in emphasis over the next two decades, but to James McAndrew must go great credit for putting the second Army War College on a sound and solid base.[21]

If subsequent assignments are criteria, the two classes that graduated while McAndrew was Commandant were to have great influence on the United States Army as it approached the Second World War. During the five years just prior to that war, four officers held the position of

Deputy Chief of Staff. Three of those officers were of either the Class of 1920 or the Class of 1921. George Marshall was the one exception. In every year from 1921 through 1940, at least one officer of those two classes served as a principal staff officer on the War Department General Staff—that is, as an assistant chief of staff. In those twenty years, fifty-one officers served as assistant chiefs of staff; twenty of them were from McAndrew classes.[22]

Pershing Reorganizes

McAndrew's successor was Brigadier General Edward F. McGlachlin, a field artilleryman who had commanded the artillery of Hunter Liggett's First Army in France. McGlachlin had been a prewar Commandant of the Artillery School of Fire at Fort Sill, Oklahoma, and he was a 1916 graduate of the Army War College. Other changes in personalities occurred as well. In March 1921, Warren G. Harding had become President and Commander-in-Chief. Secretary Baker departed with the Wilson administration, to be replaced by a Naval Academy graduate and former Senator from Massachusetts, John W. Weeks. On June 30 Peyton March retired from the Army to spend the next five years living and traveling in Europe. Pershing became Chief of Staff in addition to General of the Armies. By the time the Class of 1922 convened, General Haan had become ill and departed the War Plans Division. The college year 1921-22 was to be under entirely new direction.

An early decision by the new Chief of Staff was to approve a change in the name of the General Staff College back to the prewar designation of "Army War College." There were apparently three reasons for the change. Probably the most compelling was for the name to better reflect the emphasis on "command." The institution should not have the image of a school for mere staff officers. Next, the amendments to the National Defense Act of 1916 had removed the language pertaining to the "Army War College." There were no longer statutory restrictions on who could be assigned to the institution and in what work it might engage. Finally, there was convenience. "War College" in common usage had become the designation of a location, used more frequently than "Washington Barracks." The institution might as well be officially named what it was most commonly called.[23]

Within two months of assuming office, Pershing reorganized the War Department General Staff in line with his own preferences and experience, assisted by a board of officers led by Major General James G. Harbord, the former commander of the Services of Supply in France and then Pershing's Executive Assistant. Haan and Palmer were members of the board. The French "G-Staff," familiar at tactical levels, was installed at the War Department. There would be a Deputy Chief of Staff and five Assistant Chiefs of Staff: Personnel (G-1), Military Intelligence

(G-2), Operations and Training (G-3), Supply (G-4), and War Plans Division (WPD). All of the sections had a role in mobilization planning, but it was the WPD that was specifically charged with plans for "the initial strategical deployment" and for "actual operations in the theater of war." Moreover, the WPD was to be the nucleus of a general staff for a field GHQ and was to organize itself in the G-Staff pattern. The additional personnel needed to convert and expand the WPD into a field headquarters upon mobilization would be provided by the Army War College.[24]

The Assistant Secretary of War, in accord with the National Defense Act, was charged with preparation of plans and policies to provide for the mobilization of the materiel and industrial organizations essential to wartime needs, while the G-4 was charged with the plans for distribution, storage, and issue of supplies. The new organization gave staff responsibility for all schools except the "General Service Schools" to G-3. Those remained under the supervision of the WPD. Although the following year all schools were placed under G-3, the initial placement under the WPD indicates that Pershing and Harbord felt that the interests of the War College should be focused on deployment planning and theater of operations planning, not, as McAndrew had originally been directed, on mobilization planning.[25]

The staff reorganization also removed from the War Department General Staff the Historical Section of the War Plans Division and assigned it to the Army War College. The Historical Section had been established in early 1918, apparently on the initiative of Tasker Bliss, and had enjoyed phenomenal growth. At its height in June 1919 forty officers and civilians were assigned to it. About half of those were under Pershing's control at GHQ in France, including R. M. Johnston in the uniform of a National Army major. Historians of contemporary and future reputation had been recruited, including Frederic L. Paxson, Solon J. Buck, Charles C. Tansill, and Dexter Perkins. The section's contraction after the war was as rapid as its expansion had been. At the time of its transfer to the War College, it consisted of three officers and nine civilian clerks under the direction of Colonel Oliver L. Spaulding. Its capability was little more than that of preserving historical archives.[26]

The wartime romance of historian and soldier had been turbulent. Secretary Baker had discouraged an early and ambitious project to write a "General Staff History of the War of 1917," which would have included diplomatic and economic history. In France, the soldier seems to have looked upon the historian as unqualified to criticize things military, and in turn the historian seems to have believed the soldier interested primarily in justifying his own conduct of campaign. Baker's ultimate instructions were for the Historical Section to collect, index, and preserve records, and to prepare monographs of a military nature useful to the

Army. He wanted facts presented without official interpretation. Spaulding did not take exception to these instructions. A wartime brigadier general and a 1911 graduate of the War College, he understood the value of military history to military education. He saw the role of his section as preserving historical documents, making them accessible, and preparing historical studies of interest primarily to the Army. His goal was to make his section a War College Department of History.[27]

The Historical Section did not physically move to Washington Barracks but was located at 6th and B Streets, N.W. An office was maintained at the War College building, however, to enhance the section's usefulness to faculty and student research. The attachment of the Historical Section with its custody of World War records presented the college with a new and unusual opportunity. It now had the potential to become an institution of serious military research as well as a teaching institution. To reach that potential, however, would require financial support, assignment of qualified researchers, and appreciation by future commandants of the potential worth of the section. Unfortunately these three requirements would rarely be met in combination.[28]

Edward McGlachlin and the "Art of Command"

The academic year 1921-22 started auspiciously. The President, Secretary of War, and General of the Armies all attended the opening exercises. It has been written of Warren Harding that "his genius lay not so much in his ability to conceal his thought as in the absence of any serious thought to reveal."[29] He revealed little to the Army War College Class of 1922: "I pledge you now you will never be called to service during the present Administration for any war that you will not enter with all your hearts and souls as American citizens." This message apparently meant that there would be no more of this League of Nations peacekeeping talk. Or perhaps it was a pledge to what he believed to be normalcy. The General of the Armies in his address emphasized that the mission of the War College was "preparation for high command." He then added, "for which training as a General Staff officer is an initial qualification." He left it to McGlachlin to sort out those things that were "command" but not "general staff."[30]

Commandant McGlachlin reorganized the faculty divisions and the curriculum to reflect the new War Department General Staff structure, bringing back the Personnel (now G-1) Course and retaining the Command Course. The original McAndrew curriculum organization essentially was still in place, with the class studying in sequence G-2, War Plans, G-3, G-1, G-4, and finally Command. The concept of one large problem was still discernible.[31] McGlachlin attacked the problem of teaching "command" vigorously and personally. As the senior and most experienced member of the college, McGlachlin saw his role as more than that of administrator and motivator; he would also teach. In a sub-course on the "Art of Command," McGlachlin prepared and delivered four lectures which required considerable research and which reveal a high degree of analytical skill.

His first lecture addressed the problem of teaching "command." McGlachlin held that there was such a thing as the "Art of Command" and that it could be taught. He recommended that "acquirement of knowledge of the methods of General Staff work be accepted as an indispensable part." Learning by doing was the best teacher of the art of command, but it was also the "slowest and most expensive" teacher. The college would therefore attempt to teach "method." The applicatory system with its map maneuvers and war games would be used to develop "independence of action, decision and initiative, and the use of common sense developed into military good judgement." Just as the sound operational principles applied in war games had been derived from the study of military history, so principles of command could be derived from the study of the lives of good and poor commanders. The Commandant recognized a problem here; the personalities and careers of those who failed at command were seldom recorded.[32]

In his second lecture, McGlachlin attempted to isolate from a wide range of personality traits those that were most important to successful command. Through his analysis he concluded that those traits were, in order of importance, character, good judgment and common sense, and understanding of men. He stopped short on how these characteristics could be taught in one year at the War College. McGlachlin's next two lectures addressed the lives of four commanders—Moltke, MacMahon, Bazaine, and Benedek—illustrating to the students how one might deduce principles of command from the study of biography . He had Assistant Commandant Harry Smith present similar lectures on Napoleon's marshals and Instructor Walter Krueger present one on Hannibal. Thus McGlachlin took two approaches to teaching the "Art of Command": the conduct of map maneuvers and war games, and the analytical study of biography.[33] In the second approach, McGlachlin's logic was similar to that of Stephen Luce in the early days of the Naval War College when he set Mahan and Bliss to the task of deriving principles of naval warfare through the "comparative method."

Another McGlachlin initiative was to increase the number of guest lecturers. In his first year he increased to 130 from 84 the number of lectures presented. From the selection of lecturers it is apparent that McGlachlin felt a need to extend the horizons of those in his charge. With no additional time available and the topics beyond the expertise of his faculty, guest lecturers were the only means available to bring to bear disciplines other than military science on the one large problem. McGlachlin designed the lecture program "to inform and to interest, to

179

encourage study, investigation, reflection." Then, to help students stay abreast of weapon developments, McGlachlin had arrangements made for the class to visit ordnance facilities at Aberdeen Proving Grounds and the chemical warfare installation at Edgewood Arsenal, both in nearby Maryland.[34]

The McGlachlin Board

In early February, McGlachlin had to interrupt his professorial activities. The General of the Armies convened a board of officers to restudy the entire school system, naming General McGlachlin the board chairman. Underlying Pershing's action was the fact that the school system had been designed in accordance with the National Defense Act of 1920 to support an Army of 280,000. It was already apparent, however, that Congress had no intention of giving substance to the act through adequate appropriations. Regular Army strength was declining and by the end of June 1922 would be below 150,000. Pershing also had other suspicions: the school system was too "cumbersome," too much of an officer's career was spent in school, duplications and conflicts in doctrine existed among the various courses, and too much money was spent transporting officers to and from schools.[35]

Fundamentally, however, the problem was money. The Republican 66th Congress had set the tone in the last two years of the Wilson administration, appropriating just over a third of what the War Department had requested for fiscal year 1921 (July 1, 1920 to June 30, 1921) and less than half the request for fiscal year 1922. The new Harding administration continued the drive for economy. Seeking to reduce taxes and promote government efficiency, Harding signed into law in June 1921 the Budget and Accounting Act providing for a Director of the Budget, a Comptroller General, and, in each executive department, a Budget Officer. Charles G. Dawes, a Chicago banker who had been the AEF's purchasing officer in France, was appointed the first Director of the Budget. In December 1921 he submitted Harding's fiscal year 1923 estimates to the Congress. Dawes had drawn up a budget that would produce a surplus for the treasury, but it would limit Regular Army officer strength to 12,000.[36]

Pershing's decision to look for economies within the school system was triggered by a letter he received in November from Brigadier General Fox Conner (AWC 1908), the War Department G-4; by an inspection trip Pershing had made in the previous fall; and by a letter received in January from Colonel Hugh A. Drum, Commandant of Leavenworth's School of the Line. Conner had attended a six-week general officer orientation course at the Infantry School at Camp Benning. In his letter to Pershing he confined his comments essentially to what he had seen there. He had found the particular course he attended to be valuable, and he recommended that it be lengthened to three months. Beyond that, he was concerned about the advanced age of officers entering the General Service Schools at Fort Leavenworth. The age limit should be drastically reduced; the officers being trained would all be on the retired list during the ten- to fifteen-year period when they might be needed. He also knew of one officer at the War College who would reach mandatory retirement age the year after he graduated. But Conner also recognized the problem of the generation gap in officer training; for the older officers he recommended correspondence courses, which could also serve the needs of the officers of the National Guard and the Officers Reserve Corps. The G-3 at the War Department generally agreed with Conner's observations.[37]

Colonel Drum at Leavenworth, displaying less reserve than Conner, took on the entire system regardless of whether he was familiar with its parts. Building on discussions he had had with Pershing during the latter's visit to Leavenworth, Drum pronounced the system uneconomical and inefficient, comprising too many special schools, producing specialists and theorists, and tending to substitute schooling for troop training. The many years of schooling kept officers away from valuable experience with soldiers. Among the many suggestions that Drum offered was one that in effect would disestablish the War College, though Drum presented the idea as one of combining the War College and Leavenworth's General Staff School.[38]

Drum believed that those subjects taught at the War College pertaining to the theater of operations should be taught by the combined school, which would then be teaching all echelons from army corps through theater army. The School of the Line would teach division and army corps. The combined school could be in Washington or at Leavenworth, but Drum thought Leavenworth preferable. It could be called either "General Staff College" or "War College." As for those subjects being taught at the War College that pertained to war plans and projects, mobilization of industry and manpower, and the Zone of the Interior, Drum believed that they could be learned by annually detailing thirty-five officers as understudies on the War Department General Staff. Training more than thirty-five, he thought, was a waste of time and expense.[39] Either Drum was sincere in his proposals or, realizing that budget and manpower cuts were coming, he was making a power play to insure that they fell most heavily at places other than Leavenworth.

Before McGlachlin's board was handed the problem, Drum was already being counterattacked. The G-3 at the War Department, Brigadier General William Lassiter, demonstrated to Pershing that to meet the approved mobilization plan of fifty-four divisions, eighteen army corps, six field armies, an expeditionary force headquarters, a GHQ, and the War Department General Staff, 1,650 general-staff-trained officers would be required—800 graduates from the School of the Line, 500 from the General Staff School, and 350 from the War College. To meet this requirement the War College must graduate sixty-five Regular Army officers each year. Disputing the charge of inefficiency, Lassiter claimed that the General Service Schools had a high faculty-to-student ratio only because of the individual teaching nature of the applicatory method, but they still compared quite favorably with such institutions as MIT, Yale, Cornell, and the University of Minnesota. The G-3 had all the facts and figures. Finally Lassiter reminded Pershing that there were just not enough troops out there with whom officers could profitably train.[40]

Before convening the board McGlachlin surveyed his faculty for ideas and had a quick precis done on the military school systems of Britain, Japan, Italy, Chile, Argentina, and Germany, showing that officers of those armies spent more time in school than did American officers, and all had larger armies, even disarmed Germany. Regarding the school system itself, the War College faculty produced an abundance of schemes on how to save money, some practical, many not. The faculty's attitude toward the War College program, however, was consistent. Their responses provide insight into what the faculty believed it was about. The faculty had a strong sense that the War College had a responsibility to broaden the outlook of the Army's potential leadership: "Knowledge . . . of the military, political and economic situation of our own and other nations . . . [is] among the foundation stones of fitness for high command." And, "Broaden the course even more . . . [so that] the best men in the army . . . may meet here the prominent men in industrial and educational lines upon whom the [War Department] depends for help in war."[41]

Members of the faculty were unanimously opposed to Drum's understudy idea, despite its similarity to the German practice. The officers selected as understudies would either become clerks or get in the way, without gaining "any particular large vision." McGlachlin's staff was also opposed to moving to Leavenworth. In addition to the more obvious reasons for remaining in Washington (proximity to other government agencies, the War Department General Staff, the Library of Congress), the faculty feared contamination by the Leavenworth system of instruction, which, as one member put it, "leads to mental indigestion [and] nervous breakdowns and steals a man's thinking mind away from him." Like faculties elsewhere, this one saw a need for more careful selection of students. The Assistant Commandant was most severe: "After a close observation of three classes at the Army War College, I feel confident that fully one third of each class should not have been detailed to take the course."[42]

McGlachlin convened his board at the Cavalry School at Fort Riley on February 20. Serving with him were eight representatives of the major Army schools. Besides McGlachlin, two were graduates of the Army War College; Malin Craig (1910), and Hanson E. Ely (1916 and 1920), who was the Commandant at Leavenworth. Working their way east, visiting most of the larger schools, the board reconvened in Washington in late March.[43]

In Washington McGlachlin made a final and eloquent plea that the board share with him his vision of the Army War College as

> not a vocational school from which a group of officers emerge ready to carry on the peace-time administrative duties of the War Department. . . . It should become a great institute at which the broader problems of national defense are studied and discussed . . . teaching the methods of investigation to correct conclusions.

To McGlachlin, Drum's understudy idea was "unworthy of consideration." The War College should be a place where "selected, mature officers meet together and with the officers of other departments of the government and the leaders of our industrial and political life, [to] freely discuss the great problem of mobilizing the nation for war." McGlachlin went on to describe how representatives of the Navy, Commerce, Agriculture, and State Departments might gather so that "the best of their minds can be given to the problem of the nation in which they believe. . . . One year is not too much to give to the general cultural study of the great problems involved in the higher management of war."[44]

On March 30, the board submitted its conclusions to Pershing. If the General of the Armies expected a unanimous finding, he was disappointed. He received a majority report; a minority report from Colonel Harold B. Fiske, the Chief of the Training Branch of War Department G-3 and Pershing's former Assistant Chief of Staff for Training at GHQ of the AEF; a "Dissenting Opinion" from McGlachlin; and numerous lesser dissents.[45]

Either the board never intended to disestablish the War College or McGlachlin's eloquence won them over. Leavenworth, not Washington Barracks, was the loser. As Drum had sowed, so now he reaped. The majority report recommended that the School of the Line and the General Staff School be combined into a *"Command and General Staff School"* to provide a one-year course instructing in command and general staff duties from reinforced brigade through army corps level. On this McGlachlin dissented. He argued to retain the School of the Line to teach the division, and also to retain the General Staff School to cover army corps and field army. He thought a year was needed by the General Staff School, but perhaps four to six months would suffice.[46]

For the Army War College the majority report recommended that no major changes be made in the conduct of the existing course. But General Ely dissented. He recommended that the War College cover "the strategy, tactics and logistics of all units larger than an Army Corps, the organization and functioning of all establishments in a Theater of Operations and the functions of commanders and staffs of all units larger than Army Corps." All this was to be in addition to what the college was already doing. According to Ely, time could be made available by reducing the G-1 and G-4 courses.[47]

Another issue was how much time, if any, should elapse between graduation from the Command and General Staff School at Leavenworth and attendance at the War College. The majority recommended not less than two years. McGlachlin again dissented. He wanted not less than four years. He disliked the competitiveness at Leavenworth: "The tendency of close application for a period of nine months of severe competition under highly systematized and quite rigid instruction in the School of the Line is to subdue the student's independence and initiative." The General Staff School, in McGlachlin's view had also become highly competitive though not planned to be so, and it showed at the War College where there was a clear difference in attitude between those who had come directly from Leavenworth and those who had not. Those coming directly from Leavenworth were "subdued, lacking in initiative and expression, and inclined to 'play the instructor,' attempting to do what is wanted rather than come to independent conclusions on the basis of study and reason." McGlachlin wanted "collegiate students," not "academic pupils" at the War College. He believed that the "envy and jealousy of competition" at Leavenworth would be alleviated if selection to attend the War College was not made until four years later and if it depended in part on duty performance as well as on class standing.[48]

In his minority report Colonel Fiske held that the majority had not clearly distinguished between the responsibilities of the Command and General Staff School and that of the War College. He felt that too much had been given to Leavenworth and not enough to the War College. According to Fiske there should be a School of the Line at Leavenworth for the development and teaching of tactics of the combined arms. The War College should teach two courses. The first would be a staff course, training officers for all general staff positions, both on the War Department General Staff and with the General Staff with Troops. The second course would be for a small group of carefully selected colonels who would be prepared for the "highest professional duties," to include that of high command. Fiske thought the Command Course then being taught at the War College was a good start at what those select colonels would need.[49]

Fiske's was and is an interesting scheme. He wanted Leavenworth to get back to what he recalled as the days of glory before 1916, the days of the great tacticians and military historians, when men such as Arthur Wagner, Eben Swift, John Morrison, Arthur Conger, Matthew Steele, Farrand Sayre, Oliver Spaulding (and perhaps too, Harold Fiske) wrote the histories, translated the German and French texts, developed the doctrine, conducted the war games, and graced the lecture platform, assisted by bright and eager young officers such as George Marshall and Walter Krueger. Fiske envisioned Leavenworth as the intellectual center for the serious study of battle, where tactical doctrine would be developed, taught, and disseminated to the Army. The War College, for its part, would develop and teach in its staff course the management of raising, training, supplying, sustaining, and moving armies and all components of armies. For the elite of the elite, there was to be the study of high command. Fiske's concept was original and on the surface seems to have much to commend it. How it would have worked out is unknown. The American Army would continue to delineate the mission of its officer schools by branch of service and tactical echelon.[50]

The future structure of the Army school system was now up to Pershing. In May he announced his decision. There would be one school at Leavenworth, a "Command and General Staff School." Attendance would be selective; 250 officers would enter each year. Two years after graduation they would be eligible for selection for the War College. The Command and General Staff School would instruct through the level of the army corps. Pershing accepted "in principle" Ely's dissenting recommendation that the War College be responsible for the field army and all establishments in the theater of operations.[51]

When Ely recommended and, over McGlachlin's objections, Pershing approved reducing the Leavenworth schooling to one year and teaching at the War College the "strategy, tactics, and logistics" of the field army, a decision was made that was more basic than Pershing probably recognized. The War College had reopened in 1919, as it had opened in 1903, with primary emphasis on preparation for war. Now in 1922 it was decided, as it had been in 1907, that study of the conduct of campaigns should receive at least equal attention. In effect, as long as the War College and the Command and General Staff School remained one-year courses, confining boundaries were placed on the possible breadth of the Army's education system. Newton Baker had been forever impressed in 1917 and 1918 that war could not be put in compartments, that it was the business of not just the Army but of the nation. He had directed that the school system insure that future senior officers understand this. But after Pershing's decision, the study of the totality of the phenomenon of war had to compete with study of the combatant phase. Pershing's decision was not necessarily wrong, but it was limiting. To use Elihu Root's terms, Pershing moved the War College away from the study of the great problem of national defense and toward the narrower problem of military science.

NOTES

1. Vandiver, *Black Jack*, 2:1052-54. Coffman, *March*, 171, 184, 196.
2. Ibid., 197-99, 202. Statement of General Pershing, 31 October 1919, in 69th Cong., 2d Sess., *Historical Documents*, 370-81. Statement of Colonel Palmer, Ibid., 306-11.
3. HR 14560, *Historical Documents*, 242-51. Statement of General Pershing, 31 October 1919, Ibid., 410-11, 414-15. Statement of Colonel Palmer, Ibid., 340-58. Coffman, *March*, 203-04, 207.
4. 66th Cong. 2d Sess., Public Act #242, An Act to amend an Act entitled "An Act for making further and more effectual provision for the National Defense . . . approved June 3, 1916." (Hereafter *National Defense Act, 1920*) *Acts and Resolutions*, December 1, 1919-June 14, 1920, Vol. 26:424-55.
5. For March's relations with Congress, Coffman, *March*, 188-90, 194. Hewes, *Root to McNamara*, 50-52. *National Defense Act, 1920*, Sec. 5.
6. *National Defense Act, 1920*, Sec. 5a. Hewes, *Root to McNamara*, 51. Nelson, *National Security*, 301-07.
7. War Department General Order 48, 12 August 1920.
8. Annual Report of the Director, War Plans Division, General Staff, for the year July 1, 1919, to June 30, 1920, copy in AWC-CF 1919-20. *Chief of Staff Report: War Department Annual Reports, 1920*, I:190.
9. Report of Director, War Plans Division, 1920. Haan to Policy and Coordinating Committee, 12 July 1920, File 1-1 to 81, AWC-CF.
10. James W. McAndrew, "Chief of Staff," *Infantry Journal*, IX (1912): 181-214. War Department General Order 56, 14 September 1920.
11. Haan to Chief of Staff, 26 June 1919, forwarding memorandum, McAndrew to Director, War Plans Division, 26 June 1919, File 1-1 to 81, AWC-CF. Edward M. Coffman, "The American Military Generation Gap in World War I: The Leavenworth Clique in the AEF" in *Command and Commanders in Modern Warfare*, ed. William Geffen (Colorado Springs: U.S. Air Force Academy, 1964). Statement of Palmer, 10 October 1920, *Historical Documents*, 340-41.
12. Henry A. Smith, Address, 2 September 1920, AWC-CF, 1920-21, VII: "Miscellaneous Lectures." John A. Lejeune, Lecture, 18 January 1921, Ibid.
13. Smith, Address, 2 September 1920.
14. Stanley Coben, "A Study in Nativism: The American Red Scare of 1919-1920," *Political Science Quarterly*, 79 (March 1964): 52-75. Haan to Colonel Embick, 10 April 1920; Haan to McAndrew, 21 April 1920; Haan, Memorandum for consideration by General Staff College and General Staff School, 23 April 1920, File 1-1 to 81, AWC-CF. Smith, Address, 2 September 1920. Smith to Haan, 30 December 1920, File 1-1 to 81, AWC-CF.
15. Smith, Address, 2 September 1920. W. W. Hicks, Lecture: "Estimate of Radical and Revolutionary Situation in the United States," December 1920, AWC-CF, 1920-21.
16. Adjutant General to Commandant, 4 September 1920, in "Chronicle 1919/20-1930/31," 11-13.
17. March to Members of Joint Board, 13 March 1920, File 1-1 to 81, AWC-CF. "Chronicle 1919/20-1930/31," 14.
18. Coffman, *March*, 220-21. *Official Army Register*, 1921.
19. Acting Commandant to Adjutant General, 16 June 1921. "Reports of Operations, 1920-1940."
20. War Department General Order 40, 15 August 1921. Haan to Commandant, General Staff College, 15 November 1920, File 1-1 to 81, AWC-CF. Director, War Plans Division to Commandant, General Staff College, 10 March 1921, Ibid. Haan to Commandant, 5 April 1921, Ibid. Army War College, "Summary of the Courses at the Army War College since the World War," File 1-105, AWC-CF.

21. General McAndrew's illness was terminal. He died in 1922 in Walter Reed Hospital at age 60.
22. Data on assignments derived from *Army Register* for years 1921-1940 and *The War College Directory.*
23. War Department General Order 40, 15 August 1921.
24. Extracts of the Harbord Board proceedings are in 69th Cong., 2d Sess., *Historical Documents*, 568-648. War Department General Order 41, 16 August 1921.
25. Ibid. Change 2 to Army Regulation 10-15, 1 September 1922. *Secretary of War Report: War Department Annual Reports, 1922*, I:158.
26. General Order 41, 1921. "History of the Historical Section, Army War College," comp. R. S. Thomas, 1941, MHI Library. Stetson Conn, *Historical Work in the United States Army, 1862-1954* (Washington: U.S. Army Center of Military History, 1980), 15, 17-19, 27, 31, 46.
27. Ibid., 19, 29, 33, 35-37.
28. "History of Historical Section."
29. John D. Hicks, *Republican Ascendancy 1921-1933* (New York: Harper and Brothers, 1960), 25.
30. Addresses at Opening Exercise, 1 September 1921, AWC-CF 1921-22, Vol. VIII: "Miscellaneous."
31. AWC-CF 1921-22, "Outline of Course."
32. AWC-CF 1921-22, Vol. VI: "Command Course."
33. Ibid.
34. Ibid. "Chronicle 1919/20-1930/31," 18.
35. Chief of Staff to McGlachlin, 4 February 1922, in "Report of Proceedings of a Board of Officers appointed to Study the Army School System." (Hereafter "McGlachlin file," copy in MHI Library.)
36. *Report of the Secretary of War to the President: Annual Reports of War Department, Fiscal Year ended June 30, 1923*, 2. Hicks, *Republican Ascendancy*, 51-52. Coffman, *March*, 221-22, 309. Mark S. Watson, *Chief of Staff: Prewar Plans and Preparations* (Washington: Historical Division, Department of the Army, 1950), 16.
37. Fox Conner to General of the Armies, 14 November 1921, "McGlachlin file." Lassiter to Chief of Staff, 6 January 1922, Ibid.
38. Hugh A. Drum to Pershing, 27 January 1922, Ibid.
39. Ibid.
40. Lassiter to Chief of Staff, 22 December 1921, "McGlachlin file."
41. Unsigned memorandum, n.d. [February 1922]; G.E. Kilbourne to Commandant, 8 February 1922; George R. Spalding to Commandant, n.d. [February 1922]; all in "McGlachlin file."
42. Unsigned Memorandum, n.d. [February 1922]; Spalding to Commandant; H. A. Smith, The Army School System, n.d. [February 1922]; all in "McGlachlin file."
43. War Department Special Orders 29-0, 4 February 1922.
44. McGlachlin to Board, 19 March 1922, "McGlachlin file."
45. "McGlachlin file."
46. Final Report of Board, par. 2c(6), Ibid.
47. Final Report of Board, par. 4b, Ibid.
48. Dissenting Opinion by General McGlachlin, Ibid.
49. Minority Report by Colonel H. B. Fiske, Ibid.
50. For the prewar Leavenworth faculty see Nenninger, *Leavenworth* (1975), 259-78.
51. John McA. Palmer, Aide-de-Camp, to G-3, 19 May 1922, "McGlachlin file."

TEST YEARS
1923-1928

Into the 'Twenties

While General McGlachlin grappled with the problem of teaching the Art of Command and General Pershing with that of a school system that was too costly, Secretary of State Charles Evans Hughes faced the problems of world power. Having rejected the Versailles Treaty, the United States signed a separate treaty of peace with Germany in August 1921. France was left with the responsibility to enforce Versailles; the United States declined any part of it. With the European balance thus provided for, Hughes turned his attention to the maritime balance and that in the Far East. For these the United States would rely upon international agreement. On the day after Armistice Day 1921, in response to President Harding's invitation, the International Conference on the Limitation of Armaments, the so-called Washington Naval Conference, convened. War College Commandant McGlachlin, recognizing the significance of the event, requested 115 tickets to the open sessions for his faculty and students. He was given ten.[1]

Secretary Hughes had three objectives for the United States: stop the naval arms race, break the Anglo-Japanese defensive alliance, and thwart Japanese designs on China. He successfully negotiated three treaties. The Five Power Pact established a capital ship ratio of 5:5:3 for Britain, the United States, and Japan. The Nine Power Pact made formal the principle of respect for the commercial and territorial integrity of China. And the Four Power Pact, signed by Britain, the United States, Japan, and France, called for consultations in the event of aggression in the Far East. The Senate found the Four Power Pact a bit vague. In ratification it added the reservation that the United States recognized "no commitment to armed force, no alliance, no obligation to join any defense." The naval race was stopped, the Anglo-Japanese Treaty abrogated, and Japan put on a leash. Hughes had constructed a

189

diplomatic masterpiece; the United States had free security—or so it was thought at the time.[2]

In return for free security the United States agreed, as an item in the Four Power Pact, to respect the status quo in the western Pacific in regard to naval bases and fortifications. It would not fortify the Philippines, Guam, or the Aleutians. The American security frontier in the Pacific would rest upon Alaska, Hawaii, and the Canal Zone. The Navy's leadership was dismayed; the Army's less so—they had yet to find a solution to Philippine defense. But with France responsible for Europe, the Far East secured through solemn international agreement, and the Marines willing and experienced in policing the unruly republics of the Caribbean, there was apparently little need for an American army or for providing financial support to the military policy elaborated in the 1920 Defense Act. At least the administrations of Calvin Coolidge and the Republican Congresses of the mid-1920s saw little need.

In fiscal year 1924, appropriations limited the enlisted strength of the Regular Army to 125,000, and officer strength reached its lowest point in the years between the two World Wars—11,655. In fiscal year 1925 appropriations for the military activities of the War Department reached their between-wars low. After Congress established the Army Air Corps in 1926, War Department budgets were increased, but not to the degree that satisfied the needs and ambitions of the new branch. But if the decade of the 1920s was one of poverty for the Army of the United States, it was also a decade of stability. There was time for education, and to those Army officers who cared and believed that the millennium had not yet arrived, the school system became the focal point of professional interest and pride. In their view, the smaller and more obsolete the Army became, the more critical was the need for a highly schooled officer corps. They believed that one day the safety of the nation would rest on the shoulders of the Army's commanders and staff officers, and that only through intense training and formal education could the Army produce leaders able to bear that great load.[3]

The McGlachlin Philosophy

Pershing, McGlachlin, Ely, and Fiske all shared that view. They differed, though, in their judgments as to where economies might be made with least risk to serious professional education. As McGlachlin had expressed so eloquently to his board, his ambition was to expand the scope of what was already being accomplished at the War College. With a two-year interim now prescribed between Leavenworth and attendance at the War College, the first Leavenworth graduates who had not progressed beyond the study of the army corps would not arrive at the War College until the 1925-26 school year. McGlachlin had two years to phase in the instruction that he had been directed to provide on field army operations. In the interim he would try to put the War College on the broader road that he had described to his colleagues.

Despite his innovations in the study of the Art of Command and his victory over Hugh Drum's scheme to disestablish the War College, General McGlachlin could not have considered the year 1921-22 a complete success. Soon after becoming Commandant he had written Pershing that he saw his mission as furnishing the "maximum number of officers of judgement, capacity, and willingness of application" but he "should eliminate promptly the more unsuitable." Guided by that philosophy he graduated only seventy-four of the ninety-eight students who began the year, an attrition rate of over twenty-four percent. There had been one death, five reliefs due to illness, and two transfers. Sixteen officers completed the year but were not awarded diplomas. Fifteen students in the class were administrative and technical service officers and had not had the Leavenworth training of most of their line officer classmates, but they were not really the problem. Too many in the class apparently just did not have the background or wit to handle the complex problems involved in preparation for war. It was obvious that more careful selection and better preparation of students was needed.[4]

McGlachlin had good reason to complain about the qualifications of the students. When the Class of 1922 took their annual physical examinations, six were found to have conditions that precluded them from active field service; fully thirty percent of the class had less serious physical problems. Moreover, in reviewing the records of the incoming Class of 1923, McGlachlin found that a few were rated as "below average" in efficiency and many rated as only "average" even though a criterion for selection was an efficiency report record of at least "excellent." In July 1922 the War Department established the policy that an officer could not be over the age of fifty-two years at the time of entrance, and therefore would have ten years of service remaining after graduation before reaching mandatory retirement age. But almost immediately this requirement was waived. The Adjutant General suspected that the chiefs of the various arms and services who actually made the selections were being guided primarily by availability and seniority. Before the war Wotherspoon's problem had been to corral the more senior officers into the college. McGlachlin's problem was to keep them out.[5]

For the Class of 1923, the Adjutant General promised McGlachlin a smaller class, only sixty-five Army officers, of whom fifty would be graduates of Leavenworth's General Staff School and only eleven would be of the administrative and technical services. Four vacancies would be reserved for outstanding officers who had not had the opportunity to attend Leavenworth. To help improve performance and production, McGlachlin introduced into the G-1 and G-3 courses "informative phases," an idea used successfully in the G-4 course the year before. The informative phases were designed to provide the background necessary to do the applicatory work and to add "technical training . . . for duty on the War Department General Staff."[6]

As was apparent in his approach to the study of command, McGlachlin believed in the feasibility of deducing principles from historical experience. In his view the success of the applicatory method rested on an understanding of immutable principles. The previous year he had scheduled two lectures on the "principles of war" as they had been demonstrated during the First Battle of the Marne, and he had personally lectured on the thoughts of Sun Tzu. In the coming year he would have Krueger again present his lecture on "Conditions of Success in War as Illustrated by Hannibal's Campaign in Italy." McGlachlin believed, moreover, that there were "principles of supply" that could be derived through historical analysis. The G-4 division of the faculty put together a series of lectures labeled "Supply Plans, Lessons and Principles Deducible from—" that drew on British, French, and German campaigns going back to Frederick the Great and Napoleon, and from American campaigns since the Revolution.[7]

McGlachlin's approach to senior officer education gave the Historical Section the important role of preparing monographs for faculty and student study. He was able to increase the staff of the section to twelve officers, three of whom were stationed abroad to collect documents pertaining to American operations that might be in the war archives of London, Paris, and Potsdam. To Potsdam he initially sent Walter Krueger, then Lewis Sorley. General McGlachlin and Colonel Spaulding were unable, however, to fend off the Adjutant General, who demanded and won custody of those AEF records that had already been collected.[8]

During his second year McGlachlin continued to give the Command Course major emphasis. Interspersed among the other courses, the Command Course consumed eight and a half weeks. It began with wargaming the Meuse-Argonne offensive, followed by study of the German offensive of the spring of 1918, Mackensen's 1915 campaign on the Donajee, the 1916 German campaign in Rumania, and the First Battle of the Marne. Still later in the year, war games were conducted of the initial concentrations and operations of the German and French armies in 1914 and finally of the war plan the students themselves had developed during the War Plans Course, which involved an assault on Halifax. To prepare them for this planning, McGlachlin had the students study War Plan Green (Mexico), the German and French plans of 1914, and the 1918 plan of the AEF. To properly game the Halifax plan, four additional naval officers were brought in to assist the naval representative on the faculty in the joint play. In all, the students spent twenty-seven days conducting war games.[9]

In a continuing effort to broaden the outlook of his students, General

McGlachlin collected under the broad heading of "general subjects" a program of twenty-five lectures covering five areas: "The Science of Economics," "Political Science," "Fundamentals of Psychology," "Foundations of Military Strength," and "International Law." Believing that a less homogeneous student body would also tend to broaden student outlook, he had recommended to the Chief of Staff the previous winter that students from outside the Regular Army, Navy, and Marine Corps be included in each class. He suggested including Reserve and National Guard officers, officials from other government departments, and even men not affiliated with the government. He was only partially successful. The War Department saw no advantage in devoting effort to men not with the government unless they applied for commissions in the Officer Reserve Corps. During the year, however, five National Guard and five Reserve officers did attend the G-1 Course, and four National Guard and five Reserve officers attended the G-3 Course. Four of the Reserve officers remained for the seven-week War Plans Course.[10]

In the eight-week G-2 course McGlachlin came closest to achieving his hopes for a class composed of men of more varied background and experience. Five National Guard and four Reserve officers attended the course, but also present were six representatives of the Department of State and six representatives of the Department of Commerce. Among the latter was a twenty-seven-year-old assistant to Secretary of Commerce Herbert Hoover named Christian A. Herter, who would one day serve as Secretary of State. McGlachlin had expanded the G-2 instruction into what was beginning to take on the appearance of a course in national or grand strategy. In addition to the usual country studies, the class was now required to consider the sources and availability of critical raw materials and to study international trade routes and the strategic positions that controlled those routes. In the tradition of earlier years, particular attention was given to the approaches to the isthmian canal.[11]

To accommodate the addition of historical studies, informative periods, war games, and general subject lectures, other items in the curriculum had to be either dropped or drastically condensed. The ultimate casualty was McAndrew's one great problem of national mobilization. The college retained McAndrew's basic organizational structure, and the fundamental idea of preparation for war remained central, but there was no longer time for the class to work its way through all the *grosser Generalstab* steps of war preparation using the applicatory method. One year was too short to do properly all that McAndrew and McGlachlin together saw as desirable. Under the pressure of time the format of the War College was gradually changing from the magnified applicatory method to a version of the contemporary graduate school characterized by individual study and research, a gathering in seminar ("committee work" at the War College), and a reinforcing lecture program.[12] Still missing were comprehensive examinations and the writing of a major thesis. A more significant difference, however, was that solutions to problems were found by a group not by the individual. The drift toward the graduate-school format was gradual and the change far from complete, but the War College had begun moving in a direction quite different from what had become the traditional system of training officers by immersing them in the applicatory method.

In 1922-23 General McGlachlin was assisted by a faculty of sixteen officers, only two of whom remained from General McAndrew's 1919 selection. The remainder were graduates of the first three classes. The original Assistant Commandant, Harry A. Smith, had been promoted to brigadier general in May of 1922, and reassigned. He was replaced by Colonel George S. Simonds, who had graduated with the first postwar class and had been on the faculty for the past two years. McGlachlin avoided the severe student attrition of his first year. He attempted a grading system that would "reduce comparison to the lowest limit . . . and not lead to the vices of competition." He was still required, however, to submit the normal officer's efficiency report on each student. He made no attempt to determine a student's qualification by staff area or level of command. The student either completed the course satisfactorily or he did not. In the Class of 1923 only three officers, each because of physical disability, were unable to finish the course and graduate. Either the students were better qualified than those of the year before or less was expected of them. In 1922-23 McGlachlin both broadened the scope of the course and increased the productivity of the War College. He also more than tripled the operating budget, from $20,000 to $70,380.[13]

The Fiske Board

After Pershing gave his general approval to the recommendations of the McGlachlin Board, he convened another board to devise a coordinated and progressive program throughout the school system that would reduce duplication to the minimum. He appointed Harold Fiske to head the board despite, or perhaps because of, Fiske's minority opinion on the McGlachlin report. Fiske's instructions included the specific admonition that "particular attention must be given to defining the division of duties as between the General Staff Schools—namely, the Command and General Staff School at Fort Leavenworth, and the Army War College at Washington, D.C." The War College representative on the Fiske Board was Colonel Simonds, the new Assistant Commandant and an officer thoroughly familiar with the work of the college since its reestablishment in the summer of 1919. Also on the board was Colonel Edgar Collins, a 1917 graduate of the college and a member of the faculty during the McAndrew years.[14]

The Fiske Board convened at the end of July 1922. Pershing approved its recommendations in early October. Fiske's recommended program for the War College was essentially the one McGlachlin was currently conducting for the Class of 1923. The board recommended that the War College mission be stated as

> to train officers for (a) high command and staff to include units higher than army corps, (b) War Department General Staff duty and duty in the office of the Assistant Secretary of War, (c) Corps Area Command and General Staff duty.[15]

This statement made specific the various headquarters in which War College graduates would be expected to serve. The office of the Assistant Secretary of War, the War Department General Staff, and the Corps Area Commands all had critical roles in planning and preparing for mobilization. The Assistant Secretary of War by law had the primary responsibility for industrial mobilization. The nine territorial commands ("corps areas") were directly subordinate to the War Department and, in addition to peacetime training and administrative responsibilities, had the mission to plan for and be prepared to execute mobilization within their geographic boundaries. It is apparent that Pershing and Fiske now expected the War College to address the full range of mobilization problems, all the problems of preparation for war.

The new mission statement also directed the War College to address the actual conduct of field operations as viewed from the command levels of the field army, group of armies, and theater of operations. Pershing made this even more explicit in his letter approving the Fiske Board recommendations:

> The War College course will include the tactics of a typical army, acting independently or within an army group, covering phases of concentration, advance, deployment, combat and pursuit, with the general details of supply incident thereto.[16]

Hanson Ely Becomes Commandant

The restated mission and the Chief of Staff's emphasis on field army operations were to take effect with the class entering in August 1924. General McGlachlin, however, would not be responsible for their implementation. In February 1923 the War Department informed him that after the graduation of the Class of 1923 he would be reassigned to command the Panama Division. McGlachlin elected not to go to Panama; he retired in the fall.[17]

The reasons for the reassignment of General McGlachlin are not clear. They may have been nothing more than the consequence of routine reassignments to fill general officer positions. On the other hand, McGlachlin had been moving the War College in a direction not entirely consistent with Pershing's expressed interest in making the War College, in addition to what McAndrew had begun, a school for the teaching of large-unit operations. McGlachlin had not neglected military operations; indeed, he had intensified their study through increased wargaming and particularly through a wide spectrum of historical analyses. Concurrently, however, he had attempted to give substance to his conviction that fitness for high command included understanding of the political and economic aspects of war and the role played in war by people outside the naval and military professions. If McGlachlin differed with Pershing and such officers as Ely and Fiske, it was on the issue of just what constitutes fitness for high command or, using Elihu Root's term, the "great problem of responsible command."

The new Commandant was Major General Hanson E. Ely. As Commandant of the General Staff Schools at Fort Leavenworth, it was Ely who had convinced Pershing that the War College should teach field army operations and that time for this instruction could be provided by reducing the time devoted to the G-1 and G-4 courses. Ely now had the opportunity to prove his thesis. Hanson Ely was an officer with field service credentials of the highest order. As a young officer he had served with distinction during the Philippine insurrection. He had commanded a battalion at Vera Cruz. In France he had been a superb combat commander. He had led the 28th Infantry Regiment at Cantigny, where he had won the Distinguished Service Cross. He had commanded a brigade of the 2d Division at Soissons, then commanded the 5th Division in the Meuse-Argonne. He was a 1916 graduate of the Army War College, had been at the Staff College at Langres, and was a 1920 graduate of the General Staff College (Army War College).[18]

In the spring of 1923, after the War College faculty had drawn up a tentative program for the next year, McGlachlin was courteous enough to send it to Leavenworth for General Ely's comment. Ely was also a gentleman; he made no suggestions for change. He expressed the greatest interest in the mechanics of the Command Course. The 1923-24 program, although executed by General Ely, was planned by General McGlachlin. In its essentials it did not differ from the 1922-23 course. The G-1, G-3, and G-4 "informative periods" were duplicated to provide similar periods for the G-2, Command, and War Plans courses. The faculty presented all "informative" instruction sequentially between September and mid-March, dividing the year's program into an "Informative Period" and a "Practical Application Period." In compliance with Pershing's desires, "conduct of field operations" was included in both periods. Reserve and National Guard officers attended the informative phases of the G-1, G-2, and G-4 courses. Representatives of the Department of State and the Department of Commerce returned for the G-2 course of the 1923-24 year, but they attended lectures and conferences only intermittently.[19]

General Ely was most concerned with the 1924-25 course, when he would have to add all the topics recommended by the McGlachlin and Fiske boards to include operations of the field army and the army group. In his view an additional complication was that the class makeup would be far from homogeneous. Half the Class of 1925 had finished the two-year course at Leavenworth, a quarter had received Leavenworth's new one-year Command and General Staff School training, and the remainder had no Leavenworth training at all. Ely hoped that as the year progressed the more advanced students could instruct those with less training. He considered 1924-25 a "test year."[20]

The mission of training officers to serve in the office of the Assistant Secretary of War was another problem. McAndrew's program, concerned as it was with the one large problem of preparation for war, had given industrial mobilization extensive treatment. Subsequent emphasis on command and field operations resulted in less time being available for the industrial mobilization issues. The Fiske Board program, as approved in the fall of 1922 and as executed by Ely in 1923-24, gave minimum attention to the problems of the Assistant Secretary. It specified only "informative studies of the duties and functions of . . . the office of the Assistant Secretary of War," and those as part of the three-week G-4 course. During the nine weeks in which the class prepared war plans, the G-1 and G-4 divisions of the faculty were to "conduct studies of the plans for the mobilization of the manpower and material resources and their forwarding to the Theater of Operations."[21] The War College no longer had the time or the incentive to pursue in depth the subject of industrial mobilization.

The Army Industrial College

In fact, the Assistant Secretary had already begun a training program of his own. As early as 1921 the planning branch of the Assistant Secretary's office was experimenting with a sort of apprentice system for training officers of the procurement branches in mobilization matters. Later it added an "Orientation Course of Reading." In March 1923 Dwight F. Davis became Assistant Secretary. He approved sending eight officers to the Harvard Graduate School of Business Administration, beginning in February 1924. That same month he opened the Army Industrial College in the Munitions Building. It began modestly, with nine students attending a six-month course designed for "instructing officers of the procurement branches in the higher duties of their profession in connection with the procurement of supplies in time of war." The "case system" borrowed from Harvard and the Army's applicatory method were both used. By 1926-27 the Army Industrial College had expanded to a year-long course with a student body of thirty-five.[22]

As conceived, the Army Industrial College was at the same level in the Army education system as Leavenworth's Command and General Staff School. As line officers did at Leavenworth, procurement branch officers would establish by attendance at the Industrial College their eligibility to attend the Army War College. The War College, nonetheless, still retained the mission to train officers for duty in the office of the Assistant Secretary. During Ely's "test year" of 1924-25, and again in 1925-26, "Assistant Secretary of War" instruction was included as part of the G-4 course. In the 1926-27 course an "Assistant Secretary of War Course" gained independent status. Pershing's economy program may have eliminated Leavenworth's School of the Line from the educational system, but at the same time it had contributed to the birth of the Army Industrial College. Forced to include subjects no longer taught at Leavenworth, the War College could not treat adequately the problems of industrial mobilization.[23]

The Ely Years

As War College Commandant, Hanson Ely served under three Chiefs of Staff. Just after the start of the "test year," Pershing reached mandatory retirement age, Congress having failed to make any special provision for keeping on a General of the Armies. He was replaced by his deputy, John L. Hines, who two years later was in turn replaced by Charles P. Summerall. Neither Hines nor Summerall changed Pershing's guidance on the War College program while Ely was Commandant. Ely evidently had relatively free rein within that guidance—and within budget restraints. His operating budget for the "test year" was fourteen percent less than McGlachlin had enjoyed during his final year, but the major problem Ely faced during his incumbency was to implement the instructions that he himself had recommended in 1922 and that Pershing had made explicit when approving the Fiske Board findings.[24]

Ely included field army and army group operations within the Command Course. In presenting instruction on the field army, he used the analogy of the field army as a machine, the army commander being the operator. The students studied in turn the component parts of the machine, the system for control (that is, the staff), the method of communication between the commander and his staff, and the method and system by which the staff carried out the operator-commander's decisions (for example, estimates, orders, staff visits, and inspections). Next, as Pershing had directed, students investigated the tactics, logistics, and strategy of the field army. Finally, the class put the "machine" to practical use through the means of map problems, map studies, map maneuvers, terrain exercises, and tactical rides. In concept, Ely's plan did not differ basically from Eben Swift's prewar course in Military Art, although by 1925 the "machine" had grown much more complex, its staff much larger, and its methods more sophisticated.[25]

Ely followed the same procedure for the study of army group operations. The Command Course also carried the study of the organization and functions of the GHQ of a theater of operations. Ely hoped, in vain as it turned out, that the work of student committees would produce a text on GHQ operations and procedures. Command Course topics also included joint operations, the study of expeditionary forces in limited operations, and the solving of map problems based on war plans. Despite the comprehensive and elaborate approach Ely described to the War Department, he conducted fewer map problems than called for by the McGlachlin/Fiske program. In 1925 the field exercise conducted the previous year at Gettysburg was moved to Camp Dix, New Jersey, and tied to planning for the defense of Delaware Bay. The reconnaissance of the northeastern United States initiated by McAndrew was continued.[26]

The "test year" retained the idea of an "Informative Period" lasting through March. The "Practical Application Period" was renamed the "War Plans Period." If any one subject dominated Ely's program, it was war planning. Ten weeks were devoted to the subject. This emphasis had begun during the McGlachlin period when the class first attempted to construct a complete war plan. It continued in 1924-25 when the class tried its hand at a Joint Plan Red and a Joint Plan Orange, and also studied three approved Army strategic plans: Orange, Red, and Green. The college, however, did not treat strategy per se as a distinct area for investigation, nor did it give in-depth consideration to national strategy or policy. It assumed simply that a war had begun and that the object of war was obviously, victory.[27]

The curriculum became very crowded. Ely was able to reduce the G-1 course from four to three weeks, but he had to add time to the G-4 course to accommodate his obligation to the Office of the Assistant Secretary of War. He included aspects of mobilization other than industrial mobilization in the G-3 course, another practice begun by McGlachlin. An Ely innovation that further added to the workload was student preparation of an individual "General Staff Memorandum" in each of the five staff section courses. This practice was intended to train students both in the mechanics of War Department General Staff work and in how to research, prepare, and coordinate recommendations on policy to be made to the Chief of Staff. It was also designed to force the student to consider systematically current or future policy questions.[28]

General Ely continued to experiment with and modify the course during the next three years. In 1925-26, the subject of mobilization (less industrial mobilization) was taken out of the G-3 course and treated separately; the next year it was made part of the G-1 course—as it had become primarily a study of manpower mobilization. By 1926-27 only the G-1, G-4, and Assistant Secretary of War courses required preparation of individual General Staff Memoranda. The next year each student prepared only one General Staff Memorandum and that, after approval by the Commandant, in any staff area the student chose. The number of war plans actually prepared also diminished. By 1927-28 only the Red Plan was attempted, but eight weeks were devoted to it. The Camp Dix field exercise was continued in 1925-26, but in 1926-27 it was moved to Fort Adams, Rhode Island, as a sequel to a joint exercise conducted with the Navy focusing on the defense of Narragansett Bay. In 1927-28 lack of funds precluded holding both a field exercise and a strategic reconnaissance. The field exercise was canceled and a reconnaissance of the Chesapeake Bay area was substituted for the traditional reconnaissance in the northeast.[29]

Another experiment was a "Coordination Course" designed to emphasize the duties of a chief of staff and the necessity of staff coordination and teamwork. Three days were given this course in 1925-26, ten days in 1926-27. After that year the idea was abandoned. New requirements, some self-generated, had forced General McGlachlin to modify and reduce much of what McAndrew had established. Similarly, new requirements forced Ely to modify McGlachlin's program. The McGlachlin attempts to broaden the course beyond things military were gradually discarded. By 1926-27 Ely had reduced the general subject lectures involving other academic disciplines from twenty-five to fifteen; in 1927-28 they disappeared entirely. The use of historical situations was discontinued as the basis for teaching command, operations, and logistics. The historical search for principles, whether of war, command, or supply, was given up to be replaced by the consideration of hypothetical operational situations believed to be more modern, realistic, and practical. Evidently Edward McGlachlin's approach was deemed too theoretical and abstract.[30]

Understandably the Historical Section did not prosper in the post-McGlachlin atmosphere. In the summer of 1924 Lieutenant Colonel Christian A. Bach, just graduated from the War College, replaced Oliver Spaulding as chief of the section. The next summer he proposed a program that would produce a three-volume work on the World War for the general public and sixty-two monographs for use by the Army. Hanson Ely was apparently not seized with the idea. He did not forward Bach's program to the War Department until the following January and then only after a faculty review. The faculty recommendations were conservative to say the least, warning that there should be no "criticism, censure, commendations, praise, blame, or opinion." It would be dull history, if history at all. Despite the support of Fox Conner (AWC 1908), the Deputy Chief of Staff, the three-volume work was not approved and no funds were made available for additional employees at the Historical Section.[31]

In the interim a revised volume of the *Encyclopedia Brittanica* was published containing an article titled "The United States Army, 1910-1926." The article had been prepared and submitted by the Historical Section without General Ely's knowledge. Understandably, Ely was annoyed by the neglect of proper channels; apparently, he was also annoyed with the article. He instructed Bach that henceforth the Historical Section would stick to facts; the faculties of the Army service schools would derive any "lessons learned." In November 1926 Ely issued instructions that he believed would make the section a more effective supporting agency of the schools. To add to the section's troubles, the Adjutant General made another play to take over control, but this the Chief of Staff did not approve.[32] In the mid-1920s neither the Army nor the Army War College really understood how to use the Historical Section or history—or else they simply would not risk tarnishing the heroic image of the AEF.

National Guard and Reserve Corps officers continued to attend the G-1, G-2, and G-3 courses while Ely was Commandant. Each year approximately fifteen of these officers attended each of the three courses; a total of some forty-five non-regular officers per year thereby got partial exposure to the War College program. Ely recommended, with only marginal success, that the number be increased; he was an enthusiastic supporter of Pershing's "One Army" concept. In both the classes of 1926 and 1927, one Reserve officer attended the entire year. General Ely was particularly desirous of having the states' adjutants general attend those portions of the course that pertained to mobilization. During the three years 1925 through 1927, fifteen adjutants general attended the G-1 or G-4 courses. McGlachlin's program of having officials of the Department of State and Department of Commerce attend the G-2 course, however, dwindled and died during Ely's tenure. In 1924-25, the Department of Commerce ceased to participate, and six State Department officers attended only a few lectures and conferences. In 1925-26 two State Department officers were assigned to student committees but appeared only seldom. Apparently the other government departments lost interest when the G-2 course began to focus primarily on military intelligence and the "General Subjects" lecture program was cut back.[33]

In the tradition of Root and Bliss, General Ely was a proponent of stronger ties between the Army and Naval War Colleges. He was able to increase the number of naval officers in each class from three to six, and he maintained the Marine Corps quota at three. In 1927 he recommended that other service representation on each faculty be increased from one to two officers. He insisted to the War Department that the three Army War College graduates sent to take the Naval War College course each year be selected very carefully. They should not only desire the detail, but they should be from among "the ablest, most tactful, and more careful" group of officers. Finally, Ely saw great merit in the continued exchange of lecturers between the two institutions.[34]

In 1923-24 the two War Colleges began a continuing joint war game involving the defense of the Philippines. That first year only the G-2 Division of the faculty participated. The next year twenty members of the class were added to the player personnel, and in 1925-26 a majority of the class—forty-four students—was involved. By the latter year, the game play had progressed to the point that the ground situation on Luzon had stabilized, the Navy had gained sufficient superiority at sea to return to the western Pacific, and the problem had become one of landing American reinforcements on the island. Throughout the active play, communications between Newport and Washington Barracks were maintained by telegram. The two War Colleges were actually functioning as the war-gaming agency of the Joint Army and Navy Board. The war game was testing an early version of the Joint Board's War Plan Orange.[35]

In May of 1927 General Ely was able to provide his students with a rare opportunity to experience joint planning and operations when the United States Fleet held exercises off the New England coast. The Army War College provided the command and staff elements of an invading landing force assumed to be embarked with the fleet and, with the naval staff, planned the landing operations. Army War College personnel also supplemented the staff of the defending forces and the umpire staff. As noted earlier, the class continued the ground play of the exercise at Fort Adams, an Army coast artillery post at the entrance to Narragansett Bay.[36]

During his more than four years as Commandant, General Ely was assisted by a faculty numbering from thirteen to sixteen officers. After the 1923-24 academic year the entire faculty consisted of graduates of the post-1919 college, and all were included on the elite "general staff eligible list." The Assistant Commandant was the dean of the faculty. George Simonds was in his second year as Assistant Commandant when Ely arrived and in his fifth year at the college, having been a member of the Class of 1920 and then having served two years as an instructor. When Simonds left in the summer of 1924 to become commander of the Tank School at Camp Meade, Maryland, he was replaced by Herbert B. Crosby, of the Class of 1923, who had already served one year on the faculty. Crosby served two more years as Assistant Commandant, then was replaced in 1926 by Lytle Brown, who was not a graduate of the War College but, who, as Peyton March's Director of War Plans in 1918 and 1919, had been primarily responsible for devising the Army's initial postwar education system. Understandably, Ely believed that duty on his faculty had an importance "second to none in the Army." He urged that the Commandant be allowed "ample latitude" in faculty selection. He also recommended, if it could be administratively arranged, that the Commandant of the Command and General Staff School at Leavenworth be selected with the view of subsequent assignment as Commandant of the War College. That, of course, was the pattern that Ely himself had followed.[37]

General Ely also sought more influence in the selection of students. He recommended that the Commandant be allowed to scrutinize the list of tentative selectees and have the authority to eliminate those "not specially fitted" for War College work. Selection of students, whether "from the Regular Army, the National Guard or the Officer Reserve should be made with the most discriminating care and judgement." Ely believed that regardless of all other considerations," instructors and well-qualified graduates of the Command and General Staff School should "receive the preference over all others" for attendance at the War College. Ely was unable to change the selection process, however. The chiefs of the arms and services were not about to surrender that prerogative, even to an officer of Hanson Ely's reputation. The selection criteria during Ely's tour remained at the level McGlachlin had managed to obtain.[38]

The last class that General Ely saw graduate, that of 1927, consisted of sixty-nine Regular Army officers, one Reserve officer, six naval officers, and three Marines. Three of the Regular Army officers were from the Air Corps, and eleven were from the noncombatant arms. The Army War College was becoming less exclusively an institution for line officers. The ages of the Regular Army officers ranged from thirty-three to fifty-eight, the mean was forty-four. In length of service the range was from twelve to thirty-three years,with the mean twenty-two years. Only nine students in the Class of 1927 were not graduates of Leavenworth, but of those nine, four were graduates of the Army Industrial College. One student had attended both Leavenworth and the Industrial College. The tone of Hanson Ely's recommendations indicate, however, that he was still not entirely happy with the selection process for either his faculty or the student body.[39]

General Ely was Commandant from July 1923 to November 1927, directly influencing the education of five classes. Among his students was Walter S. Grant (1924), a future War College Commandant and commander in the Philippines in 1940. George V. Strong (1924) was the early war plans director for Chief of Staff George Marshall, and Adna R. Chaffee, Jr. (1925) was a pioneer of American armored forces. William D. Puleston (1925), a naval officer, became an authoritative biographer of

Mahan. Three officers among Ely's students would become associated with early American misfortunes during World War II. Naval officer Thomas C. Hart (1924) was commanding the Asiatic Fleet and Walter C. Short (1925) the Hawaiian Department on December 7, 1941. Lloyd R. Fredendall (1925) commanded II Corps at Kasserine Pass in 1943. Two officers would hold critical positions during the World War II mobilization—Brehon B. Somervell (1926) and Ben Lear (1926). Daniel I. Sultan (1926) commanded American forces in the China-Burma-India theater in 1944-45.[40]

The Question of Purpose

When Hanson Ely departed the War College, nine years had passed since the end of the Great War. Early in that period, in the winter of 1919-20, the postwar role of the Army was far from clear. But whatever its future role, Secretary Baker and Chief of Staff March, as well as General Pershing and his AEF lieutenants, were convinced that if any one thing needed to be done, it was to create a pool of highly trained staff officers. Baker and March then moved aggressively in that direction. Within nine months after the armistice an elaborate four-year program was in place to train staff officers, a program culminating in attendance at a senior college with a productive capacity three times that of its prewar counterpart. Baker and March may have moved too early; another year would pass before the outlines of America's postwar foreign and military policy would emerge.

With the rejection of the French guaranty and Versailles treaties in 1920, followed by the ratification of the three Hughes treaties of 1922, it became clear that United States foreign policy would rest on the principle of accepting no international security obligations. Concurrently, the Congress had deliberated upon military policy. The result was the National Defense Act of 1920. By mandating a military establishment of three components while at the same time rejecting compulsory military training, the Congress effectively discarded any policy calling for a force-in-being, whether in the form of a standing army or a trained citizen army. The frugality of the Harding and Coolidge administrations merely reinforced the policy (cynics might call it an absence of policy) established in 1920. Beyond garrisoning overseas possessions and manning harbor defense works, the Regular Army was engaged in two important activities. First, it was schooling itself and the two civilian components in the military art. Second, it was planning and preparing for the creation of another mass army if the need should again arise.

The need to prepare for the creation of another mass army was the stimulus behind the initial program of the General Staff College (Army War College). March and Baker saw the college as one means through which some future "Great Winter Crisis" might be avoided. Almost immediately, however, confusion had arisen as to purpose. William Haan, perhaps representative of the returning senior officers of the AEF and grimly aware of the AEF's actual performance, believed that a major purpose of the college was to train combat commanders. Since Chief of Staff March and General of the Armies Pershing evidently agreed, McAndrew and Harry Smith had to accommodate that additional mission. The war game, previously treated as a step in the mobilization planning process—the means of testing plans and determining requirements—became instead a primary method of developing commanders. McGlachlin continued and expanded this use of the war game, but at the same time, based on his more sophisticated view of what constituted fitness for high command, he broadened the program into areas beyond those concerned directly with field command.

The National Defense Act of 1920 was a major influence on the War College's programs. The dismantlement, with Pershing's encouragement, of General March's "Purchase, Storage and Traffic Division" and the designation of the Assistant Secretary of War rather than the General Staff as the central agency for industrial mobilization and materiel procurement eroded the War College's initial high interest in the problems of the "Great Winter Crisis." The birth and growth of the Army Industrial College was both an effect and a cause of the diminished interest. General Staff and War College work on mobilization became centered on manpower, not materiel, mobilization. Greater War College interest in the affairs of the corps areas was a natural outgrowth.

Implanted in the 1920 act by John McAuley Palmer and John J. Pershing was the requirement that graduation from the War College was a prerequisite for duty on the War Department General Staff. This mandate kept the War College intellectually tied to the War Department General Staff even though it had been organizationally separated. The Pershing staff reorganization that created the War Plans Division of the General Staff as an embryonic theater of operations GHQ, however, forced the War College to deal simultaneously with the problems of a field headquarters. Pershing's insistence, growing from concerns with economy, that the War College also take on the teaching of field army and army group operations further diverted War College interest toward field operations.

General Ely's problem on becoming Commandant was to balance the various demands—in fact his problem was to resolve the issue as to the very purpose of the War College. In the process of Ely's attempts, McAndrew's one great problem of preparation for war split into two segments: manpower mobilization planning, and theater of operations campaign planning. The more nebulous study of responsible command (Root's third "great problem") evolved into study of the operations of large tactical formations. McGlachlin's broad-vision approaches were all but discarded. Yet Ely could never wander too far from the immediate concerns of the War Department General Staff. By his own estimate, Ely was never quite successful in achieving the proper balance. He tinkered each year with the instruction on mobilization and the duties of the Assistant Secretary, and with the number and depth of war plans attempted and war games played. In his last year he still complained that the study of command needed reemphasis.[41] In a sense, all of Ely's four years were test years. It was Ely's successor who finally articulated the role of the War College in a way that brought an end to experimentation and set the War College on a bearing that remained relatively constant until World War II.

NOTES

1. McGlachlin to Adjutant General, 22 November 1921, AWC Files 1-1 to 1-81.
2. J. Chalmers Vinson, *The Parchment Peace: The United States Senate and the Washington Conference, 1921-1922* (Athens, Ga.: 1955).
3. Mark S. Watson, *Chief of Staff: Prewar Plans and Preparations* (Washington: Historical Division, Department of the Army, 1950), 16, in series *U.S. Army in World War II: The War Department*. John W. Killigrew, *The Impact of the Great Depression on the Army, 1929-1936* (Ph.D. Dissertation, University of Indiana, 1960), Chap. I:5-6.
4. McGlachlin to Chief of Staff, 26 July 1921, AWC File 1-1 to 1-81. AWC, "Chronicle, 1919/20-1930/31," 16-18. *Secretary of War Report: War Department Annual Reports, 1922*, I: 157-58.
5. Commandant to AG, 26 January 1922, AWC File 74-55. Commandant to Assistant Chief of Staff, G-3, 22 July 1922, Ibid. Letter, AG 210.63, 14 July 1922, Ibid. AG to Commandant, 1 August 1922, Ibid.
6. Letter, AG 210.63, 5 January 1922, Ibid. AWC, "Chronicle 1919/20-1930/31," 24.
7. AWC Course 1921-22, "Miscellaneous," Doc. 13; "Command," Doc. 12, 13. AWC Course 1922-23, "Command," Doc. 20; "G-4," Docs. 15-18.
8. Conn, *Historical Work*, 39, 47-48. AWC, "Chronicle 1919/20-1930/31," 23-50.
9. George S. Simonds, Jr., Outline of Course, AWC Course 1922-23, "Miscellaneous," Doc. 8. AWC, "Chronicle 1919/20-1930/31," 25. Edward L. King to General Ely, n.d., in Ibid., 28-37.
10. AWC Course 1922-23, "Course at the Army War College." AWC, "Chronicle 1919/20-1930/31," 25-26.
11. Ibid., 27. Among the G-2 lectures were, "Commercial Relations between States as Provocation of War," "Economic and Financial Base of War-Making Ability," and "Existing Economic Conditions in Europe," the last delivered by Secretary of Commerce Hoover. Former French Premier Georges Clemenceau also spoke to the class, AWC File 240-48. It is interesting that as Secretary of State in 1961, Herter initiated the exchange program whereby military officers would serve in the State Department and State Department officers would serve in the Department of Defense, Donald F. Bletz, *The Role of the Military Professional in U.S. Foreign Policy* (New York: Praeger, 1972), 113-14.
12. Stetson Conn, "The Army War College, 1899-1940: Mission, Purpose, Objectives" (unpublished manuscript), 8, copy in MHI Library.
13. AWC, "Chronicle 1919/20-1930/31," 21, 23. McGlachlin, address, AWC Course 1922-23, Vol. VI: "Command," pt. 2. 67th Cong., 2d sess., HR10871 in *Acts and Resolutions, December 5, 1921-September 22, 1922*, 29:410-11.
14. AG, Letter of Instructions to Board, 15 August 1922, in "Report of Board of Officers Appointed to Prepare Programs of Instruction for General and Special Service Schools," 1922, copy in MHI Library.
15. War Department Special Orders 175, 28 July 1922, par. 44. "Report of Board," 5.

16. AG, Letter, Program of Instruction for the General and Special Service Schools, 3 October 1922, par. 2, in "Report of Board."
17. *Army and Navy Journal* (3 February 1923): 556, and (31 March 1923): 749.
18. *Cullum's Register*, Vols. V and VI A.
19. Ely to McGlachlin, 29 March 1923, AWC File 1-82A and 1-82B. McGlachlin to AG, 2 April 1923, Ibid. Unsigned memo for Ely, 19 April 1923, Ibid. Parker to Commandant (Ely), Ibid. AWC, "Chronicle 1919/20-1930/31," 62-63. DeWitt to Chief of Staff, 19 October 1939, AWC File 93-12.
20. Ely to AG, 22 August 1924, 1st Indorsement to Letter, AG to Commandant, 16 August 1924, AWC File 1-82A, 1-82B.
21. "Report of Board," 10-11.
22. Industrial College of the Armed Forces, "The Industrial College of the Armed Forces, 1924-1949, Twenty-Fifth Anniversary" (Pamphlet, 25 February 1949), MHI Library. War Department General Order 7, 25 February 1924. *Secretary of War Report: War Department Annual Reports*, 1927, I:34.
23. AWC File 1-105, pars. 6-8.
24. Appropriations for War College operations for fiscal years 1923 through 1928 are included in annual appropriation acts reprinted in *Acts and Resolutions*, Vols. 29-34.
25. Ely to AG, 1st Indorsement, 22 August 1924, to letter, AG to Commandant, 16 August 1924, AWC File 1-82A, 1-82B.
26. Ibid. AWC Course 1923-24, Vol. V: "Command," Pt. 2, Docs. 48-66. AWC Course 1924-25, Vol. VII: "Command," Pt. 4, Docs. 69, 69A-H, 70, 70A-D.
27. Ely to AG, 10 July 1924, AWC File 1-82A, 1-82B. AWC File 1-105, par. 6. AWC Course 1924-25, Vol. VIII: "War Plans," Docs. 21, 23-33.
28. Ely to AG, 10 July 1924. AWC Course 1924-25, "Outline of Course," 18-19, 25, 38, 53, 59.
29. AWC Course 1925-26, Vol. VI: "Command," Pt. 4, Docs. 40A-G. Ibid., Vol. IX: "Mobilization." AWC Course 1926-27, Vol. I: "G-1," Pt. 1. Ibid., Vol. VI: "Command," Pt. 2, Docs. 25, 25A-C. AWC Course 1927-28, Vol. VIII: "War Plans," Pt. 2, Doc. 13. Ibid., Vol. VI: "Command," Pt. 2, Docs. 36, 39. AWC File 1-105, pars. 7-9.
30. AWC Course 1925-26, Vol. VII: "Coordination," Doc. 1. AWC Course 1926-27, Vol. IX: "Coordination," Doc. 1. Ibid., Vol. VIII: "Miscellaneous," Doc. 1. AWC File 1-105, pars. 7-9.
31. Conn, *Historical Work*, 55-58.
32. Ibid., 56-59.
33. AWC, "Chronicle 1919/20-1930/31," 62-63, 125, 161. Ely to AG, 11 July 1925, "Report of Operations, 1920-1940." Ely to AG, 15 July 1926, Ibid., Ely to AG, 1 July 1927, Ibid. DeWitt to Chief of Staff, 19 October 1939, AWC File 93-12.
34. Ely to AG, 1 July 1927, "Report of Operations, 1920-1940."
35. AWC Course 1925-26, Vol. VI: "Command," Pt. 3, December 26.
36. Ely to AG, 1 July 1927, "Report of Operations, 1920-1940." AWC Course 1926-27, Vol. VI: "Command," Pt. 2, Doc. 26.
37. "Administrative Staff, Faculty and Graduates, 1903-1938," AWC File 151-5. *Official Army Register, 1929. Cullum's Register,* Vol. VII. Ely to AG, 1 July 1927, "Report of Operations, 1920-1940."
38. Ibid.
39. Ibid. *Official Army Register, 1929.*
40. Chaffee's contributions are described admiringly in Mildred H. Gillie, *Forging the Thunderbolt: A History of the Development of the Armored Force* (Harrisburg: Military Service Publishing, 1947). Lear was Commanding General of Army Ground Forces replacing Lesley J. McNair in 1944. Somervell commanded Army Service Forces, 1942-46.
41. Lytle Brown, address, 2 September 1927, AWC Course 1927-28, "Lectures."

Preparation for and
Conduct of War
1928-1935

Major General William D. Connor, Corps of Engineers, replaced Hanson Ely as Commandant in November 1927 and began his third association with the War College. He had been one of William Wotherspoon's "temporary personnel" during the 1908-09 session, then had remained at Washington Barracks as Director of Civil Engineering at the collocated Engineer School until 1912, when he moved back to the War College. He was assistant director through 1916. On the faculty Connor was responsible for instruction in terrain appreciation and field engineering and was in charge of the practical exercise that required students to lay out the defense of the city of Washington. During those years he served under three presidents, William Crozier, Hunter Liggett, and Montgomery Macomb. He had known McAndrew as a student and then as a faculty colleague, and Ely as a student.[1]

Connor had graduated first in the Class of 1897 at West Point and had served in the Philippine Insurrection. In France he was Pershing's G-4 and also Haan's chief of staff and a brigade commander in the 32d Division. After Pershing's return to the United States, Connor commanded the residual American force in France with responsibility for the closing of American installations. Returning to the United States in early 1920, he served briefly as Commandant of the Engineer School and then spent a year as Assistant Chief of Staff, G-4, at the War Department. He was the first War College Commandant with postwar experience on the War Department General Staff. From 1923 through 1926 Connor was in China in command of American Army forces. When appointed Commandant of the War College, he had just completed eighteen months as commanding general of the 2d Division at Fort Sam Houston, Texas.[2]

Connor took command of the War College at a time when Americans could not have been less interested in things military or their Army. Indeed, what could be called a crusade to outlaw war had seized much of the nation; internationalists and isolationists both could agree upon this worthy goal. Two months before Connor arrived at the War College, the Assembly of the League of Nations passed unanimously a resolution declaring that war of aggression was an international crime. Before Connor completed his first year as Commandant, Coolidge's Secretary of State, Frank B. Kellogg, manipulated France into cosponsoring a multilateral treaty outlawing war as an instrument of national policy. Sixty-four nations eventually subscribed to the Kellogg-Briand Pact. Leaders of the peace movement hailed it as a diplomatic triumph. The Senate ratified the pact with but one dissenting vote, after first assuring itself that the Monroe Doctrine was not in jeopardy and that the United States was assuming no obligation to enforce the treaty. Despite the League's resolution and the outlawing of war, American Army officers continued to study the subject within their formal educational system.[3]

Pershing Reversed—In Part

All was not well within that system, however. Less than two years after Pershing's decision on the McGlachlin Board's findings, doubts were being raised as to the wisdom of his decision to reduce the Leavenworth schooling from two years to one. One year had proven to be insufficient time to teach all that was necessary regarding the operations of the reinforced brigade, the division, and the corps. This was particularly worrisome because understrength units and meager appropriations precluded large-scale exercises and maneuvers in which officers might practice their Leavenworth training. As War College Commandant, Hanson Ely had recommended against returning Leavenworth to a two-year course, primarily because the one-year course could produce a hundred more general staff offices each year. Ely conceded, however, that a two-year course had important advantages. Not only would graduates be more thoroughly trained, but since they would be fewer in number, all of them could be admitted to the hallowed "general staff eligible list," avoiding the severe morale problem among those who were denied selection. Moreover, Ely believed that the intense competition to do well at Leavenworth and thereby win selection to the important list had resulted in a situation in which "conformity to established doctrine amounts almost to religion."[4]

In December 1927 Chief of Staff Summerall reversed Pershing's decision of 1922. Beginning in academic year 1928-29 Leavenworth's Command and General Staff School program would be lengthened to two years. Summerall did not direct Leavenworth to reassume its earlier responsibility for instruction in field army operations, however. This task would remain at the War College. At the same time, Summerall authorized the Army Industrial College to enroll officers of the line branches in its 1928 course, and Industrial College students that year began to attend selected lectures at the War College. To a degree the War

College was relieved of the need to deal in depth with industrial mobilization.[5]

When the War Department directed Leavenworth to extend the length of its course, it also rewrote the official mission of the Army War College. The revised mission expanded the scope of the course and concurrently divided its activity into two categories, "to train" and "to instruct." It was implied that some senior officer duties required specific military skills. To acquire these skills *training* was necessary and appropriate. In this category of training fell "the conduct of field operations of the army and higher echelons [and] . . . joint operations of the army and the navy." But the new mission statement implied also that some senior officer duties required more than proficiency in specific military skills. They required insight and understanding. For these duties the War College could only provide instruction. In this category fell "War Department General Staff duties and those of the office of the Assistant Secretary of War." Also in the instruction category were two fields at times approached in previous War College programs but never before explicitly charged to the War College:

> to instruct in those political, economic and social matters which influence the conduct of war [and] . . . in the strategy, tactics, and logistics of large operations in past wars, with special reference to the World War.[6]

The restated mission gave belated sanction to the broader, more historically oriented program that McGlachlin had urged and attempted in 1922-23. But more than vindication of McGlachlin's philosophy was involved. Significantly, the War Department appears to have sensed that there was a distinction between training and education. For the conduct of field army and joint operations, doctrine and procedures could be learned through repeated practice. On the other hand, gaining insights from earlier campaigns, appreciating the political, economic, and social influences on war, and dealing with the complex problems faced by a capital staff could not be forced into the mold of a doctrine. In these areas the goal was more ambitious; it involved the intellect, the development of understanding, judgment, and analytical thought. In other words, it called for education.[7]

General Connor received his revised instructions in December 1927, a month after becoming Commandant. Accompanying the mission was an admonition to emphasize the conduct of field operations. The 1927-28 program devised by Ely was already in progress when Connor arrived, and he wisely attempted no immediate alterations. The opportunity to participate in fleet exercises did not present itself that year, and lack of travel funds precluded conducting the "command" or "strategical" reconnaissance in New England. Connor had to be content with a recon-

211

naissance nearer Washington. Rather than testing a war plan, the purpose of the reconnaissance was "to appreciate such features of the terrain as affect the operations of a landing in force on the Atlantic Coast in the area contiguous to Delaware and Chesapeake Bays" and then "to appreciate the terrain in the area generally west and south of the Allegheny Mountains between Washington and New York City." During the reconnaissance Connor dispersed the class from Fort Monroe to Fort Monmouth, New Jersey, and from Harper's Ferry through Carlisle, Pennsylvania, to Newark.[8]

While the Class of 1928 was in session, Connor and his Assistant Commandant, Lytle Brown, solicited from their faculty ideas as to how best to meet the requirements of the new mission. Of the varied concepts they received, Connor and Brown seem to have been most influenced by the views of Troup Miller, a G-3 instructor, and Walter C. Sweeney, the head of the G-1 division of the faculty. Miller provided a succinct and well-reasoned analysis of the curriculum since 1919. He concluded that war planning had come to dominate the course at the expense of the coverage of both field operations and command. Sweeney pointed out that all the past rhetoric about "command versus staff" and "operations" tended to obscure the fundamental problem facing the War College. That problem, as Sweeney saw it, was that the War College had two related but nonetheless distinct fields of interest. One field was the preparation for war; the other was the conduct of war. Colonel Sweeney must have consulted his Clausewitz. The translation of *vom Krieg* held by the War College library affirmed that "the activities belonging to War divide themselves into two principal classes, into such as are only 'preparation for War' and into the '*War itself.*' This division must also be made in theory."[9]

The Program of William Connor

After further faculty discussions Connor concluded that the War College program not only had to be rational, it also had to be described in a way that its rationality was apparent to students, faculty, and the controlling War Department General Staff. In March, Connor gave his instructions as to what would occur the next year. The course would be divided into two distinct phases, "Preparation for War" and "Conduct of War." The number of faculty divisions would be reduced from seven to four. The Command, Assistant Secretary of War, and War Plans divisions would be abolished. Only the G-1, G-2, G-3, and G-4 divisions would remain. In Connor's view the French-based American staff was an eminently sound system. When it functioned properly, every activity associated with the preparation for and conduct of war was performed somewhere within the staff.[10]

Connor had no qualms about eliminating the course labelled "Command." In educating a general staff officer, he believed that he was at the same time providing the education necessary to qualify an officer for higher command. The difference between the commander and the staff officer in Connor's view, was not a question of education, but of "temperament" and "natural qualities." There was nothing original in Connor's view. McAndrew had expressed similar thoughts in 1919, as had Tasker Bliss more colorfully a quarter-century earlier when he wrote, "Those things that differentiate a Napoleon from other generals cannot be acquired in any school . . . else Napoleons would be as thick in history as apple blossoms in a New England spring." Bliss, McAndrew, and Connor all implied that providing the American Army with competent leadership was as much a matter of accurate selection as of proper education.[11]

As scheduled for the Class of 1929, "Preparation for War" instruction began in September and lasted into February. During the four months before Christmas, a month was devoted to each of the "G-staff" sections in the order G-3, G-1, G-4, G-2. In each staff area the approach was basically the same. The class was divided into committees, and each committee was presented with a different problem. Through research and discussion the committee would arrive at its solution, which it would then record in the format of a "Staff Study." Subsequently each committee would present its problem and solution to the assembled class, answering questions and defending conclusions. The faculty criticized and commented upon the staff studies but did not offer "approved" solutions.[12]

During the period that the committees were researching and deliberating, they also attended lectures presented by the faculty and guests relating to the staff area being studied. The problems assigned the committees were appropriate for solution at the level of the War Department General Staff or the corps area headquarters, the two echelons responsible for mobilization planning. Industrial mobilization problems of the Assistant Secretary of War were included among those of the G-4. Staff operations at the field army and army group levels were not taken up during the "Preparation for War" phase. Armies and army groups were not active in peacetime and therefore had no role in preparation for war.[13]

The "Preparation for War" phase culminated in a six-week period immediately after Christmas during which the class prepared war plans. The faculty presented the class with three hypothetical situations, two demanding the full resources of the United States. The class was then divided into six general staff groups; of these, two groups were assigned to each situation, one to draw up the United States war plan, the other to draw up the plan of the opposing force. A seventh general staff group was organized to continue joint war-gaming with the Naval War College.

By 1929 War Plan Orange had progressed to the point that an opposed amphibious operation to recapture Luzon was under consideration.[14]

In February, after the war plans had been drafted, the class began the "Conduct of War" phase, which lasted until the end of the school year in June. During this phase the class conducted four two-sided map maneuvers, one two-sided command post exercise, and the strategic reconnaissance. During Connor's years as Commandant, through 1932, this phase varied little. The map maneuvers, all based on student war plans, dealt with situations calling for the defense of the Chesapeake and Delaware bays area, the defense of Puget Sound, and a campaign in the Allegheny Mountains, as well as the Luzon problem. The command post exercise was held at Fort DuPont, Delaware, and was an extension of the Chesapeake-Delaware map maneuver. Participating with the War College in the command post exercise were the faculty and students of the Air Corps Tactical School at Langley Field, Virginia, the Signal Corps School at Fort Monmouth, New Jersey, and the Quartermaster School at Philadelphia. The reconnaissance was held either in the Delaware Bay area or in New England, depending upon the availability of funds.[15]

The practice that Connor introduced of dividing the War College program into the two phases, "Preparation for War" and "Conduct of War," proved enduring. It lasted through five more commandants, until classes were suspended in 1940. Connor introduced another innovation that proved lasting and that was expanded under later regimes: a course called "Analytical Studies." Initially introduced in the year 1928-29 as "Historical Studies," this course was designed to meet the obligation to instruct in the "strategy, tactics, and logistics of large operations in past wars." Included within the Conduct of War phase, the course required each student group to make two histroical analyses. Campaigns assigned for investigation included three from earlier American military history—operations in Mexico in 1846-47, operations of the Army of the Potomac in 1864, and Sherman's Atlanta Campaign. One study dealt with the 1904-05 Russo-Japanese War. The remaining campaigns were from the World War and included German and French operations through the First Battle of the Marne, Tannenberg, Gallipoli, the operations of the French Fourth and Tenth Armies and the British Fourth Army in the summer of 1918, and, finally, the concentration and operations of the American First Army in the Meuse-Argonne.[16]

For the 1929-30 program the college redesignated "Historical Studies" as "Analytical Studies." Connor's change in label indicates the difficulty he was having in pulling from the students exactly what he wanted. He insisted to the class, "You must know the facts . . . facts which must be sought in a comparison of the details of many operations . . . from an analytical treatment of historical examples." Connor demanded that the students answer from their analyses questions on force ratios, how many men and weapons were required to defend a sector of specific size and configuration, and how many days and hours were needed to concentrate, move, and deploy corps and divisions. He cautioned them that "facetious anecdotes and interesting narratives do not answer these questions." Connor fully recognized that there were intangibles in war, but these he believed could be reduced to a minimum by determining through historical analyses those things that were tangible. In 1930-31, though still included within the Conduct of War phase, additional analytical studies were introduced to provide a logical link between the Preparation for War and the Conduct of War phases. Connor's idea was to have the students determine just how successful war offices and supreme commanders had been historically in actually executing the war plans drawn up prior to hostilities. But the Commandant was not interested in narrative history. His engineer's mind was taking him close to what in later years would become known as operations research.[17]

Whether the object was narrative history or operations research, the Historical Section of the War College was in a position to make a major contribution to the Analytical Studies program. When Connor became Commandant he was aware of criticism of the section to the effect that officers untrained as historians were writing history before all the data were available. He therefore invited civilian historians of reputation to act as an "Advisory Board on Historical Work." With the board's assistance, the section revised the program for producing monographs. This time the monographs would be supported by parallel volumes of documents from official sources and constitute "a complete and accurate account of the U.S. Land Forces in the World War." The Adjutant General, still jealously guarding his custodianship of Army records, was opposed to the program and, unhappily, the Historical Section was again in trouble. It had incurred the wrath of the General of the Armies by publishing a volume by Major Julian F. Barnes titled *The Genesis of the First Army.*[18]

Public reviews of *Genesis* emphasized Pershing's triumph over the French in the wartime struggle to activate an autonomous American Army. When the reviews hit the street, Pershing happened to be in Paris for the funeral of Marshal Foch. He was embarrassed and infuriated despite having reviewed the work before its publication. *Genesis* was immediately recalled and suppressed. As a result of the incident, Chief of Staff Summerall directed that henceforth no manuscript of any kind on the World War would be published without prior submission and approval by Pershing and the Chief of Staff. Summerall's decision virtually killed the new monograph program. The major task of the Historical Section became one of preparing the Army's World War records for publication.[19] Pershing's anger was misdirected and Summerall's censor-

ship decision shortsighted. The two senior gentlemen contributed neither to Connor's Analytical Studies program nor to the understanding
of a younger generation of officers of American military participation in
the World War.

In 1930-31 the college modified the purely historical flavor of the Analytical Studies program when it included two studies of a combat-
developments nature. One dealt with the organization and administration of a theater of operations and the other with the type of plans and
orders needed to launch a joint overseas expedition.

Adding "Analytical Studies" to the War College program did not end
the requirement for each student to submit an Individual General Staff
Memorandum. The schedule allowed from September to April for preparation of these papers, but no exclusive time was set aside for the work.
Connor's guidance was for students to deal with "live issues" and "contribute something of value to the betterment of the army." By introducing the Analytical Studies program and continuing the requirement for
an Individual General Staff Memorandum, Connor brought student research to a higher level than it had previously attained. Time for research remained limited, however, particularly during the Conduct of
War phase when research was competing with the traditional applicatory method.[20]

That part of the revised mission dealing with the political, social, and
economic influences on the conduct of war proved to be more difficult to
handle than the historical studies. Lieutenant Colonel John R. Brewer
had the task of lecturing on these influences. He used an "elements of
national power" approach, including as political influences a nation's
form of government, policies, and relationships between the chief executive and the military leadership. Economic influences Brewer saw as the
availability of raw materials, manufacturers, labor, capital, electric
power and communications, and transportation. Social factors he listed
were race, nationalism, religion, patriotism, and "level of civilization."
Brewer's approach was a reasonable start, but the elements of national
power were not explored in any depth.[21]

The G-2 Course carried much of this other-than-military instruction.
General Connor lent a personal hand, lecturing on "Some Aspects of the
Foreign Policies of the United States." Drawing from the work of American diplomatic historians, he concluded that there were four policies
that guided the foreign relations of the United States—avoidance of entangling alliances, maintenance of neutral rights, the Monroe Doctrine
and its corollaries, and expansion. He interpreted the policy of expansion as resulting from a need or desire for "acquisition and control of
routes of communication." Except for the policy of avoiding alliances,
Connor argued that these policies could lead the United States into war.
Both the G-2 Course and the War Plans Course made greater use of

lecturers from outside the Army, either historians or political scientists who were specialists on world regions of interest. Distinguished journalists as well as officials from the Department of State also lectured. The Class of 1929 heard five such lecturers, while the Class of 1932 heard ten.[22]

The G-2 Course in fact began to take on aspects of a course in international relations, though this does not seem to have been Connor's conscious intent. This subtle shift, taken together with the analytical investigation of national planning for past wars, can be seen now as a move toward the study of national policy and its related military strategy, however. It apparently was not recognized as such then, as the faculty made little attempt to emphasize the relationship between national and military strategy. But the more perceptive members of the faculty and student body may have begun to recognize a military interest in the ends as well as in the means of policy. They may have realized that as implementators of policy, commanders and staff officers at high levels might have a legitimate interest in the formulation of policy.

During the 1928-29 school year General Connor decided that another study of the higher military schools in Europe might be useful. He proposed to the War Department that he be authorized to make the trip and offered to do so at his own expense if the War Department would pay the expenses of his aide-de-camp, who was a linguist, and pay for any official entertaining that might be required. The War Department was too poor to support the aide, but Captain Leon Dessez took the trip either at his own expense or at Connor's. General Connor was abroad from the end of June to the middle of September 1929, visiting England, France, and Germany. He did not confine his investigations entirely to military education but looked into staff systems as well as such contemporary fields as aviation, mechanization, and motorization. The War Department had asked him also to seek information on German procedures for artillery support.[23]

Connor evidenced the greatest interest in the British College of Imperial Defence and the French Centre des Hautes Etudes. Although the American War College touched on some of the work being done at the College of Imperial Defence, Connor found his War College more comparable to French institutions, since the staff systems of the French and American armies were the same. He found that the French school did not emphasize general staff work, but it did provide strategic and grand tactical training to senior officers and thus its course was not unlike the Conduct of War phase of the War College. Whatever Connor learned abroad did not result in major change at the Army War College. In France, General Maxime Weygand had explained to Connor a five-month preparatory course provided to the French officers who were prospective students. Connor toyed with the idea of presenting a similar

217

two-month preparatory course covering the employment of heavy artillery and air forces, to be conducted at Camp Bragg, North Carolina, and Langley Field, Virginia, but in the end he settled for lectures on those two subjects. Connor returned happy with what the United States Army was doing: "All in all, I came back home with a greater feeling of satisfaction with our course at the Army War College than I had when I left. All things considered the Army War College is serving the nation and the service better than any of the institutions that I inquired into abroad would serve them."[24]

In addition to the problem of familiarizing his students with heavy artillery and air forces, Connor also was faced with the problem of having his students consider mechanized forces and their employment. In early 1929, as the result of studies and an experiment with independent mechanized forces held the previous year at Fort Meade, Maryland, the War Department directed that mechanized forces be included in the exercises of the War College. Since the United States Army as yet had no organization or doctrine for mechanized forces (nor did foreign armies), the faculty prepared a document entitled "Mission and Composition of a Mechanized Force." Connor forwarded this paper to the War Department, stating that if no better ideas were forthcoming the War College would base its instruction on its own document.[25] The War College, however, did not become an active participant in the growing debate over mechanized forces. Mechanized forces, as directed, were included in its problems and exercises, but the War College was neither proponent nor opponent of the theories of J. F. C. Fuller, Basil Liddell Hart, and their American disciples.

William Connor's years of stewardship of the Army War College were productive for the United States Army and stabilizing for the institution. Connor's typical student had participated in the writing of four staff studies having something to do with preparation for war, had attempted historical analyses of two past campaigns, and had contributed to the drafting of a hypothetical war plan. He had been involved in three month-long map maneuvers or war games, a command post exercise, and a strategic reconnaissance. He had individually prepared a study on a "live issue" for the "betterment of the army." And he had heard numerous lectures on a variety of subjects delivered by senior generals, War Department General Staff officers, the faculty, his classmates, and experts from outside the Army.

Connor left the War College to become superintendent of the Military Academy on April 30, 1932, just as advancing technology, depression, and arms limitation were becoming influences with which the Army would have to cope. Like Hanson Ely before him, Connor had the opportunity to influence five classes. Among his students were officers who would serve in positions of great responsibility during World War II, including Dwight D. Eisenhower (1928), Lesley J. McNair (1929), Roy S. Geiger, USMC (1929), Joseph T. McNarney (1930), and Thomas Holcomb, USMC (1930). Five of his students would actually command field armies in campaigns: William H. Simpson (1928), Simon B. Buckner (1929), Robert L. Eichelberger (1930), Alexander Patch (1932), and George S. Patton, Jr. (1932).[26]

The Army, the War College, and the Great Depression

The Army of the United States and the military policy as called for by the National Defense Act of 1920 had not been richly endowed by the Congresses of the Harding-Coolidge years. Nonetheless, the Army had been able to maintain its three components and to give some substance to the policy. As the decade following the World War drew to a close, however, several influences were coming together that raised serious question as to the 1920 policy. An economic theory approaching dogma, shared by Republican and Democrat alike, demanded that federal expenditures not exceed revenues. The Budget and Accounting Act of 1921, specifying a single appropriation for the military activities of the War Department and requiring a Budget Officer in the War Department, had strengthened the authority of the Chief of Staff relative to the bureau chiefs, and at the same time had provided greater visibility of how Army resources were being applied. Advancing technologies in motorization, mechanization, radio communications, and particularly in aviation were suggesting a need for revised operational doctrines and for reequipment of the Army. Items from the World War were becoming obsolete, and some stocks were becoming depleted. Finally, in the spirit of Versailles, the Hughes Pacts, and Kellogg-Briand, significant and vocal segments of American opinion insisted that security be sought through diplomatic agreement and multilateral arms limitation, not through military preparedness.

In the summer of 1929 the new President, Herbert Hoover, gathered together the civilian and military leadership of the War Department at his Rapidan retreat in the Blue Ridge Mountains of Virginia. Hoover ordered a thorough reconsideration of the Army's program. His obvious objective was to reduce the cost of the military establishment. Upon his return to Washington from the mountains, Chief of Staff Summerall charged the chief of the War Plans Division, Major General George S. Simonds (AWC 1920), with guiding the reconsideration. Surveying the War Department General Staff and the major field commanders, Simonds found little indication of a desire to abandon the military policy of the 1920 Defense Act. Douglas MacArthur, commander in the Philippines, suggested withdrawing Army forces from China, but Stuart Heintzelman (AWC 1920) at Leavenworth approached closer to the heart of the problem. To Heintzelman the Army clearly was attempting too many programs with too few dollars. It could not continue that way. The War Department must ask for a restatement of mission and policy. But more typical was the response of the Chief of Field Artillery and the Chief of the Air Corps. The artilleryman called for a ten-year program to motorize the artillery and to replace its ordnance. The aviator wanted to scrap the last year of the five-year aviation program established in 1926 and substitute a more ambitious and more expensive program.[27]

The War College, probably because Connor was abroad during these deliberations, confined its remarks to its own operations and a few minor cost-saving measures it might take. Five days after his return from Europe, Connor submitted the War College response. Citing the important positions in the Army occupied by War College graduates, Connor nonetheless recommended that the size of the class be reduced. In the efficiency reports he had rendered on the Class of 1929, twenty-three students had been considered less than "excellent." Obviously they should not have attended the War College. Implied in Connor's response was the opinion that there were a limited number of officers in the Army capable of War College work, and that number was being exceeded by the number of students selected.[28]

Simonds completed the survey and submitted his report on November 1st. By that time Wall Street had experienced its first traumatic shocks. The Great Depression, though not yet recognized as such, had begun. Federal revenues were falling, and the budget for fiscal year 1930 was already in deficit. The Simonds Report, after offering a brief strategic survey that did not claim any immediate threat to the nation's security, and after castigating the Bureau of the Budget for making changes in the War Department's program without consultation with the department, offered two plans. Plan I called for an increase in expenditures to fully support the obligations of the 1920 Act. Plan II was less ambitious. It called for a Regular Army of 14,000 officers and 165,000 enlisted men, a National Guard of 250,000, and an Officer Reserve Corps of 116,000. It would cost from $438 million to $500 million per year over a ten-year period. The trade-off between Plan I and Plan II was a longer time to mobilize and greater risk while mobilizing. Simonds warned that if the Army received less support than that called for by Plan II, then a radical revision of military policy, essentially a return to the 1916 posture, would be necessary.[29]

The Secretary of War was Patrick J. Hurley, who in early December had moved up from the position of Assistant Secretary. He and the Chief of Staff supported Simonds' conclusions. Hurley's objective in the estimates for fiscal year 1932 was to "stabilize" Army appropriations for military activities at about a third of a billion dollars, less than the Plan II level. To Hurley "stabilization" meant obtaining for the War Department a fixed budgetary ceiling and the authority to make resource decisions within that ceiling. To facilitate making these decisions, Hurley directed that research and development projects be arranged in priority and that "research and development" be treated separately from "rearmament and reequipment." When Douglas MacArthur became Chief of Staff in November 1930, he created a "General Council" chaired by the deputy chief of staff and consisting of the five assistant chiefs of staff, the executive officer to the Assistant Secretary of War, and, when matters of interest to them were being considered, the chiefs of the arms and services and the chief of the Militia Bureau. The War College Commandant was also included. The General Council was to be a body superior to the Budget Advisory Committee chaired by the G-4. The new procedures and organization brought into much clearer focus the issues of expenditures for operations as opposed to materiel, and for research and development as opposed to procurement.[30]

During the summer and fall of 1930, the War Department was faced not only with making its fiscal year 1932 estimates, but with new demands from Hoover to reduce fiscal year 1931 expenditures, the budget again having fallen into deficit. In May 1931 the President had to reconvene the War Department leadership at the Rapidan retreat, together with a congressional delegation. Hoover wanted the Army to reduce its personnel strength and the number of posts it maintained. The Army was willing to give up posts, but it was not willing to reduce its strength. The mobilization capability had to be protected. Soon after the second Rapidan conference adjourned, the War Department announced that fifty-three posts would be closed. MacArthur then disestablished the experimental mechanized force that had been activated at Fort Eustis, Virginia, only the previous fall. Later the strengths of the headquarters of the corps areas were ordered reduced by fifteen percent. The Army had remained loyal to the 1920 Defense Act and the mobilization policy it prescribed. An air force in being and modernization were secondary to maintaining the mobilization base.[31]

While MacArthur and his staff were struggling to preserve a structure that would give some meaning to the military policy of the 1920 Defense Act, events in the Far East should have raised questions as to whether this policy, even if fully supported, was adequate. In September 1931 the Japanese Kwantung Army, exploiting the so-called "Mukden Incident," began to expand its already considerable control in Manchuria. The United States responded with the "Stimson Policy" of nonrecognition of territorial change accomplished by force. In January 1932 Japanese marines, attacking from the International Settlement in Shanghai, launched what appears now to have been a punitive expedition against Chinese forces in the environs of the city. The United States dispatched the 31st Infantry from the Philippines to Shanghai to protect its citizens. It was May before Japanese forces were withdrawn.[32]

The Hoover administration continued to seek international peace through arms limitations. The Washington Treaty of 1922 had established capital ship ratios for naval forces. An effort to extend the ratio concept to other than capital ships failed in 1927, but a second effort in 1930 resulted in the London Naval Conference. Concurrently, within the League of Nations negotiations went forward to attempt an arms limitation conference that would include land forces. In February 1932, the delegations of thirty-one nations, including that of the United States, assembled in Geneva for the "Conference on the Reduction and Limitations of Armaments."

When it became apparent that the negotiations were bogging down, President Hoover proposed that each nation reduce by one-third the strength of its Army that was over and above that required for internal security. He also proposed that all tanks, large mobile guns, bombers, and chemical and bacteriological weapons be abolished. Bombardment from the air would be prohibited. How much faith Hoover had in this conference, and how optimistic he was in having his proposals accepted, cannot be demonstrated. If his proposals had been accepted, however, Hoover would have made a major advance toward solving the problem of his War Department's budget.[33] Even having such proposals under negotiation discouraged support of the established military policy.

Though Connor had left the War College in the spring of 1932, his replacement did not arrive until the following summer. He was George S. Simonds (AWC 1920), formerly an Assistant Commandant and chief of the War Plans Division of the War Department General Staff, a veteran of the Hoover budget battles, and, at the moment, the military advisor to the American delegation at the arms limitations conference in Geneva. General Simonds' problems at the War College would prove to be as much financial as academic. Appropriations for the military activities of the War Department were less in fiscal year 1933 than they had been in any year since 1923. But the New Dealers who came to Washington in the spring of 1933 were no more inclined to spend money on an army than had been the Hoover administration. The new Secretary of War, former Governor of Utah George P. Dern, supported Chief of Staff MacArthur, but he was not of the inner New Deal circles and had little real influence. The issue between the War Department and the administration and the Congress, however, was not merely one of total appropriations, but also of where cuts should be made. The War Department understandably sought to control those decisions.[34]

Critical to the citizen-army concept underlying the 1920 Defense Act was an overstrength Regular Army officer corps (overstrength in the sense that it should be larger than that required to man the Regular Army's force structure), large enough to operate the school system and to provide assistance to the reserve components and the ROTC. This officer overstrength was a favorite target of the economizers. In 1932 the House had passed a bill requiring a reduction of 2,000 Regular Army officers. In the War Department's view this reduction of some seventeen percent would have resulted in either a drastic cutback in the school system or a severe crippling of the Regular Army's ability to support the reserve components. Representative Ross Collins, Democrat from Mississippi, supported by John Nance Garner, Speaker of the House and future Vice President, challenged the basic concept of a citizen army. Collins had become a convert to the thinking of the British writer, Basil H. Liddell Hart. He opined that "defense of this country lies in the utilization of science and warfare by a comparatively small army of experts." The "air power" enthusiasts, as well as those in the Army who had little confidence in the National Guard or Organized Reserves, were not unsympathetic to Collins' view. To MacArthur's great relief, Collins' bill failed in the Senate.[35]

MacArthur could not rest easy, however. In April 1933 the new President announced that he was considering a plan to furlough on half pay 3,000 to 4,000 officers, an action which would have reduced the Army almost to caretaker status. MacArthur and Dern argued hard against the proposal, and Roosevelt backed off. Rather than MacArthur's objections, it may have been a cherished New Deal scheme that actually saved the officer corps. That scheme was the Civilian Conservation Corps. In May, Roosevelt ordered the Army to enroll 274,000 unemployed men and by July 1 establish them in work camps. Three thousand Regular Army officers were assigned directly to the project. They processed and moved more men to camps than had been moved during the comparable period of the World War I mobilization. The Army paid a price, however. The War Department had to reduce the number of Regular officers on reserve component duty from 1,600 to 700. It canceled ROTC camps that summer. It also reduced by half the number of officers attending schools. The CCC was undermining the National Defense Act of 1920. The War College was not affected, however; its students apparently were not needed or were too senior to administer company-size camps in remote regions of the United States.[36]

Roosevelt's original plan, if he had a plan at all, was to reduce Army appropriations by $90 million. MacArthur fought back hard. He gained an audience with the President and threatened to resign and to make his opposition public. By MacArthur's own account, during the audience he approached insubordination, and when it was over he threw up on the White House steps. Roosevelt cut fiscal year 1934 War Department proposals by only $45 million, but that still represented a reduction from fiscal year 1933 of $65 million. MacArthur and Dern were unable, however, to prevent Congress from including both active and retired officer pay in the provisions of the Economy Act of 1933, which required reductions in pay of up to fifteen percent. Throughout the budget process MacArthur clashed continually with the Director of the Budget, Louis Douglas, a misfit within the New Deal who insisted upon a balanced budget. Without consulting the War Department, Douglas reduced National Guard and Organized Reserve drills from forty-eight to twelve per year. The National Guard Association took up this matter directly with FDR, who restored the forty-eight drills, a result in accord with MacArthur's support of the citizen-army concept. But the War Department—and Douglas MacArthur—no longer appeared to be masters of their own house. Despite budgetary restrictions, Dern and MacArthur held to their priority, Secretary Dern insisting that "the Army school system . . . will continue."[37]

It appeared for a time that money for Army modernization might be forthcoming from the relief agencies of the New Deal. The Public Works Administration (PWA) directed by Secretary of the Interior Harold Ickes allocated $54 million in September 1933 to the War Department for construction and rehabilitation of facilities. The War Department had requested $135 million. In October 1933 the PWA allocated $10 million for Army mechanization and motorization and $7.5 million for aircraft. The Secretary of War had expected $170 million. In all, the Army received $72.2 million in 1933 PWA appropriations, much less than the General Staff's estimated requirement of $304 million. Particularly aggravating was the practice whereby Ickes, not Dern or MacArthur, specified the projects on which the money would be spent. In defense of Ickes it must be said that his job was to put men to work, not to rearm America. He favored labor-intensive projects.[38]

The New Deal programs provided other sources of money. In July 1933, $2.5 million was allocated to government arsenals under National Recovery Administration (NRA) authority for the manufacture of munitions. Pacifist groups deplored the action. The next year (and each year through 1937) the NRA appropriations bill forbade expenditure for such purposes. The War College, as well as other installations, gained from the largesse of the Federal Emergency Relief Administration. The Army received through the Civil Works Administration $1.12 million. With its share of this work-in-kind, the War College accomplished a long list of repair and maintenance projects, including renovation of faculty quarters, installation of an Officers' Mess in the basement of the main building, and connection with the District of Columbia sewer system.[39]

Otherwise the War College took its budget cuts along with the rest of the Army. Simonds' 1933 budget was fifteen percent less than Connor's last budget. By 1935 he was operating with only seventy-three percent of the appropriations Connor had enjoyed. In neither of his first two years was Simonds able to find the funds for both a command post exercise and a strategic reconnaissance. The Class of 1933 participated in the Delaware Bay command post exercise but made no reconnaissance. The Class of 1934 conducted the reconnaissance but held no command post exercise. The Historical Section had enjoyed something of a renaissance under Connor, but its staff was severely slashed as Simonds economized. The participation of reserve component officers in the G-1, G-2, and G-3 courses lessened as money grew tight. It ceased entirely after the 1932-33 school year.[40]

A limiting budget was not the only external influence that affected Simonds' direction of the War College program. While in Geneva, Simonds had observed Adolph Hitler become Chancellor of Germany and begin his attack on the Versailles system, ending German payment of war reparations. In 1933 both Japan and Germany withdrew from the League of Nations. Japan withdrew in March after a mild rebuke by the international body because of the Manchurian conquest. Germany withdrew in October after failing to win equality at the Geneva Arms Limitation Conference. By 1934 Hitler had established himself as dictator of Germany, and in March he announced that Germany would rearm. That same year Japan announced that it would not renew the Five Power Naval Treaty.

Concurrently with Hitler's rise to power in Germany, isolationism began to take center stage in the United States. The first Neutrality Act was passed in 1935. That same year the Senate defeated a proposal that the United States seek membership in the World Court. In the Western Hemisphere, Roosevelt continued the policy of his Republican predecessor of nonintervention in Latin America, announcing in his inaugural address the Good Neighbor Policy. In August 1933 he withdrew the Marines from Haiti, and in March 1934 Congress repealed the Platt Amendment, which had limited the sovereignty of Cuba. Reflecting the foreign policy approach of Roosevelt and of the Congress, War Department planners began to view passive defense of the continental United States and its possessions as the only acceptable and possible military strategy.[41] Not surprisingly, the War Department view began to influence the deliberations in the committee rooms of the Army War College.

The Simonds Years

At the War College, General Simonds continued Connor's scheme of dividing the year into "Preparation for War" and "Conduct of War" phases. As might be expected from his experience as War Plans Division chief, Simonds gave the greater emphasis to Preparation for War. In his first year he added two weeks to the War Plans Course in order to address mobilization planning as conducted by the chiefs of the arms and services and by the corps area commanders. For his second year, 1933-34, he reestablished a faculty War Plans division in which he included the Air Corps and Navy faculty members. Also that year Simonds took the significant step of having the students consider in the War Plans Course a problem involving coalition warfare, hypothesizing a situation in which the United States would align itself with Great Britain, China, and the Soviet Union against Japan.[42]

The heavy emphasis that General Simonds gave to the Preparation for War Phase, specifically to war planning, was not solely a personal preference. Douglas MacArthur, upon becoming Chief of Staff in November 1930, began to question the basic concepts of previous mobilization planning. He believed that the six field armies to be activated upon mobilization should be at least partially active in peacetime. He also wanted a mobile force of moderate size to be available in an emergency earlier than the contemplated mass army could be produced. Moreover, the mobilization of the mobile force should not have to await enactment of legislation. Finally, in MacArthur's opinion, mobilization should be geared to a war plan, and mobilization plans should be flexible enough to support any of the various color-coded war plans. Throughout the latter half of 1931, the War Department General Staff, with Simonds as head of the War Plans Division, worked in great secrecy to produce new plans reflecting MacArthur's concepts. In August 1932 MacArthur announced his "Four Army Plan." By then, Simonds was at the War College.[43]

MacArthur's scheme called for the activation of a GHQ, with the Chief of Staff assuming command of the field forces. In peacetime four of the nine corps area commanders and their staffs would act concurrently as field army headquarters; their responsibilities would include war and mobilization planning and general supervision of the training necessitated by their plans. The scheme called for an initial mobilization two months in duration that would include the Regular Army and the National Guard augmented by voluntary enlistments. The scope of a subsequent mobilization would depend upon the situation; it might require conscription.

In August 1933, a year after the first announcement, MacArthur approved "War Department Mobilization Plan, 1933," which called for an "Immediate Readiness Force" and mobilization within six months of four million men, to be prepared for combat within a year. To equip the first million men, the General Staff devised a six-year program covering the years 1934 through 1940. It included both research and development and a program to rearm and reequip the Army. As part of the six-year program, MacArthur approved in November 1933 a "Policy for Mechanization and Motorization." By September 1934 priorities were established for research and development.[44]

The reoriented and intensified planning of the MacArthur years (1930-35) had a direct and significant effect upon the War College course as administered by General Simonds. Adapting a scheme similar to that in vogue when he was on the faculty of Edward McGlachlin and Hanson Ely, Simonds divided the War Plans Course of 1934-35 into an "Informative Period" and a "Formulation of War Plans Period." Using MacArthur's Four Army Plan as the basic document, student committees during the Informative Period studied and critiqued the current war and mobilization plans of both the War Department and the corps areas. They learned war-planning procedures and studied the military geography of critical areas of the United States. As individuals they made detailed map studies of the Canal Zone, the Hawaiian Islands, and the Philippines. In committee they studied the organization of a theater of operations, then applied this knowledge to seven hypothetical theaters. Theaters assigned included northern Mexico, four within the continental United States, one in the western Pacific, and, for the first time, a European theater of operations. For Europe the assumption was that the United States, allied with Britain, France, and Italy, would face a German, Austrian, Hungarian, and Yugoslav coalition (termed the "Nazi Coalition").[45]

Divided into four groups, the class took up "Formulation of War Plans." Three of the situations presented were hardly new at the War College. They included Green (Mexico), Orange (Japan), and Red Coalition (Britain allied with Mexico, Canada, and Japan in an attack against the United States and its possessions). An entirely new situation called for a campaign against the Nazi Coalition. The student committee that was assigned this problem, however, was not required to go beyond the selection of a theater of operations, recommendations as to command arrangements for coalition warfare, and the drafting of instructions to the American force commander.

It was mid-April before the class completed the Preparation for War phase. With two weeks then set aside for the students to finish their Individual General Staff Memoranda, the class did not enter the Conduct of War phase until early May. The three months that Connor had devoted to Conduct of War Simonds had reduced by over half.[46] Indeed, Simonds not only cut back the time that had been devoted to map maneuvers or war games during the Connor regime, he also altered the method of instruction. Instead of two-sided, free-play map maneuvers, the faculty used "map problems" in which a student staff solved an initial operational situation and was then presented with subsequent situations and requirements developed by the faculty. As an experiment, the Class of 1933 conducted three types of map problems. The first type called for large student groups and required the solution of operational problems in considerable detail. The second type called for smaller groups but required less detail. Finally, the faculty drafted problems for students to solve individually. After 1933 the individual problems were eliminated. In shifting from map maneuvers to map problems, some of the dynamics of battle may have been lost, but the students (and probably the faculty) had found the earlier map maneuvers "monotonous," and the new method permitted greater faculty control in bringing out in less time the desired teaching points.[47]

General Simonds continued the "Analytical Studies" program, each student participating in two, a month being devoted to each. The historical flavor of the studies was retained. But whereas McGlachlin had turned to history in a search for principles and Connor had sought to mine operational data from history, Simonds wanted his students to discover trends. He required them to investigate operational episodes of two different periods to see if they could not detect continuities in technological development, doctrine, and method that could be projected into the near future. In addition, Simonds was not averse to having his students take on studies that the War Department General Staff needed. At the request of the War Department G-3, a special committee in the fall of 1934 conducted a study entitled "Modernization of the Army." With faculty comments added, the college forwarded this study to the General Staff.[48]

Simonds continued the requirement for Individual General Staff Memoranda. Because this program apparently had been a distraction from committee work, however, a separate two-week period, as mentioned earlier, was set aside for it in the spring. During this two weeks students were not required to be present at the War College. In 1932-33 the students chose their subjects from a list provided by the War Department General Staff. After that year the faculty, after discussion with the General Staff, assigned each student a subject. Two students, who were not to consult with each other, were assigned each topic so that solutions might be compared.[49]

The 1934-35 school year was to a degree unusual. As part of the General Staff planning for MacArthur's Four Army Plan, a GHQ command post exercise was held at Fort Monmouth, New Jersey, during late August and early September 1934. The Class of 1935 reported to the War College earlier than usual, in August, and spent several weeks wargaming the coming exercise and in other ways preparing themselves to act as assistant umpires to General Simonds, the designated chief umpire. The start of the actual War College course was thereby delayed. The lost time was made up by reducing the assigned number of Analytical Studies.[50]

Under Simonds the lecture program began to take on something of a new dimension. Previously students attended the lectures and were provided the opportunity to question the lecturers, basically a very passive learning procedure. In an effort to enliven the question period and have the students better understand what they were hearing, Simonds directed that selected readings be assigned to each student (not all students were given the same selections) prior to a lecture. The required reading had the side effect of expanding student understanding, particularly in those nonmilitary areas addressed by authorities from universities, industry, and government agencies. Undoubtedly it expanded the understanding of the members of the faculty also—they had to select the readings. In a restricted sense, the War College was beginning to offer courses as opposed to merely lectures on nonmilitary topics.[51]

The Historical Section of the War College suffered major setbacks during the budget-cutting years. Once the furor over publication of *Genesis of the First Army* had abated, the section led a life free of major controversy and had resigned itself to the major task of preparing the Army's World War records for eventual publication. General Connor's introduction of the historically inclined "Analytical Studies" course at least in theory had given the section a role in direct support of the War College curriculum. When General Simonds became Commandant, the manpower situation of the section was the best it had been since the war. Twenty-eight officers, twenty-three warrant officers and enlisted men, and twenty-three civilians were assigned to the section. Also, missions had been clarified. The Historical Section was to establish the facts of America's military history, and the General Staff, the service schools, military students, and historians were to make the deductions from those facts. The Adjutant General was to preserve the original evidence. General Simonds, however, was either unwilling or unable to protect the Historical Section from the reductions in his budget. By 1935 the section's staff had been sliced to eight officers and eight civilians. Oliver Spaulding returned that year to assume once again the leadership of the section, but by then the War College was taking little notice of its Historical Section.[52]

In January 1935 George Simonds left the War College to become MacArthur's Deputy Chief of Staff. He was replaced by Malin Craig, a graduate of both the 1910 and 1920 courses. Craig brought back the staff rides over Civil War battlefields that he himself had experienced a quarter-century before. Only now, instead of riding horses, the students rode Greyhound busses. The class studied twelve Civil War campaigns or battles with designated students making presentations at various points during the trip on the strategy and tactics that had been used. Craig spent almost $10,000 on the excursion but assured the poverty-stricken War Department that "the results obtained were most distinctly worth the time and expense involved."[53] No other type of field exercise was held.

Among the students of Simonds and Craig were a number of officers who in later years would hold positions of prominence. During World War II Jacob L. Devers (1933) and Omar Bradley (1934) would command army groups. Courtney Hodges (1934) would command First

Army. After the war, of course, Bradley would serve as Army Chief of Staff and, during the Korean War, as Chairman of the Joint Chiefs of Staff. Jonathan M. Wainwright (1934) had the unhappy task of surrendering American troops in the Philippines in 1942. Lewis B. Hershey (1934) would direct the selective service system through three wars. In the Pacific theater, William F. Halsey (1934) would become an Admiral of the Fleet and George C. Kenney (1933) would lead the Fifth Air Force. John R. Hodge (1935) would command the American military occupation of Korea after World War II.

NOTES

1. *Cullum's Register*, Vol. VIA. AWC Course 1912-1913, Vol. IV:129. AWC Course 1915-1916, Vol. 62, Pt. 5.
2. *Cullum's Register*, Vol. VIA, VII.
3. This interpretation is from Robert H. Ferrell, *Peace in Their Time: The Origins of the Kellogg-Briand Pact* (New York: Norton, 1952).
4. AG to Commandant, 24 September 1925, forwarding "A Study Relative to Length of Course at General Service Schools" and 1st Indorsement, Ely to AG, 6 November 1925, File 74-50.
5. AG to Commandant, 22 December 1967, Ibid. *Secretary of War Report: War Department Annual Reports, 1928*, I:55.
6. AG to Commandant, 22 December 1967, File 74-50. Army Regulation 350-5, Change 5, 30 January 1931, par. 3f(1).
7. For discussion of distinction between military training and military education see Bletz, *Military Professional*, 133-34; also R. L. Gidding, "The Neglected Task of Officer Education," Air University Quarterly (July-August 1965): 51-59.
8. AWC Course 1927-28, Vol. VI, Pt. 2, Docs. 36 and 39.
9. Troup Miller to Assistant Commandant, 20 February 1928, File 1-82A. W. C. Sweeney to Assistant Commandant, 27 February 1928, Ibid. Carl von Clausewitz, *On War*, translated by Col. J. J. Graham, new revised ed., with introduction and notes by Col. F. N. Maude, 3 Vols. (London: Kegan Paul, Trench, Truber & Co., 1908), I:84.
10. W. D. Connor, Directive for the Course, 1 March 1928, File 1-82A.
11. John L. DeWitt, Orientation, 4 September 1928, AWC Course 1928-29, "Lectures." McAndrew, Address, n.d. File 24-A-23. Report of Brig. Gen. Bliss, 11 November 1903, 90.
12. AWC Course 1928-29, Vol. I: "G-1," Vol. II: "G-2," Vol. III: "G-3," Pt. 2: "Committees," Vol. IV: "G-4."
13. Ibid.
14. Commandant to AG, 30 June 1929, "Report of Operations, 1920-1940," Report for 1928-29.
15. AWC Course 1928-29, Vol. V: "Conduct of War." AWC File 1-105, pars. 10-13.
16. AWC File 1-105, pars. 10-21. AWC Course 1928-29, Vol. V: "Conduct of War."
17. AWC File 1-105, pars. 11-12. AWC Course 1930-31, Vol. V: "Analytical Studies," Doc. 1A.
18. Conn, *Historical Work*, 60-63.
19. Ibid., 62-63, 64-65, 68-69. "History of Historical Section," R. S. Thomas, comp., 3.
20. AWC Course 1930-31, Vol. V: "Analytical Studies," Doc. 1A. File 1-105, par. 12.
21. AWC Course 1928-29, Vol. VII: "War Plans," Doc. 6.
22. Connor remarked that his lecture was "in accordance with the policy of having the instructors take a somewhat more active part in the work of the College." Historians cited by Connor include Justin Smith, James Rippy, Arthur Schlesinger, Charles Beard, John Foster, Carl Fish, and John Latane, AWC Course 1928-1929, Vol. II: "G-2," Doc. 15. AWC Course 1928-29, "Lectures." AWC Course 1931-32, "Lectures."
23. Connor to AG, 10 November 1928, File 241-64. Connor to AG, 29 November 1929, Ibid. Connor, "Notes on European Trip, 1929," Ibid.

24. Connor, "Notes on Trip." Connor to AG, 7 April 1930, (not sent). File 1-83.
25. R. M. Ogorkiewicz, *Armoured Forces: A History of Armoured Forces and their Vehicles* (New York: Arco, 1970), 86-87, 188. War Department, "Report of a Board on Mechanized Force, 1928," copy in File 84-20. "G-3 Study on Mechanization, 1928," copy in File 84-17. Connor to AG, 12 March 1930, forwarding AWC, "Mission and Composition of a Mechanized Force," File 84-26.
26. McNair would command Army Ground Forces and McNarney, an Air Corps officer, would be Marshall's Deputy Chief of Staff and later military governor of the American zone of occupied Germany. Holcomb would be Commandant of the Marine Corps, and Geiger would command Fleet Marine Forces in the Pacific.
27. Killigrew, *Impact of Depression*, Chap. II, 1-15, 18. Watson, *Prewar Plans*, 23-24. War Department, "Report of the Survey of the Military Establishment by the War Department General Staff, 1 November 1929," copy in File 12-20.
28. Connor to AG, 20 September 1929, File 12-20.
29. Killigrew, *Impact of Depression*, Chap. II, 18-28. War Department, "Report of Survey, 1929." Marvin A. Kreidberg and Merton G. Henry, *History of Military Mobilization in the United States Army, 1775-1945* (Washington: Department of the Army, 1955), 437, 460-61, 551.
30. Killigrew, *Impact of Depression*, Chap. III, 1-4, 18-24. Watson, *Prewar Plans*, 38-39. *Chief of Staff Report: War Department Annual Reports, 1931*, 70-72. Dorris C. James, *The Years of MacArthur, Vol. I: 1880-1941* (Boston: Houghton Mifflin, 1970), 366-67.
31. Killigrew, *Impact of Depression*, Chap. III, 9-12, Chap. IV, 9-21. Ogorkiewicz, *Armoured Forces*, 188.
32. Christopher Thorne, *The Limits of Foreign Policy: The West, the League, and the Far Eastern Crisis of 1931-1933* (New York: Capricorn, 1973). James, *MacArthur*, I:374-75.
33. Sir John W. Wheeler-Bennett, *The Pipe Dream of Peace: The Story of the Collapse of Disarmament* (New York: H. Fertig, 1971), 11, 40-41.
34. Appropriations for military activities, as requested by the War Department, allowed by the Bureau of the Budget, and approved by the Congress, are displayed in Killigrew, *Impact of Depression*, App. I. James, *MacArthur*, I:362. Killigrew, Chap. X, 2-8.
35. Ibid., Chap. V, 5-23. James, *MacArthur*, I:356-62.
36. Killigrew, *Impact of Depression*, Chap. X, 8-14, Chap. XII, 18-27. Kreidberg and Henry, *Mobilization*, 461-63. James, *MacArthur*, I:417-27.
37. Killigrew, *Impact of Depression*, Chap. X, 9-25 (Quotation of Dern cited on 16). James, *MacArthur*, I:425, 427-29.
38. Killigrew, *Impact of Depression*, Chap. XI, 1-31. James, *MacArthur*, I:430-31. Kreidberg and Henry, *Mobilization*, 451.
39. Ibid., 453. Watson, *Prewar Plans*, 34. James, *MacArthur*, I:431. AWC, "Chronicle of the Army War College, 1899-1946," Vol. III, Chap. XXXII.
40. Appropriations for War College operations for fiscal years 1932 through 1935 are included in War Department annual appropriation acts reprinted in *Acts and Resolutions*, Vols. 37-40. File 1-105, pars. 14-15. E. H. Humphrey, General Orientation, 10 September 1934, AWC Course 1934-35, Vol. VII: "Miscellaneous," Doc. 1. Conn, *Historical Work*, 70-71. AWC, "Report of Operations, 1920-1940," Reports of 1932-33 and 1933-34.
41. Watson, *Prewar Plans*, 87-88. Stetson Conn and Byron Fairchild, *The Framework of Hemispheric Defense* (Washington: Office of the Chief of Military History, Department of the Army, 1960), 3-4, in series *U.S. Army in World War II: The Western Hemisphere*.
42. File 1-105, pars. 14-16. Leon B. Kromer, General Orientation, 1 September 1932, AWC Course 1932-33, Vol. VIII: "Miscellaneous," Doc. 1. Meeting of 3 May 1933, "Minutes of Faculty Meetings," File 241-50. AWC Course 1933-34, Vol. VII: "War Plans," Doc. 14.
43. Kriedberg and Henry, *Mobilization*, 424-26. Killigrew, *Impact of Depression*, Chap. VIII, 7-20. James, *MacArthur*, I:367-68. Meeting of 9 December 1932, "Minutes of Faculty Meetings," File 241-50. "Development of Four Army Organizations," File 52-60.

44. Ibid. Kreidberg and Henry, *Mobilization*, 426-49. James, *MacArthur*, I:367-68. Kent R. Greenfield, Robert R. Palmer, and Bert I. Wiley, *The Organization of Ground Combat Troops* (Washington: Historical Division, Department of the Army, 1947), 3-5, in series *U.S. Army in World War II: The Army Ground Forces*.
45. File 1-105, par. 16. AWC Course 1934-35, Vol. VIII: "War Plans," Pt. 1, Docs. 1, 4-6, 8. Ibid., Pt. 2, Doc. 16.
46. Ibid., Doc. 22. File 1-105, par. 16.
47. File 1-105, pars. 14-15. AWC Course 1932-33, Vol. VI: "Conduct of War," Doc. 1. AWC Course 1934-35, Vol. V: "Conduct of War," Pt. 2.
48. File 1-105, pars. 14-16. AWC Course 1933-34, Vol. V: "Conduct of War (Analytical Studies)," Pt. 1. AWC Course 1934-35, Report of Special Committee: Modernization of the Army, 19 November 1934.
49. File 1-105, pars. 14-16. AWC Course 1934-35, Vol. VI: "Individual General Staff Memorandum Period."
50. File 1-105, par. 16.
51. Ibid. George Grunert, Lecture, AWC Course 1934-35, Vol. II: "G-2," Pt. 2, Doc. 1.
52. Conn, *Historical Work*, 68-72, 77.
53. AWC Course 1934-35, "Conduct of War Course: Field Exercise, Civil War." Grunert to Assistant Commandant, Report on the AWC Field Exercise, FY 1935, File 6-1935-12. Craig to AG, Report of 1934-35, AWC "Report of Operations 1920-1940."

Toward Rainbow
1935-1940

Malin Craig was the first of four commandants to direct the work of the five War College classes in session between 1935 and 1940. He served as Commandant for less than a year. In October 1935 he replaced Douglas MacArthur as Chief of Staff. After Craig's departure, Colonel Walter S. Grant (AWC 1924), the Assistant Commandant, acted as head of the college for the remainder of the 1935-36 year, was then promoted to brigadier general, and served as Commandant for the 1936-37 year. In the summer of 1937 Grant was replaced by Major General John L. DeWitt (AWC 1920) who supervised the work of the classes of 1938 and 1939 but departed in the fall of 1939. Brigadier General Philip B. Peyton (AWC 1931), like Joseph Kuhn in 1917, was left with the task of graduating the last prewar class and closing the classrooms.

The relatively short tenures of the last four commandants before America began its mobilization in 1940 may explain in part why no truly fundamental changes were made in the War College program after the departure of General Simonds. A more significant reason, however, is that during these five years the War Department General Staff was attempting, in what seems to have been almost desperation, to reconcile the eroded mobilization base with the ever more threatening international situation. The struggles at the War Department with the problems of mobilization planning, modernization, rearmament, and, toward the end of the period, with a revision in national strategy all affected the Army War College. The commandants and their faculties were in a race to keep up. In their efforts to remain relevant and current, they made numerous adjustments to the program, but their changes were essentially piecemeal and patchwork. The period of stability that the Army and its education system had enjoyed since passage of the 1920 Defense Act was over.

The influence of Malin Craig on the Army War College came not from his brief tour of duty as Commandant but rather from the four years that followed when he was Chief of Staff. In his career Craig had commanded a corps area and an overseas department. He was a former Chief of Cavalry and G-3 of the War Department General Staff. He was the first Chief of Staff of the Army to have taken every step on the educational ladder designed by William Harding Carter at the turn of the century and so elaborately reestablished by Peyton March after the World War. As Chief of Staff he was an evangelist of realistic planning. Over the next four years he had the War Department revise most of the planning accomplished during the MacArthur period and supervised the early stages of rearmament. General Simonds had reoriented the War College program to follow MacArthur's concepts. Much of what Simonds had put in place would have to be redone.[1]

In Search of Neutrality

General Craig's outlook as Chief of Staff can be interpreted as either realistic or pessimistic. If the latter is the more accurate, Craig had a great deal to be pessimistic about. The inability of Franklin Roosevelt's first two administrations to overcome the enduring Depression; the breakdown of the international system based on Versailles, the Nine Power Treaty, and Kellogg-Briand; and the growing movement to seek American security through neutrality and isolation all buffeted upon Craig's Army. Only a month before Craig became Chief of Staff, Roosevelt signed into law the Neutrality Act of 1935, and on October 3, 1935, the day after Craig took office, Mussolini invaded Ethiopia.

In February 1936 Congress extended the Neutrality Act to be effective through May 1937. The next month Hitler ordered the German Army into the Rhineland. In July civil war broke out in Spain. By joint resolution in January 1937 Congress placed an arms embargo on all parties to that conflict. In August Mr. Roosevelt declared, "I hate war. I have passed unnumbered hours . . . planning how war may be kept from this nation." The plans to which FDR devoted those unnumbered hours apparently did not include any for a major strengthening of the Army. Although Congress appropriated for fiscal year 1936 sufficient funds to permit the War Department to attain the goal of an Army of 165,000 men, sought since the Simonds' survey of 1929, the Commander-in-Chief allotted funds for only 158,000.[2]

In May 1937 Congress passed the third Neutrality Act, continuing the arms embargo but giving the President discretionary authority to permit trade with belligerents in other materials on a "cash and carry" basis. The already gravely wounded Versailles system received further blows the next year when German troops moved unopposed into Austria in March and, with French and British compliance at Munich, into the Sudetenland region of Czechoslovakia in October. Then in March

1939, in direct violation of the Munich agreement, Hitler dismembered the remainder of Czechoslovakia.[3]

Command, Mobilization, and Combat Developments

After becoming Chief of Staff in 1935, General Craig found in the mobilization plans of Douglas MacArthur a "lack of realism." The assessment was accurate. Despite MacArthur's vigorous and not entirely unsuccessful efforts to protect the mobilization base from the fiscal conservatism of the Hoover administration, the anti-military inclinations of the New Deal, and the isolationist attitude of the Congress, the base had eroded to such a condition that the early large mobilization contemplated in MacArthur's plans was infeasible. Moreover, the dynamic international situation called for a new national strategy, but that new strategy by all outward signs appeared to be a deeper retreat into isolation. Military policy and war planning would have to be adjusted.[4]

MacArthur's plans had called for a decentralized mobilization that put major responsibilities on the staffs of the corps area commanders, four of whom were to act concurrently as field army commanders. By 1933 it had become apparent, however, that the headquarters of those commands contained too few trained staff officers to competently perform mobilization planning. Since 1927 responsibility for training officers for the corps area staffs had rested at Leavenworth, to be supplemented by instruction at the War College. The physical plant at Leavenworth was limited, however, and during the Depression years the War Department saw little prospect of expanding it. The only available means to increase Leavenworth's production was to have it return once again to a one-year course, thereby doubling its annual output of trained staff officers. Beginning with the 1935-36 school year, the Command and General Staff School reverted to a one-year program. As a result the War College in the future would receive less-thoroughly prepared students. The War College would also have to present some of the instruction that could no longer be provided at Leavenworth. Moreover, beginning with the school year 1935-36, the War Department increased from seventy-five to ninety the number of Army officers in each class.[5]

With the Class of 1937 the War College began to teach those aspects of the organization, functions, operations, and tactics of the field army and group of armies previously taught at Leavenworth. Some thought was given to having prospective students study these matters individually before reporting to the War College, but Commandant Grant made the firm decision that "the principle heretofore prevailing that no work, prior to the date of reporting should be required . . . will be adhered to."[6]

General Grant elected to label the instruction he was to provide on large-unit operations as "command." The classes of 1937 and 1938 devoted three and a half weeks immediately after their arrival to a "Preliminary Command Course." In 1938-39 General DeWitt incorporated the Preliminary Command Course into the Conduct of War phase presented later in the year. He then reconstituted the Command Course that Connor (with DeWitt as his Assistant Commandant) had eliminated in 1929. The new Command Course consumed four and a half weeks. To allow time for this field army and army group instruction, the college scheduled only one theater-of-operations map problem and eliminated the two weeks dedicated to the preparation of the Individual General Staff Memorandum. Henceforth the students had to meet that requirement during whatever time they could make available.[7]

And a Course on Mobilization

Chief of Staff Craig's early doubts as to the feasibility of MacArthur's 1933 mobilization plan reached the point of decision in late 1936. Craig directed that funds be shifted from research and development to the acquisition of materiel, and in December he directed that work begin on a "Protective Mobilization Plan." The plan, if executed, would immediately mobilize the Regular Army and the National Guard as a covering force ("Initial Protective Force") for the defense of the United States. The plan was announced to subordinate commanders in February 1937 and its troop basis approved in April. By midsummer of the next year, 1938, the plan was essentially complete, and in December General Craig formally approved "Protective Mobilization Plan—1939." It had been two years in preparation.[8]

With a new concept for mobilization and with plans under almost frantic revision at the War Department, it was difficult for the War College to keep current its treatment of mobilization. The course on this subject that had been so carefully constructed by General Simonds to support MacArthur's plans was completely disrupted. The faculty tried to keep the Class of 1937 up-to-date, and it had the Class of 1939 study the fragments and drafts of Craig's Protective Mobilization Plan as they became available. For the 1938-39 year, Commandant DeWitt decided to reinstitute the Mobilization Course that General Connor had abandoned in 1929. DeWitt's organizational change may have lent emphasis to mobilization, but it did not represent any major change in the substance of the instruction.[9]

The War Department's plans for mobilization were built around a trained nucleus of Regular, National Guard, and Reserve officers and units. The plans depended upon the Army's ability to acquire and train manpower rapidly, and its ability to procure and receive materiel. Planning materiel procurement for a mobilization was the responsibility of the Assistant Secretary of War, not the Chief of Staff. But the Assistant Secretary's plans had to be based on requirements calculated by the

General Staff. Requirements in turn were based not only on how many units the General Staff planned to mobilize, but on how those units were to be organized and equipped. Decisions on how to organize and equip units are the end product of the combat-developments process; they are also expressions of more fundamental decisions—on how units are to fight and at what level of technology.

In the late 1930s the General Staff had a severe intellectual problem. Much of the technology that was hardly beyond the stage of promise at the end of the World War had been incorporated into significant capabilities fifteen years later. If mobilization planning was to go forward, far-sighted decisions had to be made in the areas of aviation, mechanization, motorization, communications, and chemical warfare, and in anti-aircraft and anti-tank weapons and methods. With inadequate funds for research and development, field testing, and pilot production, making these decisions was extremely difficult.[10]

In the pre-World War II American Army, combat developments was not a formal process; indeed, the term was not yet coined. It was within the branch schools and at the War Department in the offices of the chiefs of the arms and technical services that most combat-development work was performed. Coordination among these elements varied from nonexistent to sporadic, and the War Department General Staff was not in the habit of forcing resolution of combat-developments issues. At the Army War College, activity in combat developments had been minor, confined essentially to issues assigned student committees as part of their "preparation for war" studies. But this does not mean that the War College had been unaware of or uninterested in new combat methods and advancing technology.

"Aeronautics," for example, had been the subject of a Wotherspoon lecture as early as 1906. In the 1920s the military application of aviation had been a frequent subject of committee investigation as well as lecture. Before his court-martial for insubordination in 1925, General William Mitchell had discussed his theories of airpower with the Class of 1922. The college had studied and criticized the analyses and findings of various boards appointed to deal with the use of air forces—the "Lassiter Board" of 1923, the "Drum Board" of 1933, and the "Baker Board" of 1934. The impact of mechanization and motorization also was featured in all courses from 1928 forward. The debate as to whether a mechanized force should be established independent of the traditional arms went on in the War College committee rooms as it did elsewhere. A student committee in 1932, for example, considered that question. It found MacArthur's decision to have the individual arms develop mechanization within their traditional missions to be sound. The committee report was signed by its chairman, a major of cavalry, George S. Patton, Jr.[11]

By the mid-1930s however, the War Department General Staff was

237

beginning to take more interest in combat developments, particularly with regard to combined-arms formations. And the General Staff began to call upon the War College to assist in the research effort. In 1935-36, at the direction of the War Department, a student committee conducted a study seeking improved organization of the infantry division and of the echelons above the division. The next year, the War Department having accepted a new concept of a smaller triangular division for field test, it directed the college to conduct a study of the proper organization of the corps and the field army consisting of the smaller divisions. Concurrently another committee studied the cavalry division to determine if it too should be organized in the triangular mode. In its last prewar year, 1939-40, again at War Department direction, student committees conducted studies leading to revision of the doctrinal *Field Service Regulations.*[12]

General Staff Work

The Assistant Chief of Staff, G-3, tasked the War College in 1935-36 with reviewing and critiquing the maneuvers and command post exercises held the previous year. By 1937-38 the command post exercise conducted at the War College no longer had as its primary purpose the training of student officers as commanders and staff officers, but rather the purpose of refining the techniques so that the command post exercise would better serve the training of higher staffs. The Class of 1939 produced a manual covering the conduct of command post exercises and maneuvers by field armies and higher units. The Class of 1940 prepared detailed plans for the summer maneuvers of Third Army.[13]

It was not only the War Plans Division and the G-3 Division of the War Department General Staff that turned to the War College for assistance in the increasingly busy late 1930s. In 1937-38 the Assistant Chief of Staff, G-2, requested War College committees to study and report on the Army's foreign language translation capability and its military attache system, and to develop an index guide for use by attaches in information collection. The next year the G-2 asked for a study on the collection of military information by nonmilitary personnel.[14]

Although the War College had been organizationally severed from the General Staff since 1919, as World War II approached the College became increasingly involved in the actual work of the War Department General Staff. It was reverting to the adjunct of the General Staff that Elihu Root and Tasker Bliss had once envisioned.

Foreign Relations and New Strategy

By the mid-1930s the War College also began to take an increased interest in the changing international situation. In 1935 Commandant Craig introduced a program initially called "Current Events" and later

"Foreign News." Neither title really described what Craig had in mind. Placed under the direction of the G-2 Division of the faculty, the program divided the class into five groups and asigned to each group a number of nations of the world, not including the United States. A group's task was to keep itself informed on events and trends within the assigned nations, analyze each nation's actions in the context of its longer-term interests and policies, and identify conflicts of interest with other nations. The ultimate question to be addressed was how other nations' actions, policies, interests, and conflicts influenced the security of the United States. Periodically each student group would brief the entire class on its conclusions—in not more than fifteen minutes. From September through March these briefings were held twice a week.[15]

In February 1936 the War Department (at whose instigation is not clear) queried the War College as to the desirability of introducing a course in foreign relations. Colonel Grant, the Acting Commandant, did not encourage the idea. Taking inventory, he found that the college program included four lectures on foreign relations, seven lectures, during the G-2 Course, that were partially on foreign relations, and five committee problems on foreign relations. Adding "Foreign News" to this inventory, Grant concluded that he was already presenting a foreign relations course. But "Foreign News" was not a popular program with the students. Many thought it a bother and felt that they were perfectly capable of analyzing international events without their classmates' assistance. Perhaps because the current Chief of Staff had introduced the program while Commandant, it was not dropped; but in 1936-37 it was reduced to four months. The Class of 1940 had to endure it for only a month.[16]

As Colonel Grant had pointed out, the "Foreign News" program, which was eventually termed "Current News of International Affairs," was not the only effort the War College made to have its students better understand the dynamics of the international scene. In 1936 Professor H. P. Willis of Columbia University lectured on "Economic and Financial Causes of War," and Harold Sprout, a future distinguished historian of the American Navy, addressed "Some Aspects of the Neutrality Problem." That same year, Analytical Studies topics included "National, Economic and Military Objectives in War." In 1937-38, at the request of the War Department, a special committee of the Class of 1938 studied the Spanish Civil War—its causes, the effects of external assistance, and its military lessons. Another Analytical Studies issue was "Overseas Possessions and their Influence on the Strategic Position of the Mother Country." Analytical Studies committees of the Class of 1940 investigated the "Influence of Seapower on the Causes and Conduct of War" and the "Influence of Public Opinion on the Conduct of War." In 1940 four Foreign Service officers (the first since 1926) joined the class for the G-2 Course. Indeed, Colonel Grant's point that he offered the equivalent of a course in foreign relations, had some validity, but the college's effort was rather loosely constructed and without any clearly defined overall objective.[17]

The same international unrest that lay behind the college's awakening interest in foreign affairs stimulated consideration of strategic alternatives. Until the late 1930s, reflecting both the strength of the nation's isolationist thrust and General Craig's realistic appraisal of the state of the mobilization base, the War Department had tacitly accepted a military strategy limited to the passive defense of the United States and its overseas possessions. As noted earlier, General Simonds had begun to require detailed individual map studies of the Canal Zone, Panama, and the Philippines. In 1936 Alaska was added to the list. In 1937 a special committee was formed to study the land, water, and air transportation systems of the United States and "their peace and war organization for defensive war on the continental United States."[18]

But in March 1937, four months before the incident at the Marco Polo Bridge outside Peking that began the Sino-Japanese War, the Joint Army and Navy Board began reconsideration of the 1928 War Plan Orange, the plan that the Army and Naval War Colleges together had so conscientiously war-gamed throughout the 1920s. At the Army War College in the spring of 1937, during the Formulation of War Plans Course, the faculty again assigned the Orange situation to a student group and for the second time presented a European problem. For the latter problem, Germany, Italy, Austria, and Hungary were assumed to be aligned against France, the Soviet Union, Czechoslovakia, and Rumania. Britain and the United States, initially neutral, were assumed to enter the conflict only after a German invasion of Czechoslovakia. The remaining planning groups addressed the usual Plan Green and plans involving the defense of the continental United States against various coalitions. The unwritten message in this breakout of assignments appears to have been that the strategic options were to fight overseas with allies or to fight at home alone.[19]

Increased interest in a strategy more dynamic than continental defense became evident in 1938. The War College changed its studies of American overseas possessions from individual to group efforts that year and had the military geography of Brazil and Argentina investigated with the same thoroughness. The war plans assigned the class were the same as those of the year before except that the European problem was dropped (perhaps reflecting the neutrality legislation) and in its place a situation was introduced that called for a major overseas expedition in the Western Hemisphere, termed Plan Purple. Moreover, at levels above the War College planners were stirring. In February 1938 the Joint Army and Navy Board approved a revised Plan Orange. On the initiative of the State Department, a Standing Liaison Committee came into being in April 1938 to coordinate the military and naval arms with diplomatic policy.[20] It was the Sudetenland crisis of the fall of 1938, however, that appears to have been the true catalyst to revised strategic thinking.

Reflecting State Department concern that Hitler or Mussolini might attempt to exploit the situation of ethnic groups in South America, as Hitler had that of the Sudeten Germans in Czechoslovakia, Deputy Chief of Staff George Marshall directed the War College to determine the force required to protect Brazil from German and Italian machinations. Marshall stressed to Commandant John L. DeWitt that the task was urgent and must be done in the utmost secrecy. Within ten weeks a special War College committee produced a plan for a rapidly deployable Hemispheric Defense Force of 112,000. The college submitted the results of its study to the War Department at the end of March 1939. Early in May 1939 the Joint Board began exploratory study of what was to result in the "Rainbow" series of plans with which the United States entered the Second World War. Fundamental to each of the five Rainbow plans was an aggressive defense of the Western Hemisphere. Rainbow marked the end of acceptance of a passive continental defense strategy. The War College had contributed to its demise.[21]

Last Days of the Historical Section

As the clouds of war gathered in the late 1930s, the War College's Historical Section seems to have been rediscovered. In 1937 the section received 2,100 official and unofficial requests for information. In 1938, over the objections of the Adjutant General, *Genesis* was republished and made public. Interest in what had occurred from 1917 through 1919 was becoming more widespread as expectations of a new war sharpened. Once mobilization began in 1940, the Historical Section was deluged with inquiries. But by that time the War College had suspended classes and the Historical Section, perhaps gladly, was essentially on its own. It remained so until 1947 when it became the World War I Branch of the Historical Division of the War Department Special Staff. This new Historical Division, under the direction of a general officer, had been created in 1945.[22]

The Final Distractions

The threatening international environment finally forced the nation to take some tentative steps toward rearmament and modernization of its forces. In 1938 the Congress authorized a twenty-percent increase in the Navy, and Roosevelt at long last allowed the Army to reach its long-held goal of a Regular Army strength of 14,000 officers and 165,000 enlisted men. But in February 1939, Craig and Deputy Chief of Staff George

Marshall were asking for a further increase of 40,000. By the summer of 1938, a shortage of officers had developed to participate in maneuvers and to supervise the intensified summer training of the reserve components. The summer of 1939 promised to be even busier. To help relieve this shortage in the summers of 1938 and 1939 the War Department did not convene the Class of 1939 until September 15, and graduation was scheduled in June a week earlier than had been the practice. General DeWitt reduced the Conduct of War phase to six weeks. Four weeks were devoted to the Command Course. During the remaining two weeks the class was divided into three groups. One group drafted a command post exercise, one participated in a map problem, and the third prepared presentations to be delivered during the historical ride.[23]

The 1939-40 session experienced even more disruptions from the worsening international situation and the Army's early efforts at rearmament. In September 1939, just before the class assembled, Germany invaded Poland, igniting the Second World War. That same month the Navy withdrew its officers from the Army War College, presumably to help meet the needs of the expanding fleet. General DeWitt departed in November to take command of the IX Corps Area. In April 1940, Hitler's armies overran Denmark and Norway; in May they invaded Belgium and the Netherlands and pinned the British Expeditionary Force against the Channel at Dunkirk.

At the Army War College the historical ride was canceled and on June 8 a third of the members of the Class of 1940 received orders for duty on the War Department General Staff. The remainder of the class was formed into five groups corresponding to the five sections of the General Staff for a "Special Course," actually to perform studies for the General Staff. These studies ranged from the problem of pilot procurement for the Air Corps to supply and evacuation procedures in mechanized warfare. One nine-man group of War College personnel was put to work on the Rainbow-4 plan.[24] In the summer of 1940, the War Department announced that the War College session for 1940-41 was suspended, an announcement made annually thereafter throughout the war.[25]

Among the graduates of the last five classes in session before World War II were many officers who distinguished themselves as combat commanders of divisions and corps and as staff officers at all levels. At a higher echelon Mark W. Clark (1937) commanded Fifth Army and Fifteenth Army Group in Italy. Walter B. Smith (1937) was Eisenhower's Chief of Staff, and Hoyt S. Vandenberg (1939) lead Ninth Air Force in Europe. Members of those classes would continue to serve in even more influential positions after the war. Smith became Ambassador to the Soviet Union. During the Korean War, J. Lawton Collins (1938) was Chief of Staff and Charles L. Bolte (1937) Vice Chief of Staff of the Army. Vandenberg was Chief of Staff of the Air Force, and Clifton B.

Cates (1940) was Commandant of the Marine Corps.

In the Far East Walton H. Walker (1936), Matthew B. Ridgway (1937), and Maxwell D. Taylor (1940) commanded Eighth Army in Korea. George E. Stratemeyer (1939) commanded Far East Air Forces. Ridgway served also as Commander of the Far East Command, followed by Clark. William K. Harrison, Jr. (1938) was chief of the truce team that finally brought about an armistice in the Korean War. After the Korean War Ridgway was Chief of Staff of the Army, as were Taylor and Lyman L. Lemnitzer (1940), Lemnitzer subsequently becoming Chairman of the Joint Chiefs of Staff and NATO's Supreme Allied Commander, Europe, a position held also by Ridgway and Alfred M. Gruenther (1939). A few members of these pre-World War II classes also held pivotal positions during the early development of the Southeast Asia problem. Collins was Special U.S. Representative to the Republic of Vietnam in 1955-56, and Samuel T. Williams (1938) was Chief of the Military Advisory Group. Taylor was Chairman of the Joint Chiefs of Staff, 1962-64, and Ambassador to the Republic of Vietnam in 1965.

The Second Army War College: What Was Taught

In 1903 when Tasker Bliss was in the process of opening the first session of the Army War College, the session without students, he posed for himself three very basic questions. What shall be taught? How shall it be taught? How shall the teaching be extended to the greatest number? Without question the version of the Army War College from 1919 to 1940 came much closer to providing satisfactory and definitive answers to those questions than had the version of 1903 to 1917. The organizational divorce of the War College from the War Department General Staff mandated by the National Defense Act of 1916 was a major step in promoting clarity of purpose. The theory of the War College as "great adjunct" to the General Staff was not seriously reconsidered after 1919. The congressionally authorized overstrength of the officer corps of the Regular Army shielded the War College further from temporary emergency demands made on the Army. And between 1919 and the late 1930s, the nation placed few demands on the Army, support of the Civilian Conservation Corps being the single major exception.

The Army therefore enjoyed between the two world wars its first prolonged period of stability since the outbreak of the war with Spain in 1898. For the first time the Army had the opportunity to take stock of itself and its profession and to move forward with the professionalizing reforms that Elihu Root had begun. The experience of the World War had all but silenced the skeptics who saw little value in continuing postgradaute military education. The Army's officer education system, with the Army War College at its apex, was the mainstream and focus of the Army's interwar activity. Progression through that system became an imperative to career success. In the mind of the officer, the Army War College had become important.

The answer to Bliss's question as to what shall be taught remained open throughout the years of McAndrew, McGlachlin, and Ely, but William Connor was able to formulate the answer to general agreement with his organization of the program into "Preparation for War" and "Conduct of War" phases. Issues persisted, however. The appropriate division of effort between the War College and Leavenworth's Command and General Staff School recurred each time the War Department changed the length of the Leavenworth course, for reasons not directly related to the War College. It was an issue at other times also. Colonel Dana T. Merritt of the Inspector General's Department, for example, criticized both institutions in 1933 for duplication of effort. Simonds at the War College and Heintzelman at Leavenworth, however, were not inclined to accept the judgment of an Inspector General over their own. Heintzelman claimed that at Leavenworth the "whole two year course deals with the division." In his view it was utterly impossible to cover properly the command and general staff of a division in one year. Simonds agreed; he found no unnecessary duplication.[26]

Critics in search of economies, such as Pershing, Drum, and Merritt, had no difficulty finding duplications in the Command and General Staff School and War College programs. At Leavenworth the faculty found it simply could not teach division and corps operations without to some degree addressing field army operations. Attempts to draw a rigid line between the two schools on the basis of command echelon proved futile. A more fundamental difference in the purposes of the two institutions, moreover, was omitted in these dialogues.

Leavenworth was a school whose primary purpose was to train officers for duties at grades two or three levels above those they currently held. Its purpose was to train commanders and staff officers for a mobilized mass army, not for the Army of the day. The War College had a similar purpose in its "Conduct of War" phase, but the purpose of its "Preparation for War" phase was to prepare officers for their next immediate assignment, or at least a near-term assignment, as a general staff officer at the War Department or major subordinate command level who would be engaged in intense mobilization planning.

The underlying but unspoken curricular issue at the War College throughout the years between the world wars was therefore how best to balance the need to prepare students for an early general staff assignment with the need to prepare them for an assignment in the unknown future after mobilization, an assignment that would probably include command or general staff duty at field army level or higher. The initial post-World War analysis had held that the Army's greatest failing had been failure in preparation. It was this failing that Newton Baker and

Peyton March had directed McAndrew to correct. In subsequent analyses the AEF veterans, Haan, Pershing, and to a degree Palmer, pointed to additional failings in command and staff performance in the theater of operations, that is, in the actual conduct of campaigns. McAndrew, then McGlachlin and Ely, were directed to correct those additional failings. In the late 1920s Connor found a reasonable balance between the two tasks. George Simonds, however, had to respond to General MacArthur's emphasis on war and mobilization planning; he had to deemphasize instruction in the conduct of war. John DeWitt attempted to restore the balance by reconstituting the Command Course. He was not quite successful. Preparations for the war that was fast approaching overtook his efforts.

Other issues arose within the two purposes represented by the major phases of "Preparation for War" and "Conduct of War." The degree to which the War College should enter into questions that involved the use of advanced technology was a question that plagued the "Conduct of War" phase. The War College appeared to respect the primacy of the branch schools in determining the effect of new technology, just as the General Staff appeared to respect the primacy of the chief of the arms and services. The War College's war games, map exercises, map problems, and command post exercises were not at the leading edge of tactical innovation. What combat-developments work the War College attempted, or accomplished, was done at the direction of the War Department and under the "Preparation for War" label. After McAndrew, war games took on the purpose of training commanders and staff officers rather than that of testing war plans. The incentive to use war games as instruments of analysis and innovation was then lost.

The War College of 1919-40 displayed periodically some sense that it was obligated to the Army and its students to provide an understanding of the political, economic, and social influences on the conduct of war. The War Department made this mission explicit to General Connor, and he took the mission seriously. There is no evidence, however, that it was taken seriously enough that an attempt was made to include political scientists, economists, and sociologists permanently on the faculty. Guest lecturers had to suffice. International relations, moreover, received considerably more emphasis than domestic political, economic, or societal influences. And despite Commandant Grant's protestations otherwise, the college presented no structured course in international relations. Nonetheless, a War College student of the 1930s, if he was at all alert and interested, had the opportunity to broaden his understanding of the international environment and the role of force in that environment. The opportunities presented themselves not only in the G-2 Course but in the Analytical Studies and War Plans Courses.

Those courses led logically to consideration of national military strategies. The college did not, however, fully exploit the opportunity, though beginning with Simond's emphasis on war planning and culminating in the war planning exercises associated eventually with the Rainbow plans, alternative strategies were weighed by War College committees. Strategy per se, however, was not a subject of investigation. It was not seen as an academic discipline to be approached from a theoretical or historical base.

Nor did the War College as an institution or its faculty and students habitually challenge the established military policy of the United States. Mobilization of a mass army around a nucleus of the Regular Army, National Guard, and Organized Reserve Corps, as set forth in the National Defense Act of 1920, became and remained the foundation of War College "Preparation for War" studies. Challenges to this policy were coming from elsewhere, however. Air power proponents, both within and without the Air Corps, and the few proponents of forces-in-being, such as Ross Collins in the House of Representatives, seriously questioned the 1920 policy. But the War College saw its mission as preparing officers to carry out the policy despite all obstacles, not as encouraging or preparing officers to make recommendations that might lead to better policy.

Like its pre-World War predecessor, the Army War College deserves good marks for its attempts to have students think in terms of joint Army-Navy operations and include in their deliberations their best understanding of the potentialities of air power. Work with the Naval War College on Plan Orange war-gaming was continuous through the 1920s and did not cease until the superiors of the two institutions began to differ on the appropriate United States strategy in the Pacific. Naval and Air Corps officers were on the faculty and among the student body, and each year's class included students from the Marine Corps. Judging by the responsible positions that those officers from the other services subsequently held, it is evident that the other services sent to the Army War College some of their best.

Lesser marks should be given the War College of 1919-40 for its treatment of coalition warfare. The almost complete neglect of that subject seems strange, since the United States Army had participated in a major coalition effort in France and lesser coalition efforts in Italy, northern Russia, and Siberia. But other than periodic lectures by the aging Tasker Bliss on his experiences on the Allied Supreme War Council, little was done in this area until General Simonds introduced planning problems in coalition war, first hypothesizing a situation in Northeast Asia and then one in Europe. The explanation for the neglect of coalition warfare appears to be that the American Army had found its experience with allies in World War I extremely distasteful. Even an officer as astute as Fox Conner, when lecturing to the War College in the 1930s, termed fighting with allies a "dubious luxury" and opined that unity of command was possible only in matters of strategy, not of tactics.[27] Wherever Eisenhower, Bedell Smith, and Alfred Gruenther learned the value of multinational headquarters, they did not learn it as students at the Army War College.

The War College did not seem to recognize how fundamentally the role of the War Department General Staff changed during the two decades between the World Wars. As the Prussians conceived it and as John MacAuley Palmer explained it to the Congress, the general staff officer was to be a specialist in military operations. The General Staff, Palmer insisted, was a generalship staff, not a staff of generalists. Palmer's concept was gradually and almost imperceptibly lost in the way the Pershing/Harbord copy of the French General Staff evolved. The American General Staff became more than the military planning and advising body called for by the National Defense Acts of 1916 and 1920. It became involved additionally in matters beyond the traditional *grosser Generalstab* functions of strategic planning, combat developments, military education, and force readiness. It became deeply concerned with the management of resources—of men, materiel, and money—probably an inevitable result of the lean years of the Republican era and the Depression, isolationism, and neutrality. Only the G-2 and War Plans divisions of the General Staff had the luxury to remain somewhat removed from the budget battles. The officer who served on the American General Staff, in addition to being a specialist in military operations, also had to be a man who understood all the political and economic influences on resource allocation.

The War College did not clearly define for itself the evolving General Staff problem of resource management nor the new requirement it placed on the General Staff officer. It did not, therefore, attack the problem directly. It is true that the Budget Officer of the War Department made an annual address to the class and explained in rather mechanical (and probably boring) detail the budgeting process, the role of the Budget Advisory Committee, and, after MacArthur, the role of the General Council in making fiscal decisions. The problems presented to the student committees during the "G-Courses," however, were of a narrow, single staff-section nature, not designed to force the student to think in terms of the War Department as an entity. The students were not forced to consider strategy, war planning, operational doctrine, research and development, training, and fiscal and materiel-acquisition management all as related parts of the larger and more complex problem of preparation for war. McAndrew's one large problem might have evolved into this had it been allowed to mature. But War Department pressures for more instruction in tactics and in command took precedence. In sum, requirements planning and all that flows from it did not constitute the major thrust of the War College program between the world wars.

The Second Army War College: How It Taught

Whatever the strengths and weaknesses of the second Army War College's answer to Bliss's question as to what shall be taught, the college's answer to his next question—How shall it be taught?—was remarkably similar to Bliss's own answer to that question. The method of instruction and the educational philosophy remained consistent with the learning-by-doing inherited from Bliss and the applicatory method inherited from the old Infantry and Cavalry School. McAndrew reinstituted these methods in 1919 along with the first Army War College habit of committee study. The same method was used whether the problem at hand was a current issue facing one of the War Department General Staff divisions, the drafting of a mobilization or war plan, or the conduct of a war game or command post exercise. Students were expected to learn and gain understanding from each other and from the experience of participating in collective problem-solving exercises.

The role of the faculty was to devise and pose the problem and then to monitor and guide only as necessary the committees' research, analyses, and presentation of solutions. Lectures, whether presented by faculty members or by authoritative guests, were introductory or supplementary to the problem-solving.

This method of instruction was time-consuming. A more intensive lecture and directed-reading program would have enabled the college to cover a broader spectrum of subject matter. It might also have alleviated the students' frustration at never being quite able to deal with their assigned problems to a satisfying depth before their committee was disbanded, the class reorganized, and new problems assigned. Committee solutions by their nature also tend toward a not-very-innovative common denominator. Nonetheless, learning by doing, learning through group interaction, had advantages. Deeper, as opposed to broader, study was possible. Insights and innovations were brought forth for discussion even though they did not appear in formal committee reports. To the officer corps of the United States Army of the 1920s and 1930s, committee problem-solving had particularly strong advantages. Branch of service parochialism was broken down and, importantly, each student could arrive at a measure of the intellectual strengths and weaknesses of his colleagues, assessments that could be relied upon during the mobilizations and wars to come.

The committee method also tended to blur the distinction between faculty member and student, and it encouraged cooperation rather than competition among students, goals that commandants from James

McAndrew through Philip Peyton considered to be of critical importance to the health of the War College and the United States Army. Competition to enter the War College was intense; the system made it particularly so at the Command and General Staff School. The leaders of the War College understood this and accepted it as necessary up to the point of entering the War College, but from that time on they made great effort to eradicate competition and to encourage willing cooperation among officers, whether members of the faculty or the student body. It is on this point that the War College philosophy deviated most markedly from both lower-level military education and from civilian graduate- and undergraduate-level education. It deviated for sound reasons. These officer students were expected to provide the leadership of the Army in those most serious of endeavors, the preparation for and conduct of war. They were not necessarily expected to think alike, but their thinking was expected to be guided by mission rather than ambition. Whatever motivation to greater individual scholarly effort grades or class standings might have provided, the War College willingly sacrificed that to accommodate what it believed to be a higher goal.

The Second Army War College: Who Was Taught

To give effect to this educational philosophy, the selection of students was critical. McGlachlin, Ely, and Connor, like Wotherspoon before them, struggled to have the personnel managers of the arms and services understand this truth.

Hanson Ely, as we have seen, was never completely satisfied with the student body assigned. In the fall of 1927, just before William Connor replaced Ely, the War Department issued revised instructions as to the qualification of officers selected to attend the War College. Each class was to consist of ninety Regular Army officers and ten officers from the Navy and Marine Corps. Of the ninety officers, ten would be from the noncombatant branches. The Air Corps would receive a quota of two or three. Officers selected were to have efficiency reports of at least "Above Average," were to be graduates of the Command and General Staff School, and were to be listed as General Staff eligible. Each year no more than three nongraduates of Leavenworth would be admitted. Officers of the combat arms could not be over age fifty-two.[28]

After a year's experience, Connor began to hammer at the War Department to strengthen the entrance requirements. His first complaint was that the one hundred students of the yearly class, when supplemented temporarily by fifteen officers from the reserve components, overcrowded the facility. He had officers sitting at field desks in the hallways. He recommended that the number of Regular officers be reduced to seventy-five. The War Department accommodated him; the Class of 1930 had only seventy-five Regular Army students. The overcrowding undoubtedly troubled General Connor, but he was also attempting to improve the quality of the student body. As noted, in 1929 he had complained that twenty-six percent of that year's class had turned in a less-than-excellent performance. But throughout the early 1930s the composition of the classes remained much the same. In 1936 Regular Army attendance was again set at ninety students, an increase made in part to allow Air Corps students, but also to help attain the number of qualified General Staff officers needed for the mobilization requirements of MacArthur's Four Army Plan.[29]

The chiefs of the arms and services had the responsibility to make the actual selections within their quotas and within policy guidelines of the Chief of Staff, though until 1932 the Secretary of War reserved to himself the selection of ten members of each class. The chiefs did not always follow the guidelines. Commandant Grant was unhappy in 1937 because seven officers in the Class of 1936 were not graduates of the Command and General Staff School, and thirteen more nongraduates were included in the Class of 1937. Eight of these were Air Corps officers and two were of the Corps of Engineers; the remainder were from the administrative and technical services. General Grant refused to recommend these officers for the General Staff Eligible List because he considered "the Leavenworth course as the substructure of the War College course." He was most annoyed when the selection board for the elite list overrode his recommendation and selected a number of those officers nevertheless.[30]

The chiefs of the arms and services deserve some sympathy, however, for failing to follow the guidelines. There were other demands for quality officers and for other career development assignments such as command and reserve component duty and technical assignments for engineers, aviators, ordnance officers, and other specialists. The Assistant Secretary of War at the same time was interested in enhancing the prestige and desirability of attendance at the Army Industrial College. In 1930 the War Department stipulated that selection for the War College from the purely procurement branches had to be made from among Industrial College graduates, and that half of the officers selected from branches with both procurement and operational functions (such as the Corps of Engineers, Air Corps, and Signal Corps) had to be graduates of the Industrial College. In 1931 the Secretary of War reserved two spaces for Industrial College graduates. In 1932 a policy was announced that each year two Industrial College students would go directly from the Industrial College to the War College. Some line officers looked upon all this with suspicion, speculating that the Industrial College was being used as an easy route to the War College by undeserving officers (especially by competing line officers).[31]

Perhaps the most difficult obstacle put in the way of the personnel managers was the policy announced in 1928 that at least half of the War College selectees be available upon graduation for assignment to the War Department General Staff. This was made additionally complex the next year when the War Department decreed that no officer could serve more than four consecutive years in the District of Columbia, including duty at the War College and the Industrial College. Apparently designed to inhibit political connections and to prevent the creation of a War Department clique, this policy was in effect an extension of the Manchu Law to officers other than those on the General Staff. These two policies reduced further the pool of officers available for selection to the War College. The problem was only partially eased by eliminating the requirement for two years of service between graduation from Leavenworth's Command and General Staff School and attendance at the War College. Selection now had to be made from among officers already on the General Staff Eligible List, in their second year at Leavenworth, or attending the Industrial College. In 1938 the War Department added another criterion: selectees must have demonstrated "high qualification as commanders." It is understandable that some arms and services were at times hard-pressed to meet their quotas without stretching the guidelines.[32]

It was the problem of age, or more exactly over-age, that proved the most difficult to solve. In 1930 the War Department raised the maximum age at attendance from fifty-two to fifty-four. The next year it went back to fifty-two with the further stipulation that it was desirable that graduates not be over forty-four since at that age they would still have half their service before them. The age criterion for the combat arms was tougher: half of the selectees had to be under forty-four. By 1932 this policy had brought the average age of graduates still on active duty down to forty-nine. In 1936 the War Department reduced the maximum age to fifty with half the class required to be under forty-three. Finally, in 1938, the War Department arrived at a scheme of reducing the maximum age by a year for each succeeding class, so that by 1946 there would be no student officer over forty-four. The policy was apparently producing the desired result. The last pre-World War II class, that of 1940, had no student above age fifty. The concern regarding age was based on an apparently widely held assumption that the energy of a combat commander dissipated after his forty-sixth birthday. More empirically based, perhaps, was the observation that the Army had developed a highly educated retired list. But students of the post-World War institution never reached the youthfulness of the prewar college.[33] It would not be surprising if deserving officers of high potential never attended the War College. Arranging one's career to meet all the prerequisites and assignment criteria at the proper age was a difficult and probably vexing chore.

Lowering the age of War College selectees was one way the number of graduates on active duty could be increased to meet the Army's needs for staff officers trained in the intricacies of war planning and mobilization. But the number would still be insufficient to reach the goal set by War Department calculations. Even if the facilities at the War College could be enlarged, commandants were reluctant to increase the size of the class for fear of compromising the high standards for selection. Troup Miller (AWC 1925), whose views as an instructor in 1929 had influenced Connor's restructuring of the course, was in 1936 commanding the 11th Cavalry in California. He offered the War Department a way out of its dilemma, suggesting through channels that the War College offer a two-year extension course to Regular officers who had missed selection for the resident course and to reserve component officers. But Colonel Ned B. Rehkopf, Acting Commandant, quickly rejected Miller's suggestion. According to Rehkopf there were several objections. Among these, there was no way that the courses of the "Conduct of War" phase could be taught with extension methods; the War Plans course was too confidential; and only at the War College were adequate research materials available. Moreover, Rehkopf believed that attendance at the Army War College should remain competitive. To make it less so was to compromise standards. The War Department agreed; it did not approve instituting an extension course.[34] It did not believe that Miller had found the answer to Bliss's question as to how to extend the teaching to the greatest number.

Though mistakes in student selection were undoubtedly made, the system appears to have been working well by the mid-1930s. Selected were officers who throughout their prior service had demonstrated not only effectiveness, but initiative and potential. Moreover, unlike the students selected for the 1903-17 classes, they were officers who were already thoroughly grounded in the military art through World War I service, attendance at the schools of their arms and services, and survival of the trials of the Command and General Staff School.

The War Department appears to have exercised even more care in the selection of faculty. McAndrew had the opportunity to set a high standard with the original faculty, and if his successors were not provided quite as great an opportunity, standards nonetheless remained high. Of General Ely's thirteen-member faculty of 1924-25, all but two would eventually serve as general officers. The faculty rosters between the wars contained the name of Stanley D. Embick, Walter Krueger, William H. Simpson, Joseph T. McNarney, Charles L. Bolte, and J. Lawton Collins. They also included four future commandants: Simonds, Craig, Grant, and DeWitt. Continuity on the faculty was provided by three-year overlapping tours and by often selecting the Assistant Commandant from among former faculty members. A legitimate criticism of the college might have been the danger of inbreeding, though there appears to have been no real alternative as long as the War College program was to deal primarily in purely military problems.

The second Army War College, like its predecessor, failed to produce a Clausewitz, Mahan, Liddell Hart, or Quincy Wright. It contributed only marginally to any body of theory on the phenomenon of war. But that had not been its aim. Its aim had been utilitarian—to produce competent, if not necessarily brilliant, leadership that could prepare the Army for war and fight a war successfully if it came. Through the interwar period graduates of the Army War College increasingly began to dominate in numbers the War Department General Staff and the roster of the commanders of the major army commands. Graduates of the late 1920s and the 1930s, with the notable exceptions of George Marshall and Douglas MacArthur, filled practically all of the Army's high command and staff positions and many of those of the Army Air Forces during World War II. To prepare the Army for war and for fighting a war successfully proved to be a practical and a correct goal. The United States in 1940 needed not military theoreticians but able military practitioners.

James McAndrew had indeed built a new edifice, but he had built it on the foundation of the old. As a minimum the first Army War College had helped prevent any repetition of Tampa-Santiago; the second had helped prevent another mobilization crisis like that of 1917-18. With the assistance of the second college, the United States Army produced a body of leadership that successfully fought a global war, that contributed to the stabilization and reconstruction of a devastated Western Europe and Japan, and that would then contribute to the containment of a Soviet Union that appeared to threaten all that had been won between 1940 and 1945. The stability of the 1920s and 1930s would not return. It would be a full decade before the Army War College would again receive students. When that occurred in 1950, the United States Army would be part of an even more uncertain and complex world, a world that called for a military leadership of even broader vision and more precise judgment.

NOTES

1. For Craig as realist, Kreidberg and Henry, *Mobilization*, 467-68, 474-76.
2. For neutrality legislation, Robert A. Divine, *The Illusion of Neutrality* (Chicago: University of Chicago Press, 1962), 114-17, 158-61, 170-71. Quote from campaign address, Chautauqua, N.Y., August 14, 1936. Kreidberg and Henry, *Mobilization*, 437, 451, 460-61, 551.
3. Divine, *Neutrality*, 193-95, 200-18.
4. Watson, *Prewar Plans*, 30.
5. MacArthur, letter, Development of Four Army Organization, 18 August 1933, copy in AWC File 52-60. Kreidberg and Henry, *Mobilization*, 470. Stuart Heintzelman (Commandant, Command and General Staff School) to Simonds, 28 November 1933, AWC File 1-83. AG to Commandant, Command and General Staff School, 2 January 1935,

AWC File 74-50. AG, letter, Directive Army War College Class, 1935-1936, 28 November 1934 as amended by G-1 resume, February 1935, AWC File 74-55.

6. AWC File 1-105, par. 18. AWC Course 1936-37, Vol. VI: "Preliminary Command Course," Doc. 2.

7. Grant, Memorandum for Directors, 30 January 1936, AWC File 74-50. AWC File 1-105, pars. 18-19. AWC Course 1937-38, Vol. VI: "Preliminary Command Course," Pt. 1, Doc. 1. AWC Course 1938-39, Vol. XI: "Individual General Staff Memorandum," Doc. 4. DeWitt, Report of Operations, 21 June 1939, AWC, "Report of Operations 1920-1940."

8. Development of the PMP is in Kreidberg and Henry, *Mobilization*, 476-92.

9. AWC Course 1938-39, Vol. VIII: "Mobilization," Docs. 1, 2.

10. Kreidberg and Henry, *Mobilization*, 468-69, 474, 478-79.

11. AWC Memorandum, Assignment of Subjects, 1 November 1906. Mitchell, lecture, "Tactical Application of Military Aeronautics," 1921, AWC File 97-100. "War Department Committee Report on the War Organization of the Air Service," 24 April 1923, copy in AWC File 97-34. "Report of the Special Committee, General Council, on Employment of Army Air Corps under Certain Strategic Plans," 12 October 1933, copy in AWC File 97-78. "Final Report of the War Department Special Committee on the Army Air Corps," July 1934. This last study was led by former Secretary of War Newton D. Baker; members included Dr. Karl T. Compton and James H. Doolittle. AWC Course 1931-32, Vol. III: "G-3," Doc. 14.

12. Craig, letter, Reorganization of Division and Higher Units, 5 November 1935, AWC File 7-1936-5. Chief of Staff, letter, Organization of Corps and Army, 28 October 1936, AWC File 52-78. AG to Commandant, Organization of the Cavalry Division, 12 October 1936, AWC File 52-77. AWC File 1-105, par. 20.

13. AWC File 1-105, par. 17. AWC Course 1936-37, Vol. V: "Conduct of War," Pt. 2, Docs. 22, 23. AWC File 6-1937-8. DeWitt to AG, 21 June 1939, AWC, "Reports of Operations 1920-1940." AWC Course 1938-39, Vol. VII: "Command Post Exercise." AWC Course 1939-40, Vol. IX: "Preparation of Field Maneuvers."

14. AWC File 2-1938-12. Watson, *Prewar Plans*, 47. AWC File 1-105, par. 19.

15. AWC Course 1935-36, Vol. II: "G-2," Pt. 1, Doc. 2. AWC Course 1936-37, Vol. II: "G-2," Pt. 2, Doc. 2.

16. AG to Commandant, 11 February 1936, AWC File 1-83. Grant to AG, 13 February 1936, Ibid. "Student Criticisms for 1936-1937," AWC File 47-116A. AWC File 1-105, pars. 18, 21.

17. AWC Course 1935-36, Vol. V: "Conduct of War," Pt. 1. Report of Committee No. 2, AWC File 2-1938-2. Report of Committee No. 2, AWC File 5-1938-2. AWC Course 1939-40, Vol. V: Analytical Studies, Docs. 5, 6.

18. Watson, *Prewar Plans*, 88, 92. AWC Course 1935-36, Vol. VI: "War Plans," Pt. 1, Doc. 6. Report of Committee No. 9, AWC File 6-1937-9.

19. For development of War Plan Orange see Louis Morton, *Strategy and Command, The First Two Years* (Washington: Office of Chief of Military History, Department of the Army, 1962), 22-44, in series *U.S. Army in World War II: The War in the Pacific.* For Army and Naval War College gaming of Plan Orange, AWC File 242-1 through 242-8. AWC Course 1936-37, Vol. VIII: "War Plans," Pt. 4, Doc. 18.

20. Watson, *Prewar Plans*, 89-90, 94. Kreidberg and Henry, *Mobilization*, 541-42, 557. Conn and Fairchild, *Hemispheric Defense*, 1-4. AWC Course 1937-38, Vol. II: "G-2," Pt. 2, Docs. 23, 23A. AWC Course 1937-38, Vol. VII: "War Plans," Doc. 4. AWC File 5-1938-22/z.

21. Kreidberg and Henry, *Mobilization*, 558-60. Watson, *Prewar Plans*, 94-103. Development of the Rainbow plans is in Maurice Matloff and Edwin M. Snell, *Strategic Planning for Coalition Warfare, 1941-42 - 1943-44* (Washington: Office of Chief of Military History, Department of the Army), 5-10, in series *U.S. Army in World War II: The War Department.* AWC File 1-105, par. 20.

22. Conn, *Historical Work*, 115, 162.

23. Watson, *Prewar Plans*, 29-30, 78, 92, 126-28. AWC File 1-105, par. 21. AWC Course 1938-39, Vol. V: "Analytical Studies," Doc. 1. Ibid, Vol. VI: "Command," Pt. 1, Doc. 1. Ibid., Vol. IX: "Historical Ride."

24. AWC File 1-105, par. 21. Ned B. Rehkopf, General Orientation, AWC Course 1939-40, Vol. X: "Miscellaneous and Special Course." Philip B. Peyton, Report of Operations, 25 June 1940, AWC, "Report of Operations 1920-1940." War College Group, War Department General Staff, Northeastern Brazil Theater, Rainbow No. 4," Copy in AWC File 39-52.
25. AWC "Chronicle," Chaps. 41 (1942-1943), 43 (1944-1945).
26. Heintzelman to Simonds, 28 November 1933, AWC File 15-22. Simonds, Response to 12 October 1933 Letter of Colonel Dana T. Merrill, AWC File 15-22.
27. Fox Conner, lecture, "The Allied High Command and Allied Unity of Direction," 6 April 1937, AWC Course 1936-37, Docs. 24, 29.
28. Letter, AG 210.63, 1 November 1927, AWC File 74-55.
29. Connor to AG, 10 October 1928, Ibid. Letter, AG 210.63, 11 December 1928, Ibid. Connor to AG, 20 September 1929, AWC File 12-201. AG, Directive Army War College Class, 1935-1936, 28 November 1934, as amended by G-1 resume, February 1935, AWC File 74-55.
30. Letter, AG 210.63, 11 December 1928, AWC File 74-55. Letter AG 210.63, Ibid. Grant to Assistant Commandant, 16 April 1937, AWC File 29-80.
31. Letter, AG 210.63, 19 November 1930, AWC File 74-55. Letter AG 210.63, 10 October 1931, Ibid., Letter AG 210.63, 1 March 1932, Ibid. S. E. Reinhart, Policies Governing the Selection of Officers to attend the General Service Schools, 2 May 1936, AWC Course 1935-36, "Individual General Staff Memorandum."
32. Letter, AG 210.63, 11 December 1928, AWC File 74-55. Letter, AG 210.45, 22 August 1929, Ibid. Letter, AG 210.63, 10 October 1931, Ibid. Letter, AG 210.63, 25 August 1938, Ibid.
33. Letter, AG 210.63, 19 November 1930, Ibid. Letter, AG 210.63, 10 October 1931, Ibid. Letter, AG 210.63, 3 November 1932, Ibid. Letter, AG 210.63, 7 April 1936, Ibid. Letter, AG 210.63, 25 August 1938, Ibid. *Official Army Register, 1940*, Reinhart, Policies Governing Selection. Maxwell D. Taylor, Oral History Transcript No. 1, 25, MHI. McGlachlin to Chief of Staff, 30 September 1921, AWC File 68-44.
34. Miller to Commandant, 22 June 1936, AWC File 1-83. Rehkopf to AG, 3rd Indorsement, 1 July 1936, Ibid.

Decision To Begin Anew
1941-1950

The suspension of War College sessions in the summer of 1940 was an action called for by the Protective Mobilization Plan. The decision not to continue classes has been subject to historical criticism, the argument being that in view of the war's high demand for staff officers at the upper echelons, the War College should have continued to produce them. The opposing argument is that the War Department had no real choice. The demand for quality officers was so great that they could not be spared either to administer or to attend the War College.[1]

The war also affected other military educational institutions. The Army Industrial College shortened its course in 1940, then suspended operations the next year. It reopened in 1944 with its focus on training officers for the approaching problem of the termination of munitions contracts. At Leavenworth the Command and General Staff School discontinued its regular course in February 1940. It then initiated intensive abbreviated courses designed specifically to provide general staff officers at division level. It conducted twenty-seven such classes during the war, graduating some 1,800 officers. The Air Corps Tactical School was closed in 1940, but the Army Air Forces inaugurated a Staff Officers Course comparable to Leavenworth as an element of the Army Air Forces Schools at Orlando, Florida. The Navy had originally planned to close the Naval War College, but decided to keep it open for the purpose of training reserve officers in a five-month course at the command and staff school level.[2]

The major educational innovation of the wartime period was the activation in June 1943 of the Army and Navy Staff College. Suggested by Army Air Forces headquarters, this institution was the first truly joint-service school in the United States. The War Department warmly supported the idea; the Navy was less enthusiastic, but concurred. Supervised by the Joint Chiefs of Staff, the Army and Navy Staff College presented a twenty-one-week course for officers of the four services in the ranks of colonel and lieutenant colonel. Portions of the course were presented at Leavenworth, Orlando, and Newport, with the final two months in Washington where the class was organized into committees to plan in detail a major amphibious operation. The college graduated twelve classes of some thirty to forty officers each. Representatives of the State Department attended the last five classes. The Commandant of the Army and Navy Staff College during its entire wartime existence was Lieutenant General John L. DeWitt, who from 1937 to 1939 had been Commandant of the Army War College.[3]

Plans for Postwar Education

Shortly after the capitulation of Japan in August 1945, Army Chief of Staff George Marshall, who intended to retire from active service, queried his designated successor, Dwight Eisenhower (AWC 1928), as to Eisenhower's preferences on the postwar assignments for senior general officers. Eisenhower was still in Europe and apparently was not familiar with plans for the postwar Army. Among other questions, he asked Marshall when the Army War College would be reactivated. He also solicited Marshall's views as to whether Robert L. Eichelberger (AWC 1930), commanding Eighth Army in the Pacific, would be an appropriate replacement for DeWitt. At this point Eisenhower apparently felt that there was a need for both an Army War College and the new Army and Navy Staff College.[4]

On the question of a replacement for DeWitt, Marshall wrote Eisenhower that this question had already been settled between himself and the Chief of Naval Operations, Ernest J. King. DeWitt was to be replaced by Vice Admiral Harry W. Hill. Marshall also told Eisenhower that if a Joint Army and Navy War College could be created, then perhaps neither the Army War College nor the Naval War College should be retained. Eisenhower cabled back, agreeing that if the Army and Navy Staff College was put on a really sound basis there would be no need for the Army War College. The Marshall (and now Eisenhower) view that a strengthened Army and Navy Staff College could replace the Army War College became a basis of much of the Army's planning for its postwar educational system.[5]

The Army Air Forces came forward with an even more elaborate plan. Assuming that the Army Air Forces would become an autonomous and equal service after the war, an Air Training Command study of January 1944 recommended postwar air force schools at three progressively higher levels in the traditional pattern of the Army system. At a still higher level the study recommended a combined services war college. The Air Training Command concept was further developed at Headquarters, Army Air Forces, which added an "Air College" on a level equivalent to that of the Command and General Staff School at

Leavenworth and proposed that all of the Army Air Force schools be controlled by one command to be known as the "Army Air Forces University." Above the Air College, Army Air Forces recommended there be a joint war college, a joint industrial college, and an Army-Navy-Air Staff College.[6]

The Navy was also planning for its postwar educational requirements. In March 1943 a board headed by Rear Admiral William Pye recommended that the Navy's General Line School, Command and Staff Course, and Naval War College course all be expanded. The Naval War College should control the Command and Staff Course and also present an advanced course for selected senior officers just prior to their assuming positions of higher command in the fleet. The Pye Board recommended creation of a "College of National Defense," which would enroll students not only from the Navy and War Departments but also from the Departments of State, Commerce, and Treasury—and from the committees of Congress.[7]

While the services were considering these unilateral plans for postwar military education, more significant investigations were being made as to the desirability and structure of a single military establishment. In April 1944 the Joint Chiefs of Staff convened a joint Special Committee for Reorganization of National Defense, chaired by retired Admiral James O. Richardson. The Richardson Committee gave some consideration to military education, recommending in its report of April 1945 joint education and training at all levels. As a follow-on to this recommendation, the Joint Chiefs of Staff charged General DeWitt and his faculty at the Army and Navy Staff College with drawing up a plan for postwar joint education. Upon its completion the DeWitt plan was further refined by the Joint Secretariat, and it was approved by the Joint Chiefs of Staff in June 1945, several months before Marshall and Eisenhower began to correspond on postwar Army education.[8]

The Joint Chiefs of Staff plan called for joint training at all levels. At those service schools that instructed officers with more than six years of service, at least thirty percent of the student body should be from services other than the one conducting the course. The same would be true at the command and staff school level; moreover, an officer should attend the command and staff school of his own service before attending that of another service. The JCS plan proposed two institutions at the highest level, an Army-Navy Joint College located in Washington and the Army Industrial College, converted into a joint establishment. Both would be under the control of the Joint Chiefs. The Army-Navy Joint College, as the JCS conceived it, would offer instruction in social, political, and economic affairs related to the conduct of war and also instruction on joint military operations at a high level. Its emphasis would be on subjects of broad national interest related to the conduct of total war.

The JCS recommended that if the State Department established an educational institution, it should be located near and preferably in the same building as the Army-Navy Joint College.[9]

The emphasis that the Joint Chiefs of Staff intended to place on joint operations and on a more extensive background for senior officers in the political, economic, and social factors of war were of course outgrowths of the experiences and trials of the Second World War. The ideas, however, were hardly new. A primary objective of Root and Bliss for the Army War College in 1903 had been to improve Army-Navy cooperation and planning. Edward McGlachlin in 1922 had taken bold steps toward making the Army War College an institution with more than military interests. His successor, Hanson Ely, spoke of the Army War College as "national." A main purpose in William Connor's trip to Europe in 1929 had been to investigate Britain's new Imperial Defence College.[10]

Louis Johnson, Assistant Secretary of War in 1939, had recommended to President Roosevelt a National Defense College patterned on the French institution established in 1936. Johnson suggested that the proposed college address "broad political, financial, economic, and demographic problems relative to national defense and the effect of these on national strategy." Chief of Staff Marshall had referred Johnson's proposal to the War Plans Division at the time, but that body was not enthusiastic. Marshall therefore recommended merely that the Joint Planning Committee, the working element of the Army and Navy Joint Board, be made a full-time duty for assigned officers. Marshall also referred the proposal to Commandant DeWitt at the Army War College, suggesting that DeWitt institute a series of special conferences and lectures that would include nonmilitary participants. In his response DeWitt related the demise of McGlachlin's program and recommended that each year two or three representatives of the State Department and two from the Department of Commerce attend the full course at the Army War College. DeWitt also informed General Marshall that the War Plans Division had studied the question in 1934 without tangible result, and that a student committee of the Class of 1939 had addressed the question in the Analytical Studies Course and had recommended a "College of National Policy and Defense."[11]

The Gerow Board

When Eisenhower assumed Marshall's mantle as Chief of Staff in November 1945, the Joint Chiefs of Staff had already agreed to the establishment of a joint war college and a joint industrial college. The Army and Navy Staff College, under its newly assigned Commandant, Admiral Hill, was a month away from graduating what was to be its last class. On Capitol Hill the Congress had begun hearings on unification of the armed forces, and it was already apparent that deep and real differ-

Emory Upton—A leading military theorist of the post-Civil War period and Assistant Commandant of the Artillery School, 1877-80, Upton was a strong advocate of professional military education. (US Army Military History Institute)

Stephen B. Luce—Impressed by the program of the Army's Artillery School, Luce was able to found the Naval War College in 1884. (US Naval War College)

Arthur L. Wagner—Pioneer military educator, Wagner served on the faculty of the Infantry and Cavalry School from 1886 to 1897 and as Senior Director of the Army War College 1904-05. (US Army War College)

Eben Swift—Colleague of Wagner at the Infantry and Cavalry School, Swift introduced Leavenworth methods at the Army War College during 1906-10. (US Army War College)

Elihu Root—As Secretary of War, 1889-1904, Root included among important Army reforms the establishment of a progressive system of officer professional education culminating in the Army War College. (US Army Military History Institute)

22 Jackson Place, Washington, D.C.—Location of the Army War College, 1903-07. (US Army Military History Institute)

The Army War College Board appointed by Root in 1902. Major General S. B. M. Young is at the head of the table, Brigadier General Tasker H. Bliss is second from the left and Brigadier General William H. Carter second from right. (US Army Military History Institute)

Tasker H. Bliss—A member of Luce's original faculty at the Naval War College, Bliss became the founding President of the Army War College in 1903. (US Army Military History Institute)

Army War College, Washington Barracks, D.C. (now Ft. McNair)—As it appeared shortly after construction was completed in 1907. (US Army Military History Institute)

Officers Mess and faculty quarters, Washington Barracks, 1907. (US Army Military History Institute)

William W. Wotherspoon— Picture made at Gettysburg encampment 1910. Wotherspoon served almost continuously at the Army War College from 1904-12, the last three years as President. (US Army Military History Institute)

Class of 1909 during historical ride in the Virginia countryside. (US Army Military History Institute)

Near Keedysville, Maryland, in 1908 Major William D. Conner lectures on the problem of the defense of Washington (US Army Military History Institute)

The Class of 1920—Thirty members of this class had served as general officers during World War I; its graduates held numerous high command and staff positions until the eve of World War II. (US Army Military History Institute)

James W. McAndrew—First Commandant after World War I, McAndrew sought a "completely new edifice." (US Army War College)

Edward F. McGlachlin, Jr.—As Commandant 1921-23, McGlachlin had short-lived success in broadening the scope of the Army War College. (US Army War College)

William D. Conner—Commandant, 1928-32, Conner divided the War College program into two phases, "preparation for war" and "conduct of war." (US Army War College)

George S. Simonds—Served on the faculty 1920-21, as Assistant Commandant 1922-24 and as commandant 1932-35. While Commandant, Simonds emphasized mobilization planning. (US Army War College)

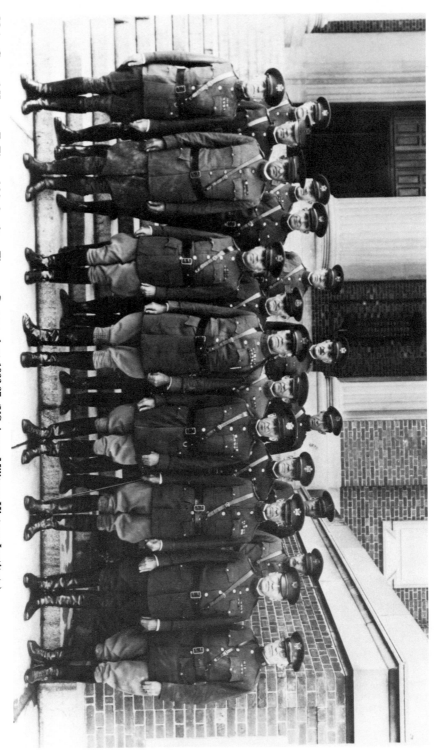

Major General Hanson E. Ely and his faculty—Ely was Commandant 1923-27. (US Army Military History Institute)

Joseph M. Swing—First Commandant after World War II, Swing forcefully rejected ideas of the Army War College as an "advanced Leavenworth." (US Army War College)

Arthur G. Trudeau—Deputy to Commandants Swing and Edward M. Almond, 1950-52. Trudeau's initiatives had a lasting influence on the Army War College. (US Army War College)

Grant Hall, Fort Leavenworth, Kansas—Location of the Army War College during academic year 1950-51. (US Army Command and General Staff College)

Carlisle Barracks, Pennsylvania—Academic area as inherited by the Army War College in 1951. (US Army Military History Institute)

Graduation ceremony, Class of 1952—First graduation of a class at Carlisle Barracks. (US Army Military History Institute)

Root Hall, 1951-66—Built for the Medical Field Service School, after 1951 the building contained the War College auditorium, library and faculty offices. (US Army Military History Institute)

Auditorium in "old" Root Hall with lecture in progress. (US Army War College)

Student committee in session in "old" Bliss Hall. (US Army Military History Institute)

College Arms, Carlisle Barracks—Student housing area constructed in the early fifties. (US Army War College)

Bliss Hall, 1951-66—A converted stables, this building provided student office space and committee rooms. (US Army Military History Institute)

Four Commandants of the third Army War College—Left to right Max S. Johnson (1955-59), Eugene A. Salet (1964-67), Clyde D. Eddleman (May-October 1955), and William F. Train (1962-64). (US Army Military History Institute)

DeWitt C. Smith, Jr.—Served as Commandant longer than any of his predecessors (1974-77, 1978-80). Smith led the War College through the post-Vietnam era stressing diversity and individual responsibility. (US Army War College)

ences existed between the Army and the Navy as to what form unification should take. Within the Army no detailed plans had been drawn as to what the peacetime officer education system should be. Eisenhower did not inherit either detailed plans or a definitive program. The JCS plan for joint officer education also fell far short of being a definitive program. If the approaching 1946-47 school year was to be productive, early decisions had to be made. On November 23, 1945, Eisenhower approved the appointment of a War Department Military Education Board, with the Commandant of the Command and General Staff School, Lieutenant General Leonard T. Gerow (AWC 1931), as President. Eisenhower gave Gerow a month and a week to come up with a plan for the postwar educational system of the Army.[12]

Gerow's instructions directed him to address specifically the question of the advisability of reopening the Army War College. He was to assume two alternate eventualities: that the Army and Navy Staff College would be retained, and that it would not be retained. Assisting Gerow were three major generals, each representing one of the three major commands into which the Army had been organized since 1942: the Army Ground Forces, the Army Air Forces, and the Army Service Forces. Major General William G. Livesay, of the Ground Forces, was a 1933 graduate of the Army War College, the other two representatives had not attended the War College. With his report due by January 1, time compelled Gerow and his colleagues to incorporate into their recommendations many of the concepts put forth earlier in study efforts of the Army Air Forces, Army Ground Forces, and the Joint Chiefs of Staff.[13]

Gerow not only lacked time, he also lacked critical information on the size and structure of the postwar Army, as well as on the future organization of the national defense establishment. The board attempted, therefore, to devise a scheme that would work regardless of whether the Army Air Forces became an autonomous service, regardless of what structure was erected to provide unity of effort to the military services, and regardless of how the Army might be organized below the War Department level. The board proposed that most of the officer education system be decentralized to the three major subordinate commands. The Army Ground Forces system would consist of basic and advanced branch school courses and a "Ground College," the system taking the officer through the levels of the division and the corps. The Service Forces system would be similar but would be capped by a "Service College." The Army Air Forces system would consist of an Air Tactical School, an Air Command and Staff School, and an "Air College," graduates of the system being prepared for duty at the headquarters of Air Force units at the wing level and higher.[14]

Above the three colleges of the major commands, the Gerow Board recommended an "Armed Forces College." Gerow did not know whether the Navy would agree to participate in this venture as an equal partner. He suspected that it would not. But if the Navy did participate, the Armed Forces College would be controlled by the Joint Chiefs of Staff (or by whatever defense coordinating agency emerged from unification legislation). If the Navy did not participate, the Armed Forces College would be under War Department control. In the case of Army officers, students at the Armed Forces College would be graduates of one of the three major command colleges. The proposed Armed Forces College would address the problems of field armies, army groups, strategic and tactical air forces, and supporting service forces. It would also instruct on joint airborne and amphibious operations. The scope of the proposed ten-month course would extend through the level of the theater of operations. The college would offer a three-month associate course, but no extension courses. Since the Armed Forces College would include as part of its curriculum the instruction that had been presented by the wartime Army and Navy Staff College, the latter institution could be disestablished.[15]

Gerow was not asked to make recommendations on educational institutions beyond those that would be under the control of the War Department, but his board nonetheless presented a plan for an elaborate system of high-level joint institutions to be controlled by the Joint Chiefs of Staff. The plan called for a "National Security University" to coordinate the work of four, or perhaps five, colleges complete within themselves: an "Administrative College" instructing in manpower and personnel management, an "Intelligence College" addressing national-level intelligence affairs, an "Industrial College" with a role similar to that of the Army Industrial College, and a "National War College" to prepare officers to serve with the Joint Chiefs of Staff and at the War and Navy Department levels. The fifth recommended college was a "State Department College." The board did not explain this last institution in detail, merely recommending that the State Department be urged to establish it and that its course of instruction be coordinated with the other four colleges. Of the four proposed colleges, only at the National War College would a prerequisite for attendance be graduation from the "Armed Forces College."[16]

Having divided the former missions of the Army War College between the proposed colleges of the "National Security University" and the "Armed Forces College," the Gerow Board recommended that the Army War College not be reestablished. Though expressing a preference that all the colleges of the university be under one roof, the board recommended that if such was not practical, the facilities of the Army War College should be made available to the university. The board recommended further that the "Armed Forces College" be located at Fort

Leavenworth and the Ground College at Fort Benning, Georgia.[17]

The recommendations of the Gerow plan, despite the recommendation calling for disestablishment of the Army War College, were in fact a strong endorsement of what the Army War College had been attempting throughout the interwar years. Moreover, they vividly demonstrated how extremely ambitious the War College program of the 1930s had been. Gerow in essence recommended that the Conduct of War phase of the former Army War College program be expanded into a full ten-month course at the Armed Forces College. The Preparation for War phase would be expanded also, and the responsibility for presenting it would be divided between the Administrative College and the National War College and, to a degree, the Industrial College and the Intelligence College. The fundamental Gerow criticism of the old Army War College was not that it contributed too little, but that it attempted more than it alone could do. Another interesting feature of the Gerow recommendations was the implication of the need for specialized study by those officers who were to serve at the national level. The board saw a need for officers versed in manpower mobilization problems, just as before the war a need had been seen for officers knowledgeable of the problems of industrial mobilization. The board perceived a need also for specialized study of politico-military affairs, national strategy, and intelligence. Without stating it explicitly, Gerow and his colleagues were in fact suggesting that the traditional concept of the general staff officer as a mere specialist in military operations was no longer adequate.

The Gerow Board did not meet its suspense date of January 1. Soon after convening it asked for and received an extension until January 25. Its final report, however, was not submitted until February 5, 1946. As far as the higher-level educational institutions were concerned, it is difficult to conclude that the Gerow Board exercise had any real effect. Marshall and Eisenhower had been considering closure of the Army War College long before the board was convened. Steps were already underway to transform the Army and Navy Staff College into a higher-level institution along the lines of General DeWitt's earlier recommendations. Major General Alfred M. Gruenther (AWC 1939) had been brought back from Austria in the fall of 1945 and assigned as Admiral Hill's deputy to assist in the transformation.[18]

While the Gerow Board was still in session, Hill submitted a curriculum to the Joint Chiefs for approval. Eisenhower concurred in Hill's plan. Remarking that the new joint institution was to be the capstone of the military educational system, Eisenhower offered to turn over the Army War College building whenever Hill was prepared to accept it. Then, on the 4th of February 1946, the War, Navy, and State Departments jointly and publicly announced the establishment of the National War College; the first class was to assemble in September. In April the

War Department dutifully and formally relinquished control of Elihu Root's building to the joint college. At the same time the Army Industrial College was transferred to the joint control and direction of the Under Secretary of War and the Assistant Secretary of the Navy, the school to be considered equal to the National War College and redesignated the Industrial College of the Armed Forces. In July the Industrial College was moved to the site of the former Army War College, now officially named Fort Lesley J. McNair. Its first Commandant was an Army War College classmate of Gruenther's Brigadier General Edward B. McKinley. None of the other three colleges of Gerow's "National Security University" were activated.[19]

Neither did Gerow's "Armed Forces College" materialize in the form he visualized. With the Army and Navy Staff College converted into the National War College, the services recognized the need for a joint school focusing on theater of operations and joint task force problems. But the Armed Forces Staff College that evolved to meet this need was only a shadow of the Armed Forces College that Gerow had recommended. By April 1946 Eisenhower and the Chief of Naval Operations, Chester A. Nimitz, agreed that a five-month course would be adequate. In June the two chiefs appointed a committee consisting of Vice Admiral Forrest P. Sherman, Lieutenant General Wade H. Haislip (AWC 1932), and Hill and Gruenther from the National War College to recommend a curriculum. Nimitz offered Navy facilities at Norfolk, Virginia, as the site of the new school, but Eisenhower and Nimitz differed on the exact role the new school should play. Nimitz wrote Eisenhower in early June that in his view the new institution should teach joint techniques and procedures. It should be a school to train staff officers, not to develop commanders. "Staff" should appear in its title. Eisenhower's reply indicated a broader approach. As the Army War College had come to believe during the era of William Connor, Eisenhower saw the functions of command and staff as "inseparable." Moreover, as the only existing school concerned with the levels of the theater of operations and the joint task force, the school could not avoid dealing with command functions at those levels. Eisenhower believed further that graduation from the school should be a prerequisite for attendance at the National War College. The more limited Nimitz approach won out. Established two weeks after the Eisenhower-Nimitz correspondence, the institution was named the "Armed Forces Staff College." It offered the agreed-upon five-month course and made no provision for an associate course or other special means by which officers of the reserve components could participate. It accepted its first students in January 1947.[20]

The structure of a postwar educational system was not the only organizational issue facing the Chief of Staff in the spring of 1946. Closer to home was the problem of the War Department itself. Its postwar organization was the subject of heated debate even before the war ended. In May 1946, under the guise of decentralizing the War Department, Eisenhower abolished the Army Service Forces, granted increased autonomy to the Army Air Forces, and reorganized the War Department General Staff. Six directorates were formed: Personnel and Administration; Intelligence; Organization and Training; Service, Supply and Procurement; Plans and Operations; and Research and Development. Additionally, Eisenhower organized in his office an Advisory Group under Lieutenant General Wade Haislip to study Army organization and management problems. In effect, with the exception of the new Research and Development Directorate, Eisenhower had returned to the Pershing staff organization that Marshall had abandoned in 1942. The Operations Division that had acted as Marshall's operating and strategic command post during the war lost its primacy to become but one staff element among equals. Within the continental United States six numbered army headquarters were established, each responsible for a specified geographical area. These six headquarters answered directly to the War Department in carrying out their administrative, service, and supply functions, but they were under the supervision of Headquarters, Army Ground Forces, on training and troop matters. Headquarters, Army Ground Forces, was moved from Washington to the facilities of the Coast Artillery School at Fort Monroe, Virginia.[21]

Despite the desires of Marshall and Eisenhower for a strong joint educational system and Eisenhower's willingness to give up the Army War College and the Army Industrial College in order to encourage one, it would be mistaken to conclude that either Chief of Staff was convinced that establishment of the joint system was certain. They hedged the investment. In August 1945 General Marshall approved Leavenworth's initiating a Command Class for about fifty specially selected officers in the grade of colonel and lieutenant colonel from the Ground, Air, and Service Forces. Major General William F. Dean (AWC 1940) conducted the sixteen-week course. Its similarity to the pre-1941 War College is striking. The students were assumed to already be familiar with general staff work and, after a brief refresher phase, conducted analytical studies of World War II operations, studied the organization and functions of the War Department, and drafted theater war plans. The method of instruction was the traditional War College pattern—committee studies, map exercises, and map maneuvers. Two classes completed this course between October 1945 and July 1946. Some members of the first class had the opportunity to express their opinions on an Army educational system to the Gerow Broad.[22]

The Command Class was discontinued after the summer of 1946 when the Command and General Staff School returned to a peacetime forty-week course. The postwar Leavenworth mission, however, was greatly expanded in scope. Leavenworth now was to instruct on the employment of all field forces "within the framework of the army group." Moreover, it was to prepare officers for duty as commanders and staff officers at the "division and higher levels." In other words, the War Department asked Leavenworth to accomplish everything it had before the war regarding the division and corps, but in addition to take on the former Army War College mission relative to army, army group, and the War Department General Staff. It was to do all this in one academic year, despite the belief held before the war by many, perhaps most, experienced officers that Leavenworth should be a two-year course, as indeed for a number of the interwar years it had been. Commandant Gerow and his faculty had a probably impossible challenge on their hands.[23]

Experiments at Leavenworth

In 1919 and 1920 Peyton March had willed to the United States Army an officer educational system much more important and influential than that which had existed before World War I. The goal of George Marshall and Dwight Eisenhower in the immediate post-World War II period was to create a similarly influential joint educational system. For a number of reasons beyond their control they were not successful. Unfortunately, in the process of trying they fragmented the Army's own system at the higher levels. It was left to the institution at Fort Leavenworth to fill the gap, to put the pieces back together. Leavenworth proved unable to do so, but it was at Leavenworth where much of the thought and planning for a new Army War College took place. It was at Leavenworth that the foundation of the third Army War College was laid.

The War Department's helpful solution to General Gerow's immediate problem was to redesignate the Command and General Staff School a "college" and to separate its school year into two phases—a "common" phase and a "specialized" phase. For the ten-week specialized phase the class was divided into four groups, each group studying but one of the four principal staff areas—personnel, intelligence, operations and training, and logistics. During the specialized phase, concentration would be on the duties and functions of the general staff at army group, theater army, zone of the interior, and War Department levels, those levels that before 1940 had been the instructional responsibility of the Army War College. To present the instruction the War Department organized Leavenworth into "four schools"—Personnel, Intelligence, Combined Arms, and Logistics—a structure not unlike that installed by General Connor at the Army War College in 1928. But Leavenworth had been given a task too large to achieve in ten months. Even before the first class convened, Gerow requested the advice and assistance of experts on education.[24]

The help Gerow sought was provided by a special survey commission led by Dr. Edwin R. Henry, Chief of the Personnel Research Section of the Office of the Adjutant General. The commission visited Leavenworth during August, October, and December of 1946 and submitted its report in February 1947. The commission offered seven major recommendations. The lead recommendation was that the Command and General Staff College be reorganized into two distinct institutions. The first institution would be a "college" performing the traditional Leavenworth mission pertaining to command and general staff functions at the levels of division through field army. This "college" would offer a ten-month course with a common curriculum for all students.[25]

The second institution at Leavenworth would be a "university" made up of four "schools" which would assume the former Army War College mission as it pertained to general staff duties at the War Department level. Selected graduates of the "college," after intervening command and staff tours of duty, would return to pursue a specialized course at one of the autonomous "schools" of the "university"—Personnel, Intelligence, Training and Operations, or Logistics. Henry's group did not spell out in any detail the curricula of the four schools either as to length or content. The basic assumption behind Henry's proposed organization, however, was the same assumption that had been behind the National Security University proposal of the Gerow Board the previous winter: above field army level, staff specialization was necessary. The original Prussian idea that a general staff officer was a specialist in military operations was being replaced by a concept of staff specialization—at least above field army level.[26]

Gerow accepted the thrust of the Henry Commission findings that the preparation of general staff officers for duty at the War Department, theater, and zone of the interior levels should be separated from the preparation of officers for duty as commanders and staff officers at tactical levels. In essence, he returned to the 1903 concept of Tasker Bliss that the *Truppengeneralstab* was the true business of Leavenworth. As he had the previous year, Gerow recommended that a school of personnel and a school of intelligence be established in Washington and that the Industrial College teach a course on logistics. Gerow's superior on educational matters, the Commanding General of Army Ground Forces, General Jacob L. Devers (AWC 1933), concurred in the recommendations and forwarded them to the War Department. Receipt of the Gerow recommendations in March 1947 sparked General Staff reconsideration of the school system.[27]

Eisenhower, Bradley, and No Decision

The General Staff agreed that the current educational system was inadequate; however, opinion differed on how to rectify the situation. The Director of Organization and Training recommended that the capacity of the National War College and the Industrial College be increased. The Director of Personnel and Administration recommended that the Army War College be reestablished. The Director of Plans and Operations had no specific solution, but he insisted that higher-level training be along broad, not specialty, lines. The Director of Service, Supply, and Procurement suggested two new schools, one for intelligence and the other for personnel, administration, organization, and logistics. Confronted with this variety of staff views, Eisenhower asked General Haislip to review the problem. In August 1947, Haislip reported that he concurred in the view that a gap existed in officer education and that it could best be closed by establishment of an Army War College. Haislip urged that all possibilities be explored to activate the college at an early date.[28]

Eisenhower did not act on Haislip's recommendation. Haislip submitted his report the month after enactment of the National Security Act of 1947, legislation that had been preceded by a year-long debate over the degree to which the military services should be unified. The act of 1947 did not provide for unification. It mandated a National Military Establishment, a sort of federation of the military departments, with a presiding Secretary of Defense supported by a small staff led by three Special Assistants. The Air Force became a third and equal service, and the War Department was renamed the Department of the Army. The organization of Joint Chiefs of Staff was put on a statutory basis, and a Joint Staff not to exceed one hundred officers was authorized. The 1947 act charged the JCS with preparing strategic plans and providing strategic direction and joint logistics plans, and it authorized the JCS to establish unified commands in strategic regions. The Joint Chiefs were also charged with formulating policies for the coordination of the education of members of the military forces. At a level above the National Military Establishment, the act authorized a National Security Council to integrate domestic, foreign, and military policy. Also formed outside the National Military Establishment was a Central Intelligence Agency, and a National Security Resources Board to coordinate military, industrial, and civilian mobilization. Within the National Military Establishment a Research and Development Board was provided, as well as a Munitions Board, to plan for the military aspects of industrial mobilization.[29]

In general, Eisenhower and the Army had been and were proponents of greater unification, with the Navy opposing. It is possible that Eisenhower, in his desire for greater unification, was still hoping for a more comprehensive system of joint education. To establish an Army War College while the unification debate was still going on would appear to be downgrading rather than strengthening unification. The Navy and the recently emancipated Air Force, however, had also discovered gaps in their educational systems. As mentioned, the Naval War College had not closed during the war, though its focus had been at the command and staff school level. In its postwar reorientation, however, the Naval War College instituted a senior course for captains and commanders. In 1947 it initiated a second senior course in logistics. It was apparent that the Navy did not intend to rely on the joint schools to meet the educational needs of its senior officers. The Air War College also rose to a more elevated position than wartime planning had called for. Its program began to broaden beyond purely military concerns, with an increasing emphasis on international affairs. This was a natural outgrowth of strong convictions within the Air Force of the primacy of air power in the preventing and winning of wars.[30]

In February 1948, when Omar Bradley (AWC 1934) replaced Eisenhower as Chief of Staff, the problems of the Army's educational system were still unresolved. In March the War Department queried the National War College and the Industrial College regarding correlation of the Army school system with the joint schools. Both of the joint institutions indicated that an Army school comparable to the Naval War College and the Air War College was needed. Army students attending the joint schools needed better preparation in economics, political science, and international relations. They needed better understanding of the role of the Department of the Army and its relationship to the national defense establishment and other governmental agencies. The schools suggested a course similar to that of the pre-1940 Army War College. In June 1948 the War Department Policies and Programs Review Board recommended a full review of the entire Army educational system, and in July 1948 the Acting Director of Organization and Training on the Army General Staff, Major General Harold R. Bull (AWC 1933), recommended to Bradley that the Army War College be reestablished with an annual student capacity of three hundred officers.[31]

The Army Staff's concern was not only the gap that existed between the level of the Leavenworth course and that of the joint schools, but also the limited number of graduates produced by the joint schools. In January 1948, during his last full month in office as Chief of Staff, Eisenhower had queried the Joint Staff as to the possibility for quotas for reserve component officers, only to be told that there was simply no room. The Army's annual quota at the National War College was thirty, only a third of the output of the interwar Army War College, and only a few more than the Army War College Class of 1912. For the Industrial College the quota was fifty-seven, and for the Armed Forces Staff College, one hundred. Only one-fifth of one percent of the planned officer strength of the Army could be educated annually at the joint colleges. The Gerow Board had estimated that several hundred officers should attend each of these schools annually. The Chief of Engineers reported that whereas one in five of the eligible group of Corps of Engineers officers could attend the War College before the war, now only one in twenty-six could be selected. An Organization and Training Division staff study in 1947 found that the joint schools were producing only one-third of the graduates needed. Bull provided all of this information to Bradley, along with his recommendation to reestablish the Army War College. Bull indicated that the matter was urgent, pointing out that unless funds were requested in the fiscal year 1950 budget estimates, the opening of the Army War College would be delayed until September 1950.[32]

In January 1948, the month before Bradley replaced Eisenhower, Lieutenant General Manton S. Eddy replaced Gerow as Commandant of the Command and General Staff College. With no definitive action forthcoming from the Department of the Army on the former Commandant's recommendations to relieve Leavenworth of the specialized staff courses, Eddy moved ahead to reorganize the institution in accord with the concept of the Henry Commission. By the start of the 1948-49 school year, Eddy's faculty was arranged so that one department—that of "The Commander and General Staff"—presented all the instruction in what Eddy considered his primary mission, preparing officers to serve as commanders and general staff officers at division, corps, and army levels. Four other departments, a rather pale reflection of Henry's "university," taught the ten-week specialized courses in personnel, intelligence, organization and training, and logistics. Whether intentionally or not, Eddy had structured Leavenworth so that a separation along the lines dividing the prewar Command and General Staff School and the Army War College would be easy—if that was to be the decision.[33]

The Eddy Boards and J. Lawton Collins

Chief of Staff Bradley, however, did not accept Bull's recommendation that the Army War College be reestablished for the 1949-50 school year. Instead he approved the convening of yet another board of officers to review the Army's entire school system. Once again the Commandant at Leavenworth, now General Eddy, was designated to lead the board. Assisting him were the commandants of the Infantry, Artillery, Armor, and Engineer schools, as well as representatives of the Organization and Training Directorate of the Army General Staff and of the Office of the Chief of Army Field Forces. The latter "office" was a field agency of the Department of the Army. It had been organized in March 1948 as the successor to Headquarters, Army Ground Forces. It had no command functions, but was to provide general supervision, coordination, and inspection of all matters pertaining to the training of individuals of the field army. Three of the officers serving with Eddy were graduates of the

Army War College, but Eddy was not. One member, Major General William G. Livesay (AWC 1933), had been a member of the Gerow Board. Given a more reasonable amount of time to complete their study than Gerow had been given, the Eddy Board submitted its report in June 1949. As Wade Haislip had in the summer of 1947, and as Harold Bull had in the summer of 1948, General Eddy recommended that the Army reestablish an institution equivalent to the former Army War College.[34]

The Department of the Army had directed the Eddy Board to determine the adequacy of the entire system for the education of officers. Within that mission, however, the board had been directed to determine "specifically whether an Army War College (or other institution at a level comparable to the Naval and Air War Colleges) should be included in the Army School System." The board apparently was expected to find in favor of an Army War College because in that event it was asked to submit a plan that would include the institution's mission, scope of instruction, location, personnel requirements, costs, and prerequisites for attendance. The Department of the Army had one stipulation: "In no case will the location proposed be in the Washington area."[35]

The Eddy Board produced thirteen recommendations. Recommendation Number 6 outlined an officer's progression through four educational levels: a branch school company officers' course, a branch school advanced officers' course, a regular course of the Command and General Staff College, and finally, at the top, not an Army War College but an "advanced course of the Command and General Staff College." Both the regular and the advanced courses at the Command and General Staff College were proposed to be ten months in length. The regular course would take the officer through the division, corps, and army, and comparable levels of command within the communications zone. The advanced course would be attended only after an intervening course tour of duty. It would include instruction on the duties of commanders and staffs of higher army echelons such as the army group, theater army headquarters, zone of the interior, and headquarters, Department of the Army. The course would emphasize "Army technique necessary to carry out the army's mission as a part of the National Military Establishment." The course should be located initially at Fort Leavenworth: The first class should have one hundred officer students, but subsequently enrollment should be increased to three hundred. Students selected for the advanced course should have between thirteen and twenty-one years of service and should not have passed that critical forty sixth birthday.[36]

The rationale behind the Eddy Board recommendation for a higher-level course rested primarily on what by 1949 was widely perceived as the gap that the postwar education system had created between the instruction received at the Command and General Staff College and that received at the National War College. Eddy's group deemed a failure the attempt to fill this gap with the ten-week specialized staff courses at Leavenworth. Not only was thirty weeks clearly inadequate to study the division, corps, and army, but the ten-week specialized courses did not provide the opportunity to investigate thoroughly the problems of the commander and the entire general staff at the higher Army levels. The output of the National War College was clearly too small to meet Army requirements, and it appeared unlikely that its capacity would be increased. Even if it could be increased, the gap would remain. Army officers attending the National War College should already be competent army planners at theater level and carry with them to the National War College a broad understanding of the strategical and tactical power of land forces and their logistical requirements. This understanding they could gain neither at the current Command and General Staff College nor at the National War College.[37]

The Eddy Board report arrived at the Department of the Army in mid-June 1949. Recognizing its long-term influence on the effectiveness of the officer corps, the Organization and Training Directorate of the General Staff sought comments from thirty-eight various staff agencies and commands. Opinion that the new course was needed was unanimous, but many of the respondents objected to the name "Advanced Course, Command and General Staff College," urging instead "Army War College." Many also insisted on its physical separation from the Command and General Staff College. The Organization and Training Directorate added reinforcing rationale to support founding of the new school. In this staff division's view, the two joint colleges were evolving into agencies of the federal government increasingly interested in economic, political, and industrial matters. They were not true advanced military schools. They were no substitute for the old Army War College. The Organization and Training Directorate also argued that the meager quotas to the joint colleges precluded any reasonable selection of officers for high-level training. It calculated a need for three hundred graduates per year, whereas the National War College and the Industrial College were educating together only seventy-six Army officers annually. Highly deserving officers were being denied opportunity, and among them a general feeling of futility had developed.[38]

In August General J. Lawton Collins (AWC 1938 and member of the faculty 1938-40) replaced Omar Bradley as Chief of Staff. General Wade Haislip had become Vice Chief. In October Collins approved the Eddy report—but with modifications. The modifications, pertaining to the new senior institution, changed the whole tenor of what that institution was to be. Quite clearly it was to be an Army War College, not an advanced course of the Command and General Staff College. Moreover, the Army War College was to stand at the apex of the army educational system for officers; attendance thereat will represent completion of the formal educational requirement for the assumption of high level positions with the Department of Defense, and those governmental agencies which the army might be called upon to fill.

Although, as explained in the modifications, the Army would continue to select annually a few officers to attend the National War College and the Industrial College of the Armed Forces, attendance at the joint institutions was to receive no more than equal weight with attendance at the Army War College when officers were selected for high-level positions. Joe Collins was interested in more than gap-filling; in the future the Army would exercise full responsibility for the preparation of its own officers for service at the highest levels.[39] Collins' strong endorsement was only the first indication of the solid support this energetic Chief of Staff would provide during the early years of the third Army War College.

Collins' quick action on reestablishing the Army War College, in contrast to Eisenhower's and Bradley's reluctance to do so, might be explained by events on the unification front in 1949. The National Security Act of 1947 was amended that year, strengthening considerably the position of both the Office of the Secretary of Defense and the organization of the Joint Chiefs of Staff. A Department of Defense replaced the National Military Establishment. The service Secretaries lost their cabinet rank and their seats on the National Security Council. The Secretary of Defense was authorized a Deputy Secretary and three Assistant Secretaries of Defense, one of whom was to be the department comptroller. The position of Chairman of the Joint Chiefs of Staff was created, and Bradley was appointed to fill it. The Joint Staff was increased to not more than 210 officers. The battles between the Navy and the Secretary of Defense and the Navy and Air Force reached a crescendo that same year with the cancellation of construction of a super aircraft carrier, the affair known as the "Revolt of the Admirals," and the Navy's attack on the B-36 bomber program. In this atmosphere, a cooperative triservice effort to build a strong joint officer educational system was not very promising.[40]

On October 4, the Department of the Army convened a second board under General Eddy to recommend the location and command structure for the "Army War College," the composition and source of its staff and faculty, the curriculum, and all other details required to make the college operational by the fall of 1950. To assist Eddy, three general officers representing the General Staff and a colonel from Army Field Forces were named to the board.[41]

The second Eddy Board initially met on October 17. Its first decision, by a vote of three to two, was that the Army War College should be supervised by the Chief of Army Field Forces, as was the Command and General Staff College and the combat arms schools. The two dissenters were the representatives of the Army General Staff. They immediately submitted a minority report. They held that the Army War College should not be just one of a number of schools operating under a training agency, but should function directly under the Army General Staff. They argued that the principal employer of the graduates of the Army War College would be the Department of the Army General Staff, not the army in the field, which was the chief user of the products of the schools supervised by Army Field Forces.[42]

On the 24th of October the board submitted its first interim report to the Chief of Staff. The interim report recommended that the Army War College be established initially at Fort Leavenworth, but permanently located later at Carlisle Barracks, Pennsylvania. Eddy's first board had recommended Fort Monroe, Virginia, the site of the former Coast Artillery School, as the best location. It left it up to the Department of the Army to determine Monroe's availability, that post then being the home of the Chief of Army Field Forces. It had recommended Leavenworth as the second choice. During the staffing of the first report a number of other sites were brought up, including the former Cavalry School at Fort Riley, Kansas; Fort Myer, Virginia; Fort Meade, Maryland; a naval installation near Bainbridge, Maryland; Fort Benjamin Harrison, Indiana; and Fort McClellan, Alabama.[43]

General Eddy himself dissented on the recommendation for permanent location at Carlisle Barracks. As indicated by his earlier, probably impossible play for Fort Monroe, Eddy really wanted the War College permanently located at Fort Leavenworth. He submitted to the Chief of Staff a minority report. His arguments in favor of Leavenworth were primarily that it would be more economical and cause less disruption to station the War College there. He also believed that the subject matter of the new school would be the same as that taught by the specialized departments of the Command and General Staff College. In his minority report General Eddy outlined his preferred command structure. An "Army University" subordinate to Army Field Forces should be established at Fort Leavenworth, in command of both the Army War College and the Command and General Staff College.

The splits among the members of the second Eddy Board were resolved the next month at a conference in the Pentagon Office of Vice Chief of Staff Haislip. In attendance were Eddy, Lieutenant General Matthew B. Ridgway (AWC 1937), who was the Deputy Chief of Staff for Administration and Operations, and Major General Clift Andrus (AWC 1934), the Director of Organization and Training. Haislip's decision was to have the War College remain at Leavenworth only temporarily and to decide later on a permanent location. While at Leavenworth the War College would be a separate institution with its own Commandant, but under the "general direction" of the Commandant of the Command and General Staff College. Manton Eddy lost his battle to keep the War College at Leavenworth and to inaugurate an "Army University." Whether Eddy recognized it or not, his plan was not in accord with Collins' aim to enhance the prestige of the Army War College. The Haislip decision left both colleges subject to supervision by the Chief of Army Field Forces, and it did not provide a very clear command arrangement at Fort Leavenworth. But that could be straightened out once the War College was moved.[44]

Two weeks after General Haislip's decision the Department of the Army announced that the Army War College would be reestablished at the apex of the Army's educational system, and that pending approval of a permanent site, it would be located at Fort Leavenworth. The announced purpose of the institution would be to fill a gap between the Command and General Staff College and the joint colleges by preparing officers for duty at the headquarters of the Department of the Army, army groups, theater army, and continental armies. On February 1, 1950, General Order No. 4 made official the reestablishment of the Army War College as of January 25, 1950. Early in March the Department of the Army announced that the initial session of the revived War College would begin about October 1. The first postwar Commandant was to be Major General Joseph M. Swing.[45]

The second Eddy Board, with its president dissenting, had recommended Carlisle Barracks, Pennsylvania, as the permanent location of the Army War College. A general consensus appears to have existed among Army Staff members that Carlisle was the most appropriate and desirable of all the installations considered. The Honorable Lister Hill, United States Senator from Alabama, however, did not join in that consensus. Senator Hill thought Fort McClellan, Alabama, had virtues that had been overlooked, and he made his views known to the Department of the Army. In April the Department convened another board of officers to weigh the merits of Carlisle Barracks versus those of Fort McClellan. Led by Colonel Marion Carson of Army Field Forces, the board consisted of two Department of the Army staff officers and Lieutenant Colonel Harry H. Critz, the recently designated Secretary of the reestablished Army War College. Carson's group met briefly in the Pentagon during the first week of May, then recommended Carlisle by virtue of economy, better geographical location and communications, and earlier availability. Planning proceeded on the basis of Carlisle, but until the War College was actually operating at that place there was no guarantee that Senator Hill would remain silent.[46]

In the spring of 1950 Carlisle Barracks could hardly have been considered to be without any disadvantages, but the basic ingredients that a prestigious War College might need were there. Carlisle was located near the metropolitan centers of the east coast, convenient both to Washington and to major civilian academic institutions. It enjoyed rail service, the Pennsylvania Turnpike was under construction with its eastern terminus now but three miles from Carlisle, and Olmstead Air Force Base was on the southern outskirts of Harrisburg, only some twenty-five miles distant.

Carlisle Barracks was a historic military installation, dating back to the colonial period. It had the distinction of having been put to the torch by Jeb Stuart's cavalry during the Gettysburg campaign of 1863. From 1879 until 1918 it had been the site of the Indian Industrial School, founded and for many years led by an Army officer, Richard Henry Pratt. The Indian School won national and international notice through the exploits of the amazing Olympic athlete Jim Thorpe and its football teams coached by Glen S. "Pop" Warner. Between the World Wars Carlisle Barracks was the home of the Army's Medical Field Service School. In 1950 three military schools were operational at Carlisle Barracks: the Armed Forces Information School, training officers in the intricacies of public information duties; the Army Security Agency School; and the Army Chaplains School. The academic facilities, while hardly lavish, were adequate for the beginning of the Army War College. Moreover, Carlisle Barracks had the potential for that difficult to define but easily recognized attribute of academic atmosphere.[47]

Leavenworth Plans a War College

During the month before the Carson Board convened, General Swing and his designated Deputy Commandant, Brigadier General Arthur R. Trudeau, had arrived at Fort Leavenworth. They found curricular planning for the War College already well along. The program for the first Army War College had germinated in the fertile mind of Tasker Bliss. That of the second Army War College had emerged from the assembly of the prospective faculty by James McAndrew in Germany. The program for the third Army War College was to come from the collective wisdom of the faculty at Fort Leavenworth. Or at least that was the plan.

As early as February 1949 General Eddy had formed a committee of the heads of the specialized staff departments of the Command and General Staff College to begin the planning. Fundamental differences as to approach had arisen almost immediately. The majority recognized that the new "advanced" or "war college" course should be different from the regular course at the Command and General Staff College, that it should provide opportunity for greater initiative and freedom of thought on the part of the student, and that more reliance should be placed on learning through student investigation. Nonetheless, that same majority, perhaps reflecting the views of General Eddy, saw the course as an expansion of what the ten-week specialized staff courses were already doing. They saw a need for what Hanson Ely's faculty of the 1920s would have recognized as "informative periods," with basic information and principles being provided by the faculty from the lecture platform.[48]

Colonel George R. Barth, on the other hand, opposed the majority. He thought the Army War College should conduct its program more as a university conducts graduate study. The curriculum should not be built around the current specialized courses. Barth recommended a course in the German tradition, more akin to McAndrew's one great problem, where after a short orientation period the class would construct a basic war plan consisting of a strategic plan, a mobilization plan, and a logistical plan. The class would then coordinate the three plans and finish the course by preparing campaign plans. Finally, the student campaign plans would be war-gamed. Though Barth did not use the term, the emphasis, in his view, should be on "preparation for war." Delays at the Department of the Army obviated any need to resolve the issue during the spring of 1949, but by September, with the findings of the first Eddy Board about to be approved, planning for the advanced or war college course needed to be resumed.[49]

General Eddy convened a new board under Colonel Wayburn D. Brown. It was to plan not only the curriculum and method of instruction, but the organization of the faculty and students, the facilities needed at Leavenworth, and a tentative schedule for the 1950-51 school year. Brown's group elected not to stray far from the specialized staff courses, just as the majority of the department heads had earlier recommended. The War College faculty would remain organized around the traditional staff sections, the Department of Personnel adding "and Comptroller" to its title. The board recommended a thirty-seven-week program, with the class in session five days per week. For twenty-six weeks the students would be in class six hours a day, with four hours of outside study expected of them. For the remaining eleven weeks they would be in class for eight hours a day participating in applicatory exercises or war games, with two hours of outside study expected. The recommended curriculum was divided rather evenly between basic general staff subjects and applicatory planning, plus another large block of "general studies" consisting of a potpourri of subject matter ranging from public speaking, statistics, and communism to atomic and radiological warfare, economic warfare, and guerrilla warfare. By Brown's analysis twenty-nine percent of the year was concerned with logistics, twenty-eight percent with personnel administration and comptrollership, twenty-three percent with operations and training, and nineteen percent with intelligence.[50] This was the basic curriculum plan being worked up in detail when General Swing arrived at Fort Leavenworth in

April 1950—but the new Commandant did not like it. He figuratively, if not literally, threw it in the trash basket.

NOTES

1. Kreidberg and Henry, *Mobilization*, 611-13, 697.
2. Ibid., 612. John W. Masland and Laurence I. Radway, *Soldiers and Scholars: Military Education and National Policy* (Princeton, N.J.: Princeton University Press, 1957), 101.
3. Ibid., 103-04. T. A. Brown, "ANSCOL at the Naval War College," *Naval Institute Proceedings*, (March 1946). T. Turner, "The Army-Navy Staff College," *American Foreign Service Journal*, (March 1945): 20-21.
4. *The Papers of Dwight David Eisenhower*, Alfred D. Chandler, Jr., ed. (Baltimore, Md.: Johns Hopkins Press, 1970-   ), 7:Item 307.
5. Ibid., Items 307, 311.
6. Masland and Radway, *Soldiers and Scholars*, 129-30. James C. Shelburne, *Factors Leading to the Establishment of the Air University* (Ph.D. Dissertation, University of Chicago, 1953).
7. Masland and Radway, *Soldiers and Scholars*, 130-31.
8. Ibid., 131-33.
9. Ibid., 133-34.
10. Ely, closing address, 28 June 1926, AWC Course 1925-26, "Miscellaneous," Doc. 10.
11. Johnson to Roosevelt, March 8, 1939, copy in AWC File 93-12. DeWitt to Marshall, August 8, 1939, Ibid.
12. Masland and Radway, *Soldiers and Scholars*, 133-36. Hearings before the Senate Committee on Military Affairs, 17 October-17 December 1945, *The Department of Defense: Documents on Establishment and Organization, 1944-1978* (Washington: Historical Office, Office of the Secretary of Defense, 1978), 6-7. AG Letter, 23 November 1945; Subject: War Department Military Education Board, in *Report of War Department Military Education Board on Educational Systems for Officers of the Army*, 5 February 1946 (hereafter *Gerow Report*), 14-15.
13. Ibid. Masland and Radway, *Soldiers and Scholars*, 136-37.
14. *Gerow Report*, 5-8, 41-66.
15. Ibid., 7-11, 37-39.
16. Ibid., 7-11, 27-36. Masland and Radway, *Soldiers and Scholars*, 137-38.
17. *Gerow Report*, 10-11.
18. I. H. Edwards, Memorandum for the President, War Department Military Education Board, 12 December 1945, *Gerow Report*, 17. Board Procedure, Ibid., 19.
19. Thurman S. Wilkins, "The Postwar Military School System," *Military Affairs* 10 (Summer 1946): 42-44. Eisenhower, Memorandum for the Commandant Army-Navy Staff College, 28 January 1946, *Papers of Eisenhower*, 7:Item 682. "The Industrial College of the Armed Forces," *The Field Artillery Journal* 37 (March-April 1947): 105-07. War Department Circular No. 117, 23 April 1946. Masland and Radway, *Soldiers and Scholars*, 140-41.
20. United States Armed Forces Staff College, *Catalogue Class 53* (Norfolk, Va., 1973) I: 1-2. Eisenhower to Nimitz, Subject: Armed Forces College, *Papers of Eisenhower*, 7:Item 938. Wilkins, "Postwar School System," 45. "The Armed Forces Staff College," *The Field Artillery Journal* 37 (March-April 1947): 102-04.
21. Hewes, *Root to McNamara*, 129-62.
22. Orville Z. Tyler, Jr. "The Development of the Command and General Staff College at Fort Leavenworth, Kansas, 1937-1951." (master's thesis, American University, June 1952), 39-41. Robert A. Doughty, "The Command and General Staff College in Transition, 1946-1976" (Special study, Command and General Staff College, May 1976), 8-9. *Gerow Report*, 23.
23. War Department Circular No. 202, 9 July 1946. Tyler, "CGSC, 1937-1951," 41-47. "The Command and General Staff College," *The Field Artillery Journal*, 37 (March-April 1947): 99-101. Wilkins, "Postwar School System," 47.

24. Circular 202. Tyler, "CGSC 1937-1951," 49-50. Doughty, "CGSC 1946-1976," 11-13. Gerow to ACofS G-3, WDGS Subject: Use of Scientific and Technological Experts at the Command and General Staff College, 4 June 1946, reprinted in The Adjutant General's Office, *Survey of the Educational Program of the Command and Staff College* (hereafter *Henry Survey*), February 1947, 109-10.
25. Henry had formerly been with the Department of Psychology, New York University. Other members were Dr. Mitchell Dreese, Professor of Educational Psychology, The George Washington University; Dr. Harold A. Edgerton, Professor of Psychology, Ohio State University; and Dr. Jacob S. Orleans, Assistant Professor of Psychology, The City College of New York. Orleans later took a permanent position at Leavenworth with the unusual title of Psycho-Educational Adviser. *Henry Survey,* 2-8, 26-27, 111-16.
26. *Henry Survey,* 2-8, 26-27.
27. H. R. Bull, Acting Director of Organization and Training to Chief of Staff, Subject: Establishment of a School at War College Level, 28 July 1948, par. 2a, copy attached as Appendix F to DeVere Armstrong, "Study on the Army War College," 13 August 1953, (hereafter "Armstrong Study"), AWC File Academic Year 1954, MHI.
28. Ibid., par. 26. War Department Policies and Programs Review Board, Final Report, 11 August 1947, extract attached as Appendix E to "Armstrong Study." Masland and Radway, *Soldiers and Scholars,* 146.
29. *The National Security Act of 1947,* 26 July 1947, reprinted in the *Department of Defense: Documents on Establishment and Organization, 1944-1978* (Washington: Historical Office, Office of the Secretary of Defense, 1978), 35-50.
30. Masland and Radway, *Soldiers and Scholars,* 144-45, 148-52.
31. Bull to Chief of Staff, 28 July 1948, pars. 3-5, 11, "Armstrong Study."
32. Eisenhower to Joint Chiefs of Staff, 16 January 1948, Subject: Allocation of Quotas to the Reserve Components for the Joint Colleges, *Papers of Eisenhower,* 9:Item 1994. *Gerow Report,* 72-75. Bull to Chief of Staff, 28 July 1948, pars. 7-8, 10.
33. Eugene A. Salet, "Reorganization of the Command and General Staff College," *Military Review* (September 1948): 3-12. Salet was a member of a faculty board Eddy established to recommend organization of the college. George B. Barth, "The Department of Operations and Training," *Military Review* (May 1949): 52-55.
34. Historical Background and Authority for Reestablishment of the Army War College at Fort Leavenworth, Kansas, par. 6, "Armstrong Study," Annex 2. Masland and Radway, *Soldiers and Scholars,* 146. Letter AGPA-BG350, Subject: Department of the Army Board on Educational System for Officers, 15 June 1949 (hereafter *Eddy Report*), 11-14. In addition to Eddy, members of the board were Major Generals Clift Andrus (AWC 1934), Withers A. Burress (AWC 1935), and Douglas L. Weart, and Colonels Edward H. McDaniel, Cecil W. Nist, and Philip C. Wehle. Hewes, *Root to McNamara,* 171.
35. *Eddy Report,* 12-13.
36. Ibid., 6-9, 43-44.
37. Ibid., 36-39.
38. Clift Andrus, Director of Organization and Training, to Chief of Staff (undated draft), Subject: Report of the Department of the Army Board on the Educational System for Officers, attached as Appendix H to "Armstrong Study."
39. Modifications of the Department of the Army Board on Educational System for Officers, *Eddy Report.*
40. Public Law 216, 81st Congress, 10 August 1949, reprinted in *Department of Defense: Documents,* 84-106. For summary treatment of 1949 unification controversies see Keith D. McFarland, "The 1949 Revolt of the Admirals," *Parameters: Journal of the U.S. Army War College,* 11 (June 1981): 53-63.
41. Letter AGAO-S (4 October 1949) CSGOT, Subject: Board for the Establishment of an Army War College, attached as Appendix I to "Armstrong Study."
42. E. M. Starr and A. D. Marston to President of the Board, 20 October 1949, Subject: Minority Report on the Recommended Command Structure, Appendix K, "Armstrong Study."

43. First Interim Report of the Board of Officers to Consider the Establishment of an Army War College, 24 October 1949. Extracted as Appendix J, "Armstrong Study." *Eddy Report*, 41. "Armstrong Study," Annex 4.
44. Eddy to Chief of Staff, 29 October 1949, Subject: Minority Report on the Recommended Permanent Location of the Proposed Army War College and on a Proposed Command Structure, Appendix L, "Armstrong Study." John R. Beishline, Memorandum for the Record, 30 November 1949, Appendix M, "Armstrong Study."
45. *The Army and Navy Journal* (4 March 1950): 696. Department of the Army General Orders No. 4, 1 February 1950.
46. Report of Proceedings of Board of Officers to Establish Location of the Army War College, 2-6 May 1950, Appendix O, "Armstrong Study." Other members of the Carson Board were Lieutenant Colonels William M. Breckinridge and Arthur W. Tyson.
47. Ibid. Thomas G. Tousey, *Military History of Carlisle and Carlisle Barracks* (Richmond, Va.: The Dietz Press, 1939), 229-34, 273-353, 360-405. Richard H. Pratt, *Battlefield and Classroom: Four Decades with the American Indian, 1867-1904*, Robert M. Utley, ed., (New Haven: Yale University Press, 1964)
48. U.S. Army Command and General Staff College, Report of Committee for Curriculum for Army War College, 8 March 1949, MHI Library.
49. Ibid.
50. U.S. Army Command and General Staff College, Report of Board of Officers on Army War College, November 1949, MHI Library.

The Third Beginning
1950-1952

Major General Joseph M. Swing was a field artilleryman and a 1935 graduate of the Army War College. He had served in Washington in the office of the Chief of Field Artillery, but he had not performed duty on the War Department General Staff. For five years, from 1943 to 1948, he commanded the 11th Airborne Division throughout its campaigns in the Pacific and its occupation duties in Japan. During 1948 he commanded I Corps in Japan. In 1949 he returned to the United States and was commanding the Artillery Center and School at Fort Sill when selected to become the first Commandant of the third Army War College. At the suggestion of Lieutenant General Ridgway, Deputy Chief of Staff for Administration, Brigadier General Arthur G. Trudeau was appointed Swing's Deputy Commandant. At the time, Trudeau was commanding a constabulary brigade with the occupation forces in Germany. An officer of the Corps of Engineers, Trudeau had served as Director of Training in General Somervell's Army Service Forces and had been a pioneer architect of engineer amphibian forces during the war. After the war Trudeau served in the office of the Assistant Chief of Staff, G-1, on the War Department General Staff. Swing and Trudeau had been only briefly acquainted prior to their War College assignment.[1] Both were men with strong personalities and unusual energy. They were officers who got things done. Of the two, Trudeau probably possessed the more active intellect.

Swing and Trudeau: Getting Started
With the possible exception of the challenge faced by Tasker Bliss in 1903, the challenge to Swing and Trudeau was greater than that presented to any past Army War College leadership. Their immediate task was to prepare for the 1950-51 school year, and the worth of that first course inevitably would be measured by how firm a foundation it provided to the courses that followed. The course had to fill the often-cited

"gap" and it also had to satisfy the Chief of Staff's desire to put the War College solidly at the apex of the Army's educational system. Moreover, while the first course was in process at Fort Leavenworth, Swing and Trudeau had to insure that Carlisle Barracks was being appropriately readied and equipped to be the permanent home of the Army War College. Neither officer wasted time. Swing moved to Leavenworth in April. Before departing from Europe Trudeau took the opportunity to visit the higher military schools of France and Britain. After his return he also visited the National War College and the Naval and Air War Colleges.[2]

Immediately upon his arrival at Fort Leavenworth, General Swing created consternation among the curriculum planners. He rejected as inappropriate to a war college most of the plans that had been made over the previous six months. In Swing's opinion the faculty proposals retained too much of the flavor of the super-Leavenworth that General Eddy had been proposing and borrowed too much from the specialized staff courses of the previous Command and General Staff College course. That would not do. The new Commandant wanted distinguished guest lecturers, one or perhaps two per day, and he wanted seminars, discussion groups, and work by student committees. What Joe Swing wanted, he got. The curriculum planners began all over again. Throughout the first year they struggled to stay a few months ahead of the class.[3]

Fortunately, Swing had a flexible and energetic faculty drawn from both the faculty of the Command and General Staff College and the Army at large. The Chief of Staff saw to it that the Department of the Army gave high priority to the faculty assignment, even after June when the outbreak of the Korean War brought on partial mobilization. Like McAndrew in 1919, Swing was given almost carte blanche in faculty selection. Of the thirty-one officers of the faculty that received the Class of 1951, ten were graduates of the National War College. Three (Paul D. Adams, James F. Collins, and William C. Westmoreland) would one day wear four stars; six would become lieutenant generals; and fourteen others, either major generals or brigadier generals.[4]

To accommodate the temporary stay of the Army War College at Fort Leavenworth, General Eddy provided the top floor of the main academic building, Grant Hall. There, on October 2, 1950, the first Army War College class in over ten years convened. The class was soon being referred to by the students of the command and general staff course as "The Hundred Old Men on the Hill." But their age was advanced only in the eyes of their juniors; most were in their early forties. Only one, Colonel Thomas J. F. Trapnell, had passed the still-critical 46th birthday. Like the faculty, the students had been carefully selected for potential. Of the ninety-six Army officers in the class, forty-seven would become general officers. Dwight E. Beach and Ralph E. Haines would become generals, and four others (including Trapnell) would become lieutenant generals. The Army War College was no longer an institution attended almost exclusively by officers of the combat arms. The Army students were from all the arms and services except the Chaplains and Medical Service Corps. The class included one National Guardsman, one Navy officer, and two Marines, but no Air Force officers.[5]

Chief of Staff Collins traveled to Fort Leavenworth to help get the class off to a strong start. Although the topic of his address was "The Army and National Security," he reiterated his determination that the Army War College would occupy the apex of the educational system. He laid aside all rumors that Korean War requirements would shorten or cancel the course. What a hundred select officers would gain from a year of study was more important to the future of the Army than any contribution they might make in Korea. Collins chose to explain to the class why General Swing was selected to be the first Commandant. Collins had wanted a nonconformist in the position, and Joe Swing was the most nonconforming general officer he knew.[6]

Swing's nonconforming personality, however, contributed to a degree of friction at the highest levels at Leavenworth. As the complete revision of the planned curriculum indicated, the "general direction" authority Haislip had given to General Eddy over the Army War College was not strong enough to restrain Swing, especially after the Chief of Staff indicated his intention to give Swing a loose rein. The Command and General Staff College did have reason to feel put upon. To accommodate the War College it was necessary to reduce the size of the Command and General Staff College class. In August General Eddy departed for Europe, eventually to command the reactivated Seventh Army. Swing, as the senior officer on the post, became post commander, thereby falling heir among other things to all of Grant Hall. Swing soon changed a number of policies on how the post would operate. Moreover, disputes over doctrine arose between the two institutions. General Mark Clark, Chief of Army Field Forces, attempted to resolve these differences by charging Swing with the coordination of doctrine. Swing's promotion to lieutenant general in the spring of 1951 helped consolidate his authority. Both General Clark and Eddy's replacement as Commandant of the Command and General Staff College, Major General Horace L. McBride, were probably happy to see the War College depart for Carlisle.[7]

The Initial Program: 1950-51

In subject matter and in method, the initial program of the third Army War College was an amalgam of the second Army War College (which Swing had known), of the National War College (which through Al Gruenther had also been influenced by the second Army War College), and of whatever vestiges of Eddy's super-Leavenworth Swing had not detected. With the assistance of a member of the National War College faculty, the program began with a two-week period designed to acquaint the students with the committee-study method of instruction. As a practical exercise in the method, each student committee addressed one of several selected Army personnel problems—for example, racial segregation in the Army, the use of female soldiers, and the effect on the officer corps of the new thirty-year retirement policy. After the committees presented their solutions, the true war college course began. It consisted of thirteen courses divided into three phases.[8] The logic of the prewar division into "Preparation for War" and "Conduct of War" was either forgotten or discarded.

The first phase, "The Army and National Security," appears to have followed parts of the National War College program. But unlike the course at the National War College, the emphasis here was on the Army's role in national security. The phase consisted of two courses, each of about five weeks' duration, for which the class was divided into sixteen six-officer committees. For the first course, "National Policy," a committee addressed one of six foreign policy issues. One issue dealt with the question of German rearmament, another with an appropriate organization to carry out the military aid program to Western Europe. The remaining four issues required committee recommendations on American policy toward Latin America, the Middle East, Southeast Asia, and Northeast Asia. This "National Policy" course was the only part of the year's program that dealt almost exclusively with matters not of a purely military nature.[9]

The third Army War College had good reason to look more carefully at the world environment than had the first or second War Colleges. In the five years between the end of World War II and the reopening of the War College, the Cold War had become the accepted state of international existence. The postwar refusal of the Soviet Union to permit national self-determination in Eastern Europe and Korea, the crises of 1946 and 1947 in Iran, Turkey, and Greece, the communist coup in Czechoslavakia in 1948 followed by the Berlin blockade crisis of that same year, and the expulsion of Chinese Nationalist forces from the Asian mainland in 1949 all seemed to emphasize that the military strength of the United States was a crucial element in preventing Soviet-controlled communist expansion throughout the globe. If doubts remained as to the hostility of Soviet intentions, the blatant North Korean invasion of the Republic of Korea in the summer of 1950 tended to remove them.

The response of the United States to perceived Soviet expansionism was political, economic, and military; it was described as a policy of containment, a term first introduced in 1947 by a Foreign Service officer, George Kennan. Containment, as it had evolved by 1950, included efforts within the United Nations structure to build a world consensus against Soviet actions, the permanent stationing of U.S. naval forces in the Mediterranean and of U.S. bomber forces in the United Kingdom, the Truman Doctrine of American aid to nations threatened externally or internally by communist force, the European Recovery Program or Marshall Plan, the Berlin airlift, the North Atlantic Treaty Organization, and the commitment of U.S. ground forces to the defense of the Republic of Korea.

Those who looked beyond the single threat of Soviet expansionism understood that World War II had created great vacuums of power. Not only had Germany in central Europe and the Japanese Empire in the Far East been crushed, but the great colonial empires of Britain, France, and the Netherlands in Asia and Africa were crumbling under nationalist pressures, frequently to the accompaniment of guerrilla warfare conducted by a Marxist-inclined leadership. There were other areas of concern. India and Pakistan, newly independent, had fought one war and remained bitter enemies. British withdrawal from Palestine in 1948 had set off the first of what was to be a series of Arab-Israeli wars. A new world order was in the making, and national interest dictated that the United States take a leading role in shaping that order.[10] The American military was sharing and would continue to share in that role. The Army's future leadership at its new War College would need to understand the forces and trends shaping the new order.

As set out by the National Security Act of 1947 as amended in 1949, the governmental organization for national security was a much more complex arrangement in 1950 than it had been in 1940. This matter also deserved the attention of the third Army War College. The second course in the phase "Army and National Security" was "National Security Organization." The class, again divided into committees, was asked to provide reports contrasting the organizations of the three service departments, analyzing the structure of the Department of the Army or the Joint Chiefs of Staff, or critiquing the interservice integration of logistical support. This course included a week-long trip to Washington, where the class received eighteen briefings at the Pentagon and the State Department. Defense Secretary George Marshall addressed the class, as did Chairman of the JCS Omar Bradley and Secretary of the Army Frank Pace.[11]

The primary focus of the week in Washington, however, was on the Army General Staff, which once again had undergone reorganization. To supervise the four traditional Assistant Chiefs of Staff, G-1 through G-4, three Deputy Chiefs of Staff were now provided (a Deputy Chief of Staff for Administration, a Deputy Chief of Staff for Plans, and a Comptroller). The Congress had just passed the Army Organization Act of 1950, permanent legislation which replaced the National Defense Act of

1920. It permitted 3,000 officers to be assigned to the Department of the Army, "only" 1,000 of whom could be assigned to the Army General Staff. If a major issue arose among the students, it involved the proper positioning and role of the Comptroller of the Army. Comptrollership was hardly a traditional general staff function. Eisenhower had introduced a comptroller position into the Deputy Chief of Staff's office in 1948. Congress made it a statutory position in 1949. By 1950 the Comptroller was one of three principal deputies of the Chief of Staff. He also had concurrent responsibilities directly to the Secretary of the Army.[12]

The second phase of the year's program, lasting nine weeks, was organized around the four traditional general staff functions, as the program of the second Army War College had been. It was titled "Current Army Problems." Many of the issues addressed by the student committees would have been familiar to the students of the second Army War College. In the "Personnel and Manpower Management" course, five studies were divided among the student committees. Each problem dealt with a phase of manpower management in wartime—its procurement, development, supply, conservation, and demobilization.

In the area of G-3 responsibility, the class was organized into twenty committees, and three courses were presented concurrently: "Military Doctrine and Techniques," "Training Army Forces," and "Special Problems Relating to Future War." Each committee conducted a study in one of the three courses. In the "Military Doctrine" course, student committees were designated to address either amphibious, airborne, armor, tactical air support, or air defense operations. Other committees were asked to compare U.S. Army doctrine for army group operations with that of the former German Army or with that of the Soviet Army. The committees designated to make studies in the "Training Army Forces" course dealt either with mobilization training or with training of the reserve components. The "Special Problems" course called for two studies, one on partisan warfare and one on psychological warfare.[13]

After completion of the G-3 courses, the class was again reorganized into new committees and presented with six logistic problems encompassing mobilization requirements, interservice logistical support, logistical support of a unified command, organization for Army logistics, and the influence of atomic weapons and air transport on logistics. Two or three committees, working independently, were assigned each problem. A course on industrial mobilization followed, but as an exception to the rule it was exclusively a lecture course.

The first two phases of the program, "The Army and National security" and "Current Army Problems," although of value in themselves, were in a real sense introductory and preparatory to the final phase, "War Planning." "War Planning" consumed almost half the academic year. It began with each committee making an area assessment similar to those written by students of the first Army War College, then drafting a global strategic estimate. Two weeks were given over to each task. After the strategic estimate was completed, three courses followed in order: "Joint War Planning," "Army Planning and Mobilization Planning," and "Theater Planning." But before the class began these courses, the faculty provided a week-long presentation of an illustrative war game.[14]

The war game presented was a reconstruction of *War Game Padrone*, an exercise undertaken by the Chief of Staff's Advisory Group under General Haislip in 1948 during the Berlin blockade crisis. The philosophy of Haislip's group was that the purpose of a war plan was to set balanced, phased objectives for the peacetime military program. Moreover, if a war plan was to be realistic, its feasibility had to be tested through war-gaming. It followed, then, that a war game was a test of a plan, not a test of the skill and knowledge of the individual players. *Padrone* assumed Soviet attacks on Western Europe, the Middle East, the Mediterranean, Korea, and Alaska. It involved not only what Haislip termed the meeting engagements, but the whole sequence of problems from mobilization through demobilization.[15] James McAndrew's students thirty years before would have recognized it as the one big problem.

Indoctrinated by *Padrone* into the range and scope of war planning, the students in the joint and Army planning courses conducted studies dealing with both the short- and long-range periods. To improve their understanding of the possibilities of future technology, a field trip was made to White Sands Proving Grounds and Sandia Base in New Mexico. During the "Army Planning" course student committees were required to draft outlines of both a war plan and a mobilization plan. For the "Theater Planning" course the class was divided into six committees to study the problems of the defense of Western Europe. Some committees investigated the military problems of NATO forces; other committees studied the military problems of the forces of the eastern bloc. In support of the "War Planning" phase, the faculty drafted a text on planning procedures and techniques based upon documents already in use at the Armed Forces Staff College, the Naval War College, and the Air War College. General Swing forwarded the text to the Department of the Army. The G-3, Maxwell Taylor (AWC 1940), commented favorably upon the effort and offered suggestions that would align the text closer to procedures being used by the Joint Staff and the Army General Staff. Taylor did not indicate an intention to adopt the text.[16]

General Swing held to his purpose to provide a large number of distinguished guest speakers. Not counting orientations by the faculty, but including the briefings heard in Washington, the class attended two hundred lectures, a considerable increase over the fifty-seven to which the last prewar class had been subjected. The guest list was impressive. It included three Cabinet members, senior State Department and military officers, ambassadors, industrialists, publishers, historians, political scientists, a congressman, and even an eminent psychiatrist.[17]

In addition to committee studies and lectures, Swing used the individual research paper as an element of his educational method. The faculty specified ten topical areas of a doctrinal or organizational nature within which each student was assigned a subject. He was asked to prepare an original paper of some 5,000 words in length. The subjects were assigned shortly after the class convened, with presentation of the papers scheduled for February, about the mid-point in the course, just before the war-planning phase began. Two weeks were devoted to the presentations.[18] In sum, each student of the Class of 1951 attended two hundred lectures; participated in a committee solution to eleven studies, assessments, estimates, and plans; and prepared an individual research paper. Probably more significant to his overall intellectual development during the year, he heard, considered, discussed, critiqued, and argued the findings of other committees on subjects that he had not addressed directly himself.

Given the circumstances of a temporary location and the late hour of curriculum planning, the judgment has to be that the initial session of the third Army War College was a success. Generals Swing and Trudeau provided strong leadership, and the high quality of the faculty and the class contributed in a major way to the success of the course. The support of General Collins and the Army Staff also was critically important. Swing appears to have created the type of institution he had in mind, "a post-graduate school, contemplative in nature and mature in aspect." He attempted to provide a broad understanding of national security problems, of the Army's peacetime and future issues, and of the complexities of war planning—an integrated picture of the Army's role as an instrument of national security policy. Concurrently, he aimed to encourage creative and objective thinking.[19]

The concept of minimum distinction between faculty and student that originated in 1903 and was followed generally by the first and second War Colleges was reemphasized during the year at Leavenworth. General Swing professed that the distinction was "almost exclusively one of whether the member is assigned permanently or temporarily to the College." Trudeau went so far as to have the Fort Leavenworth telephone directory list War College personnel as "members" of the Army War College, a gesture that Tasker Bliss would have understood and appreciated. To Swing the primary duty of the faculty was to determine the nature and scope of the problems, assist with obtaining research sources, and provide general guidance. Its duty was not to offer categorical solutions or to supervise. The "mature and responsible demeanor of the members of the College" obviated the need for supervision.[20]

As the withdrawn role of the faculty demonstrates, the general approach to and methods of instruction at the third Army War College did not deviate in their essentials from those of the second. Greater differences are evident, however, in the actual subject matter addressed. The second War College had never been in the habit of investigating or having its students question national policy. Its treatment of the international environment had been essentially peripheral to its study of military intelligence matters. But in 1950 the new and leading role of the United States in the postwar world seemed to dictate at the higher military levels a broader and deeper understanding of foreign affairs and national security policy. It was not coincidence or General Swing's personal interests that resulted in the initial phase of the Army War College program being devoted to these matters. Requirements planning and preparation for war demanded it.

A second major influence evident on the curriculum of the third Army War College was the technological explosion that began during World War II and was continuing in its aftermath. Particularly disconcerting were atomic weapons aboard bombers with almost intercontinental range and the apparent potential of long-range guided missiles. Few who thought deeply on these developments had confidence in their own conclusions as to what they might mean to the future role, configuration, and tactics of land armies. But the Army War College had to address in some fashion the nature of future war. Uncertainties may have contributed to the near disappearance from the curriculum of what the second Army War College knew as "Conduct of War," with its map maneuvers, map exercises, command post exercises, terrain reconnaissances, and war games. Absent with "Conduct of War" was its companion piece of the 1920s and 1930s, a course in "Command."

In the language of the second Army War College, the emphasis of the initial session of the third Army War College was on "Preparation for War." Because of the perceived necessity to consider broader national security problems and future doctrinal issues (under the somewhat inaccurate label of "Current Army Problems"), however, the third Army War College could not require the detail in mobilization and war planning that had characterized the earlier institution. The 1950-51 program was broader than its predecessor but not as deep. This is not necessarily a criticism; there were so many more unknowns in 1950 than in 1930. Moreover, the second Army War College and the Army it served had enjoyed two decades of relative stability, a stability that still eludes the third Army War College.

Nonetheless, Swing, Trudeau, and the other members of the War College had done their work well and built a solid foundation. Although a number of adjustments and modifications were made over the next several years, the program presented at Leavenworth and the next year transported to Carlisle Barracks remained the basic program for at least the next six sessions. It filled the gap that since 1947 had so concerned the Army's leadership. Moreover, it positioned the War College to occupy with honor the apex to which J. Lawton Collins had pointed.

Readying Carlisle

Even before the 1950-51 session began at Fort Leavenworth, Generals Swing and Trudeau had begun to plan for and initiate the conversion of Carlisle Barracks into not merely an installation that would support the Army War College, but one whose name would become synonymous with the institution. Trudeau was familiar with Carlisle Barracks. As Director of Training of the Army Service Forces, he had been involved in wartime expansion of the Medical Field Service School and, because of lack of outdoor training areas at Carlisle Barracks, its removal in 1946 to Fort Sam Houston, Texas. Trudeau had been impressed at the time that Carlisle Barracks was almost ideally situated and configured for a smaller school. He was disappointed that the Carson Board had not made a stronger case for Carlisle Barracks over Fort McClellan, and he was concerned over the interest of the Alabama Senator, Lister Hill. Trudeau made his views known as best he could to those in influential positions in the Department of the Army. And through his former commander, retired General Brehon B. Somervell (in 1950 an industrialist in Pittsburgh) he made the acquaintance of the Governor (later Senator) of Pennsylvania, James H. "Red" Duff. Duff was helpful in establishing a political balance on the site question.[21]

After a visit to Carlisle Barracks in June of 1950, General Swing concluded that the anticipated composition and strength of the War College of four hundred officers and three hundred enlisted men would overtax the installation in four ways—family housing, children's schools, and hospital and recreational facilities. Of the four, family housing would prove the most difficult to solve. Family housing at Carlisle Barracks was limited to a few quarters (including that of the Commanding General) that dated back to the rebuilding of the post in the mid-1860s after the visit of the Confederate cavalry. Other quarters remained from the days of the Indian School. The Medical Department had obtained sufficient Public Works Administration money to complete in 1939 twenty units for officers and twenty-eight for noncommissioned officers. An apartment complex that could house ten families had been built in 1947. But the total was only sixty-eight sets of family quarters for officers and sixty-three sets built for warrant officers and noncommissioned officers. The town of Carlisle, with a population of only some 14,000, did not have a large rental market and therefore off-post housing was insufficient to meet the shortfall. Beyond that, what rental housing did exist was considered by the authorities of Carlisle Barracks to be exorbitantly priced.[22]

Expectations on obtaining funds for new construction were not high. Family housing was an Army-wide, indeed nationwide, problem in the postwar years. To alleviate the problem for the military services, Congress in 1949 passed the so-called Wherry Act. This act provided for low-cost (maximum $9,000) units to be built on or in the vicinity of federal property. A Wherry Act project was built, owned, maintained, and managed by a private entrepreneur. The Federal Housing Administration (FHA) guaranteed financing of responsible developers. The Army's obligation was to maintain a high occupancy rate in the units. The individual service member's obligation was to pay the monthly rent, which was pegged to his housing allowance. In theory the scheme provided housing to service families at no cost to the government beyond that of the service member's housing allowance.[23]

Of low cost and therefore small, a Wherry Act unit was not really adequate for the family of a War College student. The law had been designed for younger junior officers and noncommissioned officers, not for men with larger families and half-grown children. Nonetheless, a Wherry Act project was the quickest, probably the only, route available for the War College to provide housing for the families of its student officers. Carlisle Barracks already had one Wherry Act project nearing completion when General Swing visited in June 1950—a sixty-two-unit apartment complex named Stanwix Manor.[24]

Arranging a Wherry Act project meant navigating through a bureaucratic jungle. Approval and construction of a project involved not just the local commander and competing developers and financial institutions, but also the headquarters of a continental army, the Department of the Army, the headquarters of the Corps of Engineers district, and the FHA. Developers and contractors sometimes sought political assistance in their endeavors to win contracts, thereby adding confusion and delay to the process. General Trudeau became almost a commuter to Pennsylvania. He and the Deputy Post Commander at Carlisle Barracks, Colonel John Mesick, slashed away at this jungle throughout 1950. Approval was finally won in January 1951 for a project consisting of one hundred single units. To keep costs down, the planned size of each unit had to be reduced two feet in each dimension. Approval was not construction, however. Ten months later, when the first class arrived at Carlisle Barracks, ground had still not been broken. Due to lack of housing the size of the Class of 1952 was held to approximately 150. Student families found shelter where they could throughout south central Pennsylvania, some living as far away as Gettysburg and York.[25] Thirteen student officers chose not to bring their families to Carlisle.

By early April 1951 the three military schools at Carlisle Barracks to be displaced by the War College had moved elsewhere, and major renovation of the post began. The interwar tenant of the post, the Medical Field Service School, might be criticized with some justification by later-day preservationists for razing many of the buildings of the old Indian Industrial School, but overall it deserves praise for the period of its stewardship of Carlisle Barracks. Aesthetics as well as utility had guided the extensive construction program of the late 1930s. Much of the landscaping, emphasizing flowering trees and shrubs, was begun during the same period. In addition to the brick quarters and barracks completed earlier, a large and stately academic building containing an auditorium and library space was completed in 1941. This building General Swing chose to use as his headquarters and as office space for his faculty, retaining the auditorium and library space for their original purposes. Appropriately he named this building Root Hall.[26]

Across the street from Root Hall was a building that originally had been a stables, but in 1946 it had been converted into an academic building. It was enlarged and renovated to provide twenty-eight student committee rooms and four conference rooms. A common-room coffee shop was also provided. Swing named this building Bliss Hall. Other work went forward during the summer. The former post headquarters was converted into quarters for the Deputy Commandant. The Commanding General's quarters, which had been half of a duplex, was expanded and renovated into one set of quarters. General Swing's plans for Carlisle Barracks were ambitious, perhaps elaborate; but the place, was, after all, to be the home of the Army War College, not just another Army post. In all, the renovation of Carlisle Barracks was estimated to cost almost $569,000; for Bliss Hall alone $131,000 was programed.[27]

There were other more-academic and less-expensive suggestions being put forward to assist the War College in its move toward the apex of the Army educational system. Many of these originated in the active mind of its Deputy Commandant. With a major phase of the War College program now dealing with international affairs, Trudeau thought it desirable to broaden the faculty by adding civilian professors and representation from the Department of State. He also recommended, even before the first class convened at Leavenworth, a permanent civilian advisory group composed of distinguished educators and men of affairs. Trudeau also explored the possibilities of the Army War College becoming a degree-granting institution, or at least of having the work at the War College accepted as contributory to the granting of a graduate degree.[28]

While the 1950-51 program had not been heavily oriented toward military history, Trudeau saw great potential in a close relationship between the War College and the Army's military history community. He requested of the Chief of Military History an investigation and evaluation of the use of war games by the former German Army, specifically at the level of the army group. He suggested Carlisle Barracks as an appropriate location for the Office of the Chief of Military History. Swing, on his part, saw the possibilities of the War College, as part of its educational mission, becoming a serious research institution. He requested that the Department of the Army task the college with the study of long-range Army problems.[29] Few of these ideas reached fruition during the tenure of Swing and Trudeau, years would pass before others were implemented, and some have never been accepted; but their range is solid evidence that there was no lack of imagination on the part of the initial leadership of the third Army War College.

In mid-April General Swing authorized members of his staff and faculty to move to Carlisle Barracks as soon as their duties at Leavenworth would permit. By mid-May a nucleus of the War College began to emerge at the new station. General Swing and the college Secretary, Colonel Harry Critz, arrived in late June, in time to participate in the ceremonies that marked the bicentennial of the town of Carlisle and surrounding Cumberland County. At midnight June 30, 1951, the headquarters of the Army War College closed at Fort Leavenworth and opened at Carlisle Barracks. Most of the faculty that had been at Leavenworth moved with the college, except for those who had served several years at Leavenworth before the reestablishment of the War College and had received normal reassignments during the summer. On July 9, however, the Department of the Army announced that Lieutenant General Swing was to take command of Sixth Army in San Francisco. On the 1st of August Trudeau assumed command of the War College and Carlisle Barracks pending the arrival of the new Commandant later in the month.[30]

The Initial Year at Carlisle

In the summer of 1951, with armistice negotiations begun and the front generally stabilized in Korea, the Army began to rotate to the United States those division and corps commanders who had been in Korea most of the previous year. A number of these senior officers were reassigned within the Army's school system. One such officer was Lieutenant General Edward M. Almond, former Commanding General of X Corps. Almond was given a choice by General Ridgway, the Far East commander, of a number of assignments in the United States. Attracted by its serenity, he selected the Army War College. A division commander in Italy during World War II, Almond had been in the Far East since 1946. He had been Douglas MacArthur's Far East Command Chief of Staff and still held that title when he commanded the independent X Corps during the Inchon landing. Subsequently, the Corps made a landing on the east coast of North Korea, and its lead elements reached the Yalu River. After the Chinese entered the war, the Corps was withdrawn from North Korea by sea and redeployed in the South to become an element of Eighth Army. In his prewar service General Almond had graduated from the Army War College with the Class of 1934. He had served on the War Department General Staff in the G-2 Division, and he had graduated from the Air Corps Tactical School in 1938 and from the Naval War College in 1940. He was over fifty-eight years old when he returned from the Far East. Policy would require his retirement upon reaching age sixty.[31]

General Almond did not arrive at Carlisle until the end of August, only a few days before classes began. In most respects he was pleased and impressed with what he found. Trudeau and the faculty struck him as first-rate. Chief of Staff Collins again delivered the opening address, bringing with him as a guest retired General John DeWitt, the next-to-last Commandant of the second War College and Collins' superior when Collins was a War College student and instructor. Also appearing at the opening exercises were Harold Stassen, President of the University of Pennsylvania, and Senator Duff. Almond had no urge to make immediate changes in the program planned for the year, though it was his ultimate intention to emphasize cooperation with the other services, an area in which his experience in Korea had indicated that Army officers were deficient. Moreover, he soon arrived at the conclusion that the War College needed a capability to continually study the relationship of the United States with other nations, especially with the Soviet Union. In time he would take steps to correct these perceived shortfalls.[32]

The program presented to the Class of 1952 was structured essentially the same as the program the year before, but there were enough changes to indicate that serious thought had been given to improving its quality. The Department of the Army provided an additional week for the War College program, and this, combined with eliminating the orientation course on the committee-study method, made an additional three weeks available for substantive work. Three phases or "general fields of consideration" were retained. One of the additional three weeks was given to the "Army and National Security" phase, and two weeks were added to the "War Planning" phase. In "Army and National Security" more time was allowed for completion of committee studies, and a problem on economic policy was added to the area problems of the previous year. Work on national security organization was shortened, but studies of national intelligence organization and combined and unified command organization were added.[33]

In the "Current Army Problems" phase, the three concurrent G-3 courses were consolidated into one course. This part of the program underwent major change. Five studies requiring analyses of a World War II campaign were introduced; a sixth study required comparison of British, German, and American training methods. The course on logistics

294

was similarly changed; the World War II campaigns were analyzed from a logistical point of view. Other elements of the program remained essentially the same. The separate course on industrial mobilization was eliminated; however, members of the faculty of the Industrial College came to Carlisle and discussed aspects of economic mobilization with groups of twenty-five students during a one-week session.[34]

The "War Planning" phase was conducted much as it had been the year before. For the Joint Planning course the class was organized into twelve committees; six of them did "requirements war planning" and six "capabilities war planning." Additionally, the class was introduced to a proposed ten-year planning cycle that the JCS was then considering. As it matured, this Joint Strategic Planning System would become the backbone of future War College courses.[35]

In the theater planning exercise each committee drew up a campaign plan, an operations plan, and a base development plan; the previous scheme of committees drawing up counterplans for Soviet and Eastern European forces was dropped. The final event of the year was a war game in which student theater plans were tested; student committees represented NATO and American headquarters in Europe from Supreme Headquarters Allied Powers Europe through the United States Seventh Army. It was a one-sided game with the faculty control group acting as the opposing force.[36]

The Individual Studies Program was repeated with fifteen topic areas offered and twelve more weeks allowed for completion of the papers. Ten students (working separately) were assigned each topic. The number of lectures was reduced from 200 to 162. The class again visited Washington and made a trip to Aberdeen Proving Grounds rather than to Sandia Base and White Sands. The War College inaugurated a third field trip, this one to United Nations headquarters in New York City, where delegates from selected nations addressed the class. The Department of the Army disapproved a scheme developed by General Trudeau for trips overseas for reasons of economy and because of criticism that was already being heard regarding the costs of operating the War College at Carlisle Barracks.[37]

A comparison of the second year's program with that of the first indicates that much had been learned during that one year at Leavenworth. If the study of international affairs and national policy was to be useful, more time would have to be devoted to it. Conduct of war received some attention in the analytical study of World War II campaigns required by the Operations and Logistics courses. Preparation for war, however, remained the major thrust. The program for the 1951-52 session was less ambitious. The total number of committee problems conceived by the faculty was reduced from twenty-four to sixteen, and each student participated in nine of them rather than eleven. These reductions, together with the severe reduction in the number of lectures, seems to indicate that Swing, like Bliss before him, had tended to expect too much. If the program was to be "contemplative in nature," some time had to be available to contemplate. The concern over the impact of nuclear weapons on the future of the Army seems to have lessened, as well as concern over future doctrine in general. Either the subject had proven too complex to be handled within the context of committee study or the Korean War was demonstrating that land warfare using conventional weapons was not as yet an anachronism.[38]

Trudeau enjoyed some success in adding variety of experience to the faculty and student body, bringing a State Department representative, Frank S. Hopkins, onto the faculty as the first nonmilitary member since the War College was founded. Another State Department officer was a member of the class. Three Air Force officers were also in the Class of 1952. The Navy again provided one student and the Marine Corps two. With the class enlarged by fifty percent, one National Guard officer and two Reserve officers were able to attend the entire session. Like the first class, this one contained members of expected potential. George R. Mather and Bruce Palmer, Jr., became generals, and four other members of the class, including a future Commandant of the War College, William E. Train, became lieutenant generals. Of the 145 Army officers in the class, 53 would eventually attain general officer grade.[39]

Success of the committee problem method was dependent, of course, on the availability of reference and research material. This was not a major problem when the Command and General Staff College library was available, but it became a limiting factor when the War College moved to Carlisle. Eisenhower, in presenting the old Army War College building to the National War College, had also donated the library collection. The nucleus of a new collection, some 118,000 pounds of material, was brought from Leavenworth, but the college had to turn also to the National, Naval, and Air War Colleges for assistance. The National War College had already thinned its collection to provide a start for the Armed Forces Staff College. Three librarians transferred from Leavenworth to organize the new library, and loan arrangements were made with the Library of Congress, the library of Dickinson College in Carlisle, and the Harrisburg library. It was the best that could be done for the moment. Only time and an adequate acquisition budget could solve the problem.[40]

Library materials were not the only items that General Swing desired to reclaim from the National War College. There were also a number of artifacts, works of art, and memorabilia collected by the Army War College between 1903 and 1940 that Swing felt belonged rightfully at Carlisle Barracks. He and Harold Bull, the Commandant of the National War College, had been corresponding on this subject and by the time

General Almond arrived had reached agreement on the transfer of books, records, and miscellaneous property—except for three items: a bust of Elihu Root, a portrait of Robert E. Lee presented to the old college by the United Daughters of the Confederacy, and a portrait of William Tecumseh Sherman. General Bull was willing to give up Root, but he thought Lee and Sherman should remain in Washington. So did former Commandant DeWitt, who had been in charge when the portraits were received. In regard to Lee's portrait, historian Douglas Southall Freeman had been instrumental in having the Daughters present the portrait, and he thought it should remain in Washington. If the decision was to move Lee to Carlisle, however, Freeman was willing to give a try at persuading the Daughters of the propriety of the move. Almond was initially agreeable to the arrangements made by Bull and Swing, but in February 1952 he requested that the National War College return the bronze class tablets on which were listed the names of the faculty and students of each Army War College session since 1903. Bull was not willing to part with these. Consultation with previous commandants did not help. Hanson Ely thought the tablets should be at Carlisle, William Connor preferred they stay in Washington but promised not to object to a move, and John DeWitt preferred Washington. Decision on this difficult matter went to the Vice Chief of Staff of the Army, John Hull (AWC 1938). He ruled against Carlisle Barracks. The tablets were thus to remain in Washington; Carlisle got only the bust of Root.[41]

General Almond continued to push ahead with Swing's elaborate plans for the development of Carlisle Barracks. He pressed the Commanding General of Second Army (whose headquarters was responsible for the logistical and administrative support of Carlisle Barracks) and the Comptroller of the Army for additional funds for operations and for assistance in getting more family housing built. In the summer of 1952 work was finally begun on the Wherry Act project, to be named College Arms. Additionally, the barracks built for the 1st Medical Regiment in 1936 was being converted into student apartments. It would be named Young Hall after the president of Root's War College Board. In the welfare and morale area, the Post Exchange was renovated during the year and opened in February. Construction of a golf course began, a project that had been contemplated even before the decision to move the War College to Carlisle. Swing's program for the post, as implemented by Almond, was unfortunately not in accord with the Truman Administration's urge of austerity. In March the *Washington Evening Star* reported that the Department of Defense was unhappy over the Army's efforts to turn Carlisle Barracks into a "plushy" installation. Citing work being done on the Commandant's quarters and the Officers Club, the *Star* alleged that minor projects of less than $50,000 were being stacked together to accomplish major construction at a cost of $600,000. The Department of the Army announced that it would investigate the allegations, and War College relations with its higher headquarters became strained.[42]

Swing had requested that the Army War College be considered an agency for the study of Army problems and programs. The Commanding General of Army Field Forces, Mark Clark, and the Deputy Chief of Staff for Operations and Administration of the Department of the Army, Maxwell Taylor, agreed to accommodate him. During Almond's tenure, however, it was the Commandant who was the main inspiration of special studies. He put Colonel William J. McCaffrey, a faculty member who had been his Corps G-3 in Korea, on a project to determine whether nuclear weapons might have been used to tactical advantage during X Corps' campaign in North Korea. Additionally, Almond took a personal interest in finding ways in which the air-ground operations system might be made more responsive. He also organized a sort of strategic studies group within the faculty. In sessions held several times a week, it studied the broad national security problems of the United States. Trudeau welcomed this intellectual activity, but he admitted during the year that "we are over our heads in special studies and reports."[43]

Trudeau's earlier idea of bringing in a civilian group to advise on the college's program bore fruit in January 1952. There is no reason to believe that Almond and Trudeau sought anything other than an objective evaluation, but the group was in session only three days at the War College, and thus many of its recommendations reflected concerns and proposed courses of action already current at Carlisle Barracks. The advisory group's report therefore tended to reinforce the rationale for what Almond was already attempting or intended to attempt. On methods of instruction the group recommended fewer lectures, fewer committee problems, more extensive student reading, and a narrower focus for the individual student research paper. It also recommended greater faculty involvement in monitoring student committee deliberations and in providing constructive comment on committee reports and individual work. This would require a larger faculty. It would also require, though the advisory group did not say so, a better-prepared faculty capable of providing sound criticism on research efforts. Because of faculty and facility limitations, the advisory group recommended that the class be held to two hundred rather than increasing it to the planned three hundred, and that the number of students from other services be substantially increased.[44]

Not surprisingly, the civilian advisory group avoided criticizing instruction presented on military subjects and concentrated its suggestions on the substance of the course that dealt directly with nonmilitary affairs. It recommended expansion of the work on international relations and foreign policy and suggested study of civil-military relations. In a direct reflection of the nation's uneasiness with the inconclusive outcome of the Korean War, and perhaps because of the circumstances surrounding the relief from command of General MacArthur, the group saw a need for senior military offices to have a deeper understanding of the American system of government and of the strains on the American political processes and national economy resulting from partial mobilization and protracted limited war. Study in these areas might create duplication between the programs of the Army War College and the National War College, but the group did not see duplication as necessarily evil.[45]

A Question of Mission

General Almond either found persuasive the civilian advisory group's recommendations or else they merely reinforced his own beliefs. In February 1952 he forwarded to the Chief of Staff through the Chief of Army Field Forces a proposal for the restatement of his mission. The mission under which Swing and then Almond had been operating was that proposed by the first Eddy Board in 1949:

> to prepare officers for duty as commanders and general staff officers within the headquarters of army group and corresponding communications zone activities, the theater army, the theater, the zone of the interior army, and the Department of the Army, with emphasis on the Department of the Army.[46]

It was Almond's position that this statement reflected Eddy's super-Leavenworth orientation, was not in keeping with the Army War College's apex position, and was not "in consonance with the breadth of the curriculum and the academic maturity" developed over the past two academic years.[47]

To correct these shortfalls Almond recommended that the mission be rephrased as:

> to provide a graduate course of study designed to broaden the education of selected officers with respect to national policy, national security organization, strategic planning and employment of the Armed Forces, in order to assist in fitting them for high command and important staff assignments in the military service, with emphasis on the Army.[48]

Almond's proposal might appear on the surface to be merely an attempt on his part to win regulatory authority for doing what he was already about. But the proposal also reveals considerable clairvoyance. It shows a recognition that the year at the Army War College was only one brief event in an officer's career-long professional development, and that "to prepare officers" for the headquarters of a long list of specific commands was a dissipation of effort and probably not possible. The best Almond could promise was "to broaden the education . . . in order to assist in fitting" officers for responsible positions.

The restated mission also demonstrates that Almond understood the direction in which the unification winds were blowing; that if the Army War College did not delve into matters beyond Department of Army level, its graduates, and hence the Army, would be at a severe disadvantage when they were assigned to the Joint Staff or to the staffs of the unified commanders and defense agencies. More rather than fewer of these assignments could be expected in the future. If the Army War College was limited in the instruction it provided, graduates of the National War College, the Industrial College, and the Armed Forces Staff College would be preferred, but those institutions could not provide the number of officers that would be needed. General Mark Clark, Chief of Army Field Forces and Almond's immediate superior, did not share these concerns.

In forwarding Almond's proposal to the Chief of Staff, Clark stated his beliefs that the role of the Army War College was to complete an officer's "formal education concerning the application of military power on land," and that it should not "dwell excessively long on matters that are not primarily United States Army affairs." He recommended that the War College mission be stated succinctly as:

> to prepare officers for duty as commanders and General Staff officers at the highest United States Army levels.[49]

In April, with a decision signed by Vice Chief of Staff John Hull, the Department of the Army came down on the side of General Clark; his mission statement was approved with only a phrase added prohibiting any instruction that would duplicate that given at lower Army schools.[50]

Hull's decision was accompanied by additional guidance on the scope of the War College's program. Interestingly, this guidance reflects much of the thinking that both guided and disturbed the program of the second Army War College. "The Army War College curriculum is properly concerned with the *Army's preparation for and conduct of war*" (emphasis added). Instruction on the conduct of war should develop knowledge and capabilities "primarily as a commander of large units." Preparation for staff duties was secondary to command and should "emphasize preparation for duty in the Department of the Army." Additionally, the guidance warned that the "curriculum of the joint colleges will not be duplicated nor overlapped to any appreciable degree."[51]

The Department of the Army proved ambivalent, however. Only the month before Hull's decision it had published a circular to be brought to the early attention of all general and field-grade officers restating its position regarding the Army War College. The circular reiterated the modification to the Eddy Board report that had stated that the Army War College was at the apex of the educational system and that graduates of all War Colleges would receive equal consideration for promotion and assignment to responsible positions, even though the scope of the instruction at the National War College and the Industrial College was somewhat broader in the fields of national and joint strategy. Skeptical officers concerned with career success might have found this difficult to believe since the Army continued to send a few graduates of the Army War College to the National War College and the Industrial College.[52]

The issue of the place, role, and mission of the Army War College had several dimensions. First there was what might be called the philosophical dimension; that is, just what knowledge and capabilities were necessary for senior professional military officers? Here there were honest differences of outlook. One school of thought was traditional; it was reflected in the approach to the problem by Hugh Drum in the early 1920s, then by Manton Eddy, and now by Mark Clark. The senior military officer must remain within strict professional boundaries and not dwell on "matters not primarily United States Army affairs." The other school of thought, represented earlier by Edward McGlachlin and now by General Almond, sensed that the higher commander and staff officer should be a man who understands and appreciates the broader political, economic, and social contexts in which armed forces are employed. Formal education was required to provide this understanding.

There was also a practical dimension. A gap in fact had existed in the educational system between the Command and General Staff College and the National War College. As a joint institution the National War College could not fill that gap, and the efforts of Gerow and Eddy to fill the gap at Leavenworth had proven inadequate. Those to whom the gap was a serious concern looked favorably upon the concept of an advanced command and general staff course put forward by Eddy. Generally those favoring this approach were located at Army Field Forces, where the Army school system was viewed as a progressive, integrated whole. Their vision was properly limited to the necessities of the field forces. But at Department of the Army level, the Army was seen as having problems beyond those of its field forces. Not the least of these problems was having officers of sufficient talent and in adequate number to articulate Army capabilities and requirements in the growing number of joint and multinational headquarters, as well as in the defense agencies and the committee rooms of Congress. They feared a void at the top more than the gap.

Finally there was a prestige dimension, understandably important to faculty member and student alike of the Army War College. Here concern was whether selection for attendance at the Army War College was in truth but a consolation prize, and whether Army War College graduates would remain competitive for bigger things if they did not attend one of the senior joint colleges. At Department level also it was important that graduates of the Army War College not be considered in any way as having received a lesser education than that provided at the Naval and Air War Colleges.

Those who for whatever combination of reasons were gap-fillers could always conjure up the specter of cost-savers and unification extremists closing down or moving in on the Army War College if it duplicated to any great degree the program of the joint colleges or appeared to stray too far from Army affairs. The apex-builders, on the other hand, could conjure up the specter of ill-equipped Army officers losing the Army's shirt in the poker games of the joint staffs, defense agencies, and congressional hearings. These pressures and counterpressures on the Army War College program were endemic to the system. They could not be relieved unless the system was changed to provide more years of schooling per individual career and a joint school establishment of greatly increased production. The system has not changed. Chiefs of Staff and commandants therefore have had much less flexibility in moving the War College off the narrow path between gap-fillers and apex-builders than they themselves have probably realized.

Arthur Trudeau had departed the War College for assignment in the Far East before Hull's decision on mission turned Swing's loose rein into Almond's curb bit. Trudeau was not replaced immediately. Colonel Gordon B. Rogers, a member of the faculty since the days at Leavenworth, acted as Almond's deputy until promoted and reassigned in May. Colonel Howard Ker then acted as Deputy Commandant until Brigadier General Verdi B. Barnes arrived just prior to the opening of classes for the 1952-53 session. General Trudeau had another decade of service ahead of him when he left Carlisle Barracks. He would serve in a number of positions of high responsibility. It was as Deputy Commandant of the third Army War College in its formative years, however, that he may well have made his most enduring contribution to the future of the United States Army.[53]

NOTES

1. Biographical information is from *Cullum's Register*, Vol. IX. Calvin J. Landau interview with Trudeau, 1971, Vol. I, 40, Arthur G. Trudeau papers, MHI Collection. Trudeau to Swing, 23 March 1950, Ibid.
2. Trudeau to Swing, 23 March 1950; and Captain H. E. Eccles, USN, to B. W. Wright, 2 May 1950, Trudeau papers.
3. Clyde Patterson and Nicholas Psaki interview with Jonathan O. Seaman, 19 May 1971, Sec. II, 21-22, Jonathan O. Seaman papers, MHI Collection.
4. Trudeau interview, Vol. I, 45. Data on faculty from AWC, *Directory 1905-1980*.
5. Wade Hampton interview with James F. Collins, 1975, James F. Collins papers, MHI Collection, Sec. II, 22. Data on class from AWC, *Directory 1905-1980*.

6. Seaman interview, Sec. III, 1. For rumors see "Fate of Schools," *Army, Navy, Air Force Journal* (29 July 1950): 1276.
7. Trudeau interviews, Vol. I, 46. Seaman interviews, Sec. III, 1. Clark to Edward M. Almond, 28 August 1951, Edward M. Almond papers, MHI Collection.
8. Irving Monelova and Marlin Lang interview with Paul D. Adams, 1975, Sec. IV, 28, MHI Collection. J. Lawton Collins, *Lightning Joe: An Autobiography* (Baton Rouge: Louisiana State University Press, 1979), 92. AWC, *Curriculum, 1950-51 Course*, October 1950-June 1951. AWC, "The Committee System of Problem Solution, Problem Directive," 2 October 1950.
9. AWC, "Course Directive, Course 2," 27 September 1950.
10. John Spanier, *American Foreign Policy Since World War II*, 7th ed. (New York: Holt, Rinehart and Winston, 1977), 27-83.
11. AWC, "Course Directive, Course 3," 3 October 1950.
12. Hewes, *Root to McNamara*, 206-12. Trudeau to Clifton F. Von Kann, 5 December 1950, Trudeau papers.
13. AWC, "Course Directive, Course 4," 4 December 1950. AWC, "Course Directive, Courses 5, 6 and 7," 4 January 1951.
14. AWC, "Course Directive, Course 8," 29 January 1951. AWC Memorandum, Committee and Room Assignments, Courses 9 and 10, 8 February 1951. AWC, "Course Directive, Course 11," Part I, 26 February 1951 and Part II, 9 March 1951.
15. AWC, "Illustrative War Game," Script for First Day, 17 March 1951.
16. AWC, *Curriculum 1950-1951 Course*. AWC, "Course Directive, Course 12," 2 April 1951. AWC, "Course Directive, Course 13," 30 April-10 June 1951. AWC, "Course Directive, Course 14," 8 June 1951. Paul D. Adams to Deputy Commandant, 10 May 1951, subject: War Planning Guide, Trudeau papers.
17. AWC, *Curriculum 1950-51 Course*. Speakers included Thomas J. Watson of IBM, Robert R. McCormick of the *Chicago Tribune*, Ralph Bunche, Philip Jessup, Paul Nitze, Dean Rusk, and Generals Jacob Devers, Mark Clark, Maxwell Taylor, and Curtis LeMay. The Congressman was Dewey Short, the psychiatrist, Dr. William C. Menninger; AWC, "Guest Speakers, 1950-1951 Course." AWC, "Lectures 1939-40."
18. AWC, *Curriculum 1950-1951*. AWC, *Information and Instructions, 1950-51*. AWC, "Individual Studies," 20 October 1950-19 February 1951.
19. J. M. Swing, "Army War College," *Army, Navy, Air Force Journal*, (9 December 1950): 385, 412.
20. Ibid. Trudeau interview, Vol. I, 47.
21. Ibid., 44-45.
22. Swing to Brigadier General McGaw, CG of Carlisle Barracks, 19 June 1950, AWC Central Files 1945-1963. Tousey, *History of Carlisle*, 384-86. Carson Board Report. Briefing on Carlisle Barracks, n.d., Box: "Carlisle History," MHI Collection.
23. "Armed Forces Housing," *The Army-Navy-Air Force Register* (27 August 1959): 1.
24. Entries of 3 February 1950 and 25 June 1950, "Carlisle Barracks Diary," MHI Collection.
25. AWC Central Files, 1945-1963, Item 64. Trudeau, Remarks at Opening Exercise, 1 September 1951, "Army War College Addresses," Trudeau papers. Trudeau interview, Vol. I, 53-54. Thomas G. Fergusson interview with Edward M. Almond, 29-30 March 1975, 65, Almond papers.
26. Entries of 31 March, 9 and 16 April 1951, "Carlisle Barracks Diary." Tousey, *History of Carlisle*, 396.
27. Entry of 16 April 1951, "Carlisle Barracks Diary." Hq., Second Army to Division Engineer, North Atlantic Division, 23 January 1951, File: Establishment of Army War College at Carlisle Barracks, MHI Collection.
28. Trudeau, memorandum: Improvement of Curriculum, 6 February 1952, Trudeau papers. Trudeau to Colonel Marshall Carter, 8 May 1950, Ibid. Trudeau to Dr. J. Douglass Brown, Princeton University, 26 June 1950, Ibid. Trudeau interview, Vol. I, 50-51.
29. Trudeau to P. M. Robinett, 5 April and 1 May 1951, Trudeau papers. Trudeau interview, Vol. I, 50. Swing to Chief of Staff, 14 October 1950, Trudeau papers.

30. Letter, AWC, 10 April 1951, subject: Movement of the Army War College to Carlisle Barracks, Inc. 1. AWC General Order No. 1, 29 June 1951. Entries of 7 and 25 May, 21 June, 1 Aug. 1951, "Carlisle Barracks Diary."
31. Entries of 30 August and 4 September 1951, Ibid. Almond interview, 60-61, 63.
32. Trudeau to Almond, 30 June 1951, Trudeau papers. Almond interview, 65-67. Trudeau to Paul D. Adams, 14 December 1951, Trudeau papers. Entries of 4 and 5 September 1951, "Carlisle Barracks Diary."
33. Trudeau, Remarks at Opening Exercise, 1 September 1951. AWC, *Curriculum 1951-1952 Course.*
34. Ibid. AWC, "Directive for Course 4," 31 October 1951. AWC, "Course 5, Logistics," 26 November-21 December 1951. AWC, "Course 6, Manpower," 3 January 1952. AWC, *Curriculum 1951-1952 Course*, 8. AWC, "Economic Mobilization for Defense and War," 17-20 December 1951, prepared by Industrial College of the Armed Forces.
35. AWC, *Curriculum 1951-1952 Course.* AWC, "War Planning General Directive," 25 February 1952. AWC, "Supplemental Information on War Planning," 26 February 1952.
36. AWC, "War Planning General Directive," 25 February 1952. AWC, "Course of Instruction, Course 10, Theater Planning, 1951/52." AWC, Memorandum, "Committee Assignment of Students for War Game," 28 May 1952.
37. AWC, "Individual Studies Directive for Course 3," 29 October 1951. Trudeau, Remarks at Opening Exercise, 1 September 1951. Entry for 4 April 1952, "Carlisle Barracks Diary." Trudeau, Memorandum for the Faculty Board, 30 October 1951, Trudeau papers. Trudeau to Colonel James A. Bassett, 24 March 1952, Ibid.
38. AWC, *Curriculum 1950-1951 Course.* AWC, *Curriculum 1951-1952 Course.*
39. Data from AWC, *Directory 1905-1980.*
40. Trudeau interview, 48-49. Colonel Critz to Colonel Mesick, 30 March 1951, File: Establishment of Army War College at Carlisle Barracks. Hq. AWC ltr., subject: Movement of the Army War College to Carlisle Barracks, Pa., 10 April 1951, Ibid. Lowell G. Smith and Murray G. Swindler interview with Clyde D. Eddleman, 11 February 1975, Sec. 3, 14, MHI Collection. Paul D. Adams interview, Sec. 4, 28. Entry of 7 May 1951, "Carlisle Barracks Diary."
41. Bull to Almond, 20 August 1951, Almond papers. Vice Chief of Staff to Commandant, 7 March 1952, AWC Central Files 1945-1963.
42. Almond to Lieutenant General Edward H. Brooke, 8 November 1951, Almond papers. Almond to Comptroller of the Army, 29 October 1951, AWC Central Files 1945-1963. Entries of 19 September 1951, 19 February and 23 June 1952, "Carlisle Barracks Diary." Carlisle *Sentinel*, 6 February 1952. Swing to McGaw, 12 October 1950, Trudeau papers. Swing to Chairman, Joint Welfare Board, 12 October 1950, Ibid. Trudeau interview, 52. *Washington Evening Star*, 2 March 1952. *Sentinel*, 17 March 1952. Almond interview, 64-65.
43. Clark to Almond, 28 August 1951, Almond papers. Taylor to Trudeau, 3 August 1951 and Trudeau to Taylor 11 August 1951, Trudeau papers. Deputy Chief of Staff for Operations and Administration, Memorandum, 15 August 1951 attached as Appendix U, "Armstrong Study." Trudeau interview, 55-56. Almond interview, 66. Trudeau to P. D. Adams, 14 December 1951, Trudeau papers.
44. "Report of Civilian Advisory Group," January 1952. The group included Julius O. Adler, Royden Dangerfield, Hardy Dillard, William Draper, Donald C. McKay, Troy H. Middleton, Howard Petersen, and Arnold O. Wolfers.
45. Ibid.
46. *Eddy Report.*
47. Almond to Chief of Staff, 8 February 1952, subject: Mission of the Army War College.
48. Ibid., Inclosure 1.
49. Clark to Chief of Staff, 18 February 1952, 1st Ind.
50. Hull to Office, Chief of Army Field Forces, 11 April 1952, 2nd Ind., Inclosure 3.
51. Ibid.
52. Department of the Army Circular 16, 3 March 1952.
53. Entries of 8 February, 1 March, 25 April, and 21 August 1952, "Carlisle Barracks Diary."

Toward a National Perspective
1952-1957

The several years following the reestablishment of the Army War College at Fort Leavenworth and its subsequent move to Carlisle Barracks were marked by self-inquiry and by some confusion as to just what the institution should become and how it fit into the Army's overall scheme for the professional education of officers. The disapproval of General Almond's proposal for a change in mission did not settle the question. He and future commandants still had considerable flexibility if they interpreted the mission statement liberally. Some of the questioning and confusion may have resulted from the assignment of a series of short-term commandants, but it probably resulted as much from a changing national security environment and changes in the Army's internal organization. These were the years of President Eisenhower's "New Look" at defense policy, with an outcome detrimental to the Army's budget and to its confidence and morale. Concurrently the Department of the Army established the Continental Army Command to replace Army Field Forces and gave it an expanded mission in the field of combat developments. Both the New Look and the new command would directly influence the program of the Army War College.

The 1952-53 Program
Despite the narrower mission statement, Almond made no fundamental changes in the 1952-53 program. It remained divided into three parts or phases. The first phase focused on national-level security problems, the second on Army problems, and the third on war planning. Within each phase, however, were modifications that now can be recognized as symptoms of change as the program evolved over the next five years.[1]

The phase that had begun as "The Army and National Security" now became "National Policy and Security," marking the beginning of a trend away from viewing national security from the limited perspective of the Department of the Army. One of the studies in this phase required student committees to recommend United States policies toward either Germany, Spain, the United Kingdom, the Arab states, Japan, or China.[2] The pre-World War II college had never attempted such a broad endeavor.

In the second phase, titled simply "The Army," the attempt at historical analyses of World War II campaigns was abandoned. Instead and in compliance with Department of the Army guidance accompanying the revised mission statement, student committees studied the effect of nuclear weapons on Army doctrine and on the command of large military units. In line with General Almond's particular interests, other committees studied Army responsibilities in joint operations and the air-to-ground support system. The historical approach to the study of operations and logistics had lasted but one year. The War College intended to concern itself only with contemporary and future problems.[3]

Of interest, recalling the second Army War College's difficulties on how best to teach "command," was the introduction of a study with the title "Command of Large Military Units." The committee assigned to conduct this study attempted to investigate the personalities, characteristics, attitudes, and qualifications of successful large-unit commanders, exploring additionally their application of the principles of war and the adequacy of the command and staff organization of the United States Army. In flavor it was a return to McGlachlin's short-lived attempt of the early 1920s to teach command through biography and campaign analysis. It proved to be a popular study. The faculty adviser recommended that in the future an entire month be devoted to it.[4]

The entire second phase, whether covering operations, logistics, or manpower, concerned itself with problems that the Army would face in war, not with its problems in peacetime. Almost invariably there was an underlying assumption of total war conditions, although significantly, as far as subsequent trends are concerned, one committee was directed to study for the first time the peculiar problems of military operations under conditions short of general war.[5]

Although the war-planning phase remained essentially as constructed initially, the "Joint War Planning" course was renamed "Strategic Planning." Work in this course was tied directly to the "Joint Program for Planning" of the JCS, with committees preparing their own versions of the "Joint Long Range Strategic Estimate," the "Joint Strategic Objectives Plan," or the "Joint Strategic Capabilities Plan." This was an important step because for decades following the War College would habitually structure its courses on military planning to resemble the JCS system. As the course titles "Army Planning" and "Theater Planning" indicate, in this phase the class was forced to view war planning not only from the perspective of the JCS, but also from those of the Department of the Army and the European theater commander. A war game again

climaxed the phase and the year's program. The game was closely controlled, the players dealing with an initial situation and three subsequent situations designed to test student war plans for the first six
months of a war in Europe.[6]

The Individual Studies Program was continued and expanded in 1952-
53. The students selected subjects from seventy-nine topics offered by
the faculty, a number of which had been previously suggested by the
Army Staff. Field trips to Washington and to the United Nations headquarters remained on the program, although the Washington trip was
eliminated after this year. Additionally, one group of twenty-five students visited the Philadelphia Ordnance District and industrial plants
engaged in producing Army equipment. Another group of similar size
visited an aircraft factory in Hagerstown, Maryland.[7]

Problem-solving by student committees reinforced by guest lecturers
remained the primary and fundamental method of instruction. New
committees were organized for each course, varying in size to fit the
problem assigned. The committees were composed so that two students
would not serve together on a committee more than once. In a sense,
therefore, each War College student followed a program different from
that of any of his fellows. The only truly universal experience was the
lecture program. Faculty advisers were assigned to each committee,
with some faculty members advising several committees concurrently.
The faculty was not large enough for specialization; one faculty member
might be assigned as an adviser for a number of different courses.
Learning was to be accomplished through self-development through
sharing the experiences of officers with varied professional backgrounds. A committee's work generally followed a set sequence. First
the assigned problem was divided into distinct tasks; then came individual research and study, group analysis and discussion to arrive at conclusions and recommendations, a written report, and finally a formal
presentation. Except for many more lectures, the program was all very
much in the tradition of learning-by-doing instituted fifty years earlier
by Tasker Bliss.[8]

After Almond

When Edward Almond reached age sixty in December 1952, he was
retired from the Army as he had expected. He was not immediately
replaced at the War College, revealing a lack of concern by the Department of the Army that probably did not enhance the prestige of the new
institution. The Class of 1953 in fact had three Commandants. After
Almond's departure Brigadier General Barnes acted as Commandant
from December to mid-April, when Major General James E. Moore arrived. Moore left just short of two years later, in February 1955. Again a
replacement was not immediately provided, and so the Class of 1955

also had three Commandants. Brigadier General Thomas W. Dunn, the Deputy Commandant, acted as Commandant after Moore's February 1955 departure until Major General Clyde D. Eddleman arrived in May. But Eddleman remained at the War College only until October, when he was replaced by Major General Max S. Johnson. The third Army War College thus was led by six Commandants in its first five years. Johnson was the first postwar Commandant to enjoy tenure comparable to that of Ely, Connor, and Simonds of the second War College. He remained through February 1959.

The years of Barnes, Moore, Dunn, Eddleman, and Johnson at the Army War College—1953 through 1958—correspond to the first six years of the presidency of Dwight Eisenhower. They were lean and trying years for the United States Army. Eisenhower and his party had promised the American people fiscal responsibility—-demanding in sequence an end to the war in Korea, a balanced federal budget, and reduced taxes. For reasons that perhaps will never be entirely clear, the Chinese in the summer of 1953 agreed to an armistice in Korea. It appeared at the time to be a triumph for diplomacy underwritten by nuclear threat. Unwilling and probably unable to cut back the New Deal and Fair Deal programs of FDR and Harry Truman, Eisenhower's budget-balancing by necessity had to concentrate on defense spending, then seventy percent of the federal budget. Military strength, Eisenhower insisted, had to be maintained within economic realities. He thus directed his "New Look" at American defense policies.[9]

The New Look translated into reducing the defense budgets for fiscal years 1954 and 1955 by almost twenty-five percent; it also included a goal of reducing the Army's force structure from twenty to seventeen divisions. Among the numerous explanations of the New Look, that of Secretary of State John Foster Dulles in January 1954 is the best known. It was then that he outlined what came to be known as the strategy of massive retaliation. America's defense policy would emphasize air power and atomic weapons. It was a strategy designed not only to be congenial with fiscal responsibility but to answer the widespread disenchantment with the strategy of containment as exemplified by the protracted, indecisive, and frustrating Korean War. Massive retaliation may have been more rhetoric than strategy, more myth than reality, but the budget cuts were real. The Army, although hardly impoverished by the Great Depression standards of Hoover and the early Franklin Roosevelt, entered a period of severe reductions in expenditure and manpower. The contraction was accompanied by demands for strict cost justifications.[10]

Of as much concern to the Army's leadership as near-term reductions in strength and financial support were the long-term implications of the New Look. Clearly the Air Force was to have the primary combatant role, with ground forces playing but a minor and supporting part. But parochial service interest was not the sole basis for criticism of the New Look. To critics, massive retaliation was a strategy that promised in war neither defense nor victory. Designed to contain the Soviet Union through deterrence of aggression, massive retaliation was not seen as a solution to defending Western Europe against the superior numbers of the Soviet Army should deterrence fail. Critics held that even as a deterrent the strategy was seriously flawed. Nuclear retaliation as a response to local or ambiguous aggression appeared to lack credibility, particularly once the United States lost its nuclear monopoly, a condition fast approaching. Thoughtful observers were speculating already that nuclear superiority might be a dubious advantage once the Soviets possessed even a limited capability to use nuclear weapons to attack targets within the United States. In sum, critics held that the strategy of massive retaliation could produce no rational political result if brought to the test.[11]

The proponents of massive retaliation were not always consistent nor clear as to their objectives. Their words and their actions indicated that local defense and collective defense also played important roles in their strategy. By the spring of 1956 American military assistance and advisory groups were active in thirty-six nations. In addition to the collective defense obligations inherited from the Truman administration (the Rio Pact of 1947, the North Atlantic Treaty of 1949, and the 1951 treaties with Japan, the Philippines, and Australia and New Zealand), Secretary Dulles negotiated in 1953 a bilateral treaty with Korea and in 1954 a bilateral treaty with the Republic of China. After the French defeat in Indochina in 1954 came the centerpiece of Far East containment, the Southeast Asia Treaty. The United States, while not a signatory, also sponsored and encouraged the Baghdad Pact of 1955 designed to create a "northern tier" against the Soviet Union with Turkey, Iraq, Iran, and Pakistan allied with Britain. In all, the United States had some form of defense obligation to forty-two nations. Tactical nuclear weapons also began to play an increasingly important part in the Eisenhower strategy, their use contemplated as a means of offsetting the manpower superiority of the Sino-Soviet bloc.[12]

The pronouncement of the strategy of massive retaliation ignited a major public debate over national security policy. Academicians of various disciplines—physical scientists, social scientists, historians—and, of course, journalists, politicians, and members of the military bureaucracy all participated. By the late 1950s national security affairs had become a distinct field of study, almost a discipline of its own. An extensive literature resulted, with much theorizing on deterrence and escalation, and particularly on limited war. A subordinate debate centered on whether nuclear weapons could be used in limited war. The

Army War College cannot claim to have been at the forward edge of this theorizing, but the effect of that thinking upon the War College program was significant. Indeed, once the theorizing was distilled to the question of the Army's role—in general nuclear war, in limited nuclear war, and in limited conventional war—the effect was direct.[13]

To deal constructively with the intellectual problem of the Army's future role, the War College also had to address the terribly complex question of the employment of nuclear weapons in ground combat. Despite the diversion of three years of limited conventional war in Korea, the Army had been making progress in developing the weapons, organization, and doctrine that it believed would be required on a nuclear battlefield. During the 1950s the Army had under development a variety of nuclear weapons and associated surface-to-surface delivery systems, including the 280mm gun, the Honest John free rocket, and the Corporal, Redstone, and Jupiter guided missiles. For the air defense of vital areas, it was developing the surface-to-air Nike missile system. But the Jupiter and Nike systems were viewed in many quarters as duplicating and competing with Air Force programs and missions.[14]

To integrate the development of weapons, doctrine, and organizations and to provide guidance to developmental programs, the Army had begun to build a formal combat developments structure. As early as 1948 it had contracted with Johns Hopkins University to establish the Operations Research Office (ORO) to capitalize on scientific operations research methods for improving tactical doctrine. In June 1952 the Chief of Staff instructed the Chief of Army Field Forces to establish a combat developments organization within his office. This led to a combat developments element within Army Field Forces headquarters, and to combat developments departments at the Command and General Staff College and the four combat arms schools. In December 1952 a field agency of Army Field Forces, the Office of Special Weapons Development, was organized at Fort Bliss, Texas, to study the military applications of atomic energy. Army Field Forces also contracted with the ORO to organize an operations research group within Army Field Forces headquarters to work parallel with the civilian analysts of the ORO. The next year, in order to improve its capability to look at least ten years into the future, the Combat Developments Division of Army Field Forces headquarters was enlarged and renamed the Combat Developments Group.[15]

In February 1955, in a return to the organizational principle of the wartime Army Ground Forces, the Office of the Chief of Army Field Forces was reorganized into the Continental Army Command. Centralized control of combat developments was thereby strengthened further. By the late 1950s a body of doctrine on the employment of nuclear weapons had emerged from the Office of Special Weapons Development and was being incorporated into the texts and curricula of the Command and

General Staff College and the combat arms schools. Beginning in 1956 a new divisional organization with the attention-attracting name of "Pentomic" was being introduced for test. The proposed organizations were designed for the nuclear battlefield, but by eliminating numerous tactical headquarters perhaps manpower and money would also be saved.[16]

The recently reestablished Army War College was not a major participant in the debates over the New Look, nor was it yet a major participant in the debates over innovations in weapons, tactics, and organization. To deal with this latter question the Department of the Army had established combat developments arrangements that did not include the War College. Both debates nonetheless were followed closely by the faculty and students at Carlisle Barracks. The War College, moreover, like all Army activities, was affected immediately by the funding constraints of the Eisenhower budgets.

The Move to Improve: Successes and Failures

Already suspect because of General Swing's program for extensive renovation of Carlisle Barracks in 1951 and 1952, the War College became a vulnerable target for cost-savers. Acting Commandant Barnes in early 1953 directed Colonel DeVere Armstrong to summarize and document the arguments as to why the Army needed an Army War College and why the Army War College should be located at a separate installation such as Carlisle Barracks. Additionally, Barnes directed Armstrong to determine whether other schools or activities might be located at Carlisle Barracks in order to more efficiently use the post overhead and thereby reduce the per capita cost of producing a War College graduate. After two months' work Colonel Armstrong concluded that the reasons for reestablishing the Army War College and locating it at Carlisle Barracks remained sound. He also determined that the per capita costs at Carlisle Barracks compared favorably with those of the other higher-level educational institutions of the armed forces.[17]

While Armstrong was studying the recent past and present, another faculty member, Colonel James H. Polk, was looking toward the future. Polk, who had just graduated from the National War College, was directed to undertake a study to determine what actions might be taken to insure that the War College would become and remain an essential step in the educational system and that its graduates would be assured a "high degree of acceptance." The ideas that Polk discussed were not original; many had been floating about since 1950, and some were reflections of the second Army War College or practices of the National War College. The value of Polk's study was that he discussed these ideas from both desirability and feasibility viewpoints, thereby providing the new Commandant, General Moore, with a compendium of initiatives from which he might choose.[18]

In Polk's view, if the War College was to reach its potential, high academic standards must be retained and attendance must remain extremely selective. Polk believed that reserve component officers should be permitted and encouraged to attend at least portions of the program. He recommended that the college sponsor a professional journal or periodical and that the faculty and students be encouraged to write for publication. The faculty should be expanded to include civilian professors. Polk recommended further that a permanent board of civilian consultants be established. He discussed a number of other actions that he did not recommend because of fiscal, facility, and faculty limitations. Among the items considered and rejected was moving the Office of the Chief of Military History to Carlisle Barracks, creating a special short course for senior officers of the reserve components, participating in the combat developments program of Army Field Forces, initiating an annual strategic seminar with distinguished civilians participating, and affiliating with the national educational community in order to permit the awarding of academic degrees.[19]

General Moore began action on a number of the initiatives that Polk (and Trudeau before him) had suggested. A second civilian advisory group was convened at Carlisle in January 1954. Among its members was a future Secretary of State, Dean Rusk; a former commandant of the National War College, Harold Bull; and a professor from Dartmouth College, John W. Masland, who in a few years would publish a definitive study on American military education. The thrust of the group's report was that the Army War College should endeavor to become the intellectual center of the Army. With Polk's findings generally reinforced by the civilian advisory group's report, General Moore requested of the Department of the Army that two civilian professors, an economist and a political scientist, be authorized to join the faculty from June through December 1954 to assist in the preparation and presentation of the national and international affairs portion of the program.[20]

The tale of the request for authority to hire civilian professors is a case study in the ability of a bureaucracy to kill a proposal without ever disapproving it. The need was obvious. The War College was attempting to teach a course without a faculty trained in the disciplines involved. Moreover, there was precedent: the National War College had been bringing five scholars onto its resident faculty each summer and fall for its comparable course. After seven endorsements to the request by Second Army, Army Field Forces, and Department of the Army, and subsequent correspondence between Department of the Army and the Civil Service Commission, the hiring was approved in April 1954—much too late, as the potential faculty members had already committed themselves to their universities.[21]

In December 1954 General Moore tried a different approach. Instead of requesting two professors for six months each, he requested authority to hire one, an educational specialist, for the full 1955-56 academic year. In late March 1955 the Civil Service Commission granted authority, but again approval came too late to obtain the man sought. In 1956 a permanent educational specialist position was authorized, but at a civil service grade level too low to attract the quality desired. The position remained vacant until it was eliminated by a manpower utilization survey in 1961.[22]

The civilian advisory group also seconded Polk's recommendation that the War College sponsor a professional journal. Throughout the remainder of 1953 the question was explored, first by the officer in charge of publications and then by a committee consisting of Armstrong, Colonel William P. Yarborough (AWC 1953), and Lieutenant Colonel John F. Davis, Jr. In May 1954 the committee recommended that a quarterly journal be published under the title *Army War College Forum*. Hopes for approval, however, were not high. A similar request by the National War College had been turned down by the Army Chief of Staff the previous May, and a second proposal to the Joint Chiefs of Staff had been pending since November. General Moore apparently felt that the case for a journal was not strong enough to pass muster before the Adjutant General's Publications Board and its monitor, the Bureau of the Budget.[23]

In January 1955, just before his departure, General Moore allowed the question to be reopened, and a survey was made to determine the opinion of graduates and former faculty members on the need for a journal. Leavenworth, Maxwell Air Force Base, and Fort Benning were visited to learn the experiences of the *Military Review*, the *Air University Quarterly*, and the *Infantry Quarterly*. With this additional information Colonel Frederick W. Ellery (AWC 1953) again recommended in April 1955 that the War College sponsor a journal, but the subject was not taken up by the Faculty Board until October, after General Eddleman had been replaced by General Johnson. In November the Faculty Board recommended that a journal be published, but Johnson took no further action.[24]

General Moore had problems other than those connected with obtaining the services of civilian scholars and founding a journal. It was his lot to head the War College during the unsavory period of McCarthyism. On Washington's Birthday, 1954, the *Washington Times-Herald* headlined a column by Westbrook Pegler, "Communist Teaching U.S. Army." Pegler's column had to do with two lectures delivered at the Army War College, one in 1951 and another in 1952, by Mr. Jay Lovestone, an American labor leader and admitted former communist. That Lovestone was now an outspoken anti-communist did not impress Pegler. Unlike in 1919, the Army in 1954 was too busy defending itself against the Red-hunters to concern itself with defending the United States from domestic Reds. McCarthyism had no lasting effect on the Army War College. There were no book burnings, but to protect its library against the rummagings and attacks experienced by the overseas libraries of the State Department at the hands of Senator McCarthy's minions, precautionary measures were taken. Using the House Committee on Un-American Activities "Guide to Subversive Organizations and Publications" and the Attorney General's list of organizations considered "to have interests in conflict with those of the United States," an Army War College "Special Reference File" was established. Here were listed suspect library holdings. The fly leaves of these books were stamped with a notice referring the reader to the Special Reference File.[25]

Although unsuccessful in hiring civilian professors and in establishing a professional journal, General Moore was able to organize a research group dedicated to the conduct of advanced studies. General Almond had used faculty members on a part-time basis to accomplish such a purpose, but if the effort was to yield useful results a dedicated group was necessary. The 1954 civilian advisory group had encouraged this idea also in its admonition that the War College endeavor to assume intellectual leadership within the Army. Happily this scheme did not require direct funding support nor dealings with the Civil Service Commission, but merely authorization for enlarging the faculty and the assignment of qualified officers. The former proved easier than the latter.[26]

Moore's request for authorization was forwarded to the Department of the Army in 1954. He proposed that the group perform long-range studies on strategy and on land power, complementing rather than duplicating the combat developments program of Army Field Forces and the Operations Research Office of Johns Hopkins University. General John E. Dahlquist (AWC 1936), Chief of Army Field Forces, added a strong positive indorsement to Moore's request, stating that the Advanced Studies Group of the Army War College would serve "to round out the combat developments organization." Either through oversight or with intent, Dahlquist missed the point. The War College had in mind an independent group with the liberty to think conceptually in the long range. It did not want its study group thought of as one more element in a rigidly structured combat developments apparatus nor tied to a mechanistic process. This difference in outlook would one day cause difficulties. As a result of Moore's request and Dahlquist's support, the Department of the Army authorized an Advanced Studies Group of five officers, one colonel and four lieutenant colonels.[27]

The group was established in late September 1954 with the initial three members taken from the faculty already at Carlisle. They were relieved of other duties, including that of acting as faculty advisers to student committees. The Career Management Division of the Adjutant

General's Office, however, did not immediately assign additional officers to the War College, leaving the instructional side of the faculty under-strength. Initially led by Colonel C. B. Beasley with Colonels Lynn D. Smith (AWC 1952) and William P. Yarborough as members, the group launched into a study "to determine a desirable, feasible, and acceptable organization and deployment for the United States Army to be used to deter aggression and war or to fight successfully under all conditions of limited and global hostilities." It was a tall order for only three officers, but the War College had at least entered the field of advanced research.[28]

One officer who was impressed by the potential of an advanced studies element and who took seriously the comments of the civilian advisory group and the emerging results of Professor Masland's research on military education was the college's Secretary, Colonel James A. Berry. Throughout the fall of 1954 Berry offered suggestions on how to improve the quality of graduates, increase the effectiveness of the program, and enhance the prestige and usefulness of the institution so that it might assume a position of intellectual leadership. The goal, as Berry saw it, was to instill in the students habits of "skeptical inquisitiveness about fundamental values." It was necessary therefore to have the students probe problems in much greater depth—but that would require more time.

Berry's proposed solution had several facets. First, much of the mere transfer of knowledge, the "What" of the program, could be accomplished before the student's arrival at Carlisle Barracks through the means of an extension course made available to aspirants. Students would then be prepared to attack immediately in committee the "Why" of complex Army problems. Second, the resident program itself should be extended from one to two years. After 1959, Berry reasoned, the Army would have the quantity of War College graduates that it professed were needed, 1,588 officers. After that year it would only be necessary to maintain the pool, not enlarge it. A two-year course with each class half the size of the current class would permit greater selectiveness in who would attend and increased depth of inquiry. Third, a journal should be published to stimulate both aspirants and graduates to greater intellectual curiosity and more careful consideration of fundamental principles and values. Fourth, procedures for faculty selection and training should be improved. Finally, the scope of work of the Advanced Studies Group should be expanded, but it should be outside the formal combat developments program of the Army Field Forces.[29]

Colonel Berry's design for intellectual leadership apparently did not leave Carlisle Barracks. Indeed, the War College was having enough difficulty just maintaining the status quo, particularly in obtaining faculty. During the 1951-52 school year eight faculty members had been promoted to brigadier general and transferred without replacement. In

1952-53 the same thing occurred with three faculty members. The school year 1953-54 began with the faculty short seven of its authorized forty-four members. That same year the class had been expanded from 150 to 200 students, but additional faculty were not authorized until the next year, and even after authorization six faculty positions were unfilled when the 1954-55 program began. Then in June 1955 half of the faculty members were ordered to other stations. An additional problem, already mentioned, was the Career Management Division's failure to provide immediately for the needs of the newly organized Advanced Studies Group. If the War College enjoyed high priority in the Army's scheme of things, that priority was not or could not be met by those responsible for officer assignments.[30]

Despite the personnel problems, Army Field Forces and its successor after February 1955, Continental Army Command (CONARC), increasingly began to look to the War College for the accomplishment of important studies. In November 1954 Army Field Forces directed the Army War College to conduct a study on the structure of the Army for the 1960-70 decade. In August 1955 CONARC requested that the War College analyze an Air War College study addressing the future role of the Air Force, with the view of conducting a similar study for the Army. CONARC apparently believed that to be an appropriate task for the Advanced Studies Group. The War College believed otherwise, proposing instead that students perform the requested study as part of the Individual Studies Program, just as they performed studies of interest to the Army Staff. CONARC accepted that approach. By the end of August 1956 CONARC and the War College had agreed upon twelve topics pertaining to the role of the Army. These were arranged in priority—the top three being "Land Power as a Deterrent to War," "Land Power in Limited War in Selected Areas," and "Nuclear War and the Army."[31]

According to CONARC these studies should "present and justify a factual, bona fide restatement of the truism that the Army is indispensable to national security." That a truism by definition does not require justification escaped the author of the directive. The War College was uncomfortable with the task; it seemed that CONARC was not only directing a study, but directing its conclusions as well. The War College did not want to ask that of its students, nor would it do more than encourage members of the class to undertake the studies. Students of the Class of 1957 selected four of the twelve studies, "Land Power as a Deterrent to War," "A Philosophy of Landpower," "Fundamentals of Military Power," and "Recruit Training for the Future Army." The results submitted in March did not impress the faculty. The Deputy Commandant, Brigadier General Edgar C. Doleman (AWC 1951), tended to fault the faculty for the poor results, believing that the scope of the studies had not been clearly delineated. In September the better efforts were forwarded to CONARC, reluctantly and somewhat apologetically, with a promise to do better next time.[32]

If the leadership at the War College truly desired to win intellectual leadership for the college, the delayed and less-than-priority attention it gave to CONARC's request for studies on the role of the Army may well have been an opportunity lost. The question of the Army's role fundamentally was an issue of strategy, as was the national debate over security policy and the sometimes bitter interservice disputes. Considering the great difficulty that the Department of the Army and its supporters were having in establishing the role of the Army within the Department of Defense and with the American public, the War College might have been able to make a valuable contribution to the content of the Army's case and perhaps also to the national debate.

Concurrently, CONARC was moving to bring the War College into its combat developments fold. After discussion and correspondence during the summer of 1955, CONARC published a memorandum in October entitled "Development of Joint and Unilateral Army Doctrine, Procedures, Tactics and Techniques," designed to give direction to the Army's schools on the doctrinal aspects of the combat developments program. The War College's share was the development of doctrine and procedures relating to the army group and the theater army in joint and unilateral operations. Brigadier General Thomas W. Dunn, the Deputy Commandant, termed this "a new and significant" mission, for which three officers would be required. The Faculty Board considered the problem later in the month and recommended that the Commandant insist to CONARC that the new mission be confined to doctrinal and related organizational questions and exclude any study of materiel characteristics. Moreover, the War College should not become involved in matters below army group level.[33]

A third task imposed by CONARC involved civil defense. In February 1956 CONARC directed that the War College conduct continuing investigations of civil defense from both civil and military perspectives. War College objections to this mission resulted in its modification so that the college was required to conduct only those studies necessary to support its own instruction on civil defense. By the summer of 1956 the piecemeal assignment of noncurricular missions had become confusing to the degree that CONARC felt it necessary to consolidate them all into one directive, "Responsibilities of the Army War College."[34]

Receipt of this directive caused a reorganization of the faculty and at the same time set off a two-year struggle, largely unsuccessful, to increase the number of officers and administrative personnel permanently assigned to the college. A separate faculty group (Faculty Group I) was organized to handle "research, evaluation and doctrinal activities of the

College." Included in Faculty Group I was the earlier-activated Advanced Studies Group, an Evaluation Section charged with the continuing internal evaluation of curriculum and methodology, a War Games Section, and a Doctrine Section. This last element, in addition to meeting the CONARC requirements for doctrine pertaining to the theater army and army group and for studies pertaining to the role of the Army, would supervise the student Individual Studies Program. Two other faculty groups were organized to conduct designated portions of the instructional program.[35]

General Johnson insisted to CONARC that he needed increased manpower and funding support. He requested fourteen additional officers. General Willard G. Wyman, Commanding General of CONARC, strongly supported Johnson's request as it went forward to the Department of the Army in the summer of 1956. The request was returned, however, to be scaled down to a request for seven officers. It went forward again in the fall of 1957, but in March of 1958 was approved only "for planning purposes." The War College had received additional noncurricular missions but, in its view, had been denied the resources necessary to carry them out. Its situation was hardly unique in the Army during the Eisenhower presidential years. The college received scant sympathy from CONARC headquarters, which was trying desperately to juggle ends and means throughout the school system and at schools whose missions were more clearly understood than that of the War College.[36]

General Johnson was particularly concerned with being forced to shift faculty from curricular to noncurricular activities. A former assistant commandant at both the Engineer School and the Command and General Staff College, Johnson was never quite comfortable with the idea of an egalitarian military institution where little differentiation was made between faculty member and student. Johnson had been attempting to force the "faculty adviser" into a much more active role in guiding, perhaps even directing, the work of the student committees. Noncurricular missions were detrimental to the faculty adviser system he sought. Perhaps the cruelest blow occurred in late 1957, when CONARC directed the War College to prepare a text and supporting instructional material for an ROTC course on "The Role of the Army in National Defense." To the faculty this task was a gross distortion in priorities, for despite their ambitions to make the War College the Army's intellectual center, the faculty and successive commandants never deviated from the idea that development of the individual resident student was their primary task. In accord with this understanding of priority, the faculty was more comfortable when questioning the structure and content of the curriculum and the methods of instruction.[37]

Curricular Trends

During the five academic years from 1953 through 1957 under Commandants Moore, Eddleman, and Johnson, and Acting Commandants Barnes and Dunn, this continuing questioning resulted in the War College curriculum evolving generally in the direction of greater emphasis on the study of national security policy, international affairs, and joint war planning, with a lessening interest in internal Army issues. By the 1956-57 academic year almost half the program was devoted to the study of international affairs and national security policy.[38] The trend in direction is understandable. It was a direct reflection of the Army's major problem of the period—establishing its place in the declared national policy of massive retaliation. The War College was obligated to produce future decision-makers who understood the three major and related influences on national strategy and hence on the Army—the worldwide Soviet threat, the need for economy in government, and the effects of weapons of mass destruction on both international relations and military operations.

The trend toward a national perspective is discernible in the 1953-54 academic year, when the "National Policy and Security" block of instruction was extended by two weeks and relabeled "National and International Affairs." It became further evident the next year when a "National Strategy Seminar" was held in March just before the class began its work on war planning. Some fifty distinguished guests, half military officers and half civilians, participated with the class in the seminar. Promoted by Chief of Staff Ridgway, the seminar was quite openly patterned on the "Global Strategy Discussions" conducted each year at the Naval War College. There had been Army War College interest in such a program ever since General Trudeau had attended the Newport sessions in 1951. It admittedly had public relations as well as instructional goals.[39]

In 1955-56 an introductory course called "The World Scene and the Army," apparently also desired by General Ridgway, began the year's program. But it was not a success and was discontinued the next year. In 1955-56 also, the National Strategy Seminar was scheduled for June rather than March and replaced the war game as the grand climax of the year. In 1956-57 the year's program began with "American Tradition and the Communist Threat," followed by a six-week course on "International Relations" and then "Strategy and Policy Formulation." The class took the national perspective again in the last course of the year, "National Strategy," which included the National Strategy Seminar and a final consideration of the current world situation and possible developments over the next ten to fifteen years. In the five years between 1952 and 1957 the time that a class devoted to international affairs and national security problems had increased from eight to twenty weeks, while the total length of the academic year had increased from thirty-seven to forty-three weeks.[40]

For the 1953-54 year the war-planning phase was expanded by two weeks and renamed "*Strategy* and War Planning." The next year joint war planning and Army war planning, which had been separate courses, were consolidated. The emphasis of the merged course was almost exclusively on the Joint Strategic Planning System as practiced by the Joint Chiefs of Staff. A new course one week in length, "Strategy," was squeezed into this phase. Its stated purpose was to relate historical concepts of strategy to future concepts. This modest attempt at a theoretical approach to strategy was a new departure. However, it was short-lived. The next year the course was relabeled (and somewhat mislabeled) "*Military* Strategy," but the historical aspects were de-emphasized and study was directed instead at the "realities" of the nuclear age and on national objectives over the next ten years.[41]

The roots and fate of the course on strategy are interesting because they exemplify the difficulty that the War College was having in the 1950s in sorting out that which was "military" and that which was "national" and in finding the perspective that it wanted students to assume. Until 1953-54 it was thought that familiarity with strategic thinking would be a bonus benefit of the war-planning course, but the "Command of Large Military Units" study of the "Operations" course, with its consideration of the principles of war, stimulated a new interest in strategic theory and the history of strategic thought. Hence a course on "Strategy" was introduced in 1954-55. Unfortunately it directly preceded the first attempt at the National Strategy Seminar. According to the course director, Colonel Richard G. Stilwell, preparation for the seminar with its emphasis on national strategy tended to obscure consideration of military strategy. Stilwell recommended that in the future the two be separated and treated independently. That was done the next year, 1955-56. The National Strategy Seminar was moved to the end of the year, and the strategy course was renamed "Military Strategy." Stilwell was no longer in charge, however, and despite the change in title, the course retained its emphasis on national strategy. By 1956-57, Stilwell's earlier arguments for a course in military strategy were forgotten, and the course was absorbed into "Strategy and Policy Formulation," losing its separate identity.[42]

The course "Theater War Planning," followed by a war game, was retained for the classes of 1954 and 1955; however, 1955-56 saw the demise of the war game. Rather than being tested with a war game, student plans were merely critiqued. The argument for dropping the game was that it had come to dominate the course in theater planning. Plans tended to be written to accommodate the requirements of the game. A war game was reinserted into the curriculum in 1956-57, not as a device to test plans but as a means to analyze an assumed military situation ten years in the future. The theater war-planning course of that year was expanded into "Theater, Theater Army, and Army Group Planning and Operations," a late-hour reminder to the third Army War College that in fact it had been founded to fill a gap in military instruction. It was also a step consistent with the new combat-developments mission. But by 1957 the time a student devoted to war planning had been reduced from eighteen to eleven weeks.[43]

The amount of time that a student spent on strictly Army matters remained constant at about nine weeks throughout the five-year period. The "Operations" course carried what limited treatment the War College still gave to the problems of field command. The popular study "Command of Large Military Units" was repeated in 1953-54, but the next year it was transformed into "Command of Multinational Forces" and subsequently eliminated. Studies on "Command Decisions," essentially historical analyses, were introduced in 1953-54 and continued for the next two years, but they were not included in 1956-57. How to teach "command" seems to have been just as knotty a problem as it had been for the program designers of the second Army War College. In 1954-55 the "Operations" course was expanded into "Operations and Intelligence" in an effort to revive some consideration of intelligence problems below the national level.[44]

The "Manpower" and "Logistics" courses were combined into one course in 1955-56. The next year, at the direction of CONARC, a study on "General Management" was required of all committees and included in the "Manpower and Logistics" course. One week was spent on the subject, culminating in two days of analyses of case studies. Peacetime problems were beginning to find a place in the War College program. By 1956-57 only in the "Manpower and Logistics" course could be found the emaciated remains of what once had been a heavy emphasis on the problems of mobilization. In this course also could be found whatever the War College provided on the problems of administering foreign military assistance.[45]

When Collins, Swing, and Trudeau reestablished the Army War College in 1950, the perspective was to have been primarily that of the Department of the Army, and secondarily that of the echelons just below the Department of the Army down through the army group. The shift that occurred during the next six years was basically to a broader national perspective. This shift accelerated after the conclusion of the Korean War, Eisenhower's reductions in defense budgets, and the great national debate on security policy that placed in question the traditional role of the Army. Increasingly the War College turned its attention to international affairs, national security policy, and JCS-level planning. Theater war planning began to be de-emphasized, and war-gaming lost its climactic position. The study of military strategy and of the problems of field command, though experiencing promising starts, barely survived. And while the perspective of the original program was shifting, different methods of instruction were also being tried.[46]

Methods of Instruction

Committee problem-solving was the heart of the Swing method, as it had been in the second War College. In 1950-51 the class was normally organized into sixteen committees of five students each. The next year, when the size of the class expanded to 150, eight additional committees were organized. When the class grew to two hundred in 1953-54, the same number of committees were formed but with more students per committee. During a course each committee was presented with one explicit problem. Up to three committees might work on the same problem. During the year 1953-54, a total of 243 separately organized committees were active. With the courses increasing in length, by 1956-57 only 153 difference committees were formed. A student would serve on ten or eleven different committees during the year. It was a highly decentralized method of instruction, but it provided the maximum opportunity for each student to learn from his colleagues and to test and share his own career experiences. On the other hand, it did not insure that each student received equal exposure to the entire curriculum.[47]

To compensate, each committee in the early years was required to formally present its problem and solution to the assembled class. Concerned that students were spending too much effort in preparing the presentations, and that too few officers were being afforded the opportunity to make them, the faculty introduced a scheme (except for the war-planning courses) whereby students were regrouped into seminars at the end of each course. Less formal, more discussion-encouraging reports were presented to these seminars, and individual students had greater opportunity to present their own conclusions. Under this system emphasis gradually began to shift from formal, written, group reports to the informal, oral, individual reports. Other experiments were also being tried.[48]

In an effort to encourage analysis rather than fact-gathering, the scope of the committee problems was broadened to lessen the amount of detailed research. Concurrently, because of student dissatisfaction, the faculty reduced course bibliographies that in some courses had listed over sixty items. The "considerations" that committees were asked to address were broadened or in some cases eliminated altogether. In the course on the Soviet Union, group solutions were no longer required. Instead, each officer had to submit an individual summary report of about 1,000 words providing his personal assessment of the Soviet threat. In 1956-57 in the "Strategy and Policy Formulation" course, all committees dealt with the same broad problem of deriving an appropriate national strategy.[49]

The technique of case studies had been tried in the 1953-54 "Command Decisions" problems and found to be popular and useful. In 1955-56 a deliberate experiment in the use of case studies was made in the "Manpower and Logistics" course. Harbridge House, Inc., a civilian consulting firm, provided twenty-six case studies that were divided among three committees. For each case the discussion leader was either an expert from Harbridge House, one from the Army Command Management School or the Army Supply Management School, or a specially prepared member of the War College faculty.[50]

Other uses were made of outside experts. After the failure to obtain civilian professors, a system of consultants was begun whereby civilian experts (or military experts in the case of military subjects) were brought in for a few days or even for several weeks to assist committees by providing information or outlining approaches to the solution of a problem. These visiting consultants at times also conducted panel discussions which were used in lieu of or in addition to lectures. These discussions were scheduled for committees dealing in particular problem areas; a student might attend twenty-five to thirty of them during the year. Attempts were made to further exploit the knowledge of visiting lecturers by asking them to hold after-lecture conferences with several committees or with a few representatives from all committees. In 1955-56, in order to promote deeper consideration of what a lecturer had presented, those students who did not attend the after-lecture conference were gathered into groups where faculty advisers led discussions on the points made by the lecturer. These discussion groups were not popular with the students, however, and the scheme was dropped in 1956-57.[51]

In general, although the committee problem-solving method remained the fundamental means of encouraging student self-development through research, analysis, and group report writing, the instructional system was moving away from the formality of the committee method and moving toward a more informal seminar technique, a technique emphasizing individual student responsibility and requiring greater involvement by the faculty adviser. Instruction also was moving toward the consideration of broader, less precisely defined problems.

A tendency toward less-rigid structure was also apparent in the Individual Studies Program. The stated aim of that program remained constant—to apply original thought to subjects of current importance to the Army. But while some faculty members thought priority should be given to student self-improvement, others looked upon the program as an important means of solving problems of the Army Staff, and a third school thought the greatest value was to record the corporate experience of each class in support of the college curriculum. Beginning in academic year 1952-53 students were given increasing independence in their choice of a topic, and even encouraged to develop their own subjects. In 1956-57 permission was granted to a few students to engage in group research, individuals within the group investigating different facets of the same problem. Yet the Individual Studies Program, with its finite suspense dates, was apparently a major cause of tension at the War College. The consensus among the students was that the experience was valuable, however, and the faculty by and large agreed, though it was sore pressed to provide the guidance and constructive criticism necessary to make the program a complete success.[52]

Improving the Setting

During General Moore's tenure the War College moved to establish, record, and display the heritage of both the Army War College and Carlisle Barracks. After the Vice Chief of Staff in 1953 decided against moving the class plaques of the first and second Army War Colleges to Carlisle Barracks, Acting Commandant Barnes had Major Paul Goodman investigate the feasibility of having them duplicated. Goodman estimated the cost at over $5,000. Barnes saw no way of getting such a sum for that purpose and decided to have the plaques photographed and the pictures framed and hung in Bliss Hall to inspire future classes. The National War College provided the photographs on request in April 1955. That same year the Department of the Army approved a distinctive shoulder patch for the War College.[53]

The statue of Frederick the Great, which had been redisplayed at the old Army War College in 1927, was removed to storage once again during World War II. After the war it was discovered in an equipment yard at Fort McNair (formerly Washington Barracks) by retired Colonel J. E. Raymond who from 1938 to 1942 had been a member of the staff of the second Army War College. Raymond was able to arouse Chief of Staff Collins' interest in having the statue remounted. Harold Bull, at the National War College, was reluctant to relinquish Frederick, but after Bull's departure the statue was offered to General Moore, who agreed to accept it. A committee was appointed at Carlisle Barracks to select "a relatively inconspicuous site for the statue and to arrange for its mounting with minimum publicity." It was suggested that there would perhaps be less criticism if the statue of an American great captain was installed at the same time. West Point was considered as a possible source, but West Point apparently had no great captains to spare. So, since 1954 this Frederick has stood alone in an inconspicuous but serene spot, a place of greater peace than Frederick the Great probably ever knew in his lifetime and a setting of calm and dignity incomparable to the monument's fifty years in the District of Columbia.[54]

The quantity and variety of memorabilia returned to the War College caused General Moore to appoint a standing committee to catalogue, refurbish, and recommend placement of the items. The versatile Colonel William Yarborough was appointed chairman, possibly because of his adroit handling of Frederick. The Historical Committee had more ideas than money, but progress was made. A bust of Tasker Bliss done in Paris in 1918 by Jo Davidson was obtained in November 1953 on loan from the late sculptor's estate. Moore attempted to raise $1,500, first from appropriated funds and then from Second Army welfare funds, to purchase the bust, but he was unsuccessful. Contact was then made with General Bliss's son, Colonel E. Goring Bliss, himself a 1925 graduate of the War College. Goring Bliss offered several times to raise the necessary funds from among the friends of his late father. It would not have been difficult; Tasker Bliss's friends included such men as Bernard Baruch. At one point, Goring Bliss and Colonel Yarborough tentatively agreed to establish a "Tasker Bliss Memorial Fund," but General Moore finally was able to pry $5,000 out of Second Army for support of his historical program. The bust of Bliss was purchased and dedicated in October 1954, with Goring Bliss an honored guest at the ceremony.[55]

Other items were inspected and considered and after due deliberation placed on display or relegated to storage. A major project was decorating the student coffee shop in Bliss Hall with the coats of arms of all military units, including British units, that had served at Carlisle Barracks, and with the distinctive unit insignia of United States Army regiments. A few field pieces were obtained to decorate the post. A German "88" was obtained and sited as though to provide Frederick with overwatching fire. Efforts to obtain an Honest John rocket and Corporal and Redstone missiles were unsuccessful; subsequent classes and the Carlisle Barracks landscape have been denied that inspiration.[56]

Overall, the mid-1950s were years of both consolidation and trial. Unfortunately, the momentum engendered originally by Swing and Trudeau slowed with the criticism of costs. Those who were sensitive to such criticism, as Trudeau put it, "ran for cover." Nonetheless, the faculty continued to conceive of ways to improve the institution, and facilities at Carlisle Barracks continued to be improved. Tolerable, if not fully adequate, housing was provided; the library was expanded; a nine-hole golf course was completed; and a swimming pool was planned.

The Members

After 1955 the selection process for students was centralized so that students were selected by board action rather than by the Career Management Division and the chiefs of the administrative and technical services. Representation from the other services did not reach the figure of ten students from each service that Almond had requested, but by 1956 four Air Force, two Navy, and four Marine Corps officers regularly joined each class, and quotas were available for five representatives from the civilian departments of the federal government. Design of the curriculum was left essentially to the commandant, though curriculum review and approval was delegated from the Army Staff to CONARC in 1955. The authorities at Carlisle Barracks appreciated independence, but that independence left the college without any really highly placed advocate.[57]

The War College of the early and middle 1950s had as members many of the officers who would occupy senior command and staff positions in Southeast Asia a decade or more later. William Westmoreland was an instructor from 1950 to 1952, as was Richard G. Stilwell from 1953 to 1956. Bruce Palmer and John Heintges were in the Class of 1952, and Creighton Abrams was in the Class of 1953. With Abrams were Julian Ewell, William McCaffrey, William Peers, and William Yarborough, the latter remaining three years on the faculty. Others were Stanley Larsen and William B. Rosson of the Class of 1954, Joseph McChristian and John Tillson of 1955, and Walter Kerwin, James Hollingsworth, and Willard Pearson of 1957.[58]

Southeast Asia was not a major topic for study during the period, although it was a subject of an area study in Swing's initial year and by 1955-56 it was included along with the Middle East as a possible theater of operations in the war-planning course. Western Europe was the region of primary interest, and there is little indication that the French Army's experience in Vietnam was studied in depth. "Counterinsurgency" was not yet an operative term. The lack of interest in the French experience has been explained by what might be called the "No More Koreas" syndrome. In the years immediately following the Korean War, it seemed most unlikely that the United States would again attempt a land campaign on the Asian mainland. Moreover, Vietnam was seen as a French problem, not an American one. The lack of interest in the French campaigns is also an indication that the Army War College approached its studies from a base of contemporary issues and problems perceived to be in need of early solution. Its approach was not from a base of either history or theory. As Professors Masland and Radway were to comment, the level of abstraction was not high.[59]

NOTES
1. AWC, *Curriculum, August 1952 to June 1953*.
2. AWC, "Course Directive, Course I, Parts 2 and 3," 19 September 1952.
3. AWC, "Course Directive, Course II, Part 3, Operations," 26 January 1953. AWC, "Course Directive, Course II, Part 1, Logistics," 17 November 1952. AWC, "Course Directive, Course II, Part 2, Manpower," 5 January 1953.
4. AWC, "Course Directive, Operations," 26 January 1953. William W. Whitson, *The Role of the United States Army War College in the Preparation of Officers for National Security Policy Formulation* (Ph.D. dissertation, Fletcher School of Law and Diplomacy, 1958), 414-15.

326

5. AWC, "Course Directive, Logistics," 17 November 1952. AWC, "Course Directive, Operations," 26 January 1953.
6. AWC, "Course Directive, Course III, Part 1, Strategic Planning," 24 February 1953. AWC, "Course Directive, Course III, Part 3, Theater Planning," 1 June 1953. AWC, "Course Directive, Theater Planning, Guide for the Conduct of a War Game," 22 October 1952. AWC, "Special Directive, War Game," 1 June 1953.
7. AWC, "Directive, Individual Studies," 5 September 1952. Whitson, *Role of War College*, 284.
8. Ibid., 253-54.
9. Spanier, *American Foreign Policy*, 103-08. Lee Douglas Kinnard, *President Eisenhower and Strategy Management: A Study in Defense Politics* (Lexington, Kentucky: The University of Kentucky, 1977), 2-6, 23-26. Robert A. Divine, *Eisenhower and the Cold War* (New York: Oxford University Pres, 1981), 17-19, 27-31. Samuel F. Wells, Jr., "The Origins of Massive Retaliation," *Political Science Quarterly* (Spring 1981).
10. John Foster Dulles, "The Evolution of Foreign Policy," *Department of State Bulletin*, 30 (25 January 1954): 107-10. For the origins of the New Look see Kinnard, *Eisenhower and Strategy*, 26-36. On massive retaliation see Paul Peeters, *Massive Retaliation, the Policy and its Critics* (Chicago: Henry Regnery Co., 1959); Urs. Schwarz, *American Strategy: A New Perspective* (New York: Doubleday, 1966), 84-94; and, more recently, Wells, "Massive Retaliation." For the reaction of the then Army Chief of Staff see Matthew B. Ridgway, *Soldier: The Memoirs of Matthew B. Ridgway*, as told to Harold H. Martin (New York: Harper and Brothers, 1956), 288-94.
11. For early criticism of the Eisenhower strategy see Edward L. Katzenbach, "The Diplomatic Cost of Military Penny Pinching," *The Reporter* (2 February 1954): 18-21; Chester Bowles, "Our Present Foreign Policy," *Commonweal* (30 April 1954): 86-95; Bernard Brodie, "Unlimited Weapons and Limited War," *The Reporter* (18 November 1954): 16-21; and William W. Kauffman, "The Requirements of National Security," Memorandum No. 7, Princeton Institute of International Studies, 1954.
12. Spanier, *American Foreign Policy*, 107, 112-13, 115. John Foster Dulles, "Challenge and Response in United States Foreign Policy," *Foreign Affairs* (October 1957): 31-33. Kinnard, *Eisenhower and Strategy*, 86-89.
13. For the extent of the literature on limited war see Department of Army Pamphlet 20-60, *Bibliography on Limited War* (Washington: GPO, 1958) and Morton H. Halperin, *Limited War in the Nuclear Age* (New York: John Wiley and Sons, 1963), 133-84.
14. "The Case for Tactical Atomic Weapons," *Army* (March 1956): 24-25. Maxwell D. Taylor, "The Army in the Atomic Age," *Quartermaster Review* (January-February 1956): 4-5, 152, 155-56, 159. "This is a Look at the New 'Atomic' Army—," *U.S. News and World Report* (25 January 1957): 50-53.
15. Hewes, *Root to McNamara*, 244, 259-60.
16. Ibid., 261-70. Lionel C. McGarr, "U.S. Army Command and General Staff College Keeps Pace with the Future," *Military Review* (April 1957): 6. William R. Kintner and George C. Reinhardt, *Atomic Weapons in Land Combat* (Harrisburg, Pa.: Military Service Publishing Co., 1953). Maxwell D. Taylor, *Swords and Plowshares* (New York: W. W. Norton, 1972), 171.
17. DeVere Armstrong, Memorandum for Commandant, 13 August 1953, Subject: Study on the Army War College, File: Academic Year 1954.
18. James H. Polk, Memorandum from Director, GS Group, to Commandant, 25 June 1953, Subject: Projects to Enhance the Prestige of the Army War College, File: 1954.
19. Ibid.,
20. Second Civilian Advisory Group Report, February 1954, AWC Library. James A. Berry to Commandant, 16 November 1953, Subject: Resident Civilian Professors on Army War College Faculty, File: Educational Specialist for USAWC.
21. Chairman, Curriculum Group, to Commandant, 20 November 1963, USAWC Historical File: 1959-1963.
22. Ibid., Moore to Director of Civilian Personnel, 28 December 1954, USAWC Historical File: 1959-1963.
23. Secretary to Chief, Reproduction Division, 30 July 1953; Secretary to Colonels Armstrong, Yarborough, Davis, and Haley, 6 November 1953. Secretary to Commandant,

14 October 1953; Report of Committee Periodicals, 2 March 1954; all in File: AWC Periodical.

24. John W. Yow to Secretary, 17 January 1955, Subject: Survey of Former Faculty and Graduates; F. W. Ellery, Memorandum for Record, 20 January 1955, Army War College Periodical; Ellery to Acting Commandant, 20 April 1955; Minutes of Faculty Board Meeting, 2 November 1955, 25 and 26 October 1955; all in Ibid.

25. Westbrook Pegler, "Communist Teaching U.S. Army," *Washington Times-Herald*, 22 February 1954. John F. Davis, Jr., Memorandum for Record, 23 February 1954. Library Committee to Commandant, 21 January 1953. Librarian to Assistant Secretary, 8 February 1954, Subject: Communist Books. AWC, Memorandum, 8 February 1954, Subject: Defense Against Communist Propaganda. Secretary to Commandant, 5 March 1954, Subject: Defense Against Communism.

26. Report of Civilian Advisory Group, February 1954.

27. AWC Letter, 17 March 1954, Subject: Army War College Advanced Study Group, OCAFF 1st Indorsement, 29 March 1954 signed by Dahlquist, and 2nd Indorsement, Hq., Dept. of Army, 14 June 1954, AWC File 30-10: Support Requirements.

28. Moore to Chief, Career Management Division, 23 September 1954 and AWC Memorandum, Advanced Study Group, attached to memorandum, Secretary to Deputy Commandant, 22 October 1954, Subject: The Near and Long Range Future of the ARWC (hereafter "Berry Study"), MHI. AWC, Memorandum for Staff and Faculty, 3 December 1954, Subject: Terms of Reference, Advanced Study Group, MHI.

29. "Berry Study." Whitson, *Role of War College*, 179-80, 188.

30. Acting Commandant to Chief, Career Management Division, 5 August 1953, in "Berry Study." Whitson, *Role of War College*, 198-99, 234.

31. Berry, Memorandum for Record, 17 November 1954. CONARC, Letter, 19 August 1955, Subject: Analysis of Air War College Study; AWC, Letter, 25 October 1955, Subject: Analysis of Air War College Study; Hq., CONARC to Commandant, 31 August 1956, Subject: Doctrinal Studies Depicting the Role of the Army in Modern Warfare; all in File: Doctrinal Studies Depicting the Role of the Army.

32. Ibid. Director Course 10 to Deputy Commandant, 6 August 1957; Doleman to Commandant, 2 April 1957; AWC to Commanding General, CONARC, 4 September 1957; all in File: Doctrinal Studies.

33. CONARC Memorandum No. 18, 7 June 1955, Subject: Development of Joint and Unilateral Army Doctrine, Problems, Tactics and Techniques; CONARC to AWC, 5 October 1955 and AWC to CONARC, 17 January 1956, Subject: Development of Joint and Unilateral Army Doctrine; Minutes of Faculty Board Meetings of 25 and 26 October 1955, Topic 5, 2 November 1955; all in File: Doctrinal Studies.

34. Hq. CONARC, Letter, 14 February 1956; Hq. CONARC, Letter, 1 June 1956, Subject: Responsibilities of the Army War College; all in File: Doctrinal Studies.

35. AWC, Faculty Memorandum No. 41, 12 July 1956.

36. AWC to Hq. CONARC, 5 July 1956, Subject: Responsibilities of the Army War College; Wyman to Chief of Staff, 10 August 1956, Subject: Army War College Support Requirements; AWC to Hq. CONARC, 21 November 1957, Subject: U.S. Army War College Support Requirements with 4th Indorsement, Hq. Dept. of the Army, 14 March 1958; all in File 30-10.

37. Draft letter (not sent) Johnson to Commanding General, CONARC, 29 October 1956; CONARC to AWC, 12 September 1957, Subject: Development of ROTC Manual; File: Doctrinal Studies.

38. AWC File: Course Material—Summary of Curricula, 1950-1964.

39. AWC, *Curriculum August 1953 to June 1954*. AWC, *Curriculum August 1954 to June 1955*. AWC, "Course Directive Course 8, Strategy," 14 March 1955. Richard G. Stilwell, Final Report on Course 8, 6 May 1955, Final Report National Strategy Seminar, 29-31 March 1955. Trudeau to Captain J. M. Sweeney, USN, 18 June 1951, Trudeau papers.

40. Lowell G. Smith and Murray G. Swindler interview with Clyde D. Eddleman, 1975, Sec. 3, 18, 22, MHI. AWC, *Curriculum August 1955 to June 1956*. AWC, "Course Directive Course 1, World Scene and the Army," 22 August 1955. AWC, "Course Directive Course 1, American Tradition and Communist Threat," 17 August 1956. AWC,

"Course Directive Course 2, International Relations," 24 September 1956. AWC, "Course Directive Course 3, Strategy and Policy Formulation," 31 October 1956.
41. *Curriculum 1953-54.* AWC, "Course Directive, Course 8, Strategic War Planning," 11 March 1954. AWC, "Course Directive, Course 9, Joint and Army War Planning," 4 April 1955. AWC, "Course Directive, Strategy," 1955. AWC, "Course Directive, Course 7, Military Strategy," 27 February 1956.
42. AWC, "Course Directive, Strategic War Planning," 1954. AWC, "Course Directive, Course 7, Operations," 1 February 1954. AWC, "Course Directive, Strategy," 1955. Whitson, *Role of War College* 414-15. Stilwell, Final Report on Course 8, 1955. AWC, "Course Directive Military Strategy," 1956. AWC, "Course Directive, Strategy and Policy Formulation," 1956.
43. AWC, "Course Directive, Course 10, Theater War Planning," 10 May 1954. AWC, "Course Directive, Course 10, Theater War Planning," 16 May 1955. AWC, "Course Directive, Course 9, Theater War Planning," 23 April 1956. AWC, "Course Directive, Course 7, Theater, Theater Army, and Army Group Planning and Operations," 22 April 1957.
44. AWC, "Course Directive, Course 4, General Army Orientation," 16 November 1953. AWC, "Course Directive, Course 7, Operations," 1 February 1954. AWC, "Course Directive, Course 7, Operations and Intelligence," 31 January 1955. AWC, "Course Directive, Course 2, Operations and Intelligence," 8 September 1955. AWC, "Course Directive, Course 4, Operations and Intelligence," 2 January 1957.
45. AWC, "Course Directive, Course 3, Logistics and Manpower," 17 October 1955. AWC, "Course Directive, Course 5, Logistics and Manpower," 7 February 1957.
46. Whitson's 1958 dissertation, cited earlier, contains detailed analyses of the evolution of the third War College's programs and methods during its first seven years. It has been most helpful in preparation of this chapter.
47. Whitson, *Role of the War College*, 272-74.
48. Ibid., 253-54, 289.
49. Ibid., 338-39, 350-51, 364-66. AWC, "Course Directive, Course 4, The Communist Bloc," 1 December 1955. Course Directive, "Strategy and Policy Formulation," October 1956.
50. AWC, "Course Directive, Operations," 1954. AWC, "Course Directive, Logistics and Manpower," October 1955. Whitson, *Role of the War College*, 278-80.
51. Ibid., 241-45, 281-83.
52. Ibid., 290-99. AWC, "Course Directive, Individual Studies, 1954-55," 10 September 1954. AWC, "Course Directive, Individual Studies," 24 August 1956.
53. Goodman to Acting Commandant, 19 February 1953; Colonel C. H. Clarke, National War College to Berry, 13 April 1954; Historical File 1957-58. Quartermaster General to Commandant, 28 November 1955, Subject: Shoulder Sleeve Insignia for the Army War College, Historical File 1954-55.
54. Raymond to Commandant, 3 May 1958; Johnson to Raymond, 27 May 1958; Secretary (Colonel Childs) to Colonels Otto and Yarborough and Major Southard, 23 October 1953, Subject: Disposition of the Statue of Frederick the Great; Historical File 1945-1953.
55. Secretary to Colonel Yarborough, 15 February 1954; Undersecretary of the Army to Comptroller of the Army, 14 December 1953; Moore to Commanding General, Second Army, 10 February 1954; E. Goring Bliss to Colonel John F. Davis, Jr., 12 April 1954; Yarborough to Commandant, 9 June 1954, Subject: Tasker Bliss Memorial Fund; Moore to Commanding General, Second Army, 30 August 1954, Subject: Army War College Historical Development: Moore to E. Goring Bliss, 13 October 1954; all in Historical File 1957 and 1958.
56. AWC Historical File 1957 and 1958.
57. Trudeau to Colonel James A. Bassett, 24 March 1952, Trudeau papers. Eddleman interview, Section 3, 20-21. Whitson, *Role of War College* 189-90, 207-08. Almond to Reuben E. Jenkins, Assistant Chief of Staff, G-3, 22 January 1952. Trudeau papers.
58. USAWC, *Director 1905-1980.*
59. Roland D. Tausch interview with James Polk, 1971-1972, 41. Masland and Radway, *Soldiers and Scholars*, 381.

National Strategy and Military Program 1957-1961

Whatever the level of abstraction achieved or not achieved at Carlisle Barracks, by 1957 the third Army War College had all but abandoned the gap-filling role and was nearing the apex. Its movement in that direction, however, had not gone unnoticed outside the Army. As early as 1953 Lieutenant General Harold Craig, U.S. Air Force, Commandant of the National War College, recognized that he had competitors not only at Carlisle Barracks but also at Newport and at Maxwell Air Force Base. The duplication at those places of a large part of his curriculum appeared to be dissipating his own unique mission, and it was perhaps denying the National War College its full share of the best-qualified students.

Defending the Apex

In June 1953 General Craig initiated a series of actions designed to restore to the National War College its position of unquestioned preeminence over the war colleges of the separate services. His first step was a request to the Joint Chiefs of Staff that a review be conducted of all the war colleges. The JCS declined to make the broad review that Craig desired but did agree to a review of the *joint* colleges. For that purpose it established a six-member board headed by the President of Williams College, James P. Baxter.[1]

The Baxter Board recommended in June 1955 that the services send more senior officers to the National War College and that each of its classes include a proportion of graduates from the services' war colleges. The services balked, however, insisting that the selection of officers to attend the various war colleges was strictly the prerogative of the individual services. In September, Craig's successor, Vice Admiral Edmund Woolridge, appealed directly to the Chairman of the JCS, Admiral Arthur Radford, who in turn asked the service chiefs to review again their selection procedures for the joint colleges. But the service chiefs held firmly to their earlier positions. Radford then urged the formation of an ad hoc committee to look for ways to improve the joint institutions.[2]

In response to Radford's request, in May 1956 the JCS formed a committee of four distinguished retired officers, one from every service, headed by General Charles L. Bolte, former Vice Chief of Staff of the Army and an instructor at the Army War College from 1938 through 1940. In July the Bolte Committee reaffirmed in essence the Baxter recommendations that the JCS should establish selection criteria for the joint colleges and that a substantial number of the members of each National War College class should be graduates of the services' war colleges. This time the service chiefs agreed. Consequently in 1957 the Department of the Army began to send a few officers who had attended the Army War College three to seven years earlier to each session of the National War College. The action was taken despite the recognized morale problem that the practice created among the officers who weren't selected, and despite the belief that no real need existed for an officer to spend a second year undergoing a war college experience. Additionally, the partial success on the part of the National War College in regaining a unique position was of course a setback to those in the Army who were endeavoring to raise the sights and prestige of the Carlisle institution.[3]

The reopening of the issue of the relationship between the Army War College and the National War College appears to have stimulated, if it did not initiate, another intensive internal review of the Army War College curriculum during the 1956-57 school year. Perhaps also contributing to the decision for review was the pending publication of a Dartmouth College study of military education by Professors John Masland and Lawrence Radway in the work *Soldiers and Scholars*. In the authors' words, they had set themselves to the task of appraising "the contribution these schools [the senior service colleges] are making to the preparation of their graduates for assignments in which they participate in the formulation of national security policies at the highest levels." Constructive and generally favorable, *Soldiers and Scholars* nonetheless pointed out among its criticisms the need to approach advanced education in a more relaxed manner. The curricula of the colleges were held to be too rigid and the colleges too concerned with form and technique. Masland and Radway attributed these weaknesses to tendencies among senior officers to associate education with training and to attempt to differentiate between the "need-to-know" and the "nice-to-know," practices dangerous in higher education where the aim is, or should be, to raise the intellectual level of the individual.[4]

Most influential on the perceived need to redesign or at least review the curriculum at the Army War College, however, was the ordered thinking of the Army's Chief of Staff, General Maxwell D. Taylor. Ever since his return from the Far East in 1955 to replace General Ridgway,

General Taylor had been attempting to convince the Joint Chiefs of Staff and the Secretary of Defense of the critical need for a guiding document which Taylor called a "National Military Program." He had worked personally at drafting such a document even before he formally became Chief of Staff. He was not enjoying great success, however, in having a National Military Program either considered or adopted by the administration, despite the crises of 1956 in which British, French, and Israeli forces invaded Egypt, Russian forces went into Hungary, and Nikolai Bulganin threatened his own version of massive retaliation. It is hardly surprising and more than coincidental that the curriculum of the Army War College began to mirror Taylor's approach to the problems of national security.[5]

By academic year 1956-57 the War College had adopted a scheme whereby all courses and studies lead to the derivation of a recommended national strategy for the approaching decade. In 1957-58 this theme was reinforced. Added to it that year was the derivation of a military program to support that national strategy. The 1957-58 curriculum had the clearest logic of any War College program since the "preparation of war" and "conduct of war" structure of the 1930s. The curriculum was divided into two parts, "The United States and Its National Strategy" and "Military Doctrine, Strategy and Readiness." The first part culminated with each committee drafting a recommended national strategy for the United States; the second part, with the drafting of a National Military Program. Then, in a short summation period, which included the National Strategy Seminar at the end of the year, the two were put together and offered to the distinguished civilian and military guests for comment and criticism.[6]

A Benchmark Program: 1957-58

The new unifying theme of national strategy and national military program introduced in 1957-58 did not require major modification of the first part of the year's instruction. This first phase lasted seventeen weeks and ended just before the Christmas holidays. The trend toward less-formal, more-individual presentations continued, as did the trend toward fewer formal committee-written reports. The periodic rearranging of the committees into seminar groups for discussion and informal presentation of papers increased. The only formal committee report required was the national strategy draft itself. Guest consultants and lecturers were used extensively.[7]

The second part of the course, however, commonly called the "military phase," underwent major revision to meet the new theme. No longer was the phase divided into studies concerning the internal problems of the Army and studies concerning war planning. Gone was the traditional structure of approaching problems in sequence from the viewpoint of each of the four functional staff areas. The military phase began with a course titled "The Army in Combat," in which committees investigated possible doctrinal and organizational concepts for the next ten years.[8]

"The Army in Combat" was followed by a course in war-gaming. For the majority of the class the course was a series of seminars led by representative of the war-gaming elements of various headquarters and agencies, including the Office of the Chief of Naval Operations, Supreme Headquarters Allied Powers Europe, CONARC, RAND Corporation, and the Operations Research Office. Forty-eight students were selected early in the year to assist the faculty in developing an analytical war game, exercising it, and presenting its results to the class. The evidence is strong, however, that by the late 1950s the War College had fallen far behind in the increasingly sophisticated art of war-gaming. For the next two years war-gaming continued to enjoy separate course status, but the game was hand-computed and after 1960 was discarded as too detailed and time-consuming for the benefits derived.[9]

In 1957-58 the war game was followed by a course titled "Theater, Theater Army, and Army Group Operations." This course was all that remained of the war plans phase that had been a major element of the Swing-Trudeau program. The class was organized into nine committees, with each committee required to develop a conceptual basis for theater, theater army, and army group war plans in a specific theater and for a specific type of war. For Europe the scenarios considered were general war, non-atomic war, and limited atomic war; for the Middle East, general war and contingency operations; for the Far East, general war; and for Southeast Asia, limited atomic war and limited non-atomic war. The ninth committee developed a concept for organizational and operational doctrine pertaining to the army group. The conceptual bases called for by this course were a far cry from the detailed war plans once required of Army War College students.[10]

Having previously arrived at a national strategy and having just completed two courses that involved future concepts of land warfare, the students were now prepared in theory to draft "A United States National Military Program." This they did in the next course, "Military Strategy." Each committee, assuming a JCS perspective, prepared a military strategic concept and its supporting requirements, the paper being written as if to provide guidance to the military departments and subordinate unified and specified commands for the short, middle, and long terms. Guidance on the air defense of the United States and on civil defense was to be included. The faculty provided a detailed format for the National Military Program, although the committees were not required to adhere to it. The college informed its students, however, that the description of contents included in the format was considered to be "in consonance with the views of the Chief of Staff."[11]

Included in the format were strategic appraisals and the resulting military objectives, military strategies, and basic military undertakings essential to the achievement of national objectives in all world regions of importance to the United States. Estimates had to be made of the total forces required, as well as estimates of how many of those forces could be supplied by allies. The format included provisions for research and development, reserve component forces, aid to allies, logistical support for US and allied forces, and the mobilization and training base. The rationale for the need for a National Military Program was definitely that of General Taylor, and the document was to be thought of as one that might be prepared by the JCS, forwarded to the Secretary of Defense, and then if approved sent on to the National Security Council. The Joint Strategic Objectives Plan (JSOP) being used by the JCS contained, according to the War College, only portions of the information required by a true National Military Program.[12]

Each committee had twenty-five days to prepare the document, a period during which they also attended sixteen lectures and five panel discussions by operating officials of all services, both chiefs and officers at the second and third operating levels. The committees were expected to draw on all the studies they had previously completed on national strategy and future operations. This exercise was by far the most comprehensive and detailed requirement placed on the committees during the year. It was in effect the practical application of all that had gone before. If General Taylor had been unable to convince his colleagues on the JCS of the worth of a National Military Program, he had at least provided the War College with a theme for its program and provided future high-level staff officers with a logical approach to the intellectual problem of determining the nation's defense needs.[13]

"Military Readiness" was the course that followed the drafting of the National Military Program. It was misnamed. Its stated purpose was to appraise the *nation's* ability to support the national strategy and required military program, and the course contained additionally a number of studies on diverse topics which, although important, only indirectly pertained to military readiness. Among the topics considered were several that hinted at the gathering momentum of a new trend, one toward giving more attention to developing the managerial skills of senior officers. Written into the "Military Readiness" phase were discussion topics on "Management," "Management within the Army," and "Army Budgeting." Among the lecturers was the Comptroller of the Department of Defense.[14]

Concurrently with these many courses the students had been preparing their individual studies, in 1957-58 labeled the "Thesis Program." The evidence is strong that a serious attempt was made that year to improve the quality of the products of the program. The criterion was to "satisfy the normal standards of graduate or professional work," and six additional weeks were allowed to complete the papers.[15]

The last three weeks of the year, the students were engaged in the course "National Strategy and Supporting Military Program," culminating in the four-day National Strategy Seminar. Before the guests' arrival for the seminar, the class spent two weeks reviewing their national strategies and military programs, adjusting them to recent changes in the international situation and to the realities brought out by the "Military Readiness" course. By 1958 the number of guests invited to the seminar had grown to eighty. As in earlier years each student committee was reinforced by a proportional number of guests, and with its guests it continued to consider and refine its national strategy and military program. During the four days of the seminar, lectures were presented by representatives of the Central Intelligence Agency, the Department of State, and the Council of Economic Advisors, as well as by the Chairman of the Joint Chiefs of Staff and the Secretary of the Army. The final lecturer was Chief of Staff Maxwell Taylor, whose topic was "Preparations for Limited War." It was an appropriate subject. The next month American forces landed in Lebanon in accordance with the "Eisenhower Doctrine," and before the summer was done there was another crisis in the Formosan Straits. Before Christmas, Khrushchev would issue an ultimatum on Berlin.[16]

The 1957-58 program was decidedly a benchmark in the evolution of the program of the third Army War College. It was the culmination of all the trends underway since 1951, and it was the base upon which the programs of the 1960s would be built. Minor adjustments would be made the following year and also for the 1960-61 year, but the program remained essentially unchanged through 1963. More significantly, the curriculum theme of a "National Strategy and Its Supporting Military Program" would remain in place for more than a decade.[17]

The Williams Board

The 1957-58 program was subject to an external review earlier than the War College probably wanted or expected. On December 23, 1957, the Department of the Army established an Officer Education and Training Review Board chaired by the deputy commanding general of CONARC, Lieutenant General Edward T. Williams. Serving with Williams were two major generals, five colonels (four of whom were either 1955 or 1956 graduates of the Army War College), and one lieutenant colonel. For the first time since the Eddy Board of 1949, an investigation of the entire officer education and training system was to occur. Williams convened his board in early January 1958, and it remained in session until July.[18]

On its own initiative, the board set out some "provocative thoughts" and a frame of reference to guide its work. The provocative thoughts included some questions to be answered. First, should the current objective of the school system—to train officers for wartime duties—be expanded to include training for peacetime management of men, materiel, and installations? Second, should the Command and General Staff College and the War College shift emphasis to the "broad educational function of advancing the art and science of land warfare?" Third, was the current scheme of systematic progression from the training of branch specialists to the education of generalists still sound?[19]

The board's frame of reference stipulated an environment of continuing world tension in which immediately ready land forces were critical to the deterrence of war. The board saw a continuation of the trend toward closer integration of civil and military authority in the formulation of policy; it also felt that moves toward greater unification of the military services would continue. The board noted the increased interest and competence of civilian scholars in the fields of national military policy, military strategy, and grand tactics, and it saw a need to meld military thought with this academic thought.[20]

The Board produced a number of findings and recommendations on the overall school system that were of interest to the War College. Within the office of the Deputy Chief of Staff for Operations at Department of the Army and within the G-3 Section of CONARC, the staff elements that were charged with supervising the school system were undermanned and organizationally buried. They needed to be strengthened because the school system, in the board's view, should enjoy a priority second only to that of the operational forces. If the schools were to be charged with a combat developments mission, as they then were, they should be provided additional personnel. The board saw a distinction between education and training: It believed the War College's mission to be exclusively within the range of education, while Leavenworth was concerned with both education and training. The board also reaffirmed that the objective of the entire school program should be to prepare officers for wartime duties, with emphasis on the art of command.[21]

The Williams Board report discussed thoroughly the Army War College but made few specific recommendations for change. The wisdom of the decision to reestablish the college in 1950 was confirmed, as was the correctness of the subsequent shift in emphasis from operations of larger Army units to national military power and joint military strategy. The board recognized the opposing gap-filler argument that a significant portion of the program should be devoted to the operations of the army group and theater army and to training officers for duty on the Department of the Army staff. It also recognized the thinking of some that the War College, as it had in the early 1920s, should relieve

337

Leavenworth of the task of teaching operations of the field army and the theater army logistical command. The board rejected those approaches, however, as it did a criticism that the college did not prepare officers for specific duty assignments, an idea that the board found "unsound, unrealistic, and probably infeasible."[22]

The role of the War College, as the Williams Board saw it, was "to elevate and to project the level of thinking to encompass the political, military, economic, and psychological intangibles and realities that shape the course of modern history," keeping in mind nonetheless that the college was an Army institution, educating Army officers, and that the perspective, therefore, must be that of the Army. The board concluded that the 1957-58 program had struck a good balance that should remain appropriate for the immediate future, as long as the role and mission of the Army were stressed within the study of national strategy.[23]

The Williams Board did recommend a restatement of the War College mission, primarily to clarify it and to bring it into consonance with what was actually going on at Carlisle Barracks. The restated mission had four parts reflecting, first, the professional development being sought; second, the doctrinal responsibilities assigned; third, the college's research and study responsibilities; and, finally, its interservice, interdepartmental, and interacademic responsibilities. The professional development to be sought was the preparation of officers for the highest command and general staff positions in the Army and for other high positions that the Army might be called upon to fill in joint and combined commands, the Department of Defense, and other national governmental agencies.[24]

The proposed mission statement reflected in detail the CONARC letter of 1956 on Army War College responsibilities. The doctrinal responsibilities pertaining to the army group and the theater army were retained, and curriculum coverage at these levels was to be provided. The Board considered that appropriate since the operations of the theater army and the army group were of a "strategic nature." The Board warned, however, against too much curricular emphasis at that level; the program should not be reduced to one of "military mechanics."[25]

The board recommended that the War College continue to develop studies relating to strategy, organization, and equipment for current and future Army forces. While recognizing that the faculty and student body of the War College collectively represented a great store of experience and knowledge the board did not consider the War College an appropriate agency for the Department of the Army staff to call upon in expectation of solutions to current problems. In other words, the college should not be allowed to become an extension of the staff, though the informal relationship as exemplified by the individual studies or thesis program should continue.[26]

The fourth element of the restated mission had to do with developing interservice and interdepartmental understanding and supporting academic exchange with selected civilian institutions. The board had few suggestions on how to carry this out. It recommended that more Navy, Air Force, and Marine Corps officers be included in each class so that non-Army representation would be present on all committees. Also, it recommended an increased number of faculty members from the other services and the cultivation of closer ties with the Naval and Air War Colleges.

The mission statement recommended by the Williams Board was confirmed in Army regulations in December 1958. In July 1960 the regulations were again changed, making even more explicit the missions of preparing officers from the other services for high-level positions and of developing interacademic understanding with educational institutions and other activities having interests in common with the War College.[27]

The Williams Board stated unequivocally that the Army War College had reached the apex of the Army educational system, was the equal of the National War College, and should remain so. The board implied its disagreement with the JCS decision on the report of the Bolte Committee that resulted in four or five Army War College graduates being sent each year to the National War College. If more than that number were sent, the board believed that the whole issue of the relationship between the two institutions should be reexamined. The Williams Board considered again General Gerow's idea of a National Security University and concluded that it might have application in the future. The idea of a National Security University composed of all five senior service colleges was also considered and found to have some merit, but the board noted that it was "not propitious for the Army to introduce and support this proposal at this time."[28]

The pressures for including ever more topics in the War College program and the criticism of a lack of depth in what was already being covered led the Williams Board to consider extending the program to two years. It concluded that the extension was feasible but not desirable. Arguments in favor of retaining the one-year program were the traditional ten-months-at-a-time pattern of Army professional education and training and what was referred to as the "optimum learning period for mature students." Given that the physical plant at Carlisle Barracks had a finite capacity, the compelling argument seems to have been that the output of the college would be halved, and selection for attendance correspondingly restricted. The board apparently did not think it necessary to defend its logic that two hundred shallowly educated officers per year were of greater value to the Army than one hundred officers educated in greater depth.[29]

The question of the size of each class in fact received greater attention than the length of the program. Carlisle's facilities limited the class to two hundred, but that number was also considered the maximum that could be managed using the educational techniques preferred, and the maximum that would allow every student to come into academic and social contact with every other student, a goal that every War College since the days of Bliss's collegium had believed to be of great importance. The Williams Board thought it virtually impossible to determine finitely the number of War College graduates needed by the Army; position surveys seemed useless, wastes of effort. But the board was willing to accept as a planning base the figure of 1,558 approved by the Vice Chief of Staff in 1955. As far as could be determined the current stockage was 2,000, and by 1963 it would stabilize at about 2,500. Nonetheless, the board recommended that the annual production of Army graduates from all the senior service schools remain at 278, of which the Army War College would produce about 185. As the board reported, "Our aim should be to educate as many officers as possess the necessary potential." The number should not be increased, however, since to do so would dilute the existing quality.[30]

The board recommended that the composition of each class remain at seventy percent combat arms officers and thirty percent officers from the administrative and technical services. The presence of the latter officers was deemed important as much for the varied knowledge and experience they brought to the college as for their own enlightenment. The Williams Board recommended that the annual selection board process begun in 1955 be continued. It recognized that pressures for a larger class would increase once the new enlarged academic facilities under construction at Leavenworth began to produce more officers eligible for selection to the War College. Nonetheless, it rejected abridged courses as a means of relieving the pressure. Such courses were "incompatible with the educational objectives."[31]

Similarly, nonresident courses were rejected because of a number of administrative complications having to do primarily with classified material and the educational limitations of this method of instruction. Basically the board simply saw no need for "universal" education at the levels of the Command and General Staff College and the War College. Competition among officers to attend the higher colleges was accepted and thought desirable. The board did recognize, however, that there might be a number of advantages in a nonresident program. It could give those not selected to attend the resident class an opportunity to achieve the educational objectives of the War College, and it would provide a means whereby influential industrial and professional leaders could be provided an appreciation of the Army concepts of sound military policy. Finally, such a program could serve to keep graduates current. Curiously, the board apparently saw no requirement to provide senior reserve component officers an opportunity to undergo the War College experience.[32]

With regard to faculty selection and training, the Williams Board had very little to offer. It confined itself to a recommended goal that the faculty should be able to provide intellectual challenge and leadership to an increasingly better-qualified group of student officers. Moreover, the faculty should be of a quality to encourage rapport and interchange with leading institutions dealing with national strategy. The board also suggested that the tours of duty of the faculty, particularly those of the commandant and the deputy commandant, be stabilized at three years, and that the tours of the commandant and the deputy commandant be staggered to provide continuity in leadership. As a way to increase the academic and professional prestige of the War College, the board asked the Department of the Army to consider filling the position of commandant with an officer in the grade of lieutenant general or general. That the National War College habitually was headed by a lieutenant general or vice admiral may have influenced that recommendation. One intriguing idea that the board noted with interest was a proposal of having the outgoing Army Chief of Staff, Vice Chief of Staff, or CONARC Commanding General serve as War College commandant as his last tour of active duty.[33]

As a final recommendation, the Williams Board asked the Department of the Army to consider correlating the course at the Army War College with a graduate study program leading to a master's degree in international relations or government affairs. The board confessed that it was not able to pursue this idea thoroughly, but it appeared that academic credit might be awarded for work done at the Army War College or that the work done there might supplement off-duty work done for credit under the supervision of a university faculty. The board recognized the desire of a number of officers to earn graduate degrees as a measure of their intellectual development and as an indicator of professional achievement. The idea, the board suggested, might have merit.[34]

The importance to the Army War College of the findings of the Williams Board did not stem from any suggestions for change or for new direction. Indeed, criticism of the War College was mild and confined to a few remarks pertaining to strengthening instruction in logistics above theater army level and in industrial mobilization. The value of the Williams Report, rather, was that it confirmed the direction in which the War College had moved since its reestablishment. It brought into the open issues that had long surrounded the War College, and it supported the War College's position on those issues. Additionally, it encouraged a few of the ideas that had been previously considered but not yet tried. The Williams Board had conducted an audit of the third Army War College and its first eight years and had not found them deficient. It provided a vote of confidence in the college and a firm base on which to build.[35]

The Post of Carlisle Barracks

The Williams Board also enthusiastically endorsed the decision that had brought the Army War College to Carlisle Barracks, and it considered a single-mission post dedicated to the support of the War College to be a decided advantage worth the higher overhead costs. The board suggested that a long-range plan be initiated for the development of the facilities at Carlisle Barracks and that this plan be given high priority in the Army's military construction program. Despite General Swing's renovation, the War College basically was confined still to the facilities built for the smaller Medical Field Service School before World War II. That does not mean that commandants after Swing had been inactive in developing the post, however, for by the summer of 1960 construction of several new facilities had begun and many more additions were planned that dwarfed in ambition anything Swing had attempted.[36]

A twenty-five-bed infirmary was under construction, and a new chapel center was planned. Those two facilities would eliminate the short nine-hole golf course within the confines of the post proper, but Second Army had provided a $24,000 welfare fund grant, and plans had been approved to begin a second nine holes adjacent to the nine that General Swing had negotiated. Other recreational facilities included a six-lane bowling alley to be completed in October 1960 and a barn near the golf course that had been converted through a self-help program into a stable with paddock and riding ring.[37]

Family housing remained a problem, lacking in both quantity and quality. During 1959 the Army acquired a strip of land along the northern boundary of the reservation adjacent to Highway 11. A five-unit apartment house converted from an old mill stood on this property, as well as a commercial building and three large residences—Herman House, Wilson House, and the house on the so-called Barnitz Estate which had been renamed Sumner Hall and was being used as a supplementary guest house. In all there were now 377 units of on-post housing. Negotiations were underway for the government to purchase the two Wherry projects, Stanwix and College Arms. After transfer of title, plans called for complete renovation of fifty of the College Arms units and partial renovation of the remaining fifty. A portion of the newly acquired acreage had been named Marshall Ridge after the Chief of Staff who in 1945 had seen no need to reactivate the Army War College.

342

Thirty-six sets of quarters were planned for this land, but funds were not yet available.[38]

Another strip of land had been acquired along the road leading into the post to permit landscaping and a more attractive entrance. For future years the 1960 master plan called for construction of an eleven-unit building to house female officers, a ten-unit bachelor officers' quarters, a commissary, a post exchange, a noncommissioned officers' open mess, and a gymnasium. Perhaps most importantly, a new academic building to replace Root Hall and the inadequate Bliss Hall was planned, but again funds were not yet programmed. Construction of this building was estimated to require over $2 million.[39]

The physical development of Carlisle Barracks into an essentially self-contained installation dedicated solely to the support of the Army War College converted the college into an institution distinctly different from the pre-World War II version located in the District of Columbia. The students of the earlier college were apartment-dwellers and streetcar-riding or traffic-fighting commuters; only faculty resided at Washington Barracks. While some social and recreational activity was centered at the college, basically the students were socially part of the larger but physically dispersed military community of the nation's capital. The War College was what happened during duty hours. At Carlisle Barracks the Army War College became much more than a committee room, a lecture hall, an academic exercise. It became a socializing experience comparable to that of attendance at the Military Academy or the Command and General Staff College. To the great majority of the postwar Army War College students and faculty, the War College experience was by no means confined to duty hours; it was all day and seven days a week. William Wotherspoon would have found it unnecessary to expend so much of his energy combating branch parochialism if he could have had as his ally a community like that built during the 1950s at Carlisle Barracks.

The value to the officer corps of this total immersion at the War College cannot be quantified, but it is almost universally remarked upon by those who have experienced it. It is often expressed in the comment that the greatest benefit of the college year is the contacts made and the friendships formed. This expression might appear on the surface to be a sad commentary on the curriculum and instruction at the War College, and an even sadder commentary on the intellectual curiosity of the commentator. On closer examination, however, the expression points up an important but sometimes overlooked truth. The Army War College is, after all, a professional school; to enhance the professional corporateness of the officer corps is a legitimate—even critical, though unwritten—mission of the Army War College. If successive commandants and faculties have not always expressed this truth, the evidence is overwhelming that they have sensed and understood it. The development and distinctiveness of Carlisle Barracks have been major contributors to the successful accomplishment of this unstated mission.

As with most benefits there were costs. The commandant became not only college president, but installation commander and community leader. The obligations of these latter roles could not be delegated completely, and to the extent that they could not, the commandant was diverted from his educational role. Communities also require social organization. This is particularly true of military communities, in which the makeup of the community is constantly changing. It is even more true of the Army War College, where much of the population remains for but one year. As a result there grew up at Carlisle Barracks a number of unofficial but recognized organizations and activities dedicated to the social, religious, and recreational life of the community and to its service and support. Differing only in degree from that of any Army post, or indeed of any well-ordered American town or neighborhood, the unofficial side of life at Carlisle Barracks became highly organized and extremely active. The argument in favor of all this activity was that only with community organization could an atmosphere be created that encouraged intellectual pursuits and permitted the student officer to know all his colleagues, keep himself in appropriate physical condition, and reduce the competing concerns of husband and father. In these terms, whether these unofficial organizations and activities, at other institutions called extracurricular activities, were too distracting from the academic program becomes a value judgment varying with the individual officer considered.

Defense Reorganization Act of 1958

For deliberations regarding the Army War College, the Williams Board may have been convened a year too early. In April 1958, while the board was still in session, President Eisenhower requested of the Congress legislation that in his view would improve the effective direction of the defense establishment. By summer the Department of Defense Reorganization Act of 1958 had emerged from Capitol Hill. The President signed it into law on August 6th. Its purpose and eventual effect was to strengthen further the centralized authority of the Secretary of Defense and his office over the individual services. With regard to military operations, the chain of command ran from the President through the Secretary of Defense, and now through the Joint Chiefs of Staff to the unified commanders. Eliminated was the former scheme whereby one service acted as executive agent. To assist the Joint Chiefs in their expanded planning and operational responsibilities, the law increased the Joint

Staff from 210 to 400 officers. The Joint Staff subsequently was completely reorganized along staff lines familiar to Army officers since the 1921 Pershing-Harbord reorganization of the War Department General Staff, although the law prohibited the formation of an "Armed Forces General Staff." The authority of the Chairman of the JCS over the Joint Staff was increased, and unified commanders were given full "operational command" over the forces of the several services assigned to them. With regard to research and development, authority was centralized in a new position, the Director of Defense Research and Engineering.[40]

Though perhaps not clearly or universally understood at the time, the role of the separate services had been markedly diminished. As Eisenhower put it in asking for the legislation, the services' primary functions were now "managing the vast administrative, training and logistics functions of the Department of Defense." Moreover, the services were now limited in their authority over the development of new weapon systems. In the case of the Department of the Army, its role had become analagous to that of the World War II Army Ground Forces and Army Service Forces. In a sense the Department of the Army had become a great support command.[41]

If the full implications of the legislation had been understood by the Williams Board and the Army War College, it would have been clear that there were four directions the War College program might follow. First, it could prepare its students for Department of the Army duties, for management of "vast" support functions. Second, it could prepare its students for service on the joint staffs assisting the JCS and the unified commanders, emphasizing joint military strategy, planning, and operations. Third, it might adopt the philosophy of the gap-fillers and concentrate on preparing officers for duty with the largest Army units— theater army and army group, and perhaps field army. Finally, it could attempt to do all or a combination of these things. The mission recommended by the Williams Board would have the War College attempt all.[42] Achieving the proper balance among the four would be the large issue faced by War College curriculum planners over the next two decades.

The effect of the Defense Reorganization Act of 1958 first became apparent at the Army War College in changes to the curriculum for the year 1960-61. That year marked a distinct shift toward having the students assume the perspectives of the JCS and the unified commanders. Whereas the second (military) phase of the 1959-60 program had consisted of the four courses "War Games," "Theater Operations," "The Army in Combat," and "Military Readiness," the phase was now reoriented to stress joint operations and procedures. War-gaming lost its separate course status. Only in one course, "Concepts of Future Land Warfare," was there any real emphasis on the operational problems of the army in the field.[43]

The Graduate Degree Program

Another indication of the direction the War College was taking was its reaction to the Williams Board suggestion that the awarding of an advanced degree be considered. In its response to this suggestion, the War College pointed out to the board that the question was almost perennial. General Trudeau, in December 1951, had corresponded on the matter with officials of The George Washington University and had directed two officers of the faculty who possessed Ph.D. degrees to advise him on the possibilities. In January 1952 the President of The George Washington University proposed to Trudeau a collaborative program leading to a degree of Masters of Arts in International Relations. Trudeau formed a committee of five officers to consider the proposal, but by the time the committee had completed its work, Trudeau had departed. The committee recommended that the university's proposal be declined, and General Almond approved that recommendation. The committee recommended further that the Faculty Board consider the advisability of seeking legislation that would enable the War College to become a degree-granting institution. But the Faculty Board advised no further action on the proposal. By that time General Almond was in the midst of his difficulties in having the War College mission broadened. On seeking legislation, Almond's decision was blunt: "As far as I am concerned the subject is dead."[44]

General Moore reopened the issue in October 1954, specifically as to whether the War College should seek academic accreditation. The Faculty Board advised him to wait until the outcome was known on a similar request by the National War College. In May 1955, when it became apparent that the National War College was not meeting with success, the Faculty Board recommended no further action. In August, while General Eddleman was Commandant, the decision was made once again to drop the effort.[45]

In 1956 a student again suggested a degree program, and an investigation was made of an arrangement between the Naval War College and Boston University whereby faculty members of the Naval War College were working toward advanced degrees. In June of the next year, following comments by the Dean of the School of General Subjects of Columbia University on the feasibility of a degree program, interest was renewed and an approach was made to the accrediting authority, the Middle Atlantic Association of Colleges and Secondary Schools. The association's response was not encouraging. The painstaking, laborious

346

process was described, and the experience of the National War College was cited. For a third time, the subject was shelved.[46]

When the Williams Board dusted it off once again, the War College reviewed for the board all its past study and explained to the board that two courses of action were possible, but that neither was attractive. The first course was to enter a collaborative agreement with a university; the second was to seek accreditation together with enabling legislation. The War College listed as disadvantages possible outside pressures to make the War College conform to procedures inappropriate to its mission and its student body, imposition of academic reuqirements on the thesis program, and the possibility that academic qualifications would be required of the faculty, thereby reducing the pool of potential faculty members. The overriding consideration, however, seems to have been the suspected distraction of the time and effort required of those participating in the program.[47]

The issue would not remain dormant, however. On December 30, 1959, it was surfaced again, this time by CONARC. Major General William P. Ennis, Jr., was now Commandant. CONARC suggested a cooperative degree program with The George Washington University. Ennis's initial reaction was negative. In his reply to CONARC he cited past considerations and stressed the difficulties in meeting the university's residency requirements, either through having War College students travel to the Washington campus or having university faculty members travel to or reside in Carlisle. He recommended no further consideration. By the next month, however, Ennis had begun to change his mind. He had an officer visit the university to discuss what might be arranged, and on February 24, 1960, referring back to the university's proposal of eight years before, he made a counterproposal.[48]

Ennis suggested a program that would lead to the degree of Master of Arts in International Affairs. He proposed that the university grant fifteen semester-hour credits (the number the university had offered in 1952) for work done in the War College program, and six additional semester hours for the thesis. The nine hours remaining to reach the thirty required by the university for the degree would be earned through courses offered by university faculty at Carlisle. Since degree candidates would have spent at least one tour of duty in a foreign country and thus could be presumed to have a working knowledge of a second language, Ennis proposed that the language requirement be waived. Ennis then wrote CONARC, saying that he had reconsidered, now saw no "impingement upon academic sovereignty," and had entered into negotiations with The George Washington University.[49]

Throughout the spring of 1960 negotiations between the two institutions continued. Two deans of the university visited Carlisle to learn more about the War College program, and in June the university's Deans' Council met with General Ennis and his staff at Carlisle Barracks. That meeting resolved most problems. The university would now allow only nine rather than fifteen semester-hour credits for War College work, however, citing a tightening of policy by the Middle Atlantic Association since 1952. Six semester hours' credit would still be given the thesis. Ennis no longer insisted upon "exclusive jurisdiction" over the paper, agreeing that it should be "mutually acceptable in form and quality." Eight additional semester hours could be earned from a course offered by the university in the fall and one offered in the spring. The remaining seven semester hours required would be earned in a six-week summer session offered by the university after the War College program was completed. During this session the university would also administer a comprehensive examination. The university, probably naively, waived the language requirement as Ennis had suggested.[50]

The War College also had to sell the program at Headquarters, Department of the Army. Since the program would require Army money and the summer session would take officers out of the regular assignment pattern for six weeks, there would probably be opposition. But the War College had powerful supporters. The Deputy Chief of Staff for Personnel, James F. Collins (formerly of the War College faculty at Leavenworth), and the Deputy Chief of Staff for Operations, John E. Oakes, both favored the program. The Chief of Research and Development was now Art Trudeau; apparently he was still an active and effective lobbyist for the War College—and for a degree program at minimum cost to the individual officer. On August 31 the Chief of Staff, General Lyman L. Lemnitzer (AWC 1940), personally gave his approval. Then a very unexpected thing occurred. All planning had been based on the assumption that a maximum of fifty faculty members and students might sign up. By September 2nd, despite a personal cost of $210, an astounding total of 203 had tentatively committed themselves. The university had believed that one faculty member could coordinate the program and teach the courses at Carlisle. Now the university was in a scramble to find additional faculty members, and the Army looked to find additional money. The program appeared to be in jeopardy.[51]

Another problem created by the unexpectedly heavy enrollment involved the summer session. The Army was in the process of purchasing the housing built under the Wherry Act, and a major renovation of those quarters was scheduled for the summer of 1961. But, with so many officers remaining on the post for the summer session of the degree program, and with the new War College class coming in immediately after their departure, either the renovation could not go forward or the new class would not have housing immediately available. It was not until December that a solution was found, with the War College making a number of compromises. The summer session would begin on 15 May before the War College program was actually completed, and the arrival of the Class of 1962 would be delayed by a week.[52]

The officer probably most responsible for overcoming all the problems and getting the degree program started was the Deputy Commandant, Brigadier General Bruce Palmer, Jr. (AWC 1952). Assisted by a project officer, initially Colonel Richard J. Long (AWC 1959) and then Colonel Harold E. Nelson (AWC 1960), Palmer was not only able to win agreement on solutions to the numerous early problems, but to resolve amicably issues that repeatedly arose which basically stemmed from the difference of perspective of the Army officers and the university officials involved. By the end of September 1960, the program was in place, with 184 officers (including Palmer) enrolled in six courses offered by the university.[53]

Separation from CONARC

The move into a cooperative graduate degree program is evidence that the War College had become an institution different from the Army's other professional schools. When General Haislip had supported General Eddy in 1950 and placed the Army War College under the supervision of Army Field Forces, it seemed a reasonable decision. Haislip could not predict then just what the main thrust of the War College program would be, although the two colonels from the Army Staff had pointed out in their minority report that the War College's work would be more closely allied to that of the Army Staff than to that of the Army in the field. After the Williams Board put its seal of approval on the War College's 1957-58 program that stressed national strategy and a national military program, it became even more apparent that the mission of CONARC and that of the Army War College had become increasingly dissimilar over the years.

General Johnson had the question of the relationship to CONARC studied in 1956 and found that the problem was not that CONARC interfered with or hampered the War College's endeavors; CONARC Headquarters routinely and without modification annually approved the War College curriculum. The problem was that the CONARC staff was without capability to provide support, assistance, or guidance to the War College in the accomplishment of its mission. Upon the initiative of the War College, the matter was discussed by Chief of Staff Lemnitzer, the Commanding General of CONARC, and the War College Commandant. As a result Lemnitzer directed in June 1960 that the War College be placed under the direct supervision of the Department of the Army, with the Deputy Chief of Staff for Military Operations exercising staff responsibility. The War College was to continue to answer to CONARC, however, in the exercise of its combat developments mission.[54]

As the decade of the 1950s came to a close, the Army War College appeared to have found its place. The issue of gap-filling or apex-building seemed to have been settled. If the relationship of the Army War College to the National War College was something of a compromise, the Army War College certainly was not the advanced course of the Command and General Staff College that Manton Eddy had recommended. The reasons for the continued trend toward the broader study of national security affairs stemmed from the Army's almost desperate efforts to establish its proper role in the defense policies of Dwight Eisenhower. The problem facing Eisenhower's administration was to adjust to the long-term realities of a bipolar world while at the same time maintaining a defense program whose costs were not detrimental to the nation's economy. How to solve this problem was the subject of continuing intragovernmental and public debate. Among the leading proponents of a policy other than the one adopted by the administration had been two strong Army Chiefs of Staff, Ridgway and then Taylor, to whom massive retaliation was not just unsound strategy but a threat to the Army's very existence.

Both Chiefs of Staff directly and indirectly influenced the Army War College to concentrate on the study of national security policy as the means of understanding the most critical issue facing the Army. To understand the issue required an appreciation of international relations and a grasp of the future capabilities of not just Army weapon systems, but also those of the Air Force and the Navy. Maxwell Taylor in particular presented, with his National Military Program, a disciplined way to get at the issue. The reorganization of the Defense Department in 1958 reinforced the trend toward emphasis on the problems of joint and unified commands. As the Army War College looked to the approaching 1960s, it believed itself to be on the correct bearing, confident that its graduates would go on to responsible assignments able to articulate the Army's case. The Army War College, with an increasingly sophisticated program built about a rational theme and supported by an improved and improving physical plant, had every reason for optimism.

NOTES

1. Masland and Radway, *Soldiers and Scholars*, 387, 486-90.
2. Ibid., 491-93.
3. Ibid., 494-96. Paper, Statistical Comparison, File 701-14.
4. AWC, "Comprehensive Review of Curriculum," 13 September 1957. Masland and Radway, *Soldiers and Scholars*, 368-69, 506-08.
5. Maxwell D. Taylor, *The Uncertain Trumpet* (New York: Harper and Brothers, 1959), 29-49. Taylor's "National Military Program" is reprinted on 30-34. Divine, *Eisenhower*, 79-88. Spanier, *American Foreign Policy*, 104, 120-23.
6. AWC, *Curriculum, August 1957-June 1958*. AWC, "Course Directive, Course 3: Strategy and Policy Formulation," 7 November 1957. AWC, "Course Directive, Course 7: Military Strategy," 19 March 1958 and "Course 7, Annex 4: National Military Program (NMP)", 19 March 1958. AWC, "Course Directive, Course 9: National Strategy and Supporting Military Program," 28 May 1958.

7. *Curriculum, 1957-58.* "AWC, Course Directive, Course 1: National Interests and National Power of the US and USSR," 21 August-24 September 1957. AWC, "Course Directive, Course 2: International Relations and U.S. Foreign Policy," 24 September 1957. "Course Directive, Course 3."

8. *Curriculum, 1957-58.* AWC, "Course Directive, Course 4: The Army in Combat," 16 December 1957.

9. AWC, "Course Directive, Course 5, Part I: Analytical War Game," 23 August 1957. AWC, "Course Directive, Course 5, Part II: War Games," 3 February 1958. AWC, *War Games Brief Anthology,* 6 January 1958. AWC, Talking Paper for the Military Education Coordination Conference, 20-21 May 1964, Tab A-3, File 203-3.

10. AWC, "Course Directive, Course 6: Theater, Theater Army and Army Group Operations," 10 February 1958.

11. AWC, "Course Directive, Course 7: Military Strategy," 19 March 1958.

12. Ibid. AWC, "Course 7, Annex 4: National Military Program (NMP)," 19 March 1958.

13. "Course Directive, Course 7."

14. AWC, "Course Directive, Course 8: Military Readiness," 29 April 1958.

15. AWC, "Course Directive, Course 10: Thesis Program," 21 August 1957.

16. AWC, "Course Directive, Course 9: National Strategy and Supporting Military Program," 28 May 1958.

17. AWC, *Curriculum, August 1958-June 1959.* AWC, *Curriculum, August 1960-June 1961.*

18. Department of the Army, *Report of the Department of the Army Officer Education and Training Review Board,* 1 July 1958 (hereafter *Williams Board,* 1-2, 60, 74-75.

19. Ibid., 76.

20. Ibid., 5-7.

21. Ibid., 10, 15, 47, 55-56, 105, 128, 137, 152, 221-31, 256-59.

22. Ibid., 12, 29-30, 103-04.

23. Ibid., 186, 190-91.

24. Ibid., 29, 44, 189.

25. Ibid., 44, 189, 193-94.

26. Ibid., 29-30, 191-92.

27. Ibid., 30-31, 44, 53, 198. AR 350-104, 15 December 1958. AR 350-104, 29 July 1960.

28. *Williams Board,* 25, 29-30, 53, 68, 92, 187-88, 194-95.

29. Ibid., 196-97.

30. Ibid., 19, 150-51, 156-67, 198.

31. Ibid., 20, 49-50, 158-59, 186.

32. Ibid., 31, 153, 200.

33. Ibid., 16, 31, 53, 198-99.

34. Ibid., 31, 200-01.

35. Ibid., 13-14, 53, 213-17.

36. Ibid., 188-89.

37. L. M. Scarborough, Memorandum for MG Thomas W. Dunn, Subject: Preface to Briefing Notes, n.d. [August 1960], File: Post Activities, 1960.

38. Ibid. AWC, Historical Files, 1959-1963.

39. Scarborough, Memo for Dunn.

40. Eisenhower, Message to Congress, 3 April 1958, reprinted in *Department of Defense: Documents,* 175-86. Department of Defense Reorganization Act of 1958, 6 August 1958 (72 Stat. 514), reprinted in Ibid., 188-230.

41. Eisenhower, Message, 3 April 1958, 182. Hewes, *Root to McNamara* 297-98.

42. *Williams Board,* 44.

43. AWC, *1959-1960 Curriculum,* 1 July 1959. "Course Directive: Theater Operations," 23 November 1959. "Course Directive: Army in Combat," 25 January 1960. "Course Directive: Military Readiness," 7 March 1960. *1960-1961 Curriculum,* 1 June 1960. "Course Directive: Introduction to Joint Operations," 16 November-1 December 1960. "Course Directive: World Wide Strategic Military Capabilities," 2 December 1960. "Course Directive: Concepts of Future Land Warfare," 26 January-8 March 1961.

44. AWC, Brief Study of Subject of Masters' Degrees at AWC, n.d. [January 1960] 1, 2, AWC Central Files.

45. Ibid., 2.
46. Ibid., 2-3.
47. Ibid., 3-4.
48. Letter, CONARC to AWC, 30 December 1959 with 1st Ind., AWC to CONARC, 7 January 1960; Memorandum, Commandant to Deputy Commandant, 4 January 1960; Ennis to Dean G. L. Angel, College of General Studies, The George Washington University, 24 February 1960; all in AWC Central Files.
49. Ibid. Letter, AWC to CONARC, 29 February 1960, Subject: Academic Credit for Attendance at Senior Service Schools. AWC Central Files.
50. Richard J. Long, Memo for Record, 29 March 1960, Subject: Graduate Degree Program; Ibid., 11 April 1960, Subject: Negotiations with The George Washington University; Ibid., 20 April 1960; Subject: Negotiations with G.W.U.; Ibid., 23 June 1960; Subject: Meeting of the Deans' Council, The George Washington University, at Carlisle Barracks, Pennsylvania, 22 June 1960; all in AWC Central Files.
51. J. F. Collins to Ennis, 14 June 1960; Don H. McGovern, Memorandum to Commandant, 2 August 1960, Subject: Telephone Call from Colonel Landrum, DCSOPS, DA; Colonel H. E. Nelson to Acting Commandant, 31 August 1960, Subject: GWU Trip Report; Palmer to Admiral Colclough, The George Washington University, 3 September 1960; Harold E. Nelson, Memo for Record, 9 September 1960, Subject: Telecon: Colonel H. E. Nelson/Colonel Jack Wilhm, 9 September 1960—The George Washington University Program; all in AWC Central Files.
52. Colonel L. M. Scarborough, Memo for Record, 13 September 1960, Subject: USAG Support to George Washington University Program; Palmer to Dean Archibald M. Woodruff, 21 December 1960; all in AWC Central Files.
53. Nelson to Deputy Commandant, 29 September 1960, Subject: GWU Registration, AWC Central Files.
54. Commandant to Deputy Commandant, 21 January 1956, Subject: Staff Study; C. H. Blumenfield, Study, 8 February 1956, Subject: Advantages and Disadvantages Associated with Placing the Army War College Directly under the Department of the Army, AWC Central Files. DA General Order No. 19, 16 June 1960. Army Regulation 350-104, 29 July 1960. Change 2 to Army Regulation 10-7, 29 September 1960.

In Defense
of the Generalist
1961-1966

The assumption of power by John F. Kennedy's administration in 1961 seemed to the Army to signal a new national strategy, a new appreciation of what land forces contributed to national security, and even a renaissance in Army fortunes. Both Kennedy and his Secretary of Defense, Robert S. McNamara, embraced the strategy of flexible response so compellingly argued by Maxwell Taylor in his 1959 book, *The Uncertain Trumpet.* In his budget message to Congress in March 1961, for example, Kennedy declared that the defense posture of the United States must be flexible enough to permit a response "suitable, selective, swift, and effective." He promised to set no arbitrary ceilings on the defense budget. In April testimony before the Senate Subcommittee on Department of Defense Appropriations, McNamara included among his proposals increases in nonnuclear capabilities in order to provide limited war forces with a greater degree of versatility.[1]

Secretary Robert S. McNamara
Before any real changes could be made in force structure, however, the administration found itself swept up in a series of foreign policy crises. In April there was the embarrassing Bay of Pigs affair. In June, Kennedy experienced his somber Vienna meeting with Nikita Khrushchev, followed in August by the Soviet construction of the Berlin Wall. As one measure for meeting the renewed Soviet challenge on Berlin, the administration began a major expansion of the Army. Draft calls were increased in July, and three active Army divisions that had been employed as training divisions began conversion into operational units. With a goal to increase the active Army from some 875,000 to one million, Seventh Army in Europe was reinforced by 43,000 troops, and in September 46,000 Army reservists were brought on active duty. The next month two National Guard divisions were mobilized.[2]

Berlin was not Kennedy's only problem. Khrushchev's statement in early January 1961 that the Soviet Union would lend its support to wars of national liberation was taken with serious concern by the new administration. Laos, the Congo, and Vietnam were perceived as immediate Soviet targets. In October 1961 the President sent General Maxwell Taylor to Saigon to see what might be done to bolster the increasingly threatened regime of President Ngo Dinh Diem. Soon after Taylor's return the assistance program to Diem was substantially increased. In November, Secretary McNamara announced that "anti-guerrilla" forces of the United States had been enlarged by 150 percent. In January 1962, Kennedy established the interdepartmental Special Group (Counterinsurgency) with Taylor at its head. By March the Special Group (CI) was successful in having published a National Security Action Memorandum directing widespread training in counterinsurgency. By July the Joint Chiefs could report that all war colleges had added counterinsurgency to their curricula and that nine special counterinsurgency courses for officers had been established. One of these courses was presented by the Army War College during a three-week period in June and July in a special "Senior Officers Counterinsurgency Course." Forty-seven Army officers ranging in rank from lieutenant colonel to brigadier general attended. Lecturers included General Taylor. Also in July the Joint Chiefs created on the Joint Staff the position of "Special Assistant for Counterinsurgency and Special Activities." On the Army Staff a "Special Warfare Directorate" came into being. The Special Forces headquarters at Fort Bragg was expanded into the Special Warfare Center.[3]

Concurrently, Secretary McNamara was installing within the Department of Defense what was claimed to be a more rational system to control and integrate planning, programming, and budgeting. The keystone to the system was to be a "Five Year Force Structure and Financial Program." As the name implies, this was a force program with attendant costs projected for the next five years. It was organized into nine "program packages" so arranged that functional appropriations in theory could be related to major military missions and objectives. It was a systematic and centralized approach to the problems of defense resources management. The Army, along with the other services, found other aspects of McNamara's stewardship less appealing.[4]

The new Secretary began to take full advantage of the authority provided by the Defense Reorganization Act of 1958. Important decisions on force structure and weapon-system development were made increasingly often within the secretariat of the Department of Defense. The Kennedy administration has been characterized as imbued with scientific optimism. Nowhere was this characteristic more evident than in the staff elements that McNamara created to assist him in the making of decisions, initially the Systems Planning Directorate and the Weapons Systems Analysis Directorate of the office of the Defense Comptroller.

By 1965 these elements would be consolidated into the Office of an Assistant Secretary of Defense (Systems Analysis). The relatively young men schooled in economics or operations research who populated these staff elements soon became the "whiz kids" who, in the view of the services, enjoyed an influence far out of proportion to their experience and wisdom. If McNamara had launched a managerial revolution within the defense establishment, the language of that revolution was the language of economic and cost-effectiveness analysis and of operations research. It was a language in which few of the products of the Army school system were fluent.[5]

The Regime of William Train

The War College Commandant when the McNamara revolution began was Major General Thomas W. Dunn, then in the second (and last) year of his tour of duty at Carlisle. Acknowledgement of the McNamara ideas on strategy and management appeared in the War College curriculum of that academic year, 1961-62, during the phase "National Strategy," when the students were required to determine the costs of their National Military Program. Dunn was succeeded by Major General William F. Train in May 1962. It was Train to whom fell initially the major task of adjusting the War College's program to the McNamara era. Train was a 1947 graduate of Britain's Imperial Defence College and a 1952 graduate of the Army War College. He was the first graduate of the post-World War II Army War College to return as Commandant. His experience in military education also included two years (1955-57) as Assistant Commandant at the Command and General Staff College.[6]

The attempt to cost out the student-derived National Military Program became more sophisticated in 1962-63, and considerable effort, not altogether successful, was made to establish the relationships between the War College's now traditional National Military Program, the Joint Program for Planning of the JCS, and the new five-year program procedures of Mr. McNamara. A basic introduction to the new management procedures was included in the course "United States Preparedness for War." In this course the students were also familiarized with two management techniques, the Program Evaluation and Review Technique (PERT) and the Critical Path Method.[7]

Counterinsurgency was also included in the War College program in 1962-63. As a distinct second phase of the course "United States Global Strategic Concepts," two weeks were devoted to the study of counterinsurgency. In the following course, "Strategic Military Capabilities in Selected World Areas," two committees were required to assume the role of "country teams" and to prepare detailed counterinsurgency plans for selected countries. With the intense high-level pressure to emphasize training in counterinsurgency, the War College appears to have been somewhat sensitive as to its coverage. It found it necessary to publish a separate document listing all the subjects and topics included in its curriculum that could be considered as relating to counterinsurgency. The War College can be given good marks for its responsiveness in including instruction in the two new arts introduced by the Kennedy administration—counterinsurgency and planning, programming, and budgeting—but it can hardly be categorized as an intellectual leader in these arts. It was definitely a follower. It relied almost exclusively on outside lecturers and consultants.[8]

That same year the War College was attempting to respond also to the recommendations of a civilian advisory group that General Dunn had brought in during the winter of 1962. Like the predecessor advisory groups of 1952 and 1954, this group was more inclined to comment on the "nonmilitary" phase of the course. It believed that since officers attending the War College had little experience in those things studied during the nonmilitary phase, every effort should be made to compress the military phase in order to provide greater breadth and depth to the nonmilitary. The advisory group was critical of what it saw as insufficient analysis of the interests and attitudes of major allies of the United States. The group also recommended treatment of the "Sino-Soviet bloc" rather than of the Soviet Union alone. Finally, it suggested that more attention be given to the impact of science.[9]

The War College took these suggestions seriously, and they were reflected in the 1963-64 program. The nonmilitary phase, "National Power and International Relations," was expanded by a week to include a course called, "The United States and the North Atlantic Community." In the second "military" phase of the program, "Concepts of Land Warfare" became "Science, Technology, and Future Military Power" and no longer dealt exclusively with future concepts of *land* warfare. Additionally, a guest lecture series was inaugurated called "Frontiers of Knowledge." One lecture was presented each month for seven months, each guest lecturer attempting to survey advances in a particular field. Technology and the physical sciences were part of the program, but these evening lectures, to which spouses were invited, also addressed progress in the life sciences, behavioral sciences, and social sciences.[10]

General Train additionally had to cope with a major reorganization of the Army that occurred in the summer of 1962 shortly after his arrival at the War College. Instituted by Mr. McNamara, this reorganization created two new functional commands to complement CONARC. One was the Army Materiel Command (AMC), which consolidated the materiel research and development, procurement, and wholesale logistic support functions of the Technical Services. The second was the Combat Developments Command (CDC), which inherited from CONARC the responsibility for the development of qualitative materiel requirements, operational doctrine, and tactical organizations. The following March the Army Staff itself was reorganized, and a new entity was created, known as the Office of the Assistant Chief of Staff for Force Development (ACSFOR). This staff section assumed a number of the functions formerly the responsibility of the Deputy Chief of Staff for Military Operations, including training and force development, the latter encompassing combat developments.[11]

These reorganizations affected the Army War College primarily in the relationship between research and teaching. The Doctrine and Studies Group of the Army War College, the current version of what had begun under General Moore as the Advanced Studies Group, was renamed the Institute of Advanced Studies. It remained at the War College but became a subordinate element of the new Combat Developments Command. This move was not unique to the War College; the former combat developments elements at all the schools became CDC institutes or agencies. The War College Commandant served concurrently as Commanding General of the institute, but in that role he was subordinate to the Commanding General of CDC. Responsibility for the War College on the Army staff was transferred from the Deputy Chief of Staff for Military Operations to the new staff element ACSFOR. These reorganizations at the War College, as well as at the lower schools, in effect organizationally separated the development of doctrine from instruction in doctrine; put more broadly, they separated research from teaching.[12]

If General Train had a major criticism of the Army War College as he found it, the criticism was that the college had become too inward-looking, concentrating its endeavors exclusively to the benefit of its annual resident class and neglecting other constituencies within the Army. He directed a number of programs be undertaken that in effect would expand the War College's audience. At Train's direction the college faculty drafted programs that would serve officers of the reserve components, officers who were selected to attend the war colleges of Canada, France, and the United Kingdom, civilians appointed to responsible positions within the Department of the Army, and officers considered for but not selected to attend the War College. In all but the last endeavor his programs were implemented.[13]

Attendance of reserve component officers during portions of the War College program had been a practice throughout the 1920s until the shrunken budgets of the Great Depression put an end to it. Colonel Polk in the 1950s had suggested the practice be resumed. In early 1963, Train resurrected the idea and recommended to the Department of the Army that he be allowed to initiate a course for general officers of the Army's reserve components. Train's rationale was that the reserve components were receiving almost no benefits from the Army War College, and with only two inactive duty officers in each annual class, the resident stu-

357

dents learned too little of the capabilities and problems of the reserve components. His concept was for a two-week course during which the reserve component officers would join the resident class student committees, would attend regularly scheduled lectures and discussion periods, and would hear additional lectures especially prepared by the faculty. He suggested that sixteen officers attend the course, so that one reserve component officer could be assigned to each student committee.[14]

In March 1963 the Department of the Army approved Train's concept, and the first Senior Reserve Component Officers' Course (SRCOC-1) was scheduled for January 29 through February 12, 1964. The success of the course exceeded the most optimistic expectations. The officers who attended, the resident students, the Army Staff, and the War College faculty all agreed that the program should continue. Train himself thought the course had been so worthwhile that he recommended, over his faculty's initial objections, that two "SRCOC's" be scheduled for the following year, and he considered the idea of recommending a similar course for active-duty general officers. Two senior reserve component officer courses were in fact approved for the 1964-65 year, one to be held in the fall and one in the spring.[15]

The concept of the War College providing an orientation for newly appointed civilian officials of the Department of the Army received the support of Secretary of the Army Stephen Ailes, and the first orientation was held in June 1964. Tailored for the individual official, the program was a mixture of participation in resident class seminars and special faculty seminars. Train's objective was to provide the civilian appointee facts about Army history, traditions, roles, and missions, but, above all, to enable the civilian official to gain in an informal atmosphere an appreciation of the professional Army officer. The course for those few officers selected to attend foreign war colleges was five days in length. It was designed to provide those officers, just prior to their departure, with an understanding of their own Army's War College, its objectives, methods, and program.[16]

A move with even greater potential for influencing the officer corps was the assumption by the Army War College in 1963 of the responsibility for compiling the Contemporary Military Reading List. This list, published annually by the Adjutant General to provide recommended reading on international and military affairs, was designed to guide self-development on the part of individual officers. It also guided acquisitions by the worldwide Army library system. In the fall of 1962 the War College had begun the practice of providing officers selected to attend the Army War College with a reading list of some two dozen items divided into seven categories. The War College suggested, but did not require, that the incoming student read at least one book from each category before arriving at Carlisle. To compile this list a faculty "Reading List Panel" was formed each year. In March 1963 the function of this panel was expanded to include recommending changes to the Adjutant General's annual Contemporary Military Reading List. Thereafter, the Adjutant General's Office followed without exception the War College's recommendations. Thus the War College began to exert an influence on the holdings of Army libraries and on what serious officers would read.[17]

General Train attacked head-on a concern of commandants and faculties since the incumbency of General Swing: Did the Department of the Army practice of student selection truly reflect its policy that the Army War College was at the apex of the officer educational system? Train pointed out to his superiors that graduates of the National War College were being selected for promotion to general officer earlier and at a higher rate than were graduates of the Army War College. This led him to suspect that officers with the top thirty-five records were being sent annually to the National War College. On the other hand, Train noted that the selection rate for promotion from brigadier general to major general was higher among Army War College graduates, a fact Train naturally attributed to the more pertinent education received at Carlisle Barracks. In effect, General Train's argument was that the Army's more talented officers were receiving a lesser educational experience. The personnel managers accepted the logic; they changed the system to provide equal distribution of talent among the several senior service colleges. The effect was immediate. The number of officers eventually selected for promotion to general officer from each of the Classes of 1965 and 1966 was twice the number selected from the Class of 1964.[18]

General Train also suggested that the maximum number of years of service of officers selected to attend the senior service colleges be reduced from twenty-two years of service to twenty, so that the Army would receive at least three full duty tours from each graduate before mandatory retirement at thirty years of service. The Department of the Army, however, did not approve this recommendation.[19]

During General Train's incumbency much progress was made in the continuing development of the physical plant at Carlisle Barracks. The new chapel center was completed at the end of 1963 and dedicated the following spring. Construction of thirty-six sets of officer quarters on Marshall Ridge began in the summer of 1963, with occupancy commencing the next summer. Most important, and a personal triumph for General Train, was the new academic building to replace old Root and Bliss Halls. This project was successfully inserted as a change to the military construction appropriation for fiscal year 1965. Train then brought Lieutenant Colonel Wilfred C. Washcoe onto his staff as project officer for the new building. Washcoe was an imaginative officer experienced in the interior design of Army academic buildings. Ground was broken for construction of the new building in February 1965, the cost now approaching $5 million.[20]

Included in the plans for the new building were facilities to house the Institute of Advanced Studies (IAS) of the Combat Developments Command. After its conversion from the Doctrine and Studies Group of the Army War College, this organization had been considerably strengthened. Sixteen officers were assigned to the institute, and CDC had negotiated a contract with a research firm known as Operations Research Incorporated (ORI) to provide a scientific support group in residence at Carlisle Barracks. This support group provided expertise in academic disciplines ranging from chemistry and mathematics to political science and history. Combat Developments Command had accomplished immediately what the War College had never been able to do or to bring itself to do—invite civilian scholars to Carlisle Barracks on a permanent basis. Within a year IAS had grown to twenty officers and ten contract scientists.[21]

Initially the institute remained closely involved with the work of the War College. It managed both the "Frontiers of Knowledge" lecture series and the course "Science, Technology, and Future Military Power." It also provided faculty advisers to student committees and to the thesis program. It soon became apparent, however, that the volume of studies required of the institute by Combat Developments Command and the Army Staff would preclude intensive work by the institute on behalf of the War College. The Department of the Army had organizationally separated the research element from the War College, and now workload was separating it intellectually. By April 1964 General Train found it necessary to establish a new research group within the War College, the "Committee for Strategic Analysis."[22]

Establishment of the Committee for Strategic Analysis was based on the premise that there was a clearly identified requirement for the Army War College to assume intellectual leadership in the specific art of military strategy. The initiative in this critical field of military interest, according to the authorizing regulation, needed to be "recaptured and sustained." Three officers were assigned to the committee, Colonel Donald S. Bussey and Lieutenant Colonels Nels A. Parson (AWC 1963) and Charles M. Fergusson, Jr. (AWC 1963). An immediate endeavor was to establish or maintain contact with other military and civilian organizations engaged in strategic analysis. For the longer term the committee conceived a project to produce a book in which the principles of modern American military strategy would be derived. Before the Class of 1965 had even arrived at Carlisle Barracks, Parson was soliciting volunteers from it to participate in a special thesis program to work on the project.

The isolation of military strategy as a unique area of competence of the Army War College was hardly a "recapture." It was actually a new departure for the institution. Only twice before had the Army War College attempted to present a course entitled "Military Strategy," once in 1956 and once in 1958. Neither course had survived the end-of-year curriculum review, and both had been concerned with what properly could be called national strategy. Now, in 1963-64, the college introduced a course entitled "Strategic Military Concepts and Capabilities" and dedicated a small group to the investigation of military strategy.[23]

Formation of the Committee for Strategic Analysis represented a new departure in another sense. It was an early indication of an increasing specialization within the faculty. General Train had inherited the perennial question of the need for civilian faculty members; the civilian advisory group of 1962, like its predecessors, had recommended that the War College obtain for its faculty experts in economics, political science, and international affairs. From 1960 through 1963 the issue had remained somewhat dormant. Research Analysis Corporation (RAC), which replaced the Operations Research Office (ORO) in 1961 as the Army's primary contractor for operations research support, had provided an economist in residence for the War College, Dr. Lawrence J. Dondero. In addition, Colonel Bussey, asigned to the faculty since 1959, had considerable academic and practical experience in international affairs. The War College felt that Dondero and Bussey partially filled the requirement, and that any shortfall could be made up through the use of temporary consultants. A suggestion by one faculty member, Lieutenant Colonel Franklin M. Davis, Jr., that civilian academicians be offered one-year fellowships at the War College was not pursued. Unfortunately, Dondero departed the War College in 1963, and RAC was unable or unwilling to provide a replacement. Even though the faculty's composition remained what it had been since 1950, a homogeneous body of carefully selected Army officers, by the early 1960s there appears to have been a growing sense that faculty specialization and an expertise beyond that gained in the Army school system and through career experience was a necessity for the future.[24]

The Class of 1964 was the fourteenth to graduate from the Army War College since World War II. In those fourteen years the trend in the program had been away from the operational problems of an army in combat, away from the internal problems of the Department of the Army, away from the problems of war and mobilization planning, and toward the consideration of national security affairs in the broadest sense of that term. The activism and globalism of the Kennedy foreign policy and its search for options in response to perceived threats ranging from general nuclear war to communist-supported insurgencies served to reinforce the trend. The Army War College of 1964 was hardly the contingency planning agency and school of the military art that the first Army War College was, nor the investigator of the problems of preparation for and conduct of war that was the second. It was even different in major ways from the Army-oriented institution of Swing and Trudeau.

But the 1963-64 program of the Army War College seemed to be resting on a sound base. The curricular theme of a national strategy and its supporting military program appears to have been able to accommodate the innovations of counterinsurgency and planning, programming, and budgeting. The suggestions of the 1962 civilian advisory group, where deemed appropriate, had been worked into the curriculum. The college was beginning to reach out to a larger audience, and tentative steps had been taken to establish the War College as an institution with a unique competence in the field of military strategy. Moreover, the soundness of the thrust of the War College's program had been confirmed as late as 1962 by the so-called Eddleman Committee, which had been convened by the Department of the Army to review the program of the Command and General Staff College. But the trend of the Army War College was not being universally applauded. Over the next several years there would be a growing volume of criticism of what the War College was attempting to do and the way in which it was doing it.[25]

The criticism did not begin suddenly. As early as 1961 a member of the Army War College faculty, Colonel Russell Fudge (AWC 1954), lamented in the magazine *Army* that fundamental thinking in the field of strategy was being done by scholars, not military officers. Fudge suggested a scheme whereby military study fellowships would be offered at the War College, allowing officers to engage in one or two years of research on military subjects of their own choice. The War College learned in May 1963 that civilians within the office of the Secretary of Defense were criticizing the joint and individual service war colleges for duplication of effort. The specter of centralized Department of Defense control over military education was raised. In January 1964, in a thesis similar to that of Fudge, Robert N. Ginsburgh, an Air Force officer, criticized the military colleges in a *Foreign Affairs* article for not standing at the "frontiers of knowledge." Several months later the War College learned that the Deputy Assistant Secretary of Defense (Education), Dr. Edward L. Katzenbach, Jr., was expressing his opposition to the cooperative graduate-degree programs now being conducted at all the War Colleges in conjunction with The George Washington University. Katzenbach was said to believe that the time could be better spent on matters more closely related to the respective missions of the service colleges. It was further understood that Katzenbach, also an officer of the American Council on Education, believed that the degrees being awarded were of questionable value anyway. Lieutenant Colonel Charles M. Fergusson, recently appointed to the Committee for Strategic Analysis at the War College, added to the dialogue in April 1964 with an article in *Mili-*

tary Review calling for greater attention at the War College to strategic thought and study.[26]

Army War College-70

General Train departed from the War College in June 1964 and was replaced by Major General Eugene A. Salet. Salet was a 1955 graduate of the National War College and a 1959 graduate of the Department of State's Senior Seminar in Foreign Policy. He had also attended the Harvard Advanced Management Course. As a lieutenant colonel he had participated in the reorganization of the Command and General Staff College that Manton Eddy had carried out in 1948. A few months after his arrival, General Salet directed that an extensive study be made of all facets of the War College's program. This effort came to be titled "Army War College-70," as it was intended to produce a five-year program to provide guidance for actions that would prepare the War College for the 1970s.[27]

General Salet assigned responsibility for the study to an ad-hoc committee lead by his Deputy Commandant, Brigadier General Ward S. Ryan (AWC 1958), and he provided Ryan with some definite ideas as to the direction he thought the college should take. These ideas were officially expressed to Lieutenant General Ben Harrell, the Assistant Chief of Staff for Force Development and Salet's superior, early in November. They dealt primarily with strengthening the faculty. Salet recommended that fifty percent of the faculty members serve three years, that another twenty-five percent serve four years, and that the remaining twenty-five percent be quasi-permanent under a system similar to that of the permanent professorships at the Military Academy. His goal was to change the faculty from a "management" type to one of "management, teaching, writing, and publication," though he assured Harrell that he did not intend to do away with the guest speaker program. The faculty should possess higher academic qualifications, but Salet did not believe that the War College should seek academic accreditation. As one means of improving faculty quality, Salet recommended that "chairs" be established to which outstanding retired general officers or distinguished civilian educators would be appointed. Finally, Salet informed Harrell that he would soon propose that six "fellowships" be authorized to enable selected students to remain at the War College an additional year to conduct original research.[28]

In his guidance to Ryan, General Salet expressed a preference for a faculty of generalists but recognized the need for some specialists. He wanted "capable officers with graduate degrees," a faculty with credentials that would warrant academic accreditation if that were sought in the future. He saw a particular need for a Chair of Economics. He envisioned the faculty as being organized into two departments, a Department of National Strategy and a Department of Military Strategy. Following an idea that Eddleman had championed in 1955, he thought that each faculty member should make a formal presentation to the class at least once during the year. Salet suggested that the curriculum provide more emphasis on the strategic employment of the Army, include more case studies, and require more individual work by the student. He also saw a need for group or collective research, however, and again expressed his confidence in the scheme of one-year fellowships.[29]

From October through February, Ryan and his group visited the Military Academy, the Woodrow Wilson School of Public and International Affairs at Princeton, and the Mershon Center for Education in National Security at Ohio State University. They also invited to Carlisle singly and in small groups a number of consultants. At West Point they studied the system of permanent professorships and had explained to them all the problems of accreditation. At Princeton the message was clear: The quality of a program depended upon the quality of the faculty. They were advised to rely less on lectures and more on research as an instructional mode. The people at Princeton were not optimistic that the War College could attract a top-quality civilian faculty even with academic chairs. The Army would have to develop its own scholars as it had for West Point.[30]

Dr. Ivan Birrer, the longtime educational advisor at Leavenworth, visited Carlisle in January. He warned against too much enthusiasm for academic degrees; rather, the faculty should earn its reputation in its own areas of military scholarship. Birrer thought that the War College should go ahead and establish the academic chairs but that at least initially the department heads should be designated the occupants. Birrer was forthright in relating that the Army-wide impression of the War College was that it was a leisurely, expensive institution which suffered from a lack of clearly defined goals and purpose.[31]

Dr. Alain Enthoven, the Assistant Secretary of Defense (Systems Analysis), and his assistant, William K. Brehm, were invited to Carlisle to express their views. Implied in Enthoven's recommendations was the view that the Army's staff procedures and decision-making processes were antiquated. The core of the War College course should be "Military Science and Strategic Studies," supplemented by courses on economics and "Decision-Theory and Systems Analysis." He challenged the view that Army officers needed broadening: They were already broad-minded men; what they lacked was the experience of concentrated study in depth. Enthoven's recommendations tended to confirm an opinion expressed earlier by representatives of the Research Analysis Corporation. Those men had warned that the Army could not continue to "hire out its staff work" over the long term. "An organization can lose its decision-making authority if it lacks the means to make those decisions."[32]

Retired general officers were also asked to visit Carlisle. Two of the more thoughtful were General Garrison Davidson, a former Commandant at Leavenworth and Superintendent at West Point (as well as Commanding General of Seventh Army) and Lieutenant General Arthur Trudeau, who had never lost his interest in the War College. Davidson thought the Army reorganization that had separated the development of doctrine from its teaching was a serious error. Trudeau seemed to agree. He expressed the view that research fellowships were not needed; what was needed was to make the Institute of Advanced Studies more responsive to the needs of the War College. Davidson concurred: The IAS was becoming an extension of the Army Staff and the Commandant was losing control of it.[33]

Davidson's was something of a lonely voice when he expressed the views that in the future senior officers would have to be more specialist than generalist and that the War College should recognize this truth when designing its program. Davidson and Trudeau were in agreement that greater faculty tenure was mandatory and that there must be greater rewards for faculty duty—for example, the Deputy Commandant should be selected and promoted from among the department chairmen. The two generals also agreed that the cooperative degree program should be continued only if the courses offered by the university became more allied to the work of the War College. As he had in 1951, Trudeau again recommended that the Office of the Chief of Military History be moved to Carlisle Barracks to help make that place the Army's true intellectual center.[34]

General Salet also queried a number of senior active-duty officers for their views on the War College's future. Lieutenant General Dwight Beach (AWC 1951) favored the idea of having civilian scholars serve at the War College during their sabbaticals, but he was indifferent as to the future of the degree program. Lieutenant General Bruce Palmer expressed doubts in regard to a tenured faculty, but he liked the idea of academic chairs to be occupied by retired officers for limited periods. Major General William Rosson (AWC 1954) favored a teaching faculty with fewer guest lecturers. He was against the degree program because he believed officers entered it for selfish motives. Rosson was alone among those queried in believing that all the war colleges should become joint institutions.[35]

Before the Army War College-70 project could be brought to completion, however, the War College was growing increasingly aware that the Office of the Secretary of Defense was taking a greater and more critical interest in military education. In August 1964 President Lyndon B. Johnson in an address to the National War College and the Industrial College had mentioned the need for a systematic review of military education. From the Army War College-70 research effort, Salet learned

365

that Deputy Secretary of Defense Cyrus Vance was preparing the terms of reference for this study. The officials in the Defense Secretariat apparently believed that the war colleges placed too much reliance on guest speakers and that their curricula were providing only a panoramic view of national security affairs at the expense of close study of professional military matters. It was understood that they were in favor of more instruction in systems analysis and more emphasis on joint military planning, together with better coverage of the linkage between politics and the use of military force.[36]

In late December, General Salet was informed of the contents of a soon-to-be-published article by Dr. Katzenbach that was highly critical of the war colleges. In his budget message to Congress in January, the President again mentioned an impending review of military education. Then in February, the Commandant of the Marine Corps, General Wallace M. Greene, Jr., published an article in which he recommended more rigorous, challenging, and professionally oriented courses at the war colleges and singled out the cooperative degree programs for elimination. Katzenbach's article, "The Demotion of Professionalism," appeared in March. The same month the War College learned that the Joint Chiefs were establishing an ad-hoc committee to study the joint colleges with a view to making their programs more difficult. The Army Staff was also reacting to the Department of Defense criticism: In late January, General Harrell had informed General Salet that a "new Williams Board" was being considered to review the entire Army school system.[37]

The barrage of criticism, together with the impending Department of Defense and Department of the Army reviews, probably influenced General Salet to commit himself to Army War College-70 reforms earlier than he may have intended. By late December he had formally requested that six one-year fellowships be established and solicited possible volunteers from the incumbent class. He also requested that the criterion of the possession of a baccalaureate degree be added to the requirements for selection to attend the War College. He approved a plan whereby seventeen selected faculty positions would require advanced degrees in specific disciplines, a considerable move toward faculty specialization. In a press interview the week after the release of the Marine Corps Commandant's article, he publicly declared that significant changes were in prospect at the Army War College, that the pendulum had swung too far in the curricular emphasis on economic, societal, and political considerations, and that the hard core of the program must be the military. He mentioned measures being considered to increase the prestige and stature of the faculty, including selective tenure, academic chairs, platform teaching, and stimulus to publish on military subjects. The Commandant expanded on these concepts in an article in *Army*.[38]

At Department of the Army, General Salet's plans met with less than unqualified approval. On the 18th of January, General Harrell disapproved the recommendation to establish fellowships (the stated reason was budgetary), and five days later he disapproved the recommendation to make the baccalaureate degree a prerequisite for selection to the War College. General Salet also had difficulty obtaining the support of the Assistant Chief of Staff for Force Development in matters not connected with Army War College-70. In October a field trip to the Caribbean had been recommended for the Class of 1965, both for its prestige and its educational value, but it was turned down. When the trip was proposed again for the Class of 1966, Salet once more came away empty-handed. The travels of the Army War College classes remained limited to the annual trip to the United Nations headquarters and the family outing and tour of the Gettysburg battlefield for the Carlisle Barracks community that had been originated by the Armed Forces Information School. A limited number of students did visit Redstone Arsenal, however, at the invitation of its Commanding General in the spring of 1965.[39]

Despite the confusion of the variety of advice Salet and Ryan were receiving from their consultants and from their faculty, four common themes seem to have emerged. First, there was the idea that a distinct field of study existed which the Army War College should be uniquely equipped to handle. This field of study needed more precise definition, but its center of gravity was military affairs, more specifically, the development and employment of land forces. Second, there were specific qualifications and skills required of the senior commander and staff officer that the War College had an obligation to develop. Like the field of study, these qualifications and skills were not yet defined. Third, the Army War College could not fall back on external resources to accomplish its purposes. Complete reliance could not be placed on long- or short-term civilian professors, consultants, guest lecturers, a cooperative degree program, or a combination of those means. A fourth theme, a corollary to the third, was that the success of the War College's program was dependent upon Department of the Army support of a range of policies, primarily in the manpower and personnel areas, that would provide a qualified investigative and instructional faculty.

With uneven success, the final recommendations of Army War College-70 at least indirectly addressed the issues raised by each of the four themes. Recommended as the field of study of special interest to the Army War College was the study of military strategy, a confirmation of the view put forth by General Train several years before. The report recommended a restated War College mission that added to the previous "emphasis on Army doctrine and operations" an emphasis on "Army strategic concepts." Army War College-70 envisioned and recommended a much more active research and publishing program in the field of military strategy, including both faculty and students. As to the qualifications required of graduates, General Salet recommended an exploratory investigation by the Human Resources Research Office (HumRRO), an Army contract research agency. He had already made tentative arrangements for this investigation. In his report General Salet insisted that the War College was engaged primarily in the development of commanders and only secondarily in the development of staff officers. Moreover, its development of staff officers was not confined solely to staff officers for the Department of the Army, Joint Staff, and Department of Defense in Washington, but for all major Army, joint, and combined headquarters.[40]

As to faculty, in something of a reversal from Salet's earlier ideas, the report rejected the temporary or permanent employment of civilian professors and a semi-tenured faculty along the lines of the Military Academy. The field of study of the War College was seen as too dynamic for that, needing constant refreshment with operational experience. Recommended instead was a policy of three-year tours of duty for most of the faculty and a four-year tour for individuals in seven designated key positions with an option of a fifth year. Unless The George Washington University could make the courses it offered in the cooperative degree program more supportive of the War College curriculum, abandonment of that program was recommended. The Army War College-70 report included a proposed faculty selection and development program that would seek to use the quasi-permanent West Point assistant professors at various stages of their career, would more systematically select faculty members from the classes of all the senior service colleges, would assign to the War College each year the one colonel whom the Army had sent as a fellow to the Harvard Center for International Affairs, and would require advanced degrees. Additionally, manpower authorization should be approved to permit three officers each year to spend a year of study at one of eleven civilian institutions before coming onto the faculty. A faculty orientation program was also recommended.[41]

The ideas expressed in Army War College-70 were reflected in a rearrangement of the faculty. The former four faculty groups were reorganized into three departments—a Department of Strategy, a Department of Strategic Appraisal, and a Department of Military Planning. The heads of these departments would occupy academic chairs named respectively for Elihu Root, Dwight D. Eisenhower, and John J. Pershing, even though the latter two could hardly be considered as having been strong proponents of the Army War College. The position of Director of Instruction and Research was created to supervise and coordinate the three departments. Within that office was a Research and Publications Section to coordinate the conduct of faculty and student research and to assist in publication of the results in professional journals. As a start, "United States Army War College Occasional Papers" were to be reproduced locally and distributed to the Army's leadership and within the Army school system. Rather than ask again for the six one-year post-graduation research fellowships that had been refused him, Salet now recommended four.[42]

Army War College-70 recommendations were also reflected in the proposed 1965-66 curriculum submitted concurrently with the study. From the start of the study General Salet had favored evolutionary change; the proposed curriculum was not revolutionary. The curricular theme of a national strategy and a supporting military program remained. Also retained were the eight courses of the previous two years, though the titles of four of them were altered to include the word "strategic" and the titles of two changed to include the word "Army." Course requirements also were changed, however. Whereas seven committee reports and only one individual report had been required in the previous year, now three of the courses required individual reports, three required a combination of individual and group reports, and only two required committee reports alone. Also, more faculty lectures were scheduled than in previous years. Other changes included the elimination of the "Frontiers of Knowledge" lecture series, which some had found beyond comprehension, the addition of a week-long "Command and Management Seminar," and a major revamping of the Thesis Program. In line with the new emphasis on research, the Thesis Program became the "Individual Studies Program." It consisted of three elements, allowing the student a choice between writing a graduate-school-variety thesis, a more narrowly focused individual research paper, or two essays written specifically with a view to publication.[43]

The response of the Assistant Chief of Staff for Force Development to Army War College-70 was not enthusiastic. Pending the results of the Department of the Army's comprehensive review of the school system, General Harrell declined to endorse any of Salet's long-term proposals, including the restatement of mission and the HumRRO survey. Nor would he support faculty tours of duty in excess of three years, believing that the result would be retirement tours for academically inclined colonels. Nor did he see any reason to send prospective faculty members off for year of civilian schooling. The Army had plenty of officers with graduate degrees, and he thought that Army War College-70 overemphasized the need for graduate degrees anyway. General Harrell advised a cautious approach to faculty research, citing the danger of a publish-or-perish syndrome distracting from teaching. Somewhat inconsistently, he also questioned the value of a teaching faculty. Faculty members might be chosen because of their instructional ability rather than because of their broad experience, and the guest speaker program might be diluted. The value of individual student work, as opposed to committee work, he also doubted; it might jeopardize the ability of students to learn from each other. The cooperative degree program should be eliminated—the sooner the better. Systems analysis needed no great emphasis; it was a technique for managers, not commanders. Finally, General Harrell offered the view that in the 1950s the Army War College had taught its students to communicate with the civilians in the State Department, and now in the 1960s it seemed inclined to teach its students how to communicate with the civilians in the Defense Secretariat. In General Harrell's opinion, if an officer was expert in his own profession, he could hold his own in either arena.[44]

The Haines Board

In view of General Harrell's response to Army War College-70, it was apparent that any major moves would have to await the outcome of the long-promised Department of the Army review of officer education. The board to conduct that review was appointed in June 1965 and convened in July. Its president was Lieutenant General Ralph E. Haines, Jr., a graduate of Swing's 1951 Army War College and of the 1958 National War College. There were nine other members of the Haines Board, four of whom had graduated from the Army War College, two as recently as 1962. Charged with reviewing the entire officer school system and given only six months for the task, the Haines Board did not investigate in detail all the recommendations of Army War College-70, but General Salet made sure that the board knew of them and understood the rationale behind them.[45]

In preparation for the Haines Board review, the War College drew together in a formal document all that had been learned in its own study and in the process strengthened its defenses against Katzenbach-type criticism and suggestions. In fact, the War College "positions" for the Haines Board's review came close to being a defense of the status quo as modified by Army War College-70. As Salet saw it, the fundamental point at issue between the War College and Dr. Katzenbach was that the latter called for a narrow concentration of study in civilian disciplines having application at departmental level, while the War College believed in a broader education to prepare an officer for worldwide high command and staff positions. To Salet, Katzenbach was suggesting that an unacceptable specialist or "technologist" approach replace the generalist approach.[46]

Actually, in a number of ways what Dr. Katzenbach suggested in his article paralleled what Army War College-70 recommended. Both urged a more professionally military program of study. Both saw a teaching faculty as a virtue. Both called for more serious research, and both were disillusioned with the cooperative graduate-degree program. But the War College was adamant on the generalist-specialist issue, even employing the curious argument that changing to a specialist approach would constitute an indictment of the Army's current leadership. Haines attempted to resolve this issue. In his report he held that "both the specialist and generalist concepts have merit . . . [and] it is possible to combine both in the same program." Specialization, according to Haines, could be centered on a program of elective courses.[47]

The Haines Board report was published in February 1966. In July, after comments by interested headquarters, schools, and agencies, General Harold K. Johnson, the Chief of Staff, announced his decisions on its recommendations. The electives program was one of two significant recommendations on the War College that Johnson eventually approved. The other was the initiation of an extension program, reversing the Williams Board findings. Johnson directed that the electives be in place for the 1967-68 school year and that the extension program be offered in the 1968-69 school year. Another major recommendation, but one on which Johnson withheld a decision, was that the instruction at the War College and at the Command and General Staff College be monitored by the Combat Developments Command. The War College, however, had made strong representations in its comments on the board's report that the War College should remain directly under the Department of the Army, using arguments similar to those that influenced General Lemnitzer to remove the college from CONARC's supervision in 1960.[48]

In approving the Haines Board recommendations, the Chief of Staff reaffirmed that all the senior service colleges were at the same educational level. Gap-filling versus apex-building was no longer a big issue. The curriculum at the Army War College should be military-oriented with emphasis on the Army's role and on strategic concepts and doctrine. In support of this orientation the individual research papers were to be limited to subjects of direct interest to the Army. Also, more use should be made of case studies. The remainder of the approved recommendations had to do with the faculty. The faculty should include more specialists; the fields of research and development, logistics, project management, and operations research and systems analysis, particularly needed representation. The Harvard Fellow in International Affairs was to be assigned to the faculty after completion of his work at Harvard. Finally, the War College should obtain the services of a well-qualified educational advisor.[49]

In general the Army War College program had survived without any immediate, revolutionary effect both the Army War College-70 study and the Haines Board review. Yet there was one more trial to overcome: another formal review, this time by a committee appointed by the Assistant Secretary of Defense (Manpower), entitled the "Officer Education Study." For the Army War College this review occurred in December 1965, only three months after the visit of the Haines Board. The committee was provided the Haines report and acknowledged that it was of considerable value to its own study, but it felt that the two studies were complementary rather than duplicative. The report of the Officer Education Study proved anticlimactic. It had only two broad recommendations of interest to the Army War College. One was that the responsibilities for education and training of the Office of the Secretary of Defense, the Joint Chiefs of Staff, and the services be clarified. From the point of view of the services, there was no confusion; responsibility for professional education belonged with the military professions, not with temporary appointees of the Department of Defense. The second recommendation was that another study, under JCS direction, be made of the senior service colleges. Here there was clearly a cloud on the horizon. Even though the services were assured that the Department of Defense did not desire to take over education, the JCS group would be asked to investigate whether any of the senior service colleges should be placed under the direct control of the Office of the Secretary of Defense and whether there should be a core curriculum common to all the senior service colleges. In effect, however, the Army had preempted the study with its Haines Board; as far as the Army was concerned, it had already looked into the topics the Assistant Secretary wanted the JCS to investigate. In the fall of 1966 the Officer Education Study was of little moment to the Army War College. The problem at hand was to implement the decisions of the Chief of Staff on the Haines Board recommendations and the decisions of the Commandant on the Army War College-70 recommendations. There was much work to be done.[50]

NOTES
1. *Congressional Record*, March 28, 1961, 4717-18. William W. Kaufmann, *The McNamara Strategy* (New York: Harper and Row, 1964), 60.
2. Ibid., 67, 70, 258.
3. Ibid., 60, 70. Taylor, *Swords and Plowshares*, 225-51. Douglas Blaufarb, *The Counterinsurgency Era: U.S. Doctrine and Performance, 1950 to the Present* (New York: The Free Press, 1977), 67-82. AWC, Course Directive, Senior Officers Counterinsurgency Course (SOINC), 18 June-6 July 1962.
4. Hewes, *Root to McNamara*, 306-10. Charles J. Hitch, *Decision-Making for Defense* (Los Angeles: University of California Press, 1965), 27-39.
5. Term "scientific optimism" is from "From John F. Kennedy to Jimmy Carter," *The Wilson Quarterly* (Spring, 1981): 73. See also Henry Fairlie, *The Kennedy Promise: The Politics of Expectation* (Garden City, N.Y.: Doubleday, 1973). Henry Beecher, "Pentagon Whiz Kids," *The Wall Street Journal*, 24 September 1963, 18.
6. AWC, *1961-1962 Curriculum*, 1 July 1961. Course Directive Course 7: US National Strategy and a Supporting Military Program, 12 April 1962.
7. AWC, *1962-1963 Curriculum*, 1 July 1962. Course Directive Course 7: United States Preparedness for War, 20 March-19 April 1963.
8. AWC, Course Directive, Course 4: U.S. Global Strategic Concepts and Military Capabilities, Part II: Counterinsurgency, 3 December 1962. Course Directive, Course 5: Strategic Capabilities in Selected World Areas, 19 December 1962. AWC, *Curriculum Coverage of Counterinsurgency*, 26 November 1962.
9. Report of Civilian Advisory Group, 1962.

10. AWC, *1963-1964 Curriculum Pamphlet*, 1 July 1963. Course 1: The World Environment and International Relations, 20 August-16 September 1963. Course 2: The U.S. and the North Atlantic Community, 17 September-10 October 1963. Course 3: The Communist Powers, 11 October-8 November 1963. Course 4: The Developing Areas, 12 November-6 December 1963. Course 7: Science, Technology and Future Military Power, 1-28 April 1964. Directive: Frontiers of Knowledge, 29 August 1963.

11. The reorganization of the Army was a result of what was known as "Project 80." The staff reorganization was the result of "Project 39a." Hewes, *Root to McNamara*, 316-65.

12. Department of the Army General Order No. 19, 22 April 1963. AWC, Talking Papers for the Military Education Coordination Conference, 20-21 May 1964, Tab X, File 203-03 (1964).

13. Entry of 26 April 1963, Deputies Meeting, File 203-03.

14. Train to DCSOPS, 10 January 1963, Subject: USAWC Program for Senior Officers of the Reserve Components, USAWC Historical Files, 1959-63.

15. Creighton Abrams to Commandant, 2nd Indorsement, 8 March 1963 to Letter Abrams to Commandant, 19 February 1963, File 203-03. AWC Circular 621-1, 15 January 1964, Announcement of Special Course of Instruction, 29 January-12 February 1964, File 205-02. W. H. S. Wright to Train, 25 February 1964, File 1003-16. Train to Ben Harrell, 29 April 1964, Ibid. Commandant to Deputy Commandant, 15 April 1964, File 1003-15. CONARC Circular 350-12, 12 June 1964, Subject: Reserve Component Officers ACDUTRA at the Army War College, File 1003-15. Memorandum for Record, 6 February 1964, Subject: Possible Future USAWC Program, A SRCOC for Regular Officers, File 1003-01.

16. Talking Papers for 1964, Tab S and Tab T, File 203-03.

17. AWC Memorandum No. 49, "Reading List Panel," 10 September 1962. Army Regulation 28-86, "Contemporary Military Reading List," 6 March 1963. AWC Memorandum 350-2, "Reading List Panel," 19 May 1964. All in File 205-01.

18. Train to LTG T. W. Parker, 12 March 1963, File 205-03. Parker to Train, 28 March 1963, Ibid. AWC, *Directory 1905-1980*.

19. Train to Parker, 12 March 1963. Parker to Train, 28 March 1963.

20. Entry of 20 September 1963, Minutes of Deputies Meetings, File 203-03 (1945-1963). Train to Chief of Chaplains, 20 March 1964, File 206-01. Entries of 26 June 1963 and 29 July 1963, Minutes of Deputies Meetings, File 203-03. District Engineer to Commanding General, Carlisle Barracks, 1 June 1964, Subject: Completion Date for Family Housing, File 1503-01. Entries of 7 May 1963, 26 June 1963, and 8 July 1963, Minutes of Deputies Meetings, File 203-03. Train to Dwight Beach, 31 January 1964, File 205-02 (1964). "Army War College Starts Expansion," *The Journal of the Armed Forces* (February 13, 1965): 1, 24. Talking Papers for 1964, Tab A-4, File 203-03.

21. Talking Papers for 1964, Tab X, File 203-03 (1964). Talking Papers for 1965, Tab T, File 203-03 (1965).

22. Ibid.

23. AWC Circular 15-1, 9 April 1964, Subject: Establishment of USAWC Faculty Committee for Strategic Analysis, File 205-02 (1964). File 1003-12 (1964). AWC Circular 621-34, 20 October 1964, Subject: Presentation of Special Thesis Plan: Principles of U.S. Military Strategy, File 205-02 (1964).

24. Bruce L. R. Smith, *The Rand Corporation: Case Study of a Nonprofit Advisory Corporation* (Cambridge, Mass.: Harvard University Press, 1966), 2-3. Paul Dickson, *Think Tanks* (New York: Atheneum, 1971), 149-50. Chairman, Curriculum Group to Commandant, 20 November 1963, USAWC Historical Files, 1959-63.

25. The Eddleman Committee (U.S. Army Command and General Staff College Educational Survey Committee) was chaired by General Clyde D. Eddleman, former Commandant of the War College. It visited the War College in October 1962. File 203-03 (1964).

26. Russell D. Fudge, "Paging Colonel Mahan," *Army* (January 1961): 58-64. D. F. Halpin to Commandant, 21 May 1963, Subject: Remarks by Chairman, JCS, and J-1 at the Military Education Coordination Committee, File 203-03 (1945-1963). Robert N. Ginsburgh, "The Challenge to Military Professionalism," *Foreign Affairs* (January 1964):

261. Chairman, Curriculum Group to Commandant, 20 April 1964, File 203-03 (1964). Charles M. Fergusson, Jr., "Strategic Thought and Studies," *Military Review* (April 1964): 9-24.

27. Salet to LTG Ben Harrell, 12 November 1964, File: USAWC-70 Project.

28. Ryan to "All Members of the Faculty," November 1964, File 205-06 (1964). Salet to ACSFOR, 6 November 1964, Subject: U.S. Army War College Activities, File: USAWC-70 Project. Salet to LTG Harrell, 12 November 1964, Ibid.

29. Salet's marginal notes on Ryan to Commandant, 19 November 1964, Ibid. Eddleman interview, 23.

30. Salet to Lampert, 5 September 1964, File 205-02 (1964). Memorandum for Record: Visit of LTC John Mastin, Office of the Dean, USMA, 6 October 1964, File 205-06. Memorandum for Record, 6 November 1964, Subject: Staff Visit to U.S. Military Academy, 29-31 October 1964, Ibid. Ryan to Chairman, Curriculum Group, 29 December 1964, Subject: Mershon Center for Education in National Security, Ibid. Salet to Dr. Edgar S. Furness, Jr., Mershon Professor of Political Science, 31 December 1964, Ibid. Memorandum for Record, 22 December 1964, Subject: Visit of Deputy Commandant to Princeton, 15 December 1964, Ibid.

31. Birrer to Deputy Commandant, 13 January 1965, File: USAWC-70 Project.

32. Enthoven to Salet, 15 February 1965, Ibid. Memorandum for Record: Visit of RAC Representatives, 13 January 1965, Ibid.

33. Davidson to Ryan, 17 February 1965, Ibid. Memorandum for Record: Visit of Generals Trudeau and Davidson, 18 February 1965, Ibid.

34. Ibid. Davidson's views on specialization by senior officers are expressed further in Garrison H. Davidson, "Tomorrow's Leaders—Their Education, Training and Nurture," *Army* (October 1964): 28-29.

35. Beach to Salet, 19 January 1965; Palmer to Salet, 26 January 1965; Rosson to Salet, 15 January 1965; all in File: USAWC-70 Project.

36. Director, Committee for Strategic Analysis, to Deputy Commandant, 30 December 1964, Subject: Civilian Attitudes Toward the Military Profession, File 205-06.

37. C. S. Pond to Commandant, 29 December 1964, Subject: Forthcoming Article in the Naval Institute Proceedings by E. L. Katzenbach, File 205-06. "Marine Commandant Proposes School Changes," *The Journal of the Armed Forces* (6 February 1965), 2. Edward L. Katzenbach, "The Demotion of Professionalism at the War Colleges," *USNIP* (March 1965): 34-41. W. C. Esterline to Acting Commandant, 2 March 1965, Subject: JCS Study on Making Joint Curriculum More Difficult and Challenging, File 1003-03. Harrell to Salet, 23 January 1965, File 205-06.

38. Salet to Harrell, 24 December 1964, File: USAWC-70. Ryan, Memorandum for Record, 29 December 1964, Subject: Interview with General Harrell on Fellowships, Ibid. AWC Circular 621-52, 29 December 1964, Subject: "USAWC Fellowships," File 205-02. Salet to ACSFOR, 31 December 1964, Subject: Additional Prerequisites for Attendance at USAWC, File 205-06. Ryan to Fergusson, 29 December 1964, Subject: Graduate Degrees for USAWC Faculty, Ibid. "Army War College Starts Expansion—Major Changes at Top School Seen," *Journal of the Armed Forces* (13 February 1965): 1, 24. Eugene A. Salet, "The Army War College Looks to the Future," *Army* (March 1965): 28-35.

39. AWC Circular 621-5, 18 January 1965, File: USAWC-70. Harrell to Salet, 23 January 1965, File 205-06. Salet to Harrell, 11 September 1964, File 1000-09. Harrell to Salet, 9 October 1964, Ibid. Salet to Harrell, 4 November 1964, Ibid. AWC, Minutes of the 32nd Meeting of the Curriculum Board, 30 June 1965, File 1003-03. AWC, Talking Papers for 1965, Tab R, File 203-03.

40. Salet to ACSFOR, 15 March 1965, Subject: Conclusions and Recommendations from Staff Study, "U.S. Army War College 1970," 1, File: USAWC-70. Tabs 1B, 1C, and 2A to Ibid.

41. Tabs 1E, 1G, 2C, and 2E to Ibid.

42. Tabs 1B, 1F, and 2D to Ibid.

43. Tab 2B, Ibid. AWC, *Draft USAWC Curriculum Pamphlet, 1965-66*. Chairman Faculty Group IV to Chairman Curriculum Group, 12 June 1964, Subject: Student Comments on Frontiers of Knowledge Program, File 1003-26.

44. Harrell to Commandant, 7 April 1965, Subject: Conclusions and Recommendations from Staff Study, "U.S. Army War College 1970," File: USAWC-70.
45. Department of the Army, *Report of the Department of the Army Board to Review Army Officer Schools* (hereafter, *Haines Board*), 3 vols., February 1966, I: 105-06, 108-10.
46. USAWC, *Positions for the Department of the Army Board to Review Army Officers Schools*, 21 September 1965 (hereafter, *AWC Positions*), 173.
47. Katzenbach, "Demotion of Professionalism." Salet to Harrell, 15 March 1965. *AWC Positions*, 80. *Haines Board*, 489.
48. Department of the Army Letter, 20 July 1966, Subject: Report of the Department of the Army Board to Review Army Officers Schools, February 1966 (Haines Board); Salet to DCSPER, 13 April 1966, 1st Ind. to Letter, DCSPER, 22 March 1966, Report of the DA Board to Review Army Officer Schools; all in File 1003-16.
49. Department of the Army Letter, 20 July 1966.
50. Office of Assistant Secretary of Defense (Manpower), *Officer Education Study*, 2 vols. (July 1966), I: 95-99, Annex A.

Prelude to Change 1966-1970

In the fall of 1966 the Army War College was emerging from two full years of both self-inspired and externally generated review and examination. The process had begun in the early fall of 1964 when General Salet launched his Army War College-70 project, had continued with an aggressive defense of the generalist approach against the attacks of the Katzenbach school, and had extended through the Haines Board deliberations and the period of negotiations that followed Haines's recommendations. Finally, there had been the rather cursory review by the Assistant Secretary of Defense (Manpower) group. The four academic years (1966-67 through 1969-70) that followed the two years of examination were, at least in the eyes of the faculty, very much years of transition as the college attempted to put into place the varied and sometimes conflicting measures dictated by Army War College-70 and the Haines Board. Viewed in retrospect, these four years also appear as a prelude to even more fundamental changes that were to occur throughout the decade of the 1970s.

Army War College-70 Actions

As has been mentioned, General Salet did not wait for final approval of Army War College-70 before making changes in the college's organization and program. In academic year 1965-66 he reorganized the faculty into three academic departments, established three academic chairs, created the position of Director of Instruction and Research, directed the publication of "occasional papers," and designated certain faculty positions as requiring advanced academic degrees.

Of more significance to future academic programs, General Salet also added to the curriculum of the 1965-66 year the "Command and Management" seminar.[1] As it was presented, "Command and Management" turned out to be more concerned with economic analysis, systems analysis, and automatic data processing than with "command"—at least "command" in the sense that an officer of Ben Harrell's outlook understood the term. The seminar, at least in title, appears to have been an attempt to reconcile the modern management methods of Secretary McNamara's Department of Defense with the venerable admonition of Secretary Root that the Army War College was founded to study the great problem of responsible command.[2]

In his reorganization of the faculty, General Salet also abolished the Committee for Strategic Analysis. This decision in part may have been taken because a manpower survey had held that the committee's functions properly belonged to the Institute of Advanced Studies. It was an unfortunate decision because the three-man committee under Colonel Bussey had been highly productive during the 1964-65 school year. One member of the committee, Lieutenant Colonel Nels Parson, with fourteen students organized into a special thesis seminar, produced in July 1965 a four-volume manuscript in which were derived, compiled, and discussed a long list of "tenets" of the military strategy of the United States. The work was admittedly incomplete; a continuing effort at synthesis was badly needed. Nonetheless, it was the first attempt by the War College, and a potentially successful one, to produce a major work on military strategy, that field of study that General Salet claimed as the special province of the Army War College. With the inactivation of the committee in March 1965 and Parson's reassignment in July, however, the project was never completed. Also in 1965 Lieutenant Colonel Fergusson, the third member of the Committee for Strategic Analysis, authored a manuscript addressing the question "What does it mean to win?"—a topic suggested to General Salet by Chief of Staff Johnson in the summer of 1964. Even after disestablishment of the committee, Fergusson continued this effort, and the results were forwarded to General Johnson in August 1965. Comparable initiatives were not taken after the committee disbanded.[3]

The concept of occasional papers bore fruit in September 1965 when papers by two students, Colonel Leilyn M. Young and Lieutenant Colonel George E. Wear, were published as "Occasional Papers of the Army War College" and distributed to the Army's senior leadership, graduates and past faculty of the college, and throughout the Army school system. The reaction to the papers was generally favorable, though a former member of the 1950-51 faculty, General Paul D. Adams, who a few months earlier had written to the Haines Board that the Army War College had become somewhat sterile, too academic, and out of the mainstream of military life, cautioned that occasional papers were no true substitute for a professional journal.[4]

"Occasional Papers" enjoyed sufficient success, however, that four essays by students of the Class of 1966 were published in April of that year under a new title, *The United States Army War College Commen-*

tary. Salet decided to delay requesting approval of *Commentary* as an officially sponsored Army publication in order to allow *Commentary* time to mature and to avoid administrative problems involved in obtaining such approval. At Department of the Army headquarters, the Chief of Information recommended that future issues of *Commentary* be classified as "For Official Use Only." He saw public relations problems ahead if controversial articles not necessarily in accord with Defense Department or Army policies were published openly. Salet would not accept this stricture, but he indicated that distribution would be limited to within the Army.[5]

The Chief of Information also discouraged another idea that would have made work performed by students at the Army War College widely available in academic circles. The War College had proposed that student theses be registered with and reproduced by University Microfilms, Inc., as were doctoral dissertations, thereby making them available to scholars worldwide. The Chief of Information, however, pointed out that all theses would then have to be cleared at Department of the Army level. The Army Staff and certainly the office of the Chief of Information were not prepared to take on this workload. So the War College dropped the idea. Nonetheless, Salet's desire that members of the War College write for publication did meet with success after the Commandant began to ask for monthly reports on what was being published. He was informed in December 1966 that members of the 1965-66 War College had published ninety-two articles in twenty-three different publications and journals. Concurrently, Salet was encouraging the faculty to join and participate in the activities of various professional associations and learned societies.[6]

In contrast to these efforts to increase recognition and expand the constituency of the Army War College, Salet recommended, after the 1964-65 experience, to reduce the number of Senior Reserve Component Officer Courses (SRCOC's) from two to one per year. His rationale was that while one SRCOC per year was very beneficial to the resident class, two per year were distracting. The high level of success of the first three SRCOC's, however, made the Assistant Chief of Staff for Force Development extremely reluctant to reduce their frequency. The alternative of one SRCOC per year with double the number of participants was suggested, but the War College argued that it did not have the physical facilities to accommodate that number of participants at one time. In the end ACSFOR relented, and beginning in 1965-66 only one SRCOC of sixteen participants was to be held each year.[7]

Improving the quality and prestige of the faculty was a major thrust of Army War College-70. In May 1966 General Salet recommended to the Department of the Army that officers assigned to the faculty be authorized to wear a distinctive collar insignia (the torch of enlightenment held aloft by a mailed fist) in lieu of insignia of branch. There were precedents in the collar insignia worn by permanent professors at West Point and by officers detailed to the General Staff Corps and the Inspector General's Corps, but Salet's superiors disapproved the recommendation. Salet thereupon authorized a special pocket insignia for local wear at Carlisle Barracks to distinguish faculty from students and staff. The concept of an egalitarian institution as espoused by Bliss and Swing was eroding.[8]

General Salet took another step to increase faculty prestige in August 1966. Each member of the faculty was designated a "director" of a specific field of study, for example, "Director of International Relations Studies," "Director of National Defense Organization Studies," and "Director of Force Development Studies." At the same time, the State Department member of the faculty became "Diplomatic Advisor to the Commandant." In all, twenty-seven directorships were designated. This step was more than a prestige measure, however. It was a recognition, belated perhaps, that the range of interest of the War College had become so broad that specialized faculty expertise was mandatory. But General Salet was not naive; he understood that more than insignia and titles were needed if the faculty was to win the prestige he wanted it to have. Its members would have to be experts able to exercise intellectual leadership in the classroom.[9]

Haines Board Actions

Action to carry out the Haines Board recommendations began in earnest in the fall of 1966 under the direction of the recently arrived Deputy Commandant, Brigadier General Robert B. Smith (AWC 1959). Smith isolated forty-one separate tasks to be accomplished. As a rough measure of importance, sixteen pertained to faculty requirements, selection, and development. During the Army War College-70 study the War College itself had rejected adding more civilians to the faculty or attempting to adapt the West Point system of tenure. But the Haines Board had not supported the Army War College-70 scheme of extended tours for selected faculty positions; indeed the Chief of Staff had approved stabilized three-year tours for all faculty members only as an objective, not as a policy. The Chief of Staff also approved only as an objective a recommendation of Haines (and also of Katzenbach) that students serve an intervening tour of duty before coming onto the faculty. By 1966 the War College was experiencing, as were all Army activities, the competition of the Southeast Asia war in the assignment of personnel.[10]

General Johnson did approve, however, the recommendation that certain specialties be included on the faculty and, in approving the introduction of electives, also agreed that civilian professors might be placed on contract for short periods to teach these courses. The original War

College idea of six one-year research fellowships emerged from the Haines Board exercise warped and diluted as approval for four additional faculty members to conduct research pertaining to the curriculum. Expansion of the faculty was further implied by approval of the concept that the faculty assume a more active teaching role, the inauguration of an extension program in 1968-69, and the addition of a Comparative Military Strategy Seminar as well as an expanded Command and Management Seminar to the 1966-67 curriculum.[11]

General Johnson reaffirmed that the Army officer assigned annually as a Fellow at the Harvard Center for International Affairs would subsequently serve at the War College, but Haines had recommended no other special means of faculty development. General Salet therefore initiated a series of faculty seminars to which outside experts were invited in order to instruct the faculty in such arts as the conduct of seminar discussions, the preparation of case studies, and the use of war games. In sum, the results of all the deliberations connected with Army War College-70 and the Haines Board as pertained to the faculty were meager at best. The source, qualifications, and tenure of the faculty would remain essentially as it had been since 1950, only now the problem was made more difficult: Vietnam, not the school system, had become the prestigious place for officers to serve. It was up to the War College to provide whatever additional faculty training was required and to somehow turn the War College faculty into an assignment that quality officers would seek.[12]

Other than the possibility of obtaining civilian professors for the planned electives program, the only concession made to bringing civilians onto the faculty was the approved Haines Board recommendation that an educational advisor be permanently assigned to the faculty. This step, of course, had been considered ever since the years of Trudeau and had nearly been accomplished under General Moore. Salet had not sought the position—he felt that the services of ad hoc consultant groups were all that was needed—but the Haines Board overrode him. The college therefore sought candidates with a Ph.D. degree in the field of education to be hired at the civil service grade of GS-15. Throughout the fall and early winter of 1966, contact was made with a number of schools of education asking for recommendations, but as the year closed the Department of the Army had not yet formally authorized the position nor provided the necessary funds.[13]

The Chief of Staff decisions on the Haines Board recommendations came too late to have a significant effect on the 1966-67 curriculum, but the War College did make adjustments based on a draft of the Haines Board report. The War College understood that it had the support of Haines in presenting a curriculum with greater "military and army emphasis," but it was not yet clear just how this new emphasis should be expressed. In fact, the 1966-67 program retained the same curricular theme that had been in place since 1957-58, and it presented the same eight courses of the previous three years. The Command and Management Seminar, however, was now scheduled "horizontally" instead of "vertically"—meaning that the student attended the seminar once a week for a period of twelve weeks rather than devoting one full week exclusively to the subject. As in the previous year, the seminar was more management than command; problems of field command were not addressed. An additional "horizontal" seminar lasting fifteen weeks was also introduced, the Comparative Military Strategy Seminar.[14]

For only the third time since the War College was reactivated in 1950, a block of instruction appeared in the War College program labeled "military strategy." The course of that title in 1955-56, however, had been subsumed by a search for national objectives of the future, and the course by that title in 1957-58 was but a derivation of the National Military Program. The 1966-67 military strategy seminar in fact most closely resembled the strategy course presented by Colonel Stilwell in 1954-55. It began with consideration of the objectives of war and the nature of military strategy, then progressed from a study of the military strategies of World War I through the strategy of flexible response and contemporary military strategic concepts. The course also addressed arms control and disarmament and the military strategies of the Soviet Union and the People's Republic of China, and it ended with an analysis of alternative military strategies. Unlike Stilwell's course, it was a pure seminar course; no guest lecturers were scheduled, and considerable reading was required as well as a written precis of the discussion and conclusions of the seminar. Two faculty members, Colonel Charles W. Fletcher (AWC 1958) and Lieutenant Colonel Donald E. Fowler (AWC 1964), conducted the seminar sessions, each officer taking two groups of about twenty-five officers each day that the seminar was conducted. The Comparative Military Strategy Seminar was a showpiece not only of the new emphasis on things military, but also of what was meant by a teaching faculty.[15]

The absence of guest lecturers for the military strategy seminar was deliberate and part of the methodology changes that General Salet desired. He had directed that the number of lectures be reduced to as few as two per week. One reason for the reduction was to allow two full and uninterrupted days each week for research and study ("R&S Days"). He was interested not only in promoting the research and publication program but also in encouraging wider student reading. For those students whom he could not entice into the library, he brought the library to the student, placing a selection of books in each committee room and establishing a browsing room in Bliss Hall to encourage what was termed "impulse reading." He also made available machines that were advertised to double one's reading rate and comprehension.[16]

With teaching methods changing, that old standby of the first, second, and early third Army War Colleges, the war game, was not able to make a comeback despite the declared emphasis on the Army and things military. As late as the 1964-65 year, Colonel Kenneth W. Kennedy (AWC 1962) and Lieutenant Colonel Frederick J. Kroesen, Jr. (AWC 1962), were endeavoring to find a way to use computer assistance in the analysis seminar in which theater of operations concept plans prepared by students were tested, but the effort was not crowned with success. Although an introduction to the concepts of politico-military simulations was included in the Command and Management Seminar in 1966-67, the case study had become by far the more fashionable teaching technique. It had been suggested to the Army War College-70 study by Dr. Enthoven, and its use had also been recommended by the Haines Board.[17]

The War College of the mid-1950s had used with profit the case study method. Use of the method had declined, however, when the War College failed to train new faculty members in the technique. Its reintroduction in the late 1960s was therefore a new start. For the 1966-67 program, four case studies were attempted. The first, a case study of the 1965 intervention in the Dominican Republic, was prepared at the War College and incorporated into the course "Strategic Implications of the Developing Areas." The three other case studies had been prepared elsewhere and were adapted to War College use. Two of them were used in the Command and Management Seminar, one prepared at the Military Academy on foreign military assistance and another provided by the Combat Developments Command comparing the M-14 and AR-15 rifles. Preparation of case studies was included as a student option in the Individual Research Program for 1966-67. Twenty-four students chose to make the effort. The Department of the Army had not yet authorized the four additional faculty members that Haines had recommended for this work.[18]

In addition to including the preparation of case studies, the Individual Research Program for 1966-67 retained the three options of a thesis, an individual research paper, or two essays. In accordance with a Haines Board recommendation, topics selected had to address military problems rather than the broader area of national strategy and security. To provide greater visibility to what was being written, General Salet directed Army-wide distribution of a list of the titles, accompanied by an abstract of each paper.[19]

In November 1965, while the Haines Board was still in session, responsibility at the Army Staff level for individual training had been transferred from the ACSFOR to the Deputy Chief of Staff for Personnel. Included in the transfer was staff responsibility for the Army War College. Lieutenant General James K. Woolnough became General Salet's immediate superior. In commenting upon the 1966-67 curriculum General Woolnough was supportive. His only reservations concerned the greater emphasis to be placed on individual work as opposed to committee work. Woolnough, like Harrell before him, saw the value of student discussion and exchange and did not want it compromised.[20]

General Woolnough also renewed consideration of more field trips, suggesting that for academic year 1967-68 the War College initiate visits to activities both in the United States and overseas. Accordingly, the War College began planning for one field trip within the United States for each student (in addition to the trip to the United Nations headquarters) to take place in 1966-67, for small group trips overseas in 1967-68, and for a class overseas trip in 1968-69. The planning proved to be for naught, however. Funds to support the additional trips were not forthcoming, probably because of the Department of the Army's unwillingness to risk public criticism for promoting junkets. Moreover, ambassadors and overseas commanders are rarely supportive of programs that increase the volume of visitors into their territories. Plans for the traditional trip to the United Nations headquarters also caused concern in 1966-67 when the declining state of passenger rail service in the United States was brought home to the War College. Busses had to be used for the first time. The amenities of the club car had been greatly appreciated in years past and would be missed. Despite forebodings, however, Greyhound apparently came through in good style.[21]

Demise of the Degree Program

In 1966-67 the cooperative graduate degree arrangement with The George Washington University was discontinued. The declared reason was the added student workload created by the increased emphasis on research and publishing, the addition of the two "horizontal" seminars, and the planned introduction of electives. Actually the relationship between the two institutions had never been an easy one. Each institution had its own requirements that it could compromise only so far. In renegotiating the contract with the university in 1963, General Train had to accept what many felt was a downgrading of the degree title from Master of Arts to Master of Science. He also had to accept a tuition increase, the second since the initiation of the program. The university in turn had to accept a curtailment in the length of the trimester. The War College had come to the position that it neither encouraged nor discouraged student participation in the program, a position somewhat curious since the Army still saw fit to pay a portion of the tuition costs. Nonetheless, the program remained extremely popular, and General Train still felt the university courses complemented the War College program.[22]

During General Salet's tenure as Commandant, the degree program became a lightning rod for criticism of the War College from both outside and inside the Army, including from within the War College. It was difficult for him to respond to the allegation that the War College demanded so little of the student that an advanced degree could be earned at the same time. The Army War College-70 study considered the issue, and in the spring of 1965 Salet decided to allow the program to expire after completion of its coming summer session. His colleagues at the other senior service colleges, all of whom now had comparable programs with The George Washington University, closed ranks with him and unanimously agreed that the programs should be abandoned. The commandants believed that the popularity of the program stemmed solely from their students' perception that possession of a graduate degree improved the chances of career progression. A perception so widely held was perhaps not altogether in error.[23]

Despite Salet's conviction that The George Washington University program was too costly, competed unduly for the student's time, and was not responsive to the needs and purposes of the War College, he was the first of the several war college commandants who broke the solid front. He was given to understand that the Chief of Staff wanted the Haines Board to reconsider the issue and to look for alternatives to merely continuing the present arrangements or killing the program altogether. Thus the program won at least one more year of life. The Haines Board report, however, was not much help. It simply recommended that the program be discontinued "unless the incursion on student time can be eliminated." General Salet's negotiations with the university proved fruitless. The War College wanted the university to eliminate two of its courses, "Organization and Functions of the United Nations" and "Cultural Contact and Change in Developing Areas," substituting in their place courses entitled "Economics of National Defense" and "Selected National Strategies." The War College also wanted the university to offer a reading course built around important publications in the field of international relations and national security. University officials declined to offer the "Economics of National Defense" course, deeming it inappropriate to a degree in international affairs. They were also reluctant to accept a reading course.[24]

With the university unwilling or unable to accept General Salet's recommendations, the Chief of Staff decided to allow the program to expire in the summer of 1966. From the inception of the program through the time the Class of 1966 graduated, 478 officers had earned master's degrees and eighty-seven were still enrolled in the program and completing the degree requirements. In the meantime, despite their strong stand to the contrary in 1965, all the other senior service colleges had reached an accommodation with the university and continued their programs. The Industrial College actually integrated university courses into its core curriculum.[25]

In retrospect the root cause for ending the degree program at the Army War College appears to have gone almost unrecognized, obscured by all the discussion of workload, student motives, degree titles, and costs. The fundamental reason for the program's demise, for a number of reasons not then clearly seen, was that the central position the War College had given to the study of international relations since the advent of the Eisenhower administration was simply no longer appropriate; hence, also no longer appropriate was a degree program complementary to that emphasis. The end of the degree program was in fact one symptom of a slow but basic reorientation of the War College that had begun about 1963 and that would continue for almost five more years before becoming fully evident.

Evaluating Students

While the Army War College-70 and the Haines Board studies had treated at length issues involving faculty and curriculum, neither study had challenged existing procedures for selection of students or questioned qualification criteria. The Haines Board, however, had recommended that every Army school derive a "Commandant's List" of the upper ten or twenty percent of each class and from this list designate "Distinguished Graduates" and "Honor Graduates." The scheme was reminiscent of the practice of the old School of the Line that Commandant McGlachlin in the early 1920s had objected to and had held responsible for creating unhealthy competition. The War College took exception to this recommendation, at least in part. It was willing to go along with a Commandant's List, but not with any finer discrimination.[26]

The Department of the Army already required the War College to submit academic efficiency reports, essentially a narrative of a student's performance during the year and remarks on his potential as demonstrated by his academic work. To arrive at this report a system of feeder reports had evolved whereby those members of the faculty who had closely observed a student during the individual research program, committee work, or seminar discussions provided a narrative input at least four times per year. During the year 1965-66 the feeder report format was revised in a way that allowed numerical scoring, weighting, and totaling, and from the result a class academic order of ranking could be derived. This was only an experiment, but it was considered a successful one, and a tool was now available to produce both a Commandant's list and a Distinguished and Honor Graduate designation if that was to be the decision.[27]

The Deputy Chief of Staff for Personnel supported the War College position that at most there should only be recognition of the top ten or twenty percent of a class. In any event, the only recommendation that reached the Chief of Staff was one that declared written examinations at the War College to be inappropriate; students were to be evaluated on the basis of individual research papers, committee and seminar participation, oral presentations, and frequent faculty observation. General Johnson approved this recommendation as advisory to the Commandant. In other words, no change in existing procedures was directed.[28]

How to provide the Department of the Army an evaluation of the work of a War College student was one of those issues that never seem to be settled to anyone's complete satisfaction. There was broad consensus, but not complete unanimity, that academic grades per se would discourage original and critical thinking. At the same time, however, there was a sense that those officers who made the greater effort and contributed the most should be recognized and rewarded. The War College had gotten into the habit of including remarks such as "definite general officer material," "general officer material," and "potential general officer material" on academic efficiency reports. These were sweeping judgments, but in the Class of 1965 fourteen percent were judged as "definite," fifty-seven percent as general officer material without an adjective, and twenty-five percent as "potential." The remaining four percent apparently had not impressed the War College; their reports were silent as to whether they were or might be general officer material. How much weight promotion boards gave to these remarks cannot be known and undoubtedly varied from board to board, but this kind of judgment could certainly have been perceived by the students as much more threatening than any system of letter or numerical grades. In November 1966 General Salet announced the policy that on feeder reports either the comment "general officer material" would be made or there would be no comment at all pertaining to general officer potential. No variations of the expression or adjectives were allowed. The student evaluation issue was not settled, however. It would return.[29]

Still Another Review

Despite all the review activity that had gone on over the previous two years, in the fall of 1966 General Salet thought that another objective outside review would be useful. He also reversed an earlier recommendation of the Army War College-70 study and directed that measures be taken to form a permanent Board of Visitors. Both of these decisions were made over the objections of his faculty. They felt that academic year 1966-67 was only a transition year and that another review should not occur until all the recommendations of the Haines Board had been put in place, including the elective courses and the extension program.[30]

General Salet was not dissuaded, however, and in February 1967 an eight-man mixed civilian and military consultant group met for three days at Carlisle Barracks. The group included former Secretary of the Army Stephen Ailes and two men who had been consultants to the Army War College-70 study, retired General Bruce C. Clarke and Professor Lawrence I. Radway. It will be recalled that the latter, together with Professor Masland, did the Dartmouth surveys of military education in the 1950s. General Haines was a member of the group, as was Brigadier General Melvin Zais, the Director of Individual Training in the Office of the DCSPER.[31]

The group offered more reassurance than new ideas. Essentially it gave a stamp of approval on the measures underway to put into effect the findings of the studies of the previous two years. The group implied that little had been accomplished to increase the expertise of the faculty. The West Point system of tenure was again discussed, as was the desirability of retaining some faculty members on active duty beyond their mandatory retirement dates. The consultants expressed some concern that with the addition of the electives, student workload might become too great. They warned once again that the requirement for individual work should not be allowed to degrade the exchange between students. General Clarke attempted to convince his colleagues that the program should be structured formally around the problems of raising, training, organizing, equipping, transporting, employing, and maintaining Army forces. His proposal in essence was a version of McAndrew's one great problem of 1919-20. Clarke was unsuccessful; his colleagues had no quarrel with the existing decade-old curricular theme. Professor Radway, however, picked up on the item of raising Army forces. Perhaps more sensitive than the others to the undercurrents on American campuses in 1967, he suspected that there might be serious problems in this area over the next twenty years. He advised the Commandant to give the question "close and substantial attention."[32]

New Root Hall and Other Amenities

When the consultant group visited Carlisle Barracks, the Class of 1967 was in residence in the newly completed academic building. Classes had assembled in the modern facility for the first time after the Christmas break. The building had been under construction for almost two years but represented only the first phase of what was to be a four-phase project. With faculty and student offices, space for the Institute of Advanced Studies, and seminar rooms now provided in the new building, the old converted stables known as Bliss Hall could be razed to make room for the next two projects, a new library below ground level, and a new auditorium. The fourth phase of construction was to be a physical conditioning facility (a gymnasium) to be built at the opposite end of the complex from the auditorium. This last phase had not yet been approved, nor had funds for it been provided. The former Medical Field Service School academic building that General Swing had named Root Hall could be diverted to other purposes as soon as the library and auditorium were completed. The new building was officially dedicated as Root Hall in April. On hand as honored guest and speaker for the ceremony was Major General Ulysses S. Grant, III, retired, son-in-law of Elihu Root and a member of the War College Class of 1934. Seminar rooms within the building were named in honor of senior Army commanders of American wars. The War College graciously named one of the rooms for Nelson A. Miles, the implacable foe of Elihu Root and all his ideas for a general staff.[33]

During his tour as Commandant, General Salet officiated at a number of other dedication ceremonies. Public rooms in the Officers' Club were named for distinguished graduates of the War College representing all four services—Eisenhower, LeJeune, Halsey, Vandenberg, and Pershing (a drop-out of the Class of 1905 but later anointed an honorary member of the Class of 1925). Dedication ceremonies were held for each of these rooms with either a member of the family or a representative of the service present. Former President and Mrs. Eisenhower traveled from their Gettysburg farm to be present at the dedication of the Eisenhower Room and of the General Dwight D. Eisenhower Chair of Strategic Appraisal.

General Salet was also successful in accomplishing what had eluded his predecessors Generals Swing, Almond, and Barnes. He was able to retrieve from the National War College the bronze plaques on which were listed the names of the members of the classes of 1905 through 1940. Vice Admiral Fitzhugh Lee, Commandant of the National War College, returned the plaques—with ceremony—on August 25, 1965.[34] They were then mounted in permanent public display on the exterior walls and pillars of the recently completed Root Hall.

McCaffrey Consolidates

General Salet departed the War College in August 1967, soon after the arrival of the Class of 1968. He was only the second Commandant (the other being Max Johnson) since the reestablishment of the War College in 1950 to have served through three complete academic years. To consolidate the Haines Board recommendations would be the responsibility of the new Commandant, Major General William J. McCaffrey. McCaffrey had been with the War College both as a faculty member and as a student in its earliest days at Carlisle Barracks, from 1951 to 1953. The contrasts between the War College of 1967 and that of those earlier years were striking. A modern, well-designed academic building was in use, and a new library and lecture hall were under construction. Faculty and student housing now approached adequacy, although student families still had to tolerate the limitations in space imposed by the now defunct Wherry Act. And the other amenities provided by the post of Carlisle Barracks had either been improved or expanded.

The academic program General McCaffrey inherited had been recently blessed by the consultant group and reflected the results of a debate of three years' duration, but the curricular theme remained as it had been formally established for the Class of 1958. Despite the persistence of the curricular theme, however, there were indications that the emphasis on international and national security affairs had passed its zenith. The time devoted to these matters had increased incrementally over the years since 1958 to the point that by 1965-66 they constituted fifty-one percent of the program. In 1967-68 the portion was reduced to forty-one percent.[35]

The time made available by that reduction was devoted to a new five-week course labeled "Army Internal Defense and Development Operations," a course which consolidated most of the instruction on counterinsurgency that had been included previously in several courses. (The terms "internal defense" and "internal development" had become the official substitutes for what had first been known as "counterinsurgency" and sometimes as "stability operations.") The Chief of Staff had directed that the subjects be integrated into curricula throughout the Army school system. The subject matter was not to be set aside for unusual emphasis and special courses, but rather treated as a third and normal Army mission along with conventional land warfare and land warfare in a nuclear environment.[36]

Somewhat outside the main curricular theme were the two "horizontally scheduled" seminars. The Military Strategy Seminar scheduled for the fall was a reflection of General Salet's claim that military strategy was the true core of the War College program. The Command and Management Seminar in the spring was expanded from twelve to fourteen sessions but continued to deal with management processes, analytical techniques, information systems, and planning, programming, and budgeting. The Individual Research Program retained its four options, and available topics continued to be confined to the military field.[37]

As directed by the Chief of Staff, the electives program was inaugurated in 1967-68. Three of the courses offered in the fall related broadly to national security affairs, "Social Factors and National Security," "Political Systems and National Security," and "Economics of National Security." Six civilian instructors were employed to teach the three courses, three of them were members of Operations Research Incorporated (ORI), the firm on contract to provide scientific support to the Institute of Advanced Studies. A fourth elective offered in the fall was "International Law and National Security," a course desired by the Judge Advocate General of the Army and for which he provided the officer instructor. A fifth fall elective course was one recommended by the Haines Board, "Communicative Arts." It was offered again in the spring and taught by contract professors.[38]

Except for Communicative Arts, the electives taught in the spring provided additional depth to the topics covered in the Command and Management Seminar. Three courses were provided, "Analytical Techniques of Management," "Military Information Systems," and "Resource Management and Control." The latter two were conducted by military officers of the War College staff and faculty.

The Haines Board had proposed elective courses as a way out of the generalist-specialist dilemma. As the term "specialist" had normally been used in the generalist-specialist debate, the three management courses of the spring were specialist courses. They and the Command and Management Seminar apparently were the War College's acknowledgement of the McNamara revolution in defense management. Interestingly, none of the courses offered as electives in this first year pertained to combat operations of the Army or even to operational planning. It is difficult to conclude that they supported the objective of Army War College-70 and of the Haines Board that called for the War College program to become more oriented on the Army and military subjects.[39]

The student of the Class of 1968 appears to have been busier than his counterparts of the preceding years; at least his time was more rigidly scheduled. During a typical week he was engaged in the study of one of the "vertical" courses of the common curriculum with all the required readings, lectures, committee discussions, and perhaps a case study it involved. He attended one two- to three-hour session of a "horizontal" seminar and another two- to three-hour session of an elective; both required additional preparatory reading and study. In what time remained in the week, he performed research and other tasks leading to the production of a thesis, individual research paper, essay, or case study. The War College program had become formal and highly structured. Whether it yet remained, as General Swing had once insisted, "contemplative in nature" is problematical.

The subject matter of the curriculum had shifted also from Army-oriented problem-solving and war-planning to a study of broader national security affairs. It now also included no small amount of instruction in modern management techniques. The instructional method of problem-solving by small committees of varying complement had given way to standard-sized seminar groups. All students now received essentially the same exposure to the entire curriculum, the only variation provided by a limited number of elective courses.

The experience the student brought to the War College also had changed since the early 1950s. While the average age of the students had remained essentially the same (forty-one and forty-three years), the average length of service had increased from fifteen to twenty years. The percentage of students with graduate degrees had grown from fourteen percent to forty-nine percent. In 1953 only twenty-six percent of the students had served on very high level staffs (JCS, Department of Defense, Department of the Army, major Army command, unified command); by 1966, however, eighty-six percent had performed this duty. One the other hand, those who had held command positions at battalion level or higher had declined slightly from sixty-nine percent to sixty-seven percent.[40]

General McCaffrey's principal task during the two years that he was to serve as Commandant was to implement fully the approved recommendations of the Haines Board. The core of the curriculum did not require major alteration, although for the year 1968-69 the college consolidated the nine courses into seven. A significant innovation of the Haines Board, however, had been the recommendation to introduce elective courses. In 1968-69 the same eight electives that had been offered in 1967-68 were repeated, but War College curriculum planners were working not only to expand the number of elective courses but to better integrate the entire program—the common courses, the elective courses, and the individual research program. Six additional electives were added for the 1969-70 year, although elective course offerings remained limited to the fields of international relations and management.[41]

During General McCaffrey's second and last year as Commandant, he initiated a program called "Elements of Command" a revisit to Secretary Root's third great problem of responsible command. In this program the student, representing the Army's future leadership, was to gain insights into the problems of higher command through interaction with the Army's current leadership. General officers who were holding or had recently held positions of high responsibility were invited to Carlisle Barracks to meet informally with a small group of students (sixteen, one from each student committee). A ninety-minute session was held late in the afternoon, followed by an informal dinner, and then by another hour-and-a-half session in the evening. The guest and the students were encouraged to delve into any subject they thought needed airing and discussion. The relaxed conversations were privileged and therefore unrecorded, but by 1969, the fifth year of U.S. Army troop commitments to Southeast Asia, there were enough problems and uncertainties facing the Army that these discussions could not have failed to enlighten both student and guest. "Elements of Command" became a fixed feature in the War College resident program.[42]

General McCaffrey pursued the scheme of permitting students and faculty members to draw upon the wisdom of men with extensive experience when he revived the idea of using academic chairs to attract distinguished retired officers onto the faculty. In June 1968, when he learned that General Harold K. Johnson, the Chief of Staff, would soon retire from active service, McCaffrey proposed that Johnson spend the next year at Carlisle Barracks, suggesting that the War College could assist him in arranging his papers and in writing, and that in turn General Johnson would be asked to conduct seminars and to make himself available to faculty members and students. An academic chair would be created for him, the General Omar Bradley Chair of Military Strategy, and a set of quarters would be provided. General Johnson responded that he did not believe his presence at Carlisle Barracks would be appropriate. He might be a thorn in the side of the incoming Chief of Staff, and he was not sure that he would have wanted his predecessor as Chief of Staff in the position. However, General Johnson did not completely close the door on the idea.[43]

The next month, independently of General McCaffrey, retired Air Force General C. P. Cabell, a member of the Board of Consultants to the National War College, proposed to the commandants of all the senior service colleges a concept of a "Distinguished Officer in Residence" (Cabell also referred to it as "Warrior in Residence"). Cabell's concept differed from that of McCaffrey only in that he suggested a two-year period in residence.[44]

In August, General Johnson informed McCaffrey that after additional consideration he believed he would be interested in a year's association with the War College, but under the condition that he not be recalled to active duty for the purpose. General McCaffrey then formally recommended the concept to the Department of the Army. In response, the Deputy Chief of Staff for Personnel, General Connor, informed McCaffrey that he had discussed the matter with the new Chief of Staff, General William C. Westmoreland, and the conclusion was that the time was not propitious to implement such an ambitious project. It was an opportunity lost. The War College faculty and the Class of 1969 were not able to experience an attainable close association with the officer who had been the Chief of Staff of the Army throughout the period of the commitment of United States forces to Southeast Asia and one whose military experience had included the campaign on Bataan in 1942 and the early campaigns of the Korean War. The War College subsequently established a General Omar Bradley Chair of Nonresident Instruction for the active-duty chairman of that department.[45]

Nonresident Instruction

The second large effort resulting from the Haines Board recommendations was to establish a nonresident program. The board's primary rationale for what it termed an extension program was to add depth to the educational base of the active Army. The board held that an extension

393

program would increase the value to the Army of the many dedicated officers who failed to be selected for the resident class. That active-Army officers had a high interest in professional education beyond the Leavenworth level was evident. During the previous three years, 643 active-Army officers had enrolled in the correspondence course of the Industrial College, and 405 had graduated. Moreover, the board believed that an extension program would fill a schooling void for officers of the reserve components. At the time the Haines Board was meeting, the resident class of the Army War College included only two reserve component officers. The board's idea, at least initially, was that the War College would offer only selected courses from the resident program and that completion of these courses would not be considered the equivalent to graduation from the resident program. Completion would, however, be recognized by a diploma and be duly noted in the individual's personnel records. Enrollment would be voluntary.[46]

As it invariably had in the past when the idea of an extension program had been broached, the War College opposed the proposal. The War College did not believe that the need for an extension program justified the costs required in additional personnel to prepare, conduct, and administer the program. Nor did it believe that the level and nature of its curriculum lent the program to extension methods. If the proposal was approved, moreover, the War College preferred to conduct seminars at senior Army headquarters worldwide using War College faculty and materials. After failing to dissuade the Haines Board, the War College softened its position. It in effect became neutral, arguing that only the Department of the Army was in a position to determine if an extension program was really necessary. If one was necessary, then the War College must be provided additional faculty and funds. Meanwhile, the War College began to plan the course, appointing in July 1966 Colonel Thomas H. Reese (AWC 1963) as the project officer.[47]

In September the War College informed the Department of the Army that it would need an additional seven officers and eleven civilians to conduct the extension program. The Department of the Army responded to the request with something less than alacrity. The first chairman of the new Department of Nonresident Instruction, Colonel Urey W. Alexander (AWC 1958), was not assigned until July of the next year, 1967. The new department was officially organized the following month. Another year would pass before the department received all its personnel, and another two years before the authorized educational specialist was hired. Nor could space be found for the new department in Root Hall, the main academic building. The department had to take up its work isolated in the old Medical Field Service School building, the former Root Hall now known as Upton Hall.[48]

Basic decisions on the nature of the new program remained to be made, and on this the War College took the initiative. Two alternatives were considered. The Army War College's nonresident program, like the nonresident program of the Industrial College, could be opened to all interested personnel, or it could be made to resemble the resident program, highly competitive and selective. The War College decided upon the latter course of action and successfully persuaded the Department of the Army of its correctness. Basically the War College believed that if any real return was to result from this effort, the program had to be exacting, paralleling the resident program as closely as possible. The image of the Army War College was also of concern. It dictated that nonresident as well as resident students be carefully selected with consideration of their past records and potential service.[49]

During the fall of 1967 the War College and the Deputy Chief of Staff for Personnel reached agreement on a number of aspects of the program. It would be under DCSPER auspices rather than that of CONARC, and it would not be part of the school system of the U.S. Army Reserve. In March 1968 decisions as to eligibility and selection were officially announced. Selection criteria were modified but slightly from that for the resident program. Two more years of eligibility were allowed, up to twenty-five years of service. General officers would be accepted. Officers of services other than the Army would not be accepted, at least initially, until more experience with the program had been gained. Moreover, nonresident students would not incur, as did resident students, any additional service obligation.[50]

The program to be offered would be based on the 1968-69 resident program with its three major fields of study—strategic appraisal, strategy, and military planning—and would require approximately two years to complete. The standard curricular theme of a military program to support a national strategy would be followed, but no elective courses were to be offered. The program would consist of three courses corresponding to the three fields of study, subdivided into sixteen subcourses, each further subdivided into "lessons." Each lesson would require fifty to one hundred pages of reading and study. It was thought that a lesson would require three to seven hours of work and that a student could spare that amount of time each week to devote to the program. All but a few subcourses would require a written submission; a 3,000- to 4,000-word paper would be required at the conclusion of each of the three courses. The program would be progressive; the subcourses and lessons would have to be taken in sequence.[51]

The Haines Board had visualized phases of the program being accomplished in residence at Carlisle Barracks. It was thought that resident phases would both increase motivation and strengthen the curricular theme. Resident phases would also permit committee work, lectures, and access to the War College library and to classified material. Finally, resident phases would provide opportunities for the faculty to observe and evaluate the students. Since the resident phases would be the most expensive part of the program and have the greatest effect on the routine of the War College, many at the War College doubted that they would in fact be worth the costs. Although two resident phases were planned, one in the summer at the end of each year's work, the first resident phase held in the summer of 1969 was viewed as strictly an experiment. After that first resident phase a determination would be made whether to have a second, and in the case of future classes, whether to have resident phases at all. Despite the active planning and work that had gone into constructing the nonresident program, the War College retained serious doubts as to whether a nonresident program was really desirable or feasible. The primary concern was that somehow the new program might degrade the resident program.[52]

A problem foreseen clearly by the planners of the nonresident program involved the evaluation of the students' written responses. Any idea of "objective" examinations of a multiple choice or other variety had been rejected early as inappropriate to War College level work. Devising statements of requirements to be placed on the students therefore became a critical task. On the advice of HumRRO, the War College asked the Education Testing Service of Princeton, N.J., to assist. The college contracted with the Education Testing Service to review nonresident material to insure that the key issues and arguments that the War College wanted to impart were brought out in the material and responded to by the students.[53]

Subjective evaluation of student responses of course also required a faculty with a comprehensive understanding of the subject matter. Colonel Reese had initially recommended a Department of Nonresident Instruction that would have been responsible only for coordinating and administering the program, with the three established academic departments selecting and preparing the substantive material and evaluating student work. Reese therefore recommended additional personnel be assigned to each department. This scheme of organization was rejected, however, apparently because of the concern that the resident program might thereby be degraded and because of the tentative status of the nonresident program. The Department of Nonresident Instruction was therefore established not just as an administrative, coordinating agency but also as a teaching department, preparing all course material and evaluating student responses.[54]

This structure may have been a wise choice in the short term. It undoubtedly made for more efficient administration, particularly in the critical early stages. Maintaining this organization over the long term had unfortunate results, however. Although college policy stated that the established academic departments were to provide support to the

Department of Nonresident Instruction, they had no real responsibility for the new program and took secondary interest in it except during the summer resident sessions when they were required to provide faculty advisers to student committees. Thus two War College faculties began to evolve, the traditional faculty oriented on the resident class, and the faculty of the Department of Nonresident Instruction oriented on the nonresident class. Hard-to-obtain faculty expertise in essence had to be duplicated. The nonresident class may have suffered by not having greater contact with the specialists on the resident program faculty, but the greater loss was probably to the older departments themselves. They were denied the discipline of having to produce a complete course of instruction without the crutch of guest lecturers and group discussion, and they were deprived of interaction with classes whose members soon proved to include experienced and competent talent in fields of importance to the War College.[55]

The first nonresident class, the Class of 1970, began its work in September 1968 with two hundred officers, half selected from among active-duty applicants and half from among those of the reserve components. Three separate Department of the Army boards, one for the active Army, one for the Army Reserve (USAR), and one for the National Guard, made the selections. Of 229 active-Army officers applying, one hundred were selected; of 219 USAR officers, eighty-three were selected; and of forty-nine National Guard officers, seventeen were selected. Attrition had been expected, but it proved to be much higher than any but the most pessimistic had forecast. By the end of the first year, twenty-seven percent of the active Army students, fifty-three percent of the National Guard students, and eleven percent of the USAR students had been disenrolled.[56]

Disenrollment most frequently took the form of voluntary withdrawal by students who had fallen behind in submitting responses to requirements. Few disenrollments were involuntary due to inadequate responses. The basic cause of the inability to stay current was that a student's involvement in this program was an activity added to his normal work. The War College program had to be completed during what otherwise would have been leisure time. For officers on active service, the program was in addition to a primary duty. In the case of officers of the reserve components, it was in addition to civilian professional or business pursuits. National Guard officers and officers of the USAR with troop unit assignments faced a particularly difficult problem: Their War College work was added not only to their civilian obligations but also to their obligations toward their military units. Recognizing these difficulties, the Department of the Army adopted a liberal deferment policy, that is, a policy of allowing a student to drop back to the next class when official duties, transfers, or unusual personal circumstances made

397

it evident that he would be unable to stay current.[57]

The program was in fact demanding. Those students who might have expected objective examinations that characterized the extension courses of the Industrial College and of some of the lower-level Army schools found the repeated requirements for analytical and expository writing much more exacting. Some officers apparently did not have either the educational or practical experience to meet these demands easily or well. Rewards for completing the program also varied. Officers of the active Army were suspicious that despite all their work they would receive little recognition for it in future assignments or promotions. Some National Guard officers did not feel that the level of the War College program was truly pertinent to their situation. The highest organizational level of the National Guard was the division, and that level they had already studied in the Leavenworth courses. Officers of the USAR probably had the greatest motivation. With troop unit assignments scarce and difficult to obtain, completion of the War College program provided a means of earning retirement points. Moreover, graduation from the War College would probably be seen as an advantage in the competition for the more desirable mobilization designee positions.[58]

Attrition in the second year of the program understandably was lighter. Most of those who could not or would not do the work had already withdrawn. At the graduation of the first class in July 1970, of the two hundred who had begun the program almost two years before, 122 received diplomas—fifty-two from the active Army, sixty-two from the USAR, and eight from the National Guard. Included in the class were one major general and two brigadier generals. That first class deserves much credit for changing the attitude of both the War College and the Department of the Army toward the nonresident program. Much less homogeneous than a resident class, the first summer session in residence had proven to be a stimulating experience for both the class and the faculty. The mixture of active Army and reserve component officers and the increased understanding thereby gained among the three components was a benefit that had been underestimated. Doubts as to the value of the resident phases were forgotten.[59]

Through the nonresident program the War College had increased its total annual production by fifty-four percent and its annual production of active-Army graduates by twenty-eight percent. Of more significance to the Army, however, was that for the first time since its initial class entered in 1904, the War College was offering an equivalent program to an appreciable number of the non-active-duty members of the officer corps. Yet, whether the nonresident program was to be considered the equivalent of the resident program remained an issue. Neither the Department of the Army nor the War College had begun the new program believing or officially recognizing that it was truly equivalent. The War

College, in fact, was prone to wash its hands of that question, holding that equivalency was a Department of the Army problem.[60]

The introduction of elective courses into the resident program in 1967-68 and the initiation of the first nonresident program in September 1968 met the two principal and direct charges to the Army War College posed by the approved recommendations of the Haines Board. It might appear that with these two actions the War College had accommodated to the Haines group's benchmark effort. But such a judgment would be premature. In fact the implications of the Haines Board were more fundamental, and the immediate actions resulting from its findings were to prove only a prelude to even deeper questioning of past practices in the development of the Army's senior leadership.

NOTES

1. AWC Circular 614-2, 12 May 1965, File 201-45.
2. AWC, "Command and Management Seminar," 7 September 1965.
3. Bussey to Commandant, 6 August 1964, Subject: Committee for Strategic Analysis Publications, File 1003-01. Nels A. Parson, ed., *The Future Profile of United States Military Strategy*, 4 vols., July 1965, File 1003-08. Fergusson to DIR, 30 March 1965, Subject: The Study: "Military Strategy and National Objectives," File 205-06. Salet to Harold K. Johnson, 20 July 1964, Ibid.
4. AWC Memorandum 310-1, 29 March 1965, USAWC Occasional Papers, File 205-01. DIR to Commandant, 1 November 1965, Subject: USAWC Occasional Papers, File 205-03. Adams to Salet, 6 October 1965, Ibid. Adams to Haines, 20 July 1965, Ibid.
5. AWC Memorandum 310-3, 10 August 1966, *U.S. Army War College Commentary*, File 201-45. DIR to Commandant, 31 May 1966, Subject: Official Recognition of the *USAWC Commentary*, File 205-03. Keith L. Ware to Salet, 19 May 1966, Ibid.
6. Chester M. Freudendorf to Information Officer, USAWC, April 1966, File 1003-12. AWC Memorandum 310-2, 16 April 1965, USAWC Research and Writing Program, File 205-01. DIR to Commandant, 1 December 1966, Subject: Publication by 1966 War College Class and Faculty, File 205-22. AWC Memorandum 621-1, 24 March 1965, Faculty Participation in Professional Associations or Societies, File 205-01.
7. Salet to Harrell, 11 May 1965, File 201-45. West to Salet, 8 June 1965, Ibid. Michael S. Davison to Salet, 21 July 1965, Ibid.
8. Salet to DCSPER, 27 May 1966, Subject: Branch Identification, Faculty, USAWC, File 716-03. J. K. Woolnough to Salet, 30 June 1966, Ibid. AWC Memorandum 670-1, 14 November 1966, Faculty Identification Badge, File 201-45.
9. AWC Memorandum 600-2, 15 September 1966, Reorganization of USAWC Faculty, File 201-45. Minutes of the Second Meeting, AY67, of the Curriculum Board, 3 and 6 August 1966, 9 August 1966, File 1003-03. Salet to Deputy Commandant, 23 August 1966, Subject: Haines Board Recommendations and AWC-70 Projects, File 1003-03.
10. Smith, Memorandum, 6 September 1966, Subject: Haines Board and "USAWC 70" Projects, File 1003-03. AWC, Talking Papers for 1965, Tab K, File 203-03. Salet to ACSFOR, 15 March 1965, Tab E. *AWC Positions*, p. 297. *Haines Board*, p. 83. Department of the Army Letter, 20 July 1966, 4, 16. Katzenbach, "Demotion of Professionalism."
11. Department of the Army Letter, 20 July 1966, 4. Smith, Memo., 6 September 1960, Tab D.
12. Department of the Army Letter, 20 July 1966, 4. *Haines Board*, 83. DIR to Deputy Commandant, 19 September 1966, Subject: Periodic Instruction of Faculty, File 1003-03.
13. *AWC Positions*, 104. Department of the Army Letter, 20 July 1966, 16. Letters in File 1003-08. DIR to Deputy Commandant, 29 November 1966, Subject: Educational Advisor, File 1003-03.

14. *Haines Board*, 76. AWC, *Curriculum Pamphlet*, 1 July 1966. AWC, "Directive, Command and Management Seminar," 18 January 1967.
15. AWC, *Curriculum Pamphlet*, 1 July 1966. AWC, "Directive, Comparative Military Strategy Seminar," 22 August 1966. AWC, Notebook for Seminar on Comparative Military Strategy (Record Copy), 1966, File 1003-08.1.
16. Salet to Deputy Commandant, 23 August 1966. DIR to Directors, 16 March 1966, Subject: Bliss Hall Initial Distribution and Impulse Reading for AY1967, File 205-22. Secretary to Commandant, 22 August 1966, Subject: Reading Improvement Program, File 1003-03.
17. AWC Circular 350-28, 28 September 1964, File 205-02. AWC, *Analysis Seminar Control Manual*, 18 February 1965, File 1415-06. AWC Talking Papers for 1965, Tab U. File 1003-12 (1966). Enthoven to Salet, 15 February 1965, File: USAWC-70. DA Letter, 20 July 1966, 4.
18. AWC, Instructional bulletin 9, 13 January 1966, Use of Case Studies, File 1003-03. DIR to Deputy Commandant, 21 October 1966, Subject: Use of Case Studies AY67, Ibid. DIR to Deputy Commandant, 30 November 1966, Subject: Case Studies AY68, Ibid.
19. AWC, "Directive, Individual Research Program, 12 August 1966. Smith, Memo, 6 September 1966.
20. Department of the Army General Order 37, 16 November 1965. T. J. Conway to Salet, 19 November 1965, File 201-45. Woolnough to Commandant, 13 May 1966, 1st Indorsement to Salet to DCSPER, 19 February 1966, Subject: USAWC Curriculum Academic Year 1967, File 1003-03.
21. Smith, Memo., 6 September 1966. Smith, Memorandum, 23 August 1966, Subject: Class Trips, AYs 68 and 69, File 1003-03. DIR to Chairman, Joint Advisory Group, 12 October 1966, Subject: Field Trips, File 1001-19. CG, Military Traffic Management and Terminal Service, to Salet, 29 August 1966, File 716-03. AWC Circular 621-31, 22 September 1966, Administrative Instructions for 1966 UN Trip, Ibid.
22. AWC, Talking Papers for 1964, Tab G, File 203-03.
23. AWC, Talking Papers for 1965, Tab H, File 203-03. President, Naval War College, 2 June 1965, Subject: MECC Report: Review and Approval, File 203-03.
24. AWC, Talking Papers for 1965, Tab H. Salet to Schomberg, 8 July 1965, File 205-03. *Haines Board*, 77. Salet to Harrell, 15 March 1966.
25. AWC Information Office, News Release, 25 March 1966, File 260-27. Salet, Commandant's Welcoming Remarks to Class of 1967, 8 August 1966, File 205-03. *AWC Positions*, 242. McCutcheon for Commandant, n.d. [November 1965], Subject: Position Paper for the Interim MECC Discussion on the GWU Program, 10 December 1965, File 203-03. DCSPER, Message, 25 January 1966, Subject: George Washington University Graduate Study Program at the U.S. Army War College.
26. *Haines Board*, 84. Salet to DCSPER, 13 April 1966, 1st Ind. to DCSPER to Commandant, 22 March 1966, Subject: Report of the Department of the Army Board to Review Army Officer Schools, File 1003-16.
27. AR 623-106, Personnel Efficiency Ratings - Academic Reports, 26 February 1967. AWC, Talking Papers for 1964, Tab D. File 203-03. Secretary to Deputy Commandant, 3 October 1966, Subject: Haines Board Recommendations, File 1003-03.
28. Zais to Salet, 30 September 1966, File 205-03. Department of the Army Letter, 20 July 1966, 17.
29. Chairman, Curriculum Board to Commandant, 9 December 1965, Subject: Distinguished Graduate Program, File 1003-03. AWC Memorandum 623-1, 25 November 1966, Subject: Personnel Efficiency Ratings, File 704-03.
30. Salet to Deputy Commandant, 23 August 1966. Chairman, Curriculum Board to Deputy Commandant, 24 October 1966, Subject: Review of Curriculum, USAWC, File 228-08. Deputy Commandant to Curriculum Board, 4 November 1966, Subject: College Consultants, Ibid.
31. Deputy Commandant to Commandant, 9 December 1966, Subject: USAWC Consultants and Board of Visitors, Ibid. Salet to DCSPER 9 March 1967, Subject: Report of Consultant Group, U.S. Army War College, 1967, Ibid. Other members of the consultant group were Howard L. Rubendall, Dickinson College; Ralph L. Powell, American

University; and Brigadier General John R. Jannarone, USMA.
32. Ibid. Radway to Salet, 22 February 1967, File 208-08.
33. AWC, Memorandum for All Students, 15 December 1966, Subject: Move to Academic Buildings, File 1503-01. USAWC Pamphlet, "Dedication of Root Hall, Saturday, April 29, 1967, File 201-45. Train to Beach, 31 January 1964, File 205-02. AWC, Proposed Talking Paper on USAWC for Use in Discussion with General H. K. Johnson, 19 January 1965, File: USAWC-70.
34. Acting Deputy Commandant to Information Officer, 21 March 1966, Subject: Naming Various Public Rooms at CBOOM, File 1503-01. AWC, Memorandum for All Student Officers, USAWC Class of 1967, 24 August 1966, Subject: Eisenhower Dedication, File 403-02. Salet to Lee, 12 August 1965, File 205-03.
35. AWC, *Curriculum Pamphlet Academic Year 1968*, 1 July 1967. AWC, Minutes of the 10th Meeting of the Curriculum Board, 28 November 1965, 2 December 1966, File 1003-03. AWC, *Curriculum Pamphlet Academic Year 1966*, 1 July 1965.
36. AWC, Directive Course 5: Internal Defense and Development Operations (Stability Operations), 16 December 1967. AWC, Memorandum for Record, Curriculum for 1967, 13 February 1966, File 1003-03. DCSPER to Commandant, 22 November 1966, Subject: Department of the Army Board to Review Army Schools, File 1003-16.
37. AWC, Directive: Military Strategy Seminar, 21 August 1967. Salet, Commandant's Welcoming Remarks to the Class of 1967, August 1966, File 205-03. AWC, Directive: Command and Management Seminar, 20 March 1967. AWC, Directive: Command and Management Seminar, 22 January 1968. AWC, Directive: Individual Research Program, 14 August 1967.
38. AWC, *Curriculum Pamphlet 1968. Haines Board*, 489-90, 494, 801. AWC, Directive: International Law and National Security Elective, 24 January 1968.
39. AWC, *Curriculum Pamphlet 1968*.
40. Figures compare Class of 1953 with that of 1966. AWC, *Positions*, 162, 273-74.
41. AWC, *Curriculum Pamphlet Academic Year 1969 (Resident)*, 1 July 1968. Deputy Commandant to Chairman, Department of Research and Studies, 26 August 1968, Subject: Study of Electives Program, File: Course Correspondence 1969. Deputy Commandant to Director of Instruction, 13 December 1968, Subject: Electives Program, AY 70, Ibid. AWC, *Curriculum Pamphlet 1970 (Resident)*, 1 July 1969.
42. Director of Instruction to Curriculum Board, 11 June 1970, Subject: Final Report on 1970 Elements of Command Discussion Series, Curricular Materials Files, 1970.
43. McCaffrey to H. K. Johnson, 3 June 1968, Cooling Material, MHI Collection. Johnson to McCaffrey, 26 June 1968, Ibid.
44. C. P. Cabell to McCaffrey, 17 June 1968, Ibid.
45. Summary of Telephone Conversation, McCaffrey-Johnson, 8 August 1968, Ibid. McCaffrey to Connor, 10 August 1968, Ibid. McCaffrey to Johnson, 19 September 1968, Ibid.
46. *Haines Board*, 494-95, 536, 538, 540.
47. Director of Instruction and Research to Cmdt., 22 December 1965, Subject: Title for USAWC Class. File 204-58. AWC, *Positions*, 427-28. Salet to DCSPER, 13 April 1966. DIR to Reese, 18 April 1966, Subject: Planning for N-RI at USAWC, File 1003-26/ NRI.
48. AWC, Briefing, U.S. Army War College Correspondence Course, 15 July 1968, 3, File: Non-Resident. Interview with Albert P. Holmberg, 11 December 1981. Holmberg has served as educational specialist on nonresident instruction from August 1969 to the present.
49. Briefing, Correspondence Course, 4-5.
50. Ibid., 7-8. McCaffrey to DCSPER, 11 December 1967, Subject: U.S. Army War College Correspondence Course, File: 1002-02. Department of the Army Circular 350-63, 28 March 1968.
51. Briefing, Correspondence Course, 5, 13, 19. AWC, *Curriculum Pamphlet Academic Years 1969 and 1970 (Nonresident)*, 1 July 1968.
52. *Haines Board*, 528, 534. Briefing, Correspondence Course, 17, 21-22, 31. Holmberg interview.
53. Briefing, Correspondence Course, 17-19.

54. Reese to Deputy Commandant, 31 October 1966, Subject: Status Report Relative to USAWC Nonresident Instruction, Tab C, File: Nonresident. Ibid., Tab D. Briefing, Correspondence Course, 18. Holmberg interview.
55. Briefing, Correspondence Course, 12. AWC, Policy Statement of Deputy Commandant, 13 July 1967, cited in Ibid., 28.
56. Ahern to Deputy Commandant, 12 September 1969, Subject: Expansion of NRI Course, Tab A, File: 1003-11.
57. Holmberg interview. Briefing, Correspondence Course, 11.
58. Ibid. Holmberg interview.
59. Ibid. USAWC, Pamphlet, "Nonresident Course - Graduation, 2 July 1970."
60. Briefing, Correspondence Course, 10.

The Change in Theme
1967-1971

In the early 1960s, with the New Look a memory and its companion piece, the strategy of massive retaliation, discredited, the officer corps of the United States Army regained confidence and sense of place despite its difficulties in adjusting to Secretary McNamara's scientific methods of management. The struggle for adjustment was evident at Carlisle Barracks throughout the 1960s as the War College attempted to resolve the questions posed by Tasker Bliss so long ago—what should be taught and to whom and how many. By the late 1960s and early 1970s, however, the war in Southeast Asia, to which the Army was the nation's largest institutional contributor, was creating another crisis in confidence. The question of what should be taught, fleetingly believed to have been settled by General Haines and his colleagues, reappeared in more critical form. In the process of resolving this most basic issue, the War College was to abandon the curricular theme that had guided its academic program for a decade and a half.

An Attempt at Expansion
In 1958 the Williams Board, when addressing the question of the adequacy of the annual production of graduates by the Army War College, had relied upon a stated requirement by the Army to have 1,558 senior service college graduates on active duty. This figure had been derived by the DCSPER in 1954. But in 1965, at a time when there were 3,718 senior service college graduates on active duty, the DCSPER increased the figure to 5,050. The Haines Board report pointed out the difficulties in determining this kind of stockage objective and implied that the figure of 5,050 was not substantiated. The figure included twenty percent of the colonels of the professional and administrative services, all the colonels of the other branches, and an arbitrary figure of 560 lieutenant colonels.[1]

Haines therefore recommended that "no fixed stockage figure be established" but that the current output of the senior service colleges be maintained. As Haines saw it, the purpose of the War College was to "foster excellence of a few, rather than raise the average of all." His solution may have been both reasonable and practical, but in an era of quantitative analysis it would not stand up to the argument of those who viewed the War College as an expensive enterprise that should have a finite quantitative goal as well as qualitative objectives. Chief of Staff Johnson withheld his decision on this recommendation, asking the DCSPER to reevaluate the stockage question.[2]

The DCSPER completed his reevaluation in 1967 and produced the figure of 2,882 as a reasonable stockage objective. Working from this figure, and assuming there would be no increase in production by the joint or other senior service colleges, the DCSPER computed that the Army War College needed to expand so that it could graduate 312 officers per year rather than the current 205. The War College was then asked to determine its capability for expansion.[3]

The War College responded that the size of the resident class could be increased to 255 without major additions to the academic plant. Facilities would be crowded, however, and housing on post would not be available for the fifty additional students. Moreover, the faculty would have to be increased by nine and the support staff by ten. Root Hall, the new academic building, had been designed so that a fourth floor could be added, and if this were done then the academic facilities could accommodate a class of 350. To reach the inventory objective of 2,882, a catch-up period of five or ten years would be necessary, during which the size of the class would be larger than that required merely to sustain the inventory. The War College proposed a construction program that would provide for the addition to Root Hall and additional family housing, suggesting that funds for the required construction should be included in the fiscal year 1970 construction appropriation. In the meantime, the resident class for 1968-69 should be increased by nineteen, from 205 to 224, thereby making full use of Root Hall.[4]

The Department of the Army agreed to the War College's plan. It directed that the Class of 1969 be increased by eighteen Army officers and by a third representative from the Department of State. It authorized the faculty to be increased by five officers. The Department of the Army, CONARC, and CDC all agreed on the desirability of adding the fourth floor to Root Hall and assumed that the additional space could be made available for the Class of 1973. The Department of the Army contemplated a more gradual catch-up period of fifteen years.[5]

Construction of additional family housing, in the view of the War College, would require obtaining additional land. Coveted were eighty-four acres of a 180-acre tract owned by Cumberland County. Most of this 180-acre tract was being leased out for farming, but also located there was the county home for the elderly. In June 1968 the War College presented its plan to the county commissioners and shortly thereafter made the plans public. Some members of the community objected. They pointed out that as late as 1961 the War College had given up land that would have met the requirement, land now being used by Dickinson College for athletic fields. Some citizens also expressed great concern for the peace and quiet enjoyed by the residents of the county home. The local resistance and Department of the Army priorities delayed submission of the construction projects until fiscal year 1971. The War College argued that construction of additional family housing was not entirely dependent on an enlarged class; it held that a hundred more sets of quarters were needed whether the student body expanded or not.[6]

In June 1969, his interest raised during a visit to the War College, General Bruce Palmer, Vice Chief of Staff and former Deputy Commandant, asked for a comprehensive briefing on the previously approved expansion plans. Present at the briefing were most of the principals of the Army Staff. No one was enthusiastic about going ahead with expansion. The staff had little confidence in the DCSPER stockage figures derived two years earlier. Moreover they expected that the Army was about to enter a period of contraction as the Southeast Asia war wound down and the so-called Nixon Doctrine of reliance on the indigenous manpower of allies took effect. After the meeting the DCSPER, Lieutenant General Albert O. Connor (AWC 1952), informed the Army Staff and the War College that he would not pursue expansion. He would, however, continue the attempt to gain Department of Defense approval for additional family housing. The War College included a project for fifty sets of quarters in the program for fiscal year 1971. But the Office of the Secretary of Defense disapproved, arguing that plans for expansion had been deferred and, moreover, that the unit cost of the proposed construction was too high. The Department of the Army accepted the disapproval.[7]

With plans for near-term expansion of the resident class of the War College in effect dead, attention turned to expansion of the nonresident class as an alternative, a course of action that would require construction of neither housing nor academic facilities. In November 1969 Major General George S. Eckhardt, who had replaced General McCaffrey in July, recommended that the active Army quota for each nonresident class be increased from 100 to 124, beginning with the class that would enter in the summer of 1970. The DCSPER, by then Lieutenant General Walter Kerwin (AWC 1957), felt that the increase should be held in abeyance "until we see a marked improvement in the number and quality of applicants" from the active Army for the nonresident program. Kerwin had a point; only 316 applications had been received in 1969, and of those qualified, fifty percent had been selected. This compared to a selection rate of only five percent for the resident class.[8]

The conference of June 1969 at which General Palmer decided not to push for expansion of the War College proved to be of long-term significance to the college. The decision reflected immediate and highly practical concerns. The officers who were involved in the decision anticipated another historical reduction of the Army after a period of active campaigning. They were concerned over a smaller Army's ability to support an expanded War College with the increases required in faculty, staff, student body, and budget. They were also concerned over the reaction of their civilian superiors to proposals for an expanded institution when an unquestioned need for more War College graduates could not be demonstrated. But the effect of the decision on the Army's educational system was more far-reaching and more fundamental. The Army War College would remain dedicated, as General Haines had put it, to fostering "excellence of a few."

Yet increasing the output of the War College was another issue that would not go away. It rose again when General Eckhardt revived an idea that had last been studied by General Salet's staff—offering a program for foreign officers. Eckhardt proposed that a nonresident course for allied officers be initiated in academic year 1971-72. General Kerwin, however, did not favor the idea. He reasoned that any available resources should be applied to reducing the shortfall of graduates on duty in the United States Army. He also questioned whether a program centered on United States foreign policy was really appropriate for foreign officers.[9]

The disapproval of the foreign officer proposal redirected attention to the need to increase the number of American graduates. Colonel Richard L. Morton (AWC 1966) of the faculty was assigned the perhaps impossible task of determining how the student body might be enlarged without any expansion of existing facilities or additional resources. Morton concluded that under these guidelines only a modest increase was possible. The most stringent limitation to increasing the size of the resident class remained the shortage in family housing. In academic year 1969-70, sixty-one students were living off post, and although Carlisle Barracks had requested construction of more housing in fiscal year 1972, there was no assurance that funds for that would be forthcoming. The housing shortage might be further aggravated because the War College was considering reestablishing a cooperative graduate degree program, and thus portions of the resident classes would overlap during the summers as officers began or completed work on their degrees. Morton considered the alternative of enlarging the nonresident classes, but he pointed out that the Department of the Army had not yet "committed itself to what degree of academic comparability it will assign" to the War College's nonresident instruction.[10]

Based on Colonel Morton's study, General Eckhardt recommended increasing each resident class by sixteen students and, for the second time, recommended expanding each nonresident class from 200 to 224. He also asked the Department of the Army to support the fiscal year 1972 request for more family housing at Carlisle Barracks. But the Vice Chief of Staff would not approve an increase in the size of the resident class. Because of declining Army strength, the number of senior service college graduates that the Army needed on active duty was again under study. Moreover, it was General Palmer's opinion that student officers who did not live on post contributed too little to the overall War College experience. He also disliked the practice of student officers commuting to Carlisle Barracks from homes in the Washington area, the so-called "road-runners." This time, however, Eckhardt did win approval for increasing the size of the nonresident class. General Kerwin also promised his support of the program for additional housing. Eckhardt assured Kerwin in turn that a hundred sets of quarters could be sited at Carlisle Barracks without purchasing additional land.[11]

The Institute of Advanced Studies

Another issue between the War College and the Department of the Army, second only to that of expansion and increased production, involved the Institute of Advanced Studies (IAS). In question was its relationship to the War College and the relationship of the War College to the Institute's superior headquarters, the Combat Developments Command. The Army War College-70 study had highlighted this issue for General Salet in assessing how the work of the Institute might be better integrated with that of the War College.

Salet may have also considered the warning of Generals Gar Davidson and Art Trudeau that separating the teaching of doctrine from its development was a poor idea, but of more immediate concern was how the War College could make better use of the Institute's people, including those of the ORI scientific support group. The Commandant wanted the Institute to participate more actively in the teaching, writing, and publishing activities of the college. When Salet challenged the Institute on this point, it responded that since 1963, at the instigation of General Train, it had provided faculty advisers for Course 3, "Strategic Threat of Communist Powers," and had developed and was still responsible for conducting Course 7, "Long Range Strategic Study." In regard to Course 7 the Institute might better have remained silent. A student panel of the Class of 1966 appointed at the close of the academic year to comment on the curriculum had found Course 7 to be something less than satisfactory.[12]

The Institute pointed out accurately that it was deeply involved in the CDC program. The combat developments process had become very formal, consisting of sequential steps beginning with concept studies from which flowed doctrinal and derivative studies. This formal process led eventually to the production of doctrinal field manuals, tables of organization, and statements of qualitative materiel requirements. The role of the Institute of Advanced Studies in the process was primarily, but not exclusively, to develop concept studies looking twenty years into the future. In 1966 it was working on a concept study, "Army 85," and a doctrinal study, "Theater Army 75." At the same time, however, the Department of the Army and Headquarters, Combat Developments Command, were becoming increasingly dissatisfied with the ability of the process to provide definitive guidance to the Army's program for materiel research and development.[13]

In April 1967, in an attempt to strengthen CDC's capability, the Department of the Army authorized a new element, the Institute of Land Combat, to be established elsewhere within CDC. Its mission was to produce a comprehensive concept study—"Land Combat Systems Study, 1990." The Institute of Land Combat was to work closely with two other new agencies, the Threat Forecast Group of the Office of the Assistant Chief of Staff for Intelligence, and the Advanced Materiel Concepts Laboratory of the Army Materiel Command. The combined efforts of this triad were to result in a conceptual Army force structure for the 1990s, a "Land Combat System, 1990" or LCS-90. To produce LCS-90 would require a massive effort, sustained for years, using the most advanced analytical techniques and computer-assisted land warfare simulations. In scope and sophistication it was an effort far beyond the limited resources of the Institute of Advanced Studies at Carlisle Barracks, which did not even own a computer. Moreover, the Institute of Land Combat would be led by a major general with no competing duties, responsible exclusively to the commanding general of CDC.[14]

The creation of the Institute of Land Combat, which at its zenith would be manned by a force of over two hundred, removed from the Institute of Advanced Studies one of the major reasons for its existence, the conduct of long-range conceptual combat developments studies. What remained for the Institute of Advanced Studies appeared to be the conduct of strategic studies. Essentially, the Institute of Advanced Studies had become an agency looking for a mission—and a staff sponsor. Several years earlier, in 1964, a Department of the Army "study of studies" had suggested placing the IAS under the DCSOPS, but in the interim a new element had been created on the Army Staff known as the Office of the Assistant Vice Chief of Staff. In February 1967 this new staff element was charged with the responsibility for longer-range studies. General Salet therefore recommended to General Ben Harrell, at that time the commanding general of the Combat Developments Command, that the Institute of Advanced Studies be detached from the

Combat Developments Command and placed directly under the Assistant Vice Chief of Staff.[15]

General Salet's recommendation was not acted upon; instead, in November 1967 the Chief of Staff directed a special study to reexamine the role of the Institute of Advanced Studies. By that time General Salet had been replaced by General McCaffrey, and General Harrell by General Harry W. O. Kinnard (AWC 1956). General McCaffrey saw correctly that a change in the mission of the Institute of Advanced Studies was inevitable. He recommended to Kinnard that the IAS concentrate its efforts on long-range strategic studies that would provide policy guidance to the more detailed concept studies being produced by the Institute of Land Combat.[16]

General Kinnard visualized the role of the Institute of Advanced Studies differently. In his view the IAS should be used to examine critical areas isolated by the various concept studies. Besides, the IAS had at least three years of work remaining to develop Army 85 conceptual objectives. After that the IAS should concentrate on derivative or follow-on studies that expanded upon the LCS-90 concepts as they pertained to operational echelons above, and perhaps including, the field army. Clearly, in Kinnard's scheme, the IAS would no longer be the lead horse of the CDC team. Moreover, Kinnard believed, as had Haines, that the whole arrangement would be smoother if the War College and the Command and General Staff College were placed under the command of CDC. This would help solve the problem created by the separation of the development of doctrine from the teaching of doctrine. There was a scent of the old gap-filler philosophy in Kinnard's proposal; teaching tactical doctrine had not been and was not currently what the War College was about. General McCaffrey was no more enthusiastic about the proposal than had been General Salet.[17]

As for the Institute of Advanced Studies, it would of course have to continue those tasks assigned it by the commanding general of CDC, but a more prestigious, or at least more visible, future appeared to rest with the surviving element of its truncated mission, the conduct of strategic studies. A demonstrated capability in this field would not only make the institute a more valued partner to the Army War College but also might appeal to the strategist of the Army Staff, the Deputy Chief of Staff for Operations. So the Institute began to incline in that direction.

The issue persisted, however, as the Combat Developments Command continued to evaluate its overall organization. Near the closing months of General Eckhardt's term, CDC reached the decision that the Institute of Advanced Studies and the Institute of Land Combat should be merged, although how this was to be done and where the combined agency was to be located was not yet worked out. In the meantime, a growing percentage of the effort of the Institute of Advanced Studies was originating with the Army Staff and involving questions of strategic options and the Army's contribution in a spectrum of conflict ranging from very low intensity to nuclear operations.[18]

Professionalism, Leadership, and Army Tasks

If the status and future role of the Institute of Advanced Studies remained uncertain when General Eckhardt took command at the War College, all indications were that the Army War College itself would enjoy a period of stability. By the summer of 1969 many of the activist and centralizing civilian managers who in the early 1960s had promised revolutions in strategy and in the ways of military management had departed the Pentagon somewhat confused by the results of their efforts. Behind McNamara's desk now sat former Congressman Melvin Laird, a consummate politician with a much firmer grasp of political and bureaucratic realities. The sense of the administration that Laird represented was simply that the economic, the social, and especially the political costs of continuing to pursue United States objectives in Southeast Asia with American troops were much too high. The battles in Southeast Asia with American troops were far from over, but President Nixon had promised withdrawal and withdrawal had begun. Laird sought respite, not reform.[19]

At the War College the innovations that had begun in 1964 with General Salet's Army War College-70 project and had continued for the next five years through the implementation of the Haines Board recommendations had run their course, being either accommodated or discarded. Eckhardt appeared to face little unfinished business. At Department of the Army, attention was increasingly being directed from the conduct of the war in Southeast Asia to the rebuilding of a postwar Army. The Army's senior leaders had experienced similar situations earlier in their service—after World War II and after Korea. But the rebuilding this time would prove to be of different scope and of greater difficulty. The five years of war in Southeast Asia, still continuing, had taken from the Army a toll that only the most pessimistic had suspected. The Vietnam War would rob the War College of the stability expected and launch it into three consecutive years of consuming investigative effort.[20]

Truly objective political, military, and social histories of what is called the Vietnam era are probably several generations in the future. It is ventured here nonetheless that future historians will conclude that the American Army was simply not prepared, organizationally or intellectually, for protracted warfare. Despite the Army's embracing of limited war theory in the late 1950s, that theory had not been thought through, at the War College or elsewhere, to the point of understanding that inherent in limited war is a high probability of protracted war. Protracted war in turn places the highest premium not on raising, training, and deploying an army, but in the broadest sense on sustaining it. Manpower and personnel policies, and leadership practices, need to be peculiarly designed to hold up over an extended period.

Future historians will find that the appropriate design did not exist when American troops were sent in strength into Vietnam beginning in 1965. Compounded by the political decision not to make available the manpower or unit assets of the reserve components, the experienced talent of the active Army was soon spread dangerously thin as expansion went forward. The system of manpower procurement and discharge on a two-year basis and individual rotation into and out of the active theater on a one-year basis mandated the maintenance of a large training establishment within the United States, and in effect the conversion of the strategic reserve in the United States and the deterrent army in Europe into replacement depots for Southeast Asia.[21]

The noncommissioned officer structure, that critical connection between officer and soldier upon which morale and discipline ultimately depend, was the first element to feel the pressure. Inadequate in number for the tasks it was being called upon to perform, eroded by battle casualties, faced with repetitive duty tours in Vietnam, and asked to lead soldiers who were perennial recruits, the near exhaustion of the noncommissioned officer corps appears now to have been inevitable. For many of the same reasons, the officer structure began to show signs of strain. The dilution of talent required junior officers to be promoted into positions of responsibility for which they had no maturing experience. Moreover, the manpower procurement system effectively denied to the Army any real access to that sector of the nation's youth with the greatest potential for intelligent leadership, to the detriment of both the Army and the colleges and universities themselves.[22]

The objective future historian will conclude that it is exaggeration to characterize the American Army of the late 1960s and early 1970s as in a condition of widespread breakdown in discipline. The Army accomplished too much worldwide during those years for that characterization to be historically correct. Nonetheless, it will not be exaggeration to conclude that the Army's leadership structure was under heavy stress and that standards of discipline had declined to the point that breakdowns within some units were possible and, under certain circumstances, probable. The most tragic example of breakdown occurred in mid-March 1968 at the Vietnamese village of Son My.

Not until approximately a year later did the Department of the Army learn of the Son My incident (or, as it became better known, My Lai). In November 1969 the Chief of Staff of the Army, General Westmoreland, jointly with Secretary of the Army Stanley R. Resor, directed Lieutenant General William R. Peers (AWC 1953) "to explore the nature and scope of the original U.S. Army investigation(s)" into the incident.[23] Criminal investigations of the affair itself had been underway for some months under the auspices of the Office of the Provost Marshal General. The "Peers Inquiry" was completed in mid-March 1970. Shortly after forwarding his formal report, General Peers submitted a separate memorandum to General Westmoreland providing the Chief of Staff with Peers' own personal views "regarding the ethical and moral standards required of U.S. Army officers and noncommissioned officers."[24] Although Peers had intended only that the memorandum assist General Westmoreland in better understanding the formal report, it in fact deepened the Chief of Staff's concerns regarding the moral and ethical climate within the U.S. Army. General Westmoreland saw a need for nothing less than "a thorough review of certain areas and practices within the Army" and an analysis that might lead to prompt and corrective action.[25]

On April 18, 1970 General Westmoreland charged the Army War College with the task of conducting the analysis, which came to be called the Professionalism Study. His choice of the War College to perform the task was logical. Present at Carlisle Barracks were several hundred mature officers, many with experience encompassing service in at least two wars, the great majority with past service in Vietnam in assignments varying in place, time, and duty performed. Moreover, there were at Carlisle Barracks officers experienced in the conduct of analyses, representing an institution that had long claimed to be educating men to think critically and objectively. More importantly, the War College included officers who cared deeply about the officer corps of the Army.[26]

General Westmoreland allowed the War College slightly more than two months to complete the study; he wanted the results by the first of July. General Eckhardt understandably gave the effort top priority, organizing the study team around a nucleus of officers assigned to the Department of Research and Studies. Students with qualifications that would contribute to the study were pulled out of class. Problem definition and data accumulation had to be done expeditiously (perhaps hurriedly), and the limited time for analysis did not permit extended periods of contemplation. The study team queried and received replies from some 420 officers, for the most part students at the War College, the Command and General Staff College, and the Infantry, Artillery, Armor, Transportation, and Chaplains schools. A stratified random sample of the officer corps was not attempted, an omission that later caused criticism of the findings. In addition to qualitative (content) and quantitative analysis of the responses, small group discussions led by two-man teams from the War College were conducted with some 250 officers at six Army posts. Tentative conclusions were discussed and tested in seminars at the War College.[27]

The report of the War College study group was presented to the Chief of Staff as scheduled on July 1, 1970. The overview conclusion was that while officers prized high ethical standards and values, they also perceived that the officer corps in its daily performance of duty fell far short of those same high standards. The study group did not attribute the shortfall in performance to social phenomena caused or released by the Vietnam era, nor to accelerated commissioning and promotion during the buildup of forces. If there was one primary cause of the condition, the study group felt that it was related to "prevailing institutional pressures" that encouraged untoward and unhealthy "striving for success." According to the War College study, institutional systems pertaining to the selection, reward, promotion, and education of officers were in need of correction, even of overhaul. The message of the study was clear: the Army as an institution had serious and fundamental problems. As Elihu Root had reason to state in 1899, the machine was defective.[28]

General Westmoreland, despite misgivings among some of his senior staff, took the findings of the study seriously. Many of the institutional changes recommended by the War College group began to be implemented. On other recommendations more deliberation was directed. One recommendation the Chief of Staff did not accept. The War College had proposed that the findings of the study be disseminated to the officer corps. This was not done; two years would pass before the study was released. But, at the least, General Westmoreland had discovered, or had seen confirmed, that at the War College there was a body of officers who would tell him the facts as they saw them, no matter how unpleasant those facts might be. His choice of a review agency had been not only logical but wise. In January of the next year he was back to ask the War College to undertake another major study. The subject was the validity for the years ahead of the Army's concept of leadership—particularly in view of the impending demise of selective service.[29]

The research effort for what became the study "Leadership for the 1970's" was organized, as had been the effort for the Professionalism Study, around a nucleus of officers assigned the Department of Research and Studies, Colonel LeRoy Strong (AWC 1966) and Lieutenant Colonels D. M. Malone (AWC 1970) and Walter Ulmer (AWC 1969). Sixty students from the Class of 1971 volunteered to participate in the study. Eighteen were selected who provided a variety of military and academic backgrounds. Members of the War College staff were also used. Recognized civilian authorities in the field of leadership behavior and related fields contributed their assistance. Liaison was established with other Army elements having a continuing interest in the study of leadership—the Military Academy, the Infantry School, the Human Resources Research Office, and a new agency organized in May of 1971 at

Fort Bragg, N.C., the CONARC Leadership Board. Teams from the study group visited seventeen Army installations.[30]

With the experience of the professionalism analysis of the year before, and with more time available to study the leadership problem, "Leadership for the 1970's" proved a more technically supportable product than the the Professionalism Study. Through scientifically designed and tested questionnaires and group interview techniques, data were collected from 1,800 individuals ranging in grade from recruit to general officer. Eight to ten percent of the general officers of the Army were contacted. The study confirmed that the leadership principles long taught by the Army were overwhelmingly accepted as valid at all levels, but that there were marked deficiencies between the principles and their application. How well leadership principles were being applied and their relative importance varied with the perspective of each grade level.[31]

The War College study group did not make specific recommendations as to courses of action; rather, it presented for the Chief of Staff's consideration eight "solution concepts." The conclusions and solution concepts did not create among the Army Staff the same degree of controversy that had marked the reception of the Professionalism Study. The methods and findings of the study group were immediately incorporated into the seminar program to be conducted by the CONARC Leadership Board at installations worldwide during the summer and fall of 1971. Moreover, the study introduced to a much broader base within the Army the value of contemporary scientific approaches to the study and teaching of leadership. For the second consecutive year the War College had demonstrated its ability to provide assistance to the Army Staff on matters of central concern, and to do so without any degradation in the performance of its instructional mission.[32]

General Eckhardt departed the War College in March 1971, before "Leadership for the 1970's" was completed. In May he was replaced by Major General Franklin M. Davis, Jr. (AWC 1960). General Davis had been assigned to the faculty after his graduation until September 1962 and most recently had been serving in the Office of the DCSPER. He knew of the two major studies undertaken by the War College in 1970 and 1971, the second now nearing completion. Even before arriving at Carlisle, Davis had expressed the view that the Army War College should be a main source for changing the Army as it might need to be changed for the 1970s and beyond. An annual major study by the War College, if well done, might be one means of initiating change. Davis recommended, as a follow-on to one of the solution concepts of the Leadership Study, that the War College study for 1971-72 be an investigation of leadership modes (attitudes, values, and concepts) of the Army's senior officers, colonels and above. The proposal was not received enthusiastically by the members of the Army Staff with whom General Westmoreland consulted. In their view, introspection was now approaching self-flagellation, and it was time to get on with preparing for the Army's future. The Chief of Staff accepted this view but supported the idea of the War College annually conducting a major study.[33]

In place of another leadership study, the Chief of Staff asked the War College to determine how the Army could most effectively support national strategy during the next decade, or, as it came to be named, "Army Tasks for the Seventies." This study required different disciplines from the earlier two studies, and while the Director of the Department of Research and Studies retained overall control, a new faculty member with a Ph.D. degree in political science, Colonel Donald F. Bletz, was made study director. Also on the study team was Lieutenant Colonel William P. Snyder (AWC 1971) and two students of the Class of 1972, Lieutenant Colonels Charles Debelius and Francis Nerone. Dr. Donald D. Penner, a productive consultant on the Leadership Study and now a member of the War College faculty, also joined the study team.[34]

In the course of the study some four thousand respondents were contacted, ranging from officer candidates to War College students. The Command and General Staff College and the Military Academy were both brought into the study process. Interviews were conducted with scholars, senior military and civilian officials, and futurists throughout the United States. Findings of the study were divided into three parts: international tasks, domestic tasks, and internal Army tasks. From the vantage of the early 1980s, the conclusions of this predictive study have proven on the whole to be sound, though specific events such as the Watergate affair, the 1973 Arab-Israeli War, and the sudden and complete collapse of the army and government of the Republic of Vietnam could hardly have been predicted. The study was not of the type to provide specific recommendations for action; it was meant to educate and enlighten.[35]

In May 1972 General Westmoreland, in company with his DCSOPS, Lieutenant General Richard G. Stilwell (AWC faculty 1954-56), and his DCSPER, Lieutenant General Kerwin, visited Carlisle Barracks and were briefed on the study results. The report was then printed. Once again whether to release a War College study became an issue. Since some findings were not entirely in accord with current administration and Defense Department policies, General Stilwell had to oppose its release. General Kerwin, on the other hand, while understanding Stilwell's concerns, argued that the study could not meet its educational and intellectual objectives if it were not widely disseminated. The issue was not an easy one to resolve. It was not until December 1973 that the markings "FOR OFFICIAL USE ONLY" could be removed from the document.[36]

The three studies conducted by the War College during the years 1970 through 1972 represented a new departure in the role of the third Army War College. For the first time since the days of hemispheric defense planning in 1939-40, the War College was making a direct contribution in areas of central concern to the Army Staff, producing the long-range studies that General Swing had solicited without reverting to the "great adjunct" to the General Staff that Root and Bliss had established. The results of these studies were quite properly not accepted without question by the Army Staff, but nonetheless the War College was being heard by those in a position to take action on the problems investigated. The War College had demonstrated that it was competent to marshal the military experience it represented and to apply the resources and methods of several academic disciplines to important Army concerns. It had come closer than ever before to being the intellectual center that had been its ambition since its doors opened at Leavenworth in 1950. However, the problems involved in having two of the three studies released and disseminated demonstrate vividly the difficulties that any government institution must overcome if it is to join in public dialogue and exert influence beyond the perimeter of its own department.

The Military History Research Collection

With considerably less drama than accompanied the three major investigative efforts of the War College, and with less trauma than accompanied the search for the rightful place of the Institute of Advanced Studies, a third research-oriented activity evolved at Carlisle Barracks during the 1960s. This was the Military History Research Collection (MHRC) established initially in May 1967 during General Salet's tenure. Early in that year, with construction of the new academic complex nearing completion, General Salet recommended and Chief of Staff Johnson approved conversion of the library space and other facilities of Upton Hall (the new name for the old Root Hall) into a repository for a collection of items supporting the study of military history. The research collection was organized initially as an element of the War College under the supervision of the college secretary, with Colonel George S. Pappas (AWC 1966) the director. The nucleus of the collection, moved into the building in the fall of 1967, was 20,000 bound volumes transferred from the library of the Army War College and 30,000 older volumes that had once belonged to the Army War College but which since 1946 had been in the library of the National War College. The concept was to centralize at this facility items dispersed in other Army libraries as well as personal papers and private collections.[37]

Actually, Salet's ambitions for the facility extended beyond the field of military history to the broader area of military art and science. With the larger objective in view, he established in June 1967, at least in name, the "U.S. Army War College Research Center," to include both the Military History Research Collection and the Army War College library. This center was to include the historical collection and the results of all research done at the War College; it would be open, within security limitations, to both military and civilian researchers. General Salet's successor, however, did not push this concept. He felt that before attempting to present a full-blown research center analogous to those of major universities, the Military History Research Collection should be adequately staffed and provided time to grow, time to become well established and recognized in its own right.[38]

Under Pappas's direction more than 300,000 items were collected by 1971. The MHRC received a healthy boost in 1970 when General of the Army Omar Bradley designated it as the repository for his papers and memorabilia. To accommodate the donations the Omar Bradley Museum and Foundation was formed and ambitious plans were conceived to enlarge the facility physically, a project that unfortunately would mean demolishing an old and historic Indian School building being used as the post gymnasium and named for Jim Thorpe. The Bradley Museum, housed in a section on the ground floor of Upton Hall, was dedicated on May 7, 1970, the twenty-fifth anniversary of VE Day. The MHRC also inaugurated an "oral history" program, initially known as the "Senior Officer Debriefing Program." Resident War College students were encouraged to conduct and record interviews of retired general officers as a way to meet their student research requirement. By 1971, eight retired general officers had participated in the program.[39]

The coupling at Carlisle Barracks of the Army's historical program and the War College's educational program was a concept General Trudeau had recommended on several occasions since 1950. Until the late 1960s the project had never progressed to the stage that organizational arrangements needed to be addressed. The subordination of the historical program to the second Army War College had proven to be less than productive, and since World War II the Army's historical program had grown into a mature, quasi-independent, and respected activity. Moreover, if the MHRC was to prosper, it needed to be supervised, encouraged, and funded by those most interested and qualified in the pursuit of military history, specifically the Office of the Chief of Military History. The organizational solution, arrived at while General Eckhardt was Commandant, was for the Military History Research Collection to become a field activity of the Chief of Military History and a tenant activity of Carlisle Barracks under the command of the Commandant of the Army War College. Both the Commandant and the Chief of Military History became responsible for the health and growth of the activity. The collection itself and the professional staff remained organizationally and physically convenient to support the War College but could also support historical research throughout the Army, indeed nationwide and

417

worldwide, under the technical direction of the Chief of Military History.[40]

Parameters

Another idea of General Trudeau dating back to the early years of the third Army War College was the need for the War College to publish a professional journal. It will be recalled that General Salet had directed the publication of an unofficial journal initially by distributing occasional papers and then in 1966 by establishing the unofficial *US Army War College Commentary.* Until 1970 *Commentary* continued to be published only occasionally as worthwhile material became available. Between 1966 and 1970 seven issues of *Commentary* were published, including a special edition in December 1967 that contained eight articles devoted to the subject of internal defense and development operations. General McCaffrey was advised by his staff not to attempt to raise *Commentary* to the level of an official journal, the argument being that such a step would require separate budgeting for the journal and review of the articles by the Department of the Army. General Eckhardt, however, apparently did not find those arguments convincing; in September 1970 he took the step that had been contemplated for so many years, formally requesting sanction to publish an official War College journal.[41]

Eckhardt proposed that the new journal be published triannually, with each issue to contain eighty pages of text. The title was to be *Parameters: The Journal of the US Army War College* (*Commentary* was already the title of a well-established public affairs journal). Authority was requested to print 5,000 copies of each issue, 4,400 for official use and 560 for free distribution. Over 3,500 copies would go to current and former members of the War College. Seven hundred copies would reach a civilian audience through distribution to libraries and to National Strategy Seminar guests. The remainder would be distributed to headquarters and schools throughout the Army. In December the Department of the Army approved publishing *Parameters* for a three-year period. The first issue appeared in the spring of 1971. It contained four articles written by students of the Class of 1970, three of whom were by then on the faculty, and two articles by other members of the faculty, including Ambassador Hermann F. Eilts, Diplomatic Adviser to the Commandant.[42]

The Vietnam Current Affairs Panel

Parameters provided one way that the work going on at the Army War College could be made available to a wider audience. In 1969 another way was discovered, quite by accident and certainly not at the instigation of the War College. Despite its relative seclusion in the primarily agricultural Cumberland Valley of Pennsylvania, the Army War College could not avoid, even if it had so desired, the domestic turmoil created by the Southeast Asia war. In October 1969 the War College was invited—perhaps more accurately, received a demand—by student groups at Dickinson College to send representatives to a "teach-in" on Vietnam. Some fifteen to twenty War College student and faculty volunteers participated. They later had no illusions that minds either at Dickinson or at the War College had been changed by the War College's participation, but the experience was considered successful. When a similar invitation was received from nearby Shippensburg State College, two groups of about ten officers participated. The Dickinson and Shippensburg exercises proved to be only a warm-up for things to come.[43]

Encouraged by the Department of the Army (and perhaps even by higher authority), the War College continued to accept invitations to have its representatives appear on civilian campuses to discuss the war with many—and to listen to the shouts and epithets of many others—concerned about America's role in Southeast Asia. Two "Vietnam Panels" were formed, a primary panel and an alternate panel employed in the event of duplicate scheduling. In May 1970 the primary Vietnam Panel had to make an unscheduled appearance even at the main entrance to Carlisle Barracks when less-than-peaceful elements of a student peace demonstration demanded an audience. The panel's presence and willingness to discuss the issues apparently had a salutary effect on a situation that otherwise might have degenerated to an affair with property damage or personal injury.[44]

The primary Vietnam Panel was composed of five officers, two faculty members and three students. Included was an officer of the Judge Advocate General Corps competent to discuss the legalities of American involvement, an officer of the Chaplains Corps to discuss the moral and ethical aspects, and an officer who had studied counterrevolutionary war to the depth that he had authored a book on the subject. The panel's approach to the discussions was to stay with documented facts, to explain the legitimate strategic interests of the United States in the future makeup of Southeast Asia, and, above all, to avoid becoming provoked. The last was not always easy. There were some very hostile elements among the audiences.[45]

Opinion at the War College varied on the panel's activity. Some believed that it was a duty of those who had served in Vietnam in reasonably responsible positions to attempt to correct the many misconceptions held to be truths on American campuses. Others felt that where there was no willingness to listen there was no point in speaking. A third group felt that it was not the place of military officers to participate in what had become a new type of American political process. In 1971, however, the Vice Chief of Staff approved continuation of Vietnam Panel activity. While initially the panel had to deal with large audiences, heated discussions, and polarized viewpoints, once the troop withdrawal from Vietnam was well underway the audiences became smaller, as well as more interested and more civil. The Vietnam Panel transformed into the "Current Affairs Panel." Reorganized annually, the panel then normally consisted of a faculty adviser and five students from the resident class. Its challenge as the Vietnam issue receded was one of overcoming indifference rather than one of keeping public discussion rational.[46]

Visible Accomplishments

Although without the stability and perhaps the serenity that General Eckhardt may have anticipated, the two academic years of his incumbency, 1969-70 and 1970-71, were years of visible accomplishment at the Army War College. A number of projects conceived earlier reached fruition, and new programs were begun. In addition to the establishment of *Parameters* and the conduct of the important professionalism and leadership studies (the latter still underway when Eckhardt departed), the first nonresident class graduated and the next two enrolled. In February 1971 the annual Senior Reserve Component Officer Course was doubled in size from sixteen to thirty-two officers, providing both a senior National Guard and a senior Army Reserve officer to join each student seminar group for the two-week period.[47]

General Eckhardt was also able to complete a project begun by General McCaffrey at the instigation of the superintendent of the Military Academy. In the fall of 1968 the superintendent proposed that members of West Point's tenured faculty be allowed to attend the War College during a one-year sabbatical. McCaffrey favored the proposal, suggesting that the academy representative assume teaching duties as well as attending lectures and discussions. In December 1969 the DCSPER approved the scheme. Colonel William F. Luebbert of the Military Academy faculty was thus assigned to the War College during the 1970-71 academic year as "Fellow in Computer Science." He was considered a member of the War College faculty but also attended classes and received credit as graduating from the War College. Luebbert was a good choice as the first "USMA Fellow"; the two years previous he had been a consultant to the War College in its endeavors to obtain computer support for the academic program.[48]

General Eckhardt was able to reap the rewards of another project begun by his predecessors. General Salet had started the process when he requested funds to refurbish as "representational housing" the large home acquired in 1958 with the land adjacent to Carlisle Barracks. Officially called Sumner House but more popularly known as "The Castle," this imposing home had been used since its acquisition as a bachelor officers' quarters and guest house. Salet, recognizing its suitability for the unusual amount of official entertaining required of the Commandant, proposed that it be converted into quarters for the Commandant.

420

But General Salet did not win immediate approval. General McCaffrey continued the effort to refurbish the home, believing that it would be appropriate quarters for former Chief of Staff Johnson if he were to join the faculty. Although the Johnson project fell through, McCaffrey was eventually successful in obtaining funds for renovation. General Eckhardt was the first Commandant to occupy the Castle, moving in during the fall of 1969.[49]

Despite the continuing and vexing problem of the shortage of family housing, the development of Carlisle Barracks begun by Generals Swing and Trudeau had resulted in a first-class academic plant. In addition to Root Hall, the new library and the new auditorium (named Bliss Hall) were in use. During General Eckhardt's term the chapel center was expanded and an enlargement of the hospital was approved. The Department of the Army, as it had promised, submitted to the Department of Defense a request for an additional sixty sets of family quarters. General Eckhardt also resubmitted the request to add the fourth floor to Root Hall. His plan was to move the library to the fourth floor and to use the evacuated space below ground level for an activity known as the Operations Group which had been present at Carlisle Barracks since January 1963. Subordinate to the War College, the Operations Group was concurrently a field operating agency of the Department of the Army Deputy Chief of Staff for Operations. Its value to the War College was as a source of current worldwide operational data and intelligence. General Eckhardt's plans also called for a computer center located in this space.[50]

In Pursuit of a Computer

The acquisition of automatic data processing support for the War College is a tale of prolonged frustration. The proliferation and high cost of this equipment throughout the defense establishment had resulted in approval authority for its acquisition being centralized in the office of the Defense Comptroller. At Department of the Army level the Comptroller of the Army, the Assistant Vice Chief of Staff, and the Assistant Secretary of the Army (Financial Management) all had responsibilities relating to these systems. General McCaffrey attempted to penetrate this thicket as early as the fall of 1967, his first year as Commandant. His proposal was to establish a "USAWC Research and Education Computer Center" which could serve both the War College and the Institute of Advanced Studies. General McCaffrey was reassigned before any decision was made on his request. When action was taken, the decision was negative.[51]

The best that those who controlled computer acquisition would do for the Army War College was to include it in a consortium to be called SHARESIMCOM (Shared Simulation Computer). SHARESIMCOM allowed the Army War College, together with the other four senior service colleges, the Armed Forces Staff College, and the Marine Corps Command and General Staff College, to share time on the West Point computer facility and the computer facility of the Rome, New York, Air Development Center. During academic year 1968-69 some limited use was made of this capability in support of two elective courses and individual student research projects. By 1970-71 the consortium arrangement was working well enough to support the military planning courses of both the resident and nonresident classes. The arrangement was far from satisfactory, however. No classified information could be transmitted over the leased lines, and use of the computer at West Point was based on the premise of no interference with cadet instruction.[52]

Because of the limitations of the SHARESIMCOM arrangement, General Eckhardt continued the efforts McCaffrey had begun to obtain a computer facility at Carlisle Barracks. By combining the needs of the War College with those of the Operations Group, approval was finally won to bring a computer to Carlisle from the National Security Agency at Fort Meade, Maryland. The DCSOPS provided the necessary funds for site preparation, and installation was expected in time to support the 1971-72 academic year. The schedule was almost met. Early in January 1972 installation was complete in the subbasement of Root Hall. In April the facility became available for academic use. Almost five years had passed since General McCaffrey had begun the project. General Eckhardt's successor performed the ribbon-cutting chore.[53]

Changing the Theme

The basic academic program that General McCaffrey left to General Eckhardt did not change materially during academic years 1969-70 and 1970-71, although the number of elective courses offered increased to twenty-one. The official announcement of these offerings categorized six of them as management courses, five as political science, and three as communicative arts. One course was in the field of law. Two courses each were presented in economics and sociology. Only two courses were considered "military."[54]

Within the common curriculum and in direct response to the Professionalism Study of the year before, a week in February was devoted to a "Military Professionalism Seminar." Two innovations within certain courses are also worth noting. In Course 5, "Joint Strategic Military capabilities," a political-military game, an exercise in crisis management, was introduced with the assistance of the Studies, Analyses, and Gaming Agency of the Joint Staff. In Course 6, "Joint Strategic Military Planning," students were still required to derive force-level objectives for the midrange period; analyzing costs of the alternative force levels was now greatly facilitated by use of the "Army War College

Force Costing Model" programmed in the West Point computer. This model permitted for the first time rapid manipulation of force elements in terms of program year and costs.[55]

The relative stability of the curriculum during the years of McCaffrey and Eckhardt did not necessarily indicate complete satisfaction with the program. Indeed, there was a growing dissatisfaction. Increasingly questioned was the concept of "national strategy." As expressed to the War College in the 1967 review by outside consultants, national strategy was in fact an abstraction. To derive something as finite as a costed force program from an abstraction did not appear to make good sense. Moreover, a national strategy could too easily be converted into dogma; the intervention in Vietnam was cited as a tragic example of following the national strategy of containment to an illogical conclusion, an example of dogma discouraging careful assessment of national interests. A challenge of the utility of the concept of a national strategy was also a challenge of the underlying curricular theme that had served the War College since 1957-58.[56]

The experience with elective courses, moreover, indicated that here was a potential for a much more flexible curriculum. As envisioned by the Haines Board, electives had been no more than a compromise between the generalist approach so vigorously defended by General Salet's faculty and the specialist approach attributed to the followers of Dr. Katzenbach. Now doubts along the lines suggested earlier by General Gar Davidson as to the value of generalists were being expressed throughout the Army. The findings of the Professionalism Study certainly reinforced these doubts. At the least the traditional generalist thrust of the War College program no longer appeared inviolate. Electives offered the opportunity to accommodate the movement toward specialization. Finally, there remained the heirs of the Advanced Leavenworth, Manton Eddy persuasion. The Army War College in their view should never have launched off in pursuit of national strategy and a broad generalist education in the first place.

The element of the War College responsible for the continuing evaluation and development of the curriculum was the Department of Research and Studies. In February 1970, reacting to a staff effort about to begin in the office of the DCSPER designed to update the Haines Board findings and entitled "Military Education of Career Officers," this department initiated a formal review under the rubric of "USAWC Mission and Curriculum Study." The study was to evaluate the contemporary and future (next ten years) environment in which War College graduates would serve, derive from the evaluation the desirable characteristics of War College graduates, and then correlate the mission and curriculum with those characteristics. The department had planned to finish its effort in June but, in part due to the higher priority of the

Professionalism Study begun in April, did not present the results of its study until November. A recommended revised mission statement for the War College was forwarded to the DCSPER in January 1971. It was another six months, however, before the War College and the DCSPER could reach agreement on the revised statement.[57]

In the meantime, work went forward on a revised curriculum. The resulting proposal was a major departure—nothing less than a new curricular theme stated rather ponderously as "Issues, Alternatives, and Perspectives in National Security Affairs: Insights and Knowledge for Continuing Professional Development." The revisers pointed out a number of implications in their new theme. More emphasis would be placed on developing the ability to derive transferable concepts and more time needed for grounding in theory and concepts to provide guidelines to analysis. Less time would be available for lengthy formal reports and more time allowed for frequent seminars to isolate and explore issues and principles, with closer faculty observation of assumptions and judgment criteria. Less emphasis should be given to the sequential arrangement of courses, to the assembly of course data in solution format, and to the final capstone course.[58]

According to the reviewers, subjects that needed increased attention were human behavior, management, military capabilities (including those of allies and adversaries), reserve forces, alternatives and trade-offs in the application of U.S. military power, military application of technology, national intelligence capabilities and activities, and trends and issues in contemporary American society. It was a large order, and they did not provide a companion list of subjects that required less emphasis. Interestingly, the planners did eliminate from the mission statement concern with "higher tactics," a topic personally inserted by Chief of Staff Johnson when he approved Haines's recommendations. The term, it was argued, was ambiguous. What the planners had conceived, they now had to make specific. The initial result was the resident course curriculum for 1971-72.[59]

The program for 1971-72 turned out to be something of a hybrid. Clearly recognizable were some of the new ideas, but just as clearly visible were many of the old. The year began as it had in the past with the study of international relations, but the faculty did not intend, as it had in the past, for this study to lead to derivation of a national strategy. The "Command and Management Seminar," for the previous five years scheduled horizontally, became a course in its own right, was retitled "National Defense Decision-Making and Management," and was scheduled to follow international relations. A Department of Management was created out of the Department of Military Planning to conduct this course.[60]

The next two courses encompassed what had been addressed the previous year, and they again led to a five-year objective force program. In concept the students were expected to use the decision-making theory they had learned in the previous course presented by the new Department of Management. They were aided by an improved force-costing model programmed on the recently acquired computer.[61]

The "Military Strategy Seminar" remained unaltered as a horizontal course except that added as its second of three phases were ten sessions on Internal Defense and Development Operations. The first phase of the seminar remained the only part of the resident program that consciously attempted to build from a historical base. The "Human Dimensions of Military Professionalism" seminar received additional emphasis in 1971-72. An outgrowth of the Professionalism Study of 1970, it now drew also from the Leadership Study of 1971, addressing not only elements and standards of military professionalism but consideration of tenets of the behavioral sciences.[62]

Only two additional elective courses were added to the offerings, but in the late afternoons of the second two weeks in August (five sessions each week) were offered four "workshops" on practical speech communications, techniques of research and analysis, automatic data processing, and expository writing. The Individual Research Program received a new name, "Student Research Program," since the college was now encouraging studies performed by small groups rather than by individuals. Oral history interviews continued as an option for resident students. The final course of the year, the former "United States National Strategy and a Supporting Military Program," became a simple review and summing up, "National Security Issues," to prepare the class for the end-of-year symposium with the distinguished invited guests.[63]

The curriculum planners were not unaware of the implications of their new theme. They recognized that the old theme had been under stress for a number of years. The seminars on "Military Strategy" and "Command and Management," the so-called "horizontal seminars," had never fit easily, nor had instruction in "Internal Defense and Development Operations," nor had elective courses; now there was also the seminar on the "Human Dimensions of Military Professionalism." But if the planners were aware of the most basic implication of all, they did not mention it. In discarding the theme of "National Strategy and Its Supporting Military Program," they discarded the mechanism that for fourteen years had organized, unified, disciplined (and justified) the War College program. Depending upon one's perspective, the result would be either refreshing change in the status quo or the opening of Pandora's box.

NOTES

1. *Haines Board*, 545-46.
2. Ibid., 548, 559. HQ., DA, Letter, 20 July 1966, 7.
3. Zais to Commandant, 30 November 1967, Subject: Increase in Student Quotas, File 206-06.
4. Paul Murray to Commandant, 5 April 1968, Staff Study, Subject: Expansion of USAWC Student Body, Ibid. McCaffrey to DCSPER, 19 April 1968, Subject: Increase in Student Quotas, Ibid.
5. Zais to Commandant, 25 April 1968, Subject: Increase in Student Quotas, Ibid. Hannum to Commandant, 24 June 1968, 1st Ind. to McCaffrey to DCSPER, 19 April 1968, File 1002-07. McCaffrey to DCSPER, 8 March 1968, Subject: Increase in Student Quotas, File 1003-07. Zais to Commandant, 20 May 1968, Subject: Allocation of Resident Student Spaces for the U.S. Army War College, Ibid.
6. Nick Turo, "County May Block War College Bid to Buy 84 Acres," *Carlisle Sentinel*, Carlisle, Pa., Tuesday, September 17, 1968, Clipping in File 1003-11. McCaffrey to E. K. Masland, 6 December 1968, File 205-03. Masland to McCaffrey, 12 March 1969, Ibid. Ambrose, Memorandum for Record, 17 April 1969, Subject: Meeting with Mr. Schaffer of *Lawrie and Green* Regarding Land Acquisition, File 1003-06.
7. In addition to Palmer and Connor this meeting was attended by Lieutenant Generals William DePuy, Arthur Collins (AWC 1953), Harry Lemley, and Jean Engler. The War College was represented by Brigadier General M. J. L. Greene, the Deputy Commandant; Greene, Memorandum for Record, 18 June 1969, File 1003-07. A. O. Connor to Vice Chief of Staff, 27 June 1969, Subject: Expansion of the U.S. Army War Colege, File 1003-11. Ambrose, Memorandum for Record, 2 December 1969, Subject: New Family Housing Units and Land Acquisition, File 1003-16.
8. G. W. McIntyre to Deputy Commandant, 5 August 1969, Subject: Expansion of Nonresident Course, File 1003-03. Greene to Chairman, Department of Nonresident Instruction, 8 October 1969, Subject: Expansion of NRI Course, Ibid. Eckhardt to DCSPER, 18 November 1969, Subject: Expansion of U.S. Army War College Nonresident Classes, and 1st Ind., Kerwin to Commandant, 15 December 1969, Ibid.
9. Kerwin to Eckhardt, 9 February 1970, File 1002-07.
10. Robert A. Martin to Morton, 18 February 1970, Subject: Increase in USAWC Student Body, File 1011-04. Morton to Deputy Commandant, 26 February 1970, Subject: Increase in USAWC Student Body, Ibid.
11. AWC, Minutes of Deputies Meeting, 10 April 1970, File 1011-04. Summary of Telecom, 15 April 1970, Ibid. "AWC Expansion Denied," *Army Times*, 29 April 1970. Kerwin to Commandant, 13 April 1970, Subject: Family Housing Requirements at Carlisle Barracks, File 1011-14. Eckhardt to Kerwin, 27 May 1970, Ibid. 12. Salet to Deputy Commandant, 23 August 1966, Subject: Haines Board Recommendations and AWC-70 Projects, par. 3, File 1003-03. J. R. Wendt to Deputy Commandant, 26 September 1966, Subject: Integration of IAS and USAWC Effort, File 201-45. Train to Deputy Commandant, 8 February 1963, Subject: Responsiblity for Conduct of Instruction, USAWC, 1963-1964, File 1003-03. DIR, Memorandum for Faculty, 22 June 1967, Subject: Summary of Views Expressed by Informal Panel of Students—USAWC Class of 1966, Ibid.
13. J. R. Wendt to Deputy Commandant, 26 September 1966. The combat developments process is described in USACDC, manuscript, *Today's Vision—Tomorrow's Victory* by Mary C. Lane and John B. Kelly (Ft. Belvoir, 1966): 45-52, and Army Regulation 71-1, 27 May 1966, *Army Combat Developments*, par. 3, 14. HQ, USACDC, Letter, 7 October 1966, Subject: The Institute of Land Combat, File 201-45.
14. USACDC, General Order No. 114, 18 April 1967, Ibid. Army Regulation 71-1, 16 September 1968, *Army Combat Developments*, pars. 1.8, 4.6.
15. Salet to Harrell, 12 May 1967, File 201-08. HQ., DA, Chief of Staff Memorandum 320, 16 February 1967, Ibid.
16. Office of the Chief of Staff, 9 November 1967, Subject: Special Study: Reexamination of the Role of USACDC Institute of Advanced Studies, Ibid. Guest to Commanding General, IAS, 31 October 1967, Subject: Future of IAS, File 1003-23. McCaffrey to Kinnard, 14 November 1967, File 201-45.

17. Kinnard to McCaffrey, 4 December 1967, File 201-08. USACDCIAS, 15 January 1968, Change 1 to IAS Memorandum 10-1, 20 September 1967, *Organization and Functions Manual*, File 205-02. McCaffrey to Kinnard, 13 June 1968, File 201-45.
18. Eckhardt to Wermuth, 3 February 1971, File 1001-07. Eckhardt to Davis, 4 March 1971, Ibid. AWC, Strategic Studies Institute, *Abstracts of Studies and Other Publications*, 1 April 1981, 8-10, AWC Library.
19. Melvin R. Laird, *Final Report to the Congress of Secretary of Defense Melvin R. Laird before the House Armed Services Committee*, January 8, 1973 (Washington: GPO, 1973), 12-18. For a recent and measured evaluation see the chapter on Laird in Lee Douglas Kinnard, *The Secretary of Defense* (Lexington, Ky.: University Press of Kentucky, 1981).
20. William C. Westmoreland, *Report of the Chief of Staff of the United States Army, 1 July 1968 to 30 June 1972* (Washington: Department of the Army, 1977), 75.
21. Ibid., 5-6, 27, 34, 48. Tausch interview with James H. Polk, 1971-1972, 28, 44.
22. Westmoreland, *Report of Chief of Staff*, 5-6, 10.
23. W. C. Westmoreland and Stanley R. Resor, Memorandum for Lieutenant General William R. Peers, 26 November 1969, Subject: Directive for Investigation, reprinted in Department of the Army, *Report of the Department of the Army Review of the Preliminary Investigations into the My Lai Incident* (Hereafter *Peers Inquiry*) 3 vols. (14 March 1970) 1: Chap. 1, 6.
24. W. R. Peers, Memorandum for Chief of Staff, U.S. Army, 18 March 1970, Subject: The Son My Incident, reprinted in W. R. Peers, *The My Lai Inquiry* (New York: W. W. Norton, 1979), 246-49.
25. Ibid., 249. W. C. Westmoreland to Commandant, 13 April 1970, Subject: Analysis of Moral and Professional Climate in the Army, reprinted in AWC, *Study on Military Professionalism* (30 June 1970) (hereafter *Professionalism Study*), 53-54.
26. Ibid.
27. Interview with D. M. Malone, June 1981. Malone was one of the officers pulled from the class. D. M. Malone, "The Trail Watcher," *Army* (May 1981): 21-22. *Professionalism Study*, Annex A, 1-16.
28. Malone, "Trail Watcher," 26. *Professionalism Study*, iii-vi, 30-37. Root, *Colonial and Military Policy*, 8.
29. Peers, *My Lai*, 249-50. Malone, "Trail Watcher," 22.
30. AWC, *Leadership for the 1970's: USAWC Study of Leadership for the Professional Soldier* (1 July 1971): 1-9. Script for Multimedia, Leadership for the 1970's, 23 June 1971, 1-2, Malone Files.
31. Ibid. AWC, *Leadership*, vi, 10-40.
32. Ibid., vii-viii, 54-62. AWC, Script, 2.
33. Davis for General Magathan and Colonel Bresnahan, 2 April 1971, Subject: Ideas, 2, Cooling material, MHI. AWC, *Leadership*, 56-57. Albro, Memorandum for Record, 31 August 1971, Subject: CSA SEE ME Concerning Army War College Study Proposal, File 1001-04. DR&S to Commandant, 17 September 1971, Subject: U.S. Army War College Study Assignment, Ibid.
34. Davis, Memorandum, 8 October 1971, Subject: U.S. Army War College Study Assignment, Ibid. AWC, *Army Tasks for the Seventies: The Decade of the Seventies, Perspectives and Implications for the United States Army* (June 1972), vi.
35. Ibid., vi-ix, 152-72, Appendix II, Appendix IV, 3-4.
36. DR&S to Commandant, 27 March 1972, Subject: Gen. Westmoreland's Visit To Discuss "Tasks" Study, File 1001-04. Dir., Study Team to Commandant, 31 May 1972, Subject: Printing of Army Tasks for the Seventies Study, Ibid. Trussell to Commandant, 17 July 1972, Subject: Stilwell Memorandum on the USAWC Study, "Army Tasks for the 70's," Central Files 1969-75. Barrett to Commandant, 28 November 1973, Subject: Release of USAWC Study, Ibid. AWC, Memorandum, 17 December 1973, Subject: Army Tasks for the Seventies, File 1001-04.
37. Pappas, *Prudens Futuri*, 272-73, 283. *Army War College Commentary* (October 1970): 86-90. George S. Pappas, "Preserving the Past for the Future," *Army* (September 1971): 30-33.

38. Pappas, *Prudens Futuri*, 273. Secretary to Commandant, 12 January 1968, Subject: U.S. Army War College Research Center, File 206-06. Greene to Commandant, 23 January 1968, Subject: U.S. Army War College Research Center, Ibid.
39. Eckhardt to Westmoreland, 9 March 1971. *Commentary* (October 1970), 90-93. Davis to J. L. Collins, 17 September 1971, File 1001-07. CG, Carlisle Barracks to CG, First Army, 20 February 1973, Subject: Demolition of Indian School Gymnasium, File 1002-01.
40. Eckhardt to Westmoreland, 9 March 1971.
41. *U.S. Army War College Commentary* (December 1967). AWC, Memorandum, 310-3, 10 August 1966, Subject: U.S. Army War College Commentary, File 205-03. Director of Research and Publications to Commandant, 6 October 1967, Subject: Authority to Publish USAWC *Commentary*, File 205-02. Thomas J. Cleary to Deputy Commandant, 13 May 1968, Subject: Naval War College Review, Ibid. Eckhardt to Adjutant General, 22 September 1970, Subject: Initiation of New Periodical, reprinted in AWC, *Parameters Study: Final Report* (3 March 1975), AWC Library.
42. Ibid. Director of Research and Studies to Commandant, 3 September 1970, Subject: Initiation of New Periodical, reprinted in Ibid. U.S. Army Publication Agency to Commandant, 9 December 1970, 1st Ind. to Eckhardt to Adjutant General, 22 September 1970, reprinted in Ibid. *Parameters* (Spring 1971).
43. John J. McCuen, "Dialogue Reestablished," *Army* (November 1971): 14-20. Interview with Zane E. Finkelstein, 23 March 1982.
44. Ibid., McCuen, "Dialogue."
45. Ibid. Primary panel members were Henry A. Barber III, John J. McCuen, Zane E. Finkelstein, Albert F. Ledebuhr, and Robert L. Schweitzer.
46. Finkelstein interview. Palmer to Eckhardt, 1 February 1971, File 1001-07. USAWC Current Affairs Panel, Final Report Academic Year 1974, Central Files 1974.
47. Eckhardt to Westmoreland, 9 March 1971, File 1001-07.
48. DI to Deputy Commandant, 31 October 1968, Subject: Sabbaticals for USMA Professors at USAWC, Central Files Academic Years 1972-1975. Alexander to Deputy Commandant, 22 January 1970, Subject: Sabbaticals for USMA Professors at USAWC, Ibid. Koster to Commandant, 19 January 1970, Subject: U.S. Army War College Fellowship for USMA Faculty Member, Ibid. Eckhardt to Koster, 27 January 1970, Ibid.
49. McCaffrey to Connor, 10 August 1968, Cooling Material. Greene, Memorandum for Deputy Post Commander, 11 August 1969, Subject: Quarters Assignment, File 206-06.
50. Eckhardt to Westmoreland, 9 March 1971.
51. McCaffrey to AVCS, 27 November 1967, Subject: USAWC Research and Education Computer Center, File: Acquisition of ADPE. McCaffrey to Connor, 6 June 1969, Ibid. Robert C. Moot, Assistant Secretary of Defense, to ASA(FM), 16 September 1970, Subject: ADPE Support for the U.S. Army War College, File 201-02.
52. Charles S. Moody, Memorandum for Record: Trip Report on NATSIMCOM Meeting at USMA, 24 March 1969. File: ADPE. HQ., USMA, Letter, 5 March 1970, Subject: SHARESIMCOM Technical Memorandum, Ibid. Commandant to DCSPER, 1 July 1969, Subject: Army War College Report of Accomplishments in the Use and Management of ADP, File: Course Material, 1969. AWC, Research and Education Computer Center, *Computer Time-Sharing: User's Manual*, 24 June 1970. DNRI to Secretary, 4 March 1971, Subject: ADP Support for NRI End of Course Resident Phase, File 201-02.
53. Eckhardt to Director, Management Information Systems, DA, 19 February 1971, Subject: Request for Second Generation ADP Equipment, File 201-02. USAWC Ops. Gp. to Chairmen, 22 March 1971, Subject: Status of Computer Acquisition, Ibid. AWC, 10 January 1972, Minutes of Deputies Meeting 4 January 1972, File 211-02. AWC, 17 April 1972, Minutes of Deputies Meeting 13 April 1972, Ibid.
54. AWC, *Curriculum Pamphlet Academic Year 1971 (Resident)*, 1 July 1970.
55. AWC, Memorandum, 1 February 1971, Military Professionalism Seminar, Malone Files. *Curriculum Pamphlet 1971*. AWC, *Military Costing Guide*, 3 March 1971.
56. Report of Consultant Group, 1967.

57. DR&S to Deputy Commandant, 31 March 1970, Subject: Study of the Mission of the Army War College, File: 1970 Mission Study. AWC to DCSPER, 14 January 1971, Subject: Request for Change in AR 350-5, cited in Eckhardt to Davis, 4 March 1971, File 1001-07. LTC Ulmer, Talking Paper, 26 July 1971, Subject: Reaction to the USAWC Mission Statement Received from DCSPER-DIT by Letter, 16 July 1971, File: 1970 Mission Study.

58. AWC, USAWC Mission Study: Consolidated Major Program, 1970, File: 1970 Mission Study.

59. Ibid. Ulmer, Talking Paper, 2.

60. AWC, *Curriculum Pamphlet Academic Year 1972 (Resident)*, 1 July 1971. Secretary to Department Chairman, 15 December 1970, Subject: Realignment of USAWC Faculty, File 714-02. Eckhardt to Westmoreland, 9 March 1971.

61. *Curriculum Pamphlet 1972.*

62. AWC, Directive: Military Strategy Seminar, Phases I and III, 2 October 1970-29 March 1972. AWC, Directive: Military Strategy Seminar, Phase II, 31 January-14 February 1972, 31 January 1972. Directive: Human Dimensions of Military Professionalism Seminar, 23 August 1971-8 October 1971, 6 August 1971.

63. *Curriculum Pamphlet 1972.* Directive: Practical Speech Communications Workshop, 16-27 August 1971, 1 August 1971. Directive: Techniques of Research and Analysis, Ibid. Directive: Automatic Data Processing, Ibid. Directive: Expository Writing, Ibid.

Wresting the Mantle
1971-1974

Major General Franklin M. Davis replaced General Eckhardt as Commandant in the spring of 1971. He would serve as Commandant until June 1974, through three full academic years. During that period the Army would undergo another major reorganization, a move that affected the War College in several important ways. Davis's tenure would be remembered by those who served at Carlisle Barracks as one in which an important goal, one initiated personally by the Chief of Staff of the Army, General William C. Westmoreland, was to "wrest the mantle of contemporary military thought." In pursuit of this goal General Davis set a small group of energetic and talented young faculty members to the task of drafting a long-range development plan for the Army War College, an effort that resulted in the most systematic and scientific (and perhaps most controversial) internal review of the Army War College and all its works that had yet been attempted.

The Contrast, 1971 vs. 1962

General Davis was a 1960 graduate of the Army War College and had remained on its faculty for academic years 1960-61 and 1961-62. The nine years that had elapsed during his absence had been eventful years for the nation, the United States Army, and the Army War College. Overshadowing most of those years was the protracted war in Southeast Asia. The Army bore a major burden of that war and was still carrying it in 1971. Concurrently the Army was preparing itself for what did not appear to be a very promising postwar future.

When Davis left the War College in 1962, it was just beginning to adjust to the two innovations of Secretary McNamara's regime: counterinsurgency and scientific management. In 1971 counterinsurgency by another name was a significant element in the program, and instruction in management had become a major effort. Additionally, as a result of the Professionalism Study, the behavioral sciences were receiving in-

431

creasing attention. The War College program had been under almost continuous review during those nine years, and as a result of one of those reviews, that of the Haines Board, a nonresident program and elective courses had become standard features of the program.

With two nonresident classes enrolled in addition to the resident class, the student body of the War College now totaled over 500. Class was in session at Carlisle Barracks throughout the year except for two or three nonconsecutive weeks during the summer. The faculty had correspondingly been increased in size and reorganized into five teaching departments: the Department of National and International Security Studies, the Department of Strategy, the Department of Military Planning, the Department of Management, and the Department of Nonresident Instruction. In addition was the Department of Research and Studies. Each department head occupied an academic "chair," and the Director of Instruction held the General George Marshall Chair of Military Studies. For academic year 1971-72 General Eckhardt had created the Henry L. Stimson Chair of Political Science, the first chair that would serve the original purpose of attracting civilian academicians onto the faculty.[1]

Of necessity, the elective program had finally broken down the barriers to having resident civilian professors on the faculty. In addition to the political scientist who was to occupy the Stimson chair, approval was being sought for an economist and a behavioral scientist. The faculty remained primarily military, but officers with subject-area expertise were now being recruited in addition to officers of generalist reputation. The solution to the problem of the status of the Institute of Advanced Studies was still pending when General Eckhardt departed. Another unresolved question was whether to offer an allied officers' course. DCSPER had this question under study.[2]

The physical plant at Carlisle Barracks had undergone extensive growth over the past decade, but some major construction projects were still awaiting approval and funds. In December 1970 General Eckhardt had submitted to the Department of the Army proposals to add the fourth floor to Root Hall and to build the "physical conditioning laboratory" adjacent to Root Hall. If built, the new gymnasium would permit destruction of the Indian School gym and subsequent expansion of the Military History Research Collection and the Bradley Museum. A proposal for sixty sets of family quarters was awaiting Department of Defense approval.[3]

Soon after General Eckhardt's departure, but a month before General Davis actually assumed command, Davis visited the War College to become familiar with the curriculum proposed for the next resident class, that of 1972. He approved the new curricular theme and the program proposed to support it. Even while approving the 1971-72 resident curriculum, however, General Davis expressed his view that the War College needed a longer-range guiding program looking five, ten, and fifteen years into the future, and even a broad concept for twenty years in the future. At this time, however, the entire Army officer schooling system was under another comprehensive review—this one initiated by General Westmoreland.[4]

The Norris Review

In November 1970 General Westmoreland had directed Major General Frank W. Norris (AWC 1956), who had just completed three years as commandant of the Armed Forces Staff College, to make a personal examination of the Army's school system. Norris was not to head the customary board of officers but he was to examine the school system in terms of policy and philosophy. His review was to be subjective, providing a synthesis of existing ideas and thoughts rather than developing new concepts. Norris was to isolate the more critical educational issues and to recommend any changes in the school system that might better prepare officers for the challenges of the 1970s.[5]

General Norris's schedule did not allow a close examination of the Army War College until the summer of 1971, after General Davis had replaced General Eckhardt. Throughout the summer and fall of 1971 Norris maintained close coordination with the War College. By the end of November he had completed his year-long review and published his report. According to the report the Army War College was "generally . . . in good shape." Norris refuted the criticism that an educational gap existed at the War College; he believed that the scope of the college's program did in fact prepare officers for their probable assignments as commanders and key staff members of major military and departmental headquarters. If there was an educational gap in the system, Norris believed that it existed at Leavenworth. The Command and General Staff College, in his view, should adopt the educational approach of the War College, becoming more than a one-course, one-curriculum school.[6]

General Norris gave the 1970-71 study on mission and curriculum high marks as a professional, in-depth piece of work that had resulted in a sound, expertly designed, and well-conducted program for academic year 1971-72. Looking ahead, General Norris had several cautions, however. He believed that as the curriculum evolved, the level at which management sciences were presented must be closely monitored to avoid too great an emphasis on technique. Moreover, nothing could become obsolescent faster than an issues-oriented curriculum. Future curriculum reviews must therefore avoid mere marginal adjustments and deal with the fundamental premises of a War College education.[7]

Norris found the nonresident program also to be expertly designed as well as academically demanding. He thought it one of the most impressive activities at the War College despite (or perhaps because of) its high noncompletion rate, then approaching forty percent. Norris believed that the nonresident program was a distinct asset which deserved emphasis and support. For assignment purposes completion of the nonresident program should be considered fully equivalent to completion of the resident program. Norris argued that the nonresident graduate had received equal educational benefit and that therefore the entry on an officer's personnel record form should be the same for both the resident and nonresident class graduate.[8]

General Norris felt that the consideration of long-term issues of fundamental importance to the Army as a whole was a function entirely proper for the War College. He commended the impressive results of the Professionalism Study and the Leadership Study, which he categorized as landmark efforts that could not have been performed by any other agency. Again, however, he issued a warning. The War College should not be used to solve specific problems of immediate concern to officers of the Army Staff; the War College should not become their catch-all; only the Chief of Staff, the Vice Chief, and the DCSPER should have the authority to assign studies.[9]

The Norris report included an annex in which were included "good programs" that had been uncovered during the review. His aim was to highlight effective programs at one school for the consideration of all. Cited was the faculty chair program of the Naval War College. As for the academic chair program at the Army War College, General Norris remarked that it was promising, but that it had not achieved its potential.[10]

Norris mentioned another promising War College effort, the recently reinstated cooperative graduate degree program. It will be recalled that the contract with The George Washington University was allowed to lapse in the summer of 1966. General Salet discovered then that the solid front he thought he had built with the heads of the other senior service colleges had collapsed. None of the other colleges terminated, as promised, their arrangements with the university. It soon became evident that some officers (of all services) selected to attend the Army War College thought they were being denied an opportunity offered officers at the other senior service schools. With the encouragement of General Bruce Palmer (the Deputy Commandant when the George Washington program was initiated and since 1968 the Vice Chief of Staff of the Army), first General McCaffrey and then General Eckhardt had explored reinstituting a cooperative graduate degree program.[11]

As a first step, in the spring of 1969 General McCaffrey arranged for a team representing the American Council on Education to evaluate the program of instruction of the War College to determine how many semester hours of credit might be recommended to a degree-granting institution for the completion of War College work. The results were somewhat disappointing; the team recommended only three to twelve semester hours in the fields of either international relations or public administration. In the following year, General Eckhardt began preliminary negotiations with a number of institutions with a view to reinstituting a cooperative degree program. That same year, 1969-70, seventeen members of the War College were attending classes during off-duty hours at Shippensburg State College, an institution within reasonable commuting distance of Carlisle. The year of General Norris's review an interim arrangement was made with Shippensburg State College, and fifty-five members of the War College were enrolled in a degree program. Unlike the earlier program with The George Washington University, there was no contractual obligation between the government and the degree-granting institution. The War College acted merely as the liaison between the military student and the school.[12]

General Norris, as part of his review of the education system, examined the Army's advanced civilian degree program. He did not favor what he termed a "sheepskin sweepstakes," but nonetheless he pointed out that the officer corps could not be faulted for following promotion board returns. On the latest selection list for brigadier general, the officer without an advanced degree was the exception rather than the rule. Norris recommended, as a principal means of providing officers with an opportunity to earn advanced degrees, that cooperative degree programs such as that of the Army War College be expanded. The problem at the War College itself would become smaller. Norris noted that ten years earlier twenty-six percent of the War College students had arrived with master's degrees; now fifty-five percent arrived with them. He anticipated that in another ten years seventy-five percent would have already earned at least a master's degree, and that the increase would be primarily in management fields.[13]

The faculty at the Army War College had approached that percentage already; Norris found that seventy-three percent had master's degrees. He believed the faculty to be of high caliber, citing favorably the War College's aggressive and comprehensive faculty recruitment. Listed as a "good program" was the War College's system for the development of faculty expertise. Norris used it as the basis of his recommendations for the entire school system. For each subject area the War College had designated a "director of studies" or "faculty expert". It set quality objectives for each of these positions in terms of required military experience and civil education. The college then supported the expert through library acquisitions and by funding membership in learned societies. Opportunity was made available also for the expert for travel and research in his particular field or specialty.[14]

Other War College activities that General Norris listed as "good programs" were the Military History Research Collection and its Senior

Officer Debriefing (or oral history) Program, the War College's system for student evaluation, and the use of the Education Testing Service to review the materials and requirements of the nonresident course. General Davis nominated one of his own early innovations for the "good program" list, a practice he called "Commandant's Dialogues." The title was descriptive; the program involved the Commandant meeting informally in the evening at his quarters with seven or eight students to discuss one or two fundamental Army questions or practices. Davis found these sessions valuable as a source of student feedback and a worthwhile experience in interpersonal communications. But Norris did not choose to include the program on his list.[15]

The Long Range Development Plan

General Norris's report did not precipitate any major changes at the Army War College. It served rather to confirm the position of those who believed that the War College was moving in the right direction. General Westmoreland, however, apparently had a broader vision of what the Army War College should be. In strong guidance to General Davis he proposed that the War College be developed into a focal point or "center of contemporary military thought."[16] Immediately after the Norris report was submitted, therefore, General Davis returned to his earlier idea as to the need for a long-range plan to guide the future War College. On December 3, 1971 he formally directed his deputy, Brigadier General W. C. Magathan, to "take the necessary action to institute a long-range development plan and related concepts, broad policies, and where appropriate and practical, programs" for the War College.

General Davis translated Westmoreland's guidance into two mutually supporting but distinct objectives. The first was to insure that the War College provided the best professional education possible that would embrace the conduct of national security affairs and the art and science of what Davis called "professional generalship." The second was to take those steps necessary to develop at Carlisle Barracks, allied with the War College, a "center of contemporary military thought." His instructions to Magathan were in essence a restatement of Elihu Root's admonition of 1901 that the Army War College was to be a place for the study of the great problems of national defense, of military science, and of responsible command.[17]

The terms, "center for contemporary military thought" and "professional generalship," became almost code words for the War College's objectives during Davis's term as Commandant. Davis defined "professional generalship" as "the totality of those personal, military, and spiritual qualities that senior officers must bring to positions of high responsibility in order to perform with competence, professionalism and human understanding."[18] He did not have as ready a definition for "center of contemporary military thought." General Westmoreland apparently had in mind a formal structure, perhaps similar to the United States Naval Institute, but the concept would take some sorting out and some careful study. In the meantime a long-range development plan could be developed to guide the War College toward its educational objective.[19]

General Magathan chose to use the Department of Research and Studies rather than a faculty committee to draw up the requested plan. He believed, probably correctly, that a faculty group would consume too much time. It was important to get General Westmoreland's approval of the plan before his four-year tour as Chief of Staff expired during the approaching summer. Lieutenant Colonels Walter Ulmer (AWC 1969) and D. M. Malone (AWC 1970) and Dr. Donald D. Penner became the primary authors of the plan. They proved to be as responsive to the time constraints as General Magathan had hoped. The decision not to have representation from the teaching departments among the planners, however, would have repercussions.[20]

Within a week after their appointment, the team members produced a draft general concept, and by March they were able to brief General Westmoreland on the outlines of a development plan. They were not really starting from scratch. The genesis for a revised War College program lay in at least four sources. The "Professionalism Study," the "Leadership Study," and the ongoing "Army Tasks for the Seventies Study" all pointed to areas with which the Army War College should concern itself in the future. Moreover, the 1970 "Mission and Curriculum Study" was in essence the first step in long-range development planning.[21]

In arriving at their plan the study team dealt with the entire War College, including its support structure and physical plant, as a single integrated educational system. Within this one large system four subsystems were chosen for investigation and possible change: the curriculum structure; the process of evaluation and feedback as it pertained to students, classes, and programs; faculty selection and use; and the organization of the college. The study team argued that these four subsystems were so interdependent that the success of the long-range development plan depended upon acceptance of the modifications recommended in all four areas. By April the plan had taken definite form. The theme on which it was built was "the optimization of the learning opportunity ... by tailoring the USAWC education to individual education needs." The term "tailoring" joined "professional generalship" and "center of contemporary thought" in the popular lexicon of the Army War College.[22]

General Westmoreland visited Carlisle in May, was again briefed on the progress of the study, and expressed his concurrence in the plan as presented by General Davis and Colonel Malone. (Colonel Ulmer had been reassigned from the War College the previous month.) In regard to the structure of the curriculum, the study group believed that the primary weakness in the current curriculum (1971-72) was its rigidity. Except for the research program and two electives, all students took the same course. The program was not adjustable to the specific needs of the individual student. A second weakness was the multiple simultaneous demands placed on a student by having him address concurrently the main course, a weekly seminar, a weekly elective, and his research project. Additionally, repetition of essentially the same instructional methodology throughout the year was thought to be less than stimulating.[23]

To correct these weaknesses the plan called for distilling and shortening the present curriculum into a "common overview," expanding and upgrading the elective courses, and adding a period of "applicatory experiential group learning." Gradual change would be made in the curriculum structure so that by the year 1975-76 a trimester structure would be in place. The first trimester, the period from August to Christmas, would be devoted to the common overview attended by all students and entitled "National and International Security Affairs." Two horizontal seminars would also be conducted during this period, the "Military Strategy Seminar" of twelve weeks, and a four-week seminar on "commandership," leadership, and executive development. Just before the Christmas break, a symposium with outside guests, similar in format to the traditional National Strategy Seminar, would be held to cap the common overview. The emphasis of the symposium would not be on a military program to support a national strategy, however, but on the domestic and international aspects of national security affairs.[24]

The second trimester, January through mid-March, would be devoted exclusively to elective courses. A wide variety were to be offered, from which a program could be tailored to each student's individual professional needs. The remainder of the year would be devoted to intensive group study of selected contemporary military and national security problems. As described in the draft plan the group problem-solving phase was to be a return (although the plan's authors apparently did not realize it) to the committee study system of the second Army War College and of the initial years of the third Army War College. The problems envisioned for study and report appear, however, to have been at a somewhat higher level. Even the old practice of interchange and presentation between committees or study groups was revived. Finally, just before graduation, another symposium would be hosted during which contemporary national security problems would be discussed with outside experts. Since the discussion topics were to be the problems investigated during the group problem-solving phase, the student groups would be responsible to nominate the experts to attend the symposium.[25]

With the heavy emphasis to be placed on "tailoring," the planners were convinced that an "inventory and feedback" system was absolutely critical to the success of the overall War College program. "Inventory and feedback" systems were therefore designed to measure both student progress and system development. The data gathered through these efforts would not only support the student in his personal and professional development, but also serve War College and Department of the Army educational and personnel management programs. Six major assessments would occur sequentially as the student moved through the academic year, beginning with a baseline inventory and concluding with a value gained inventory.[26]

The baseline inventory would assess the student's skills, abilities, and characteristics before he arrived at the War College. A self-appraisal, it would assist the individual in taking stock of himself and assist the War College in planning an individualized development program.[27]

An "optional personal inventory" would begin immediately after the student's arrival at Carlisle. As the title indicated, it would be strictly voluntary; a student could withdraw at any time. The inventory would be designed to measure an individual's attitudes, values, goals, and personality and would be supported by a coaching program with trained faculty counselors. Results of the inventory would be provided only to the student and to his faculty counselor at the student's request.[28]

A "professional self-assessment" would occur during the common overview phase. In addition to the traditional group solution required by the courses of this phase, an individual examination would be administered. Each student would compare his solution with an "expert solution" provided by the faculty department. The student could assess thereby the degree of his own understanding of the field of study with that of an expert faculty member. The examination paper would then be forwarded anonymously to the faculty department so that the department could make a determination in the aggregate of how well the class had achieved the learning objectives of the courses.[29]

During the electives, or "Individual Selective Concentration Phase" of the year, "academic assessment" would be administered as it is commonly done in graduate school, that is, by written or oral examination or term papers. No grades, scores, or transcripts would be recorded, however. This assessment would serve the student by providing him with an expert evaluation of his work, and it would assist the instructor in determining the effectiveness of his efforts and in developing future course content and instructional methodology. Though the planners did not mention it, there was ample precedent for this type of assessment in the methods of evaluation of the written work of the students in the nonresident classes.[30]

An "experiential assessment" scheme was planned for the group research or problem-solving phase of the year's program. Now the student would be evaluated in the manner he would encounter in duty assignments after graduation. He would be evaluated by the study team leader (a faculty member), by his peers, and by experts in the subject area in which the research was conducted. The faculty team leader would provide each student with an evaluation similar in format to the standard officer efficiency report; however, this evaluation would go only to the student and would not become in any sense a matter of record. Anonymity would also prevail in the appraisals by peers; they would go only to the student being appraised. Subject-area evaluation would deal solely with the study team's product, not with the accomplishment of any individual team member. From the total "experiential assessment" effort, the individual would gain insights into how he works as a team member and colleague, the team leader would receive information upon which to base future study methodology, and all members of the team and the War College would have a basis for judging the conclusions of the research.[31]

The "value gained" inventory at the end of the academic year would attempt to determine the total effect on the student of the War College experience. The student, now almost a graduate, would have a starting point for planning his continuing individual development. The War College would gain even more from this final inventory: it should learn the degree to which curricular objectives had been achieved. The method of conducting the "value gained inventory" would be equivalent to the baseline inventory at the beginning of the year.[32]

In designing the "inventory and feedback" system, the long-range development planners were fully aware of the dangers of introducing what might be considered grading, the anxieties that might be created and the unhealthy competition that might follow. They were therefore careful to design a system that in their view would avoid the pitfalls of grading while at the same time providing the student, the faculty, the War College, and the Army some measure of what was or was not being accomplished, a measure that the planners felt was completely missing and sorely needed. To facilitate individual student development without appearing threatening, the "developmental coach" was introduced as a key figure. Specifically trained for the task, the coach was to be the communications link between the assessment system and the student. The planners of 1972, however, did not contemplate that the assessment system could be completely introduced into the program immediately. A three-year period from 1973 through 1975 was believed necessary as a period of experiment, test, and gradual introduction. Not until academic year 1975-76 would the system be completely in place.[33]

Fundamental to the success of the "inventory and feedback" system was a highly qualified teaching faculty that could provide the required range of subject-area expertise—and from about fifteen members of the faculty, the necessary skill in counseling or "coaching." The idea of replacing a "coordinating" or "management" faculty with a "teaching faculty" was of course hardly new. General Salet had taken the important first step of relating faculty positions ("directors") to certain areas of expertise, but his own staff did not fully support his idea of a faculty of specialists or a tenured faculty, and General Harrell had actively opposed the idea. The Haines Board recommendations on faculty, moreover, were weak and grossly underestimated the effect of electives on faculty composition. Even the mild Haines suggestion that some faculty members be given longer stabilized tours could not be supported by the Department of the Army. General Eckhardt had attempted to build upon the Salet directorship scheme, had met with some success, and had been commended in the Norris report for his efforts. Nonetheless, as late as 1972 the War College planners could still categorize the faculty as "coordinating" without drawing serious rebuttal.[34]

The Long Range Development Plan contemplated a faculty part military and part civilian, with both long-term and short-term members, some of whom would be authorized by manpower allocation documents and some of whom would be "special." The faculty would have educational and subject-area expertise and would be the product of a careful and continuing process of selection and development. Expertise was to be the overriding criterion; to be a "real leader" or a "damned good man" would not be enough, nor would academic degrees alone. The traditional requirement that only graduates of a senior service college were eligible to become military faculty members would be waived in order to get the necessary subject area or educational expertise. Faculty selection, recruitment, and development in large part would be delegated to the department chairmen, with a senior faculty board and the Commandant having final approval authority. Once brought onto the faculty, an officer or a civilian academician would be given the time and the monetary support to pursue further his area of specialization. The plan proposed some seven different levels of stability for faculty members.[35]

Finally, the Long Range Development Plan proposed changes in the college organization and certain titles in order to align functions with proposed curricular and other changes, and to emphasize the teaching role. To this end, each teaching department was to be provided an executive officer and a civilian administrator to relieve the faculty from administrative chores. The Department of Strategy would be combined with the Department of Military Planning to form a "Department of Strategy and Planning." At its own request, The Department of National and International Security Studies was to delete "Studies" from its title and substitute "Affairs." The Department of Research and

Studies would be retitled the "Department of Institutional Research." It would continue to coordinate the publication and student research programs but would give added emphasis to educational research and to planning, coordinating, and supervising the proposed program for inventory, assessment, and student guidance.[36]

A major organizational innovation was the establishment of an office of the Director of Academic Affairs, or DAA. The Deputy Commandant would serve concurrently as the DAA, with a high-grade civil servant acting as his deputy director. An experienced educator and administrator would be brought in to fill the deputy position, thereby providing a stability and continuity that had been lacking. The office of the DAA in effect was to perform the functions that heretofore had been those of both the Director of Instruction and the Educational Adviser. The title of "Commandant" was to become "President," a return to the practice of the first Army War College. More compatible with civilian academic nomenclature, it was believed that the new title would ease relationships with the academic community. General Davis did not disapprove the change in his title, but he held the change in abeyance until the development plan was fully implemented.[37]

As comprehensive as the Long Range Development Plan appeared to be, its concentration was solely on the War College's resident program. The nonresident program was mentioned only in passing even though there were more nonresident students than resident students. As was the habit, the Department of Nonresident Instruction apparently was expected to adapt itself as best it could to whatever changes were made in the resident program. The Institute of Advanced Studies (renamed after General Davis's arrival the "Strategic Studies Institute") did not figure in the plan, nor did the Military History Research Collection, although both had the capability to make major contributions to educational excellence. Despite these omissions, the Long Range Development Plan was the most scientific and systematic review of the Army War College program yet attempted. Particularly significant was the underlying philosophy that a single course of instruction, common for all students, was no longer an appropriate response to the demands of the great problems of national defense, of military science, and of responsible command.

After General Westmoreland's approval of the plan in May, the month before he was to retire, the War College was able to move ahead with the first stage of its implementation. In July, Lieutenant Colonel Benjamin E. Doty (AWC 1970) was appointed project officer to coordinate its implementation. Since the success of the scheme depended upon obtaining personnel with the proper qualifications, the first order of business was to win Department of the Army approval of the manpower requests. After some initial difficulties the DCSPER agreed in September to support a "three-tiered faculty," a term first used in the Norris review. The majority of the faculty would be assigned for a three-year stabilized tour; a few would be tenured to the degree that renewable two-year extensions would be approved. In a scheme similar to that of the first Army War College whereby non-General Staff Corps officers would be assigned as instructors for one year, a third group of faculty members would be assigned for two years or less. The DCSPER cautioned, however, that Army and career development needs might cause exceptions to the policy. The Department of the Army also approved having executive officers assigned to the teaching departments. During this same period, the fall of 1972, the War College was able to extract from the DCSPER a "policy continuity" letter which put the Department of the Army on record as supporting the objectives and philosophy of the Long Range Development Plan.[38]

No reorganization took place before the academic year began, but the office of the Director of Academic Affairs (DAA) was organized in February 1973. In a change to the original plan, the Deputy Commandant did not become the DAA; that position, pending the authorization and hiring of a civilian, was filled by Colonel Henry A. Barber, III, formerly the Director of Instruction. The Department of Research and Studies, for a brief period renamed the "Department of Institutional Research," went out of existence in February. In another significant change to the plan, the functions of that department were assumed by the office of the DAA.[39]

No radical changes were either proposed or carried out in the curriculum for 1972-73. The "Human Dimensions of Military Professionalism Seminar" was combined with the course "National Defense Decision Making and Management" to create a new course, "Management and Executive Development." A four-week "Military Jurisprudence Seminar" was added and horizontally scheduled to provide instruction in international, civil, and military criminal law. The number of electives grew to twenty-seven. As in previous years, electives were presented in both the fall and the spring. Thought was given to changing the name of the end-of-the-year symposium to "National Issues and Alternatives Seminar" to reflect the earlier change in curricular theme, but the title remained "National Strategy Seminar." In the area of inventory and assessment, a peer rating system was experimented with on an optional basis during the elective course "Interpersonal and Small Group Communication." Peer ratings were not all that new an idea. As early as 1959 an instructor, Lieutenant Colonel Arthur S. Collins (AWC 1953), had made a strong but unsuccessful argument to have them introduced together with more formal student counseling and guidance.[40]

What was scheduled for 1972-73 in the Long Range Development Plan had been accomplished, but to a casual observer it would appear that little had changed that year at the Army War College. This would seem especially so when compared to events that year at the Naval War College. The new President of that institution, Vice Admiral Stansfield Turner, almost overnight had altered radically not only the substance but the methodology of the Naval War College's senior course. Moreover, Turner and the Navy chose to give wide publicity to the changes being made. With the service journals editorializing on Turner's bold new approach, there was official and unofficial speculation as to whether the other senior service colleges would do well to follow Turner's lead. General Davis was forced to become somewhat defensive of his slower (and in his mind much more prudent) design for change. He explained in letters and when possible in briefings what it was he was about, and in February 1973 Lieutenant Colonel Doty published an article in *Army* magazine entitled "Opening Some Windows at the Army War College," a title somewhat insensitive to the feelings of those who had been responsible for the Army War College's earlier and recent programs. In sum, Admiral Turner's activities lent urgency to getting on with the Long Range Development Plan.[41]

A Center of Contemporary Military Thought

The Long Range Development Plan addressed General Davis's first objective, education in professional generalship. Movement toward the second objective outlined by General Westmoreland—creating a center of contemporary military thought—was a bit slower getting off the mark. In the fall of 1971, when General Westmoreland had outlined his ambitions for the War College, he had advised Davis to contact retired General Charles H. Bonesteel, III, former commander of United Nations Forces in Korea and an officer with broad politico-military experience and reputation for scholarship. Davis met with General Bonesteel in January 1972 to explore how the War College might proceed to develop a formal institute that would "wrest the mantle" (apparently Westmoreland's term) of contemporary military thought from those who currently held it. Exactly who was wearing that mantle was not precisely defined.[42]

Bonesteel suggested to Davis that about ten years would be required to build an institute such as that described. A focus on military strategy would be too narrow. In Bonesteel's judgment the very meaning of military power was changing. The world—and the United States—was in the midst of a social revolution; social power increasingly was becoming the determinant of affairs. It was a legacy of McNamara's approach to national strategy to consider the United States and the Soviet Union as two competing weapon systems when, in fact, the world was a complex of competing cultures, social systems, and values with commonalities as well as differences. Any useful effort to "wrest the mantle" would have to be multidisciplinary. Complete reliance on the Army's budget to support the endeavor would guarantee failure. Bonesteel saw a complicating factor in the Army's public image; in 1972 that image was so poor that something had to be done soon if the Army was to regain its legitimate influence. He suggested that as an early step in that direction the Army War College host a conference to which would be invited distinguished individuals with an interest in and an understanding of civil-military affairs.[43]

Bonesteel's discourse was sobering; it made clear the true dimensions of any effort to "wrest the mantle." At Carlisle Barracks the subject in fact remained dormant until June 1973, when it was reopened with a staff paper written by faculty member Colonel Niven J. Baird (AWC 1972). After discussing the pros and cons of establishing a quasi-official organization somewhat akin to the United States Naval Institute and with the title "Omar N. Bradley Center for Defense Studies," Baird concluded that an entity separate from the War College was not appropriate, that any effort to "wrest the mantle" should be in direct support of the War College's teaching mission. He proposed instead a sort of "wrest the mantle" program encompassing greater faculty stability, increased publication by members of the War College, individual and institutional affiliation with learned societies, and periodic War College sponsorship of the annual conventions of such societies. A project officer should be authorized whose single duty would be to guide both this program and the implementation of the Long Range Development Plan. Baird's paper did not have great influence.[44]

Actually there were a number of activities going on at Carlisle Barracks that had the potential to contribute to the objective of creating a center for contemporary military thought, but they were not pulled together into one comprehensive plan or program. In the past, various student research and studies programs had been looked to as a source for advanced military thought. When General McCaffrey was Commandant, however, that effort received a setback when the Department of the Army declined to provide funds for travel in connection with the studies. Later, Secretary Laird felt that the military school systems could be made into a more widely used source of fresh ideas and directed each service to set up a system for circulating abstracts of student papers and of recognizing deserving authors. Thus in academic year 1971-72 the Army War College forwarded to the Department of the Army thirty-six of the sixty-two items of student work completed that year. During academic year 1970-71, in another project, the Department of Strategy carried out a publishing effort similar in format and purpose to that of the Parson Committee of 1965. Under the direction of the department chairman, Colonel James H. Short (AWC 1967), six faculty members and seven students of the Class of 1972 prepared a text on military strategy edited by Colonel Wilmer F. Cline, USAF (AWC 1968), a faculty member formerly with the History Department at the Air Force Academy. Designed primarily to support the "Military Strategy Seminar," the work consisted of fifteen chapters by the end of the year. It represented a considerable body of contemporary military thought. Also in 1972 General Davis obtained permission to continue publishing *Parameters.*[45]

During the 1972-73 academic year the long-considered concept of having civilian scholars at the War College for a year's residence showed tangible results. In addition to the occupant of the Stimson Chair of Political Science attached to the Department of National and International Security Studies, an economist was brought into the Department of Management and a behavioral scientist into the Department of Research and Studies. The Military History Research Collection also established a visiting professorship, a Chair of Military History Research. In addition to his research activities, the occupant was asked to offer an elective at the War College in the field of military history.[46]

Beginning with the year 1971-72, the Department of the Army initiated a program whereby Army officers with appropriate experience and academic credentials who had been selected for senior service college attendance could, rather than attending a war college, volunteer for a year's work at the Ph.D. or fellowship level at universities or at such places as the Hoover Institution on War, Revolution, and Peace. These few "Research Associates" were attached to the Army War College, attended two National Strategy Seminars and, as an observer, attended the end-of-course resident phase of a nonresident class. They were also required to visit the Army War College one additional time during the year and to keep the War College informed on the progress of their research. The program's underlying purpose was to improve the dialogue between the Army (and the Army War College) and that part of the academic community interested in national security affairs.[47]

The greatest potential for converting the Army War College into a center for contemporary military thought, however, resulted from a major reorganization of the Army beginning in the early spring of 1973. Termed STEADFAST, this reorganization affected the War College in two ways. First, after a decade of serving the Combat Developments Command, the Strategic Studies Institute (formerly the Institute of Advanced Studies), reverted to being an integral part of the Army War College, as had been the Doctrine and Studies Group and, before it, the Advanced Studies Group from which the Institute of Advanced Studies had sprung. Second, the War College itself was removed from the supervision of the Department of the Army DCSPER and placed under the supervision of the DCSOPS.

The scheme that in 1971 would have merged the Institute of Advanced Studies with the Institute of Land Combat had been aborted by a reorganization of CDC. In that reorganization the Institute of Land Combat was disestablished and replaced with a smaller agency which, in addition to conducting the LCS-90 study, was somehow expected to perform all the combat developments functions pertaining to the echelons above the division. In the same reorganization the Institute of Advanced Studies was renamed the Strategic Studies Institute (SSI) to better reflect the nature of the studies it was to perform. The SSI evolved thereafter in many respects into a field agency of the DCSOPS. When STEADFAST disestablished both CONARC and CDC in 1973 and erected in their places a "Training and Doctrine Command" and a "Forces Command," the issue arose as to where organizationally to place both the SSI and the Army War College.[48]

After its divorce from CONARC in 1960 and its successful resistance to the advances of CDC in the late 1960s, the War College now had to persuade the STEADFAST planners that a forced marriage with the Training and Doctrine Command (TRADOC) was inappropriate. Since TRADOC was to direct both the Army's school system and its combat developments, there was, at least on the surface, a reasonable argument that both the War College and the SSI should join TRADOC. (Army reorganization planners over the years seem to have had difficulty distinguishing between vocational training and graduate education.) Using rationale similar to that used by Generals Max Johnson, Salet, McCaffrey, and Eckhardt before him, General Davis argued strongly that the War College should remain directly under Headquarters, Department of the Army. Davis also feared for the future of the Long Range Development Plan in TRADOC's hands. There were gap-fillers among the STEADFAST planners who thought that the War College should concentrate, if not confine, its instruction on the operations of echelons above the division. Davis apparently found allies. With the SSI and the Operations Group already serving primarily the DCSOPS and with the field of military strategy claimed as the special province of the War College, the Department of the Army decided that the educational institution at Carlisle Barracks should retain its independence.[49]

In January the SSI rejoined the War College, and control of the War College passed from the DCSPER to the DCSOPS, then Lieutenant General Donald H. Cowles (AWC 1958). STEADFAST reduced the personnel strength of most Army headquarters and agencies, but the SSI was an exception; it was actually authorized a higher level of manning, ostensibly to better serve both the DCSOPS and the Army War College. With its increased strength and dedication to research, and as part of the Army War College, the SSI seemed to provide a unique capability for leading the War College to the Westmoreland goal of becoming a center for contemporary thought.[50]

447

The Program of 1973-74

Soon after the War College passed to the control of the DCSOPS, Brigadier General Henry C. Newton, USAR Retired, arrived at Carlisle to survey the DCSOPS' new responsibility. Newton had been a consultant to the Haines Board and the educational adviser to the Commanding General of CONARC. He provided General Cowles with an encouraging report of what was occurring at the War College and lent his support to the Long Range Development Plan. He suggested that a permanent Advisory Board be appointed for the Army War College, that the title of the Commandant be changed to "President," and that the number of full-time civilian faculty members be increased. General Davis did not concur in having an Advisory Board, nor in changing his title, but he agreed that more civilian professors were needed, perhaps up to fifteen percent of the faculty. Newton was against having foreign officers enrolled, arguing that the problems of safeguarding classified information and the prospect of inhibiting the candor of guest lecturers made their presence "utterly impossible." Davis did not comment; the matter was again under consideration at the Department of the Army.[51]

Academic year 1973-74 was a transition year in the move toward the ultimate 1975-76 program called for by the Long Range Development Plan. In preparation, the Department of Strategy was combined with the Department of Military Planning to form the Department of Military Planning and Strategy. General Davis still refused to allow the Department of National and International Security Studies to substitute "Affairs" for "Studies" in its title. The term "executive development" had fallen into disrepute, and General Davis had changed the name of the course presented by the Department of Management from "Defense Management and Executive Development" back to "Command and Management"; similarly, the name of the department was changed to the "Department of Command and Management." The concern over "command" versus "management" seems not unlike the earlier concern of the second Army War College over "command" versus "staff." A position of Professor of Military History was added to the Department of Military Planning and Strategy; Dr. Charles S. Hall, formerly the Educational Advisor, was appointed to the position. Within the office of the DAA were created two new positions, the Director of Inventory and Assessment and the Director of Military Research Programs.[52]

During the fall of 1973 applications were received and interviews conducted to bring on board the civilian Director of Academic Affairs. In the interim, Colonel Harold B. Birch served in that capacity. The DAA was to be both an experienced administrator and an experienced educator, a Ph.D. degree being required in one of a number of appropriate disciplines. He was to act as the senior staff officer to the Commandant and Deputy Commandant in all academic matters. Selected for the position in January 1974 was Dr. Charles S. Hersh, formerly a professor of political science at American University and then with the Office of Special Studies of DCSPER, Department of the Army. Dr. Hersh assumed his new duties in May 1974.[53]

The principle change in the 1973-74 transition year was to reduce the time devoted to the common curriculum from forty-one to thirty-one weeks. The extra weeks, consuming April and May, were given exclusively to the Military Research Program. Group research was preferred and encouraged, although individual research was permitted if a student had justifiable reasons and appropriate qualifications. Three courses were presented during the period of the common curriculum, "The United States and the World Environment," "Command and Management," and "Strategic Military Studies." In substance these were the first five courses presented the year before. The extra weeks for research were found in part by eliminating Course 6: "National Security Issues," and by reducing by a week each the time allotted to the Department of National and International Security Studies and the Department of Command and Management. The Department of Military Planning and Strategy bore the brunt of the time sacrifice. It lost three weeks from its previous year's allocation; additionally, it had to absorb the remains of Course 6, and in its "Military Strategy Seminar" had to provide instruction in Internal Defense and Development Operations. The end of a dedicated course in the latter topic in 1973-74 came twelve years after "Counterinsurgency" had been so urgently introduced.[54]

The "Military Strategy Seminar" was repeated, and once again horizontally scheduled, as was the "Military Jurisprudence Seminar." The "Elements of Command" program, now conducted by the Department of Command and Management, was continued, and an "Elements of Management" program of similar format was added. The number of elective courses grew from twenty-seven to thirty. Nine were categorized as political science, seven as management, three as behavioral science, two each as economics and sociology, and one each as law and communicative arts. One elective course on "futurism" was classified as interdisciplinary. Two electives were offered in military history and two in military strategy. In this transition year the overall program was decidedly multidisciplinary, and the trend was definitely not toward a more strictly military program. If any disciplines tended to be dominant, they were political science and management.[55]

In 1974 the title of the symposium that for twenty years had climaxed the resident program caught up with the change in curricular theme that had occurred in 1972; it became the National *Security* Seminar instead of the National *Strategy* Seminar. Although the idea of two symposia, as called for by the original Long Range Development Plan, was abandoned, the format of the one that was held reflected the thinking behind the plan. It was to act as a test of the results of student research efforts. In plenary session two student study groups especially formed for the purpose presented the results of their work; one paper was on domestic, international, and defense issues and alternatives, the other on a proposed national strategy for the period 1990-95. Four other student study groups presented papers in smaller sessions attended by interested guests. An SSI team presented a paper, as did two students on the results of individual work. Additionally, five lectures by guest speakers were scheduled. It was a busy week.[56]

The inventory and assessment portion of the Long Range Development Plan got off to a bad start. The baseline survey questionnaire sent to the incoming students of the Class of 1974 reached them before the *Curriculum Pamphlet*; hence it made little sense to the recipients. Then the college failed to inform the students how they compared individually with the class profile—nor were faculty advisers provided this information. Four faculty "coaches" had been selected and trained, each to work with fifteen volunteer students. Without the baseline survey, however, a coach could hardly conduct a meaningful counseling program. Moreover, it was then decided that the coaches would not even be allowed to see the academic feeder reports prepared on their students as the year progressed. If the War College really intended to have an inventory and assessment program, it had lost a year in getting one started.[57]

The nine weeks dedicated to the Military Research Program and the revised format of the National Strategy Seminar represented steps in the direction of the goal of a center for contemporary military thought. Additionally the Department of Military Planning and Strategy continued work on the military strategy text. By the end of academic year 1973-74, this work had grown to six volumes of twenty-six chapters, and a seventh volume was planned. An argument can be made, however, that effort directed at distillation and synthesis of the earlier chapters would have been more useful than the continuing addition of more chapters.[58]

Colonel Joseph E. Pizzi (AWC 1965), the Director of the Strategic Studies Institute, had to overcome shortages in both the funds and the officer and civilian professionals authorized his enlarged agency. Nonetheless, in addition to performing major and "quick reaction" studies for the DCSOPS, he was able to form in 1973 a small group that he hoped could carry out investigations on its own initiative without having to respond to guidance and suspense dates imposed by higher headquarters. In April 1974 Pizzi also had the SSI host a Security Issues Symposium to which twenty military and civilian officials in policy positions were invited to hear and comment upon papers presented by guests and by SSI researchers. These papers were published the following year under the title *New Dynamics of National Strategy: The Paradox of Power.*

The SSI also began to publish "Military Issue Research Memorandum" pamphlets, developed on the initiative of members of the institute or as derivatives of directed studies. These were single-issue analytical efforts for distribution within the Department of Defense, designed to raise new issues or provide new insights on old issues. Five were published in 1973, twenty-two in 1974. Faculty members other than those assigned to the SSI also began to contribute to this series.[59]

Publication of the *Leadership for the 1970's* study in 1971 did not end the War College's research and analysis efforts in that area. Using a massive amount of data collected during a worldwide survey and seminar program by the CONARC Leadership Board from the fall of 1971 forward, the War College conducted a range of quantitative analyses of the Army's current leadership practices. This work led to publication of a monograph series from June 1973 through August 1974, disseminated to the Army under the collective title *U.S. Army War College Studies of Leadership for the Professional Soldier.* After six monographs were published, further analytical work using the CONARC data base was transferred to the U.S. Army Personnel and Administrative Center at Fort Benjamin Harrison, Indiana. If in the early 1970s the Army War College fell short of becoming a "center for contemporary military thought," the evidence is nonetheless convincing that it had become an intellectually aware and active institution with interests covering a wide spectrum, from small-unit leadership to military strategy to national security affairs in the broadest sense.[60]

In his role of Commanding General of Carlisle Barracks, General Davis was not able to move ahead those construction projects pending when General Eckhardt departed. The sixty sets of family quarters were advertised for bid in June 1972, but all bids were too high and therefore rejected in August. Neither would the Department of Defense approve the construction of the new gymnasium. Expansion of the Military History Research Collection and the Bradley Museum was thereby stalled. The plan for the fourth floor for Root Hall was not yet dead, but neither was it moving forward. Inside Root Hall, however, a closed circuit television was installed during the summer of 1973, and by the fall of 1974 most seminar rooms contained remote teletype terminals connected with the central computer.[61]

General Davis retired from active service and departed Carlisle Barracks in June 1974. Implementation of the Long Range Development Plan that had begun with the instructions received from General Westmoreland in 1971 was progressing, albeit unevenly. The faculty had been reorganized, and the just-completed curriculum represented the planned second stage in conversion to the "tailored" concept. But the inventory and assessment system originally thought to be critical to the entire scheme was in serious difficulty. Additionally, although progress had been made in faculty selection and development, this progress could be reversed any time the Army's personnel managers withdrew or were unable to provide their support. Tentative steps had been made in the direction of creating a center for contemporary military thought, but no formal or effective program for wresting the mantle had emerged.

NOTES

1. AWC, Memorandum 10-1, 22 March 1965, Subject: Discontinuance, Redesignation and Organization, File 204-58. Secretary to Department Chairmen, 15 December 1970, Subject: Realignment of USAWC Faculty, File 714-02. *The Army War College Commentary* (October 1970): 94-95.
2. AWC, Commander's Narrative Analysis: Appropriation—OMA FY 1973, File: ADP Budget FY72. Eckhardt to Davis, 4 March 1971, Inc. 1, File 1001-07.
3. Ibid., Tab B, 2.
4. Davis, 2 April 1971, Ideas, par. 5.
5. Major General Frank W. Norris, *Review of Army Officer Educational System*, 3 vols. (Washington: 1 December 1971), I: 1.1., 1.6, App. A.
6. Ibid., 7.1, 3.2-3.4, 6.1-6.6.
7. Ibid., 7.1.
8. Ibid., 7.3.
9. Ibid., 7.2.
10. Ibid., III: 6-7, I: 7.4.
11. Ibid., II: 8.7. Interview with Dr. Charles S. Hall, November 1981 (Hall was Educational Advisor to General Eckhardt).
12. Strong to Commandant, 9 April 1969, Subject: Suggested Guidelines for the Commandant's Entrance Interview with the ACE Team, File 1003-06. Acting Deputy Assistant Secretary of Defense (Education) to Director of Individual Training, DA, 26 May 1969, Subject: Graduate Level Accreditation, File 206-06. Morton to Deputy Commandant, 26 February 1970. Hall Interview. "AWC Expansion Denied," *Army Times* (29 April 1970). Norris, *Review*, II: 8.7, 8.15.
13. Ibid., I: 8.5, 8.9, 14.11; II: 7.1.
14. Ibid., I: 7.1, 10.1; III: 22-26.
15. Ibid., I: 13.1-13.3; III: 57-60, 150-51, 189. Davis to Norris, 14 September 1971, File 1001-02.
16. Davis, 2 April 1971, Ideas. Davis to Deputy Commandant, 3 December 1971, Subject: Long-Range Development of the U.S. Army War College, Malone Files. Davis to MG Warren K. Bennett, 10 December 1971, Commandant's File, 1971.
17. Ibid.
18. Davis to Matthew B. Ridgway, 26 May 1974, File 1010-04.
19. Davis to Bennett, 10 December 1971. Malone Interview.
20. Ibid. Magathan for Commandant, 9 December 1971, Subject: Study Team USAWC Long Range Development, Malone Files.
21. AWC, Study IV: Draft General Concept, 15 December 1971, Ibid. AWC, Minutes of Deputies Meeting, 5 April 1972, File 714-02.
22. Malone Interview. AWC, Long Range Development Plan (Draft), 30 October 1972, Chap. I: 9-13, Chap. II: 12-13, Malone Files. Commandant, Armed Forces Staff College to Chairman, JCS, 14 July 1972, Subject: Report of the 1972 Military Education Coordination Conference, File 1011-05.
23. AWC, Minutes of Deputies Meeting, 13 April 1972, File 714-02. Long Range Development Plan (Draft), 30 October 1972, Chap. II: 10-11.
24. Ibid., 17-23.
25. Ibid., 23-37.
26. Ibid., Annex C, 1, 7.
27. Ibid., 7-14.
28. Ibid., 14-18.
29. Ibid., 18-21.

30. Ibid., 21-23.
31. Ibid., 23-26.
32. Ibid., 26-28.
33. Ibid., 2-7, 29-33. AWC, LRDP Draft Planning Schedule—Revision No. 4 (1 October 1972), C-Inventory & Feedback, Malone Files.
34. AWC, Faculty Selection and Development (Draft), 14 November 1972, 1, Ibid.
35. Ibid., 1-18.
36. AWC, Briefing, "Policy Planning Toward 1980: Concepts for Maintaining Educational Excellence," n.d. , Commandant's File, 1972. Chairman, DNISS to Commandant, 5 April 1972, Subject: Organization of DNISS, File 407-01.
37. AWC, Briefing, "Policy Planning." Davis to LTG Donald H. Cowles, 18 April 1973, Incl. 1, 2, Commandant's File 1973.
38. Batiste to LTC Benjamin E. Doty, 17 July 1972, Subject: Detail of USAWC Faculty Officer, File 714-02. Seitz to Commandant, 29 September 1972, Subject: Personnel Policies and Procedures to Support the USAWC Long Range Development Plan, Ibid. Batiste to Dept. Chairmen, 2 October 1972, Ibid. Seitz to Commandant, 31 October 1972, Subject: Policy Continuity for the USAWC Long Range Development Plan, Commandant's File 1972.
39. AWC, 15 December 1972, Minutes of Deputies Meeting 13 December 1972, File 101-02. AWC, Memorandum, 6 February 1973, Subject: Disestablishment of Department of Institutional Research, File 207-01.
40. *Curriculum Pamphlet 1972 (Resident)*. AWC, *Curriculum Pamphlet Academic Year 1973 (Resident)*, 1 July 1972. DR&S to Deputy Commandant, 18 April 1972, Subject: Peer Rating Research, Central Files 1967-75. A. S. Collins to Commandant, 6 August 1959, Subject: Thoughts on Policies at the USAWC, File 245/4.
41. For details on changes at the Naval War College see Stansfield Turner, "Naval War College 1972-1973: The Report of the President," *Naval War College Review* (September-October 1973): entire issue. E. C. Meyer to CG, 19 September 1972, Subject: LRDP Outline (Draft), Commandant's File 1972. Davis to Kerwin, 3 October 1972, File 1011-04. Frank [Davis] to Don [LTG Cowles], 20 November 1972, Ibid. Benjamin E. Doty, "Opening Some Windows at the Army War College," *Army* (February 1973): 21-23. Stansfield Turner to Davis, 5 December 1973, File 1001-02.
42. Davis to Bennett, 10 December 1971. Davis to Bonesteel, 24 November 1971, Subject: Institute of Strategic Thought, File 1001-07. Davis, Memorandum for Record, 1 February 1972, Subject: Visit with General Bonesteel on 28 January 1972. Commandant's File 1972.
43. Ibid.
44. Baird, Memorandum, 18 June 1973, Subject: Wrest the Mantle, Commandant's File 1972.
45. AWC, Memorandum for Record, 27 September 1968, Subject: Policy on Student Travel in Support of Their IRP Activities, File 204-58. DOD Directive 5010-26, 15 October 1969, Subject: Effective Use of Research Output Developed in Certain Military Service Schools, File 1011-03. DCSPER to Commandant, 28 November 1969, Ibid. Chairman, DR&S to Commandant, 7 July 1972, Subject: Commandant's Board for Reviewing Student Research Papers, Ibid. AWC, 15 December 1972, Minutes of Deputies Meeting 13 December 1972, File 211-02. AWC, *Military Strategy: Studies in Military Strategy by Faculty and Students, United States Army War College*, ed. William M. Whitesel and Wilmer F. Cline (Carlisle Bks.: 1974), vii, AWC Library. Letter, DAAG-PA, 15 December 1972, Subject: Approval of Periodical, *Parameters: The Journal of the Army War College*, File 206-06.
46. AWC Memorandum 614-2, 7 July 1972, Subject: USAWC Staff and Faculty Assignments—AY 1973, Central Files. The three scholars were Drs. Raymond A. Moore, Harry B. Keller, and Donald D. Penner. Dr. Theodore Ropp was attached to the MHRC, Weighley to Davis, 22 November 1972, File 201-02.
47. Ulmer, Memorandum for Record, 8 April 1970, Subject: ODCSPER Proposal for "Alternate Educational Experience in Lieu of Attendance at SSC," Central Files 1972-75. AWC Circular 351-54, 12 December 1973, Subject: Army Research Associate Program—FY 75, Ibid. Westmoreland, *Report of Chief of Staff*, 120.

48. AWC, SSI, *Abstracts*, 1 April 1981, ii, 8-12. Henry C. Newton to Chief of Staff, 26 March 1973, Subject: Visit to Army War College, File 1011-14.

49. Eckhardt to Kerwin, 5 February 1970, File 207-01. Kerwin to Eckhardt, 20 February 1970, Ibid. AWC, Talking Paper, 26 July 1972, Subject: Placing USAWC Under a Headquarters Other than DCSPER, Ibid. Davis to Kerwin, 11 August 1972, Ibid. Kerwin to Davis, 22 August 1972, Ibid.

50. Letter, DAAG, 16 January 1973, Subject: Transfer and Reorganization of U.S. Army War College, Ibid. HQ., DA, DCSMOPS General Order No. 3, 30 January 1973, Ibid. HQ, DA, DCSMOPS, General Order No. 5, 22 February 1973, Ibid.

51. Newton to Chief of Staff, 26 March 1973. Davis to Cowles, 13 April 1973, File 1011-04.

52. Davis to Deputy Commandant, 18 October 1972, File 1011-04. Chairman, DNISS to Commandant, 13 February 1973, Subject: Organization of DNISS, File 207-01. George E. Allen to Gen. Meyer, 11 April 1973, Subject: Department and Course Titles, Ibid. DAA to Deputy Commandant, 11 April 1973, Ibid. DAA to Deputy Commandant, 10 May 1973, Subject: Reorganization, Ibid. AWC, Memorandum 10-6, 14 May 1973, Subject: Department Functions and Titles, Ibid. Barber to Directorate of Academic Affairs, 15 June 1973, Ibid.

53. Batiste to M. J. L. Greene, 15 October 1973, File 1010-07. Birch to Commandant, 31 October 1973, Subject: Interviews for Civilian DAA, Ibid.

54. AWC, *Curriculum Pamphlet Academic Year 1974 (Resident)*, 1 July 1973.

55. Ibid.

56. DAA to Commandant, 21 May 1974, Subject: Concept and Schedule for NSS 74, File 1011-03.

57. Malone to Gillert, 30 January 1974, Subject: Implementation of the Long Range Development Plan, Malone Files.

58. *Military Strategy* (1974).

59. Davis to Cowles, 9 November 1973, File 1001-02. SSI, *Abstracts*, i, 13-33. Director, SSI to Commandant, 1 March 1974, Subject: Security Issues Symposium, 21-23 April 1974, Central Files 1967-1976. AWC, Pamphlet, "Security Issues Symposium, 21-23 April 1974: Changing Dynamics of National Security: Agenda and Information" (Carlisle Barracks: 1974), Central Files 1974. *New Dynamics in National Strategy: The Paradox of Power* by members of faculty, U.S. Army War College, foreword by General Maxwell D. Taylor (New York: Crowell, 1975).

60. USAWC, *Leadership Monograph Series: Studies of Leadership for the Professional Soldier*, "Monograph #1: Demographic Characteristics of U.S. Army Leaders" by Donald D. Penner, Dandridge M. Malone, Thomas M. Coughlin, and Joseph A. Herz (Carlisle Barracks: January 1973): i, v-vi. Other monographs in the series were "Satisfaction with U.S. Army Leadership," "Junior NCO Leadership," "Senior NCO Leadership," "Company Grade Officer Leadership," and "Field Grade Officer Leadership."

61. AWC, 16 May 1972, Minutes of Deputies Meeting 10 May 1972, Central Files 1972. AWC, 31 August 1972, Minutes of Deputies Meeting 18 August 1972, Ibid. AWC, 31 October 1972, Minutes of Deputies Meeting 27 October 1972, Ibid. Louis F. Dixon to Commandant, 15 June 1973, Subject: Technical Inspection and Acceptance of USAWC Closed-Circuit Television System, File 1010-07. AWC, Summary of the Secretariat Semi-Annual Review 1 Jan-30 June 1973, Tab A, Ibid. Smith to Reinzi, 5 December 1974, File: Terminals 1972.

Mode of Association
1975-1980

Major General DeWitt C. Smith, Jr. served as Commandant of the Army War College from July 1974 until July 1977, when he was promoted to lieutenant general and assigned to the Army Staff as the Deputy Chief of Staff for Personnel. In July 1978 he was placed on the retired list at his request because of his health, but he was immediately recalled to active duty in the grade of major general and again appointed Commandant of the War College. He retained that position for another two years, reverting to the retired list in July 1980. During the year Smith was in Washington, Major General Robert G. Yerks, who had been Smith's deputy at Carlisle during 1974-75, served as Commandant. The six years spanning Smith's two tours as Commandant constitute twenty percent of the existence to date of the third Army War College.

Environment for Learning

Smith had been a member of the Army War College Class of 1966, a year in which the institution was struggling to contain and reconcile the many and conflicting pressures of the Department of Defense, the Haines Board, and Commandant Salet's own Army War College-70 project. The program that Lieutenant Colonel Smith experienced during his student year was tightly scheduled and highly structured; it allowed little opportunity for individually motivated study and reflection. Carlisle Barracks life, like the curriculum, was also highly structured—regulated and formal. In Lieutenant Colonel Smith's view, the environment for learning was not what it could or should have been.

His views on the importance of an environment for learning had not changed when Smith returned to the War College eight years later. Perhaps he best expressed his feelings late in his second tour of duty as Commandant when he quoted Woodrow Wilson to the Class of 1979. A college, Wilson had said, "is not only a body of studies but a mode of association." The evidence is convincing that Smith shared Wilson's understanding. His concern for the total living and learning environment of Carlisle Barracks and the Army War College guided Smith's actions throughout his five years as Commandant.[1]

In the early months of his command, Smith made a number of decisions, perhaps minor in themselves, that had important effects. A long-standing post directive entitled "Youth Regulations," designed to control the behavior and contain the exuberance of the many children living at Carlisle Barracks, was rescinded. Parents and the children themselves would henceforth be responsible for their behavior; no longer would youngsters be singled out as a problem to community living. The open spaces of Carlisle Barracks were to be played in, and the grass to be walked on. As with the first and second War Colleges, civilian clothes became the habitual dress of faculty and students. Targeting what Edward McGlachlin had once called "the vices of competition," Smith eliminated from individual academic reports forwarded to the Department of the Army any comment as to "general officer potential."[2]

In reflecting upon his student year and what had transpired in the eight years since, Smith was struck with how much of what had passed for wisdom at the Army War College in 1966 had turned out to be quite wrong. More sobering, many of the fundamental issues that the Army had been forced to face in the intervening years had not been addressed at all by the Army War College of 1966. If the understanding of a bipolar world gained by his classmates had proven faulty, the understanding gained of the social problems within the United States that had affected the Army so profoundly had been nil. The lesson Smith derived from this experience was the need to open the War College to as many differing viewpoints as possible. Some faculty members may have considered this thrust for diversity to be overdone, but to Smith diversity was what the United States and education itself were all about.[3]

Smith's years of service also had led him to believe that far too many American officers were in the habit of searching for "approved" or "school" solutions to clearly defined issues. They failed to appreciate that the essence of the problem facing those in positions of high responsibility was that issues were seldom if ever clearly defined and that unequivocal guidance from higher authority was rarely forthcoming. If the War College presented issues as being clearly defined and provided approved solutions, it would perform a disservice to the student officer. Moreover, Smith's reading of military history indicated to him that command failures had been due more often to personal limitations than to technical incompetence. These views undergirded Smith's conviction that the War College program must stress the development of the individual officer's capacity, not the acquisition of information or technical skill. Put another way, the focus must be on education in the broad sense—not on training.[4]

General Smith was an officer with an unusual, even extraordinary, sensitivity to the post-Vietnam and post-Watergate milieu in which the Army was and would be operating. He was also an officer with a sense of history. Within a span of but a few years the United States had experienced two unprecedented and shocking historical events. America had fought an unsuccessful war, and a President had been forced to resign his office for reasons of misconduct. These events occurred against a backdrop of what many observers believed to be an ongoing national revolution in social values and behavior. Smith felt, more acutely than many among his peers and faculty, that for at least the remainder of the decade the Army would be at a crossroads in its relationship to the society it served.

Whether Smith was correct probably cannot yet be conclusively determined, but he saw indications that a number of things could happen. The nation's leadership—its elected and appointed officials and its opinion-setting sector—could lose confidence in its Army, a much more profound problem than one of mere public image. Conversely, the Army's officer corps could lose confidence in the nation's institutions, public and private, and their ability to respond resolutely whatever the threat to the nation's interests and safety. If the result was not alienation of the officer corps from the larger society, it might well be intellectual isolation if the officer corps turned inward, concerning itself only with the technical facets of its profession. Finally, and here perhaps indicators were stronger, the officer corps could lose faith in itself, faith in its own leadership and in its corporate worth, allowing the erosion of that vital bond of mutual trust and respect so carefully and painfully nurtured since the years of William Sherman and John Schofield, a process in which the Army War College had played no small part. Whether the probability of any or all of these things occurring was high or low, the results would be so tragic to the nation that in Smith's view the possibilities had to be faced. One institution positioned to deal with these matters was the Army War College, where each year gathered a large segment of those officers who would lead the Army in the near future.

To DeWitt Smith, therefore, the mode of association and the avoidance of intellectual insularity at the Army War College were more important to the fundamental purpose of the college than whatever subject matter a curriculum might dictate or whatever instructional methodology was currently popular. In the pursuit of these objectives and the War College's fundamental purpose Smith was aware that he might open the institution to criticism for fostering breadth at the expense of depth and for lack of focus and rigor. In his view, however, focus and rigor flowed from personal commitment and the interaction of teacher and student. Neither could be forced in an environment truly educational. If a few failed to gain from the War College experience what was available, this was unfortunate, but a price worth paying. In an era of distrust, officers had to be trusted.

General Smith's belief that mature officers must see and consider seriously a wide range of viewpoints of course had precedent, exemplified particularly by the broad objectives championed by Edward McGlachlin in the early 1920s. Indeed, with his philosophy and his desired mode of association, Smith brought the Army War College back to what Generals Swing and Trudeau had begun at Leavenworth three decades earlier, back to an institution where faculty members and students enjoyed "membership," where the student was considered a mature officer experienced in his profession, and where the formal instruction characteristic of other Army schools was deemed inappropriate. In a sense, one could say that Smith was reaching for the collegium envisioned by Tasker Bliss.

Problems with the Program

General Smith's immediate problem upon arrival was to implement an instructional program which he had played no part in designing and which was yet to be tried, representing as it did the final stage of a five-year plan. Moreover, it was a program that had become the subject of increasing controversy at the War College since the early winter of 1973-74.[5]

During the planning for the 1974-75 curriculum, General Davis had decided that it was unnecessary to wait until 1975-76 to install the ultimate trimester scheme. It could be done a year earlier. The first phase, the "Common Overview," would be reduced from the thirty-seven weeks of the previous year to twenty weeks, concluding just before Christmas with a "Key Issues Conference" to which a few outside guests would be invited. The second portion, the "Individual Concentration Phase," was scheduled for twelve weeks during which some fifty to sixty elective courses would be offered. The third phase, ten weeks long, would include two weeks for a "Field Studies Program" (trips) and eight weeks for the "Military Research Program." The traditional year-end symposium, now called the "National Security Seminar," would follow.[6]

The first issue the curriculum planners had to resolve was how to distill the Common Overview into the new truncated version. To avoid creating a "pressure cooker," General Davis allowed classes to be scheduled only three afternoons each week, with no session to continue after 1530 hours. Reducing the number of guest lecturers was also desired, but Davis had directed that "lecturers of stature" be retained in the program. The problems resulting from shortening the Common Overview led General Davis to suggest requiring advanced reading by the student before he arrived at Carlisle. Some of the faculty advised against this; in the end a copy of the Contemporary Military Reading List (still drafted annually at the War College) was provided each student with the suggestion that he read one book from each of the list's several categories.[7]

Another issue arose when the Department of Military Planning and Strategy objected to the policy of the Department of National and International Studies which eliminated the requirement for students to draft a national strategy. It was argued that without such a document there would be nothing upon which to base a military strategy. The Department of Military Planning and Strategy apparently had overlooked or had never agreed to the change in curricular theme that had occurred just before the 1971-72 year. A compromise was reached, probably not wholly satisfactory to either party, by which a national strategy would be produced but not as a "solution-oriented requirement." The remaining two phases of the course did not present as many difficulties, though some elective course instructors objected to having their courses reduced in length from fourteen to twelve weeks.[8]

The Inventory and Assessment Program received the most criticism from the faculty. Counseling was a heated topic. The faculty had been given no part in designing the elaborate system, probably did not understand it, and objected to what they felt was the excessive time and resources it required. Argument over the new trimester program continued even into the early fall after the Class of 1975 had convened. Colonel Malone, one of the original architects of the Long Range Development plan, was called in to brief the Curriculum Board. Doubts were expressed regarding the very existence of a Long Range Development Plan in published form. The challenge was technically correct, the Long Range Development Plan existed as partial drafts, briefings, and in Doty's article in *Army*. General Magathan's decision not to involve the faculty in the planning had come home to roost. By the summer of 1974 there were few individuals remaining at Carlisle Barracks who felt any intellectual commitment to the Long Range Development Plan. Those few did not include the Commandant, the Deputy Commandant, nor the Director of Academic Affairs—all of whom were recent arrivals.[9]

The new Commandant in particular was not comfortable with the Long Range Development Plan. More accurately, he was not comfortable with the idea of any fixed plan that might tend to constrict or limit the flexibility of the educational processes at the War College. Rather than adhering to a "plan," Smith wanted the year at the War College to be guided by a broad objective and conducted in accordance with what he termed a "philosophy for learning." The broad objective could be stated simply as having the officer student leave the War College better prepared to contribute to the wise and responsible use of military power. The philosophy for learning stressed that the officers who came to the

459

War College were not homogeneous, but individuals with varied personal backgrounds and professional needs.[10]

By the Christmas break of academic year 1974-75, many among the faculty and the resident class had become convinced that the pace of the Common Overview phase was too fast, that the advertised year of contemplation and relaxed study at the Army War College was not materializing. In the endeavor to find more time (and to save money), the travel or "field studies" program became the first casualty.

Travel by the class, particularly overseas, had been an ambition of past commandants if for no other reason than because the National War College provided its classes such opportunity. In 1970 General Eckhardt had proposed a scheme whereby the class would be divided into groups to make trips categorized as "Command Associated" (meaning to United States unified commands overseas), as "Third World," and as "Student Initiative." But the price tag of $300,000 was too much for the Department of the Army. A lesser program followed that would involve half the class visiting Ottawa as the guests of the Canadian Armed Forces and half visiting Panama. Additionally, five trips, not including the traditional trip to the United Nations headquarters, would be scheduled within the United States; each student making one. The trips within the United States would be to installations and activities of the other services, such as the submarine bases at New London and Charleston, an aircraft carrier underway, and the headquarters of the Strategic Air Command and the North American Air Defense Command.[11]

General Palmer had supported this latter program, and funds were made available for the classes of 1972 and 1973. But by 1973-74 travel money again had become short, and General Davis preferred to use what funds were available to support travel connected with the newly installed eight-week Military Research Program. Nonetheless, despite the perennial difficulty in getting funds, travel to Latin America had been programmed for the Class of 1975. In the summer of 1974, however, the Curriculum Board agreed to recommend that the trip be canceled to make available two more weeks of study at Carlisle Barracks. Skeptical of the relative educational value of the proposed trip, General Smith approved the board's recommendation.[12]

The same month that General Smith assumed command of the War College, a group at the Pentagon called the "Committee on Excellence in Education" began to take an interest in the programs of the senior services colleges. The committee was composed of the Secretaries of the three military departments and William K. Brehm, Assistant Secretary of Defense for Manpower and Reserve Affairs. It was led by the Deputy Secretary of Defense, the Honorable William D. Clements. Since the military education systems of the services represented a substantial taxpayers investment, the committee believed that it had an obligation to know more than it did about professional military education.[13]

The committee's subsequent endeavors at self-education brought them to Carlisle Barracks in August 1974. General Smith's instruction of the committee proved uneventful. The committee apparently was sincerely interested in learning. But Smith was not naive and knew that more could be heard from this group. In December he attended an "extra-ordinary" meeting of the Military Education Coordination Conference, a body composed of the commandants and presidents of all the senior service colleges. The meeting was called in part because of the concerns of some over the effects of a reduction in funds to support the senior institutions. Particularly concerned were the heads of the National War College and the Industrial College, who suspected a move in the name of economy to at least partially consolidate those two institutions. Smith frankly and correctly suspected that there were latter-day Hugh Drums among his colleagues who, if cuts and consolidations were to come, would endeavor to have them occur at institutions other than their own. The next month the Army War College learned that another visitation by the Committee on Excellence would be made to Carlisle in the spring. Word also came that the committee had received such advice as to subordinate the three service colleges under one elevated National War College (or University). Another scheme suggested was to combine the Army War College and Command and General Staff College experiences, and beyond that just send a very few selected officers to civilian graduate school.[14]

By the spring of 1975 the committee had arrived at its concept of proper programs for the senior service colleges. Fundamentally it felt that the senior college of each service should serve as a center of learning for that service's primary function. The several colleges should present first what the committee called a "core curriculum," that is, subjects of common interest to all the services. Thereafter, each college should confine its instruction to subjects pertaining only to its own service, subjects which the committee called "mission-specific." In June 1975 it directed a number of "initiatives," some to be studied by the services, others to be implemented.[15]

The curriculum ideas of the Committee on Excellence in Education may have had some influence on General Smith's staff, but they apparently had little influence on the Commandant himself. General Smith had no major quarrel with the subject matter of the curriculum as he found it, though the 1974-75 experience convinced him, as it did the majority of the faculty, that some substantial restructuring of the program was necessary. Smith also believed that officers should leave Carlisle with a better understanding of two institutions which, whether the military professional liked it or not, had great influence on America's military policy—the Congress and the media. Smith felt too that the

461

national perspective so long a characteristic of the War College program needed to be tempered by greater consideration of the operations of commanders and staffs of major commands and military formations not located in Washington, particularly those commands that were actively contributing to deterrence and would be the first called upon to fight.[16]

Revising the Program

The 1975-76 program was therefore significantly altered from the trimester scheme called for by the Long Range Development Plan and attempted in 1974-75. The puzzle faced was how to provide the time for the Common Overview that the 1974-75 experience had indicated was necessary, add those subjects that Smith believed important, and yet avoid a return to the one-college, one-course structure of 1971-72. The solution was to make participation in the Military Studies Program voluntary and to equate participation in that program with completion of one or more elective courses. This decision was not taken hastily. A committee was formed consisting of the civilian scholars resident at the War College who had experience with graduate-level research. The quality of research papers prepared in earlier years was also examined. The committee concluded that it was unreasonable to expect, in the limited time available, the depth of original research associated with a Ph.D. dissertation or even with a master's thesis required by a strong university.[17]

The faculty was also unhappy with the Military Studies Program. The Long Range Development Plan held the faculty leader of a study team responsible for the quality of the product; in 1974-75 faculty leaders in some cases had to finish the project individually after the students departed. Moreover, the Department of the Army was reluctant to provide money for numerous research trips, and manpower reductions had eliminated the typing pool that had given administrative support to the endeavor. Since approximately two-thirds of the class already had advanced degrees, writing another thesis-type paper at the War College, if the purpose was training officers in research methods, was somewhat redundant. By making the studies program voluntary, giving participants credit for elective courses, and permitting year-long work on the project, those students who either individually or as members of small groups desired to research and write had the opportunity to do so. The option of participation in the oral history program of the Military History Research Collection remained.[18]

With time in the 1975-76 program no longer scheduled exclusively for the Military Studies Program, the Common Overview was extended by seven weeks and the Individual Concentration Phase, or electives, by one week. Despite the logic of the decision, it did represent a step back from the ultimate individually tailored program that General Davis and the authors of the Long Range Development Plan had envisioned. The program now consisted of two phases, a "Common Overview Phase" and an "Electives and Studies Phase."[19]

The 1975-76 program contained other innovations. The Department of National and International Security Studies introduced "Specific National Issues Seminars" of fifteen hours each and four intensive theoretical seminars addressing ideology, sociology, the military and society, and political order. The Commandant personally participated in this seminar program. He also initiated "Discussions with the Commandant" a somewhat broader version of the "Commandant's Dialogues" introduced by General Davis. An "Army Review Week" was added to the program. Principals on the Army Staff who had been requesting platform time at the War College were then given their opportunity. The week was not a success and was discontinued, although individual lectures that appeared worthwhile were integrated into later programs. Fifty-four electives were offered this year, a threefold increase over 1973-74. The electives supported thirteen of the advanced specialities of the new Officer Personnel Management System (OPMS) being introduced into the Army. Each student was required to take four electives but was permitted to audit additional courses if he desired.[20]

In 1976 the War College collected data on the assignments received since graduation by members of the resident classes of 1971 through 1975. While the data demonstrated that a large percentage of these assignments were to the Department of the Army, Joint Staff, and Department of Defense, they also showed that the majority of assignments were elsewhere. The data confirmed Smith's view that a gap existed between the course at Leavenworth, which traditionally had not included instruction above the level of the army corps, and the War College program that since 1958 had assumed a national perspective. Left unaddressed were all the command echelons in between and the functions they performed, the more significant of those being capabilities planning and, if war came, military operations.[21]

For several years it had been evident that the gap was widening. Since the activation of TRADOC in 1973, its commander, General William E. DePuy, had been moving to lower the tactical echelon addressed by each school in his system. He believed it was time that the school system ceased to support the National Defense Act of 1920; officers should be trained for their currently held grade. The glimpse at modern battle provided by the 1973 Arab-Israeli War demonstrated vividly that there was much to be learned and relearned about the complexities of modern land warfare and the effects of the increased range, accuracy, and lethality of a new generation of weapons. Moreover, in General DePuy's view, there would be no time in the next war for deliberate mobilization; it would be, to use the popular but inelegant term, a "come-as-you-are war." At Leavenworth the center of emphasis was shifting down to the level of the reinforced brigade and the division.[22]

General Davis had been aware of the gap and the TRADOC shift. For academic year 1974-75 he had approved inclusion of two new elective courses, "Grand Strategy" and "Tactical Command." One department chairman suggested that the study of division and larger unit tactics be included in the Common Overview as a "horizontal" course. Davis agreed in principle, thereby reversing his earlier position taken when arguing against reforms of the Admiral Turner variety and against War College subordination to TRADOC. Davis's position then had been that the teaching of tactics had no place in the War College program. In March 1974 he decided that War College students should have the opportunity to study "war-fighting" (once known by the less redundant term, "Conduct of War") at the levels of the corps, joint task force, and above. Because there was something of a jurisdictional dispute between the Department of Command and Management and the Department of Military Planning and Strategy, Davis charged the Strategic Studies Institute with defining the War College's responsibilities, including curriculum effort, need for simulations and war games, and possible War College proponency for large-unit doctrine. On this last point, Davis seemed to imply that the SSI should reassume the role of doctrine development that it had lost in the STEADFAST reorganization.[23]

The SSI response to Davis's charge did not result in any change to the 1974-75 curriculum beyond that already planned. Not until 1976-77 was a move toward "war-fighting" discernible. General Smith redesignated the Department of Military Planning and Strategy the "Department of Military Strategy, Planning, *and Operations*." Under its new title the department restructured its portion of the Common Overview into five phases, including a historically oriented evolution of military strategy, derivation of a midrange military strategy for the United States, force planning, capabilities planning and military operations, and an introduction to war-gaming. Despite the reappearance after long absence of the study of capabilities planning, military operations, and war games, the Common Overview portion of the redesignated department's 1976-77 program could not yet accurately be called a course in "war-fighting." But if that was the direction the War College was to move in the future, a structure to accommodate it was now in place. More significant to future and possibly greater emphasis on military operations was the thrust of six elective courses added to the department's slate, courses which reinforced and went into greater depth on its five phases of the Common Overview. "Conduct of War" was returning to the Army War College.[24]

The rebirth of war-gaming after its demise at the War College in the mid-1960s resulted from a realization that computer-supported war games were being used extensively throughout the Army as a tool for training lower-echelon commanders and staffs, for assistance in force structuring, for testing war plans, and for making combat-development decisions on doctrine, organization, and materiel needs. The prevalent observation was that too few senior officers really understood the tool; they either accepted the results of war games without question or dismissed them categorically. War-gaming instruction was reinstituted in 1976-77 with the modest objective of helping to correct those attitudes.[25]

At the same time, however, planners realized that a versatile war-gaming capability at the War College should serve many purposes. It could support the increasing interest in providing more and deeper instruction in military planning and operations; indeed, it was difficult to see how the War College could serve this interest at all without a war-gaming capability. War-gaming could also assist the decision-making instruction presented by the Department of Command and Management, and it could add new dimensions to the studies program of the Strategic Studies Institute. Additionally, a versatile war-gaming capability could serve the Army worldwide by testing the operational plans of major Army commands, a service that the Naval War College had provided for the Fleet for many years. In this latter role a danger was also recognized—the war-gaming capability could evolve into an agency quasi-independent of the War College, beyond the Commandant's full control and removed from the educational process like the Institute of Advanced Studies during the years of the Combat Developments Command. Further, there was a danger that the war-gamers could become more enamored of technique than teaching.[26]

Colonel Raymond M. Macedonia from the Class of 1976, an officer with extensive war-gaming experience, was retained on the faculty and appointed Director of War Gaming Studies. In 1976-77 he presented the orientation instruction on war-gaming during the Common Overview and taught the elective course. He also drew up a five-year plan which, if supported adequately by manpower authorizations, funds, and proper personnel assignments, would result in a true war-gaming capability at the War College. General Smith approved Macedonia's plan, and the inevitable struggle for people and money began. The DCSOPS, Lieutenant General Edward C. Meyer, who had been General Davis's Deputy Commandant during 1972-73, was generally supportive—and his support was to prove crucial. The scheme received additional important support from the findings of the Department of the Army "Review of Education and Training of Officers (RETO)" conducted during 1977-78.[27]

RETO was undertaken at the direction of the Chief of Staff of the

Army on August 31, 1977. It probably had its genesis at Headquarters, TRADOC, as the reasons given for its formation and many of the considerations in its deliberations reflected the concerns and thinking of General DePuy. Brigadier General Benjamin Harrison, for several years previous the Assistant Commandant at Leavenworth, was designated chairman of the study group, and about thirty officers were assigned to assist him. Seven lieutenant generals were appointed as a consulting and advisory board. Among them was DeWitt Smith, who in August 1977 had been promoted and designated the DCSPER. Harrison formed a team of three officers for the review of the War College and general officer education programs. The RETO study group submitted its' report ten months later, at the end of June 1978.[28]

As literature, the RETO report is a curious piece of work. Amid exhortations that an army's role is to fight, one finds the peculiar vocabulary and manner of expression of both the behavioral scientist and the systems analyst. If the reader can survive this whipsawing and persevere, however, the message of the report as it pertains to the Army War College is clear. The War College should concentrate on military operations at the level of the Army corps and above. The instructional program should derive from what War College graduates would be expected to be and to do in their future assignments. The behavioralists were confident that the "to be" could be scientifically determined. The systems analysts were confident that the "to do" could be scientifically determined. Both groups were confident that an instructional program could be scientifically designed to provide the behavior patterns and skills so determined. Since the Army had never before been able to determine even how *many* War College graduates were needed, this optimism has to be admired. However, there can be little argument with the logic that the program's content and method should derive from the requirement.[29]

At the time of this writing it is not possible to measure what will be the long-term effect of the RETO on the Army War College. The study group made no recommendations that caused immediate change in the War College program. One item highlighted as a weakness was that the gap the Army War College was reestablished to fill in the late 1940s had now widened, according to RETO, to a "disconnect." This "disconnect" had been created, of course, by TRADOC's decision to deemphasize instruction in corps operations at Leavenworth. Though the RETO report did not cite the earlier gap, it in fact recommended that the War College become the advanced general staff school that Manton Eddy had wanted and that Joe Swing and J. Lawton Collins had thwarted in their thrust toward the apex. Indeed, RETO went back to earlier years in another significant way. In addition to the Command and General Staff course, a "Combined Arms and Services Staff School" was now to be phased in at Leavenworth with a mission not unlike that of the School of the Line that Pershing disestablished in 1923. As a result of the RETO, the DCSOPS rewrote the mission statement of the Army War College "to reflect increased instructional emphasis on the integrative aspects of joint and combined land warfare," but by the end of the decade the new statement had not caused any major program alterations.[30]

As mentioned, the RETO report improved the fortunes of those at the War College who were trying to build a strong war-gaming capability. That capability had experienced slow growth; during 1977-78 a theater-level war game was added to the Military Planning and Operations course. However, despite the backing of the new Commandant, Major General Robert G. Yerks, and the support of General Meyer, efforts to locate and have qualified personnel assigned were not crowned with complete success. The RETO group recommended that the War College manage an Army-wide "Tactical Command Readiness Program" for field commanders at corps level and above as part of the continuing education and training of general officers. A war-gaming capability was essential to this mission. The RETO group also recommended expanded war-gaming support of the War College program. Whether done by luck or design, placing war-gaming on the altar of "readiness" went far to assure Department of the Army support. The Chief of Staff, General Bernard W. Rogers (AWC 1960), approved the recommendations.[31]

In academic year 1978-79 a war game at Joint Task Force level was added to the theater-level game of the previous year. In 1979-80 a three-day, two-sided, computer-assisted game sited in Central Europe and a three-day, two-sided game pitting a United States corps against a Soviet combined arms army in the Golan Heights were conducted. The latter year new computer graphics equipment was obtained and the "McClintic Theater Model" developed. In the opinion of its proponents, this model had the capability to revolutionize war-gaming. At the least it moved the Army War College again to the forefront in the art of war-gaming, a position it had not occupied since the 1930s. The Tactical Command Readiness Program recommended by the RETO and directed by the Chief of Staff was attempted in 1980. Commanders and staffs of several operational headquarters were provided the opportunity to test their contingency plans.[32]

By 1979-80 the "Military Planning and Operations" course included study not only of the defense problems of Allied Forces Central Europe but also those of Allied Forces Northern Europe and Allied Forces Southern Europe. Two days were devoted additionally to investigation of the deployment planning of the recently created Rapid Deployment Force.[33]

The resident class programs for academic years 1977-78 through 1979-80 followed the pattern established in 1976-77, with a Common Overview phase and an Electives and Studies phase. In 1978-79 the term "elective" was dropped, and the second phase was renamed "Advanced Courses and Study Projects," a change intended to better describe the relationship of the elective courses to those of the Common Overview. By whatever name, "elective" or "advanced," the offerings remained essentially the same, with fifty-five to sixty made available each year. Participation in individual or group study projects remained voluntary.[34]

Disappointed at his inability to attract more U.S. Senators and Representatives to the War College to discuss in seminar congressional approaches to military affairs, General Smith tried a "Congressional Day" in 1977. He invited a number of legislators to come to Carlisle as a group. But legislators are busy men, and there is little home district influence in a War College class, so the results were disappointing. In 1979 Smith therefore arranged to have the students make two one-day trips to Washington to familiarize themselves with the concerns of Congress through group discussions with Senators, Representatives and their staff aides. The next year a single two-day trip was made, and sessions were added with selected executive departments and agencies. Visits also were made that year to private organizations such as the United States Chamber of Commerce, Common Cause, and the *Washington Post* Publishing Company.[35]

The Inventory and Assessment scheme that had been a major component of the Long Range Development Plan inaugurated and approved by General Davis experienced something of a rebirth after its earlier inauspicious start. Although the War College had accepted the pre-session and post-session baseline inventories as useful in measuring the success of its program, other features of the Inventory and Assessment idea had not taken hold. Within its own courses the Department of Command and Management began to experiment again with the concepts of self-assessment during the 1977-78 and 1978-79 years, and student response was favorable. By the end of the decade, the department's experimentation, perhaps bolstered by the behavioralist tone of the RETO, led to consideration of establishing an "Assessment Center" at the Army War College. The objective would be to reveal or to reinforce "awareness of personal characteristics, strengths, and values."[36]

Corresponding Studies

In 1975 General Smith moved the Department of Nonresident Instruction from its crowded and windowless office space in the basement of Root Hall into office space comparable in efficiency, comfort, and status to that of the other teaching departments. He redesignated the department and its program "Corresponding Studies." "Nonresident" was not really accurate, since the members of these classes did spend four important weeks in residence at Carlisle Barracks. The program they pursued *corresponded to* that of the resident class and in fact was more academically demanding, with heavier requirements for original individual written work.[37]

Since its establishment, this department had tended to adapt its own program to that of the resident class as changes occurred. The Nonresident Class of 1973 was the first to be provided a separate subcourse on "Command and Management." The Corresponding Studies Class of 1978 was the first to address command and management problems during their resident phases. The writing of individual research essays was made voluntary with that same class, and during the end-of-course resident phase, the 1978 class participated in a crisis-management politico-military simulation. The Corresponding Studies Class of 1980 conducted a theater-level war game in addition to the politico-military simulation. The Department of Corresponding Studies was never able to find a truly satisfactory way to provide elective courses in its program, although it gave that problem much attention. Alternatively, it attempted to provide greater depth in the required courses, which corresponded to the Common Overview courses of the resident program. The Corresponding Studies program remained academically demanding, and the attrition rate stayed high.[38]

The composition of the Corresponding Studies classes changed slightly during the latter half of the 1970s. Beginning in 1975 two Department of the Army civilian employees were enrolled each year. In 1977 an officer of the U.S. Marine Corps Reserve was enrolled, followed by two more officers from that component the next year. The Corresponding Studies classes also increased in size. By the mid-1970s the professional education systems of all the services were under heavy budgetary attack at the department level. The activities of the Committee on Excellence in Education and of the RETO study group were in part responses to these attacks. Among other cost-saving measures, the Secretary of Defense directed that for fiscal year 1979 the Army War College reduce its resident student population by fifteen percent. Despite General Smith's objections the number of active Army officers in the resident Class of 1979 was reduced to 189 from the 216 in the Class of 1978. The Corresponding Studies Class of 1980 was increased to compensate for the reduced resident class. The Corresponding Studies Class of 1980 graduated 107 active Army officers, compared to sixty-five the previous year. Fifty-nine USAR officers were also graduated, as were nineteen officers of the National Guard.[39]

Non-Curricular Changes

While General Smith was Commandant he initiated no formal, sweeping internal reviews on the order of Army War College-70 or the Long Range Development Plan. Nor did General Yerks during academic year

469

1977-78. The technique used, rather, was to examine without fanfare each facet of the War College's operations, soliciting varied opinion from both faculty and student. In the course of these examinations past habits of the War College were confirmed or modified, experiments attempted, and new programs initiated.[40]

Even the name "Army War College" came under scrutiny, but this was not a new subject. As early as 1962 General Train, noting the passing of the "War" Department and the "War" Office, speculated on whether perhaps "War" College had also become an anachronism. In 1967, near the end of General Salet's tour, alternative names were again considered. General McCaffrey and General Eckhardt also received suggestions and recommendations for change. During the Vietnam era the word "war" was held to be an unnecessary irritant and a source of misunderstanding of the War College's true function. General Davis was informed that the name of his institution offended both youth and academia. Yet he decided that no change in name was desirable. General Smith, after reviewing all the earlier considerations and receiving literally dozens of suggestions as to possible alternatives, agreed. Local citizens who found the name objectionable continued, however, to suggest a change.[41]

Smith had under review another program about which the Committee on Excellence in Education also was expressing doubts, the cooperative degree program. Revived in 1969, this program was well-established by 1974. In 1971-72 the War College had conducted a student workload study in order to determine, among other data, just how much student effort this program diverted from War College work. The study found that the average student in the degree program devoted fifteen hours to it each week; however, except for some time that might otherwise have been spent on the War College's research program, the fifteen hours were taken from extracurricular activities or other free time. The data from the workload study were used by General Davis to defend the degree program at the Department of Defense and to respond to inquiries resulting from Admiral Turner's reforms at the Naval War College, Turner having terminated the degree program there.[42]

In 1974-75 almost ninety students were pursuing master's degrees in the cooperative degree program, eight at the Capitol Campus of Pennsylvania State University, the remainder at Shippensburg State College. The most popular fields of study were public administration and communications. Students in the program took courses during two nine-week terms held the summers before and after their ten months at the War College. During these terms they received eighteen semester hours of credit. While the War College was in session, twelve additional semester hours could be earned, six to nine of them being awarded for performance of War College work.[43]

The Department of the Army had put certain restrictions on enrollments in the cooperative degree program. It would not support sending an officer to Carlisle early or having him remain after the War college course was finished if he already had a master's degree. Neither would it support his pursuit of a degree deemed not needed by the Army or not related to the officer's future assignment. General Smith's position on the cooperative degree program was not complicated—the program was valuable for the individual but it should not interfere with the main Army War College experience. The Committee on Excellence in Education, however, took exception to the additional eighteen weeks some officers were spending at Carlisle and suggested that arrangements be made so that more credit could be given for War College work. Pursuit of a similar goal was just what had put the War College and The George Washington University at odds and had led to the demise of the earlier program. For academic year 1976-77 the civilian institutions did find it possible to reduce the length of the summer sessions from nine to six weeks by giving more credit for War College elective courses, provided that the student accomplished certain additional work. This compromise proved acceptable to all parties. That year about two-thirds of the War College students who did not already have advanced degrees took advantage of the arrangement, but participation dropped by ten percent. By 1979-80 enrollment in the cooperative degree program was down to thirty-three students. The program was no longer the major issue it had been in 1960-61 when almost two hundred had participated.[44]

General Smith, the Committee on Excellence in Education and Smith's predecessor, were in accord that the proper role of the faculty was teaching. The Long Range Development Plan had created momentum in this direction. Smith won agreement from the Army's personnel managers that approximately five of his military faculty, those who possessed hard-to-find specialities, should serve five-year tours; that some fifteen faculty members should be on indefinite tenure until mandatory retirement at thirty years of service; and that the remainder of the faculty should be assigned for three-year stabilized tours. He asked for exception to the age limit on Army-sponsored graduate education as a means of faculty development. He also recommended that the Army War College have more voice in and derive more benefit from the Army's Senior Fellow program, which annually sent officers for a year's study at the Brookings Institution, the Council on Foreign Relations, and the Department of State Senior Seminar in Foreign Policy. On these last two items he got sympathetic responses but no firm commitments.[45]

The two policies that probably did more to increase the quality of the faculty than any other were the willingness (initially by General Davis) to accept officers who were on their "terminal assignment" prior to retirement, and General Smith's willingness to accept officers who were not senior service college graduates or who were less senior in grade, provided that they had the appropriate background and met his "whole man" criterion. At the end of academic year 1977, one department chairman could report that he had realized the long-sought goal of a true teaching faculty—but the chairman hastened to point out that before the next academic year began half the department would either be reassigned or retired.[46]

Except for General Train's complaint in 1963 that the National War College was receiving priority in talent, Army War College authorities perceived fewer problems with the Army's policies on student selection than they did with those pertaining to faculty acquisition. In 1971 General Davis had recommended that the number of naval officers in each resident class be increased from ten to sixteen to permit one naval representative in each student seminar group. The Navy was unable to meet an expanded annual quota, however, and beginning in academic year 1976-77 it even reduced the number of its representatives from ten to five. One of the resulting vacancies was filled when General Smith invited the United States Coast Guard to provide a student each year. General Davis in 1972 had arranged also to have the number of reserve component officers in each resident class increased from four to eight. In 1977 Smith doubled this number to sixteen.[47]

The War College gave increased attention to the role of the reserve components throughout the period 1975 through 1977. This was in part a reflection of the "Total Force Concept" introduced by Secretary of Defense Laird and later supported by Secretary of Defense James R. Schlesinger, and in part a reflection of General Smith's own belief that regular Army officers knew much less than they should about the reserve components. In both the "Command and Management" and the "Strategic Military Studies" courses of the resident program, greater academic focus was given to Army Reserve and National Guard forces. Since academic year 1972-73, a USAR officer and a National Guard officer had been assigned to the Department of Nonresident Instruction. In 1976 General Smith designated these two officers his advisors on matters pertaining to their components. He invited senior officers from the reserve components of the other services to attend the annual Senior Reserve Components Officers Course (SRCOC). By 1979-80 these classes had grown to forty-five attendees, thirteen of whom were from the reserve components of the Navy, Air Force, Marine Corps, and Coast Guard.[48]

Greater involvement by reserve component officers (including those of services other than the Army) in the work of the Army War College was one of a number of actions deliberately initiated to bring to the War College a wider range of viewpoints, an objective General Smith thought extremely important. He expanded the "Elements of Command" program initiated by General McCaffrey to include men of professions other than the military and relabeled it the "Distinguished Guest Seminar." Three additional lecture programs were begun. The "Elements of Management" series initiated in 1974 was converted into the "Brehon B. Somervell Management Lecture Series" in 1976. The success of this program led the Department of Command and Management to begin the following year the "Creighton B. Abrams Command Lecture Series," and the Department of Military Planning and Strategy to begin the "Elihu Root Lecture Series on Military Strategy." Guest lecturers in the latter series were drawn not only from among senior American military officers, but from civilian experts, and probably most importantly, from strategists outside the United States. As far as the students were concerned, these three programs were voluntary, but the programs also had the equally important objective of faculty development. The guest lecturers were asked to remain for two days, and much of their time was spent in informal but detailed discussions with appropriate faculty members.[49]

Since the late 1960s the class trip to New York City had taken on a different character. Originally a visit solely to United Nations headquarters and concerned exclusively with international affairs, as late as 1967 the three and a half days in the city had been spent at the UN building listening to the viewpoints of representatives of various nations. In academic year 1973-74 only a day and a half were spent at the UN, with another half day spent attending a panel discussion on urban problems (of which New York City had plenty) by officials of metropolitan governments and federal agencies. In academic year 1974-75 only one day was spent at the UN, the panel discussion on urban problems was repeated, and another half day was spent in small group visits to fourteen governmental and business agencies. The Department of National and International Security Studies expanded the small group visits to twenty-four for the academic year 1975-76 trip. Visits were arranged to offices of domestic and multinational corporations, the financial community, governmental agencies (at all levels), management and research firms, media organizations, and labor unions. The UN and the urban-problem panels also remained on the schedule. It was an unusual opportunity for military officers to hear different viewpoints, but it was neither free nor easy. The Committee on Excellence in Education had put a limit of $50,000 on class field trips that year, and General Smith had to call on all his not-inconsiderable persuasive powers to obtain the additional $26,000 needed.[50]

General Smith was initially suspicious of the program of the Current Affairs Panel. The year before he arrived the panel had made twelve appearances on nine different campuses, and the feeling was that a true dialogue was being reestablished. Larger audiences were now attending the discussions, and the tone was much more objective and academically oriented. The number of invitations was increasing, and the problems of the Middle East, energy supplies, the volunteer Army, the Army's social problems, and the strategic balance between the United States and the Soviet Union had replaced Vietnam as the agenda items of interest. Once convinced that the panel was not being used to propagandize for the Army nor to present an Army position, Smith saw it as an important means of feeding into the Army the opinions currently held on the campuses of the nation's colleges and universities—as one more way of bringing different viewpoints into the deliberations of the Army War College.[51]

The annual year-end National Security Seminar had been a primary means of exchanging viewpoints with a representative cross-section of American society since the seminar's introduction in 1955. General Smith was not sure, however, just how representative this cross-section was. The goal had long been to bring in distinguished men from various sectors—government, business, law, education, agriculture, journalism, labor, and so forth. Smith thought the representation should be even wider, broadened to include more members of minority groups, more women, and some younger people. Perhaps past guest lists had been more distinguished than representative. The habit of years would not be changed quickly, but the composition of the group did begin to change, even to include some young graduate students. The thrust of the seminar also changed. Rather than ask the guests to critique War College student research efforts (as called for by the Long Range Development Plan), the National Security Seminar became a less structured, more issue-oriented symposium in which domestic national issues were discussed one day, international issues the next, and defense and Army issues the third.[52]

After reviewing plans for the physical development of the post of Carlisle Barracks, General Smith concluded that the long-sought, multimillion-dollar physical conditioning facility was something that the Army War College could survive without. He had it deleted from the master plan for Carlisle Barracks, and in 1976 Jim Thorpe Hall was renovated at much less expense. In this decision Smith was influenced by more than the monetary savings involved. He felt deeply that the remaining physical evidence of Richard Henry Pratt's lifetime work, that enlightened and noble social experiment, the Indian Industrial School, should be preserved. Smith intended to honor the historic buildings of Carlisle Barracks, not preside over their destruction. As he put it, "Only grass will grow on Indian Field."[53]

International Fellows

Of all the schemes contemplated to bring different points of view to Carlisle Barracks, none was more difficult to implement than one involving having officers from armies of other nations at the War College on a resident basis. The step had been often considered and just as often rejected. General Smith's immediate predecessor studied the issue and calculated that it would cost more than a quarter of a million dollars annually, a cost that might have killed the idea if it otherwise had been universally supported. But Smith instituted another review of the issue in 1974. He solicited the opinion of his faculty on the idea as early as the fall of that year and, if he did not meet unanimous opposition, he found a strong consensus that it should not be done. The faculty believed, as had General Newton, that the problems of having to deny foreign officers classified information and the inhibiting effect those officers would have on the candor of guest lecturers and group discussions were problems without solution.[54]

Smith understood but was not impressed by these arguments; he considered them minor compared to the benefits that would accrue. The problem of handling nationally classified materials was overcome every day in multinational headquarters and at such service schools as Leavenworth and the Armed Forces Staff College. And, by Smith's reasoning, not only would the participation of foreign officers in the War College program foster international understanding, but the injection of foreign views was healthy for any profession. Moreover, alliances could no longer be considered "dubious luxuries" as Fox Conner had called them in the 1930s. The late twentieth century was an era of formal and informal alliances. No longer could either military operations or military training take place in national isolation. Smith was convinced that a foreign officer program at Carlisle Barracks would benefit both foreign and American officers—and probably the American officer the most.[55]

By 1976 General Smith had tentative approval from the Departments of the Army, Defense, and State. Specific planning began. The ultimate solution to the perceived problems had some precedents in the experience of the Corresponding Studies program, which had demonstrated convincingly that much could be accomplished without dealing constantly in classified information, and in the USMA Fellow program, which provided an example of a status between faculty and student from which both the War College and the individual could profit. As for costs, the solution was to have either the Military Assistance Program or those nations that desired to participate pay the bill. The result was the International Fellows Program.[56]

In the concept of a "fellow," as opposed to a "student," much would depend on the officer's own initiative. Based on his experience, preferences, and skills, the International Fellow would in essence design his own program, attend selected classes of the Common Overview, pursue electives that interested him, and participate in study, research, writing, and possibly in teaching. Direction for the program was found by looking from the perspective of what the foreign officer could do for the United States Army War College rather than the converse. To insure that only the most able and promising officers participated as fellows, arrangements were made whereby the Chief of Staff of the Army personally invited his counterpart of a selected foreign army to designate and send the fellow. The officers selected were to be in the grades of lieutenant colonel through brigadier general.[57]

In academic year 1977-78 one officer each from six nations— Australia, Canada, the Federal Republic of Germany, Japan, the Republic of Korea, and Mexico—participated as International Fellows. They were the first foreign officers to serve at the U.S. Army War College since the Comte de Chambrun was on the faculty in 1919-20. By the close of the 1979-80 year, twenty nations had sent thirty-two officers to Carlisle. In 1979-80 sufficient International Fellows were present to attach one to each student seminar group. As General Smith had predicted, the benefits to the War College were significant; a dimension had been added to the educational environment that broadened substantially the academic outlook of the students and the faculty. Some of the severest critics of the idea became the strongest supporters of the International Fellows Program.[58]

Research and Publications

The growth of a sophisticated war-gaming capability was not consciously connected to the earlier ambition to make the War College a "center for contemporary military thought." Talk of "wresting the mantle" subsided after 1974, although those projects able to contribute movement toward that goal were continued. General Smith had the status and health of the War College journal, *Parameters*, reviewed in February 1975. Later that year he won Department of the Army approval for its quarterly publication and expanded circulation. Its appearance and format were revised, and those items that might be considered in the category of alumni news were no longer included.[59]

Parts of the strategy text continued to be used to support both the resident and corresponding studies programs, but no additional chapters were added. It was Smith's view, however, that a more definitive strategy text was needed. In 1975-76 the Department of Command and Management undertook a similar project. Led by Colonel Ray L. Cook, who acted as editor and a primary author, the department published a three-volume text entitled *Army Command and Management: Theory and Practice.* Faculty members and students contributed. This text has since been revised annually.[60]

The War College continued its interest in the study of Army professionalism. Two additional professionalism studies were undertaken during the 1970s. Designed both to update and to test the conclusions of the earlier study hastily performed at General Westmoreland's request, the two studies had influence on the War College program and were important not only to the students but to the Army.

The DCSOPS continued to keep the Strategic Studies Institute actively employed, assigning to it six to eight major studies each year. In a sense this work by the Institute was a partial return of the War College to the status of an adjunct to the General Staff as originally envisioned by Elihu Root. Additionally, the military and civilian analysts of the Institute continued to produce numerous special studies, occasional papers, and Military Issue Research Memorandums (in 1979-80 relabeled *Strategic* Issue Research Memorandums). Although these papers did not receive wide public distribution, they did receive selected distribution to key offices within the Army and the Department of Defense. It is impossible to tell the extent of their influence. Individual attitudes are seldom changed by a single document, and seminal works are rare. Even if the only results, however, were to call the attention of the Department of the Army to future issues and to raise the level of consciousness on recognized issues, the effort was probably worthwhile.[61]

The Strategic Studies Institute continued the practice begun in 1974 of hosting symposia at Carlisle Barracks. The papers presented at the 1975 symposium were published the next year under the title *National Security and Detente.* The 1976 symposium had as its theme "Strategy, Alliances, and Military Power: Changing Roles." In 1977, in addition to the "Security Issues Symposium," a "Military Policy Symposium" was hosted with the focus on inter-American security.[62]

The Military History Research Collection continued to expand its holdings. As the reputation of the facility spread, it began to attract an increasing number of scholars from throughout the United States and from abroad. Its support of the War College increased; instructors were provided from its staff for courses of both the Common Overview and the elective phase. In view of the expanded role of the Military History Research Collection, its director, Colonel James B. Agnew, suggested a change in name. In 1977 it thus became the United States Army Military History Institute. The Harold K. Johnson Chair of Military History was created the next year for the annual visiting professor.[63]

The Vietnam Study

In contrast to the first Army War College's neglect of analyses regarding the experience of the Philippine Insurrection, the Army War College of the late 1970s took great pains to understand the unhappy period of American involvement in Vietnam. In academic year 1975-76 Colonel Dwight L. Adams (AWC 1968) introduced an elective course into the resident program entitled "The Vietnam War: Lessons Learned." That year and subsequently the course was popular. Adams brought to Carlisle a number of the men who had participated in making the decisions—both in Vietnam and in Washington—entailed in the Southeast Asian operations; they came to discuss those decisions with the class. Also invited were men who had been public supporters or critics of U.S. political and military policies.[64]

Even before he became Commandant, DeWitt Smith had felt that the military establishment should take the initiative in conducting a thorough analytical review of the strategy and policies underlying the conduct of the Vietnam War and then publish the results openly and candidly. As he was to state later, it was "absolutely imperative that we study how it is that you can win so frequently, and so well, in a warfighting sense, and yet lose a war in a strategic or political sense." Within a year after becoming Commandant, Smith had initiated what came to be called the "Viet Nam Lessons Learned Study."[65]

The initial efforts of this study fell to Colonel Donald Esper (AWC 1972), a member of the Advanced Analysis Group of the Strategic Studies Institute. Throughout 1975-76 Esper conducted a bibliographic survey pertaining to the Vietnam involvement, which in the spring of 1976 Smith approved as Phase I of the study he had in mind. Not surprisingly, Esper's survey produced a list staggering in length and in range of quality and usefulness. Concurrently, staff officers assigned to Department of the Army DCSOPS also had suggested an analysis of the Vietnam experience, a suggestion strongly endorsed by Walter Kerwin, then Vice Chief of Staff of the Army. The Army Staff was not unanimous in seeing value in such a study, however. In fact, opposition was at times bitter. There were those who felt that the Army should get on with the solution of issues current and future, specifically the defense of Western Europe. There were others, found for example at the Center of Military History, who had doubts as to the worth of the final product because of the continuing controversy and internal Army sensitivity surrounding the Vietnam episode.[66] Moreover, by the fall of 1976 it was becoming apparent that the contemplated Vietnam study could overwhelm the manpower resources of the Strategic Studies Institute, perhaps even those of the entire War College. In April 1977 the DCSOPS, Lieutenant General Edward C. Meyer, approved a recommendation from his staff that a commercial contractor be selected to conduct the study under the direction and control of a team of SSI officers. The study advisory group with responsibility for monitoring the overall effort was to be chaired by the Commandant of the Army War College.[67]

While the Department of the Army staff was deliberating on whether to solicit the assistance of a contractor, a formal study group of SSI officers was formed at Carlisle Barracks under Colonel Thomas A. Ware. This team had the task, first, of organizing the study effort, and then of drafting a contract proposal. Ware had hoped originally that the contract could be let in September 1977, with a target publication date of May 1978. He proved more than a little optimistic. As it turned out, the contract was not let until August 1978, with a projected publication date of December 1979. Among other staff delays, the War College's proposal had rested in the office of the General Counsel of the Army for more than six months. Either it was considered a staff action of very low priority or it was deliberately delayed.[68]

In June 1978 Colonel Sanders A. Cortner (AWC 1972) took over the task from Ware, who was scheduled to retire the following month. For the next year Cortner acted as the Vietnam Study Group coordinator and the contracting officer's representative. The work was published in June 1980, just prior to General Smith's departure from the War College and five years after he had first assigned Colonel Esper to the project. Consisting of eight volumes plus an omnibus executive summary, the study is organized much as Ware originally envisioned. It is measured and sober, designed, so its authors claim, not to startle but to inform. Nonetheless it is critical, particularly of what it calls the "American Way of War," which has become in the authors' view "increasingly dominated by managers, technicians, and logisticians." The work deserves the attention of those who attempt to explain the Vietnam effort.[69]

When General Smith departed the Army War College in the summer of 1980, his service as Commandant totaled five years, a longer period than that of any of his predecessors. he had accomplished most of what he had set out to do with the institution, and he had not allowed advice and criticism from either the Department of Defense or the Army's training establishment to divert him from his purposes. The faculty had been made more stable and now contained greater variety and expertise than it ever had before. The instructional program and its supplementary activities gave more attention than ever before to the sensitive and important relationship between the professional military officer and the society he served. The study of military operations had been reinstituted as a principal concern. Officers from the reserve components had become important contributors to the faculty and to the resident and corresponding studies classes. A Vietnam study had been completed, although the single comprehensive public volume that Smith had desired had not resulted. The International Fellows Program was an established and respected part of the Army War College scene.

Probably most satisfying to General Smith was that during a period which he sincerely believed to be extremely critical for the officer corps of the United States Army, he had instilled among the members of the Army War College a mode of association that is the hallmark of a profession in the most fundamental sense. The character of that mode of association was the truest measure of the value of the educational experience. In the immediate post-Vietnam years the United States Army and the republic were well served by the Army War College.

NOTES

1. DeWitt C. Smith, Jr., to "Class of 1970," n.d. [June 1979], Box 1972-1980, Smith Papers, MHI.
2. Smith, Commandant's Welcome to the Resident Class of 1975, 5 August 1974, 6-7, Ibid.
3. AWC, Extracted Remarks of Major General DeWitt C. Smith, Jr., Before the U.S. Army War College, Carlisle Barracks, Pa., 27 November 1974, 2, Ibid.
4. The interpretation of Smith's concerns are based on review of his public statements and correspondence during the period 1972-80 contained in Smith's Papers, MHI; on author's service on AWC faculty 1974-77; and on Smith interview, June 1982.
5. AWC, Minutes of First Meeting of Curriculum Board, AY75, 16 July 1974, File 1003-06.
6. Birch, Memorandum, 19 December 1973, Subject: AY75 Planning Conference with Commandant, File 1011-10. AWC, *Curriculum Pamphlet (Resident) Academic Year 1975*, 1 April 1974. DAA to Commandant, 18 March 1974, Subject: AY75 Individual Concentration Phase, File 1001-07. DAA, Memorandum, 26 March 1974, Subject: Policy Guidance for Implementing AY75 ICP, Ibid.
7. Birch, Memorandum, 19 December 1973. Birch, Memorandum, 27 December 1973, Subject: AY75 Planning, File 1011-01. DAA to Commandant, 18 April 1974, Subject: Advanced Readings for USAWC Students, Central Files 1974-75.
8. AWC, Minutes of 17th Meeting of Curriculum Board, 17 April 1974, Ibid. Chairman, DNISS to Commandant, 24 April 1974, Subject: Final Y Directive, U.S. and the World Environment Course, AY 1975, File 1011-01. Hall Interview.
9. Minutes of the First Meeting of the Curriculum Board, Ibid. AWC, Minutes of the Fifth Meeting of the Curriculum Board, AY75, 16 October 1974, File 1003-06. Minutes of the Third Meeting of the Curriculum Board, AY75, 24 September 1974, Ibid.
10. AWC, Extracted Remarks by Smith, 27 November 1974, 2, Ibid.
11. Eckhardt to Kerwin, 19 October 1970, File 1002-02. AWC, Memorandum 351-3, 10 August 1971, Subject: CONUS Field Trip Program, Ibid. AWC, Memorandum, 16 September 1971, Subject: Field Trip Program, Ibid.
12. AWC, 8 February 1972, Minutes of Deputies Meeting, File 206-06. J. W. Enos to Commandant, 1 February 1972, Subject: SAC/NORAD Field Trip Report, 17-19 January 1972, File 1001-06. W. R. O'Connell to Commandant, 17 May 1972, Subject: Report of the Norfolk Trip on 7, 8, and 9 May 1972, Ibid. Bolte to Commandant, 11 October 1972, Subject: Trip Report, Ottawa, 3-5 October 1972, Ibid. AWC, 9 November 1972, Minutes of Deputies Meeting, File 206-06. Davis to Cowles, 9 November 1973, File 1001-02. AWC, *Curriculum Pamphlet (Resident), AY 75*. AWC, 26 July 1974, Minutes of Second Meeting of the Curriculum Board AY 75, File 206-06. Smith interview.
13. David H. Roe, Memorandum for Record, 8 July 1974, Subject: Meeting of the DOD Committee on Excellence in Education, 3 July 1974, File 1974-75.
14. Smith to Cowles, 26 September 1974, File 1974-75. Smith to Cowles, 8 January 1975, File 1011-06. Cowles to Smith, 31 January 1975, Ibid. Colonel Paul R. Lunsford, Record of Telecon Lunsford-Waldman, 26 February 1975, Subject: Continuing Interest in Professional Military Education by Clements Committee, Central Files 1972-1975. The advice mentioned was attributed to Adam Yarmolinsky. Interview with DeWitt C. Smith, June 1982.
15. Hersh to Commandant, 22 April 1975, Subject: Areas Tentatively Planned to be Covered or Discussed with General Fred C. Weyand during his visit to the Army War College, Tab H, File 1001-06. End-of-Year Report AY 76 (Draft), Tab U.

16. Smith to Cowles, 8 January 1975. Hersh to Commandant, 22 April 1975, Tab A. End-of-Year Report AY 76 (Draft), Tab A.
17. AWC, *Curriculum Pamphlet (Resident) AY 75*. AWC, *Curriculum Pamphlet 1976*. Hersh Interview.
18. Ibid.
19. AWC, *Curriculum Pamphlet, 1976*.
20. Ibid. End-of-Year Report AY 76 (Draft), Tabs B, C, F.
21. Hersh Interview. Hq, DA, *Review of Education and Training for Officers* (hereafter *RETO Report*), 5 vols. (Washington: Department of the Army, 1978), 2:F-1-4,5.
22. The views of DePuy were reflected later in *Field Manual 100-5, Operations* (Washington: Department of the Army, 1 July 1976). See also William E. DePuy, "The U.S. Army: Are We Ready for the Future?" *Army* (September 1978): 22-29. Gillert to Commandant, 4 March 1974, Subject: Curriculum Development—Tactics, File 1001-07.
23. Ibid., with marginal notes of Davis. Davis to Kerwin, 3 October 1972. Davis to Kerwin, 11 August 1972. Davis, Memorandum, 27 March 1974, Subject: Curriculum Development with Respect to Large-Unit Operations AY 75, File 1001-07. Hersh Interview.
24. Interview with Niven J. Baird, March 1982. AWC, *Curriculum Pamphlet (Resident) AY 75*. AWC, *Curriculum Pamphlet, Academic Year 1977*, 2 May 1976. AWC, Directive: Strategic Military Studies; Phase I, Evolution of Military Strategy, 17 August 1976. Ibid.: Strategic Military Studies; Phase II, Midrange Military Strategy, 27 September 1976. Ibid.: Military Strategy, Planning and Operations: Force Planning, 4 February 1977. Ibid.: Military Planning and Operations, 14 February 1977. Ibid.: War and Politico Military Gaming, 7 March 1977. AWC, Syllabus, Command of Major Units in Land Warfare, 14 March 1977. Ibid.: Military Operations in the Pacific, 17 March 1977. Ibid.: Problems in Land Warfare: The Defense of Central Europe, 1 March 1977. Ibid.: Problems in Land Warfare: Warsaw Pact Strategy, Plans and Operations in Central Europe, 15 March 1977. Ibid.: Analytical War Gaming, 19 March 1977.
25. Raymond M. Macedonia, draft manuscript, "War Gaming and Politico-Military Simulation at the US Army War College," December 1980, in possession of author.
26. Interview with Raymond M. Macedonia, August 1981.
27. Ibid.
28. *RETO Report*, 1:v-viii, I-1 to I-7. The leader of the War College team was Colonel Bobby B. Porter (AWC 74). Representative of the War College during the review was Colonel Niven J. Baird.
29. *RETO Report*, 2: F-1-1 to F-1-35.
30. Baird Interview. *RETO Report*, 2: F-1-8. Office of DCSOPS, DA, "Review of Education and Training for Officers: Implementation Plan," 21 Nov. 1979, 15-17, 25. AR 10-44, *Organization and Functions: United States Army War College*, 1 February 1980.
31. Macedonia, "War Gaming." AWC, *Curriculum Pamphlet, Academic Year 1978*, 20 May 1977. Macedonia Interview. DCSOPS, "Implementation Plan," 25, 33.
32. AWC, *Curriculum Pamphlet Academic Year 1979*, 10 July 1978. Macedonia, "War Gaming." Annual Report AY 80, Annex C and K. Macedonia Interview.
33. "Annual Report AY 80," Annex C. *Curriculum Pamphlet, AY 80*.
34. *Curriculum Pamphlet, AY 77. Curriculum Pamphlet, AY 78. Curriculum Pamphlet, AY 79. Curriculum Pamphlet, AY 80*. "Annual Report AY 80," Annex C.
35. AWC, "Directive: The United States and the World Environment," 8 August 1978, 8, 67-69. In 1979-80 six senators, fourteen representatives, and five staff aides participated in the program, "Annual Report, AY 80," Annexes B and I, Appendix B.
36. "Annual Report, AY 80," Report for Commandant and Annex D. AWC, "Directive: Self Assessment/Executive Skill Development," 7 August 1978.
37. Belser, 27 February 1975, Subject Change in Department Name, Box 1972-1980, Smith Papers.
38. AWC, *Curriculum Pamphlet (Nonresident) Academic Years 73 and 74*, 1 July 1973. AWC, *Curriculum Pamphlet, Corresponding Studies*, 1 July 1976, 11, 14. AWC, "Course Directive, End-of-Course Resident Phase, Class of 1978," 17 July 1978. AWC, "Course Directive, End-of-Course Resident Phase, Class of 1980," 1 July 1980. Attri-

tion in the Corresponding Studies Class of 1980 was twenty-two percent, "Annual Report AY 80," Annex E.

39. AWC, *Directory 1905-1980*.
40. Smith, Extracted Remarks, 27 November 1974, 2-6.
41. AWC, 8 March 1973, Summary of Action on Alternative Names, File 228-08. IO to Commandant, 24 March 1975, Subject: Name Change from AWC to Army University, Ibid. Javitch to Senator Hugh Scott, 11 June 1975, copy in Ibid.
42. Hersh to Commandant, 22 April 1975, Tab G. DR&S to Deputy Commandant, 11 Nov. 1971, Subject: Student Workload Study, Central Files 1971 & 1974. Ringenbach to Commandant, 5 May 1972, Subject: Trip Report (Dr. Nathan Brodsky, OSD), File 1001-06. Davis to Kerwin, 8 October 1972.
43. Hall to Commandant, 4 April 1974, Subject: Statistics on 1975 Participation in USAWC Advanced Degree Program at SSC and PSU/CC, Central Files 1971 & 1974. R. S. Nichols, 4 December 1974, Subject: The USAWC Cooperative Degree Program - AY 76: Analysis and Recommendations, Ibid.
44. Nichols, Memorandum for Record, 5 December 1974, Subject: DA Policy on the USAWC Cooperative Degree Program, Ibid. Smith to Cowles, 8 January 1975. End-of-Year Report AY76 Draft, Tab M. USAWC, "Annual Report Academic Year 1980," Annex M.
45. Ibid., Tab P. Department of the Army, Chief of Staff Regulation 1-27. Senior Fellow Program, 11 October 1974, Central Files 1972-1975. Smith to Cowles, 19 February 1975, Ibid. Cowles to Smith, n.d. , Ibid. Hersh to Commandant, 22 April 1975, Tab C.
46. Davis to Cowles, 18 April 1973, File 1002-07. AWC, "A Report by the Commandant on Academic Year 1977," May 1977, Tab D, Smith Papers.
47. O'Connell to Commandant, 26 May 1971, File 206-06. Davis to Kerwin, 7 July 1971, Ibid. Kerwin to Davis, 26 October 1971, Ibid. Davis to CDR Laske, 14 February 1974, File 1001-02. "Report by Commandant, AY 77," Tab B.
48. Acting DAA to Commandant, 25 April 1974, Subject: Possibility of Employing Reserves in Total Force Concept, Central Files 1974. End-of-Year Report AY 76 (Draft), Tab K. Holmberg Interview. AWC, "Annual Report Academic Year 1980," Annex E.
49. End-of-Year Report AY 76 (Draft) Tabs D, H. AWC, 7 March 1975, Minutes of 11th Curriculum Board Meeting, AY 75, File 206-06. "Report by Commandant, AY 77," Tabs E, F. AWC Pamphlet, "Brehon Burke Somervell Management Lecture Series," AY 1981. AWC, Pamphlet, "Creighton W. Abrams Command Lecture Series, AY 1977."
50. End-of-Year Report AY 76 (Draft), Tab C, USAWC Pamphlet, "Schedule for Field Trip, United Nations and Urban Affairs, 30 September-3 October 1973."
51. USAWC Current Affairs Panel, Final Report Academic Year 1974, Central Files 1974. Smith to Cowles, 24 January 1975 with inclosure "Campus Today: Experiences of the U.S. Army War College Current Affairs Panel," File 412-03. Lewis Sorley to Commandant, 8 October 1974, Subject: AY 75 Current Affairs Panel, Ibid.
52. AWC, *Curriculum Pamphlet, Bicentennial Class 1976*, 2 May 1975, 22. AWC, Pamphlet, "National Security Seminar, National Security Issues Pamphlet," 27 May-6 June 1975. AWC, *Curriculum Pamphlet Academic Year 1980*, 1 August 1979, 14. Ibid., Biographic Sketches, 21st Annual National Security Seminar, 3-6 June 1975. Ibid., Guest List, 25th Annual National Security Seminar, n.d. [June 1979].
53. Smith, Memorandum for Deputy Commanding Officer, 2 December 1974, Subject: Master Plan for Carlisle Barracks, Box 1972-1980, Smith Papers.
54. AWC, 15 December 1972, Minutes of Deputies Meeting, 13 December 1972, File 206-06. Davis, Commander's Analysis - OMA FY 73. Interview with Charles S. Hersh, March 1982. Smith interview.
55. Ibid.
56. Ibid. Smith, "Report by Commandant, AY 77," Tab X.
57. Ibid. Hersh Interview.
58. AWC, *Directory 1905-1980*. Smith, "Report by Commandant, AY 77," Tab X. AWC, "Annual Report Academic Year 1980," Report for Commandant. Remarks to author by Colonel William F. Schless, Colonel Dwight L. Adams, and Dr. Charles S. Hersh.

59. The review of *Parameters* was led by Colonel Erwin R. Brigham, AWC, *Parameters Study: Final Report* (3 March 1975). "Report by Commandant AY 77," Annex U.
60. Smith interview. *Army Command and Management: Theory and Practice 1976-77*, Raymond L. Cook, ed. (Carlisle Barracks: 1976): iii. *Army Command and Management: Theory and Practice, A Reference Text for the Department of Command and Management 1980-81*, (Carlisle Barracks: 1980).
61. AWC, SSI, *Abstracts*, 1981, 23-78. "Report by Commandant, AY 77," Annex N. AWC, SSI, "Current Projects," 25 February 1980. "Annual Report AY 80," Annex R.
62. End-of-Year Report AY 76 (Draft), Tab L. The proceedings of the 1977 symposium were published as what was to be the first in a series, *Studies in U.S. National Security*, under the title *Strategies, Alliances and Military Power: Changing Roles* (Leyden: AW Sutleff, 1977), James A. Kuhlman, ed.
63. "Report by Commandant, AY 77," Annex W. Interview with Colonel Donald P. Shaw, March 1982.
64. AWC, Syllabus, The Vietnam War, 20 February 1976-20 May 1976.
65. Donald Esper to Sandy Cortner, 2 June 1982, subject: Vietnam Lessons Learned Study Effort. Smith, July 1977, as quoted in Thomas A. Ware, Memorandum for Record, 28 June 1982, subject: Chronology of and Plans for the Vietnam Lessons Learned Study (VNLES), Inc. 4. Copies of above in possession of author.
66. Esper to Cortner, 2 June 1982. Ware to "Sandy," 12 May 1982, subject: Genesis of VNL Study, copy in possession of author.
67. Ibid. Ware, Memo for Record, 28 June 1982.
68. Ibid. Ware to "Sandy," 12 May 1982.
69. Ware, Memo for Record, 28 June 1982. The BDM Corporation, *A Study of Strategic Lessons Learned in Vietnam*, 8 vols. and Executive Summary, (Washington: 1979), copy in AWC Library. One work drawing on the study is Harry G. Summers, *On Strategy: The Vietnam War in Context* (Carlisle Barracks: 1981); Colonel Summers was a member of the Strategic Studies Institute.

Of Responsible Command

The Department of the Army selected Major General Jack N. Merritt, a 1970 graduate of the Industrial College of the Armed Forces, to replace General Smith. At the time of his assignment Merritt was serving as the Commandant of the Field Artillery School. At the Army War College, plans for the 1980-81 academic year were all but complete when Merritt arrived at Carlisle Barracks, and he apparently had no instructions from his superiors that required early or major changes in the institution's programs. Moreover, within six months after General Merritt assumed leadership of the War College, the administration of Ronald Reagan took the reins of government in Washington.

President Reagan believed he had a mandate to correct as soon as possible the condition of military superiority that some believed the Soviet Union had achieved during and after the Vietnam War. Merritt thus appeared to be destined to lead the War College into another period during which a review of American security policies would be high on the nation's agenda. It was therefore not a propitious time to alter materially either the theme or the substance of the War College programs as they had developed throughout the 1970s.

The 1980-81 academic year went forward essentially as planned.

During the concluding months of the Carter administration, however, the Iranian revolution, the subsequent hostage crisis, and the Soviet occupation of Afghanistan stimulated real concerns as to the ability of the United States to project meaningful military power into the region of the Persian Gulf. These concerns had led President Carter to establish a so-called "Rapid Deployment Force" and the services to take renewed interest in the art, science, and processes of contingency planning. This subject began to receive an instructional emphasis not seen at the Army War College since the years of William Wotherspoon. The entire resident class of 1981 participated in a four-day exercise in contingency planning and a new advanced course on the subject was added to the curriculum, a course for which students would receive double credit.[1]

Evident also was a desire on the part of General Merritt and his superiors to accelerate and strengthen the trend begun by his predecessor to reinstitute war-gaming as a basic method of Army War College instruction. Ambitions for the growing war-gaming capability extended beyond merely an improved instructional methodology. The capability was seen as a means by which the college might serve a much broader and larger constituency than its own student body. In May 1981 Merritt won Department of the Army approval to renovate the Old Mill Apartments into an "Army War College War Gaming Center." In part the justification for the proposed center was that it would provide a war-gaming program for senior field commanders and their staffs and that War College simulations could be used to test actual contingency plans, as had been recommended by the RETO and tried the previous year.[2] Probably without realizing it, General Merritt and his war games director, Colonel Macedonia, were at long last beginning to fulfill the promise Tasker Bliss had made to General Young in 1903 to the effect that periodically officers responsible for executing war plans would be assembled to study them through the "working out of a great war game."

But as the War College entered the 1980s, there was a more fundamental issue under debate than the extent of war-gaming and contingency-planning instruction, one which had been most sharply drawn during the dialogue between Manton Eddy and Joe Swing at the third beginning of the Army War College and which had continued in the correspondence between Mark Clark and Edward Almond in the early 1950s. Stated in its simplest form, the issue was how to make the War College experience relevant to the students' future duty assignments. It was not a new issue of course; it had been dominant and the debate acrimonious during the tenure of Eugene Salet in the mid-1960s when the contemporary generalist approach came under critical attack. The issue was exhumed again with the maturing of TRADOC and the deliberations of the RETO in 1978. Essentially, the question was whether the third Army War College had strayed and remained too distant from the study of the conduct of military operations. Put another way, which of the three great problems set forth by Elihu Root should take precedence—that of national defense, of military science, or of responsible command? Following from this fundamental issue was another perennial: Was study at the Army War College sufficiently deep and rigorous?

How the future leadership of the Army War College reacts to those fundamental and time-worn issues remains to be seen, but past experience provides some indications. If experience repeats itself, the Army War College will not enjoy complete freedom of action, nor will the resolution of the issues be solely the prerogative of the Army. Perhaps the most significant continuity in the War College's history is that the institution had to repeatedly accommodate to pressures external to itself and the Army. What has truly counted in the evolution and development of the Army War College has not been the imagination and energy of its Commandants and faculties. Rather it has been the position of the United States in the world's power structure, the Army's position as a national institution, the role of armies and the military profession in national affairs, and the changing nature of war itself. Whatever those responsible for the Army perceived, correctly or incorrectly, to be its more glaring shortfalls during any selected period has been the direction followed by the Army War College. A concluding review of the War College's history will illustrate the point.

The very founding of the Army War College was a reaction to environmental change. In the last decades of the nineteenth century, professional education for the Army's officer corps and proposals for the revamping of its systems of command and staff were already active issues. The military memory of the great American Civil War, the emerging phenomenon of professionalization within American society, the concurrent military professionalization throughout the Western World, the end of the frontier mission of the United States Army, and the early emergence of the United States as an influential world power all were factors leading to the establishment of the institution. The college was a logical outgrowth of the success initially of the Artillery School, then of the Naval War College, and finally and most importantly of the Infantry and Cavalry School. The Army War College was not the result of the inspiration of one farsighted man or of even a small group of such men.

America's brief war with Spain resulted in the United States' becoming an imperial power. But the near tragic display of military incompetence in that war made it clear to those who would see that something had to be done to make the American Army capable of serving as an effective instrument of that power. In 1899 the responsibility for what should be done happened to fall to a newly appointed Secretary of War, Elihu Root, a man who happily possessed an unusual ability to judge and amalgamate concepts and the political acumen to give them flesh. Drawing upon the terrible lessons of the war with Spain, Root was able to convince a reluctant Congress and perhaps equally reluctant officer corps that the Army needed to adopt new ways to provide direction and to instill competence. The Army War College was to be a vital part in these endeavors.

Under the guidelines laid down by Root, Tasker Bliss began the War College as an adjunct to the new War Department General Staff, emphasizing the great problem of national defense and following the patterns established by the Prussian *grosse Generalstab* and the Naval War College. Within but a few years, however, new pressures began to alter the scheme of Root and Bliss. They grew from the foreign policies initially of Theodore Roosevelt and subsequently of William Howard Taft and Woodrow Wilson. These policies moved attention away from defense planning in the broad sense to a focus on contingency planning for the projection of power overseas. A second pressure came from Chief of Staff J. Franklin Bell, who was convinced that at least equal War College emphasis must be given to the study of the military art, following the design developed earlier at Fort Leavenworth. Bell's interest was in the great problem of military science.

Commandant William Wotherspoon and his contemporaries accommodated these pressures, bringing the first Army War College to the zenith of its effectiveness as a professional military school in the years between 1909 and 1912. After 1912, however, internal strife within the War Department, congressional hostility toward the General Staff, Wilson's forays into Mexico, and the outbreak of the European war all were exacting distractions. Despite the last-hour efforts of Secretary of War Lindley Garrison and Assistant Chief of Staff Tasker Bliss, the War College failed to prepare senior officers adequately for America's entry and participation in the World War. Particularly apparent was their inability to anticipate the need to plan and execute a national mobilization. The World War experience demonstrated that more must be expected of senior commanders and staff officers than proficiency in the military art and contingency planning.

When Secretary of War Newton Baker and Chief of Staff Peyton March reopened the Army War College in September 1919 as the "General Staff College," they directed the first Commandant, James McAndrew, to provide a program that would instill in the senior officer corps the staff skills necessary to rapidly and efficiently construct a mass army prepared for total war. Baker and March reoriented the War College toward the great problem of national defense, then defined in terms of raising, training, equipping, and employing a mass army built upon the foundation of the provisions of the National Defense Act of 1920.

Until the outbreak of World War II, the War College never completely abandoned the Baker and March purpose, although emphasis on industrial mobilization lessened with the growth of the office of the Assistant Secretary of War and the new Army Industrial College. Moreover, at the insistence of Chief of Staff John J. Pershing, the institution (after one year again called the "Army War College") reembraced the study of the military art. It took on once again the tasks of instruction in higher tactics, a return to the great problem of military science.

If an acceptable balance between emphasis on the great problem of national defense and the great problem of military science was ever reached between the two world wars, it was probably in the early 1930s when Commandant William D. Connor accepted a program of two equal parts, the Clausewitzian "preparation for war" and "conduct of war." Although Connor's theme survived in its essentials until 1940 when the War College recessed as America's rearmament efforts intensified, its survival was not assured. The effects of the Great Depression and the nation's embracing of disarmament, neutrality, and isolation as its national security policy forced Chiefs of Staff Douglas MacArthur and Malin Craig to give high priority to mobilization planning. In turn the War College in the late 1930s shifted its emphasis toward "preparation for war."

At the close of World War II, Chief of Staff George Marshall and his successor, Dwight Eisenhower, perceived the prewar deficiencies in senior officer education to have been a lack of emphasis in two areas, joint service problems and the political influences on military operations. They proposed to correct these deficiencies with a joint-services educational system that would include at the highest level participation by officers from the Department of State. To this purpose Chief of Staff Eisenhower sacrificed the Army War College, its real estate, its library, and its mission. He also created a wide gap in the progression of professional military education that the new National War College, the Armed Forces Staff College, and the postwar Army Command and General Staff College could not fill. In 1950, almost concurrently with the outbreak of the Korean War, Chief of Staff J. Lawton Collins moved to fill that gap by reactivating the Army War College. At the same time, however, Collins directed that the Army War College would constitute the apex of the Army's educational system. Inherent in Collins' instructions was the issue of balance between emphasis on the great problem of national defense and the great problem of military science.

Commandant Joseph Swing, the first Commandant of the third Army War College, rejected the idea of an advanced command and general staff college, with the apparent blessing of Collins. In effect he opted for emphasis not on the great problem of military science but on that of national defense. He began the reactivated War College with a program balanced in emphasis on national security affairs, Army internal problems, and war planning. The second Commandant, Edward Almond, endeavored to win an even broader mission for the War College in its focus on national defense. Primarily due to the opposition of Chief of Army Field Forces Mark Clark, he was unsuccessful. Clark feared the broader mission would cause neglect not only of Army problems, but also of the great problem of military science.

The frustrations of the inconclusive Korean War and the economic goals of the Eisenhower administration led to the "New Look" and the strategy of massive retaliation. With only slight exaggeration it can be said that the Army's primary problem in the post-Korea era was no longer national defense, military science, or responsible command; it was institutional survival. Under the influence initially of Chief of Staff Matthew Ridgway, but more directly under the influence of Chief of Staff Maxwell Taylor, the Army War College in the last half of the 1950s assumed a perspective more national than Army. By 1958 requirements planning, or as it was termed at the War College, "A National Strategy and Its Supporting Military Program," had become the formal theme of the War College program. The object in essence was to produce senior officers who could articulate and justify a critical role for the Army in national security affairs based on an understanding of the great problem of national defense in terms beyond that of the Army.

The theme perhaps survived beyond its usefulness. It was not officially abandoned until 1971, and vestiges of it can still be found as the 1980s begin. By the mid-1960s new pressures for change were bearing down on the Army War College. Not coincidentally, these pressures occurred just as the office of Secretary of Defense Robert McNamara grew in number, authority, and inclination to deal in matters heretofore reserved to the military and naval professions. McNamara, or at least his disciples, saw the great problems differently than had Elihu Root. The great problem was now perceived to be efficient management and rational decision-making. Criticism of the Army War College program from this quarter created resistance and probably slowed or diverted the internally generated move toward change initiated by Commandant Eugene Salet. A vigorous War College defense of what was called generalist education resulted, but Department of Defense criticism had its effects nonetheless. The most enduring were a claim on military strategy as the peculiar province of the Army War College and increased attention within the program to management science and techniques.

In an attempt to compromise what was seen as a generalist versus specialist dispute, the Haines Board in 1967 called for the initiation of elective courses. The Army War College did not recognize the full implications and potential of elective courses, as perhaps the Haines Board had not, until the early 1970s. The overarching 1958 curricular theme was then finally abandoned. The opportunity now presented itself to provide a program that could be tailored to the needs of each individual student. Such tailoring was the fundamental feature of the Long Range Development Plan championed by Commandant Franklin Davis. But tailoring, if carried to its logical conclusion, meant that each student would be allowed to determine for himself the great problem to be addressed.

Individual tailoring and therefore the Long Range Development Plan stumbled on the old issue of great problem definition. Erosion in professionalism, as indicated by the Professionalism and Leadership Studies of 1970 and 1971, and the possible long-term effects on the Army of the unsuccessful Vietnam War and the tawdry Watergate affair, led Commandant DeWitt Smith to direct unprecedented attention toward the place and perspective of the military professional in this dynamic and unsettling environment. Smith also shared the growing sentiment, both within and outside the War College, that Elihu Root's second great problem, that of military science, had too long been neglected. As the decade of the 1970s closed, the applicatory method of Arthur Wagner and Eben Swift was having a rebirth at the Army War College—in the form of the computerized war game.

But no matter the pressures, from the Secretary, Chief of Staff, or Commandant, the War College has never deviated from the belief that its primary, overriding obligation was to the United States Army. Only secondarily has the War College felt an obligation to the student as scholar, to a larger body of scholarship, or to the advancement of a field of knowledge or discipline—be it military art and science, strategy, national security affairs, or professional generalship. This focus of obligation is the fundamental that has differentiated the Army War College from the civilian graduate institutions which at times it has attempted to emulate, and to which both friends and critics frequently and mistakenly have compared it.

This focus of obligation helps explain why the Army War College has produced few if any noted military theoreticians. The quantity demand of the United States Army has not been for theoreticians but for capable practitioners. From Root forward, the United States Army and its War College have seen the function of armies as being prepared to conduct and win campaigns; the time for theory is long past once the troopship sails. While it is true that the War College's superiors from time to time have looked to the War College for the performance of research and analyses, the studies performed at the institution, whether by faculty, students, or the variously named dedicated analytical elements, most frequently have had the same focus of obligation as that of the program of instruction—to provide the United States Army with practical solutions to what were perceived as immediate Army problems.

The periodically expressed desire to create a center for contemporary military thought, to engage in public dialogue on national defense issues, to "wrest the mantle," seems to have been more a response to an institutional version of what John Adams called the "passion for distinction" than a response to a real need of the United States Army. What was to be done with the mantle once wrested, and what great benefit would thereby accrue to the Army, were points never explained. Perhaps there would be benefits and perhaps there is a need, but they are yet to be demonstrated by the Army War College. With its historical focus of obligation, therefore, the value of the Army War College to the Army and to the nation cannot be measured by its scholarly production. Its value is in the influence of the studies it has forwarded to its superiors and in the performance of its graduates as serving Army officers in assignments worldwide in peace and war.

But the War College cannot take all credit, nor does it need to accept all blame, for graduate performance. A year of War College work is too short to produce judgment, character, and virtue where none existed before, and it comes too late in an officer's life to change dramatically his personality and system of values. At best the bad can be dampened and the good reinforced. This fact, if indeed it is a fact, seems to have been understood best by the less optimistic leaders of the earlier War College who elected not to attack directly Root's third great problem, that of responsible command.

Secretary Root did not define responsible command. It seems safe to say, however, that the performance of Nelson Miles as Commanding General of the Army was Root's vivid example of what the conduct of responsible command was not. Root must have sensed that responsible command involved more than tactical competence and charismatic leadership—because Miles possessed both. To Root, responsible conduct of command must have included a better appreciation than Miles displayed of the place of a military professional in the deliberations of a republican society, of political primacy in war, and of the need for what years later Professor Huntington, in his often-cited discussion on military professionalism, would describe as the "corporateness" of the officer corps.[3] Root's establishment of the Army school system demonstrated that he valued military competence but expected more than that from the senior officers that the system would eventually produce.

No problem has perplexed the leaders and teachers of the Army War College more than Elihu Root's problem of responsible command. The first Army War College did not attack the problem directly. Bliss merely assumed that it was temperament and genius that discriminated between the great captain and the usual commander. Eben Swift set for the college the modest goal of producing "safe" commanders. The second Army War College was forced by William Haan and then John Pershing to introduce "Command" as a course of instruction, but based on their AEF experience these two gentlemen saw the problem primarily as delineating the responsibilities of the commander from those of his staff officers—making the French staff system work. Commandant James McAndrew tied instruction in command to instruction in the military art, and Edward McGlachlin added biographical studies in an attempt to find the key. Hanson Ely fretted with the problem but confessed that he did not solve it to his own satisfaction. William Connor simply dismissed the problem, holding that training for staff constituted training for command, an argument that Chief of Staff Eisenhower was to use with Admiral Nimitz when the Armed Forces Staff College was founded.

Like the first Army War College, the third Army War College, as it moved through the 1950s toward its national perspective, also did not attack directly the problem of responsible command. Only when the War College came under attack in the mid-1960s was the problem rediscovered. Commandant Eugene Salet used the problem as a justification for generalist education and as a counter to outside pressures for more training in scientific management methods. Commandant William McCaffrey instituted the "Elements of Command" discussions in the late 1960s. In the early 1970s the Professionalism and Leadership Studies generated an unprecedented and continuing interest in leadership practices and ethics—and caused the behavioral sciences to assume a place in the War College curriculum.

By the early 1970s it was realized, moreover, that only a small percentage of each class would ever become commanders of large formations or organizations and that specialization would be the path of a military career. Commandant Davis reconciled this by rationalizing that if all graduates were not to become generals, at least they would serve around generals and therefore needed to assume the perspective of a general.[4] Davis found "management" and "executive development" to be expressions inadequate in describing what was needed or desired. An important element in his program became "*Command* and Management," and electives began to appear with "command" in their titles. Now, as the 1980s begin, the Army War College is to be the proponent of a "Tactical *Command* Readiness Program."

The periodic directives from above, and calls from below, to teach "command" and the constant manipulation of, or tinkering with, curriculum hours are symptoms of the basic difficulty of forcing the problem of responsible command into a course that can be formally taught and thereby learned. The problem is simply not easily isolated and defined. Yet throughout the records of the many administrations of the Army War College there is a prevailing sense that the problem of fostering responsible command was paramount. There is the sense that responsible command was understood to be more than operational competence, more than staff and management skill, more than academic understanding of human and organizational behavior, more than an appreciation of international affairs and civil-military relations, more even than is encompassed in the overworked term "professionalism." But if responsible command is more than all these things, it must too include all these things.

Attempts to handle (not necessarily consciously) the great problem of responsible command may well have been a driving force behind what came to be the traditional format of the War College year, behind the "collegium" of Bliss, the "membership" and "a year contemplative in nature" of Trudeau and Swing, and the "mode of association" of Smith.

493

In other words, behind all the efforts to congregate the Army's experience, recognized talent, and best minds, there was created an ethical and intellectual milieu where officers through close daily association might enlighten and strengthen each other, bringing each officer out of intellectual isolation and nurturing a sustained concentration of mind.

The format not infrequently has been criticized and on occasion scoffed at in the name of rigor and relevance, but it is interesting and significant that it has never been abandoned but rather has been periodically reinforced. Command is a highly individual and personal responsibility, but it is a responsibility that can be carried out successfully only in the closest association with others who share similar standards and goals. Like command, learning is an individual responsibility which can be carried forth best in association. Creating the milieu for learning and enlightenment is the first and great task of an educational institution. Perhaps this, then, is what the Army War College has truly been about these past eighty some years, and in the process has been dealing with, even though not fully understanding, Elihu Root's greatest problem—that of responsible command.

NOTES
1. *Curriculum Pamphlet, AY80.* AWC, *Curriculum Pamphlet, AY 1981*, 1 August 1980. AWC, *Instructional Text: Contingency Planning*, 1 February 1981. AWC, *Directive: Advanced Courses*, 20 November 1980.
2. Macedonia interview. Morris J. Brady to Jack N. Merritt, 29 May 1981, copy in possession of author. Merritt, Memorandum, 29 May 1981, subject: Charter for the Establishment of a Department of War Gaming, copy in possession of author.
3. Huntington, *The Soldier and the State*, 10, 16-18.
4. Franklin M. Davis, Jr., "The Dilemma of the Senior Service College—A Commentary," in *The System for Educating Military Officers in the United States*, ed. Lawrence J. Korb, Occasional Paper No. 9, International Studies Association (Pittsburgh: University of Pittsburgh, 1976), 107-15.

Appendix

Chronology

1867 General Grant reopens Artillery School at Fortress Monroe.

1875 Artillery School program lengthened to two years.

1877 Emory Upton assigned to faculty of the Artillery School.

1881 General Sherman directs that an Infantry and Cavalry School be established at Fort Leavenworth.

1884 Naval War College authorized.

1885 First session of Naval War College; Tasker Bliss assigned to its faculty.

1887 Infantry and Cavalry School program lengthened to two years.

1893 Arthur L. Wagner becomes head of Department of Military Art at Infantry and Cavalry School; is joined by Eben Swift.

1898 Artillery School and Infantry and Cavalry School inactivated due to war with Spain.

1899 Eilhu Root appointed Secretary of War, recommends an Army War College be established.

1900 Root appoints Ludlow Board to draft terms of reference for Army War College. Congress appropriates $20,000 to support the college.

1901 War Department General Order Number 155 directs establishment of a progressive system of officer professional education to include an Army War College; system to be supervised by a War College Board.

1902 Congress fails to act on a General Staff bill. War College Board formed with Samuel B. M. Young as president. General Service and Staff College opens at Fort Leavenworth. Congress authorizes $400,000 for a war college building at Washington Barracks, D.C.

1903 General Staff Act passed; Army War College formed as adjunct to the War Department General Staff with Tasker Bliss its first

President. First session conducted without students. Cornerstone of building dedicated. J. Franklin Bell becomes Commandant of General Service and Staff College.

1904 First War College class convenes with nine students at 22 Jackson Place. Bell reorganizes General Service and Staff College into "Infantry and Cavalry School" and "Army Staff College."

1905 First War College class graduates in May. Bliss departs. Second class of seven students convenes.

1906 J. Franklin Bell becomes Chief of Staff. Eben Swift assigned to War College faculty, initiates course in "military art" to include historical rides.

1907 Class of sixteen students convenes in new building at Washington Barracks. Program extended from seven to twelve months with course on "military art" a major feature of the curriculum.

1908 Infantry and Cavalry School at Fort Leavenworth redesignated the "School of the Line." War College and Leavenworth conduct two-month preliminary courses for prospective War College students. Building dedicated.

1909 Fort Leavenworth discontinues its preliminary course for War College students. War College personnel participate in major Army maneuvers in Massachusetts.

1910 Ten-week field officer course established at Fort Leavenworth to qualify officers for War College. War College class participates in summer Camp of Instruction at Gettysburg.

1911 War College program reduced from twelve to ten months.

1912 At direction of Secretary of War Henry Stimson, the War College Division produces "Report on the Organization of the Land Forces of the United States." War College begins attempt to write a history of the Civil War. Largest pre-World War I class (twenty-nine) graduates.

1913 War College entrance examinations initiated for officers who are not graduates of the Army Staff College.

1914 United States occupies Vera Cruz in April; War College students ordered to join their regiments.

1915 War College begins work on a "comprehensive military policy"; Secretary of War Lindley Garrison cancels historical ride so that work may be completed.

1916 Newton D. Baker becomes Secretary of War. Crisis on Mexican border causes class to be dismissed two months earlier than planned. National Defense Act of 1916 effectively separates War College from the General Staff. Class of 1917 convenes two months late because of mobilization on Mexican border.

1917 In February class diverted from studies in order to prepare training literature based on European War. In April the United States enters World War I; War College classes suspended the following month.

1918 War College Division of the War Department General Staff redesignated War Plans Division.

1919 Postwar school system includes "School of the Line" and "General Staff School" at Fort Leavenworth and "General Staff College" at Washington Barracks. Based on guidance of Secretary Baker and Chief of Staff Peyton March, Commandant James W. McAndrew attempts "a completely new edifice," stressing mobilization and war planning.

1920 First postwar class graduates seventy-five Army officers and three officers of the Marine Corps. War Department directs greater emphasis on "command." Congress enacts National Defense Act of 1920.

1921 Chief of Staff John Pershing redesignates General Staff College the Army War College. Edward F. McGlachlin replaces McAndrew. Historical Section of the War Plans Division transferred to control of War College.

1922 McGlachlin Board and Fiske Board review Army school system. Pershing consolidates programs at Fort Leavenworth into a single year "Command and General Staff School." Twenty-four percent of War College Class of 1922 fails to graduate.

1923 "Informative Phases" introduced into staff courses. Army and Navy War Colleges begin joint war game of Plan Orange. McGlachlin attempts to broaden program to include nonmilitary subject matter.

1924 Hanson Ely replaces McGlachlin. Program divided into "Informative Period" and "War Plans Period." Army Industrial College established.

1927 Class participates in joint exercise with the U.S. Fleet.

1928 Program of Command and General Staff School expanded to two years. War College introduces a "Historical Studies" course.

1929 Commandant William D. Connor eliminates Command Course and Mobilization Course; directs that program be presented in two phases, "Preparation for War" and "Conduct of War." Class participates in Command Post Exercise at Fort DuPont, Delaware. "Historical Studies" becomes "Analytical Studies."

1932 George Simonds replaces Connor; stresses war planning in support of Chief of Staff Douglas MacArthur's "Four Army Plan."

1934 Class at Fort Monmouth, New Jersey, during August and September to participate in GHQ Command Post Exercise.

1935 Command and General Staff School reverts to a one-year program. War College class increases from seventy-five to ninety Army officers. Commandant Malin Craig reintroduces historical rides (in busses).

1936　"Preliminary Command Course" introduced at beginning of the academic year. War Department directs War College to conduct combat developments study of the infantry division and the echelons above division.

1937　War Department directs War College to conduct combat developments study of cavalry division, corps, and field army.

1938　Class of 1938 convenes late and graduates early in order to participate in summer training of the reserve components. Mobilization Course reinstituted.

1939　Navy withdraws students from Army War College to meet needs of the fleet. Command Course reinstituted. At direction of Chief of Staff George Marshall, War College drafts plans for a Hemispheric Defense Force. War College committees revise *Field Service Regulations* and manuals for command post exercises and major field exercises.

1940　Historical rides canceled. War Department announces in June that classes at Army War College are suspended.

1943　Army and Navy Staff College activated, presents twenty-one-week course.

1945　Marshall informs Eisenhower of tentative plans for a postwar Army and Navy War College. On becoming Chief of Staff Eisenhower convenes Gerow Board to plan postwar Army education system.

1946　Gerow Board recommends a "National Security University" of five colleges, to include a "National War College." Army and Navy Staff College converts into the National War College; Army Industrial College becomes Industrial College of the Armed Forces. Eisenhower presents Army War College building to the National War College. Command and General Staff School at Fort Leavenworth reverts to peacetime forty-week course.

1947　Armed Forces Staff College activated at Norfolk. General Wade Haislip recommends to Eisenhower that Army War College be reestablished.

1948　Army Staff recommends Army War College be reactivated.

1949　Chief of Staff Omar Bradley appoints Eddy Board to study education system; Board recommends Army War College be activated to fill gap between Command and General Staff College and the National War College. Recommendation approved by Chief of Staff J. Lawton Collins.

1950　Army War College reopens at Fort Leavenworth as apex of Army education system. Commandant Joseph Swing rejects Eddy Board concept of an "advanced command and general staff course." War College made subordinate to Army Field Forces.

1951   Army War College moves to Carlisle Barracks, Pennsylvania. Swing replaced by Edward Almond. Annual class trip to United Nations headquarters initiated.

1952   War College criticized for high costs associated with rehabilitation of Carlisle Barracks. Construction begins on Wherry Housing Act project to be named "College Arms." Department of the Army disapproves Almond's request for a broader mission.

1953   Eisenhower becomes President; introduces the "New Look" placing in question the role of land forces.

1954   War College forms Advanced Studies Group of three faculty members.

1955   Continental Army Command (CONARC), successor to Army Field Forces, begins practice of charging War College with combat developments studies. College organizes a Doctrine Section. In March the first National Strategy Seminar is hosted.

1956   National Strategy Seminar is made climax of the year, replacing a major war game. Department of the Army initiates procedure of selecting War College students by action of a Board of Officers.

1957   International affairs and national security policy now consume twenty of forty-three weeks. Influenced by Chief of Staff Maxwell Taylor, War College formally adopts curricular theme "National Strategy and Its Supporting Military Program."

1958   Williams Board reviews officer training and education; endorses War College program.

1960   Cooperative program initiated with The George Washington University leading to award of master's degree in international affairs. Except for combat developments mission, responsibility for War College transferred from CONARC to DA Deputy Chief of Staff for Operations (DCSOPS).

1962   War College "Doctrine and Studies Group" redesignated "Institute for Advanced Studies" and transferred to the control of newly formed Combat Developments Command (CDC). Instruction in counterinsurgency introduced.

1963   Operations Group, a field agency of DCSOPS, formed at Carlisle Barracks. War College placed under supervision of DA Assistant Chief of Staff for Force Development (ACSFOR). COL Otho C. Van Exel and LTC Frederic E. Davison, first black students, graduate.

1964   Initial two-week Senior Reserve Component Officers' Course held. Commandant Eugene Salet launches "Army War College-70" project.

1965   Department of Defense functionaries become publicly critical of programs of the senior service colleges. Haines Board convened to review Army officer education system. Faculty reorganized into academic departments. War-gaming disappears from curriculum; "Command and Management Seminar" added. "Occasional Papers of the Army War College" published. War College transferred from supervision of ACSFOR to that of the Deputy Chief of Staff for Personnel (DCSPER).

1966 Chief of Staff Harold Johnson approves recommendations of Haines Board that War College offer elective courses and an extension program. "Comparative Military Strategy Seminar" added to curriculum. "Occasional Papers" retitled *Army War College Commentary.* Faculty specialists designated "directors." Program with The George Washington university terminated.

1967 New academic building, Root Hall, occupied. Five-week course, "Army Internal Defense and Development Operations," inaugurated. First elective courses offered. Military History Research Collection established at Carlisle Barracks.

1968 Initial Nonresident Instruction (later redesignated Corresponding Studies) course begins its program.

1969 Department of the Army disapproves previously agreed-upon plan to expand size of resident class and facilities of the War College. "Vietnam Panel" (later "Current Affairs Panel") established. LTC Frances C. Chaffin and LTC Shirley R. Heinze, first women students, graduate.

1970 Chief of Staff William Westmoreland directs War College to undertake a major study on military professionalism. "Military Professionalism Seminar" added to the required curriculum. "USAWC Mission and Curriculum Study" initiated. First West Point Fellow joins faculty of War College.

1971 Westmoreland directs War College undertake "Leadership for the 1970's" study. Curriculum theme adopted in 1957-58 abandoned as recommended by Mission and Curriculum study. Department of Management created. "Command and Management Seminar" becomes a full course entitled "Defense Decision-Making and Management." "Military Professionalism Seminar" retitled "Human Dimensions of Military Professionalism." Cooperative degree program initiated with Shippensburg State College. Commandant Franklin Davis directs drafting of a Long Range Development Plan. Institute of Advanced Studies renamed the Strategic Studies Institute. First edition of *Parameters* published, replacing *Commentary.*

1972 Chief of Staff approves concepts of the Long Range Development Plan to be implemented over a five-year period. Instruction of the Department of Management consolidated into one "Management and Executive Development" course. Twenty-seven elective courses offered.

1973   Strategic Studies Institute assigned to the War College. Department of Management and "Management and Executive Development" course become "Command and Management." War College publishes monograph series on leadership. Director of Academic Affairs established as a civilian position. Separate course on internal defense and development operations disappears. War College transferred to DCSOPS supervision.

1974   Trimester scheme of Long Range Development Plan instituted a year earlier than programmed. DeWitt Smith becomes Commandant, immediately places emphasis on enhancing the environment for learning. Department of Defense "Committee on Excellence in Education" reviews War College program.

1975   Trimester scheme modified, making Military Studies Program voluntary. Nonresident Instruction program becomes "Corresponding Studies." Long Range Development plan lapses as guide to War College planning.

1976   Senior Reserve Component Officers' Course expanded to include officers from components other than those of the Army. Interest in study of military operations revived; war-gaming instruction reintroduced. Approximately sixty elective courses being offered.

1977   International Fellows Program initiated. "Review of Education and Training of Officers" (RETO) conducted by the Department of the Army.

1978   RETO report published; recommends War College place additional emphasis on military operations and manage an Army-wide "Tactical Command Readiness Program." Number of Army officers in Resident Class reduced by fifteen percent; Corresponding Studies Class increased to compensate.

1979   COL Evelyn P. Foote, first woman faculty member assigned to duty in July.

1980   General Smith departs after having served a total of five years as Commandant. Chief of Staff Edward C. Meyer directs additional emphasis on joint planning for contingency operations.

1981   Department of the Army approves establishment of a War College Department of War Gaming and a "Center for War Gaming" at Carlisle Barracks.

Notes on Sources

Most of the sources from which this history was constructed are located in the United States Army Military History Institute, Carlisle Barracks, Pennsylvania. Among the Institute's holdings are the "Curricular Archives of the Army War College" which contain a broader range of material than the name indicates. From the 1907-17 period are mimeographed transcripts of lectures, addresses, problems and exercises, and directives and memoranda arranged chronologically and bound separately by year. From the 1919-20 year are mimeographed instructional materials and student monographs organized in bloc category and labeled "General Staff College, 1919-1920." Similarly, from the 1920-40 period material is arranged and bound by year and by separately designated courses of instruction. Also included from this period are files containing internal and external War College correspondence, instructional and source material, and studies by student committees and individual officers, all of which are arranged topically and indexed in "Army War College Reference Cards, 1920-1940." A convenient aid to using the "Curricular Archives" is *A Suggested Guide to the Curricular Archives of the U.S. Army War College, 1907-1940* (U.S. Army Military History Research Collection, 1973), compiled by Benjamin F. Cooling.

For the post-World War II period, curricular material is filed in boxes by year and course. In addition and filed separately are studies prepared by individual students and student committees, major college studies and publications, and correspondence files. Separate files contain the correspondence and unclassified work of the Institute of Advanced Studies during the period in which it was not an organic element of the Army War College. Material that relates specifically to the Army War College is also to be found in the files of the post of Carlisle Barracks. Included are scrapbooks of press clippings pertaining to the War College.

The collection of the Institute also contains the personal papers of a number of individuals who were closely affiliated with the War College, including those from the early career of Tasker Bliss. The papers from Bliss's later years are in the manuscript collection of the Library of Congress. Also present among the Institute's holdings are the papers of Samuel B. M. Young, but they are much less useful than those of Bliss. The papers of Arthur G. Trudeau, Edward M. Almond, and DeWitt C. Smith were especially helpful.

The library of the Military History Institute contains many volumes that had been the property of the pre-World War II Army War College. This collection is an important indication of what was readily available to the students and faculty of those years and also contains documents of more direct significance. Among the latter is "The Army War College: Memoranda Pertaining to the Establishment and Operation of the Army War College, compiled and arranged by M. Barstow Mercer under the direction of Brigadier General W. W. Wotherspoon, President, Army War College, Washington, 1907," the earliest effort to record the story of the War College. Since Mercer was the chief civilian clerk of the institution during its formative years, his compilation was invaluable in reconstructing that period.

Building on Mercer's initial efforts is a bound mimeographed volume of 1919, "A Chronicle of the Army War College," edited by Colonel George P. Ahern. It covers the pre-World War I College. Apparently the War College intended to keep Ahern's work current; two additional "Chronicle" volumes are available covering the years 1919-31 and 1932-46. The latter two volumes are not so complete nor as carefully prepared as Ahern's but contain important information.

Also in the Institute's library are bound mimeographed and transcript items of interest covering specific events or practices. These include "Album, Ceremonies at the Laying of the Cornerstone of the U.S. Army War College Building at Washington Barracks" (1903), "Programme at the Ceremonies Unveiling the Statue of Frederick the Great, Saturday, November 19, 1904," "Dedication of the Army War College, November 9, 1908," and General Pershing's "Address at Graduation Exercises, Army War College, Washington, D.C. at 11:00 a.m., June 28, 1903." The bound files "Manual of the War College Division, General Staff, U.S. Army" (1915) and "History of the General Staff and Organization Charts" (1903-37) were helpful.

The United States Army since World War I has periodically convened boards of officers to conduct comprehensive reviews of its educational system. Reports of these boards (copies are available in the Institute library) were influential and provide good insight into the thinking of the time. "Report of Proceedings of a Board of Officers Appointed to Study the Army School System" (1922) and "Report of Board of Officers Appointed to Prepare Programs of Instruction for General and Special Service Schools" (1922), the McGlachlin and Fiske Boards respectively, set the tone for the period between the world wars. In the immediate post-World War II period, the Gerow Board's "Report of War Department Military Education Board on Educational Systems for Officers of the Army" (1946) and the Eddy Board's "Report of the Department of the Army Board on the Educational System for Officers" (1949) were pivotal studies. Important for later years are the Williams Board's "Report of the Department of the Army Education and Training Review Board" (1958), the Haines Board's "Report of the Department of the Army Board to Review Army Officer Schools" (1966), the report of Major General Frank W. Norris, *Review of Army Educational System*, 3 vols. (1971), and Headquarters, Department of the Army, *Review of Education and Training for Officers*, 5 vols. (1978).

Internal reviews conducted by the War College also provided insights. For the period of the early 1950s, particularly useful were James H. Polk, Memorandum from Director, GS Group, to Commandant, 25 June 1953, Subject: Projects to Enhance the Prestige of the Army War College; DeVere P. Armstrong, "Study on the Army War College," 13 August 1953; and James A. Berry, Memorandum, Secretary to Deputy Commandant, 22 October 1954, Subject: The Near and Long Range Future of the ARWC. All three studies are in the "Curricular Archives." The results of the Army War College-70 project were not consolidated into one document. The best summary of the outcome of that effort is in USAWC, *Positions for the Department of the Army Board to Review Army Officer Schools*, 21 September 1965. Similarly, the results of the "1970 Mission Study" and the "Long Range Development Plan" that immediately followed exist only in files under those labels. Colonel Dandridge M. Malone provided me additional documents on the Long Range Development Plan, which are cited as "Malone Files."

The oral history program of the Military History Institute has produced transcripts of interviews by War College students with numerous senior Army personages. Useful interviews were those of Generals Paul D. Adams, Edward M. Almond, James F. Collins, Clyde D. Eddleman, James H. Polk, Jonathan O. Seaman, Maxwell D. Taylor, Arthur G. Trudeau, and Dr. Ivan Birrer. The value of these interviews varies with the interests and skill of the interviewers, and they must be used with caution since recollection of events that occurred several decades earlier not infrequently departs from what the documentary evidence indicates. A guide to the oral history transcripts is a pamphlet compiled by Charles R. Shrader, *Senior Officer Oral History Program, 1971-1981*, Carlisle Barracks: United States Military History Institute, 1981.

Interviews, discussions, and conversations were held with a number of current and former members of the faculty who had long service at the Army War College. Included were Lieutenant General DeWitt C.

Smith, Jr., Colonels Dwight L. Adams, Niven J. Baird, Donald S. Bussey, Zane E. Finkelstein, Raymond E. Macedonia, Dandridge M. Malone, William F. Schless, Donald P. Shaw, and LeRoy Strong, Drs. Charles S. Hall and Charles M. Hersh, and Mr. Albert P. Holmberg. My personal experiences as a faculty member (1974-77) undoubtedly influenced my perceptions of the institution.

Volumes that influenced or provided information on the Army War College include Emory Upton, *The Armies of Asia and Europe*, New York: 1878; Theodore Schwan, *Report on the Organization of the German Army*, Washington: 1894; Henry Spenser Wilkinson, *The Brain of an Army: A Popular Account of the German General Staff*, London: 1895; John W. Masland and Lawrence I. Radway, *Soldiers and Scholars: Military Education and National Policy*, Princeton: 1957; and William W. Whitson, *The Role of the United States Army War College in the Preparation of Officers for National Security Policy Formulation*, Ph.D. dissertation: 1958.

Articles that describe the prospective or contemporary Army War College include Arthur L. Wagner, "An American War College," *Journal of the Military Service Institution*, 10 (1889): 288-96; Edward Field, "Wanted: A War College," *New York Times* (August 9, 1896): 24; William H. Carter, "Recent Army Reorganization," *United Service*, 2 (August 1902): 113-120; "Functions of the Army War College," *Army and Navy Journal* (April 7, 1906): 883; Eben Swift, "Military Education of Officers in Time of Peace," *Journal of the U.S. Artillery*, 33 (May-June, 1910): 285-96; Lytle Brown, "The United States Army War College," *The Military Engineer*, 19 (July-August, 1927): 294-97; Oswald H. Saunders, "The Army War College," *The Military Engineer*, 26 (March-April, 1934): 101-14; Joseph M. Swing, "Army War College," *Army, Navy, Air Force Journal* (December 9, 1950): 385; Eugene A. Salet, "The Army War College Looks to the Future," *Army* (January 1965): 28-35; Benjamin Doty, "Opening Some Windows at the Army War College," *Army* (February 1973): 21-23; and Franklin M. Davis, Jr., "The Dilemma of the Senior Service College—A Commentary," in *The System of Educating Military Officers in the United States*, 107-15, edited by Lawrence J. Korb, Pittsburgh: International Studies Association, University of Pittsburgh, 1976.

Articles critical of the war colleges of all the services during the 1960s include Robert N. Ginsburgh, "The Challenge to Military Professionalism," *Foreign Affairs* (January 1964): 255-68; "Marine Commandant Proposes School Changes," *The Journal of the Armed Forces* (February 6, 1965): 2; and Edward L. Katzenbach, "The Demotion of Professionalism at the War Colleges," *United States Naval Institute Proceedings* (March 1965): 34-41. In this category also belongs Stansfield Turner, "Naval War College 1972-1973: The Report of the President," *United*

States Naval War College Review (September-October, 1973): 1-17.

Among edited volumes of writings, personal reports, and memoirs, several were important. For the period before the founding of the Army War College, they include John D. Hayes and John B. Mittendorf, eds., *The Writings of Stephen B. Luce*, Newport, R.I.: 1975; and John M. Schofield, *Forty-Six Years in the Army*, New York: 1897. For the period of the founding of the Army War College, there are three volumes by Elihu Root—*Establishment of a General Staff in the Army*, Washington: 1902; *Five Years at the War Department, 1899-1903, As Shown in the Annual Reports of the Secretary of War*, Washington: 1904; and *The Military and Colonial Policy of the United States*, edited by Robert Bacon and James B. Scott, Cambridge, Mass.: 1916.

Official documents are cited throughout the chapter notes, but particular attention is drawn to the following documents of the United States Congress—House Committee on Military Affairs, *Hearings to Increase the Efficiency of the Military Establishment of the United States*, 2 vols., 64th Congress, 1st sess., 1916; Senate Committee on Military Affairs, *Hearings on the Reorganization of the Army and Creation of a Reserve Army*, 64th Congress, 1st sess., 1916; House Committee on Military Affairs, *Hearings on a Bill to Reorganize and Increase the Efficiency of the U.S. Army and Other Purposes*, 66th Congress, 1st sess., 1919; Senate, *Reorganization of the Army, Hearings before a Subcommittee of the Committee on Military Affairs*, 66th Congress, 1st and 2nd sess., 1919. House, *An Act to Amend an Act entitled "An Act for Further and More Effectual Provision for the National Defense, approved June 3, 1916,"* 66th Congress, 2nd sess., 1920; Senate, *Creation of the American General Staff, Personal Narrative of the General Staff System of the American Army by Major General William H. Carter*, Document 119, 1924.

Documents of the War Department included the annual reports of the Secretary of War, the Commanding General of the Army, and the Chief of Staff of the Army. Though rarely critical of War Department practices, these reports reflect problems and recommended solutions as perceived by the Department at the time, *War Department General Order Number 155*, 27 November 1901, is the initial chartering document of the Army War College.

Biographical data were obtained from the annual editions of the *Official Army Register*; George W. Cullum's *Biographical Register of the Officers and Graduates of the United States Military Academy at West Point, New York*, 9 vols., New York: 1868-1956; and *Directory, U.S. Army War College, 1905-1908*, Carlisle Barracks: 1980. Also available was material collected by the library of the Military History Institute and filed in its biographical section.

Certain biographical works contributed to better understanding of major personalities influential on the Army War College. These include Stephen E. Ambrose, *Upton and the Army*, Baton Rouge: 1964; John D. Hayes, "Stephen B. Luce and the Beginning of the Naval War College," *Naval War College Review*, 23 (1971): 51-59; Eben Swift, "An American Pioneer in the Cause of Military Education: Arthur L. Wagner," *Journal of the* Military Service Institution, *44 (1909): 67-72; Philip C. Jessup, Elihu Root*, 2 vols., New York: 1938; Edward Ransom, "Nelson A. Miles as Commanding General, 1895-1903," *Military Affairs*, 29 (1965-66): 179-200; Eugene V. Andrews, *William Ludlow: Engineer, Governor, Soldier*, University Microfilms: 1976; Frederick Palmer, *Bliss— Peacemaker: The Life and Times of General Tasker H. Bliss*, New York: 1934; Edgar F. Raines, *Major General J. Franklin Bell and Military Reform: The Chief of Staff Years, 1906-1910*, University Microfilms: 1977; Edward M. Coffman, *The Hilt of the Sword: The Career of Peyton C. March*, Madison: 1966; Frank E. Vandiver, *Black Jack: The Life and Times of John J. Pershing*, 2 vols., College Station, Texas: 1977; and D. Clayton James, *The Years of MacArthur, Vol. I: 1880-1941*, Boston: 1970.

Secondary works that were used are cited in the chapter notes, but certain historical studies should be highlighted as the subjects they address were of particular influence on the Army War College.

For the period of the late nineteenth century, these include Trevor N. Dupuy, *A Genius for War: The German Army and General Staff, 1807-1945*, Englewood Cliffs, N.J.: 1977; Richard A. Andrews, *Years of Frustration: William T. Sherman, The Army and Reform, 1869-1883*, University Microfilms: 1968; Russell F. Weigley, "The Military Thought of John M. Schofield," *Military Affairs*, 23 (1959): 77-84; Ronald Spector, *Professors of War: The Naval War College and the Naval Profession*, Newport, R.I.: 1977; Timothy K. Nennenger, *The Fort Leavenworth Schools: Post Graduate Military Education and Professionalization in the United States Army, 1880-1920*, University Microfilms: 1974; Elizabeth Bethel, "The Military Information Division: Origins of the Intelligence Division," *Military Affairs*, 11 (1947): 17-24; and Allan R. Millett, *Military Professionalism and Officership in America*, Columbus, Ohio: 1977. For the period of the Spanish-American War and the Philippine Insurrection, special mention is made of Graham A. Cosmos, *An Army for Empire: The United States Army in the Spanish-American War*, Columbia, Mo.: 1981; David M. Trask, *The War with Spain in 1898*, New York: 1981; and John M. Gates, *Schoolbooks and Krags: The United States Army in the Philippines, 1898-1902*, Westport, Conn.: 1973. Works on the U.S. Army during the early decades of the twentieth century include James L. Abrahamson, *America Arms for the New Century: The Making of a Great Military Power*, New York: 1981; James E. Hewes, Jr., *From Root to McNamara: Army Organization and Administration, 1900-1963*, Washington: 1975; Philip L. Semsch, "Elihu Root and the General Staff," *Military Affairs*, 27 (1963): 22-26; Edgar F. Raines, *Major General J. Franklin Bell and Military Reform: The Chief of Staff Years, 1906-1910*, University Microfilms: and Allan R. Millett, "The General Staff and the Cuban Intervention of 1906," *Military Affairs*, 31 (1967): 113-19.

Works that were particularly useful for the period just prior to the entry of the United States into World War I include John P. Finnegan, *Against the Specter of a Dragon: The Campaign for American Military Preparedness, 1914-1917*, Westport, Conn.: 1974; George C. Herring, "James Hay and the Preparedness Controversy, 1915-1916," *Journal of Southern History*, 30 (1961): 383-404; Marvin A. Kreidberg and Merton C. Henry, *History of Military Mobilization in the United States Army, 1775-1945*, Washington: 1955; and John McA. Palmer, *America in Arms: The Experience of the United States with Military Organization*, New Haven, Conn.: 1941.

Understanding of the performance of the officer corps during World War I was provided by two studies of Edward M. Coffman—*The War to End All Wars: The American Experience in World War I*, New York: 1968; and "The American Military Generation Gap in World War I: The Leavenworth Clique in the AEF," in *Command and Commanders in Modern Warfare*, 39-48, edited by William Geffen, Colorado Springs: 1969. For the period between the two World Wars, I drew heavily on John W. Killigrew, *The Impact of the Great Depression on the Army*, Ph.D. dissertation: 1960; Albert A. Blum, "Birth and Death of the M Day Plans," in *American Civil-Military Decisions A Book of Case Studies*, 63-96, edited by Harold Stein, Birmingham, Ala.: 1963; and Stetson Conn, *Historical Work in the U.S. Army, 1862-1954*, Washington: 1980.

Studies that should be singled out as providing understanding of post-World War II developments are L. Douglas Kinnard, *President Eisenhower and Strategy Management: A Study in Defense Politics*, Lexington, Ky.: 1977; William W. Kaufmann, *The McNamara Strategy*, New York: 1964; the previously mentioned *From Root to McNamara* by James Hewes; Douglas Blaufarb, *The Counterinsurgency Era: U.S. Doctrine and Performance*, New York: 1977; and Robert A. Doughty, "The Command and General Staff College in Transition, 1946-1976," Special Study, Fort Leavenworth, Kans.: 1977.

Special mention is made of the 1967 volume by George S. Pappas, *Prudens Futuri; The U.S. Army War College, 1901-1967*. In addition to being a history of the Army War College, this work also serves as a contemporary account of the institution during the mid-1960s.

Notes By The Publisher

The Alumni Association of the U.S. Army War College was established by Major General Eugene A. Salet, Commandant, on 19 May 1967. Concurrently he sponsored the writing and publication of a comprehensive, bound history of the college, titled "Prudens Futuri" by Colonel George S. Pappas, USAWC Class of 1966. Until 1981 when the book went out of print, a copy was given to each newly enrolled member of the Association. Having undergone six printings without major revision nor having been brought up to date in 13 years, it was deemed to have served its purpose and a new history was decided upon.

An extensive search for a competent, willing, and motivated author was undertaken. The Board of Trustees of the Alumni Association selected Colonel Harry P. Ball, USA Retired, and commissioned him to prepare a totally new history of the US Army War College. The work would be not only the history of the institution but its history in terms of the larger framework of US Army, national and international, and educational environments. In short, the Board wanted this work to determine and depict what happened as well as why and how it happened. This volume, "Of Responsible Command", is the product. Colonel Ball was asked to prepare the book in one year, later extended to eighteen months. He has used the first twelve chapters as his doctoral dissertation in history and was granted his PhD at the University of Virginia in 1983.

Copyrighted in late 1983 by the Association, the initial manuscript has undergone extensive review, revision, and editing. A copy will be given to each new Association member, continuing the custom established in 1967. It is available for sale by the Association through the Barracks Sutler, the Army War College Book Store.

Throughout the book the Army War College is variously referred to as the "United States Army War College" (its current official designation since 1957), the "US Army War College", the "Army War College" (its name when founded on 27 November 1901), or simply the "War College". The same institution is meant in every case.

511

With graduation of the 1983 Corresponding and Resident Classes, 13,125 students have been graduated. Since 1903, the graduates number officers of every component of the US Army (Regular, Reserve, Army National Guard, active and inactive), the US Navy (Regular and Reserve), the US Air Force (Regular, Reserve and Air National Guard), the US Marine Corps (Regular and Reserve), and the US Coast Guard (Regular and Reserve). Civilian representatives of the Departments of Defense, Army, State and Justice have been included among the graduates. Also included are representatives of numerous other US governmental agencies such as the Central Intelligence Agency, the Defense Communications Agency, the Defense Mapping Agency, the Defense Intelligence Agency, the Defense Logistics Agency and the National Security Agency. Faculty Fellows from the US Military Academy and International Fellows from 39 nations complete the list of graduates.

Index

513